IMITATING CHRIST IN MAGWI

To Neil,
Thank you for your care.

Todd

D1545898

T & T Clark Studies in Social Ethics, Ethnography, and Theology

Over the last half-century, there have been numerous calls for Christian theology and ethics to take human experience seriously—to delve into particular economic, sociopolitical, racial-ethnic, and cultural contexts from which theological and moral imagination arises. Yet actual theologies that draw upon descriptive-rich, qualitative methods—methods that place such particularity at the center of inquiry and performance—are few and scattered. **T & T Clark Studies in Social Ethics, Ethnography, and Theology** is a monograph series that addresses this gap in the literature by providing a publishing home for timely ethnographically-driven theological and ethical investigations of an expansive array of pressing social issues, ranging from armed conflict to racism to healthcare inequities to sexuality/gender and discrimination to the marginalization of persons with disabilities. The scope of the series projects, taken together, is at once global and intensely local, with the central organizing conviction that ethnography provides not only information to plug into a theology, but a valid and vibrant way of *doing* theology.

IMITATING CHRIST IN MAGWI

AN ANTHROPOLOGICAL THEOLOGY

Todd David Whitmore

t&tclark

LONDON • NEW YORK • OXFORD • NEW DELHI • SYDNEY

T&T CLARK
Bloomsbury Publishing Plc
50 Bedford Square, London, WC1B 3DP, UK
1385 Broadway, New York, NY 10018, USA

BLOOMSBURY, T&T CLARK and the T&T Clark logo are trademarks of Bloomsbury
Publishing Plc

First published in Great Britain 2019

Cover image: Palm Sunday in Lokung Internally
Displaced Persons Camp, 2008 © Todd David Whitmore

A catalogue record for this book is available from the British Library.

A catalog record for this book is available from the Library of Congress.

ISBN: HB: 978-0-5676-8418-9
PB: 978-0-5676-8417-2
ePDF: 978-0-5676-8420-2
ePUB: 978-0-5676-8419-6

Series: T&T Clark Studies in Social Ethics, Ethnography, and Theology

Typeset by Deanta Global Publishing Services, Chennai, India
Printed and bound in Great Britain

To find out more about our authors and books visit www.bloomsbury.com and
sign up for our newsletters.

for Susan

CONTENTS

ACKNOWLEDGMENTS

This book is a long time coming. Among the various reasons for this—the duration of fieldwork, the time it takes to learn a language for which there is no Rosetta Stone, the need for time to recover from stays in conflict and post-conflict zones, the unwieldiness of field reality when trying to convert it to prose—I think that the main one is that it takes a long time to have something to say. In his memoir-ethnography of his apprenticeship to a Songhay sorcerer along the border of Mali and Niger, anthropologist Paul Stoller writes of joining a group of elders in discussion during the early days of his research in the region as a doctoral student. "Beyond the specific teachings of Songhay kinship and cosmology, they instructed me that one can learn only when he or she is of an age such that the brain is ready to receive knowledge. . . . A man's mind can begin to receive important knowledge when he is forty years of age, but it is not until a man reaches the age of sixty that he is truly ready to learn."[1] I am sixty years old. According to the Songhay, I am only now ready to learn.

Taking this long to complete the book means that I have more than my fair share of people and organizations to thank. Because its library is the world, fieldwork requires significant stretches of time away from the academy. The Association of Theological Schools' Lilly Faculty Fellowship and the University of Notre Dame's Kroc Faculty Sabbatical Fellowship allowed me to do much of the fieldwork that has informed this book. Notre Dame's Office of Research provided a generous grant as part of their Faculty Scholarship Award Program. Various smaller, yet significant, grants from the University's Institute for Scholarship in the Liberal Arts, the Department of Africana Studies, and the Kroc Institute helped to fund travel for some of the trips. Finally, a grant from the American Academy of Religion provided needed travel funds.

China Scherz, Paul Scherz, David Clairmont, Kyle Lambelet, and Stephen Webb all provided critical feedback on a number of the chapters. There is no replacement for their wisdom and kindness. The participants in the 2014 University of Chicago Writers Group at the Society of Christian Ethics—Liz Bucar and Jonathan Rothchild, who headed up the group, and William Schweiker, Robin Lovin, Susan Ross, David Clairmont, Cristina Traina, and Melanie Barrett—read the first chapter, as did Mary McClintock Fulkerson, Ted Smith, and Courtney Davis. I figured that if I could get that chapter past these sets of eyes, then there might be something worth saying. Paul Donohue, MCCJ, who spent decades in northern Uganda, provided invaluable insight during my writing of the chapter on Comboni missionary activity in the region. Gerardo Marti, Tone Stangeland Kaufman, and Rachel Muers of the Ecclesial Practices Group of the American

Academy of Religion and the participants of the Northeastern University Workshop on Ethnography, Religion, and Ethics provided feedback on critical parts of what is now Chapter 6. Mary Moschella and Susan Willhauck, together with the group of scholars they brought together for a symposium, funded by the Wabash Center for Teaching & Learning in Theology and Religion, on teaching ethnography in theological contexts, offered many helpful insights for a piece that constitutes the concluding section of the last chapter. John Fitzgerald kept me from making too many mistakes in interpreting the apostle Paul in the appendix. Graduate students John Sehorne, Courtney Davis, Michael Yankoski, Heather DuBois, Jon Kara Shields, Janna Hunter Bowman, Lorraine Cuddeback, Ketty Anyeko, Joella Bitter, and Lindsay McClain Opiyo provided a wide range of sharp readership and academic support. I hope that the end product is worthy of this cloud of witnesses.

One cannot—or at least I cannot—do fieldwork in a warzone without ample support from practitioners of mental and spiritual health. Roger Klauer, David Stone, Michele and Jim Apostolou, Natalie Kilheeney, Nancy Gulanick, John Peterson, Jeffrey Feathergill, James Brogle, and Kearn Hinchman have kept me enough together to complete this project. I witnessed things that are rather hard to acknowledge, let alone integrate into one's psyche. This village of helpers has made that more possible than it otherwise would have been.

There are far too many Acholi to whom I am indebted to name them all. Without their hospitality, this book would not be possible. I wish to mention at least Father Joseph Okumu, Bob Okello, Opira Noah, Beatrice Noah, and the members of the Little Sisters of Mary Immaculate of Gulu. They showed me with their lives what following Christ looks like.

And thank you to my wife, Susan St. Ville, to whom this book is dedicated. The intense and intensive rhythms of fieldwork and writing do not always mesh with those of family, and she has been willing to countenance that fact more often than I can number. And she has done this while managing quite successfully her own career and vocation as theologian, therapist, and peacebuilder. On the rare days that I am fortunate enough to wake up before she does, I still, after twenty-nine years of marriage, turn toward her and think, "So this is what a sacrament looks like."

Note

1. Paul Stoller and Cheryl Olkes, *In Sorcery's Shadow* (Chicago and London: The University of Chicago Press, 1987), 13.

CHAPTER 1
IMITATING CHRIST IN MAGWI: THEOLOGY *IN MEDIA RES*

I have never seen a night sky like this. There are no cities near Magwi, South Sudan, and so no light pollution. I see now that there are stars between the main, brightest stars, and stars between the ones in between; many more and much brighter than I could have imagined. We are sitting outside in plastic chairs in something of a circle in the compound of the eucharistic center where I have been living the past two weeks. There is no electricity, and conversation has yet to be displaced by television. Father Joseph Otto and the health unit workers, Dominick, Odoch, and Kidega, bounce from topic to topic, fed by the day's events, and my attention shifts from sky to conversation to sky again.

Seemingly without topical prompt, a debate breaks out among them regarding the best direction to run during a rebel Lord's Resistance Army (LRA) attack. Though the rebels are ostensibly at war with the Ugandan government, in the complex logic of the conflict, the government of Sudan uses the LRA to fight its own rebels, the Sudan People's Liberation Army or SPLA, while the government of Uganda trains SPLA soldiers for combat against the LRA. The people of northern Uganda and South Sudan are simply caught in the middle. Though the Sudanese government and the SPLA signed a peace agreement two years ago, change is only incremental on the ground.

Dominick, a slender, lighter-skinned Madi from Adjumani, argues that it is best to run across the line of fire, to what appears to be off to the side of the attack. Father Joseph Otto disagrees. He is dark-skinned, and I can only make him out because he is very animated when he speaks. He holds up his hand in the shape of a C and presses it forward like he is holding an invisible cup.

"They attack you like this. The two sides first. They try to catch you at the back, but if you run to the side, they will catch you also. This is how they attacked in January. Ay, yi, yi," he laughs, shaking his head. "January was the worst month."

"The LRA attacked. People from all around came to our compound. They were saying, 'Father Joseph, the LRA are coming! Help us!' I did not know what to do. We could not protect them. Father Maurice was here. So I asked him what we should do. He said, 'Let's get a motorcycle and ride towards the LRA. Let's try to talk to them. Maybe they'll talk. And if they kill us, at least the others will have more time to get away.'"

The next day, Father Joseph and I drive to Torit to see the bishop. Though the Magwi County Commissioner says that they have all gone to Western Equatoria, the LRA are still around. Father Maurice saw one running from the SPLA earlier in the week, and the next week, four will be spotted on the edges of Agoro, Uganda, just south of the South Sudan border, while I am there. Father Joseph crosses himself and says a prayer before he starts the vehicle. I ask him what went through his mind when Father Maurice suggested riding a motorcycle toward the center of an LRA attack.

"We were the only ones. The SPLA was not there to protect. They did not come until after Easter. And the people, they are just people of the village. They did not know what to do. There are no activists, no community leaders. There is no one who can be in the middle and try to talk with the LRA. Someone maybe they can trust. It is hard. These LRA are not very dependable. But I am a man of peace, and so I seek to make peace wherever I am. I am a priest, and I am supposed to be an image of Christ. So we just got on the motorcycle and went."

* * *

I have done eighteen months of ethnographic fieldwork in conflict and post-conflict northern Uganda and Eastern Equatoria state, South Sudan, between 2005 and 2013, and the Acholi people and their ethnic neighbors there have taught me three main things, and these lessons, if you will, thread through this book.[1] The first is that the vocation of the Christian is to reenact and, in this way, revivify Jesus of Nazareth, in whom God and human meet as Christ. And we are to do this in a way that instigates further such reenactment and revivification in ourselves and others. When Father Joseph says, "I am a man of peace, and so I seek to make peace wherever I am. . . . I am supposed to be an image of Christ. So we just got on the motorcycle and went," he is referring to just this kind of reenactment and revivification. Among technical academic terms, that of "mimesis" best conveys the various aspects of such activity.

This is a specific lesson for the practice of theology, namely, that theology, if it seeks to signify itself as *Christian* theology, must also be mimetic—that is, it must, *as theology*, itself seek to reenact and instigate others to reenact Jesus the Nazarene the Christ. I am here categorically rejecting the idea of theology as a "second-order" form of discourse that reflects *on* the practice of the Christian community as if standing outside of, or at least at a remove from, the activity of that community. If theology is simply a second-order discourse, then, to quote Flannery O'Connor's comment on the suggestion that the Eucharist is only a symbol, "to hell with it."[2] It must be the real body and blood, our own as well as Jesus Christ's, if what we are engaged in is to be deemed Christian theology.

Theology in a mimetic mode creates all sorts of difficulties for theology as it is largely practiced in the church and the academy today. This is first of all because mimetic theology is done and can only be done *in medias res*—in the middle of things—rather than at any absolute beginning or as if at a remove high above time and the contingencies of life. Mimetic theology, therefore, is decidedly *un*systematic theology. This is not to say that a Christian community cannot develop a relatively coherent and ordered fund of wisdom that it identifies as the received tradition. To be in the middle of things is to be part of a tradition and to carry it forward. It *is* to say, however, that that tradition is constantly being interrupted by life lived, and that theology serves life and God best when it is practiced with alertness for and openness to interruption. Interruption invites, prompts, and sometimes forces re-presentation of the tradition. This is the case even when the tradition at the formulaic level appears to be merely reasserted. We can assume that Father Joseph of Magwi, South Sudan, was taught in seminary that as a Christian and particularly as a priest he is called to imitate Christ. What he did not anticipate was the way in which the interruption of a decades-long war and a specific attack by the LRA would bring him—much like the original disciples—to a far different understanding of what such imitation requires. After Peter confesses that Jesus is the Christ, Jesus responds, "If any want to become my followers, let them deny themselves and take up their cross and follow me" (Mk 8:34). So Father Joseph "just got on the motorcycle and went." Interruption and re-presentation, again and again. Mimesis is, in the words of one commentator, always "on the move."[3]

Mimetic modes of re-presentation also create difficulties for theology because, traditionally, such modes are most fully performed orally, through the use and display of the whole range of physical senses—sight, smell, hearing, touch, and even taste—in a communal setting that invites immediate interpretation and response from active listeners. In their work, *Mimesis: Culture, Art and Society*, Gunter Gebauer and Christoph Wulf put it this way:

> In oral speech, the role of context is comparably more significant and extensive and is mediated more physically than in literate speech. . . . The speaker—in particular, the performing poet—puts himself physically into his performance. His presentation is not so much the recitation of an "inner text"; it demands, on the contrary, a high level of psychological and physical involvement. When the audience takes up the rhythm of speech and representation responsively, it becomes involved in the recitation emotionally and physically. The poet's representation amounts to a kind of physical pointing that grips and involves those present. . . . Spoken and heard sounds, rhythm, schema, melody, bodily movements, and shared participation together form a kind of dance.[4]

While mimesis at its fullest is oral, physical, and immediately communal, what we call theology is—with the exception of the few conferences we attend each year—for the far greater part *written* in a manner that *suppresses the physical senses* in articles and books that we expect to be *read in isolation* in library carrels and studies. It is not incidental that two of the major intellectual forces militating against mimetic modes of knowledge—the work of Plato and the development of Enlightenment understandings of reason—arose in conjunction with the ascendance and spread of written forms of expression, particularly where the texts were increasingly meant to be read rather than heard. Although most accounts of the suppression of mimesis focus on the ancient Platonic and modern Enlightenment moments, it is also important to highlight the role of developing Christianity and the Church, not least because of their reputation as having *fostered* the *imitatio Christi*. The alternative history I will provide stresses that ongoing contestation over religious authority in the Christian community has served to limit and even suppress members' reenactment and revivification of Jesus the Nazarene the Christ.

Such suppression of mimesis has terrible costs. Theology as it is practiced today is largely—one could say almost entirely—a discipline of texts.[5] Yet, in sub-Saharan Africa alone there are 200 million people who do not read or write. In the Internally Displaced Persons (IDP) camps in northern Uganda, where I did most of my work, the nonliteracy rate was 73 percent. Among women in South Sudan, where I also lived, it is 88 percent.[6] How do these and other similarly socially located people figure in what and to whom we write? Not to undertake methodologies that gather the perspectives, judgments, and patterns of life of such people risks—I would even say virtually assures—reinforcing the patterns of political and economic dominance that coincide with the rise of literate culture.

What are the prospects of doing theology in a way that does not suppress mimesis either in ourselves or in others? To argue that the suppression of mimesis has coincided with the rise of writing intended for solitary reading is not to say that writing in itself is necessarily anti-mimetic.[7] Rather, what I want to suggest is that the incorporation of the methods of ethnography into theology can help offset the liabilities of the practice of writing. When theologians talk about theological anthropology, they almost always mean not the use of ethnographic methods to raise theological questions, but rather a theologically inflected philosophical understanding of the human person. In using ethnographic methods, I want to turn theological anthropology on its head to read "anthropological theology"—any account of "the person" must be richly informed by how persons in fact live.[8]

What is first of all helpful about ethnographic research and writing is that it can have, when done well, a certain kind of evocative and provocative vividness because it engages the physical senses. With regard to the research aspect, two ethnographic methods in particular call for our attention: participant observation and the semi-structured or open-ended interview. Participant observation is the practice of living with a community in an intensive way for an extended period of time—typically a year at minimum—with the researcher involving herself in as full a range of the community's activity as possible—work, leisure, worship, food preparation, and meals—and is considered to be "the hallmark of traditional anthropological research."[9] Participant observation—or what Loïc Wacquant aptly calls "observant participation"[10]—forces us to use our physical senses—our eyes and ears, and our senses of smell, taste, and touch—instead of shutting them out as if they are a distraction. The "semi-structured interview"—a formal term for a careful and reflective conversation—allows the members of the community to provide their own accounts of who they are in the world. It requires the theologian to be a listener and, because the interview is open-ended, a participating responder. Participant observation and the open-ended interview are particularly important because they are among the only ways to take into account the lives and narratives of largely oral—that is to say, marginalized—cultures in our theologies. Ethnographic methods—with the detailed and sense-engaged attention to the lives of other people in their own terms as much as possible—provide a way to displace ourselves and our pretentions to authority.

The sociological, epistemological, and political forms of displacement that can take place during ethnographic research—the processes are far from automatic—are concrete conditions that facilitate *theological* mimesis. We cannot reenact and revivify Jesus the Nazarene the Christ without being in some manner displaced ourselves. The practice of ethnography, with the multiple forms of displacement that it involves—displacement made possible and vivid because we have engaged the physical senses—sets the concrete conditions in which the displacement of the self and openness to Jesus Christ becomes more possible. In Walter Benjamin's words, "sentience takes us out of ourselves."[11]

The wager is that that use of the physical senses and their capacity to displace the investigator in the research phase will carry over to the writing, and to the reader of that writing. The anthropologist Clifford Geertz refers to this kind of account as offering a "thick description" of what is going on.[12] Anthropological theology turns thick description to evangelistic purpose, not in the sense of traditional missionary anthropology, where the aim is to learn about the other culture so as to convert it, but to witness to each other as theologians as we have been witnessed to in the field, to re-present what we have seen and heard, smelled and touched. *Father Joseph crosses himself and says a prayer before he starts the vehicle. I ask him what went through his mind when Father Maurice suggested riding a motorcycle towards the center of an LRA attack. "It is hard. These LRA are not very dependable. But I am a man of peace, and so I seek to make peace wherever I am . . . I am supposed to be an image of Christ. So we just got on the motorcycle and went."*

Anthropological theology seeks to displace the reader from the library carrel or study so that she can draw upon her physical senses to place herself in the descriptive scene. It is an Ignatian spiritual exercise for academics *as academics*. To be sure, there will always be the tacking back and forth between scene and analysis. Critical analysis is also what we do. But the process of tacking back and forth between field description and analysis is itself part of what it means to be "in the middle of things," and to be mimetically always on the move.

Traditional devotion, radical witness

Father Joseph crossed himself and prayed again before he started the car for our trip back to Magwi after our visit with the bishop. And I am certain that he and Father Maurice did likewise before they rode their motorcycle toward the LRA. These may be habitual gestures, but they are not empty ones. They are part of a panoply of practices dramatizing a cosmology in which God and the saints respond to our beseechments. This is the second thing that the Acholi and their ethnic neighbors taught me: the task of mimesis is not all on us.

Edith Wyschogrod writes in *Saints and Postmodernism* about the impossibility, even for saints, of imitating Christ:

> A background belief of virtually all Christian hagiography is that saints live their lives in the light of Christ's life. *Imitatio Christi* is the apothegm that illuminates saintly contemplation and the command that guides saintly conduct. But if this is the imperative under which Christian saints labor, there is an insuperable obstacle to the success of their efforts. The infinite wisdom, power, and goodness of Christ are not re-presentable even by a spiritual elite. To the extent that the earthly ministry and passion of Jesus are paradigmatic, they are so in and through their transcendent ground. Human nature, however, cannot conform itself to divine perfection. Thus *imitatio Christi* is an unrealizable imperative because the life of Christ cannot be replicated.[13]

What Wyschogrod misses in her conclusion that because perfect imitation of Jesus Christ—or any other "other"—is impossible, there is an "insuperable obstacle to the success" of mimesis is the fact that, if the saints among the Acholi whom I encountered are right, the other is also "on the move" toward us. The aim of mimesis is not perfect imitation or sameness—as distinct from likeness—but our sufficiently adequate reenactment of the other such that the other responds. In the Christian account, the defining movement toward us is the Incarnation—God's becoming human—and this crossing over, this transgressing spirit-becoming-flesh, repeats itself often enough through restored bodies taking up their pallets and walking that adherents do not hesitate to ask for more. Prayer in the Catholic communities in northern Uganda and South Sudan is this ongoing request for an encore. Sister Josephine of the Little Sisters of Mary Immaculate of Gulu, an indigenous religious order, speaks to God in the middle of the Ebola outbreak that she is trying to stem and that itself is in the middle of the two-decade war: "Even if we are suffering, we still trust in You, but now could You save us from this? This suffering, could You relieve us? Could You stop this kind of sickness?"[14]

The word "pray" or "prayer" is not part of Wyschogrod's lexicon.[15] Her project, in the face of the deconstruction of ethical theory, turns to the lives of the saints as a way to divert the trajectory of postmodernism away from nihilism. However, she identifies explicitly religious understandings of sainthood as something "in the past" that we countenance in our own accounts only at the risk of "nostalgia."[16] She therefore works hard to distinguish—separate, really—the moral practice of saints from any encounters that they might have with God or other representatives of the broader cosmos. Such encounters, she avers, are "functionally distinct from the radical altruism that is *constitutive* of saintly practice" (emphasis in original).[17] For Wyschogrod, the irreplicablity of Jesus Christ leaves the saint reliant upon only herself; the only available strategy is to enter into a "necessarily extreme" form of "self-mortification" as a means of representing "unrepresentability itself."[18] But for persons like Fathers Joseph and Maurice and Sister Josephine, whose lives we might describe as saintly, any acts of self-abnegation—"And if they kill us, at least the others will have more time to get away"—are unintelligible apart from God's self-abnegation—God's movement—on their behalf.

The degree to which Western academics will sometimes read such spirit-crossings out of religious accounts is evident in the way that Wyschogrod draws a moral of personal responsibility in a random universe from the story of Mary the Egyptian. The story itself proceeds,

> Listen to the true story of Mary the Egyptian. . . . [She] was born in Egypt and was shameful even in her youth. . . . One day . . . she went to the port where a ship of pilgrims was arriving [and] asks to go with them to Jerusalem. . . . Shortly after [she came to Jerusalem] it was the feast of the Ascension. . . . [When] she was barred entry into the Temple . . . she comes to a realization of her sins . . . cries for mercy . . . [and is able to enter]. There a statue speaks to her: "Spend the rest of your life in the desert."
>
> For more than forty years she lived nude . . . like an animal. Zozima, a saintly monk . . . give[s] her a cloth to wrap herself in. . . . [Mary prays and rises] a full two and one half feet. [Mary later dies but her body does not decompose. After another year Zozima looks for her. Led on by a bright light, he finds the body and a letter instructing him to bury her, but the earth is too hard.] A lion came up to him. . . . The lion dug out the grave . . . [and] disappeared into the great desert. Zozima returns [and] recounts the life of Mary. We pray that Mary will intercede for us. And ask God to forgive our sins. Amen.[19]

There are four salient moments of other-response in the story—the response to Mary's cry of mercy that allows her to enter the temple, the talking statue, the bright light directing Zozima to Mary's body, and the intercession of the lion, otherwise a dangerous animal, to dig Mary's grave. And, in keeping with the ethos, there is also a plea for more—the authors' prayer to Mary to ask God to forgive their sins. Yet, for Wyschogrod, the lesson to be drawn from the story is simply, "Life is transformed not because of chance events but because an individual assumes responsibility for her/his actions."[20]

The Mary the Egyptian story is apropos for the Catholicism practiced in northern Uganda and South Sudan because of the shared conviction that God can operate through objects and unusual beings. Photos, paintings, crucifixes, and the elevated Host all serve as conduits of the spirit of Jesus. The biggest celebration each year is on the regionally recognized feast day—which in lived practice lasts three days—of Daudi Okello and Jildo Irwa, the "Acholi martyrs." Daudi and Jildo were young catechists—about fifteen and eighteen years old—killed by locals in 1918. The location of their martyrdom is called *Wipolo*—"heaven" or, literally, "on top of the sky"—and pilgrims visit the site to gain a foretaste of the beatific life. Some of the relics of Daudi and Jildo are in the parish church in Madi Opei, and Father Vincentio Olim recounts their intervention during the most recent war:[21]

> You know, I asked the parents of the parish if their girls who go to our school could sleep in the church because of the insecurities of going back and forth between school and home. It was May 29, 2003. They were sleeping on the floor in between pews.
>
> Somehow, the rebels got word of this and planned a raid to abduct them. Four came in with flashlights, but somehow they did not see the girls on the floor. The rebels left.

> Meanwhile, the UPDF [government military] began firing mortar shells. They fired a bazooka into the church and it hit the floor right on the engraving in the aisle, even splitting the relics of the *Wipolo* martyrs into two, creating a second martyrdom, with fragments scattering everywhere. The ceiling. Everywhere. Yet no shrapnel hit any of the girls.

This, then, is not religion in the Weberian sense, but something else. Max Weber counterposed (his understanding of) religion—that of radical monotheism—with what he called "magic": the invocation of the power of spirits to address life here on earth. Cosmologically, for Weber, while religion worships the one God, magic appeals to a variety of lesser spirits in attempts to manipulate them for human benefit. Ethically, religion is systematically ascetic while magic is lax: it lets the believer off the hook by substituting incantation and ritual for moral reform. Magic—the less pejorative term is "sacramentality"—is the enemy of ethics. Magic is also, according to Weber, a form of captivity experienced by incapable or weak-willed Christians. He writes that in the effort to win and hold converts, priests of the Christian community had "to *compromise* with the traditional views of the laity in formulating patterns of doctrine and behavior." Such compromise meant that priests were unable to release "the faith of the masses from its *bondage* to traditions based upon magic" (emphasis added).[22] Following this interpretive lead, historians writing out of the Weberian tradition understand Catholic syncretism to be a "concession" to paganism, one which is "now all rightly disdained by intelligent persons."[23]

I draw from exemplars like Fathers Joseph and Maurice and Sister Josephine to argue that it is precisely a magical Christianity that leverages their radical witness during the overlapping wars in northern Uganda and South Sudan. Two immediate sources feed into their practices. One is the Tridentine Christianity brought by the Comboni missionaries who first evangelized the region. The Combonis, with practices such as the Adoration of the Eucharist, the devotion to the Sacred Heart of Jesus, and the veneration of saints, together with the belief in the worldly efficaciousness of such practices, brought precisely that "compromised" Christianity that Weberians disdain. More, despite protestations to the contrary on the part of the early missionaries, this strand of Christianity meshed well with the other source of magical thought in the region, traditional Acholi culture. With the latter, spirits—called *jogi*—of the dead continue to interact with the people who remain on earth. The dead are buried in family compounds so that they can continue to dwell where they always have. (To the Acholi, the idea of separate cemeteries is a bizarre one. Why cast off our ancestors just because they are dead?) Families keep ancestral shrines, called *abila*, sites where interaction with spirits is intensified. More recently, there is greater recognition of the confluences between Catholic Christianity and traditional Acholi culture. One nun told me, for instance,

> The ancestral shrine; I remember my grandfather had it in the compound, mm? So what do they believe? They believe that the spirit of those who have died a long time

ago is there. And if we seek blessing, we should ask through them. . . . They believe that those who have died long ago, they are not buried completely; they are alive.

And I think that this also could be connected with our Christianity, because we believe in the saints. The saints are our ancestors. That is why we always also pray to them, ask to God through them, mm?[24]

The actions evidenced by persons like Fathers Joseph and Maurice and Sister Josephine indicate that the Weberian opposition between magic or sacramentality on the one hand and a profoundly moral witness on the other is a false one. In fact, in this case it is precisely such magic that funds the witness.

The third and more remote source, at least in terms of historical distance, of the magical cosmology of the Catholic Christianity in northern Uganda and South Sudan is the gospels themselves. Anthropological attention to the culture of Jesus the Nazarene discloses that he, too, in the words of biblical scholar John Pilch, ministered in a "densely populated spirit world."[25] Indeed, it is precisely Jesus's engagement with spirits through healings and exorcisms that publicly leverages his authority to speak on theological matters.[26] I take this and other cultural commonalities between the world of the ancient Near East and that of contemporary northern Uganda and South Sudan to make the case that the latter can serve as "bridge cultures" to the former for the rest of us. In other words, anthropological attention to the practices of Catholic Christianity and traditional culture in the region serves not only the *practical* purpose of discerning how people like Fathers Joseph and Maurice and Sister Josephine manage to witness as they do, but also the *theological* purpose of helping to limn just what constitutes Gospel witness. From this perspective, magical Christianity is not only not a compromise, but our best bet to get the Gospel right. What we are after here is not simply a "radical" witness in the sense that it involves a willingness to risk one's life—though it includes that—but that kind of witness that goes to the *radix* or root of all there is, and that is the life, death, resurrection, and promise of return of Jesus the Nazarene the Christ as told in the gospels. In this way, reading the gospels through the lens of the beliefs and practices of Catholic Christianity and traditional Acholi culture in northern Uganda and South Sudan can serve as a theological corrective for the distortions of modern biblical scholarship. A rich sacramentality—a magical mind, if you will—is not an impediment to Christian life; rather it is one of the few things that have kept Christianity true, to whatever extent it has been, to Jesus the Nazarene the Christ.

Risk in the middle of things

"I have a favor to ask."

I say this in my most importunate voice. I am meeting with Ben Phillips, the Uganda Country Program Director for Catholic Relief Services. We have been in his office for an hour talking about the conflict in northern Uganda. The LRA, early on representative of the Acholi people of the North, has by now abducted between twenty-five and sixty-five thousand people in the region to be porters, soldiers, and sex slaves, and has mutilated or murdered thousands more. The soldiers of the Uganda People's Defense Force (UPDF), sent by the government ostensibly to protect the Acholi, have committed rights abuses of their own. It can be difficult to get around in the region, and I need Ben's help.

"Last summer CRS was kind enough to provide a car and driver to get me places around Gulu. I am wondering if it could do the same this trip in the Kitgum and Pader districts. I want to get to some more outlying areas."

"We could accommodate that. You would need to cover the cost of the driver. Also, we would need to know your views on travel with UPDF military escort. If you are unwilling to travel with escort, then you would be limited to visiting locations which CRS has assessed as being safe enough to reach without escort."

I mull over Ben's words, then answer.

"I think I'll make other arrangements. Thanks for hearing me out."

"I fully understand."

We get up from our chairs and, while shaking hands, I ask Ben, mostly out of courtesy after declining his offer, "Any final advice?"

He replies, "If you are on a road and no one is coming toward you, you are heading directly into the LRA. The people have scattered."

* * *

Anthropological theology, with its emphasis on the real body and blood of both the researcher and the persons researched, requires thick description of the attempt to practice gospel mimesis. As the actions of Fathers Joseph and Maurice and Sister Josephine evidence in a dramatic way, a life of solidarity with the poor and forgiveness of the wicked involve risks. Far from all risks will be life-threatening in the same way, but their witness makes poignant the third thing shown to me in my fieldwork: the practice of gospel mimesis takes place in a field of patterned violent mimesis, and this means that, while it is not the aim of gospel mimesis, risk is inherent in its practice. In my own case, it meant that from the start the government assumed that I was a spy and spied on me. It also meant that people marginalized and oppressed by the government regularly saw me as a resource for getting their story to the rest of the world. One man, for instance, arranged a secret meeting in the back room of a store to tell me, "I need your help. God has sent you to me. I have kept careful documentation. I have kept a diary for ten years. Everything is there. Names. Dates. . . . I can give you the names of people in the ground."

Some of the more difficult risks to assess are those that come from the institutions with whom one is seemingly allied. The early Comboni missionaries to northern Uganda and South Sudan often relied for transportation and supplies on the British who were colonizing the region; the 1885 General Act of the Berlin Conference, which divvied up Africa among the European powers, also gave the British the right to expel the missionaries—who came from Austria and Italy—if the latter did not cooperate. At first the missionaries were willing, in keeping with Daniel Comboni's theology of the Cross, to lay down their lives in the process of preaching the Gospel, and Comboni himself, the founder of the order that would then bear his name, was sharply critical of explorers like Samuel Baker. However, Comboni and his followers soon found it more "prudent to keep quiet" than protest against the colonial displacement, forced labor, and even murder of the locals.[27] There are repercussions, once one aligns one's vocation with an organizational body that is seeking to expand its operational institutional influence and authority, to imitating Christ in a way that involves the willingness to die rather than to remain silent or to take recourse in violence. This is as true in the current global political and academic context as it was in the early twentieth century: our research abroad is often premised on not disturbing the operative relations between our universities on the one hand and both domestic and foreign governments on the other.

Theology done "in the middle of things" must offer, *as intrinsic parts of that theology*, both thick descriptions of and considered reflection on the risks involved in each case. Such anthropological theology rejects the separation between "fundamental" or "foundational" theology on the one hand and "applied," "practical," or "pastoral" theology on the other. These separations, articulated with the tacit or expressed assumption of the priority of the fundamental/foundational and the derivative nature of the applied/practical/pastoral, rely on an untenable view that theology can be done from "nowhere," that is, without the shaping influence of the location in which it is done and from which it has responsibility.[28] In the case of Uganda, a theology of colonialism and neocolonialism pulses through the patterned violent mimesis evident in the country, a theology which, as Frantz Fanon first pointed out, is Manichean.[29] Laying out Manichean colonialism and neocolonialism below will enable me to provide up front a brief interpretive account of the conflict that is the setting of my research and the geopolitical backstory of everything in this book. This in turn will allow me to discuss my own social location in relation to the people of northern Uganda and South Sudan.

The global theological context of the "War in the North"

The Persian prophet Mani (AD 210–276) held, *contra* orthodox Christianity, that there was no one God, but rather that the cosmos was constructed of counterposed forces of light and darkness. The task of the adherent was to take on the quality of light and so enter into battle with darkness. St. Augustine famously first embraced and then condemned Manicheanism as a heresy. Colonialism, in contrast, whatever the claims of its practitioners to be Christian, superimposes a Manichean worldview onto society, supplementing the terms "light" versus "dark"—fortuitously allied with skin color—with those of "civilized" verses "primitive" and "modern" versus "backward." Colonial economic, political, and military power enforced this worldview through a wide range of mechanisms of regimentation of indigenous peoples, from displacement and taxation to forced labor and genocide.[30] In Uganda, the British colonized through what they termed "indirect" rule: they designated one indigenous group to rule over the others on behalf of the empire.[31] Indirect rule, together with bureaucratic order, hardened and reified ethnic differences by casting African against African.[32] The British appointed the Baganda people in the South, who already had a centralized political system that more closely resembled that of the colonizers, the administrators of the "protectorate."

Over 110 years later, a form of indirect rule continues in Uganda. After victory in a five-year bush war (1980–5), present president Yoweri Museveni and his National Resistance Movement/Army (NRM/A) chased the defeated opponents from northern Uganda back to their homes in Acholiland, raiding goods and massacring people along the way. An excerpt from an interview I gathered with an Acholi *ladit*, or male elder:

I will not forget the killing close to my house in Koc Laminatoo. Eighteen young people, who were in my neighborhood, were picked by the National Resistance Army rebels of [current Ugandan president] Yoweri Museveni, and they were supposed to have been brought to Anaka where there was a military base. The boys were asked to take hoes from my house where I had left them out after digging. And, with those hoes, they dug their own graves, on the mouth of River Ayago. And there, they got killed, one-by-one, and buried in the graves they themselves dug.

The parents and relatives of these eighteen young men were looking for them around, and they could not find where they were. They were buried on the mouth on the River Ayago—their hands and their legs having been broken, and their heads all beaten with heavy logs.

My uncle became one of the people in the area that discovered, that found, the place where the young boys were buried when he went to get some reeds to prepare a granary at home. He smelled a strong smell and he became suspicious about the smell, and he went to look at what was smelling—it was the decomposing bodies of the eighteen people who had been killed.

When my uncle saw this, along with other people that joined him in the search of the strong, smelly thing in the jungle, they went to the head of the village of Laminatoo, where we lived. The leader of the village then invited the people whose young men were lost to come and see if any of those dead were the boys they were looking for. Indeed, those who found their sons dead took the body and went home to bury.

This became a big source of fear for the people of the area. This happened in 1986. It is something that is so sad in my memory—is so sad in my life—that I have witnessed.[33]

To justify such actions and the policies which backed them, Museveni appealed to—mimicked—the Manichean colonial language of "modern" society civilizing those who are "backward." Statements from the president to this effect bookend the conflict in northern Uganda. In 1987, in reference to the battles with the Holy Spirit Movement—the precursor to the LRA—Museveni asserted, "This is a conflict between modernity and primitivity."[34] In 2006, at the installation of Sabino Odoki as Auxiliary Bishop of Gulu, and just a month before the ceasefire with the LRA, Museveni claimed, "We shall transform the people in the north from material and spiritual backwardness to modernity."[35] From the beginning of the conflict up to its end in Uganda, then, Museveni accessed the language of backward/primitive versus civilized/modern to frame events. More, his NRM/A government has received up to half of its budget from foreign aid in a way that reinforces his more than thirty-year presidency and lack of democratic accountability. What took place between 1986 and 2006 and is continuing in Uganda today is de facto indirect rule by the donor nations: Museveni serves the latter's geostrategic interests; they allow him to rule in perpetuity.

With the constant political, economic, and cultural pressure, the Acholi tried to resist the NRM/A under a series of spirit-medium leaders. The first was Alice "Lakwena" Auma.[36] The members of Lakwena's Holy Spirit Movement—smeared with shea nut oil to protect them from bullets and often armed with stones that they believed would turn into grenades—fought their way south and, strikingly, made it to within seventy miles of the capital before being routed in 1987. The movement was much like the American Indian Ghost Shirt Societies that resisted, to similar effect, settler "Manifest Destiny" expansion in the United States: under enormous pressure, these spirit-engaged cultures mutated in an effort to stave off cultural and physical extinction.

In the case of northern Uganda, it was not the last mutation to take place. By 1988, some Acholi reconstituted themselves under the spirit medium Joseph Kony into what would become the LRA. The LRA did not meet even with the kind of initial military success that the Holy Spirit Movement had managed to engineer, and most Acholi, while sympathetic to the cause, did not find further armed conflict with Museveni's forces to be wise. Citing betrayal, the leadership of the LRA turned its violence on its own Acholi people, abducting youth for its ranks and grotesquely mutilating and killing others. From another interview:

The rebels came, picked my child and me up from the house, and walked us outside the trading center with many people—women, men, old people, students, and young people who did not go to school. The rebels walked all of us across a river. There, at some point, we were made to sit down. At that point they started telling us, "If you know you are pregnant, if you know you have a baby, if you are below twelve years of age, go this way; and the rest of the people go the other way." I saw at one side a group of young people, mainly technical school students and women without babies. The rebels ordered them to lie down on their stomach. They then called the young rebels and they told them to shoot them. I heard shots. All these people were killed. A few other people that were seen alive were chopped to death with a machete.

Having killed all these young people and the women who were with them, they turned to us. "Do you see this lesson? Do you see? You have been cursing us. Some of you have been raising their breasts in curse of us. Has that curse helped you? Does that curse help you at all? Do you see our guns? These rusted guns that you despise, the guns you said are rusted, that can do nothing? Have you seen what these guns have done to you? Go tell your people this is what will happen to them."

When they finished their job, they asked us to clap our hands in thankfulness to them. They asked us to laugh at what they had done. We laughed. We followed all of the instructions they gave us for fear they would kill us also. In the end, they let us free to tell all the uncles, the aunts of all those who had been killed of what we had seen.

Adam Branch has argued, convincingly in my judgment, that the LRA leadership viewed itself as purging the enemy from within, thus making the Acholi a purer and more worthy opponent of the Museveni regime.[37] Using Rene Girard's language, in an instance of colonial mimetic "contagion," Museveni attempted to make the Acholi the national "scapegoat" for all of the social disruption and atrocities that took place in the 1980–5 bush war; however, unlike in Girard's theory, this did not lead to resolution of the conflict.[38] Rather, the LRA leaders, refusing to be so labeled, scapegoated their own people. *Do you see this lesson? Do you see? You have been cursing us. . . . Does that curse help you at all? Do you see our guns? These rusted guns that you despise, the guns you said are rusted, that can do nothing? Have you seen what these guns have done to you? Go tell your people this is what will happen to them.*

It gets worse. In 1996, citing the threatened security of the Acholi, Museveni ordered all people in Gulu district not living in towns to move to "protected" IDP camps. Refusal to go to the camps on the part of the people met with armed attack by the NRM/A's newly constituted army, the UPDF. The camps concentrated the population. By 2005, over 90 percent of the people in the north lived in them. Numerically, this constituted over a million Acholi and between 1.6 and 1.8 million people overall. The camps became LRA magnets. One peasant farmer told me, "The government soldiers who were protecting us were few. Many times when these people [the LRA] came, they [the government soldiers] ran away. They could not protect the people in the camp, and the rebels would abduct people at will. The rebels would burn houses at will. The rebels would do whatever they wanted at will."

In between massacres, even more people died in the IDP camps in northern Uganda. In 2005, the year I started going to the region, a World Health Organization study, after careful analysis of the situation on the ground in comparison with "non-crisis" levels in the IDP camps in the Acholiland districts of Kitgum, Pader, and Gulu, found that there were almost a thousand excess deaths per *week* due to such causes as AIDS, malnutrition, diarrhea, and malaria.[39] Chris Dolan of the Refugee Law Project calls the forced displacement "social torture," a "form of mass torture, whose principal victims are the population in the 'war zone', and whose ultimate function is the subordinate inclusion of the population in northern Uganda."[40]

In 2006, the LRA and the government finally agreed to a temporary ceasefire. The 2006–8 peace talks held in Juba, South Sudan, were an attempt to politically and psychologically normalize the conflict so as to make negotiated settlement possible. Even Joseph Kony—miming the dress code of the post-Westphalian international order—cut his signature dreadlocks, took off his aviator sunglasses, and showed up in a suit and tie. However, signing of the final full agreement did not, and perhaps could not, happen. Western media stress that Kony never showed up for the signing; however, Museveni did not even offer to show. When asked about the prospects of the peace talks, the latter replied, "Let me be categorical—there will only be a military solution to this problem."[41]

Violent mimetic contagion does not allow for resolution of conflict, if it does at all, without someone being killed. In December 2008, the Ugandan military, assisted by seventeen US advisors and $1 million in financial support, ended the ceasefire with "Operation Lightning Thunder," an attack on LRA bases in the Democratic Republic of Congo (DRC). It failed miserably in its objectives, succeeding only to anger the rebels, who then went on a month-long rampage, killing between 800 and 1,000 Congolese civilians—the de facto new scapegoats—whose vulnerability did not figure in operation contingency planning.

As I write (March 2018), Kony and the remaining LRA are biding their time in back bases in the DRC, South Sudan, and the Central African Republic. The United States spent $780 million in the decade between 2008 and 2017 in the effort to capture or kill Kony. At any given time, there were 150 US special forces and 1,500 Ugandan troops involved in the effort, but their governments gave up the operation in late April 2017.[42] They more than failed in their objective: the United Nations is investigating multiple reports of "rape, sexual slavery, and the exploitation of young girls" in the Central African Republic on the part of the Ugandan military.[43] Meanwhile, Museveni, who has already had the Ugandan constitution altered to allow him to remain in power even after more than thirty years of rule, attempted to push through yet another change in the founding document to permit the incarceration of protesters—under the rubric of "economic sabotage"—for six months without bail.[44] In May and June 2011, Ugandan security personnel shot and killed nine people peacefully protesting skyrocketing fuel and food prices. When priests decried the actions, they were charged with "incitement against the government."[45] Intimidation and even the disappearance of journalists who dare criticize the government continue unabated.[46] When pressed, one US State Department official said, "We're watching the situation very carefully. But we aren't considering sanctions."[47] In response to the intimidation and detention of opposition candidates during the 2016 Uganda presidential elections, the US Department of State issued a brief statement of concern, but, as before, sanctions were not forthcoming.[48] Indirect rule continues.

This is the context within which any gospel mimesis in the region takes place.

Because of the centrality in anthropological theology of the claim that where we are socially located shapes what we see and know and, consequently, how we respond, it is important in the last substantive section of this chapter to limn my own social location as an academic theologian in relation to the people of northern Uganda and South Sudan. We always enter into fieldwork from somewhere else, and reflexive awareness of that "somewhere else" on our part is necessary to avoid distorted accounts that we view and understand the field in question in the same way, with no slippage, as those who are indigenous to the region. In the case of anthropological *theology*—as distinct from anthropology as it is usually practiced—it is necessary to offer, from the start, at least an initial account of our *theo*-social location, that is to say, not just an account of our social location relative to those whom we are studying, but of all of that in relation to God.[49] For this, the stories of the rich young man and of Zacchaeus are particularly helpful.

The rich young man, Zacchaeus, and academic capital

As he was setting out on a journey, a man ran up and knelt before him, and asked him, "Good teacher, what must I do to inherit eternal life?"

Jesus said to him, "Why do you call me good? No one is good but God alone. You know the commandments: 'You shall not murder; You shall not commit adultery; You shall not steal; You shall not bear false witness; You shall not defraud; Honor your father and mother.'"

He said to him, "Teacher, I have kept all these since my youth."

Jesus, looking at him, loved him and said, "You lack one thing; go, sell what you own, and give the money to the poor, and you will have treasure in heaven; then come, follow me."

When he heard this, he was shocked and went away grieving, for he had many possessions.

Then Jesus looked around and said to his disciples, "How hard it will be for those who have wealth to enter the kingdom of God." And the disciples were perplexed at these words. But Jesus said to them again, "Children, how hard it is for a rich person to enter the kingdom of God. It is easier for a camel to go through the eye of a needle than for someone who is rich to enter the kingdom of God."

They were greatly astounded and said to one another, "then who can be saved?"

Jesus looked at them and said, "For mortals it is impossible, but not for God; for God, all things are possible."

Peter began to say to him, "Look, we have left everything and followed you."

Jesus said, "Truly I tell you, there is no one who has left house or brothers or sisters or mother or father or children or fields, for my sake and for the sake of the good news, who will not receive a hundredfold now in this age—houses, brothers and sisters, mothers and children, and fields with persecutions—and in the age to come eternal life. But many who are first will be last, and the last will be first." (Mk 10:17-31; cf. Mt. 19:16-30 and Lk. 18:18-30)

When the theology we are practicing is an anthropological one, the starting point is Jesus the Nazarene the Christ in his social location. We begin here because, following anthropology's emphasis on the particular, we affirm the significance of the fact that God chose to save humankind through this particular person at this particular time and place. We start here theologically in recognition of Christ's humanity, or more precisely, Christ's humanity-in-social-relation. Beginning elsewhere can feed a theologian's docetic temptation—the desire, however subtle or masked, to suggest that Christ only appeared to be human.

I will argue more fully in this book that Jesus's primary missions are to the poor and the wicked.[50] We can deepen our sense of how Jesus locates himself in the world by noting those to whom Jesus does not have a primary mission: the wealthy and the righteous ("I have come to call not the righteous but sinners," Mk 2:17b; cf. Mt. 9:13b and Lk. 5:32). Interpreters who seek to blunt the emphasis on the poor and to create a greater opening for the wealthy to enter the Kingdom often take one of two strategies. The first, as in the case of Max Weber, fixes on Jesus's statement that "for God all things are possible," and ignores the exchange with the rich man itself and the immediately ensuing response to Peter: all those who leave everything and follow Jesus will have eternal life, while "many who are first will be last, and the last will be first."[51] The second strategy is to note that Jesus also has positive relations with some wealthy people.[52] After all, Jesus does say only that "many" who are first will be last. Zacchaeus is the prime example cited here. He does not have to sell all of his goods, but only offer to give away half of his wealth, and Jesus offers salvation (Lk. 19:1-9).

How to make sense of the few wealthy persons who appear to make it? In light of the stories of the rich young man and Zacchaeus, together with other pericopes, it is possible to interpret Jesus's statements without distorting them by recognizing that after the categories of the poor and the wicked on the one hand and the rich and the righteous on the other, there is an important fifth player in Jesus's theo-social world: the persistent.[53] The gospels offer a number of accounts of persons who are not included in Jesus's initial understanding of his primary mission, but, because of their persistence, come to be included. Perhaps most stark is the story of the Syrophoenician—that is, Gentile—woman, who approaches Jesus to heal her daughter of an unclean spirit (Mk 7:24-30; Mt. 15:21-28). Jesus's reply is hardly an invitation to the Kingdom: "It is not fair to take the children's food and throw it to the dogs." Yet the woman persists: "Even the dogs under the table eat the children's crumbs." Jesus, in a turnabout, exclaims at her faith and heals her daughter. There are other stories of persistence: those of a Roman centurion, who recognizes his unworthiness (Mt. 8:5-13), Jairus, who begs Jesus "repeatedly" to heal his daughter (Mk 5:22-43; Lk. 8:41-56), and the unnamed and initially unseen—"Who touched me?"—woman who struggles through a crowd not just to hear but to make physical contact with Jesus (Mk 5:21-43; Lk. 8:40-56).

Despite the seeming difference in what is required of each—give all or just half of one's wealth—it is helpful to interpret the stories of the rich young man and Zacchaeus in light of the theme of persistence. The rich young man persists first of all in approaching Jesus to ask, on his knees, his initial question of what it takes to inherit eternal life (rather than to deride Jesus's message as do most of the wealthy and powerful in the gospels). Then he presses more after Jesus gives his initial response of listing most of the second table of the Decalogue. However, when the rich young man hears the more stringent demands of following Jesus, he stops persisting and turns away. Zacchaeus demonstrates his persistence first of all by making the extra effort to climb a tree in order to see and hear Jesus. Jesus recognizes the effort—a sign of interest on Zacchaeus's part parallel to the initial questioning by the rich young man—and invites him to further engagement, interestingly, by demanding to be a guest: "I must stay at your house today." Zacchaeus responds positively. He not only "hurried down" the tree and "was happy to welcome him," but then offers, without Jesus's prompting, to give away half of his wealth. In other words, though the terms of acceptance into the Kingdom are different than those of the rich young man, they are still dramatic enough to signal Zacchaeus's persistence.

The difference between the demand made on the rich young man to sell all he has for the poor and the acceptability of Zacchaeus's offer to give away half of his wealth is of a piece with Jesus's sociologically oriented two-tiered ethic, one tier shaped for those who follow him quite literally in his itinerancy and one oriented to those who remain in settled lives but who offer material support for the itinerants. While Jesus grants itinerant followers greater latitude on purity Sabbath laws—for instance, on the question of picking grain on the Sabbath—the *economic* demands are far greater—as is evidenced in his short list of what to take on the journey when he sends them out to evangelize and heal.[54] In response, Jesus commissions the itinerant disciple with the authority to more fully imitate him in his ministry (Mk 6:6b-13; Lk. 9:1-6 and 10:1-16; Mt. 9:35–10:16). Those who remain in settled lives do not have such authority, and have less leeway on ritual issues; but they also have relatively less demanded of them economically. Still, giving away half of one's income is no small life alteration, and it is clear from the Zacchaeus story that there is also the expectation of hospitality—to Jesus and to the poor and the wicked with whom he associates.

It is crucial to recognize that what prompts Zacchaeus's offer of largesse is the charge from others that he is wicked. "All who saw it began to grumble and said, 'He [Jesus] has gone to be the guest of one who is a sinner.'" It is then that Zacchaeus, in his defense, makes his offer, "Look, half of my possessions, Lord, I will give to the poor; and if I have defrauded anyone of anything, I will pay back four times as much." Jesus does not challenge the depiction of Zacchaeus as a sinner. In fact, he concludes the exchange by saying, "For the Son of Man came to seek out and to save the lost." In other words, rather than a mechanism that allows the rich person to get through the eye of the needle, the story of Zacchaeus functions to identify the wealthy as among the wicked, of a kind with tax collectors and prostitutes. This interpretation fits with the anthropological observation that in ancient Mediterranean culture, the accumulation of wealth was dishonorable.[55]

The story of Zacchaeus is of a piece, then, with those of the prodigal son, the lost sheep, and the lost coin, also prominent in Luke, and is hardly a basis on which to argue that the rich readily enter the Kingdom of God. In fact, read correctly, Zacchaeus, after giving away half of his wealth and repaying fourfold those whom he has defrauded, will no longer be whatever counts as wealthy. Otherwise, the depiction of him as one who was lost before the promise of the gift to the poor and found afterward makes no sense. It might be tempting to interpret Zacchaeus's sin not as that of being rich, but that of being a chief tax collector, because taxes were a means through which Rome oppressed the people of Israel. However, Zacchaeus does not offer to change his profession, only what he does with his income, and Jesus still offers salvation.

The reason that Jesus does not include the wealthy, although wicked, in his primary mission is that, as Weber has shown, sociologically the rich, in contrast to the poor, do not often view themselves as in need of salvation.[56] In other words, most rich count themselves as already among the righteous, and Jesus, as we have seen, did not come for the righteous. The few wealthy persons who persist—who, in other words, do not consider themselves to be righteous—gain Jesus's attention, and the offer, upon repentance and a dramatic conversion with economic consequences, of the Kingdom.

* * *

"What are you going to do for us?"

It is my last night in Pabbo camp, and I have rejoined the group of men whom I have come to call in my notes the "Teachers' Drinking Club." At 65,000 people, Pabbo is the largest of the camps, formed, like the others, when the army set up a small outpost, drew a perimeter line, and declared that everyone in the local villages had to live within it. As more people moved in, there was less room for new huts, until the point where, now, the thatch from one hut touches that of the next. The straw stalks jut out like spears, so people walk about in a permanent stoop so as to avoid getting pierced. The roofs are topped by flame-retardant United Nations powder-blue tarps because people cook in their huts, and if one dwelling goes up in flames, then four hundred do.

Each night after work, the men of the Teachers' Drinking Club sit on benches in a circle around a clay urn full of alcoholic mash and drink the brew through four-foot bamboo straws. Most of them are teachers in the secondary school. The camp has not been attacked by the rebels in two years, but a burned-out school bus three kilometers north reminds people that the rebels prefer to set them on fire than to shoot them.

"We know you have your research. But what are you going to do for us?"

Olum is the macro-theorist among the teachers. To him, it is not a matter of the rebels versus the government. "The white man gives us guns so that we keep busy killing each other." The others look away, or take another sip of their mash, but none say anything in disagreement. Perhaps they are uncomfortable because they might lose a potential patron. I have promised to see their school tomorrow before heading to Gulu. Olum is undaunted. "Then you come and steal our knowledge. You steal our culture. You come and talk to us about our knowledge and our culture and then take it all back with you. And we have nothing left. Look at us. You see how we live. What are you going to do for us?"[57]

* * *

There are debates in the United States about whether professors are paid too much, but focus on our annual income is misplaced if the main concern is with the obstacles to our following Christ. It is at this point that Pierre Bourdieu's distinction between economic and cultural capital, and his insistence, *contra* Marx, that the latter is not simply an epiphenomenon of the former, becomes important for interpreting, from the perspective of gospel mimesis, the practice of academia.[58] The pursuit of both types of capital takes place in "fields" (translated from the French word, *champs*) of engagement and competition; while capital in the economic field is constituted by money, that in the cultural field takes the form of symbolic goods, the outward signs of prestige—like endowed chairs—in particular.[59] Different forms of capital can be exchanged. For instance, an affluent person in the field of business can donate money to a university to put up a building—say, for an institute or particular school of studies—with his name on it. Though his business practice may have little if anything to do with the subject of the school, he gains symbolic capital in the academic field by the association of his name with the institute's building. Conversely, a politician can trade in her symbolic capital from being a member of a presidential administration and convert it to economic capital by leaving office and lending her name and influence to a lobbying firm. Bourdieu has not hesitated to bring his analysis of the struggle over cultural capital and symbolic goods to bear on the academy,[60] and although his focus is on French higher education, his distinctions are helpful for elucidating what is at stake for professors at US colleges and universities, particularly with those schools that are considered prestigious by such rankings as those found annually in *US News and World Report*.[61]

Within the context of relatively prestigious universities in the United States, the primary forms of cultural capital are refereed articles in elite journals and books published by university presses themselves considered to be prestigious.[62] The aim of the junior professor is to accumulate enough of these basic forms of academic capital to exchange them after six years for tenure. Bourdieu often uses terms drawn from the religious field to describe practice across the full range of social fields—for instance, he calls the exchange of one kind of capital for another, "transubstantiation"[63]—and in the context of academia in the United States, it would not be inaccurate to call tenure "academic ordination": once consecrated with tenure, a professor can be defrocked only by exhibiting behavior described in professional codes as "moral turpitude."

Until anointed with tenure, the academic's life is a series of all-or-nothing tests of worthiness: acceptance into a prestigious program, passage of exams, completion of the dissertation, the offer of a tenure-track position, promotion, and ultimately tenure itself. Bourdieu often describes competition in the various fields—whether economic or cultural—by analogy to sports (thus his reference to "fields" of competition), and the dynamic in the academic field is that, until tenure, one has to be, with few exceptions, undefeated. Lose at any one of the key transition points, and one is out of the game, or at best is cast into the academic version of limbo, adjunct status. It is worth noting that the ante is upped by the fact that the rookie player has sacrificed considerable economic capital—tuition, the loss of time earning a salary, loans that place the graduate in financial debt—in order to join the academic game in the first place. Friends of mine in the business world complain of the comfort of academic life under the protection of tenure, but they always miss the fact that we academics frontload all of our risk. Business people can and do bounce back from major losses, even bankruptcy; academics rarely do. Given the all-or-nothing dynamic of the early stages of the accrual of academic capital, the graduate student and junior professor are necessarily placed in the position of the rich young man: in order to practice a robust solidarity with the poor and the wicked, the graduate student and junior professor would have to risk *all* that they own in academic capital.

It might be objected here that one can use one's academic capital *as academic capital* on behalf of the poor and the wicked, but three factors in the modern academy work against this as a widely viable option. The first and more basic is the modern academy's turn away from the tradition of practical reason in favor of "pure" or theoretical reason, a trend that Bourdieu himself critiques.[64] In F. H. Bradley's all-too-gleeful words in 1884, practical reason in the academy "has been placed on the shelf of interesting illusions."[65] Arguments that theory-weighted scholarly books and articles will eventually have an impact, however indirect, on the lives of the poor and the wicked amount to a trickle-down theory of academic capital, with about the same impact as its namesake theory in the field of economic capital. The second factor, a function of the first but felt most immediately in the life of the junior professor, is the academy's emphasis on publishing in journals deemed to be elite and university presses: the emphasis is on writing for a small circle of persons considered experts—the already consecrated. Online journals that might reach a wider audience are suspect; similarly, more widely read nonuniversity press publishers are merely "trade" presses, and lack the necessary prestige. Third, ethnographically grounded research typically takes longer to produce—the scholar must both have facility with theory and live and interpret the complexities of life lived by a community in a particular context.[66] The junior professor, however, is on a strict timeline of advancement, and taking the time to be present with the poor and the wicked through fieldwork rather than to glean what one can from books is therefore itself a risk to advancement in virtually all academic fields except anthropology and certain types of sociology.[67] Given these factors that resist research that directly engages the poor and the wicked, combined with the all-or-nothing stakes until tenure, the likelihood at this stage of professional development of a scholarship, even a theology, driven and shaped by gospel mimesis is, at best, extremely small, and limited to only the most heroic of people or the most unusual of circumstances.

Things change with tenure, which is the context of my own theo-social location within the academy. Post-tenure, the professor has three basic options. The first is to continue in the pretenure manner of operating; that is to say, to have the accrual of cultural capital in the academic game be the prime mover of practice. Bourdieu's concept of *habitus* goes a long way toward explaining why it is that many tenured professors proceed in this way. *Habitus* is both the ingrained habit of perceiving the world in a certain way and the disposition to respond in accordance with the world as perceived. Though the term is indebted to the idea of *habitus* found, for instance, in Aristotle and Aquinas, Bourdieu places much more emphasis on how class and status in a particular field of struggle shape perception and disposition. This emendation helps explain, at least in part, the tendency of professors, despite the change in status to the tenured class, to continue to practice in the pretenure pattern of perceiving that any reallocation of time and effort to practices other than the academic game is a threat to all of one's accumulated capital. Graduate school plus junior professorship together constitute at a minimum a decade, and more often closer to fifteen years, of academic formation. As a result, the disposition to perceive the world as if the academic game is an all-or-nothing field of struggle continues. In Bourdieu's words, *habitus* is "embodied history, internalized as second nature."[68] Ongoing incentives—pay raises and promotion to full professor—work to further embed this second nature.

The second option involves the awareness that it is, to use Bourdieu's term, a "misrecognition" to perceive the academic field as somehow natural and therefore necessary in its structure, but in this case it is an awareness without the identification of a viable alternative practice. This option may be the result, quite literally, of disillusionment. The professor acts simply by ceasing to write, or at least to write as much as before. The problem here, if it is left at this, is that the professor continues to live on what he or she considers to be the ill-gotten or at least misrecognized gains of competition. Tenure here functions merely as an ongoing means for converting the symbolic capital accrued earlier in one's career into economic capital. It operates as a trust fund for oneself.

The third option is to attempt to convert at least some of the academic capital into capital usable in other ways. This is where I place efforts to practice theology as gospel mimesis. The aim of gospel mimesis is to imitate Christ in his twin missions to the poor and the wicked. However, Olum of Pabbo IDP camp argues that I am practicing otherwise: "You come and steal our knowledge. You steal our culture. You come and talk to us about our knowledge and our culture and then take it all back with you. And we have nothing left. Look at us. You see how we live. What are you going to do for us?" He is telling me that unless it is converted into forms of capital that they themselves can use, academic research on the poor is simply another instance of colonial extraction, no less so than mining for minerals, when it is the culture that one collects and bears away. Without a deeper and more steadfastly manifested love of and solidarity with the subjects of research, scholarship conducted in such settings is mere plunder, another "scramble for Africa."

To follow Christ in the manner in which Jesus invited the rich young man would require the professor to give up tenure and the salary that comes with it. If this is the sole standard, then it is as likely for an academic with his cultural capital to get through the eye of needle as it is for an economically rich man. To be sure, fieldwork that involves a high degree of risk to the life of the researcher can reflect a willingness to give up much more than tenure, and the significance of simply being present with people who are in dire circumstances should not be underestimated. Many people in the IDP camps during the conflict told me that my presence there gave them hope that they had not been entirely forgotten by the world in what was, "the world's most forgotten humanitarian crisis."[69] Still, the question remains regarding on whose behalf the risk is taken. Risk, from a gospel mimetic standpoint, is not of value in and of itself. If it is undertaken simply to accumulate academic capital, then it is done for the wrong reasons. Jesus invites the rich young man and Zacchaeus to demonstrate their faithfulness by placing their capital at the disposal of the poor.[70] Such faithfulness may also involve risk of life, but risk itself is not the point.

If, as in my case, the academic is unwilling to give up tenure—and so imitates the rich young man in turning away from Christ's invitation to sell all his goods—perhaps it is possible to persist in the manner of Zacchaeus, by offering to give to the poor half of one's accumulated capital.[71] From the perspective of an institution where only refereed articles and books count as capital, the Zacchaean option—with its conversion of half of its academic capital to forms that the community of the poor rather than the professional society can use—looks no different than the disillusionment option: both are judged simply to be a lack of adequate production. The academic Zacchaeus, like the economic Zacchaeus after fulfilling his promise to Jesus, is not a rich man. Such converted capital can take any number of forms. Given that my effort here is to set out my own theo-social location in relation to my work in northern Uganda and South Sudan, at this point I will simply describe my own attempts at—and the double *entendre* is not lost on me— conversion.

Despite many changes, Acholi work and life is, for the majority of the people, still largely agricultural, and my main effort other than writing is an attempt, however inadequate, to do theology in a mode more fitting for their economy and culture than for my own. When people have asked me, "What are you going to do for us?" I have asked in return, "What do you need?" A frequent answer: "We need oxen." Cattle theft by Museveni's NRM/A coupled with insufficient government protection from cattle-raiding Karamojong groups to the east decimated Acholi livestock holdings in the mid- to late 1980s—reducing ownership to 2 percent of what it was before[72]—and the armed conflict ensured that there would be no restocking until after the 2006 ceasefire. During this time, if they could risk moving out of the camps at all, almost all people farmed with hoes or even sticks. In 2008, I audited a course in nonprofit management, trained as an ox drover, and cofounded PeaceHarvest, a small nonprofit organization that combined livestock provision with training in agriculture and peacebuilding. We did ten one- and two-week trainings. Our focus was to train groups together that are otherwise often in conflict with each other—Ugandan/Sudanese, Christian/Muslim, female/male. The working idea was to facilitate the development of cultural and economic relationships between these groups as a means to reduce the incidence of violence when conflict does arise.

I formed the organization in light of Catholic social teaching—my main teaching and frequent writing subject—with its emphasis on positive peace as "right relationship with neighbor," and Pope Paul VI's observation and dictum, "Development is the new name for peace."[73] I also consciously designed PeaceHarvest to apply and follow Catholic social teaching's principle of subsidiarity—we used local practices as well as best practices drawn from other regions of the world; after the first two trainings, we used only local trainers. In other words, I took intellectual skills and insights that I learned through graduate school and eighteen years of university teaching, and combined them with listening-oriented fieldwork to convert my academic capital and cocreate something that contributed to the well-being not just of humanity abstractly considered, but of specific people. Catholic Relief Services invited our Ugandan manager to present on how PeaceHarvest combines agricultural development with peacebuilding at a special in-service on the topic.

Such activity does not receive any acknowledgment as academic capital in the kind of university setting I have been describing, *pace* Notre Dame's commercials about its service to the poor. The academic field does not recognize such activity as a form of currency.[74] In the meantime, founding and directing PeaceHarvest slowed the completion of this book by three to four years, which has delayed my becoming a full professor, with the bump of salary that that involves, by the same amount of time. I have made the calculation, and the total loss over the remainder of my career of being three to four years behind in salary each year runs into the six figures (and this leaves out the money I invested directly into PeaceHarvest). Using academic capital for other than academic purposes narrowly conceived has literal cost. However, it also needs to be clear that that six-figure hit is nowhere near half of my salary over that same span of time. I may be trending in a Zacchaean direction, but I am nowhere near the Zacchaean threshold. It is important, without being too much of a rigorist, to be specific about such things.

The present book is my wager that written theology, even academic theology, can be mimetic. It is intended first of all for academic theologians, and if it can move others in the profession to give away academic capital, then it will be worth the writing. I approached the editors at Bloomsbury/T&T Clark first of all because of their openness to theology that is frankly confessional—Anselmian faith seeking understanding, if you will—rather than the kind of theology described as "foundational" or "philosophical," that is, more focused on the "conditions of the possibility" of doing theology than the doing of theology itself. I also approached the editors at Bloomsbury/T&T Clark because they are not averse to the genre-warping—the admixture of thick description and analysis—that I believe is necessary to enable written theology to be an instance of the effort to imitate Christ.

Taken together with PeaceHarvest, this book is part of an effort on the part of one person in the academic field to make a Zacchaean offer. I am still well below the Zacchaean threshold of putting half of my wealth at the disposal of the poor.[75] I pray that it is nonetheless acceptable. Above all else, however, it is important not to adulterate the demands of the Gospel just so that one can be counted as among its practitioners, and this is the case whether we are talking about economic or academic capital.

Anthropological theology versus systematic/applied theology: The shape of things to come

Given the unsystematic way that anthropological theology proceeds, I should provide an overview of its modalities or moments as I practiced it, and this as a way of introducing the trajectory of this book. We can describe the modalities or moments in this trajectory as *attention, discernment, commitment,* and *return,* and the major sections of the book follow this pattern. The aim in this overall process is not to build a system of thought, but to engage you, the reader, in an alternative way of being in the world.

Attention involves the full use of the senses to attend to the way of being of a particular community. It requires placing yourself "in the middle of things" in that community. This is the practice that anthropologists and qualitative sociologists call participant observation, and it yields the kinds of insights that come from the traditional practice of ethnography. This moment of anthropological theology is critical if we are not simply to impose our own presuppositions and claims—theological and otherwise—on the community to which we are attending. In Chapters 2 and 3, I attend to the ways of being in the world of the traditional Acholi, the Comboni missionaries who evangelized them, and the women of the indigenous religious order, the Little Sisters of Mary Immaculate of Gulu, and I find that they all understand their ways of being in the world—of learning and knowing and living—in terms of imitation or mimesis.

Even in the practice of attention to the other, we cannot avoid bringing our presuppositions—what anthropologist Henrietta Moore calls "concept-metaphors and pre-theoretical commitments"—with us to the field.[76] This is why the term "description," even "thick description,"[77] does not quite do justice to the activity here. Yes, we describe in our field notes and later in our writing what we observe of the community in question, but we need to be as aware as possible that we observe through a lens crafted by the culture and training from which we come. As we will see in this book, it is often difficult for the modern or postmodern academic to let go of the metaphors and commitments that constitute that lens, but anthropological theology requires us, to the extent that we can, to try to be as aware of the metaphors and commitments as possible, and to hold them loosely. Enough time paying attention to a particular community of the "other," and our lens can, if we are fortunate, begin to shift and reshape itself. Parts of it chip and fall away, and it is another work to try to adjust to the reshaping.

The work of attending to and even actively participating in the reshaping of our worldview, in light of that of the other, is the activity of the second moment in anthropological theology as I have practiced it, that of *discernment*. When parts of our own worldview and even cosmology become challenged by that of the other, then the other's world can begin to take on a plausibility that it did not have for us before. And we need to consider whether to try to take on more fully—indeed, to embrace—for ourselves those newly plausible (to us) ways of being in the world. This moment in anthropological theology challenges traditional notions of participant observation in anthropology where the effort is to remain unchanged so as to be "objective." Anthropological theology moves with the insight that not only is it impossible to attend to the world of an other without bringing our own presuppositions, it is also evidence of a lack of attention to inhabit physically the world of an other and not have, in some way, ourselves change. All worlds have a certain plausibility—no worlds are utterly incommensurate with other worlds—and the refusal to be altered in any way by the world of the other is a failure of attention. Attention—long, deliberate attention—prompts discernment.

After paying attention to the practice of mimesis among the Little Sisters of Mary Immaculate of Gulu in Chapter 3, in Chapter 4 I consider—discern—whether an analogous practice of mimesis is fitting for academics. Traditional anthropological participant observation is anti-mimetic in the sense that it is premised on the idea of observing the other without at all becoming, as in mimesis, *like* the other. Is mimesis, in turn, anti-academic? There are enough instances of anthropologists and qualitative sociologists who operate under the metaphor of "apprenticeship"—that is, becoming like the other through imitating an exemplar—to suggest that there is some room for the mimetic scholar. In

Chapters 5 and 6, I discern how race, economics, and cosmology serve as obstacles to any crossing over into the world of the particular other whom I am considering, but also how, despite such obstacles, there are indeed "crossings," in both directions.

At some point in discernment—or, probably more accurately, at many points in the process—the anthropological theologian needs to make decisions about whether to take on herself, to the extent culturally possible and desirable, major aspects of the worldview of the other, and the practices that that may involve. I call this moment in anthropological theology *commitment*. It is not quite what some anthropologists have derogatorily called "going native," both because, given the previous formation of the theologian, going completely native is impossible, and because a key test of our ability to inhabit a worldview is the capacity to live it out in some significant way when we leave what to us has been the "field" and go home.[78]

The Little Sisters of Mary Immaculate of Gulu model for me how to imitate Christ, with all of the risks that this might involve. I tried to commit to their way by writing an article charging the Ugandan government of President Yoweri Museveni with genocide against the Acholi people, even though I knew at the time that such an article risked my being barred from the country and perhaps worse. That article is the basis for Chapter 7. Two things are worth noting about commitment as I understand it within the context of the overall approach of anthropological theology. The first is that it comes late in the process. Christians concerned with social justice often pledge to commit themselves to those who are marginalized, but with little real understanding of what that might involve. In anthropological theology, commitment—informed, steadfast commitment—follows only upon extended periods of attention to the lives and desires of the community in question and discernment about whether you can align your life and desires in a more than superficial way with those of that community. In my case, I started PeaceHarvest only after having traveled multiple times to northern Uganda over a period of three years. I wrote the article on Museveni's acts of genocide only after five years and sixteen extended trips of a month of more to the region. And it can be asked whether even this was long and intensive enough to undergird a commitment worth making. This leads to the second thing worth noting: commitment, if it is truly to be on behalf of the other and not simply an attempt to affirm one's own justice bona fides, needs to be in response to specific requests made by persons from the community in question. PeaceHarvest was in response to requests for help in reestablishing livestock agriculture in the region; the article on Museveni was in direct response to requests that I write something to "the world" about the atrocities carried out under his leadership. Commitment is not so much an application of *our* norms to *their* situation, but a willingness to take their norms seriously as the latter takes shape in the form of the request. If you live among a people long enough, particularly if you are a person of privilege living among a people who are suffering, they will make their requests known. The key is to pay attention and discern, and then be ready to respond when asked.

Although present anthropology rightfully questions drawing too sharp a distinction between the "field" and the "not-field,"[79] between the research site and the researcher's home, the fact of the matter is that most written ethnographies presuppose that separation by ending before the researcher returns home.[80] Such a representation of the ethnographic enterprise establishes, however unintentionally, an objectivized view of the research subject as "other," as somehow unrelated to us in our "normal" daily life. It is a carryover from the kind of anthropology that seeks to imitate the other by doing participant observation, but while forthrightly trying not to become like the other in any enduring way. Such an approach also masks the way in which our fates and those of the people met in the field are intertwined. Their influence on us can manifest itself in matters as seemingly trivial as the culture shock of returning home and being stunned by the wide array of options—twenty-seven different kinds of toothpaste!—in the supermarket, or it can be much more profound. If being with and imitating the other reshapes the researcher at all, then that reshaping will have manifestations when she comes back home, and this is just as much—even though it is most often left out in the writing—of the ethnographic enterprise as attention in the field. "Field" and "not-field" are always interconnected. Therefore, it is important to follow-up *attention, discernment,* and *commitment* with the fourth moment in anthropological theology, *return,* which I address in Chapter 8. My return to Notre Dame after writing the article on Museveni was a difficult one. The response to the article on Museveni by key colleagues was not receptive. They charged that detailing Museveni's human rights violations in such an overt way threatened the viability of other Notre Dame projects in Uganda. Such criticisms raised questions for me as to whether institutional self-preservation, if not aggrandizement, and risk-aversion rather than the Gospel drive the operative logic of my home culture, the one in which I work.

"Field" and "not-field" are always related. If there is any significant learning from and commitment to an other's culture, the anthropological theologian seeks to offer what is learned and partially embodied to her home culture. That is to say, upon *return, commitment* should move into a kind of invitation, an offering to our own culture what we have learned of the wisdom of the culture of the other, however difficult that process might be. And this is how Chapter 8 proceeds.

I hesitate to call these four moments or modalities of anthropological theology—attention, discernment, commitment, and return—a "method," and this for a couple of reasons. The first is that I did not set out with these moments in mind; rather, they arose in the field in the process of doing the fieldwork. The term "method" bears with it the connotation that one knows precisely what one is going to do beforehand, and that is not how the present project developed. Paying attention to the Little Sisters of Mary Immaculate and their life of *imitatio Christi* raised the question for me of whether an academic's life, *as an academic,* could take on such a shape, and this led to the stage of discernment. The sisters, though, take vows, signaling a commitment, so the question arose as to what such a commitment might look like for an academic, and I wrote the Museveni article. Given the jarring—to me—response of colleagues at Notre Dame to the article, it became clear that the return home was as much of the process as time in the field: the two were clearly interrelated, and so I had to write about both. When I think about anthropological theology as a method or approach, I think of it simply as the appropriation of ethnographic methods to raise theological questions. Someone else doing this in a different context might experience and so highlight quite different moments or modalities in the process.

The danger of hardening the four moments of anthropological theology into a strict method is evident in the "see–judge–act" method found in much Catholic social ethics. The moral methodology of "see–judge–act" provides a good point of comparison precisely because, on the surface, see–judge–act can seem a lot like the first three modalities of anthropological theology of attention, discernment, and commitment.[81] However, the see–judge–act method is indebted to the distinction, even to the point of separation into different departments or fields, between systematic and practical theology, or between fundamental and applied moral theology, or between metaethics and normative ethics. These separations presuppose that the work of the first term, whether systematic theology or fundamental moral theology or metaethics, can be conducted outside of an explicit communal context, disembodied as if from nowhere, rather than in the middle of things. Once this work is complete—that is, systematized—*then*, the operative assumption goes, we can "apply" our principles to specific concrete situations.

In the "see–judge–act" methodology, the person is to first "see" what is going on in the world, and only then judge what to do. However, the principles to be applied at the judgment stage of see–judge–act are already in place, arrived at through some other deliberation. These are the first principles, the major premises. One "sees," then, only to get the information necessary—whether gathered ethnographically or otherwise—to slide into the minor premise so that one can judge and then act. The judgment is made as if one is outside the situation, and then the act follows. Pope John XXIII describes the method in his encyclical, *Mater et Magistra*:

> There are three stages which should normally be followed in the reduction of social principles into practice. First, one reviews the concrete situation; secondly, one forms a judgement on it in the light of these same principles; thirdly, one decides what in the circumstances can and should be done to implement these principles. These are the three stages that are usually expressed in the three terms: observe, judge act.[82]

The separation of systematic theology from practical theology, fundamental moral theology from applied moral theology, and metaethics from normative ethics all have deep roots in, even as they may seek to avoid, the kind of relationship between thinking and enmeshment in the world put forward by the see–judge–act model.

In attention, discernment, and commitment, we are *already acting* in the first moment of attention, and discernment involves not us judging the situation from afar so much as careful consideration of whether we can and should more fully inhabit the world to which we are paying attention. It is not as if we never can or do make judgments regarding another culture or indeed our own, only that these judgments take place, and can only take place, within the world-enmeshed encounter with the other. See–judge–act, like any approach that makes a sharp separation between systematic and applied moments, assumes that we are the expert; attention, discernment, commitment, in contrast, begins with the assumption that the other is the expert on living, and that therefore we can learn far more from the other than simply empirical details to fit into the minor premises in our reasoning. The anthropological observer, in the words of Ruth Behar, is a "vulnerable observer."[83] Here, ethnography is not simply a method that provides information to plug into our theology; rather, ethnography *is* a way of doing theology.

Though anthropological theology is not systematic, I will try to leave enough signposts along the way indicating the various moments as moments of attention, discernment, commitment, or return so that you, the reader, can better discern the trajectory of my reasoning as I attempt to live it. Again, to this end, I divide this book into major sections in terms of attention, discernment, commitment, and return. At the same time, we need to be careful to recognize that each moment in the practice of anthropological theology bears traces of the other moments. We pay attention because we are already in anticipation of learning from the other; we discern because, on some level, we already feel called; attention bears moments of the imaginary inhabitations of the world of the other—"What would it be like . . . ?"—that lead to commitment. And the invitation to you, the reader, to inhabit likewise comes not just at the end after return, but throughout this book. Part of the art of invitation is to leave enough not pointed out so that you can also have the experience of discovery that follows from attention, discovery not of a world that did not exist before you noticed it, but discovery in the form of an invitation to participate in a world that another person or community already gracefully inhabits.

Within the fourfold pattern of attention, discernment, commitment, and return, the chapters proceed as follows. Attention to the beliefs and practices of Catholic Christianity in northern Uganda begins with an account of its two more immediate sources—traditional Acholi culture and the Tridentine Catholicism of the Comboni missionaries—and I do this in Chapter 2, "*Sequela* Comboni: Writing Theological Ethnography in the Context of Empire." The Acholi and Comboni sources contested with each other over adherents in the context of British colonization of the region, including what is now Sudan and South Sudan. The missionaries viewed themselves as following or imitating their founder, Daniel Comboni, as he followed Christ. At first, Comboni interpreted the loss of life among the missionaries—and many did die in Sudan due to fevers, dysentery, malaria, and other causes—in terms of a theology of the Cross: Christ died evangelizing; it should be no surprise that those who seek to imitate him might also. And, like Jesus of Nazareth, Comboni was, at least at first, highly critical of the violence wrought by the empire. However, over time and out of concern that they not be interned or expelled by the British colonizers, the missionaries countenanced imperial violence. Soon enough, they actively supported colonialism, and in this way, in the language of the time, they "formally cooperated with evil."

Precisely *how* the Combonis provided their support for the empire is of immediate import for anthropological theologians with a concern for the marginalized: they did so through the practice of writing. In a textbook composed for the Acholi children who attended their schools, the missionaries recast the Acholi story as one of salvation wrought by the British. While, at first, Comboni himself excoriated the early explorers, the later missionaries portrayed them as deliverers. How this came about is a cautionary tale for theologians who do their fieldwork in regions with oppressive regimes. We, too, write. We, too, have to make the choice of whether or not to curb our inclination toward truth-telling in the face of the risk of expulsion or worse. We, too, risk cooperation with evil.

So what story do we tell (as best we can)? In Chapter 3, "Bishop Negri's *Psst*: Following Jesus in the Middle of War," I let, as much as possible, the nuns of the Little Sisters of Mary Immaculate of Gulu give their own accounts of life during armed conflict. About three-quarters of the people in northern Uganda are at least nominally Roman Catholic, and during the decades-long war, the Catholic Church was one of the few nonwar infrastructures left in the region. The Little Sisters are the most direct local religious descendants of the Comboni missionaries, and their witness in the war—their willingness to lay down their lives—constitutes a retrieval of the original Comboni charism; that is, the charism before it was displaced by obsequiousness to imperial rule.

The question which shapes the chapter, therefore, is that of how it is that a Christianity that recast killers as heroes has given rise to a witness in which practitioners are once again willing to lay down their lives for the "least of these." The emic answer—that is, the answer that the Little Sisters themselves give—is that the spirit or charism of their founder, Comboni bishop Angelo Negri, and ultimately that of Jesus Christ, continues, in their words, to "animate" them. It does so through ritual objects like the rosary, relics, and the elevated Host, as well as photos, paintings, and stories of Negri and cofoundress Mother Angioletta Dognini. Dreams are also a prime venue for spirit visitation. To help illuminate how such animation takes place, I draw from James George Frazer's account of magic in *The Golden Bough*, whereby adherents' contact with and similarity to certain objects transmits what he calls "an invisible ether," and the nuns refer to as the Spirit. The sisters do not disagree with Frazer's account, only with his condescending posture toward those who believe it works. I go on to argue that the Little Sisters' practice of mimesis— their imitation of Bishop Negri, Mother Angioletta, and, above all, Jesus Christ—sits flush with how mimesis operates in the gospels. Here I trace the early oral-gestural context of mimesis to show further how the aim is not exact mimicry, but reenactment with sufficient likeness to the exemplar such that the spirit of the latter enters into the performer and in this way is made present to the audience. Through their own practices of mimesis, the Little Sisters get not just this or that teaching of the gospels right, but also how the Gospel itself works.

One area in which anthropological theology goes beyond much anthropology is to move from attention to and thick description of the other to discernment as to whether aspects of the life of the other can inform *us* how to live. The first step in this process in the present case is ascertaining whether gospel mimesis can constitute a method for scholars *as* scholars. In Chapter 4, I make the case for the affirmative by showing how such an approach is strongly analogous to the practice of ethnography understood as "apprenticeship" found in the work, for instance, of Paul Stoller, Loïc Wacquant, and Anand Pandian. The primary similarity, and what distinguishes this from most approaches to participant observation, is that the aim through such observation is precisely to become in significant ways *like* the other whom we are researching (which is not the same as the effort to become the *same* as the other). From this perspective, the effort to live among a people in their daily lives while, for the sake of a particular understanding of critical distance, steadfastly refusing to become like them in any significant way is a strange way to construct the investigative task. Critics who aver that the imitative aspect of apprenticeship sacrifices critical distance miss the give-and-take oral-gestural context of mimesis and betray a textual bias. The crux when academic mimesis turns to writing, and it is a difficult one, is how to maintain that sense of give-and-take in an article or book that is at a remove from the initial context. Apprenticeship ethnography in its written stage responds by including not just analysis, but detailed and vivid depictions of particular scenes. The aim is to create the conditions that allow the reader to enter the scene herself and in this way allow, if the conditions are right, the spirit of the other to pass to her as well.

The key difference between gospel mimesis and other modes of apprenticeship ethnography is that with the former the aim is to become more like the specific exemplar, Jesus the Nazarene the Christ. It is at this point that cultures, like that of the Acholi, that share significant characteristics with the ancient Near Eastern culture of Jesus of Nazareth can serve as what I think of as "bridge cultures" to the latter. For example, I make the case that the practices of communal property on the part of both traditional Acholi culture and the Little Sisters of Mary Immaculate of Gulu help bring light to those passages in Acts that describe early Christians as giving all that they privately own to the community to share. Modern exegetes, perhaps too influenced, even tacitly, by Western individualism, often make too little of these passages both as early practices and as models for current Christian communities. Read in light of Acholi culture and the lives of the Little Sisters, however, we can understand the early practices as constituting the most mimetically adequate form of property ownership in circumstances where the followers of Jesus, both then and now, are no longer itinerant.

In Chapter 5, "Gaps: The Limits of Mimesis," I continue to engage in discernment by limning the blockages and misrecognitions that have come to the fore when a formally educated, professionally credentialed white man from the United States seeks to become like the priests, nuns, and catechists in an East African warscape where flight from vicious rebels and forced displacement by the government army have gutted the local people and culture. Here, my whiteness is a constant sign both of the disparity of wealth and power between myself and local residents and of the local expectation that I seek not to eliminate these asymmetries, but to utilize them on behalf of the residents. By far and away, most Acholi did not want me to dismantle whiteness, but rather to serve as a good patron. In this chapter, I engage the issue of whether patronage relationships—which, while linking two persons, depends on the hierarchical ordering of their relationship in order to function—can embody Christian fellowship. In the process, I find the otherness of the other to be indelible. Christian theology underscores this truth in its insistence that the ultimate Other, Jesus Christ, is finally inimitable.

But that is not the whole story. Along with the gaps between the other and the self, there were also what we might, for lack of a better word, call "crossings," and I consider these in

Chapter 6, "Crossings: The Surprise of Mimesis." Despite our massive economic, linguistic, and cultural differences, people in northern Uganda and South Sudan repeatedly extended hospitality to me in a wide array of ways. They invited me into their modest homes, utilizing the last of their resources to offer me shelter and meals. They shared stories and songs with me about themselves and the world as they saw it. They countenanced my constant bungling of their language. Consistent with Acholi cosmology, this passing over of my mistakes and to me took place not only through living persons but also via the spirits of the dead, in this case, that of a two-year-old girl who had been murdered and mutilated. In this chapter, then, I also try to make sense of her visitation to me in a way that does justice to both Acholi culture and my own Western academic formation. Other anthropologists have had similar experiences, and I draw upon their responses to both engage and critique the discipline. I suggest that the visitation itself was, among other things, an offer of hospitality, a welcoming into a world that was foreign to me.

What way of being in the world, specifically, is being offered? If we attend to Acholi culture again as a bridge culture to the world of Jesus of Nazareth, then such spirit-crossings have implications for our understanding of the Gospel, in this case as it pertains to the relationship between justice and forgiveness. There is a fault line that splits Christian theology, and especially biblical studies, along the question of who Jesus is *for*. On whose behalf did he live and die? Liberation theology has brought the often-hidden rift to public attention by emphasizing, to greater or lesser degrees depending on the theologian, God's justice in the "preferential option for the poor." Critics counter that Jesus lived and died not specifically for justice for the poor, but for the forgiveness of sinners—even the wicked.

Here is one pertinent place where anthropology can be of service to theology. When Fathers Joseph and Maurice ride the motorcycle toward the LRA attackers, they clearly do so on behalf of the subsistence farmers and villagers under attack from the rebels. Less obvious, but no less present, is the fact that their actions also constitute an offer to the rebels to reenter the community. *Let's try to talk with them. Maybe they will talk.* In riding the motorcycle toward the LRA, the priests move both to free the peasants from the violence of an unjust world and to forgive the rebels. The act is an effort to give both groups—the poor and the wicked—more "time to get away." For the peasants, it is a reprieve, however brief, from the crush of history; for the rebels, it is an opportunity to repent and escape God's—and perhaps the government's—judgment for their acts of mutilation and murder. For both, it is a chance at new life.

Calls for forgiveness of and reconciliation with rebels who come out of the bush have been constant from religious leaders, both Christian and otherwise, and from many members of their communities in northern Uganda and South Sudan. When President Obama deployed a hundred troops as embedded advisors to the Ugandan military in an attempt to take out Kony, the Acholi Religious Leaders Peace Initiative (ARLPI), an interfaith association formed in response to the conflict, wrote in reply, "Instead of relying on military intervention, let us redouble our efforts to engage in dialogue. We believe that this is the only way to bring about a lasting solution that will foster healing and reconciliation."[84]

The witness of people like Fathers Joseph and Maurice and groups like ARLPI suggests that the trade-off between justice for the poor and forgiveness of the wicked is a false one, and prompts a rereading of scripture. There we find that Jesus had particular missions both to the poor—for instance, "Blessed are you who are poor, for yours is the kingdom of God" (Lk. 6:20-21)—*and* to the wicked—for example, "I have come to call not the righteous, but sinners" (Mk 2:17; cf. Mt. 9:13 and Lk. 5:32). How can this be? And why the split in modern theology and biblical studies?

Most biblical scholars adhere, usually tacitly, to a modern understanding of space and time as divided into discrete, uninterruptable units, an understanding due, according to Weber, to the modern quest for calculability. Such compartmentalization eclipses any cosmology or theology that allows a blurring or, worse, rupturing of the discrete units of three-dimensional space and strict linear time. The corollary is what Weber calls the "disenchantment" of the world; that is, the exclusion of spirit-interruption in human life.[85] The use of methods of calculability in the search for the historical Jesus grew out of the disenchanted world that Weber describes, such that even scholars with other theological commitments are profoundly shaped by it. The result is a Jesus whose sense of time and space is parsed into discrete units: Jesus either is a reformer who calls for social change in the here and now *or* is an "eschatological prophet" who points toward a future, if immanent, world that, at present, is elsewhere. To affirm both would constitute a contradiction, a violation of the laws of time and space. The consequence on the normative level is another parsing: Jesus is either for justice for the poor (in the here and now) or for forgiveness of sinners (in the hope for a world that is not here, but is yet to come).

With very few exceptions, the people of northern Uganda and South Sudan—whether formally educated or not—do not share the modern compartmentalization of space and time that correlates with disenchantment. Most of them practice a syncretistic blend of traditional Acholi cultural religion and Christianity. In the former, ancestral spirits continue to interact with the people who remain on earth. For Christians such as Fathers Joseph and Maurice, the sending of the Holy Spirit at Pentecost makes their reenactment and revivification of Jesus of Nazareth possible. The Holy Spirit allows Jesus the Nazarene—who lived a long time ago and in a distant place geographically—to live in them. Engagement with the spirits—including Jesus Christ in the Holy Spirit— undoes the time/space problematic that underpins the option-for-the-poor-now versus God-for-all-sinners-in-the-future-Kingdom contention. Fathers Joseph and Maurice are free, therefore, to lay down their lives for the poor *and* the wicked, both of whom suffer. Through their mimetic willingness to die for others, Joseph, Maurice, and others like them open up, however briefly, a time-space where the normal rules of violence do not apply. Their witness, if we pay attention, directs us toward Jesus the Nazarene, who, again, also ministered in a "densely populated spirit world." For Jesus, it is not a confusion to speak of the Kingdom of God both here and now as well as currently elsewhere and to come at some future time, and it is not a performative contradiction for him to have special missions to both the poor and the wicked. Given the shared cosmological presuppositions and normative commitments between Jesus the Nazarene the Christ and exemplar Christians in northern Uganda and South Sudan, the latter can serve as a cultural and theological bridge for moderns to the former. They can teach us how to be Christian.

Now comes the hard part. Is the anthropological theologian to *commit to* that world such that she is willing to lay down her life for the poor and the wicked? I went to northern Uganda and South Sudan to study traditional Acholi and Catholic religiosity in the region. However, those there told me that to truly pay attention to their world I had to attend to the violence that engulfs it. The more I paid attention, the clearer it became that between 1985 and 2006, the government and armed forces of Uganda under President Yoweri Museveni committed what can only be called genocide against the Acholi people. How is a Western scholar to try to follow Christ in this situation? In an effort to imitate the best of the exemplars I met—or at least to avoid formally cooperating by my silence with the evil of neocolonialism—I published an article in late 2010 on the abuses committed by the Museveni regime. In doing so, I knew that I was perhaps jeopardizing my ability to complete the research for this book, and perhaps my safety. The article spurred debate in the Ugandan national newspapers, a debate in which I participated, and inquiries from Ugandan officials. Acholi friends warned me to stay away, and I did for three years. In Chapter 7, I offer a compressed and updated version of the article.

Immediately after finishing the research for the article, I returned to the United States. Even with crossings from the other to the self, the ethnographer has to return to her first home, and I attend to this part of the fieldwork journey in Chapter 8, "An Offering: Bringing the Ethnographic Encounter Home." In the terms we have been using, anthropological theology follows commitment with return, and an invitation to the home community what has been learned while being immersed in the world of the other. Most ethnographic writings conclude before the return home. This is problematic in that it tends to render written ethnography as an objectivized gaze on the other rather than as an encounter between worlds.

And if the ethnographer does become shaped, to whatever limited extent, by the world of the other, the return home can be a difficult one. Such was the case for me. The publication of the article charging Museveni with genocide led to tensions with some key colleagues at Notre Dame who felt that it put other projects of Notre Dame and its affiliated institutions at risk; one colleague insisted, strongly, that I withdraw from all public discussion of governmental human rights abuses in Uganda. My colleagues suggested that our disagreements with regard to the article were simply matters of differences in prudential judgment and that we shared the same basic presuppositions and worldview, and at first I agreed. However, it later became evident to me that the overall operative institutional ethos of Notre Dame sets real limits on what its members consider just or even imaginable. It became apparent that that ethos is shaped by belief systems that have little to do with living a life that seeks to follow Christ. Commitment to the way of being in the world taught to me by the Little Sisters of Mary Immaculate of Gulu can take place only with difficulty at the university named after Our Lady.

To extend an invitation to the university community to the Little Sisters' way of being in the world, I try to give a theological account of what I thought and hoped I was doing by publishing the article. Here, I find my exemplars from outside the Christian tradition in the work and activity of anthropologists such as Nancy Scheper-Hughes and Philippe Bourgois. Jesus frequently uses outsiders to illustrate faithfulness, the story of the Good Samaritan perhaps being the most well-known. Scheper-Hughes argues for an anthropological practice that exhibits a deep "solidarity" with its research subjects, and I make the case that both her writing and her practice have close affinities with John Paul II's understanding of the charity-infused solidarity that marks the life of the Christian. What Scheper-Hughes and Bourgois have done is what I was also trying to do. I will let you decide whether I was at all successful.

It remains to address how to present the perspective of such solidarity to one's home community *in a way that it might be grasped in the home community's own terms.* Here I draw on a sports analogy because of the valuation of sports both in the United States and, more specifically, at Notre Dame: mimetic anthropological theology works, when it does, like playbooks and gamefilm in sports. The more analytic passages are like playbooks, which abstract from the immediate field of play in order to display more schematically what is going on, and this for the purpose of improving play. The thick depictions of exemplars in scenes of action work like gamefilm, which displays the practice in question in a particular instance. Anthropological theology tacks back and forth between schema and scene, playbook and gamefilm, as an invitation to join in the very serious game of the Gospel. When it works—if it works—mimetic theology is itself an integral part of practice, in this case the practice of the Gospel.

The question that arises is how theology became so detached from the concrete practice of the imitation of Christ in the first place. Addressing this question requires an historical account that is at once extensive and compressed, and I provide one in the appendix, "From Gospel Mimesis to 'Theology': How a Discipline Lost Its Senses." Most accounts of the decline of mimesis as a form of knowing in the history of ideas focus on the influence of Plato and, later, the Enlightenment, particularly Descartes and Kant. In the Christian context, however, other figures play a more important role. I highlight the writings of Paul, Ignatius of Antioch, Athanasius, and Abelard. In brief, Paul introduces theological distinctions—for instance, between spirit and flesh, faith and sight, spiritual and literal— that allow later figures to set aside as being simply "spiritual," and thus not to be literally practiced, those aspects of the life of Jesus Christ that went against their interests. By Abelard's time—and for the most part ever since then—social and ecclesiastical forces are such that those who practice what we have come to know as "theology" in the academy have little, if any, interest in writing in a mode that invites the reader to imitate Jesus Christ. That is why any effort to develop a theology in the mimetic mode must return to and retrieve the kind of mimesis as it is displayed in the gospels themselves.

Given that the Christianity of the people of northern Uganda and South Sudan provides a bridge to the gospels for the rest of us, paying attention to their history and practices—their evangelization by and indigenous appropriation of the Christianity of the Comboni missionaries—is a first step to living the Gospel.

On with it then.

Notes

1. Unless otherwise indicated, when I refer to South Sudan, it will be to the area of Eastern Equatoria where the Acholi people are prominent, an area that is roughly in the shape of a triangle with Nimule (to the west) and Labone (to the east) forming the base and Magwi (to the north) the apex.

2. Flannery O'Connor, *The Habit of Being: Letters of Flannery O'Connor*, ed. Sally Fitzgerald (Farrar, Straus, and Giroux, 1988), p. 124; 1955 Letter to "A": "[Mary McCarthy] said when she was a child and received the Host, she thought of it as the Holy Ghost, He being the 'most portable' person of the Trinity; now she thought of it as a symbol and implied that it was a pretty good one. I then said, in a very shaky voice, 'Well, if it's a symbol, to hell with it.' That was all the defense I was capable of but I realize now that this is all I will ever be able to say about it, outside of a story, except that it is the center of existence for me; all the rest of life is expendable."

3. Karla L. Schultz, *Mimesis on the Move: Theodor W. Adorno's Concept of Imitation* (Berne, Frankfurt am Main, New York, and Paris: Peter Lang, 1990).

4. Gunter Gebauer and Christoph Wulf, *Mimesis: Culture, Art, Society*, trans. Don Reneau (Berkeley, Los Angeles, and London: University of California Press, 1995), p. 47. In my judgment, Gebauer and Wulf's book provides the best historical overview of the concept and usages of mimesis.

5. For some notable exceptions, see, for instance, Mary McClintock Fulkerson, *Places of Redemption: Theology for a Worldly Church* (Oxford: Oxford University Press, 2007); Christian Scharen and Aana Marie Vigen, eds., *Ethnography as Christian Theology and Ethics* (London and New York: Continuum, 2011); Michael Banner, *Ethics of Everyday Life: Moral Theology, Social Anthropology, and the Imagination of the Human* (Oxford: Oxford University Press, 2014); Natalie Wigg-Stevenson *Ethnographic Theology: An Inquiry into the Production of Theological Knowledge* (New York: Palgrave Macmillan, 2014); Siobhán Garrigan, *The Real Peace Process: Worship, Politics, and the End of Sectarianism* (London: Equinox, 2010); Luke Bretherton, *Christianity and Contemporary Politics: The Conditions and Possibilities of Faithful Witness* (Malden, MA and Oxford: Wiley-Blackwell, 2010); Bretherton, *Resurrecting Democracy: Faith, Citizenship, and the Politics of a Common Life* (New York: Cambridge University Press, 2015).

6. Cf. dioceseofnorthernuganda.blogspot.com (November 21, 2006) and sudan.unfpa.org/souther_Sudan/index.htm. and https://www.africanlibraryproject.org/our-african-libraries/africa-facts.

7. For the postmodern turn to mimesis as an attempt to recover the performative dimension of knowledge precisely through writing, see William Schweiker, *Mimetic Reflections: A Study in Hermeneutics, Theology, and Ethics* (New York: Fordham University Press, 1990).

8. No methodology is a panacea, of course, and the discipline of anthropology is wrought with its own problems, not least of which is, for historical and institutional reasons, a largely unexamined animus against Christian theology. Still, anthropologists do not have to like our use of their methods in order for us to use them. For my criticisms of anthropology, see, "If They Kill Us, At Least the Others Will Have More Time to Get Away: The Ethics of Risk in Ethnographic Practice," *Practical Matters*, 3: *Ethnography and Theology* (Spring 2010), at http://practicalmattersjournal.org/issue/3/analyzing-matters/if-they-kill-us-at-least-others-will-have-more-time-to-get-away. This issue of *Practical Matters* focuses on the topic of theology and ethnography, and is another recent example of theologians drawing from and grappling with the methods of anthropology. With some notable exceptions, it is only

recently that anthropology as a scholarly discipline has been willing to approach even the *anthropology* of Christianity, let alone the discipline of theology. See, for instance, Fenella Cannell, ed., *The Anthropology of Christianity* (Durham and London: Duke University Press, 2006); Eloise Meneses, Lindy Backues, David Bronkema, Eric Flett, and Benjamin L. Hartley, "Engaging the Religiously Committed Other: Anthropologists and Theologians in Dialogue," *Current Anthropology* 55, no. 1 (February 2014), pp. 82–104; and Joel Robbins, "Social Thought and Commentary: Anthropology and Theology: An Awkward Relationship?" *Anthropological Quarterly* 79, no. 2 (Spring 2006), pp. 285–94.

9. Jean Jackson, "Participant-observation," in *The Dictionary of Anthropology*, ed. Thomas Barfield (Oxford: Blackwell Publishing, 1997), p. 348.

10. Loïc Wacquant, "Participant Observation/Observant Participation," in *Sociology: Introductory Readings*, 3rd ed., ed. Anthony Giddons and Phillip W. Sutton (Cambridge, UK/Malden, MA: Polity Press, 2010), pp. 69–73.

11. Cited in Michael Taussig, *Mimesis and Alterity: A Particular History of the Senses* (New York and London: Routledge, 1993), p. 38.

12. Clifford Geertz, *The Interpretation of Cultures* (New York: Basic Books, 1973), pp. 3–31.

13. Edith Wyschogrod, *Saints and Postmodernism: Revisioning Moral Philosophy* (Chicago: University of Chicago Press, 1990), p. 25.

14. Interview with Sr. Josephine, 53.

15. The words "pray" or "prayer" appear only six times in *Saints and Postmodernism*, and always in reference to others' use of the terms. Wyschogrod, *Saints and Postmodernism*, pp. 9, 10, 12, 36, 37, and 43.

16. Wyschogrod, *Saints and Postmodernism*, pp. xiv, xxiv, and 257.

17. Ibid, p. 39. Cf. 34–9.

18. Wyschogrod, *Saints and Postmodernism*, p. 13.

19. Quoted in Wyschogrod, *Saints and Postmodernism*, p. 9.

20. Wyschogrod, *Saints and Postmodernism*, p. 10.

21. The name, Vincentino Olim, is a pseudonym. I use pseudonyms throughout unless otherwise requested by the subject.

22. Quoted in Lutz Kaelber, *Schools of Asceticism* (University Park, PA: Pennsylvania State University Press, 1998), p. 105.

23. Kaelber, *Schools of Asceticism,* 105; Keith Thomas, *Religion and the Decline of Magic: Studies in Popular Beliefs in Sixteenth and Seventeenth Century England* (New York: Oxford University Press, 1971), p. ix.

24. Interview with Sister Venotrina Adiyo, 21.

25. John J. Pilch, *Flights of the Soul: Visions, Heavenly Journeys, and Peak Experiences in the Biblical World* (Grand Rapids, MI and Cambridge, UK: William B. Eerdmans Publishing Company, 2011), p. 134.

26. Weber himself recognizes the role of wonderworks in Jesus's leveraging of religious authority, but later Weberian historians skip over this fact. See Max Weber, *Economy and Society: An Outline of Interpretive Sociology*, ed. Guenther Roth and Claus Wittich (Berkeley, Los Angeles, and London: University of California Press, 1978), pp. 440 and 630–1.

27. Mario Cisternino, *Passion for Africa: Missionary and Imperial Papers on the Evangelization of Uganda and Sudan, 1848-1923* (Kampala: Fountain Publishers, 2004), p. 210, note 25.

28. On the rejection of the fundamental/applied theology split, see Fulkerson, *Places of Redemption*, pp. 9–10.

29. Frantz Fanon, *The Wretched of the Earth* (New York: Grove Press, 2005), pp. 38–43.

30. Sven Lindqvist, *Exterminate All the Brutes: One Man's Odyssey into the Heart of Darkness and the Origins of European Genocide* (New York: The New Press, 2007).

31. In formal legal terms, because of its being indirectly ruled, Uganda was a "protectorate" rather than a colony of Great Britain. In 1894, the British named Uganda a protectorate and in 1896 included the people of northern Uganda in this designation.

32. On indirect rule and its consequences, see Mahmood Mamdani, *Citizen and Subject: Contemporary Africa and the Legacy of Late Colonialism* (Princeton, NJ: Princeton University Press, 1996).

33. The geographical locations in this scene are pseudonyms in order to protect the identity of the speaker.

34. "Museveni Directs Final Lakwena Offensive," *New Vision* (November 6, 1987).

35. Chris Ocowun, "Museveni Hails Gulu Archbishop Odama," *New Vision* (October 22, 2006), p. 1.

36. *Lakwena* in the Acholi language means "messenger," a name Auma received in connection with her role as a spirit medium.

37. Adam Branch, "The Political Dilemmas of Global Justice: Anti-Civilian Violence and the Violence of Humanitarianism, the Case of Northern Uganda" (Columbia University Ph.D. dissertation, 2007), p. 22.

38. For Girard's theory of violent mimesis and the scapegoat, see Rene Girard, *Violence and the Sacred* (Baltimore: The Johns Hopkins University Press, 1979), and Girard, *The Scapegoat* (Baltimore: The Johns Hopkins University Press, 1989). My finding here is like that of Anne Llewellyn Barstow on the hunts for witches in sixteenth- and seventeenth-century Europe: *pace* Girard, the mutilations and murders did not bring a sacral reconciliation, but rather "rituals of nullity, dead ends." See Barstow, *Witchcraze: A New History of the European Witch-Hunt* (New York: Pandora/Harper Collins, 1995), pp. 153–4.

39. World Health Organization/Ministry of Health, The Republic of Uganda, *Health and Mortality Survey Among Internally Displaced Persons in Gulu, Kitgu, and Pader Districts, Northern Uganda* (July 2005), p. ii.

40. Chris Dolan, *Social Torture: The Case of Northern Uganda, 1986–2006* (New York and Oxford: Berghahn Books, 2009), p. 1.

41. Jan Egeland, *A Billion Lives: An Eyewitness Report from the Frontlines of Humanity* (New York, London, Toronto, and Sydney: Simon and Schuster, 2008), p. 211.

42. See Julian Hattem, "Joseph Kony is Still at Large. Here's Why the US and Uganda were Willing to Give Up the Hunt," *The Washington Post* (April 22, 2017), at https://www.washingtonpost.com/news/worldviews/wp/2017/04/22/joseph-kony-is-still-at-large-heres-why-the-u-s-and-uganda-were-willing-to-give-up-the-hunt/ and Jason Burke and Alon Mwesigwa, "Central Africa Fears Return of LRA After Hunt for Joseph Kony Ends," *The Guardian* (May 1, 2017), at https://www.theguardian.com/world/2017/may/01/central-africa-fears-return-of-lra-lords-resistance-army-after-hunt-for-joseph-kony-ends?CMP=Share_iOSApp_Other.

43. Zack Baddorf, "Ordered to Catch a Warlord, Ugandan Troops are Accused of Hunting Girls," *The New York Times* (May 14, 2017), at https://www.nytimes.com/2017/05/14/world/africa/joseph-kony-lords-resistance-army-uganda.html?hp&action=click&pgtype=Homepage&clic

kSource=story-heading&module=second-column-region&region=top-news&WT.nav=top-news&_r=0.

44. See Mercy Nalugo, "Museveni, MPs to Clash Over Bail Law," *the Monitor* (July 17, 2011), at http://www.monitor.co.ug/News/National/-/688334/1202200/-/bl61ecz/-/.

45. "Uganda: priests charged with incitement against government" (May 13, 2011) at http://www.catholicculture.org/news/headlines/index.cfm?storyid=10327&utm_source=feedburner&utm_medium=feed&utm_campaign=Feed%3A+CatholicWorldNewsFeatureStories+%28Catholic+World+News+%28on+CatholicCulture.org%29%29.

46. See Human Rights Watch, *A Media Minefield: Increased Threats to Freedom of Expression in Uganda* (May 3, 2010) at http://www.hrw.org/node/90067; and Human Rights Watch, "Uganda: Charge or Release Charged Journalist: Radio Reporter Disappeared After Meeting with Security Officer" (July 23, 2011), at http://www.hrw.org/en/news/2011/07/23/uganda-charge-or-release-detained-journalist; and Committee to Protect Journalists, "Uganda illegally detains journalist without charge" (July 26, 2011) at http://www.cpj.org/2011/07/uganda-illegally-detains-journalist-without-charge.php.

47. Helen Epstein, "What the US is Ignoring in Uganda," *The Monitor* (July 24, 2011) at http://www.monitor.co.ug/News/National/-/688334/1206294/-/bl38vkz/-/index.html.

48. See Ayiswa Issa, "US Govt Says Ugandan People 'Deserved Better,' Raise Concerns Continued Dr. Besigye House Arrest," *Of Uganda* (February 21, 2016) at http://www.ofuganda.co.ug/articles/20160221/us-govt-says-ugandan-people-deserved-better-raise-concerns-continued-dr-besigye.

49. It needs to be said that the question of the social location of even the Catholic academic theologian in relation to God is different than the question of her relation to the Roman Catholic Church's hierarchical magisterium. The two questions are often confused in the debate about the theologian-magisterium relationship (see John L. Allen, Jr., "Bishops' Staffer on Doctrine Rips Theologians as 'curse,'" *National Catholic Reporter* (August 16, 2011), at http://ncronline.org/news/people/bishops-staffer-doctrine-rips-theologians-curse. The matter of the obstacles to a theologian's right relationship to God is the more pressing of the two questions.

50. One could rightly include the physically afflicted (for instance, the sick and the lame) and the possessed, but these are less contended than the issue of whether Jesus went out to the poor or the wicked.

51. Max Weber, *Economy and Society: An Outline of Interpretive Sociology*, ed. Guenther Roth and Claus Wittich (Berkeley, Los Angeles, and London: University of California Press, 1978), p. 632.

52. See, for instance, John P. Meier, *A Marginal Jew: Rethinking the Historical Jesus, Volume II: Mentor, Message, and Miracles* (New York, London, Toronto, Sydney, and Auckland: Doubleday, 1994), pp. 385–6.

53. For evidence of the rich young man passage as being historical, see Gerd Theissen and Annette Merz, *The Historical Jesus: A Comprehensive Guide* (Minneapolis: Fortress Press, 1996), p. 192.

54. For the demands and allowances of itinerant discipleship, see Gerd Theissen and Annette Merz, *The Historical Jesus: A Comprehensive Guide* (Minneapolis: Fortress Press, 1996), pp. 359–72.

55. On this point, see Bruce Malina, *The New Testament World: Insights from Cultural Anthropology* (Louisville: Westminster and John Knox Press, 2001), pp. 97–8.

56. Here it is important to remember that the "Protestant ethic" to which Weber refers is not an effort to gain salvation, but a response to the belief in predestination and that one is already among the elect.

57. In this scene, I interweave what were actually two conversations, one which took place in Pabbo, and the other in Magwi, South Sudan.

58. Pierre Bourdieu, "The Forms of Capital," trans. Richard Nice, in *Handbook of Theory and Research for the Sociology of Education*, ed. John Richardson (New York: Greenwood Press, 1986), pp. 241–58.

59. See Pierre Bourdieu, *The Field of Cultural Production* (New York: Columbia University Press, 1993), pp. 29–141.

60. See, especially, Pierre Bourdieu, *Homo Academicus* (Stanford, CA: Stanford University Press, 1990).

61. See http://www.usnews.com/rankings.

62. The role of the academic as teacher is important, but in the prestigious schools that I am describing here, it is not as institutionally valued as that of researcher. If we took the terms "excellent" and "passable" as our markers of value, the excellent researcher who is a passable teacher receives tenure, while the reverse is not the case. There are noticeable differences in the policies of different universities regarding the capital value of teaching. However, on the whole, when it comes to measuring capital production, they *reward* excellent publication (with advancement) and *award* excellent teaching. Given that there are relatively few awards for teaching and that the capital value of teaching is less than that of publication, the academic field is structured so as to channel the greater effort into the latter. A senior colleague gave me blunt advice on the relative importance of research, teaching, and university service when I first arrived on campus: "Write, write, write, teach well enough, and don't be weird."

63. Bourdieu, "The Forms of Capital," p. 242.

64. Pierre Bourdieu, *Pascalian Meditation* (Stanford, CA: Stanford University Press, 2000), pp. 9–84. For my own critiques of the turn away from practical reason in the modern academy, including Catholic universities, see Todd Whitmore, "Teaching and Living Practical Reasoning: The Role of Catholic Social Thought in a Catholic University Curriculum," *Journal of Peace and Justice Studies* 11, no. 2 (2001), pp. 1–36; and Whitmore, "Practicing the Common Good: The Pedagogical Implications of Catholic Social Teaching," *Teaching Theology and Religion* 3, no. 1 (February 2000), pp. 3–19. Bourdieu is aware, as am I, of the irony and even contradiction of critiquing the academy in this way while participating in it.

65. F. H. Bradley, "Can a Man Sin against Knowledge?" *Mind* 9/34 (1884), p. 286.

66. One of the few books that draws upon ethnographic fieldwork in the doing of theology is Mary McClintock Fulkerson's *Places of Redemption* (see note 5 above). The time from the end of fieldwork until the book appeared in print was eight years. Fulkerson was tenured at the time and could afford the extra time in production.

67. Added to the fact that fieldwork adds more time to a research project is that it also takes more money to undertake ethnographic methodologies. Often, when the fieldwork is international, the amount of money is considerable. The researcher has to take the time to raise the economic capital to afford to travel to and live in often distant places where she converts the economic capital to academic capital. The extra time it takes to fund-raise for travel is a disincentive to taking on ethnographic practices.

68. Pierre Bourdieu, *The Logic of Practice*, trans. Richard Nice (Stanford, CA: Stanford University Press, 1990), p. 56.

69. There are several close versions of this quote from Jan Egeland, then UN Under Secretary General for Humanitarian Affairs, indicating that he said it several times in slightly different forms. See, for instance, Reliefweb, "War in Northern Uganda world's Worst Forgotten Crisis: UN" (November 11, 2003) at http://reliefweb.int/report/uganda/war-northern-uganda-worlds-worst-forgotten-crisis-un; and "Northern Uganda "World's Biggest Neglected Crisis," *The Guardian* (October 22, 2004), at http://www.theguardian.com/world/2004/oct/22/2.

70. Note here that it is a demonstration of faith, not an effort to get faith, and so is not works righteousness.

71. I am aware that raising the issue of how much conversion of capital is acceptable takes me along the precipice of works righteousness. However, my aim is to ask the Luther-like question of what faith active in love looks like. Jesus tells the rich young man that the kind of faith that entails following him in his itinerancy involves selling all one has. He tells Zacchaeus that it requires hospitality, and he acknowledges the latter's faith-offer to give half-earnings to the poor as an acceptable sign of faith. There is no hint from Jesus that simply giving away half or even all of one's income *earns* the Kingdom without being an act of faith.

72. See Kirsten Gelsdorf, Daniel Maxwell, and Dyan Mazurana, *Livelihoods, Basic Services and Social Protection in Northern Uganda and Karamoja* , Feinstein International Center, Working Paper 4 (August 2012).

73. National Conference of Catholic Bishops, *The Challenge of Peace: God's Promise and Our Response* (Washington, DC: United States Catholic Conference, 1983), pars. 27 and 32–3; Paul VI, *Populorum Progressio*, 76 and 87.

74. In order for PeaceHarvest to be sustainable, we need broader institutional support. I approached three entities at Notre Dame whose mission statements overlapped with that of PeaceHarvest to inquire whether it could be taken under their auspices. I volunteered to take university students on the trainings, and to teach them about Acholi language and culture. My one stipulation was that the students would have to participate in ways that actually contributed to the well-being of the people of northern Uganda. Notre Dame has many "immersion" programs to expose students to other cultures; we did not need yet another one that did simply that. I indicated that contributing to the life of the Acholi would involve more than one trip for the student. The model I recommended was for the student to go one summer, learn about the culture and needs in consultation with Acholi, come back to Notre Dame during the following school year to design a way to help address those needs, and then return the following summer to work with the Acholi to implement the project. None of the Notre Dame entities took me up on the offer. In the meantime, university administrators have signaled to me through various ways that the work of PeaceHarvest is not an appropriate use of my time.

    This is not to say that the academy could not formally recognize the creation of nonprofit organizations as valued productivity. The procedure could be much like that now employed, but instead of asking other scholars about the value of the person's written work, university administrators could invite administrators of other nongovernmental organizations—for instance, Catholic Relief Services or Caritas—to assess the nonprofit. However, given the dynamics of the academic field, this is not likely to happen in any broadly applicable way any time soon. I have spoken to the Provost about the possibility, but without luck.

75. Giving away far less than half of my academic capital might, as an indicator of my lack of faith, also indicate that I am what literary theorists call an "unreliable narrator" of the Christian story. My hope is that, like with the rich young man, the initial persistence coupled with hearing bluntly the demands of the Gospel, will, even with the turning away, provide at least a shadowed glimpse of what the life of a follower of Jesus Christ looks like. On the

concept of the unreliable narrator, see Wayne Booth, *The Rhetoric of Fiction* (Chicago: University of Chicago Press, 1983).

76. Henrietta L. Moore, "Global Anxieties: Concept-metaphors and Pre-theoretical Commitments in Anthropology," in *Anthropology in Theory: Issues in Epistemology*, ed. Henrietta L. Moore and Todd Sanders (Malden, MA and Oxford: Blackwell Publishing, 2006), pp. 443–55.

77. Clifford Geertz, *The Interpretation of Cultures* (New York: Basic Books, 1973), pp. 3–31.

78. For a complex troubling of the anthropological concept of the "field," see Akhil Gupta and James Ferguson, "Discipline and Practice: 'The Field' as Site, Method, and Location in Anthropology," in Gupta and Ferguson, eds., *Anthropological Locations: Boundaries and Grounds of a Field Science*, pp. 1–46.

79. See Akhil Gupta and James Ferguson, ed., *Anthropological Locations: Boundaries and Grounds of a Field Science* (Berkeley: University of California Press, 1997).

80. There is, of course, the possibility of the researcher deciding to stay in the researched culture permanently and not returning home. Though such instances happen, they constitute a small minority of cases.

81. See Erin M. Brigham, *See, Judge, Act: Catholic Social Teaching and Service Learning* (Winona, MN: Anselm Academic, 2013), pp. 10–12.

82. John XXIII, *Mater et Magistra*, par. 236.

83. Ruth Behar, *The Vulnerable Observer: Anthropology That Breaks Your Heart* (Boston: Beacon Press, 1996).

84. The ARLPI, "Response to the Deployment of US Military Advisors to LRA Affected Regions" (October 24, 2011), at www.arlpi.org/response-to-the-deployment-of-us-military-advisors-to-lra-affected-regions. For evidence of support for forgiveness in Uganda beyond religious leaders and northern Uganda, see Refugee Law Project and the Center for Civil & Human Rights, *Forgiveness: Unveiling an Asset for Peacebuilding* (2015).

85. Max Weber, *From Max Weber: Essays in Sociology*, ed. H. H. Gerth and C. Wright Mills (Oxford: Oxford University Press), pp. 350 and 139.

PART I
ATTENTION

CHAPTER 2
SEQUELA COMBONI: WRITING THEOLOGICAL ETHNOGRAPHY IN THE CONTEXT OF EMPIRE

The only phenomenon with which writing has always been concomitant is the creation of cities and empires, that is, the integration of large numbers of individuals in a political system and their grading into castes or classes. . . . It seems to have favored the exploitation of human beings rather than their enlightenment.

—Claude Levi-Strauss, *Tristes Tropiques*[1]

In the last dozen years or so, the idea and practice of borrowing ethnographic methods in the doing of theology have grown. Some contributors to this discussion, including myself, draw upon ethnographic methods in order to facilitate the writing of a theology that, we hope, exhibits solidarity with the poor and the marginalized.[2] Ethnography, if done well, helps to bring the lives and the voices of the poor and the marginalized into the project of theology. A key problem with the doing of theology as solidarity, however, is that writing itself has a troubled history. Levi-Strauss puts the point uncategorically: the *only* phenomenon with which writing has *always* been concomitant is the creation of empires. Theological projects seem to have a second burden of proof in that professional anthropologists themselves have, with only a few exceptions, long held that theologically oriented ethnography, most often carried out by missionaries, has been and is complicit in imperialism. John Burton writes regarding his time as an anthropology student that, "it was a moral imperative to profess a highly critical attitude towards missionaries of all devotions." Missionaries are not often the focus of anthropological writing, but when they are, according to Burton, "they are mentioned primarily as agents of colonialism."[3] While theologians are by now used to countering criticisms of religion that are rooted in secularist biases and anxieties, we are less used to addressing the problematics associated with writing itself. If we want to practice theology as a form of solidarity, however, we have to face directly the issue of writing. Our vocations depend on our discerning ways to be exceptions to Levi-Strauss's tenet. In other words, the first moment in anthropological theology, that of attention, requires attending not only to the people before us, but to the means through which we communicate their lives. The best place to begin such discernment is to investigate previous efforts to do theologically oriented ethnography. Michael Rynkiewich, an anthropologist, argues, "Anthropologists should treat missionaries as they do any other enigmatic group; they should do ethnographies of missionaries *before* justifying or condemning, if either needs to be done" (emphasis in original).[4] In other words, pay attention before moving to judgment.

The present chapter focuses on the activity of the Comboni missionaries among the Acholi people of northern Uganda in the first half of the twentieth century. However, my primary aim in paying attention to the practices of the Combonis is not to either justify or condemn *them*, but rather to ask what their practices can tell us about the liabilities of *our* doing theological ethnography. I can say in advance that, in my judgment, under immense imperial pressure combined with the hardship of outpost evangelization, the Comboni community in northern Uganda came to use writing in a way that, in the technical language of Catholic moral theology, constituted "formal cooperation with evil," in this case the evil of British imperialism.

In their own, emic terms, the Combonis assessed themselves in light of the life of *sequela Christi*—following Christ—which for members of the congregation takes place through imitating the life of their founder, Daniel Comboni. Thus, *sequela* Comboni. In the early years, this involved a willingness to lay down their lives on behalf of the people of what is now northern Uganda and South Sudan. Over time and as the result of many, even daily, decisions, however, the Combonis turned—in increments that I am sure were not fully perceptible to them—from following Christ to actively supporting the empire. It would be facile to assume that imperial pressures are any less forceful today, and my analysis in this chapter is, in part, to set up discussion in later chapters about the implications for contemporary theology.

I use the rubric of "magic" to frame the analysis. Magic as I am thinking of it here is the capacity via symbolic action to transform one reality into another and to have the new reality accepted by the intended audiences. As we will see, the Acholi people of northern Uganda had their own forms of magic; the British brought the magic of writing. Writing, in the eyes of the newcomers, converted the vast "empty" land that was Africa into parceled colonies and protectorates belonging to Europeans. The Combonis—with the Eucharist, devotion to the Cross, veneration of the Sacred Heart of Jesus, and belief in the miraculous efficacy of their practices—brought still another magic. Yet they also brought writing, and were for all practical purposes conscripted by the British to establish schools to teach writing to the Acholi for the sake of the empire.

The mission setting was, therefore, one of competing magics. When the colonial magic of writing failed to convince the Acholi that their land was under the command of the British, the latter turned to violence. The Combonis found themselves in an ongoing quandary: collaborate in the writing-violence dynamic or be expelled and thus unable to practice the magic of the Eucharist. If the choice seems easy, then we have failed to account for the fact that the Combonis considered evangelization through word and sacrament to be their vocation, one for which they were initially willing to die. Writing in the context of the empire presents *us* with issues much like those that the Combonis faced. If we are to practice what George Stocking fittingly called "the ethnographer's magic"— careful attention and interpretation with a claim to the real—without collaborating with imperial violence, then it is crucial that we learn what we can from earlier theologically driven ethnographers.[5]

In what follows, I proceed in several movements. First, I provide an overview of Acholi religiosity and the ways in which activity at clan and ancestral shrines and by free agent spirit mediums have worked the local magic. Attention to the people of northern Uganda must begin here. Then I elaborate how such religiosity has taken place through an oral/aural medium. This will allow me, in the ensuing section, to show how the British used writing in an effort to both shut down the Acholi magic and produce their own. When the colonial magic of the written word failed—as evidenced in the variety of forms of Acholi resistance—the British turned to violence. Enter the Combonis. In the ensuing sections, I show how, under imperial pressure and in response to their own sufferings, the missionaries rewrote salvation history such that the explorer, Samuel Baker, whose killings of locals Daniel Comboni initially severely criticized, becomes the new Moses and Gulu, a town constructed through forced labor, is the New Jerusalem. The Combonis did all this rather than the alternative: follow Christ in a way that likely would have brought about either their internment in or their expulsion from Uganda. In the final section, I raise in an initial way the question of the complicity of current theology in similar dynamics when we excise truths from our narratives that prevailing powers would prefer be left untold. Present-day academic theological ethnographers can—and I did—face a life situation much like that of the Combonis—curb your writing or face expulsion. It is important, then, to gain a sense of what the social pressures were like for the missionaries. But first, attention to local patterns of traditional culture.

Acholi religiosity[6]

Aya Korina[7] stomps the ground and spits holy water at me. Not Korina, really, but one of her several *jogi*, Jok Jagero, who possesses her. Although there is a four-foot clay vat of it, the water, like consecrated holy water everywhere, is not for drinking. It is for blessing and healing purposes only—and to ward off evil. Jok Jagero—"the fierce one"—spits in the other three directions, using Korina's mouth and lips as his aspergillum.

Jagero is a free *jok*—literally a free spirit—who, in contrast to chiefdom or ancestral *jogi*, is not attached to a particular shrine or natural landmark like a river or rock outcropping. He can, and does, come from great distances; most often when Korina bids, but sometimes without her asking.

Ten years ago, Korina fell sick, severely so, and went to an *ajwaka* or, as some of the early mission dictionaries translate it, a witchdoctor.[8] The *ajwaka* told her to slaughter a black male goat at a mountain called *Lacic*, and to sprinkle its blood. From the *ajwaka's* house, *Jok Jagero* lifted Korina, as she put it, "up into the sky," and placed her back on the ground at Mount Lacic. "It came as a madness," Korina told me today before being possessed, "a sort of cruelty." She slaughtered the goat, and "the gate of the mountain opened wide revealing a cave, showing me all of the items that I am showing you today."

Animal hides cover the center floor of Korina's thatch-roofed and windowless wattle and daub home; one from *dolo*, a colobus monkey, two from *noya*, a fox-like animal with "a cruelness like that of a leopard." She needs the skins of fierce animals to help bring in like-spirited *jogi*. Roots and herbs for curing ailments from anxiety to infertility trim the walls of the hut. As instructed by Jagero, she wears a garland and crisscrossing bandoliers of cowry shells. "If I do not wear them, the spirits will quarrel with me. 'Why don't you follow my law? My directive is to wear these shells. Put them on, then my spirit will be free to come.'" Such shells were first brought to northern Uganda when Arabic-speaking merchants and raiders came here from the north, using them as currency in the ivory and slave trade in the 1850s.[9]

A mushroom-shaped stool, called *adwi*, remains in the middle of the room from a curing-exorcism Korina completed just yesterday. The sick sit on the stool for three days, going outside only to relieve themselves. The *ajwaka*'s assistants aid in feeding the person. Otherwise, they form a circle around the sick, shaking *ajaa*—oil-smeared gourd rattles—dancing and carrying out call-and-response chant with Korina while she goes about her work. On the third day they shave the patient's head hair. The small inverted pot—*koro tipu*, or literally, "house in which to chase and hold the spirit"—that Korina placed on his head to draw the evil spirit out of him remains on the floor, together with scattered *nyim anyallo kweng*, a commonly eaten but also special kind of sesame seed used, when blessed, for healing the sick.

Jagero barks and whoops and says something that I do not catch. I can follow Korina's Acholi far better than I can his. But the attendants have no problem, and respond with well-timed assents and affirmations to the *jok*'s utterances and pronouncements. They, too—six of them—wear the cowry shell garlands. Jagero-Korina spins and dances facing the wall, with a *noya* skin tied around her waist and strings of bells around each ankle so that each stomp is followed by a harsh yet melodic ringing. Seven times, s/he alternates between call-and-response chant with the attendants and what to my ears—since I cannot keep up—sounds like Acholi glossolalia.

The possession lasts about half an hour. It winds down slowly; the stomps not as vigorous, the bells not as loud, the speech not as fast. Finally, Aya Korina sits down, facing me, her knees still bouncing, then slowing, then still—everything quiet except her ribs and lungs, which do quick, though not as violent, compressions that expel sharp bursts of air; the traces of Jagero as he leaves.

* * *

It is important first to limn the shape of Acholi culture and religiosity prior to colonial engagement in order to understand the impact of the Combonis' practice of mission anthropology on that culture and religiosity.[10] Okot p'Bitek's *Religion of the Central Luo* is taken by most scholars as a touchstone for what Acholi religiosity must have been like before the incursion of the British Empire. P'Bitek focuses on three types of *jogi*—that is, spirits—as they manifest themselves in different loci of religious practice.[11] The first is the chiefdom *jok*, who is called upon in an annual feast at the chiefdom shrine. Priests, male and female, officiate at the rite—an occasion when the person of the chief recedes and the emphasis is on the purification and rededication of the people to the chiefdom *jok*. The second locus of religious activity is the *abila*, the clan lineage ancestral shrine where there is a "meeting of the living and the dead." There is not, in traditional Acholi belief, a strong bifurcation between spirit and body. The ancestors, "were thought of as whole beings, not dismembered parts of man, i.e. spirits divorced from bodies." People encountered their ancestors, therefore, "as they were known before death; their voices could be 'recognized' as they spoke through the diviner."[12] Put another way, the resurrected body is a given among the Acholi, with no waiting until the eschaton. The role of the *abila*, and the ancestors who gather there, is to protect the members of the clan against whatever dangers might confront them and to bring success to their endeavors, particularly hunting. "Abila pa wora mupito an ki wan tino," a woman sings at the shrine of her clan, "Oco! Abila pa wora ogwoko an do" (*Abila* of my father that fed me from infancy; Oh *abila* of my father protect me oh).[13]

Though p'Bitek treats the free *jogi* separately from those of the chiefdom and the ancestral shrine, his accounts of all three show that the role of the *ajwaka*, the third locus of Acholi religiosity, was fluid. For instance, he tells of one case where the priestess who officiated at the annual rite of the chiefdom shrine also had oversight of a lesser spirit consulted, like the *jogi* of *ajwagi*, "for minor individual problems and sufferings."[14]When discussing the ancestral shrine, p'Bitek explicitly refers to the *ajwaka* as playing a role that closely matches, complete with shuddering, the one that Aya Korina performs for me, with the exception that Korina calls free *jogi* rather than the ancestors.

> The *ajwaka* sat by the central pole . . . she shook the rattle gourd, *ajaa*, called the names of the dead men of Pa-Cua, inviting them to come:

Ludongo Cua, Lalwak Wod Twon, bin;	Men of Cua, Lalwak, Son of Bull, come;
Awobe gutoro komgi en, gikuri;	The young men have gathered, waiting for you;
Biyu wun weng, Keny Koropil, bin;	Come all of you, Keny Koropil, come;
Aryango, Olango, Bitek	Aryango, Olango, Bitek
Awobe kuru-we en, biyu.	The young men are waiting for you here, come.

> When "they" came the *ajwaka* became very hysterical, and what she said was not clear. . . . Then the *ajwaka* calmed down, and although she now spoke very faintly, she was more audible.[15]

The precolonial Acholi respected the power of the *ajwagi*. P'Bitek elaborates, "In a significant way, their office operated as a powerful social control factor. They could always be hired by a man who had been wronged by someone stronger than him."[16] When forces or events overran the protective capacity of the *jogi* of the chiefdom or clan ancestral shrines, the Acholi turned to the *ajwaka*. And overrun the chiefdoms and clans is precisely what the British did. They brought their own magic: the power of the written and printed word. To understand the enormity of the shift from oral to written culture, it is helpful to unpack the work of three theorists who have focused extensively on this transition, Jack Goody, Eric Havelock, and Walter Ong.

From orality to literacy: Goody-Havelock-Ong and the Acholi

Aliker, kel dyanga;	Aliker, return my cattle;
Ka ilwor,	You coward,
Mony Gala	Tell the army of the white man
Cung ikura	To stop, and wait for me
Waci waromo Lamola	We shall meet at Lamola;
Iyoo, iyoo,	On the road, on the road;
Muloji lwor	Muloji is a coward
Dako loyo;	Even a woman defeats him;
Muloji lwor,	Muloji is a coward,
Muloji lwor,	Muloji is a coward
Dako loyo;	Even a woman defeats him;
Mouloji lwor,	Muloji is a coward,
Ee, Agwe pyelo i kaki	Hey, he shits his khaki trousers;
Aliker, kel dyanga.	Aliker, return my cattle.

Aliker, return my cattle. Aliker is the *rwot kalam*, "chief of the pen," whom the British installed after shipping his father, the resistant chief Awich, to prison near Kampala. In 1947, the colonial district commissioner, A. S. A. Wright, ordered Aliker to build a new road. Aliker, though the son of the venerable Awich, knew he was really a chief by imperial appointment, not by popular demand or lineage, and that his hold on his own Payira people was tenuous. So he tried to outsource the work to another clan, the Labongo.[17] But Labongo warriors blocked Aliker from approaching and killed his bodyguard. Aliker retreated and mustered British reinforcements, and together the colonizers and the Payira raided the Labongo villages, killing many of the inhabitants and stealing the cattle. A Labongo poet sung: "Aliker, return my cattle / You coward / Tell the army of the white man / to stop, and wait for me / We shall meet at Lamola."

He was not the first Acholi poet to sing defiance in the face of colonial power. Omal Lakana refused to take part in the forced labor system and the building of the town of Gulu commanded by the district commissioner:

Ee, cuna mito telo,	Ee, my penis wants to get erect,
An aito wi lela,	I am mounting the bicycle,
Alaro Gulu;	I am hurrying to Gulu;
Ee, cuna mito telo,	Ee, my penis wants to get erect,
An anongo min Dici	When I find the District Commissioner's mother,
Agero i bar Pece;	I will fuck her in the football field at Pece;
Ee, cuna mito telo	Ee, my penis wants to get erect.

The British imprisoned Lakana for two years for his insolence.

P'Bitek collected these and other song-poems called *wer* in the early 1970s and committed them to print; but how did they get passed down to p'Bitek in the first place, fifty years or more after they were initially sung, particularly given colonial efforts to exile their composers and so expunge their content from Acholi culture?[18] Oral communication is, in the words of classicist Eric Havelock, "light as air, and as fleeting." The anthropologist Jack Goody adds, "There is no store for subsequent recall." Cultural historian Walter Ong refers to the "winged words" that are "constantly moving" in oral performance and elaborates, "Sound exists only when it is going out of existence. It is not simply perishable but essentially evanescent . . . . There is no way to stop sound. . . . If I stop the movement of sound, I have nothing."[19] Havelock, Goody, and Ong have all written extensively on the relationship between oral and literate cultures, and their insights provide a way to both investigate the means of continuity in oral culture and assess the impact of the introduction of the written word in Acholiland.

Sustaining oral compositions over time, according to Havelock, requires a tradition of encoded language, what Goody calls "standardized oral forms."[20] The poet sets stock phrases to familiar rhythms and repeats them often. "Muloji is a coward / Muloji is a coward / Even a woman defeats him / Muloji is a coward." The composer sets the poem to music, frequently accompanied by the *nanga*, a cigar-box-guitar-like instrument laid flat and played in droning syncopated rhythms. The Acholi blues. Oral tradition is somatically intense. After a few bars, the audience, often dancing, knows the refrain and the song becomes call-and-response. At this point, the poet can add whatever vivid commentary he wishes. "Hey, he shits his khaki trousers." The more vivid, the more memorable.

An extended poem builds these memorable lines by parataxis; that is, the piling up of phrase upon phrase rather than by the subordination of points to a main thesis.[21] Framed by repeated incantations of the line, "Ee, my penis wants to get erect," the extended version of Lakana's poem and its threat to the sexual security of colonial mothers (and thus to the manhood of their sons who are supposed to protect them) build by working up the chain of hierarchical command. He makes the boast-threat in the first stanza to the Acholi subchief, the one who was the last to pass down the colonial order to forced labor; he makes the next boast-threats, in ascending order, to the chief, the district commissioner, and the king of England. The clear exaggeration involved in the last boast makes it all the more vivid for retelling.

Havelock describes the "performative" syntax and context of oral poetry as "a continual dynamism," "a flow of sound," and "a river of action."[22] The result is that the community that carries the song may and likely will have more than one version of it. Parts of the song placed earlier in the performance by one poet in one context may be placed later by another in a different setting. The refrains and the more memorable phrases and short sequences remain relatively unaltered, even learned verbatim, and the narratives retain a certain trajectory. But listener-participants do not learn the poems verbatim throughout, in part because of the cognitive near-impossibility of remembering the exact order and every word of a narrative performance, but also, and perhaps more fundamentally, because to perform in oral culture is at once to recite and to compose. How tightly the community controls the performances depends on a number of factors, from the size and geographical stability of the community to the presence or lack thereof of internal and external disruptions. Havelock in particular stresses the need in oral societies for regular performative contexts for the community to call forth its tradition. He identifies "ritualized utterances" in the context of "common festivals" as the bearer of memory,[23] which is less a matter of looking back at events than breathing them forth to life.

Perhaps because Havelock is a classicist describing a tradition that he knows only through texts and the oral traditions that have lived on in texts, he, while rightly discussing special festivals, misses the ordinary time means of retelling and reenacting the tradition. Among the rural Acholi, the practice of *wang oo*, the evening fire, is the center of the traditioning process. Both words in the term have multiple interrelated meanings. *Wang* can mean time, moment, or period, and *oo* translates as arrival, so that we get "time of arrival." *Wang* also means sight, appearance, opening, or passage; and *oo* can be rendered "to warm," so that *wang oo* is the warming fire where one can see and be present to others. The evening fire is the place where the Acholi gather to inform each other of the day's events, and to tell stories of origin, history, or entertainment. Parents pass out any necessary discipline. Everyone gossips. *Wang oo* is where I learned that the Big Dipper is *Cing Lyec*, trunk of the elephant, and where I first heard the story of the dispute between the brothers Labongo and Nyipir as the source of the split between the Acholi and the Alur peoples.

Around *wang oo*, the young learn not by study, but by participatory listening and observation. There are no grammars or dictionaries directing how to speak properly; rather there is what Goody terms "direct semantic ratification" in both day-to-day activities and the end-of-day *wang oo* performative context. Ong concurs, "The oral mind is uninterested in definitions. Words acquire their meanings only from their always insistent actual habitat, which is not, as in a dictionary, simply other words, but includes also gestures, vocal inflections, facial expressions, and the entire human, existential setting in which the real, spoken word always occurs."[24]

The practice of writing, particularly when it is brought from the outside by colonial powers, shocks the social latticework of performance in oral culture. Goody, Havelock, and Ong all make the case that writing and print bring profound changes, what Goody calls a "linguistic recoding," to human consciousness.[25] To understand the impact of the Comboni missionaries, therefore, we need to take into account the role of writing, particularly in imperial contexts.

The imperial magic of writing

The British explorer John Hanning Speke, in his journal from his 1860–2 trip to Uganda, relates an exchange he had with the king of Bunyoro, the region just south of Acholiland:

> The Mukama requested that I would spread a charm over all his subjects, so that their heart might be inclined towards him . . . . I said that there was only one

charm by which he could gain the influence he required over his subjects—this was, knowledge and power of the pen.[26]

How does writing come to have such "power"? Levi-Strauss gives what is perhaps the most trenchant analysis of how the magic of writing works. During a gift exchange with some Nambikwara indigenous of Brazil, he gave them paper and pencils, and later noticed them "drawing wavy horizontal lines." They were imitating his writing. The chief, however, went further. During the exchange of goods, he "read" from his piece of paper, as if checking the list of things that Levi-Strauss was giving to the Nambikwara in exchange for their offerings. Levi-Strauss interprets the chief's actions as an effort not just to mimic the physical act of reading, but to access political power. The chief sought to "astonish his companions, to convince them that he was acting as an intermediary agent in the exchange of the goods, that he was in alliance with the white man and shared his secrets." He elaborates, "Writing had, on that occasion, made its appearance among the Nambikwara but not, as one might have imagined, as a result of long and laborious training. It had been borrowed as a symbol, and for a sociological purpose, while its reality remained unknown."[27] Again, magic, as I understand it, is the capacity via symbolic action to transform one reality into another—from goats as property of Levi-Strauss to goats as possessions of the Nambikwara—and to have the new reality accepted by the intended audiences. Levi-Strauss goes on to observe that local resistance to political domination among the Nambikwara—the chief who tried to serve as access man to the power of whites "was abandoned by most of his people"—manifested itself importantly as, among other things, resistance to writing. In the end, the locals did not believe in writing's magic, at least as practiced by whites.[28]

In the case of the region that would become Uganda, the major European powers carried out the prime act of colonial magic in the form of the 1885 General Act of the Berlin Conference, twenty-three years after the explorer Speke recommended the "charm" of the "knowledge and power of the pen." The General Act parceled artificially demarcated territories to the attending conference parties in the creation of a new reality: "Africa." The particular power of the written and printed word in this case is its fixity and consequent connotation of absoluteness and, thus, transcendence. There was no power of rebuttal against an officially printed and gazetted document. The Word was God.

The magic of the written and printed word gave the colonizers the power of administration. The General Act's "Principle of Effectivity" required that the designated powers take actual possession of their granted lands via treaty with local leaders and by active administration. The British administered through "indirect rule," that is, rule through the social leadership already in place in the targeted territory, in this case, the kings and chiefs. The kings and chiefs, on this theory, collected the taxes and enforced the work necessary to build the roads and buildings that made modern administration possible. Problems arose, however, when kings and chiefs refused to cooperate or their peoples resisted.

In northern Uganda, Commissioner George Wilson described the local population as "child races to be educated firmly."[29] Chief Awich, mentioned earlier, headed the largest and strongest of the Acholi clans, the Payira. When refugees fled to Acholiland from British attack in the Bunyoro region to the south, Awich, following traditional practices of hospitality, refused to hand them over to the colonizers.[30] For his refusal, the British imprisoned him in Kampala for two years.[31]

Despite his resistance to colonial authority, Awich was the closest to a singular leader among the Acholi, so, in 1906, Commissioner Wilson appointed him "king," levied hut taxes and required pro bono work on the part of the locals. Punishment for noncompliance was swift. Comboni missionary Joseph Pasquale Crazzolara noted in his journal:

> 11 Apr. 1911—Some soldiers/police come to the mission requesting 20 porters, including an Acooli (jagang) who just happens to be around. As the latter refuses, he is beaten up. Another one, who was engaged from his very home, seems to have caused some difficulties while on the march, near Rabwon, and was pierced to death with a bayonet.[32]

The British found ruling a people as culturally independent and geographically scattered as the Acholi to be too difficult, and so—by written and gazetted fiat—ordered them to build from scratch and live in what was to become the largest town in northern Uganda, Gulu. Again, Father Crazzolara's journal narrates the scene:

> On hearing the news, the population is thoroughly shaken. They still have their grains in the fields, but orders are that they must pick up cereals not for themselves but for [the support of] Gulu town. . . . It is as if they were not in their own territory, but in a hostile one. The government has ordered to burn down any house or village of those who have made remonstrations. . . . I have seen burnt barns everywhere.[33]

When "King" Awich resisted orders, the British imprisoned him again. Commissioner R. M. Bere noted that already by this time—the British had been consistently present in the region for only fourteen years[34]—only about half of the chiefs had come to their positions by traditional means. The rest were appointed by the British after the colonizers deposed the traditional chiefs who disobeyed. The imperial dismissals of local leaders were so frequent that the Acholi developed their own term for the ersatz replacements, notable for the reference to writing as the source of usurped power: *rwodi kalam* (chiefs of the pen) as distinct from the traditional *rwodi moo* (chiefs anointed with shea oil). The explorer Speke's claim—that there is "only one charm by which he could gain the influence he required over his subjects, knowledge and power of the pen"— proved providential.

Locals put up a wide array of forms of resistance, from the more passive refusal to work to active sabotage and even outright rebellion. The most famous occasion of resistance was the Lamogi rebellion of 1911–12,[35] where the British chased an alliance of clans into the caves of the Guru Guru hills and laid siege. Even imperial-influenced reports stated that the trapped Acholi "began to suffer from dysentery and diarrhea on a very large scale, and those who attempted to approach the rivers outside the caves were shot. Many women and children died as a result of infection."[36] Ninety-one Acholi were shot and killed in the caverns; over three hundred died of dysentery.[37] Afterward, the British deported all of the involved chiefs—thirty-four of them, indicating broad support for the rebellion[38]—to prison in Entebbe to the south. The colonizers displaced the rest of the people to Gulu town with a forced march during which more Acholi died than during the siege itself.[39]

With the traditional chiefs deposed and replaced by the "chiefs of the pen," the annual rite at the chiefdom shrine lost legitimacy. With many of the other Acholi displaced from their lands, engagement with the ancestral spirits at their shrines on clan land diminished. Okot p'Bitek's insight regarding the "social control" factor of the free agent spirit medium *ajwagi* becomes pertinent: when lack of alternatives availed themselves, the weaker party in a conflict could hire the spirit medium to work her powers against the stronger.[40] The British overran the protective capacity of the *jogi* of the chiefdom and clan ancestral shrines. However, the free *jogi* of the spirit-mediating *ajwagi* remained to defend the Acholi, to give them hope and power, and this presented a problem for the British.[41] They could not, as they did with the chiefs, depose the *ajwagi* because the latter held no political power. They could not displace them because the *ajwagi* worked with free *jogi* not tied to place. They sought to root out the spirit mediums with witchcraft laws, but these worked only if people were willing to turn in the *ajwagi*—their only recourse for resistance left—to the colonial powers.[42]

The British did not quite trust Roman Catholicism to root out the *ajwaka*, not only for historical political reasons, but also because the Catholic faith, with its saints and relics, often itself verged on "superstition." However, the Brussels Act of 1890 meant that the political colonizers could not exclude Catholic missionaries from their territories, and given the limits of bureaucracy and military force, the empire needed someone who had the particular kind of wares to confront the *ajwaka* directly. The Comboni missionaries, already in southern Sudan, were ready at hand. The British allowed them in so as to disrupt Acholi magic and to bring the locals to conform to the empire.

Missionary magic

Ojara is well-off by IDP camp standards. He has three structures where he lives, a wattle and daub cooking hut, a similar storage hut, and a small brick sleeping abode. The front half of the sleeping dwelling is a sitting room—a space that is perhaps five by seven feet—with fold out chairs, and two small side tables. A suitcase rests on its side on one table, serving as a makeshift dresser. Here, he is the 1%.

A backlit clock, running when batteries are available, features the figure of Jesus pointing toward his illuminated—glowing—heart, which is garroted with a coil of thorns. The Sacred Heart of Jesus, a direct link to the Combonis.

I forget to ask Ojara where he got the clock and guess that it was either from the shop at Holy Rosary Parish in Gulu or from one of the many entrepreneurs of religious wares at the annual feast of the Acholi martyrs at *Wipolo*. There, the merchants place their items on sheets of plastic tarp laid end-to-end for stretches of fifty feet or more. Prayer books; rosaries with beads from pink to green; icons of Daniel Comboni; three-inch wood crucifixes on stands; framed depictions of Madonna and child. According to Ojara, time and money spent on the *ajwaka* is "wasted": "Only prayer to the Sacred Heart of Jesus will end this war."

The devotions which shaped Daniel Comboni grew out of very specific experiences in his life. He was praying in St. Peter's Cathedral in Rome during the Triduum in preparation for the beatification of Margaret Mary Alacoque, the French nun and mystic whose visions gave rise to the devotion to the Sacred Heart of Jesus, when his "Plan for the Regeneration of Africa" came to him as itself inspired.[43] So central was the devotion to him that Comboni named the order which he founded the "Sons of the Sacred Heart."[44] The missionaries practiced and transplanted other devotions—mediums of magic—to Acholiland as well, including the veneration of Mary.

* * *

There is only the slightest of bends in the road, but still the Toyota Land Cruiser skids to the side, pebbles flying. Father Vincentio Olim[45] is driving one hundred kilometers an hour; faster when the road is straight. He sees me put my hand to the dash to steady the ride.

I have come to visit him after joining in the celebration of the Acholi martyrs at *Wipolo*, but am regretting it at the moment. We are on our way from Madi Opei, the parish center in the far northeast corner of Acholiland, to Agoro. He is going there to perform twenty-six infant baptisms. Father Vincentio is better than many priests about getting to the outposts; still, the people are going to make the most of his visit. The priest to lay ratio is 1 to 30,000. The people of Agoro are not taking any chances that this may be the last visit for another couple of months.

It is perhaps six o'clock in the evening. At certain points the low sun catches the windshield and we, or at least I, cannot see. I make some under-the-breath utterances that mix invective with severely pared down versions of the travel prayers common out here. *God. Slow! Jesus.*

"I drive like this because I have been ambushed two times."

Father Vincentio lets me take this in, not slowing down.

The redound from a pothole jams me into the seat and then catapults my head into the ceiling. The seatbelt does not work. I tried it when we started off, but I try it again now anyway.

Vincentio looks over, "I have to get that fixed."

After a pause, he continues his earlier thread.

"The first ambush was 1997. I was traveling in a vehicle alone in the Pajule area. They attacked me at about 8:30 p.m. I jumped from the vehicle and hid in the river for about four hours. When I came out, leeches were attached all over my body.

"When I came onto the road, the first person I saw was my uncle, who was in the UPDF. He asked, 'You are the one?' I responded, 'Yes.'"

We drive by *Got Latoolim*—Mountain of the Dead Visitor—at about the halfway point. Agoro is the terminus of a north-south running road that comes to a halt at the base of the Imatong Mountains and the start of South Sudan in this sector. In 2002, one thousand LRA foot soldiers poured through a pass that the UPDF—the Ugandan military—claimed was impassable and overran the army.

"The second time was in 2003. About ten UPDF soldiers stood in the roadway and shot at us. I got out and ran into the bush and passed out. The soldiers burned the vehicle and stole some of the goods to make it look like LRA. But the soldier who took the keys later gave them, stupidly, to a Christian to give back to me. That is how I know it was UPDF."

Father Vincentio goes on, "I do not ask for any more miracles than what I have already seen. The 1997 incident, I was too young to see this way. But before the second event, a friend of mine gave me a medal with the Virgin Mary and told me to put it on the dashboard of my vehicle to protect me."

I look at the dash, partly in reaction to the comment, partly in prayer. We are still moving fast. Mary is not there now.

"In the second incident, one bullet went through the radiator, through the dashboard, deflected off the medal, and burned the skin on my left shoulder by the neck. It would have hit me. Another bullet burned the right of my abdomen and blew a hole in the seat. All of the windows were blown out. They counted ninety-seven bullet holes in the car."

He turns to me again, "I do not ask for any more miracles than what I have already seen."

* * *

Daniel Comboni was ordained in 1854, only three weeks after Pope Pius IX defined the Immaculate Conception of Mary as official church doctrine. Comboni, in his turn, consecrated Africa to the Immaculate Virgin when he made a pilgrimage to the shrine of Our Lady of La Salette in France.[46] Though immaculate virgin, Mary is also Mother of God and, more particularly for Comboni, of Jesus's Sacred Heart. In 1875, the missionary combined these two devotions—to Mary and to the Sacred Heart—to forge a new title under which to dedicate his specific vicariate in Africa: "Behold us prostrate at your feet, Mary, blessed Virgin Mother of God. Full of joy, we salute you . . . with the new and glorious title of 'Our Lady of the Sacred Heart of Jesus.'"[47]

The practical upshot of the devotions to Mary and the Sacred Heart of Jesus is that such veneration has earthly efficaciousness. When Comboni prays, he does so for the success of his mission, and is certain of the results. "Mary will be my dearest 'Mother' and Jesus will be my 'all.' In their company . . . I will succeed in giving life to the proposed Work for the regeneration of Africa."[48] The surety of success reflects the belief that this is an omnipotent God who acts through Mary and Jesus.[49] Comboni most often described this power in terms of God's "protection" of his confreres and him as they carried out their work;[50] yet, at times, that power went beyond mere protection to the effecting of great acts. "The Sacred Hearts of Jesus and Mary are enough for all, and I expect miracles through their mediation."[51] The only difference here with Father Vincentio Olim is that, at the time of the writing, Comboni *did* ask for—expect—more miracles.

The charism of religious congregations is typically interpreted as having been first displayed in the person of their founder, and the Combonis are no different. Members of the order are called upon to focus on Daniel Comboni, according to Antonio Vignato, an early superior general, so as to "study his life and virtues in order to imitate the great apostle who is Comboni, a spirituality to be inserted in our own spirituality."[52] What the order's official documents refer to as the *sequela Christi* (following Christ) is for the missionaries a matter of following Daniel Comboni.[53] Consistent with the shape of Comboni's faith life, the missionaries have stressed the efficacious power that comes from such devotion, such that miracles follow. Two miracles predominate in the literature. The first in importance is Comboni's own, which he performed eighty-nine years after his earthly death, when his relics heal a terminally ill ten-year-old girl.[54] As mentioned in Chapter 1, thirty-three years later, the relics of the Acholi martyrs protect the schoolgirls of Father Vincentio's Madi Opei parish from UPDF bazooka shrapnel: "They fired a bazooka into the church and it hit the floor right on the engraving in the aisle, even splitting the relics of the *Wipolo* martyrs into two, creating a second martyrdom, with fragments scattering everywhere. The ceiling. Everywhere. Yet no shrapnel hit any of the girls."

The second often-told miracle evidences again that, in this account of the world, the life that has devoted itself to God through Mary and the Sacred Heart of Jesus itself becomes powerful. I will let one of the missionaries tell the story:

> At the end of August 1903, Fr. Beduschi fell dangerously sick and was given the last sacraments. But Sr. Giuseppa sent word to him saying, "Father, you must not die because you must do much work here. I'll die instead of you." On the first of September, Sr. Giuseppa was stricken by a violent fever and she sent for Fr. Beduschi to hear her last confession. The suffering priest was carried to the dying sister on a litter. . . . After the sister's confession, Fr. Beduschi asked two brothers to carry him back. "No," said Sr. Giuseppa, "You must go alone, on your feet." She touched his cassock and said, "Go!" At that moment Fr. Beduschi suddenly felt invaded by a new strength; as the onlookers watched stupefied, he arose and walked. Sr. Giuseppa passed away in the evening of the same day.[55]

The Combonis, then, much like the Acholi, as we have seen, called upon spirits (and the Spirit) for their earthly powers. When the two traditions—Christian and traditional African—first confronted each other, the missionaries evangelized by presenting the

Christian god as stronger—more efficacious in this world—than the local spirits. Father Angelo Vinco, a missionary priest who had a deep influence on Comboni,[56] gave an early and indicative speech to the chiefs in Sudan, five years before Comboni himself made it to Africa:

> The God who created you and me, also create the sun, the moon, and the stars. . . . The same God who makes the grass and seeds grow—in other words, the same God who from nothing created everything in heaven and on earth. This God is, as yet, not known to you. . . . This is the God who makes the rain fall, thus preventing your fields from being scorched; He keeps you in good health; He multiplies your cattle; He gives you strength to overcome your enemies.[57]

Like the British, the Combonis enlisted, again in the words of the explorer John Hanning Speke, the "power of the pen" to manifest the power of their god.

Missionary writing and the abstraction of tradition

> **1.** The orthography adopted in this book follows that of the Rejaf Language Conference, 1928, and its suggestions. Additions, where necessary, have been made in accordance with the principles laid down by the conference. The so-called "central" vowel-type is represented in the Rejaf orthography by the symbol ö. As further vowels of this type had to be adopted, the diacritical mark ¨ has been used to distinguish them.
>
> *—Opening lines of the first chapter of J. P. Crazzolara,*
> A Study of the Acooli Language: Grammar and Vocabulary[58]

Goody, Havelock, and Ong all stress writing's ability to abstract language from its lived matrix. Written language has the capacity to be, in Ong's words, "context free."[59] In order to capture the "light as air" (Havelock) and "constantly moving winged words" (Ong) of oral culture and fix them to a page, the Comboni priest Joseph Pasquale Crazzolara followed a set of rules set out by a conference of European orthographers studying African languages. This is the same missionary who lived sufficiently in the context of Acholi life during the colonial years that he could report firsthand, "Yet now it is as if they were not in their own territory, but in a hostile one." If we are to pay attention to current Acholi Catholicism, we have to first pay attention to the earlier process of the writing of their culture by the Combonis.

The prime innovation that facilitates the process of capturing words on paper is the invention of the alphabet and its ability to convert what was fleeting sound to a more permanent visual medium.[60] Once this conversion takes place, language does not need performative reenactment to sustain a tradition. Writing itself provides a "storage" mechanism.[61] Scribes can compile long lists of objects—things sold, gifts exchanged— without reference to the occasions that make them worthy of noting.[62] In time, words and their rules themselves become listed objects, ratified not in their use, but through reference to dictionaries and grammars. Crazzolara followed rule 1 quoted above with, in numerical order, 536 more. There was no need when following such rules to refer to stolen cattle or cowards who lose control of their bowels in order to know what a verbal noun was and how to use it. And once abstracted from their lived context, words can be combined and reinserted in that context for other purposes, like the pedagogical purpose of recitative catechism.

* * *

2005. My first trip to the region. I am staying with the Comboni Missionary Sisters—first constituted as the "Pious Mothers of the Nigritia"—at their residence. The lettering on the arch over the front gate announces to visitors that they are entering the "Comboni Missionary Animation Centre." A painted cast-relief icon of Daniel Comboni stares out, though not, I think, menacingly, from a pillar to the side. He is not smiling, but his eyes are kind. The grounds are immaculate. Sister Fernanda shows me to my room and allows me to get settled before dinner. We eat late, as is the norm here, and as we finish, a strange chanting rises from somewhere beyond the back wall of the compound. Children's voices. Many of them, though all in unison. It is sing-songy, yet at the same time solemn. High-pitched voices from low-pitched souls. I try to make out what they are saying, but it is quickly clear that this is not in any language that I yet understand. *Wonwa* . . . somethingsomethingsomething . . . *polo*. I get the last because the word sounds familiar. Then *miwa* . . . somethingsomethingsomething . . . *amen*. I try to pick out more words that I recognize, even if wrongly. Something *maria* somethingsomething *gracia*. *Maria maleng* something something *amen*.

Sister Fernanda, black and gray hair, brown eyes, white veil, and light blue smock dress with white print flowers, says across the table, "Evening prayers."

"May I go see?"

"Yes."

I go through the back gate.

There they are. Perhaps one hundred fifty of them; perhaps more. Seated in six ad hoc but somehow orderly long rows under a single light bulb in front of a low-slung building on cathedral property, where they will be staying tonight. All face a single leader seated in a chair in front of them. The light crowns their heads with gold-orange. I recognize them—so many now that they have their own moniker—as "night commuters," children who leave their villages after an early supper and walk as far as twenty kilometers to the city, where they will be safer from LRA attack and abduction. At first light, they will return to their village school and start the process over. Forty thousand of them, it is estimated, all over northern Uganda.

The prayer-songs continue. More children arrive, some carrying reed mats on their heads, and join the rows, so that there are more than two hundred by the time the hour-plus para-liturgy of chant ends. The oldest are advanced high school age; the youngest are carried. A girl of sixteen tells us that this evening ritual is also taking place at St. Kizito's Counseling Centre, St. Joseph's Workshop, the Catechist Training Centre, and Lachor Hospital.

* * *

One of the first tasks which the Combonis undertook upon reaching Acholiland was to develop a dictionary so that they could instruct the locals in the catechism of the Catholic faith. The missionaries first abstracted the language from its lived context via the rules of grammar and definitions of the dictionary, then recomposed it as catechism for evangelical ends. Crazzolara's "grammar and vocabulary," with its 537 rules, is a stark crystallization of a process that the Combonis began immediately upon their arrival in Gulu. The missionaries bore a Catholicism that was well placed for the task of verbatim catechism. As recently as 1888—over thirty years after Daniel Comboni made his first trip to Africa—Pope Leo XIII argued for paternalistic forms of government in Europe on the basis of the fact that the great majority of the people there constituted the *imperita multitudo* (the illiterate masses). The pope would hardly expect different in Africa. When the missionaries brought Catholicism to northern Uganda, they brought with them, according to the Comboni historian Mario Cisternino, a Christianity "wholly and absolutely in a 'Latin' form."[63] In doing so, they brought a strong emphasis on catechesis through exact verbal recitation. Religion for the illiterate masses.[64]

The mission community superior in Uganda, Albino Colombaroli, in Cisternino's words, "forced his Missionaries to teach everything by heart, without any explanation. He himself started translating the catechism, and imposing it word for word."[65] To facilitate memorization, the missionaries had the locals chant the catechism,[66] and this, forged through life on the run in a conflict zone, gave the night commuters behind the Comboni Mission Animation Centre their haunting timbre in 2005. "*Wonwa* . . . somethingsomethingsomething . . . *polo*," is "Wonwa ma itye i polo" (Our Father, who is in heaven); "Something *maria* somethingsomething *gracia*," is "Morembe Maria ipong ki gracia" (Hail Mary, full of grace). Now as then.

Still, the Catholicism brought to the Acholi in the early twentieth century was of a mixed written–oral kind. Though the locals were instructed and responded verbally, the form of the speech was thoroughly structured by literate coding.[67] Oral remembrance, though often exact with regard to standardized and particularly vivid phrases, is not, unlike the catechism, verbatim throughout. In fact, the "flow of sound" or "river of action" (Havelock) of oral communication often does not distinguish sharply between particular words.[68] Writing simultaneously "freezes" (Goody) or "fossilizes" (Havelock) language into a seemingly fixed form and cuts up the now frozen river of action (or fossilized flow of sound) into increasingly small units, from phrases to words and even to correct vowel and consonant sounds, as in the case of Crazzolara's grammar and vocabulary, for any further utterance.[69] Learning the Catholic faith on the part of the Acholi, therefore, became a matter of learning "by heart," which meant "word for word."

The kind of instruction-from-a-distance involved in mission—bringing the teachings all the way from Rome and transplanting them to interior Africa—seemed to require the capacity to abstract language from lived context that the technology of writing offers. Writing, in Ong's words, makes language "autonomous . . . self-contained and complete." Print only furthers a text's unassailability. "Once a letterpress form is closed, locked up . . . and the sheet printed, the text does not accommodate changes (erasures, insertions) so readily as do written texts," making the printed word even more a "particularly pre-emptive and imperialist activity that tends to assimilate other things to itself." The result is what Goody calls the "orthodoxy of the book," in this case reinforcing a particular religious orthodoxy.[70]

Such an arrangement could not last, however. The very capacity of writing and print to freeze or fossilize speech in visual form facilitates critical examination—what Goody calls "backward scanning"—a process that allows what is written and printed "to be inspected, manipulated and re-ordered."[71] The nonliterate Acholi tried to place the catechetical claims in some kind of broader lived interpretive framework—typically one that they had inherited—and this led them to inspect, manipulate, and re-order the teachings they received from the Combonis. Father Joseph Zambonardi described the process in 1915: "After many months of explanations, when we wanted to summarize our teaching we heard them saying that the Father is older than the Son because no child can be older than his own father. . . . How could anyone live in Heaven without sorghum bread? Does one sleep up there? Does one go hunting?"[72]

Like with the British, then, the Combonis faced the real prospect of the failure of their magic to convert the Acholi. A 1917 epidemic in neighboring Moyo put the mission on the defensive when locals blamed the Catholic priests and their god. Father Joseph Zambonardi rebutted, "Is it the mission's fault if people die? . . . God is the master of us all, and only He can give well-being. . . . Let us therefore love Him by doing what he desires."[73] However, the charges of the ineffectiveness and even mendacity of the Christian god continued. A year later, Father Giuseppe Beduschi wrote, "One person says trembling that the 6 months spent in Gulu for Baptism causes boys and girls to starve to death! Another accusation is that death is also brought by the *waraga*."[74] Significantly, *waraga* literally means "paper," and more generally, "school," the place where paper is written upon. From the start, locals understood their misfortunes in terms of the imported act of writing. How then to respond? The missionaries had two basic options. One option was to draw upon key symbols from Daniel Comboni's spirituality of the Cross; the other was to graft the Gospel onto an imperial meta-narrative. We need to pay attention to both.

Response to mission failure, I: The Cross

Comboni interpreted ill fortune and the seeming ineffectiveness of the Christian god in terms of the Cross.[75] The Cross reveals, he repeatedly claimed, a particular understanding of God's activity in the world that is otherwise unavailable:[76] God brings success not simply in spite of, but *through*, human failure. Comboni took it as empirically verifiable that failure and death are the only true sources of success in the spread of the Gospel. "That all the works of salvation are born and grow at the foot of the cross is a fact proved by the constant experience of nineteen centuries. . . . It is through the cross and martyrdom that all the missions have been founded and prospered."[77]

Upon his arrival in Africa in 1857, Comboni had plenty of experiences to reinforce his devotion to the Cross. Between 1848 and 1862, forty-six missionaries died in the region—twenty-two in one year—mostly from illnesses ranging from malaria to fevers without identifiable sources.[78] Comboni wrote, "Here, from evening to morning, people are dying. Here, there is no time to prepare oneself for death: you have always to be ready."[79] He and his followers managed to convert only thirty families during his lifetime, indicating a rather high missionary death-to-convert ratio.[80] It seems safe to say that Comboni earned his appeal to the Cross.

In the face of death and failure, the task of the missionary, according to Comboni, is to trust in God's wisdom.[81] That trust is precisely in God's capacity—God's power—to bring about the success of the mission of evangelization. It is a trust on the part of Comboni that his followers—or even other people entirely—will continue the mission.

> The Gospel wins its victories in a very different way from the politicians. The apostle does not work for himself, but for eternity; he does not seek his own happiness, but that of his fellows; he knows that his work does not die with him and that his grave is the cradle of new apostles.[82]

Such trust in God involves a willingness to die—even, to use Comboni's words, "the slow martyrdom of privation, fatigue or the burning climate"—rather than betray one's mission.[83] Such willingness to die in evangelization, though, does not mean that the missionary does not exercise prudence; rather, it means that she or he undertakes discernment about risk within a different interpretive context, one that Comboni's writings identify variously as the "economy" or "law" of "God's Providence." In this context, sacrifice and even martyrdom are the normal means of apostolic success; in the economy of Providence, "the cross, contradictions, obstacles and sacrifices are the ordinary sign of the holiness of a work."[84]

The practical upshot of the appeal to the Cross is that the seeming failure of the Spirit to intervene on one's behalf does not, unlike with colonial magic, entail the turn to military force as backup. Comboni is clear on this point. Although historically it has been "reverenced on the standards of armies," the Cross itself involves "a strength which is gentle and does not kill." It has "great power" because, "the Nazarene . . . stretched out one arm to the East and the other to the West, and gathered his elect from the whole world into the embrace of the Church with pierced hands."[85]

The idea and practice of success through failure in the Cross provided a stark alternative to the turn to violence when colonial magic failed, and, at least at first, the missionary critique of colonialism was strong. An early letter of Comboni's to Cardinal Allesandro Barnabò makes a sharp charge against the British explorer, Samuel Baker:

> Letting the diplomats believe that the purpose of this enterprise was to introduce European civilization to these tribes and to abolish and destroy slavery there, [Baker] stationed various companies of soldiers on the principal points along the White Nile. . . . As a result of this violent invasion, the majority of the Africans of the White Nile withdrew westwards to the interior to flee the oppression of the conquerors . . . and many thousands of Africans were killed.[86]

However, soon thereafter, Comboni measured the impact of direct confrontation with the British and elected to remain silent about their atrocities. According to a private letter he wrote to Cardinal Barnabò, Comboni met with the British ambassador to Egypt but kept silent with regard to the explorer's crimes. "The illustrious Sir Bartle Frère, Her Majesty's ambassador, came to see me with his entourage. . . . However, I thought it prudent to keep quiet for the time being about the massacre of the Africans another Englishman, Sir Samuel Baker, is perpetuating."[87] Later, what was supposed to be a particular instance of prudence "for the time being" became Comboni's mission policy. "It is of supreme interest of the Mission of Central Africa that we should entertain good relations with the Khedive and the Egyptian Government [of which Baker was the representative in southern Sudan] and that maximum prudence should be used in dealing with them."[88] In the process of establishing their mission in Gulu, northern Uganda, Comboni's followers took the exercise of prudence in seeking good relations with the empire to extreme form. Father Louis Molinaro wrote in his memoirs regarding the relationship of another priest, Antonio Vignato, with J. R. P. Postlethwaite, the first district commissioner of northern Uganda. Vignato would later become the Comboni Superior General.

> How did Fr. Vignato earn the Officer's friendship? Through his humility. He didn't disdain to go up to the office on foot (half an hour's walk) when Postlethwaite summoned him, which happened often. His many years passed in the Bahr-el-Ghazal meant great experience and prudence. . . . In Venetian dialect, Vignato commented, "They say that I polish the Englishman's shoes. Not only will I polish them, but even kiss them if the Mission's survival is at stake."[89]

Once the missionaries aligned their vocation with England's effort to expand its operational institutional influence and authority, the evangelical effort to imitate Christ through a willingness to fail and even die gave way to other practices. Over time and through repeated interactions like those above with the British, the Combonis moved from Cross-defined mission to obsequious deference to the British to active support of the empire—through writing—by grafting the Gospel narrative onto the colonial one in a grand meta-narrative that, unlike verbatim catechesis, explicitly articulated how Acholi history fit within the context of a new history. This is most evident in the writing and publication of the pedagogical document, *Acholi Macon*, written by Father Vincent

Pelligrini. Published in 1949 and going through multiple editions, *Acholi Macon* saw 45,000 copies distributed among the Acholi via the school system by the 1960s, and is still used in the schools into the twenty-first century.[90] It is crucial to now turn our attention to this document and its impact.

Response to mission failure, II: *Acholi Macon*

A 1921 gathering of Combonis set out as one of its key resolutions that all converts, in the words of then Monsignor Angelo Negri, "be able to at least read the primer" before baptism.[91] Negri set up primary and secondary schools for both boys and girls in Gulu.[92] Later, as bishop in the early to mid-1940s, he founded the indigenous women's religious order, the Little Sisters of Mary Immaculate of Gulu, with a focus on teaching, and it is at this point that literacy began to spread more significantly among Catholic Acholi. Monsignor Giovanni Battista Cesana conveyed the consensus from Gulu in 1948: "Catechism is no longer enough. We must give them something more; we must give them education."[93] That same year, the Combonis brought a printing press to Gulu and, while still emphasizing English literacy, began to produce ethnographic texts on the Acholi *in* Acholi, and for consumption *by* the Acholi.[94] The following year, the Combonis, under the Archdiocese of Gulu, published Father Pellegrini's local vernacular account, *Acholi Macon*, and made it required reading in their schools.

The title, *Acholi Macon*, translates, "Old Acholi," and the first line makes clear the audience and purpose of the booklet: "We write these historical matters so that you, the new people (*jo manyen*) may know about your ancestors, so that these issues are not forgotten."[95] To make clear who these "new people" are, the present edition includes a photo of St. Joseph's Cathedral in Gulu. The photo shows Acholi heading toward the cathedral entrance flanked by its four pillars with the caption, "Abila pa Jo manyen i Gulu" (Shrine of the new people of Gulu). Traditionally, *abila* refers to the clan ancestral shrine. For the *jo manyen*, however, the cathedral has displaced the traditional shrine.

Pellegrini's reframing in terms of salvation history makes clear the supersessionist trajectory of his interpretation of local history: the new Acholi replace the old. Pellegrini, it needs to be clear, intends no disrespect toward Acholi history. On the contrary, he describes it as venerable.[96] In the background here is Thomas Aquinas's account of the relationship between the Old and the New Law, which informed the Council of Trent and, in so doing, subsequent Catholic teaching. The Old Law, as manifested in the Hebrew Bible, relates to the New Law as "imperfect" to "perfect." While the former aims for the earthly good by shaping our external acts through the fear of punishment, the latter, according to Aquinas, directs us to the heavenly good by forming our internal inclinations toward love.[97] Aquinas is clear that the Old Law is good, as is evidenced by the fact that it was given to humans by God. The important point for Aquinas is that whatever a tradition—whether ancient Israelite or "old Acholi"—adds of its own on top of the Old or Natural Law is no longer binding.[98] It is no longer necessary, or even desirable, to sacrifice to the ancestors now that the holy sacrifice of the Eucharist is available. The cathedral is the new *abila*.

Despite what Pelligrini writes about how "ancestral issues may be a source of learning" for the new Acholi, he takes the obsolescence of the *lodito* (the traditional elders) to be a given and goes on to make clear that the missionaries will serve as the relevant guides for the new Acholi. While the British replaced chiefs whom they deemed inadequate for the new order with *rwodi kalam* (chiefs of the pen) the Combonis appointed themselves the new *lodito kalam* (elders of the pen) (my term).[99] In light of previous shifts from orality to literacy in other cultures, this deliberate if not at all times conscious displacement is not surprising. Havelock writes of Plato and the impact on ancient Greek pedagogy of the turn to prose and the writing down of the Socratic discourses: "He was attacking the poets less for their poetry (one might say) than for the instruction which it had been their accepted role to provide. They had been the teachers of Greece . . . Greek literature had been poetic because the poetry had performed a social function, that of preserving the tradition by which the Greeks lived and instructing them in it . . . . It was precisely this didactic function and the authority that went with it to which Plato objected."[100] In the Acholi case, as the Comboni *lodito kalam* worked to displace the traditional elders, the school—alternately called *waraga*, literally "paper," to denote its literate basis, and *gang kwan*, or "home for reading"—began to replace *wang oo*, the evening fire where teaching and learning take place in the context of the extended family (a process that becomes more complete after the more recent displacement of the Acholi by President Museveni). Pellegrini writes as if he is retrieving Acholi tradition at the very moment that he is displacing it.

What is all the more striking about the re-narration of Acholi history in terms of salvation history in *Acholi Macon* is that there is very little reference to the missionaries themselves. The Combonis merit just two paragraphs of perfunctory description of how they settled in Gulu after the British established the town.[101] The main protagonists in bringing the new out of the old are the British. Samuel Baker, the explorer whom Comboni initially harshly criticized for killing "many thousands of Africans," now serves as a Moses figure. Arabic-speaking slave traders had preceded Baker from Egypt-Sudan. While Baker did not bring the Acholi out of Egypt on this account, he did much to get (Arabic) Egypt out of Acholiland. As governor of Equatoria in the 1860s and 1870s in what is now South Sudan, Baker, according to *Acholi Macon*, "immediately thought of visiting Acholiland so that he could stop people who were hunting for slaves." He set up a camp in northern Uganda in 1872, according to Pellegrini, in order to root out the slave traders: "You cannot narrate the kind of joy everyone had on seeing Baker," who "provided protection for the people." Baker "struggled so hard to put an end to the slave trading that the Arabs had started."[102]

Pellegrini lists a dozen chiefs who later established treaties with the British.[103] Subsequent administrators, according to *Acholi Macon*, found "the majority of the Acholi chiefs" (*rwodi Acholi mapol*) to be supportive of the new "rules of cooperation" (*cik me mer*).[104] Chief Awich, who distrusted the British and resisted the rules of the new Acholiland, was, in this account, the exception. He "started inciting" (*ocako piyo*) not only his own Payira people, but other clans as well to "start giving the government trouble" (*wek giyel government*), thereby necessitating his first imprisonment.[105] "Many chiefs," Pellegrini claims, helped the British round up Awich and his followers. The peace that followed allowed the British, the Acholi, and the missionaries together to start the "new town" (*goma manyen*) and "new mission" (*Mission manyen*) at a place they would come to call Gulu.[106] If Samuel Baker is the Moses figure in Pellegrini's re-narration of Acholi history, Gulu is the New Jerusalem.

Cooperation with evil

We have seen Comboni judgment shift gradually but definitely from condemnation of British colonialism to celebration of it, from Samuel Baker as the leader of a "violent invasion" in which "many thousands of Africans were killed," to Baker as a source of "joy" because he offered "protection for the people." The technologies of writing and print facilitated this process by abstracting Acholi language from its life setting where it had been ratified not in dictionaries and grammars but in local daily interaction. Once abstracted from its immediate life context, the language became manipulatable in the hands of those who wielded the power of the pen. The Combonis reinserted the abstracted language into an imperial life narrative. They reinvented the life of the Acholi as one indebted to the great acts and goodwill of the colonizers. The missionaries could have reinserted the Acholi language into a Gospel narrative centered, in the tradition of the early Daniel Comboni, around an interpretation of the Cross that promotes nonviolence, decries injustice, and serves as a brake on the accrual of "prudential" judgments that end in a policy of justifying, by silence and words, imperialism.[107] In their first half-century in northern Uganda, however, they selected the imperial narrative. The result was *Acholi Macon*.

It is necessary here to pause in this treatment of the Combonis from the activity of attention to that of what I have been calling discernment, that is to say, to evaluating their actions. Doing so will help in understanding when we turn in Chapter 3 to attention to contemporary Acholi Catholicism in the practices of the indigenous order, the Little Sisters of Mary Immaculate of Gulu. It will also help us understand the kind of duress the Combonis felt themselves to be under when they collaborated with the British Empire. Such duress is important to keep in mind because contemporary scholars doing fieldwork in countries where there is governmental oppression face a similar set of circumstances, as we will see in the last section of this chapter.

In order to avoid anachronistic judgment, it is important to analyze the missionaries' collaboration with the empire in Comboni-emic terms, that is, in terms that Combonis even at the time would have accepted. My aim in undertaking such analysis is less to litigate the actions of the Combonis than to set before ourselves just how difficult it is to live and write in an imperial context, now as well as then, in a way that does not further injustice. One of the key issues that framed Catholic moral analysis at the time was that of the "cooperation with evil." Medieval theologians detailed the conditions under which a person owed restitution to a victim even when someone else committed the primary act of injustice. According to Aquinas's list of conditions, a third party owes restitution to a victim when the former helps brings about the injustice, "By command, by counsel, by consent, by flattery, by receiving [some of the material goods gained by the injustice], by participation, by silence, by not preventing, by not denouncing."[108] In the eighteenth century, Alphonsus Liguori took up the list and described it in terms of "cooperation" with the injustice.[109] His further analysis of what constitutes licit and illicit cooperation with evil quickly became the standard for Roman Catholic moral theology and canon law. The key distinction is that between formal cooperation, where one affirms, at least in part, the object or aim of the wrongdoer's action, and material cooperation, where one's actions simply somehow overlap with and inadvertently aid the actions of the wrongdoer.

The Comboni missionaries in northern Uganda were aware of the formal/material distinction. During the earlier Mahdist uprising in Sudan (1881–98), the rebels captured several of the missionaries and held them for as long as twelve years. The men were tortured, the women were under constant threat of sexual assault. Most of the priests and brothers, under duress, abjured the faith—they signed a document made public stating such, thus giving their act the authority of being written and gazetted. Upon the liberation of the missionaries, the main question for Rome was whether their apostasy was formal, an affirmation in one way or another of Islam, or merely material, done with the aim of preserving their lives and no more.[110]

Liguori makes the distinction in the following way: "That [cooperation] is formal which concurs in the bad will of the other, and it cannot be without sin; that [cooperation] is material which concurs only in the bad action of the other, apart from the cooperator's intention."[111] *Acholi Macon*—again, required reading for all students in an institutional setting, the school, that functioned to displace the extended family, evening-fire context for passing on the tradition—inscribes Acholi history into a salvation history where the primary bearers of that history are the colonizers. Such a rewriting of Acholi history constitutes, in Liguori's terms and the language of the time, formal cooperation in the evil of colonialism because it "concurs in the bad will" of the British. Rather than being a Moses-like figure who delivered people from slavery, Samuel Baker owned slaves himself in Mauritius and Ceylon. He bought his Nubian troops—called "Khartoumers" after the place in which they were sold—out of slavery simply in order to make them mercenaries against other Africans. As indicated earlier, Daniel Comboni and his confreres knew about Baker's patterns of behavior.

Acholi Macon supports its presentation that there was little or no Acholi resistance to colonization by isolating Awich as the lone defiant chief, leaving the broad coalition involved in the Lamogi rebellion—the British arrested thirty-four chiefs—out of its account. This contrasts with the assistant district commissioner's own report that "the whole of the southern portion of the district" was "adopting bravado tactics." With regard to the forced labor and displacement that the British used to construct the largest town in northern Uganda, *Acholi Macon* simply states, as if it was created ex nihilo, "Gulu town started in February 1911 when Mr. Bainer and Mr. Sullivan came." The events that Crazzolara and other Combonis eyewitnessed and the insights that the former adds in his private diary—*Now it is as if they were not in their own territory, but in a hostile one . . . I have seen burnt barns everywhere*—never make it into the publicly printed booklet.[112] Again, Alphonsus Liguori delineated the distinction between formal and material cooperation in response to a longer tradition from the Middle Ages seeking to address the problem of third-party culpability in unjust acts. Aquinas included "silence" and "not renouncing" injustice in his list of third-party acts that require restitution to the victims. It is clear that the Combonis' public silence in *Acholi Macon* and elsewhere fits Liguori's understanding of formal cooperation.

It was the Combonis' judgment that the conversion of the Africans and thereby the possibility of their experiencing the beatific vision in the afterlife was more than proportionate to whatever the latter might suffer at the hands of the British in the present one. Daniel Comboni was clear: "The only thing that matters to me, I say, is that Africa should be converted."[113] However, in Catholic moral theology, then as now, it is not licit to commit an evil act or formally cooperate in such an act even in order to achieve what is taken to be a greater good. In Liguori's words, formal cooperation with evil "cannot be without sin" (*nequit esse sine peccato*). This is true even though it is likely that if the missionaries had spoken out against the colonial practices, the British would have either interned or expelled them.

At this point, it is helpful for further illumination to bring in the emic distinction between objective wrongdoing and subjective culpability. Catholic missionaries in Sudan prior to and after the formation of the Comboni order died at an extraordinary rate as a result of following their vocations. Again, twenty-two died in a single year. And again, Mahdist rebels held captive for a period of up to twelve years, threatened, and often tortured all those missionaries, male and female, who could not flee in time. For instance, the Mahdists took scissors and cut the partition between one sister's nostrils; they suspended another from a tree and beat the soles of her feet until they were "swollen and black." (It is common knowledge in the world of torture that the bottoms of the feet are one of the most sensitive areas of the body.)[114]

I hope that it is clear that what the Comboni missionaries endured during this period was more than most of us could bear. It takes no stretch of the imagination to see that the Comboni community after the Mahdist rebellion was in a state of collective shock. In its wake, they viewed the retaking of Egypt-Sudan by the British not only as a reprieve, but as a kind of liberation that they then projected onto the situation in Acholiland. Baker became Moses; Gulu the New Jerusalem. The pressures of the First World War only furthered—or as Aquinas would say, "increased"—the disposition to not speak of the British injustices. Many of the Combonis were Austrian, and thus on the "wrong" side of the war. The British arrested and interned the Austrian missionaries and required even the Italian ones to declare allegiance to the empire. Given that Italy and England were on the opposite sides of the Second World War, the years leading up to the publishing of *Acholi Macon* in 1948 provided little reprieve for the Combonis. How much such pressures mitigate the subjective culpability of the Combonis I leave open for consideration, but that there were such pressures is unquestionable. It might be tempting to heap opprobrium on the Comboni missionaries for their cooperation with evil, and to think that we would never repeat what at this distance seems to be a mistaken path, but colonial pressures continue in neocolonial form, and present us with a dilemma strikingly similar to that of the Combonis. In terms of the attention–discernment–commitment–return trajectory of the moments in anthropological theology that I set out in Chapter 1, I invite you for a moment to discern the kind of pressures and constraints that the Combonis inhabited before going on to paying attention to contemporary Acholi Catholicism in Chapter 3, because those pressures and constraints also marked my time in Uganda and South Sudan.

A contemporary dilemma

"Wait. How much longer are you here?"

Ocena Charles's question catches me by surprise.[115] We have been talking about the various practices of Acholi culture—the *otole* mock-fight dance, the fact that funerals can last days, even weeks—for more than an hour at the Victoria restaurant in Entebbe. It is why we got together. I was told that he knows something about Acholi traditions. Then he abruptly stops chewing his Tilapia, sits forward in his chair, and fires his question.

"I leave tomorrow morning," I answer.

Ocena sits back and looks out over the water of Lake Victoria, pondering my answer for a long moment. He turns to me.

"How much time do you have before you need to get back to Kampala tonight?"

Another clearly stated yet elliptical question.

"I have nothing planned. I just need to get back early enough so that I can get up on time for my plane in the morning."

He looks back out over the lake, nods his head, and then turns to me once more.

"I have some documents for you. Will you take some documents for me to the United States?"

"What kind of documents?"

"For your research." He is still speaking in code. The documents are, he says, for me, but I am to take them to the United States for him. "You can use them for your research."

He does not fully trust me yet, but he trusts me enough to be his courier.

"Yes, I will take them."

"And you know that you cannot tell anyone that they are from me."

"Yes."

"Or else the government will . . . ." He makes a slicing movement across his neck.

My risks are likely far less serious in this instance, but they are real. If I am found out, the government might not let me back in the country. Carrying what is ostensibly for my research may cost me my research. The University of Notre

Dame has funded much of my travel, and is likely to take a dim view if my project is not completed.

We get a car and driver, and Ocena explains why we are heading away from his place in Entebbe. "I have to keep the documents at my nephew's place, or else they will find them and kill me."

We drive out to a Kampala slum and he gets out of the car. I am not sure whether we have taken our circuitous route because of possible danger or simply because that is the way the streets are laid out. To our left, shacks of corrugated metal compete for coveted space. The adults continually duck their heads so as not to cut them on the edges of the roofs, and so look like they are joining the bobbing chickens around their feet.

I open the door to get out of the car, but Ocena stops me, and this time I quickly understand. My job is to ferry the documents to the United States where others can see them, but get out here and my whiteness draws too much attention.

In less than five minutes, he is back. He opens the back door, gets in, and puts a brown file folder with an elastic restraining strap around it on my lap.

"Read it later."

We drive away.

* * *

The file folder held documents that Ocena claimed undercut the predominant narrative of the conflict in northern Uganda, a narrative where the sole cause of the conflict is the madman Joseph Kony and his immediate henchmen, and the sole adequate response is a military one carried out by the enlightened "new breed" of African rulers like Ugandan president Yoweri Museveni with the support of the United States and other major Western powers. It is a soteriological narrative, furthered by such groups as Invisible Children, that Africans need saving from themselves by a force from elsewhere.[116]

My gaining access to northern Uganda for my research has depended, much like it did for the evangelizing mission of the Combonis, on my not challenging the dominant narrative. When I first arrived in Uganda in 2005, entry to northern Uganda required vetting by Lieutenant Colonel Shaban Bantariza, the Director of Public Relations and Information for the Ugandan military. The meeting was cordial. I told him my purpose, that I was a theology professor from the University of Notre Dame in the United States seeking to go to northern Uganda to study traditional Acholi culture and Christianity, particularly Roman Catholic Christianity. Lieutenant Colonel Bantariza asked if I was a journalist, and I said no. He asked if I had a camera, and I showed him my small four-megapixel Olympus C-750. He asked what I was going to use the photos for, and I replied that they would be for the classroom and my research. He accepted my response and wished me well. Things were a bit more tense with the authorities on the ground in the IDP camps where I went to live.

* * *

"You have failed to see me."

The Government Security Officer or "GiSO" of Obul IDP camp, Odoch Benedict, stops me on the main road through the camp.[117] I am the only *munno*—white person—of the twenty-two thousand people here, and not easy to miss. His presumption irritates me.

"I stopped by your compound twice. You weren't there," I answer. The GiSO's responsibility for camp security includes control of the flow of public information. He does not like my response.

"So, you have still failed to see me."

Odoch appears to be in his forties, though it is hard to tell. It is eight-thirty in the morning and his eyes are already bloodshot on yellow. He has been drinking *arege*, the clear, locally distilled cassava-based alcohol.

"I have direct contact with the President. I can call him whenever I want. If he is in London, whenever. I have been an intelligence officer for fifteen years, including in Sudan. That is why they have me here. Obul is close to Sudan. It is not even ten miles. Some people come here and say bad things about Obul. And you?" Odoch asks. "What shall I say you are doing here?"

"I am an academic. I am studying traditional Acholi religion."

"So we cooperate. I have to tell the higher command what you are up to. They already know that you are here. They wonder, 'What is the *munno* doing in Obul?' Now I can tell them what you are doing. They had some mistaken ideas."

* * *

"So we cooperate." Yet it would also seem that not publicizing the documents I received from Ocena Charles now that I had them would make me guilty of cooperation with evil not only, to use Aquinas's words, "by silence, by not preventing, by not denouncing," but also "by flattery" (of the governments of the United States and Uganda) and "by receiving," that is, by my material gain from finishing my research unimpeded, publishing the book, and being promoted within the university.

The threats to Ugandans if they challenge the dominant narrative are real. If anyone dares speak out, government personnel move in to intimidate. When CBS Radio of Uganda reported on riots in Kampala in September 2009, the government-controlled Broadcasting Council shut it down and revoked its license, charging that the station was seeking to "mobilize and incite the public."[118] After the Voice of Radio Lango station hosted an April 2010 show with opposition presidential candidate, Olara Otunnu, Museveni himself made several telephone calls to the station owner—who is also a NRM government legislator—to "ask" that the station publicly apologize, which it did. On the show, Otunnu called for open investigations into the actions of all armed groups—including Museveni's National Resistance Army, the precursor of the current UPDF government army—involved in the 1980–5 bush war in Uganda. Otunnu also charged Museveni with enabling the conflict in northern Uganda. It was made clear that failure to apologize on the part of the station would lead to its closure and, perhaps, threaten the station owner's future with NRM leadership. In October 2010, the Uganda Revenue Authority's Customs Department, under orders from an unnamed "another arm of the government," seized boxed copies of a book critical of Museveni at Entebbe International Airport where they arrived for distribution in Uganda.[119] A May 2010 Human Rights Watch report, *A Media Minefield: Increased Threats to Freedom of Expression in Uganda*, articulates the overall situation this way:

> [There have been] increasingly arbitrary state attacks on the media as the ruling party faces more and more public and open criticism. Since the previous political campaigns in 2005, at least 40 criminal charges have been levied against journalists and talk show panelists. In some cases, these threats are overt, such as public statements by a resident district commissioner that a journalist should be "eliminated," or a police summons on charges of sedition, incitement to violence, or promoting sectarianism for criticizing government action in a newspaper article. In many more cases, the threats are covert, such as phone calls—some anonymous and others from well-known ruling party operatives—intimating violence or loss of employment if a journalist pursues a certain issue or story.[120]

The tactics have continued. In May 2013, Museveni's regime sent more than fifty police officers to close two major newspapers and two radio stations for making public a letter said to be written by the government's own coordinator of intelligence service stating that there was a conspiracy to frame or kill cabinet members who do not support Museveni's son as the president's successor. When the court, which sometimes has an independent mind, withdrew the search warrant three days later, the police actually increased their presence, and detained and beat two journalists and eight civil society members who protested the closures.[121] Protest itself is a risky venture: in 2009, police shot and killed over forty people participating in public protests; in April 2011, they killed at least nine more. To date, there have been no criminal investigations into the shootings.[122] In September 2015, security forces shot five people who were protesting against government claims to what locals considered clan land.[123] Because of such government intimidation, people, through desperation, often approach persons like me to help get the word out. To such people, my protestations that I am an academic, an academic theologian at that, are irrelevant. Anthropologists often refer to the "positionality" of the researcher—his or her gender, race, nationality, and the like, and how these affect the researcher's interactions with the people researched. What I have found salient in addition, however, is how the researcher *gets positioned* by the subjects. Persons like Ocena Charles—and there were several—sought to position me as a disseminator of information that, because of government tactics, they themselves could not make public.

The government, in turn, often presupposed that I was a spy. In one of the camps, a resident warned me: "If someone comes up to you and asks how long you are staying, do not tell them. They are spies. Asking how long a visitor is staying is against Acholi hospitality. No one would ask you that except spies. Do not tell them. Just tell them you do not know. Be vague." I had been living in a wattle and daub hut, and had frequent visitors. Some were curious, others sought help of some sort or money; most of them were friends of my host. One afternoon, two men I had not seen before came to visit and sat, without asking, in some fold out chairs in front of my hut. After initial greetings and pleasantries, they asked me what I was doing in the camp. I told them. They asked how long I was staying. Having been alerted, I answered, "I am not sure." This was the second camp I had lived in, and by that time I had been told both directly and indirectly by any number of Acholi people that doing research was not enough to justify my presence in northern Uganda. How was I going to help *them*? I had been thinking about various projects—agricultural support and training among them—and testing out my ideas with the people I met. When I told my two visitors about this, one wanted to enlist me in supporting a beekeeping and honey business he sought to start. I told him that I would think about it along with the other suggestions I received. Before they left, I asked them their names—they, again in contrast to Acholi cultural practices, had not introduced themselves yet—because I wanted to remember with whom I met, particularly if they were interested in any development project I might undertake in northern Uganda. Later, I asked an active camp resident if he had heard of these two men and if they were NRM. He said that he had not heard of them, but that he would check it out. The next day he told me that they were not only NRM, but that they were not even from the camp. They had not just happened across me.[124]

This is the context—though I did not know it yet—of my dinner with Ocena Charles on Lake Victoria. When I returned to the compound at which I was staying, I opened the document packet he had given me and made a follow-up call. I was leaving the following day, and wanted to be sure that this is what he wanted transported. Most of the documents were already available on the internet, and so did not require transport in hard copy. Being on the web, they were also moot from a security standpoint, though government intelligence officers might not view it that way. The next day, in fact, intelligence officers descended upon the compound at which I was staying—which was the home of a religious community—and demanded to see the guest book and me. They had tapped our phone call. I had already left the country by the time that they arrived. Community members later told me that the intelligence officers said, "We know that he had permission from Shaban Bantariza to go to the North, but now he is talking to dissidents." In other words, they had been tracking me since I had first arrived the previous year.

Close friends warned me of the possibility that I might get into an "accident" if I sought to publish the information that Ocena Charles gave me. Maybe I would be hit by a lorry that "slipped" to the side of the road while I was riding my motorcycle. They told me that, in 1993, a Canadian graduate student doing research in the West Nile region of Uganda was brutally murdered by armed groups connected to the Ugandan government. A research assistant who worked with a number of foreign researchers was murdered in 2010, "most likely by Ugandan security," according to one source. Or perhaps I would eat some "bad food" (I am not being melodramatic here; poisoning, real and imagined, is a regular feature of Ugandan life).[125] The most probable risk for me, however, was simply that I would not be allowed to return to Uganda. The NRM has kicked out foreign journalists who have written for *The Economist*, *The Christian Science Monitor*, and the

BBC. In 2013, the government detained for three days and then deported a US filmmaker for documenting political resistance in Uganda.[126] Like the Combonis, my greatest risk was expulsion or blockage from return.

How, then, to inscribe the Acholi people?—because that is what we are, scribes: members of a professional clan that renders people into writing. We do not have a very sterling reputation in either scripture or the history of colonized peoples. Jesus says in his "woe" to the scribes, "They do not practice what they teach. They tie up heavy burdens, hard to bear, and lay them on the shoulders of others; but they themselves are unwilling to lift a finger to move them" (Mt. 23:2b-4; cf. 23:1-39; also Mk 12:38-40). Levi-Strauss warns, "The scribe is rarely a functionary or employee of the group: his knowledge is accompanied by power . . . . [He is] someone who *has a hold* over others" (emphasis in original).[127] Comboni Father Joseph Pasquale Crazzolara highlights the role of tattletales for the empire in northern Uganda. Scribes "wrote on their registers the names of the balky ones, starting from the chiefs."[128] Ocena Charles knew of my scribal power when he gave me the documents. He risked that I might register his name as a "balky one."

So again, how to inscribe the Acholi? With whose narratives from among the many that are possible? Again, inscribing well begins by paying attention, so I return to that activity in Chapter 3. I begin with the first-person narratives of the Little Sisters of Mary Immaculate of Gulu. The Little Sisters are the most direct indigenous religious descendants of the Comboni missionaries, and to tell their story is, in part, to tell of the reversal of empire-supporting Christianity in northern Uganda. During President Museveni's raid on the north and the LRA conflict that followed, the Little Sisters and the Roman Catholic Church generally were one of the few nonwar infrastructures on the ground. Through the practice of such devotions as the Adoration of the Eucharist and the veneration of their founder, Bishop Angelo Negri, they carried forward—and still do—the original Comboni charism of the willingness to die on behalf of the vulnerable. We will also see how the Little Sisters' imitation of Negri and Jesus Christ coheres with the kind of mimesis displayed in and called for by the gospels themselves.

Notes

1. Levi-Strauss, *Tristes Tropiques* (New York: Atheneum, 1981), p. 299.

2. See, for instance, Todd Whitmore, "Crossing the Road: The Case for Ethnographic Fieldwork in Christian Ethics," *Journal of the Society of Christian Ethics* 27, no. 2 (Fall 2007), pp. 273–94; Mary McClintock Fulkerson, *Places of Redemption: Theology for a Worldly Church* (Oxford: Oxford University Press, 2007); and Christian Scharen and Aana Marie Vigen, eds., *Ethnography as Christian Theology and Ethics* (London and New York: Continuum, 2011).

3. John W. Burton, with Orsolya Arva Burton, "Some Reflections on Anthropology's Missionary Positions," *Journal of Royal Anthropological Institute* 13 (2007), p. 209. For the anthropology *of* Christianity, see Fenella Cannell, ed., *The Anthropology of Christianity* (Durham and London: Duke University Press, 2006). For an anthropology that enters into conversation with Christian theology, see Joel Robbins, "Anthropology and Theology: An Awkward Relationship?" *Anthropological Quarterly* 79, no. 2 (2006), pp. 285–95. See also

Eloise Meneses, Lindy Backues, David Bronkema, Eric Flett, and Benjamin L. Hartley, "Engaging the Religiously Committed Other: Anthropologists and Theologians in Dialogue," *Current Anthropology* 55, no. 1 (February 2014), pp. 82–104.

4. Michael A. Rynkiewich, response to Charles E. Stipe, "Anthropologists versus Missionaries: The Influence of Presuppositions," *Current Anthropology* 21, no. 2 (April 1980), p. 174. Stipe's article and the responses run from p. 165 to p. 179. For nuanced essays by anthropologists on their relationships with missionaries, see also the articles in Roland Bonsen, Hans Marks, and Jelle Miedema, eds., *The Ambiguity of Rapprochement: Reflections of Anthropologists on their Controversial Relationships with Missionaries* (Nijmegen, The Netherlands : Focaal, in cooperation with the NSAV, 1990).

5. George W. Stocking, Jr., *The Ethnographer's Magic and Other Essays in the History of Anthropology* (Madison: University of Wisconsin Press, 1992).

6. I am here deliberately if momentarily reversing the Western tendency to identify its own practices as "religion" and those of indigenous peoples elsewhere as "magic." Concomitant with the development of religious freedom in Western democracy came an anxious need to identify and delimit the not-religion. "Magic" and "witchcraft" became umbrella terms to cover all cultural ritual practices that were not "religion."

7. The name is a pseudonym.

8. The first formal translation of *ajwaka* was made by Comboni Father J. P. Crazzolara: "Priest of Spirit;" also *mon ajwaka* "Female Priests of Spirits." *cf. A Study of the Acooli Language: Grammar and Vocabulary* (London: Oxford University Press, 1938; Second Edition [Revised, 1955]), p. 177. The second translation was made by Comboni Father Alfred Malandra: "Witch-doctor." *cf. A New Acholi Grammar* (Kampala: The Eagle Press, 1952; revised edition, 1955), p. 1. The third translation was made by G. A. R. Savage: "Wizard, Witch Doctor." *cf. A Short Acoli English and English Acoli Vocabulary* (Kampala: The Eagle Press, 1955), p. 1. Crazzolara arrived in Uganda in 1911, after having studied linguistics in Vienna. Malandra arrived in Uganda approximately twenty years later, but with no formal training in linguistics. Mr. Savage was a colonial officer. I am indebted to Paul Donohue, MCCJ, for these details. Donohue adds that Crazzolara's superiors "isolated him in order to marginalize him by sending him to study other African languages," in part due to Crazzolara's friendly rendering of *ajwaka* as "priest of spirits" rather than "witchdoctor." Personal correspondence, March 30, 2013.

9. Paul Donohue, MCCJ, suggests that the shells may have been present in northern Uganda even before then. Personal correspondence, March 30, 2013.

10. It is difficult to ascertain an "original" precolonial Acholi religiosity, both because of the migrations, and thus religious flux, of the peoples who would become "the Acholi" even prior to colonial contact, and because of the role of colonization itself in the formation of something like a unified Acholi identity.

11. There is a fourth kind of *jok*, one that is attached to a natural landmark but is not associated with a chiefdom or clan lineage. P'Bitek addresses this kind as part of his chapter on chiefdom *jogi*, but they are not the same, even though some chiefdom *jogi* are associated with natural landmarks.

12. P'Bitek, *Religion of the Central Luo* (Nairobi, Kampala, and Dar Es Salaam: East African Literature Bureau, 1971), pp. 96 and 104.

13. P'Bitek, *Religion of the Central Luo*, p. 94.

14. In another case, the priestess, like an *ajwaka*, divines the sources of the illnesses and troubles of the people and proffers remedies. In yet another, the *jok* of a diviner who

performs miracles *becomes* a chiefdom *jok*. See p'Bitek, *Religion of the Central Luo,* pp. 94, 76, 80, and 74.

15. P'Bitek, *Religion of the Central Luo*, pp. 95–6. The *ajwaka's* fluidity in moving between chiefdom, ancestral and free *jok* is notable given the rather strict demarcation between roles that holds today. (I asked one chief if he was concerned about *cen* (vengeful spirits) at his shrine. "No, that is the concern of the *ajwaka*. I just care for the ancestral shrine. When I die, the task will rotate to another descendent." He made clear that there is a separation of spiritual powers between him, as chief, and the local *ajwagi*. His spirits are territorial, theirs are free; his ancestral, theirs of many originations.)

16. P'Bitek, *Religion of the Central Luo*, p. 143.

17. The British administration, in its quest for hierarchical order among the decentralized Acholi chiefdoms, subordinated the Labongo people under Aliker and the Payira.

18. See Okot p'Bitek, *Horn of My Love* (Nairobi: Heinemann Kenya Ltd, 1974), pp. 12–14. I alter p'Bitek's translation of *pyelo i kaki* from "he excretes in his khaki trousers" to "he shits his khaki trousers" because *pyelo* is the cruder term for *konynye*, the latter meaning literally, "to ease oneself." Both the word *pyelo* and the context of mocking merit the cruder translation. P'Bitek does not hesitate in the second poem to translate *gero*, which means, even in a noncrude sense, both sexual intercourse and marriage, as "fuck." The defiant, mocking tone of the second poem also seems to warrant the cruder translation. Lakana composed his "penis poem" in 1918.

19. Eric Havelock, *The Muse Learns to Write: Reflections on Orality and Literacy from Antiquity to the Present* (New Haven and London: Yale University Press, 1986), p. 66; Jack Goody, *The Domestication of the Savage Mind* (Cambridge: Cambridge University Press, 1977), p. 14; Walter Ong, *Orality and Literacy* (London and New York: Routledge, 2002), pp. 76 and 32.

20. Havelock, *The Muse Learns to Write*, p. 69; cf. also p. 54 and 57; Goody, *The Domestication of the Savage Mind*, p. 113.

21. Havelock, *The Muse Learns to Write*, p. 76; Ong, *Orality and Literacy*, pp. 37–41.

22. Havelock, *The Muse Learns to Write*, p. 76.

23. Ibid., pp. 70, 77, and 79.

24. Jack Goody and Ian Watt, "The Consequences of Literacy," in *Literacy in Traditional Societies*, ed. Jack Goody (Cambridge: Cambridge University Press, 1968), p. 29; Ong, *Orality and Literacy*, pp. 46–7.

25. Without adhering to any monocausal explanation, Goody argues that the shift in the means and mode of communication brought by writing and, later, print technology has as much explanatory power as Marx's stress on the modes of production for understanding social and cultural change. Goody, *The Domestication of the Savage Mind*, p. 109; cf. also pp. 111, 128, 160–1. For Ong and Havelock on how writing changes consciousness, see Ong, *Orality and Literacy*, pp. 50–6; and Havelock, *The Muse Learns to Write*, pp. 98–116.

26. John Hanning Speke, *Journal of the Discovery of the Source of the Nile* (London: William Blackwood, 1863), pp. 535–7.

27. Claude Levi-Strauss, *Tristes Tropiques*, pp. 296, 297–8.

28. More recent anthropological work in Fiji supports Levi-Strauss's analysis. Using local materials, indigenous in Melanesia and Micronesia attempted to reconstruct—that is, imitate—modern artifacts ranging from airstrips to manifest logs in an effort to bring Western goods to themselves. Such symbolic actions are like the Nambikwara making wavy lines on paper. Martha Kaplan argues that the locals in Fiji were using magic against a prior colonial magic. Kaplan highlights the power of magic to create new social realities, and

shows that, in the case of the British colonization of Fiji, the printed and distributed Deed of Cession constituted a "magical creation of a new polity": "And from then on, everything that was official and real in the colony was made real via the printed word. If it wasn't 'gazetted,' it didn't officially exist. And one of the things that was official was the colonial state itself." Fiji resistance to colonial magic, Kaplan shows, was therefore from the start magic interwoven with political resistance.

Martha Kaplan, "The Magical Power of the (Printed) Word," in *Magic and Modernity: Interfaces of Revelation and Concealment*, ed. Birgit Meyer and Peter Pels (Standford, CA: Stanford University Press, 2003), p. 190. On cargo cults, see Lamont Lindstrom, *Cargo Cult: Strange Stories from Melanesia and Beyond* (Honolulu: University of Hawaii Press, 1993).

29. A later commissioner wrote of Wilson that he "advocated strenuous measures to bring the Nilotic tribes [of northern Uganda] under our rule and that a somewhat imposing display of force" was advisable. Cited in Mario Cisternino, *Passion for Africa: Missionary and Imperial Papers on the Evangelization of Uganda and Sudan, 1848–1923* (Kampala: Fountain Publishers, 2004), pp. 316 and 316, n. 40.

30. The possibility that the spirits of any killed returnees might visit upon the Acholi as *cen*— vengeful ghosts—also loomed.

31. Reuben S. Anywar, "The Life of Rwot Iburaim Awich," *Uganda Journal* 12, no. 1 (1948), p. 76.

32. Cited in Cisternino, *Passion for Africa*, p. 363.

33. Cisternino, *Passion for Africa*, p. 361.

34. Due to the Mahdist rebellion in Sudan, the British were absent from Acholiland from 1888 to 1898. R. M. Bere, "Awich—A Biographical Note and a Chapter of Acholi History," *Uganda Journal* 10, no. 2 (1946), pp. 77.

35. On the variety of forms of resistance by locals under imperial presence, see James C. Scott, *Domination and the Arts of Resistance: Hidden Transcripts* (New Haven: Yale University Press, 1992).

36. A. D. Adimola, "The Lamogi Rebellion, 1911–1912," *Uganda Journal* 18, no. 2 (1954), p. 175. Cisternino states that "300 and more died of dysentery." Cisternino, *Passion for Africa*, p. 375.

37. Cisternino, *Passion for Africa*, p. 375.

38. Ibid.

39. Adimola, "The Lamogi Rebellion, 1911-1912," p. 176.

40. Ibid., p. 143.

41. Heike Behrend writes, in her overview of the impact of colonialism on Acholi religiosity, "Since the colonial period, the power of the *jogi* of the chiefdoms and the clans has generally tended to fade into the background, while the free *jogi* and the witches gained ever more power." Behrend, *Alice Lakwena and the Holy Spirits: War in Northern Uganda* (Oxford: James Curry/ Kampala: Fountain Publishers/ Nairobi: EAEP/ Athens: Ohio University Press, 1999), p. 107.

42. The first missionaries to Gulu were aided in their spiritual combat by the colonial Witchcraft Ordinance of 1912, which was revised in 1921 to make punishment for practice more severe—increasing incarceration from one to five years and including penalties for possession of the objects of practice. See, A. Adu Boahen, *Africa under Colonial Domination, 1880-1935*, UNESCO General History of Africa, Volume 7, abridged edition (Berkeley: University of California Press, 1990), p. 218.

43. On Margaret Mary Alocoque, see Robert Russell, "St. Margaret Mary Alocoque and the Sacre Coeur," *Buckfast Chronicle* 32, no. 3 (Autumn 1962), p. 168.

44. The devotion remains prominent in the order, now called the "Comboni Missionaries of the Heart of Jesus."

45. A pseudonym.

46. La Salette is the site of an apparition of Mary witnessed by two children in 1846. Daniel Comboni, *Daniel Comboni: The Man and His Message*, ed. and trans. Aldo Gilli (Bologna: Edittrice Missionaria Italiana, 1980), pp. 189–90.

47. Daniel Comboni, *Daniel Comboni: The Man and His Message,* p. 192.

48. Ibid., p. 209.

49. Ibid., p. 212: "My work is in itself hard and arduous, and only God's infinite power is able to make it succeed. So all my hope is in the Heart of Jesus and in the intercession of Mary." For further references in Comboni's writings to God's power, particularly as exercised through Mary, see also pp. 189 and 193.

50. On God's protective role, particularly through Mary and the Sacred Heart of Jesus, see, for instance, Daniel Comboni, *Daniel Comboni*, p. 219: "The Scared Heart of Jesus and Our Lady of the Sacred Heart, to whom Central Africa is consecrated, they will protect our work." See also p. 194 ("guard us as your property and heritage"), pp. 214, 232 ("God should give me those who can help me . . . and should keep them safe), and p. 257.

51. Daniel Comboni, *Daniel Comboni: The Man and His Message,* p. 68.

52. Fr. Tarcisio Agostoni, *The Comboni Missionaries: An Outline History, 1867-1997* (Rome: Bibliotheca Comboniana, 2003), p. 290, referring to a letter to the Institute written by Vicar General Antonio Vignato in 1937.

53. Agostoni, *The Comboni Missionaries*, p. 486: The Comboni Rule of Life is "the concrete path of our 'sequela Christi' as followers of Comboni (sequela)." On the *sequela Christi* in the Comboni Rule, see also pp. 468 and 469.

54. Agostoni, *The Comboni Missionaries,* p. 515.

55. Giovanni Vantini, "Lul: The First Missionary Outpost in Southern Sudan in the Twentieth Century," in *White Nile, Black Blood: War, Leadership, and Ethnicity from Khartoum to Kampala*, ed. Jay Spalding and Stephanie Beswick (Trenton, NJ: Red Sea Press, 2000), p. 320.

56. Vinco taught at the Mazza Institute, to which Comboni belonged before forming his own group of missionaries. See Giovanni Vantini, *Christianity in the Sudan* (Bologna: EMI, 1981), p. 237.

57. Cisternino, *Passion for Africa*, p. 13.

58. J. P. Crazzolara, *A Study of the Acooli Language: Grammar and Vocabulary*, 1. In the earlier stages of the movement from orality to literacy, the spellings of words remain in flux. Crazzolara uses *c* to symbolize the "ch" sound, and this is still the usage with many words. However, the more common spelling of *Acooli* now is *Acholi*.

59. Ong, *Orality and Literacy*, p. 77; cf. also pp. 100 and 102.

60. See Havelock, *The Muse Learns to Write*, pp. 8–12, 58, 61–2, 106; Ong, *Orality and Literacy*, p. 84.

61. Goody, *The Domestication of the Savage Mind*, pp. 78 and 148; Havelock, *The Muse Learns to Write*, pp. 58–62.

62. On the development of lists due to the technology of writing, see Goody, *The Domestication of the Savage Mind*, pp. 74–111.

63. Mario Cisternino, *Passion for Africa*, p. 64. Cisternino is a Comboni historian in the sense that he is both a historian of and member of the order. Rev. Cisternino died in June 2011.

64. I prefer to distinguish between "nonliterate" persons in oral culture and "illiterate" persons whom a literate culture has failed to teach to read and write. Here, however, in order to indicate the parallel approach of Catholic catechesis in Europe and Africa at the time, I use Leo XIII's term, "illiterate." This also highlights the fact that European culture at the time viewed Africans not as nonliterate, that is oral, but as illiterate and therefore lesser.

65. Cisternino, *Passion for Africa*, p. 353.

66. Fr. Mario Marchetti, *Too Long in the Dark: The Story of the Two Martyrs of Paimol and the Relevance to Uganda Today* (Gulu: Archdiocese of Gulu, 1999), p. 44.

67. Oral-literate combinations of various kinds have been and continue to be common. In the early stages in the literacy of a culture, for instance, most writing intended for public consumption was read aloud. The scribe was a specialist alongside the chief, the *ajwaka*, and the poet. Even in societies that are deemed "fully literate," technologies like radio and film keep what Ong calls a "secondary orality" in play. The pertinent question is which of the two linguistic codings in the mix is dominant, and in the case of the form of catechism brought by the Combonis, it is the coding of literate consciousness. Ong, *Orality and Literacy*, pp. 133–5.

68. Goody, *The Domestication of the Savage Mind*, p. 115.

69. Ibid., p. 71; Havelock, *The Muse Learns to Write*, p. 66.

70. Ong, *Orality and Literacy*, pp. 130 and 12; Goody, *The Domestication of the Savage Mind*, p. 37.

71. Goody, *The Domestication of the Savage Mind*, pp. 128 and 76.

72. Cisternino, *Passion for Africa*, p. 433.

73. Ibid., p. 458.

74. Ibid., pp. 469–70.

75. Comboni's theology of the Cross arose out of concrete circumstances. While on a pilgrimage to the Holy Land just before his first trip to Africa, he visited Calvary. It had a profound effect on him. See Daniel Comboni, *Daniel Comboni*, p. 200.

76. Daniel Comboni, *Daniel Comboni*, p. 208: "The God-Man showed his wisdom in no better way than in making the cross." See also pp. 210 and 218.

77. Daniel Comboni, *Daniel Comboni*, pp. 213–14 and 219–20. See also p. 235. At one point, the missionary deaths prompted the pope to close down all of the missions in the region. Comboni himself had to return to Europe after only two years in the field because of severe illness. He later returned to Africa, and in 1872 became the new Pro-Vicar. But further deaths took their toll on his followers, and the Vatican then gave almost all of the Vicariate to Charles Martial Lavigerie, the founder of the White Fathers and Comboni's frequent intra-ecclesial competitor. Broken, Comboni returned ill to Europe once again. He ventured back to Africa one last time, but was too ill to stay out in the field, and had to retreat to Khartoum, where he died in 1881.

78. Giovanni Vantini, *Christianity in the Sudan*, p. 240.

79. Daniel Comboni, *Daniel Comboni*, p. 203.

80. The number of priests was so low that Mario Cisternino, himself a priest of the congregation, is forced to write, "To be honest, Comboni's priests were very few at the time: a good number had died, several others returned to Europe, and no leader had been found among the remainder." Cisternino, *Passion for Africa*, p. 212, n.29.

81. Daniel Comboni, *Daniel Comboni*, p. 211. On the theme of trust in God, see also pp. 42, 136, 203–5, 209, 232, and 236.

82. Daniel Comboni, *Daniel Comboni*, p. 136. See also p. 212.

83. Ibid., p. 220. See also p. 42.

84. Ibid., p. 221. On the "economy of Providence," see also 201–2; on the "law of God's Providence," see p. 213; on prudence, see, for instance, p. 69.

85. Daniel Comboni, *Daniel Comboni*, pp. 215–16.

86. Cisternino, *Passion for Africa*, p. 80.

87. Ibid., p. 210, note 25.

88. Ibid., p. 85.

89. Ibid., p. 410.

90. Tim Allen, "Review of Ronald Atkinson, *The Roots of Ethnicity*," *Africa* 66, no. 3 (1996), p. 474; and Behrend, *Alice Lakwena and the Holy Spirits*, p. 150. As of this writing, the most recent edition of *Acholi Macon* was published in 2006. Vincent Pellegrini, *Acoli Macon* (Gulu: Gulu Archdiocese: 2006).

91. Cisternino, *Passion for Africa*, pp. 529–30.

92. The schools were named Angelo Negri Primary and Secondary School, Mary Immaculate Primary School, and Sacred Heart Secondary School. See Sam Lawino, "Footprints of Colonialism in the North," *Daily Monitor* (July 20, 2012), at http://www.monitor.co.ug/SpecialReports/ugandaat50/Footprints+of+colonialism+in+the+north/-/1370466/1458240/-/kl62lz/-/index.html (retrieved July 28, 2012).

93. Agostoni, *The Comboni Missionaries*, p. 338.

94. See Behrend, *Alice Lakwena and the Holy Spirits*, pp. 148–50.

95. Fr. Vincent Pellegrini, *Acholi Macon*, 2. The Acholi reads, "*Lok manok man ma wacoyo kany watimo wek wunu jo manyen wungee maber lok pa kwarowu, wek kop man ducu pe dok orweny ki bot dano.*" I am indebted to Ketty Anyeko for translating key sections of the document for me. She translates much more rapidly and accurately than I can, and she saved me much time and headache. I have adjusted Ms. Anyeko's translation in a few places and in minor ways where I thought different wording conveyed the meaning more fully.

96. Pellegrini, *Acholi Macon*, 2: "*Lok pa jo macon obed pwony pi jo manyen. Ka bed buk pe kano lok man kono gin ducu ma kwarowu otimo orwenyo woko oyotyot.*"

97. Thomas Aquinas, *Summa Theologica*, Ia-IIae, q. 91., a.5.

98. Thomas Aquinas, *Summa Theologica*, Ia-IIae, q. 98.

99. Heike Behrend notes that the "feedback to the self-image of the Acholi and their ideas of their history" that resulted from the writing of *Acholi Macon*, "should not be underestimated." However, given that Behrend, by her own admission, "abstained from learning Acholi or Lwo," she has no way of knowing just what that feedback effect is given that *Acholi Macon* is written in Acholi Lwo. This severely delimits the depth of her analysis in what is in many ways a very good book. Behrend, *Alice Lakwena and the Holy Spirits*, pp. 150 and 12–13. The Combonis tried at first to convert adults, but did not have much success, so they focused on children, for whom they, the missionaries, became the spiritual parents.

100. Havelock, *The Muse Learns to Write*, p. 8. For the full exposition of Havelock's argument on this point, see Havelock, *Preface to Plato* (Cambridge, MA and London: The Belknap Press of Harvard University Press, 1963).

101. Pellegrini, *Acholi Macon*, p. 54: "*Mons. Geyer otito ki gin tic ma Mission obino ka tiyo*" and "*Lotino me lokotyeno gucako bino mapol.*"

102. Pellegrini, *Acholi Macon*, pp. 37–41. "Baker immediately thought of visiting Acholiland so that he could stop people who were hunting for slaves," in the original is, "*Baker otamo me cako limone cut, wek ecigeng ki kunnu jo yenyo dano.*" "Struggled so hard to put an end to the slave trading that the Arabs had started; his name became famous among the Acholi," is "*oyelle mada wek etyek lok ma jo Arab gu cako me cato dano calo opi; nyinge oywek mada i kin Acoli, ma giloko pire wa onyo.*"

103. Pellegrini, *Acholi Macon*, pp. 49–50.

104. Ibid., p. 51.

105. Ibid., p. 51. *Piyo*, to persuade, urge, induce, or incite, comes from its form as a verbal noun meaning to stir with a pestle. According to Pellegrini, Chief Awich was literally, "stirring things up."

106. Pellegrini, *Acholi Macon*, p. 52.

107. The Combonis also could have, as much as is possible, taught only the technology of writing—for instance, the alphabet and grammar—and allowed the Acholi to reinsert the language into their life history and practices in ways that they deemed fit. Given that the Combonis were missionaries, the likelihood of this option was nil.

108. Thomas Aquinas, *Summa Theologica*, IIa-IIae, q. 62, a. 7.

109. Alphonsus Liguori, *Theologia moralis*, ed. L. Gaude, 4 vols (Rome: Ex Typographia Vaticana, 1905–12), 2:258-70 (lib. III, sections 557–78).

110. Cisternino, *Passion for Africa*, p. 233.

111. Alphonsus Liguori, *Theologia moralis*, 1:357 (lib. II, section 63). The Latin reads: "Sed melius cum aliis dicendum, illam esse formalem, quae concurrit ad malam voluntatem alterius, et nequit esse sine peccato; materialem vero illam, quae concurrit tantum ad malam actionem alterius, prater intenionem cooperantis."

112. Paul Donohue suggests that because Crazzolara "was so isolated because of his views" by his religious superiors, he could not have felt free to publish his observations of British mistreatment of the Acholi. Personal correspondence, March 30, 2013.

113. Comboni, *Daniel Comboni*, p. 232; cf. also Comboni's letter to Cardinal Simeoni in Cisternino 143: "What I totally care for (and this has been the only and true passion of my whole life, and so will it be until death, and I will not blush about it) is that Africa should be converted."

114. Comboni, *Daniel Comboni*, pp. 215, 216, and 229.

115. I have changed the name and locations in this scenario.

116. In December 2014, citing a drop in funding, the American headquarters of Invisible Children closed, and handed over its Uganda operations to local partners. See Eleanor Goldberg, "Invisible Children, Group Behind 'Kony 2102,' Closing Because of Funding Issues," *Huffington Post* (December 16, 2014), at http://www.huffingtonpost.com/2014/12/16/invisible-children-closing_n_6329990.html.

117. I have changed the names of both the security officer and the camp.

118. Museveni reopened CBS radio, a Baganda station, in October 2010, in an effort to woo Baganda votes. The Baganda people had had a falling out with Museveni after he attempted to seize the Baganda kingdom land.

119. Charles Mwanguhya Mpagi, "Government Seizes Pro-Besigye Book," *The Monitor* (October 10, 2010), at http://www.monitor.co.ug/News/National/-/688334/1029370/-/item/0/-/7en95rz/-/index.html. The book is *The Correct Line?: Uganda under Museveni*, by Olive Kobusingye (Milton Keynes: AuthorHouse, 2010).

120. Human Rights Watch, *A Media Minefield: Increased Threats to Freedom of Expression in Uganda* (May 2010), at *www.hrw.org/en/reports/2010/05/02/media-minefield-0*.

121. Human Rights Watch, *World Report 2014: Uganda*, at http://www.hrw.org/world-report/2014/country-chapters/uganda.

122. Maria Burnett, "Dispatches: In Uganda, Killers of Protesters Remain Free," at http://www.hrw.org/news/2013/09/09/dispatches-uganda-killers-protesters-remain-free; and http://www.youtube.com/watch?feature=player_embedded&v=YFe9UQv8jOU.

123. See Julius Ocungi, "Five Residents Shot Over Amuru Land Wrangle," *The Monitor* (September 9, 2015), at http://www.monitor.co.ug/News/National/Five-residents-shot-over-Amuru-land-wrangle/-/688334/2863166/-/12guxit/-/index.html.

124. Anthropologists have been becoming more explicitly aware of the intricacies of fieldwork in politically charged postcolonial settings. In the mid-1980s, Nancy Howell approached the board of directors of the American Anthropological Association about the need to address directly the problem of risk in fieldwork. The board established an Advisory Panel on Health and Safety, and called upon Howell to chair it. The result in 1990 was *Surviving Fieldwork*, a kind of how to guide with pieces of advice not unlike the one I received from the Catholic Relief Services country director that if no people are coming toward you on the road, you are heading toward the LRA, and the people have fled. Howell dryly notes in a "by the way" fashion, "Another difficulty that anthropologists sometimes have in the field is being suspected of spying. . . . Overall, 15% of fieldworkers report that someone in the research group was suspected of spying (though only a few of these were arrested)." On the upside, she does also say that being accused of spying by the government is an "indicator of the degree of trust and good will" developed between the researcher and the local population.

Geoffrey Ross Owens provides more contextual analysis of the frequent charge of spying in an article about his expulsion from Zanzibar, "What! Me a spy?" The situation is much like that in Uganda. The ruling party "restricted opposition campaigning," and any perceived threat to its powers "prompted the government to crack down on any and all opposition activities." Though at first "welcomed" by the Ministry of Information, Owens later discovers that what, to him, were meetings about cultural matters—in this case Swahili lessons and a wedding—become the occasion for his being followed by the government. "State Security had apparently been following me since the previous year, and were convinced that I was some sort of agent sent to lend support to the opposition party. Every time I so much as greeted someone associated with the opposition, it was duly noted, providing condemning evidence that I was nothing but a troublemaker." In broadening the analysis to include the international context, Owens is spot-on: "In a world of geopolitical inequality and political tension, the role of spy is one available persona sometimes attributed to the anthropologist. . . . Anthropologists enjoy considerable economic resources, seek intimate knowledge about the communities they study, and gain prestige and privilege from their capacity to mediate between local and global contexts in which they work."

What Howell does not treat and does not occur as part of Owens's experience is the flip side to this dynamic: it is in this context of government suspicion and control that people seeking to get information out of the country come into play. They want to *enlist* us as spies.

See Nancy Howell, *Surviving Fieldwork: A Report of the Advisory Panel on Health and Safety in Fieldwork, American Anthropological Association* (Washington, DC: American Anthropological Association, 1990), 97; and Geoffrey Ross Owens, "What! Me a Spy? Intrigue and Reflexivity in Zanzibar," *Ethnography* 4, no. 1 (2003), pp. 123, 138, and 141.

125. See for instance, the exchange of views that appeared in the government newspaper, *New Vision*, "Is There a Plot to Poison Political Leaders in Uganda?" (May 26, 2007) at http://www.sundayvision.co.ug/detail.php?mainNewsCategoryId=451&newsId=567254.).

126. See BBC News, "Uganda Expels Canadian Journalist" (March 10, 2006) at http://news.
bbc.co.uk/2/hi/africa/4793500.stm; Editorial, "Hear No Evil: The Reasons for Our
Correspondent's Expulsion from Uganda," *The Economist* (March 23, 2006); and Reporters
without Borders, "Interior Ministry Deports US Documentary Filmmaker" (July 30, 2013),
at http://en.rsf.org/ouganda-us-filmmaker-snatched-by-police-in-26-07-2013,44985.html.

127. Levi-Strauss, *Tristes Tropiques*, p. 298.

128. Mario Cisternino, *Passion for Africa,* p. 361. It is noteworthy in the Acholi case that the term
for scribe—*karan*—likely comes from the Arabic "Koran," and the word for pen, *kalam,*
means "the Word of Allah" in Arabic, both terms reflecting the reality of the presence
of Arabic-speaking ivory and slave traders as the first non-blacks in the region in the
1850s and 1860s. The Acholi simply transferred the terms to the later context of British
dominance; the one constant is the oppressive use of the technology of writing.

CHAPTER 3
BISHOP NEGRI'S *PSST*: FOLLOWING JESUS IN THE MIDDLE OF WAR

So, during the war I experienced many things, but I will mention only a few. There are just too many. The first one is, I experienced deep sorrow for the loss of innocent people's lives. Abduction of both big and small children. I experienced also some deaths which were not human, that is, cutting of the parts of the bodies of people. The mouth, the hands, the legs, the ears. And then another one, another one which is very sad, also, is cooking parts of the people, like the legs, the arms, and to let those who were there, those who have been abducted, to eat. And then another experience was homeless people, because their houses were burned, or abandoned out of fear; they just fled and they left the home. Then severe hunger, which made some people to harm themselves, to commit suicide also. Because they could give nothing to their children and to see that the children were suffering like that, fed up with life, they just harmed themselves. People committed suicide because they could not bear the situation any longer. Orphans, orphans were not countable. And fear was tormenting people by day, and even at night. Mm. Peace and joy disappeared. People could not greet one another. Even if we met, we would just, just like pass one another without saying a word. Mm. No joy. At all.

And then I also came across the rebels in 1998. Mm. When we met them, I was saying the Rosary. Then one of them jumped in the middle of the road. Then I told the driver, I said, "Driver, they are the ones." I said, "They are the ones, stop." Then the driver just went with the car on the side of the road, and stopped. When he stopped, the students collected all their things and go. They all ran away. My interest was to see that nobody was there left in the vehicle. So I was just seeing that everybody should jump. After all of them had gone, what I wanted was also now to see what I could do.

By then, they had already surrounded me. So, one came, said, "Get the watch." I give. Another one came, "Give the lady bag," and I give the lady my bag. Their leader was ordering those who were in the bush to come out and collect the things from the vehicle. I was the first to get out of the vehicle. Of course I was in front, but I didn't run. And then, their commander was standing just near me there. And then he said, "Give the rosary you have in your hand." I don't know how he knew I was having the rosary because I was just doing it like this. It could not even be seen. He said, "Give the rosary here if you cannot come with us." I said, "I can help you with the rosary." Then I give the rosary to him. When I gave the rosary, he bowed down with the rosary. When he got up, he said with a very sweet voice, "You can go." Then I started going. So I believe that it was Our Lady who released me, the rosary.

And then, I developed high blood pressure, a heart problem typical at that time of war.

Now, at this difficult time, I was praying mostly the Divine Mercy . . . . I'm devoted to Divine Mercy because I know that whatever I can do cannot be up to the standard maybe God wants. So, my salvation depends on the mercy of God. I will be saved through the mercy of God, not because of what I am doing. That is why I'm devoted to the Divine Mercy.

And whenever I was troubling, I would hold the crucifix. If I entered a vehicle I would hold a crucifix like this, in front of me, I said, "Jesus you clear for me the way, you clear the way, go ahead and clear the way." And in fact I was protected many times . . .

Jesus would tell me through the Cross, "I have gone through it. And the first have already made it. Follow me." So when I see the Cross I would say, what kind of suffering has Jesus not gone through? And as I am his follower, I am also to do the little I can, too. Mine is not much if I compare my suffering to Jesus. Is the same to Mother Mary. When I say to Mother Mary, also I say, "They have gone before me. They have shown me the example; there is nothing to be done except, this is the way." Mm. So I cannot long for any other things which do not follow the way they have shown me. That is why I am devoted to the Cross. It helps me a lot. It gives me encouragement. Mm. Jesus has gone through it, so. And he also said it: "If you want to follow me, take up your cross. Then you come after me."

—*Sister Esther Arach, The Little Sisters of Mary Immaculate of Gulu*[1]

* * *

Two seemingly incompatible things are true. The Comboni missionaries in colonial northern Uganda formally cooperated with the evil of the British Empire. The missionaries also, however, brought with them and passed on a material and spiritual infrastructure that made the Catholic Church—along with its ecumenical and interfaith partners in postcolonial northern Uganda—one of the very few non-, indeed anti-, war infrastructures on the ground during the LRA conflict, enabling a powerful counter-witness to the war. The material infrastructure is relatively easy to document. Monies raised by the Combonis and the indigenous religious order that they founded, the Little Sisters of Mary Immaculate of Gulu, led to the building of a seminary; a convent; a cathedral; over two dozen parish churches; a college; two technical schools; several rural trade schools; scores of nursery, primary, and secondary schools;[2] three schools for children with disabilities; a catechist training center; a diocesan farm; three hospitals; a nursing school; an array of clinics; and a home for orphans. Throughout the war, displaced persons converged on these compounds for security, shelter, and food. One Little Sister described to me in an interview the early days of the war:

So when [current Ugandan president] Museveni took over, there were many, many displaced people who came to the seminary. There were over three thousand displaced people plus the seminarians. And we were there with them. I think that was the beginning of many of the problems. So we stay with them. Museveni took over in 1986. It was a very difficult moment. And the people were in the seminary at the same time as the parish just opposite. We were able to teach some of them. . . . Food was very difficult.[3]

And another:

Every day we experience war, war, horrible war. . . such that people came and then we had to take care of them in the mission. . . . We have to struggle to take care of them. That was in 1985. Before the LRA, yes. . . . This is when Museveni had thrown out Okello and the NRA [Museveni's army] is chasing the UNLA [Okello's troops]. The life was difficult because those who run and took refuge in the mission, we up to now accommodate them. And then this accommodation— we could not put them in our rooms [any longer]. We are sleeping in the what?—in the church. All of us. The sisters and the priests. We were sleeping in the church. . . . It was not for weeks; it was for some months. You can imagine. Lucky enough there was a bit of foodstuff in the parish, so we were able to—and those who were near sometimes go home and they bring their food here.

The people who really disturbed us, that made our life very difficult is the NRA . . . . They first of all looted, so in the course of refusal they were annoyed with us. I remember the first day when they enter, it was on a Sunday. . . . So many people run [from home], flooding the parish. I think [the NRA] wanted to kill us. Because I remember one of them . . . he was a soldier just shooting at us. . . . So you know the soldiers when they lose [their] mind. . . . None of us was injured. But the soldier opened fire just like that. Is that a miracle of God [that no one was injured]? That is a very big miracle and God made the point that those bullets should not touch us because we knew that we had to take care of those people who have taken refuge in the parish.[4]

The dynamic of ad hoc yet extensive care for the displaced continued once armed resistance from the North became organized in the form of the LRA. For instance:

As I was then in Pabbo Secondary School, I was keeping the girls in the sisters' house. I gave one big room. They just sleep together and they also cook in one of the small rooms. My aim of keeping them there [was] simply because when they move from home, the rebels keep on abducting them along the way.[5]

The material infrastructure left by the Combonis—there are few of the missionaries remaining in northern Uganda—would have been of far less consequence without the spiritual infrastructure that they handed on—a mix of devotional practices that constituted (and continues to do so) an embodied and thus lived cosmology wherein God has love and a providential design for each and every human being, particularly the marginalized. Here, what Western moderns sometimes label "conservative" or "traditional" devotions—the imitation of Christ and the saints, the Rosary, Eucharistic Adoration, mortification on behalf of those in purgatory, novenas, the Stages of the Cross—all work to leverage radical—that is, life-risking—witness (Jn 15:13). And this traditional–radical linkage—though pressed into particular poignancy by the exigencies of a conflict zone—is deliberate on the part of the practitioners. Many of the services they offered—the works of mercy to the displaced who flooded the schools and parishes— might have been ad hoc during the war, but the spiritual infrastructure that made them possible was not.

Angelo Negri, bishop of the Diocese of Gulu and a Comboni priest, founded the Little Sisters of Mary Immaculate of Gulu in 1942 to be the educators of the Acholi, particularly girls, at a time when many leaders in the Catholic Church—including some of his peers—felt that Africans—especially African females—lacked the personality traits and intellectual capacity for academic rigor. In the words of one of the sisters I interviewed, Bishop Negri, "felt that he should really do something to help raise the dignity of women in Africa. Women were also created by God and they are also intelligent. They can even learn together with the boys. They can even get a great job as men are also doing. Why should they keep oppressing them? To learn only housework?"[6]

Bishop Negri had first to educate the nuns in order for them to in turn be educators of the Acholi. He "started Mary Margaret School with the intention that, tomorrow, after the sisters [learn] there, they should be the ones to teach these girls, so that they can also learn to stand with the boys."[7] Though the Church in northern Uganda ordained African men as early as 1938, their numbers were low—kept deliberately so, I have been told—until the 1980s.[8] And while the Combonis and the archdiocese have trained over a thousand catechists, who from early on have frequently demonstrated dramatic witness in a way that continues to inform Acholi Catholic religious life,[9] the intensity (all day, every day) and duration (as long as twelve years) of the formation process of the Little Sisters of Mary Immaculate of Gulu, together with their ubiquity in northern Uganda,[10] makes their instance a particularly focused one for limning just how the religious life inculcated by the Comboni missionaries gave rise to the steady yet stunning witness of the Catholic Church in northern Uganda during an armed conflict that extended over twenty years.

Because that is the question, isn't it? How is it that a spirituality handed on by missionaries who formally cooperated with evil funded a witness that is at once dramatic in its poignancy and everyday in many of its manifestations? The question is all the more striking if we do not allow either half of it to cancel out the other. Paying attention means giving both halves their due. The subsequent witness does not undo historically nor justify morally the prior cooperation with evil, as if such cooperation is of no concern given how things turned out. In Catholic moral theology, a positive consequence does not justify an immoral act, and Daniel Comboni's own theology of the Cross insists that the missionary must not worry about consequential success in terms of numbers of baptized converts, but rather live faithfully even if it leads to one's own death, leaving the rest to God's Providence. It is also the case, however—and the discipline of anthropology has taken note of this as a small but increasing number of its scholars focus on contemporary Christian communities in the developing world as their subject[11]—that neither does the prior cooperation with the evil of colonialism erase the subsequent faithful witness to the Gospel manifested in the communities that the missionaries evangelized. We must pay attention to both.

Part of the answer to the question regarding this reclamation by indigenous Catholics of the original Comboni charism of faithful witness must be found in the twin seismic shifts of 1962: the inaugurations of both Ugandan independence and the Second Vatican Council. Independence meant that there was no longer a colonial ruler that Catholics had to flatter, and ecclesial reform pressing for indigenization gave northern Ugandans a church that they could call their own. Yet these shifts alone do not suffice for a fully adequate explanation.[12] Museveni's neocolonial government has placed ongoing pressure on local religious leaders to exercise even now what the Combonis in the colonial era had called "prudence" in their dealings with political authorities. Comboni missionaries who themselves also reinvigorated their original charism during the Amin and Museveni regimes quickly found this out.[13] As one of the few nonwar infrastructures remaining in northern Uganda during the conflict, the Catholic Church was a threat to the president. Opportunities to leave the war zone were there, sometimes offered by Museveni himself.[14] And some religious took them, either for short durations or for the full run of the war, whether because they were called elsewhere only to return, or because the stress of war wore them down, or simply for purposes of self-preservation without regard for their religious vocation. But, by far and away, most remained, and put their lives at risk on an ongoing basis in doing so. How did they manage to do it?

This chapter unfolds in two main movements. First, I draw on extensive interviews with members of the Little Sisters of Mary Immaculate of Gulu and research into their archival documents to provide a primarily though not exclusively emic—that is, in their own terms—account of how their devotional practices serve as conduits for the Holy Spirit to, in the local parlance, "animate" the sisters with the charism of their order's founder and, ultimately, Christ.[15] Such animation allows the sisters to imitate their founder and Christ in ways that move beyond mechanical external mimicry to spirit-infused re-presentation. In this section, I allow the sisters to speak for themselves as much as possible, in part for reasons of epistemically privileging their perspective, but perhaps even more so because they speak on their experiences with far more eloquence than I can. They provide the thick accounts of events. Attention here means that I try to stay out of their way as much as possible.

The practice of following and reenacting Christ for the sisters, is, like with the Combonis, not without its impediments. I will discuss how the professionalization of the sisters, enabled by their education and literacy, exacerbated what their *Chapter Documents* themselves—the sisters are their own harshest critics—refer to as self-regarding and divisive "tribalism."[16] Advanced literacy and professional certification gave the sisters access to lucrative (for the context) jobs funded by international NGOs, and some of the sisters began to divert their salaries, meant to be utilized in common in the order, to families and clans of their own ethnic group. I will highlight how the order appealed to the practice of evangelical poverty in imitation of Christ and the apostolic church as a means to curb what it sees as professionally enabled "corruption." In short, through communal mimetic practices, the sisters find a way, with a certain amount of success, to limit excesses exacerbated by literate certification culture in a time of stress. This is significant not only in light of the findings of Chapter 2 regarding the impact of literacy on mimetic oral-oriented culture, but also for the question that we will return to in Chapter 4 as to whether an academic—a modern scribe—can be a follower of Christ.

In the second movement of this chapter, I push further by offering an account of mimesis as it is understood and practiced by the community of Jesus in the gospels, and find, in the process, that the Little Sisters' understanding of what goes on in imitating an exemplar has scriptural warrant. That is to say, the sisters are spot-on not only with this or that precept of scripture, but first and foremost with regard to the *how* of living the Gospel. Their witness is therefore radical not only in the sense of their willingness to lay down their lives for the vulnerable, but also in that it goes to the root of the Gospel. Whatever level of literacy Jesus and his followers had—and this is debated among biblical scholars—it remains that the mimetic considerations of following Jesus controlled communal practices, as is evident, for instance, in the challenges to (written) Sabbath law. We will see how the Little Sisters' mimesis likewise sets limits on the influence of literate certification culture on their practices.

So, to the nuns.

Bishop Negri's *Psst*

Set on a floor-stand in a corner of the sitting room of the Mother House of the Little Sisters of Mary Immaculate of Gulu is a six-foot painting of their founder, the Comboni Bishop of Gulu, Angelo Negri—hair combed straight back, black eyebrows, precisely trimmed goatee of mostly silver-white. He is holding a streamer at waist-level that bears his motto: "Light in Darkness." The lower half of the painting features not Bishop Negri from the waist down, however, but a painted reproduction of an aerial photograph of the Little Sisters's main compound, including the Mother House, schools, dorms, and meeting rooms. A god's-eye view. Negri is looking out at the viewer of the painting, but he is clearly also watching over everything that might go on in the compound below. An archway painted over his head reads, "LSMIG Golden Jubilee in the Year 2000." The painting commemorates the fiftieth year since Negri's death.[17] Across the base of the stand, someone in the community has placed a narrow board with simple block letters painted, all caps, in red: ZEAL LOVE SIMPLICITY.

On the wall to the left of the painting is an 8 × 10-inch framed photograph of Sister Angioletta Dognini standing in a field in the full-dress dark habit of the Verona (Comboni) Sisters. Negri appointed her as the first Mother General of the Little Sisters, and they refer to her as their co foundress. The setting in the photo is fitting, given what the Little Sisters have told me about Angioletta's love of manual labor. "Mother Angioletta," one commented, "she was a hardworking person, eh? Very committed. Imagine every day she was going to the field with us. Since the Congregation started, she was going [to the field] and would come home at the same time you are coming. She was a hardworking sister, very committed, and, ahhh, she loved the Congregation."[18] It is difficult to tell when exactly the photo—black and white—was taken. Angioletta was Mother General for a significant stretch—1942 to 1973. Her gaze is kind yet no-nonsense.

On the wall to the right of the large painting is another, smaller one of Negri, this time a portrait based on a photo of him that I have seen in similar sitting rooms of the Little Sisters across northern Uganda. Looking out. Looking after.

"Our founder has a special charism," Sister Miriam Kozoa tells me in the present tense, as if he is still alive. Tinted glasses, Marian blue everyday habit, white veil. She has just stepped down as Mother General, and is part of an effort by the order to reclaim and revivify in themselves the kind of life led by Bishop Negri and Mother Angioletta, now after a generation of war.[19] "His charism is what we are living on. He imparts that charism to us, and that is why the Little Sisters of Mary Immaculate, we are who we are—because of the burning love of Christ that we have to attend to the most vulnerable people. . . . In fact, as a congregation we are trying our best to follow the footsteps of our founder, Bishop Negri."[20]

* * *

"Our founder has a special charism. His charism is what we are living on. He imparts that charism to us." How does this happen? Negri died in 1949. The Combonis and the Little Sisters have only fairly recently—the mid-1990s—attempted to write brief, article-length biographies of him and Mother Angioletta.[21] For the most part, knowledge of them is still passed on orally. Otherwise, the sisters have only photos and paintings based on photos of the two. But the photos have, the sisters claim, a real capacity to transmit an authoritative power—a charism—to them, a power that enables them to live lives of "burning love" for "the most vulnerable people." One Sister, after having told me of her various trials—government soldiers killed her mother ("One difficult thing is that I never saw the grave"), Ebola took two of her Sisters ("I found myself breaking down")—went on to elaborate on what supported her during such times: "I love our founder so much, Bishop Angelo Negri. I have not seen him, but looking at his picture, hearing about some of his stories. This kept me in this place."[22]

The sisters do not hesitate to describe Negri's character traits: "a good shepherd," "loved all categories of people without discrimination," "clever," "open-minded," "prayerful," "loving," "kind," "humble," "fair to us all," "gentle," and having a "simplicity of life" and "love for the disadvantaged."[23] Specific stories give life and context to the traits. There is one about his interceding on behalf of the local people:

> There was a chief in Pakwacika across the Nile. Very, very cruel. If somebody failed to pay tax, he will try to pull them by the hair as punishment. It was so painful. When Bishop Angelo Negri heard of this, he tried to talk to the chief very, very slowly, [telling him] that he should know how to deal with people. He should know that sometimes they can't pay the tax because of poverty. He was even teaching the chief how to pray—they would pray together—and at the same time trying to teach him how to do his administration by not frustrating people or punishing them. So eventually that chief changed.[24]

According to the stories, local chiefs were not the only leaders Negri had to overcome:

> When he was starting our Congregation, his fellow priests, they were telling him, "Don't. Don't start the Congregation for the Africans, the African girls cannot remain with that main [training]; you are wasting your time. You collect them; they all run away." But then the bishop closed the ears, said, "We are all created by God, whether black or white. We all have the same feeling; we all have the same intelligence that God has given to each one of us. So if white people can remain celibate, can consecrate themselves to God, and remain like that for the glory of God, for the good of the kingdom of God, even Africans are going to do it."[25]

Perhaps the story that most displays his love for the people of northern Uganda, such that he was willing to lay down his life for them, regards his decision to return after a trip abroad:

> He went to America to look for someone who could build the convent, because there was no money. When he was coming back, he felt very sick. Then he went to the doctors. The doctors said, "Bishop, you are very sick. Don't go back to Africa. You need to go back to Italy, so that you can live longer." And then the Bishop said, "Better to shorten my life among my sheep than to stay longer in a comfortable place in Italy."[26]

Much, and perhaps most, of what the sisters know of Negri is through a chain of witnesses: "Our older sisters, they used to teach us, those who have seen him."[27] Such character traits, given life by the stories, make Negri a "role model" for the sisters.[28]

But it is clear that for them he is more than simply an exceptionally good person. He carries the burning love of Christ for the most vulnerable in a way that shares in the traits of Christ, such that he merits veneration. "Now I've developed also a deep devotion to our founder, Bishop Negri," says one Sister. And the stories become miracle stories:

This man is working miracles in my life, especially this year. A lot of miracles—even my presence here was through him. Because I had not money [to travel]. Then I went to his tomb. I said, "I am going for the work of the Congregation. Please open the way to get transport to Kolongo." And then I waited for God. Then I got a *parapara* [driver] who said, "Sister, for 20,000 [Ugandan schillings—about $8], I can take you to Kolongo." Then I went to Kolongo. [There are] so many, so many devotees now to this man.[29]

Another Sister tells of his intervention—years after his death—in a four-year court case over disputed land claims, and the dramatic events afterward.

For four years, I was alone with the rosary and the relics of our founder, Bishop Angelo Negri. And the lawyers wanted to eat the money of the rich man, the man who was taking me to court. People said, "Sister, you are a religious, God assisted a miracle [in your winning the case]." I did not know that it was a miracle. When I finished the court, I continued to pray to our founder, Bishop Negri. Then the surveyor came and marked the land. Eight acres. The land was released. I marked the land title on the fifth of November, 2003.

I went to pray in Layibe. A melody came into my mind as I was walking. A song, to thank our founder. I said, "I don't know how to make notation of the music, and this song, if it gets lost. . . ." And I struggled. Then I said, "What can I do?" I started putting the wording down back [in my room]. I sung the wording properly. And then I said, "Tomorrow, my founder, let this thing be for your honor. Don't let me forget this song."

Immediately, I could see a cloud, a brilliant white, a different white. What is this? What is this? What is this? I was looking as the thing went oooooh, at the distant border with Sudan. And a sea of snow. What is this? What is this? What is this? And when I look at . . . I saw a big. . . . It seemed to be a mountain, very black, up there, falling at the edge of the white ocean of cloud. Very white. And is this a mountain, or is it a cloud? Immediately it came here. It came. It came on the water.

What is this, then? I started to see the what?—the cloud of the bishop, and the mitre. On that cloud, I suddenly realized, is Bishop Negri. It is Bishop Negri. Bishop Negri was transparent. Brilliant. Beautiful. He put on the *pianeta* for Mass.[30] And glittering—chit!-chit!-chit!—with something. The *pianeta*. Pulsing spots-spots. Pt!-pt!-pt! Heavenly color.

It was Negri. He gave me first Holy Communion. Confirmation. He was still. He was tall. Beautiful. Then I said, "Bishop Negri is so beautiful in heaven, it burns."

I began to see the room as it was. And I seated there. Till the cock crowed, I was sitting there. Until morning. I could not sleep.[31]

While waking visions as dramatic as this one are not everyday among the sisters, Bishop Negri, Mother Angioletta, and other heavenly figures do come to them regularly in dreams that have portent.

> Firstly, I saw [the living] Bishop Negri when I was in primary, when I was a girl, outside the gate [of the Cathedral]. And I was in love with Bishop Negri.
>
> [Later], I dreamed [I saw] Bishop Negri on a wagon in the procession of Corpus Domini [the feast of the Body of Christ]. It was a dream, that I ran from Layibe, I came before God. I saw people in procession. The seminarians and all the sisters in procession on Corpus Domini.
>
> A bishop was in white, standing on a white wagon. I saw the bishop on the walk home. Wheeewwww—he was going up [into the sky]! Wheeewwww! The seminarians were singing. They were singing. I said, "Bishop is going! Pooooh! Make the sign of the cross toward the—" It was then whooooww, whooww!
>
> As I was shouting, I hit my head on the wood [of the bed]. Then I woke up. That Sunday morning, a young man came from the chapel, told us, "Eh, Bishop Negri, who was supposed to visit us, has died." And I wept, wept, wept.[32]

And though the sisters do not venerate Mother Angioletta to the degree that they do Bishop Negri, the cofoundress nonetheless has the capacity to communicate from beyond, as in this dream:

> So when I heard from the school—I was still a student—when I heard from the school that Mother Angioletta died, ah, [I took] a breath like this. Then after four months, I had a dream at night. I saw Mother Angioletta coming. It was late evening, the sun was already set. I saw her coming in a white dress with the white cap that she used to put on.
>
> Then she was holding a very big ciborium in her hand, this big cup where they put the Host. She came and gave me the cup and she said, "Delfina, you give me some Host in this ciborium." And then I take it from her hand, I rush inside. A certain box was there. I started filling it with the Host real fast.
>
> When I came out, I didn't see her, but I found that an altar was there. And then I said, "Who has put this altar there?" Then I said, "Maybe I need to lay the altar for Mass. Maybe people are coming to celebrate Mass." And I started laying the altar. And I also put the Host there.
>
> As soon as I finished laying the altar, I saw a certain vehicle, a certain motorcycle coming with the white man. Coming very, very fast. Then he stood there and said, "Sister, where is Mother Angioletta?" Then I said, "She turned to prepare the altar, but I don't know where she went. Maybe she will come back."
>
> And then immediately I woke from sleep. Then I started thinking, "Now, Mother Angioletta died four months ago, and she came to me in a dream to bring her the Host." Then I heard in my heart that she wanted me to write the biography that is her life.[33]

Through such dreams, Bishop Negri and Angioletta exercise a capacity to communicate with the sisters, and even call them to take up specific actions or a way of life, a capacity that in other of the sisters' dreams is carried out by Jesus:

> It was in 1960 when I had the experience which led me to become a Sister. I had dreamt that I was in the chapel, praying. Then, the Divine Mercy appeared at the corner of the chapel in our place near Pabbo. He was standing on the world—globe—with rays of light; red, bluest, whitest. Shining. He did not say anything to me, but I just outstretched my hands, just like this, eh? I went to him, and he put a ring on my finger. And disappeared. So it was at this time that I confirmed that God was calling me. I was in P4 [fourth grade].[34]

Sometimes the intervening agent is anonymous, yet clearly supranatural; an unnamed divine messenger:

> I discerned this call when I was in primary. Primary five. That is when I felt that I should become a religious person. My discernment to become a sister came through a dream. I dreamt that I was just working, and I met a young man. And the young man told me that I should come and help him carry a very big pot. So I carry the pot. It was really heavy. We walk up to the cathedral. Then he says, "Now, let us put the pot down." He helped me put the pot down. Then he disappeared.
>
> This dream, I share with my mom. And my mom says, "Yeah, if that is a dream, God is calling you to do something."
>
> Another dream. I was going home. As I reach the cathedral, I was passing the door there. I saw a bright light coming from inside, but the door was closed. Yeah, the door of the cathedral was closed, and I saw a very bright light. And then in the midst of the bright light, I saw somebody. I saw only the hand of that person. I saw a hand and then feet. Then he took my hand, but I did not see who was that person. Then I woke up.
>
> And that again [was a] dream that I share with my mother. And then my mother says, "You pray. Maybe God will inspire you to do a different thing."
>
> So that is how I got my vocation.[35]

For the Little Sisters, then, Bishop Negri and Mother Angioletta are both persons to be imitated and venerable spirits who invite and enable that imitation. It is important for our understanding to keep these two aspects of their personas together. The figures visiting in the dreams are no less persons, and the embodied persons of Negri and Angioletta bear their respective charisms. This double-characteristic carries over to the various representational objects like the photographs and paintings. These, in important respects, *are* Negri and Angioletta in that, as representations of them, they participate in and serve as conduits of their charisms, even to the point where the objects "speak" to the sisters, as we saw in this chapter's opening testimony with regard to the rosary, the crucifix, and Jesus: "And whenever I was troubling, I would hold the crucifix. I would hold a crucifix like this, in front of me, I said, 'Jesus you clear for me the way.' Jesus would tell me through the Cross, 'I have gone through it. And the first have already made it. Follow me.'"

Donna Tartt's novel, *The Goldfinch*, about the hold a seventeenth-century painting of a bird by Carel Fabritius has on a boy-turned-man articulates in literary form the way in which such representational objects speak to us:

> But if a painting really works down in your heart and changes the way your see, and think, and feel, you don't think, "Oh, I love this picture because it's universal." "I love this painting because it speaks to all mankind." That's not the reason anyone loves a piece of art. It's a secret whisper from the alleyway. *Psst, you. Hey kid. Yes you.* An individual heart-shock. . . . The nail where your fate is liable to catch and snag. . . . And yes—scholars might care about the innovative brushwork and use of light, the historical influence and unique significance in Dutch art. But not me. As my mother said all those years ago, my mother who loved the painting only from seeing it in a book she borrowed from the Comanche County Library as a child; the significance doesn't matter. The historical significance deadens it. Across the unbridgeable distances—between bird and painter, painter and viewer—I hear only too well what's being said to me, a *psst* from the alleyway. . . across four hundred years of time. . . . Because, between "reality" on the one hand, and the point where the mind strikes reality, there's a middle zone, a rainbow edge where beauty comes into being, where two very different surfaces mingle and blur to provide what life does not: and this is the space where all art exists, and all magic.[36]

The role of the representational objects in the lives of the sisters—their capacity to communicate God's *psst* to them—is perhaps most evident in the practice of Eucharistic Adoration. Here, Jesus of Nazareth, born 2000 years ago, *is* the Host *now*, in front of us, and the Host *is* Jesus the Nazarene the Christ. This copresence allows the sisters to carry on colloquies with the Host as if Jesus is right there before them, because He is. As one Sister described, "As girls, we were taught what to tell Jesus when you're in front of the Blessed Sacrament. But then in the novitiate, we went deeper, because we had times for quiet whereby you allow Jesus to speak to you."[37] Another says, "The moment where I see the monstrance—Jesus in the monstrance, in the Blessed Sacrament—just like that I will be drawn. Just to be in front of the Blessed Sacrament, I feel like He's hearing me now. He is present, Jesus in the Blessed Sacrament, Jesus in the monstrance."[38] Sometimes, Jesus speaks quite specifically:

> When the Blessed Sacrament is exposed, we were told to wait on two knees. Then I also do that practice. But one day when I entered the chapel in the Motherhouse, the Blessed Sacrament was exposed, so I genuflected on both knees. Then the voice told me, "When I am on the altar exposed, you genuflect on both knees, but when I'm in the tabernacle, you genuflect with only one knee. Am I different when I'm on the altar [than] when I'm in the tabernacle?" So then I ask Him,

I say, "What message do you have for me? What do you want me to do?" [He replied,] "Worship me the way you do when I'm exposed on the altar." And from that day, I never genuflect with one leg when I'm in the church. On both knees. And when I genuflect on one knee, I am challenged, I am haunted. I feel I'm not giving enough devotion, enough respect, to Jesus.[39]

So critical is Jesus's presence in the Eucharist that the sisters, together with other of the faithful, would walk miles on roads they knew to be dangerous just to bring it back with them to locations where priests either would not or could not go to consecrate the Host. And it was the Host that gave the sisters the wherewithal to make the trip and do much else besides:

In Padibe [an outpost where some Sisters lived], there was nobody; the missionaries were in Kitgum [town]. All of them were in Kitgum. In Padibe, things were not easy, things were not easy. Many of the people there were living in the mission [as an impromptu IDP camp], so all of us were in the mission. . . .

Because the people are there we said, "Now we are sent there," which means the Congregation wants us to die together with the people. So we are not going to leave them. . . .

I cannot remember the number because all those buildings in Padibe, they were filled up. In the hospital, the health center, people were in the school, and then at the sisters's place. . . . You find people really suffered. And you could not eat twice a day. . . . During the evening they come and we eat once a day. . . .

Because there was no communication, coming from Padibe [to Kitgum] was very risky. So we were confined to Padibe. And once in a while, maybe twice a month, we foot from Padibe. We come here [to Kitgum] to get the what?—the Blessed Sacrament. When it was consecrated, then we carry it together. We move on foot.

Sometimes we were scared, but knowing we were going back with the Blessed Sacrament, we keep on praying, praying, praying. When we get tired and sit down under a tree, we pray. We were just praying, "O Sacrament Most Holy, O Sacrament Divine, all praise and all thanksgiving be every morning thine." We were just saying the name of Jesus, like that.

When we were in Padibe, at least we have one hour Adoration. We used to do one hour Adoration before the Blessed Sacrament. We would close all the doors so the people don't know where we are. We do that as a group. Because you could not predict when things may not be okay.

[The rebels] did not disturb us much, until the last moment of 1988. When we reached somewhere in the middle [between Padibe and Kitgum], that is when we met them for the first time. When we met them, they intercepted us, and moved with us. They took us and moved in the bush. We moved throughout the night until the next morning, [and] throughout the day. Then at six o'clock they released us, and we came back.

So that trauma, that trauma is still disturbing me. Sometimes now, I move to Padibe, Whenever I reach that spot where they picked me and went with me to the bush, that thing always comes back in my mind, much as I was not hurt. I was not even beaten by them. But I still think, "Why?" It all sometimes comes back. As a sort of dream. You can dream when your eyes are open. So that is still a fight. That is still a fight.

In fact, the most help that I'm getting is being close to the sacrament, the Eucharist, the Body of Christ. I know that that one is the one that sincerely is helping me to push ahead. Because I meet Christ and he is always in me. I used to say "communion"; I say now "You are with me. Everywhere I go. Whatever I do. You are here within me. I'm not praying, but the whole of you is in me. I move with you." And I say that it is really very, very important that we unite with Jesus in the Blessed Sacrament.

And it is not easy, because we need to be full in order to make others also keep hope. Without which, things will not be easy. So I praise the Lord for that. Because I know that Jesus is in me whole, not part of him.[40]

The emic answer—the one to which we must first pay attention—to the question of how the spirituality of missionaries who cooperated with the evil of the empire gave rise to the faithful witness of indigenous religious who are willing to lay down their lives for the most vulnerable is that the former are bearers and transmitters of a charism that is ultimately the charism of Jesus the Nazarene the Christ. The Little Sisters draw the same animation, therefore, from photos of Negri as they do the consecrated Host. While the worldviews and actions of the missionaries are far from irrelevant—the sisters are in the process of making the case for the beatification of Negri[41]—the gap between the best and worst of a person does not foreclose the possibility of that person passing on Christ's charism. The sisters are aware of the more imperially driven of Negri's reasons for developing schools. The short biography of him, which they made available to me, quotes him on this matter. "Our main task is to care for schools. Uganda is pushing fast in this field; the Church must be present there too. The one who has the schools today will have Uganda tomorrow."[42] For the sisters, this does not cancel out the fact that he also founded the schools because, as the sister quoted earlier says, he "felt that he should really do something to help raise the dignity of women in Africa. Women were also created by God."

The sisters' *Chapter Documents*, therefore, closely link the witness of Negri to that of Jesus Christ, even though it is only the latter who is sinless. For instance, a section of the *1985 Chapter Document* that details "the mind of the founder"—"He was humble, and loved everybody, black or white"—moves directly from the characteristics of a Sister who imitates Negri—"a sister who likes and loves to suffer for others"—to those of a Sister who imitates Christ—"He gave us the example to love one another." This is because Negri and Jesus Christ are bearers of the same charism: "When [Negri] passed by it seemed as though the living Christ was passing. He had a different unseen power that attracted everyone toward him."[43] In their *2001 Chapter Document*, the sisters note that that charism "was not yet very well defined," and so they distill their articulation of it into the simple phrase, "His burning love for the most vulnerable." Jesus Christ is the "origin of this Charism," and, for the sisters, Negri is one of its fundamental conduits.

If the fact of charism is the emic answer to the matter of how missionaries cooperating with evil pass on a spirituality that enables faithful indigenous witness, the question remains as to more precisely *how* that charism is passed, and here an initially etic or externally sourced response is helpful. Much of anthropology since James George Frazer has answered the question of charism transmission under the rubric of "magic." In *The Golden Bough*, Frazer distinguishes two ways through which practitioners of magic understand their acts to work: the "law of similarity" and the "law of contact or contagion." The law of similarity, through what Frazer calls homeopathic or, significantly, mimetic magic, works such that "the magician infers that he can produce any effect he desires merely by imitating it." In contrast, the law of contact, according to Frazer, "proceeds upon the notion that things which have once been conjoined must remain ever afterwards, even when quite dissevered from each other, in such a sympathetic relation that whatever is done to the one must similarly affect the other." Both kinds of magic "assume that things act on each other at a distance through secret sympathy, the impulse being transmitted from one to the other by means of what we may conceive as a kind of invisible ether." [44] Though *The Golden Bough* was first published in 1890, the distinction between the two "laws of magic" remains in prominent use in academic disciplines, even while Frazer's evolutionism regarding cultures is rejected. [45]

The role of the paintings, photos, and rosary crucifixes in transmitting Jesus's charism displays aspects of both "similarity" and "contact," with the movement being from the former to the latter. There is an initial act—whether through paintbrush, camera, or chisel—that produces an artifact that is *similar* to the original (or even another representation of the original); thereafter, *contact* with the artifact transmits the charism, that is, Frazer's "invisible ether" and Tartt's *psst*. Sister Margaret Aceng puts it this way in her essay for the sisters' golden jubilee:

> Within the Sisters's environments, there are holy pictures on the walls. These include the cross and the crucified Christ, pictures of Our Lady the Virgin Mary, the Pope, the Bishops, the authorities of the Congregation and other holy pictures which the Sisters deem necessary. These holy pictures purify the Sisters' environment so much that on entering the Sisters' house one feels that he/she has entered a holy place, a place where God dwells.
>
> Pictures of Superior Generals and their councilors hanged on the walls have a special significance to the Sisters. God the Father and His Son Jesus Christ whose footsteps the Sisters follow in the vows of Obedience, Chastity and Poverty do not speak and deal with the Sisters directly but through his chosen instruments—the Superiors whose presence in the pictures on our walls reflect the presence of God in our midst. [46]

In the case of the Blessed Sacrament, Jesus's words at the last supper, "This is my body" (Mk 14:22b; Mt. 26:26b; Lk. 22:15:19b), is sufficient to secure the similarity. The bread need not look like the person Jesus for Jesus to be present in it and to speak quite specifically to persons who come into contact with it. The claim of the sisters is that the transmission of Jesus's charism, sometimes through images of Negri, gives them the wherewithal to witness to the most vulnerable in a war where, again in the words of one Sister, "Peace and joy disappeared." Given that others, from many among the Acholi intelligentsia to international NGOs, either fled (in the case of the intellectuals[47]) or stayed in the major towns at the periphery of the conflict (in the case of most INGOs), it would be uncharitable—intellectually miserly, really—to not grant the sisters' interpretation of the reality and power of Jesus's charism in their lives at least initial credibility. This is all the more the case given that the sisters' sufferings during the war are much like anybody else's. Again: "And then, I developed high blood pressure, a heart problem typical at that time of war"; and, "So that trauma, that trauma is still disturbing me. I still think, 'Why?' It all sometimes comes back. So that is still a fight. That is still a fight." These are not ethereal, but flesh and blood beings, who are given life by the Spirit-*psst*.

Although the photos, paintings, crucifixes, and Host move from similarity to contact to transmit the charism, the flow is in the reverse direction—that is, from contact to similarity—in the overall formation process with the Little Sisters. Formation in this case places candidates for the order in carefully guided extended contact with the sisters (who already participate in the charism) until the candidate becomes "like" the sisters. In the words of one Sister, "You have to be guided by the sisters if you want to be a Sister."[48] The period from first vows—taken after the candidate has already spent three-and-a-half years as an aspirant, postulant, and novice—and final vows can be as long as nine years. Most of the sisters I interviewed described the formation process going back even further in their lives, to primary school (where members of the order are teachers), reporting that this is when they, as students, first sensed their desire to be like the nuns.

> I saw the way that they were dressed, and I was wondering what kind of people [they are]. For me, I thought they were angels brought from heaven. I was admiring the sisters during my P2 [second grade]. I didn't know that that was the beginning of my vocation. When I reach P4, the sister put me in charge of her things. Sister asked me to take care of her boxes. They used to have a wooden box [where] they put all the books of the children. And that is how I got in touch with this Sister. I could feel, you know, the desire, the eagerness to be with the sisters. I would feel the desire to go and pray.

Then Sister started teaching me this—it was a kind of poem. It goes like this:

> I heard a voice, how deep the sound;
> Just like the murmur of the sea.
> And in my heart an echo was found;
> The words were this: "Come, follow me."
> Were they addressed to rich or poor?
> To those of high or low degrees?

No, they were very simple;
They only meant, "Come, follow me."

And these words sink deep into my heart. "Come, follow me." Then I started watching the sisters. Every prayer time they go to visit Jesus in the church, I would run and hide behind the door, and I would peak to see what they were doing there. I would see them kneeling before the tabernacle. At the altar, they were praying. They were praying aloud. Community prayer. Then at lunchtime also, they would go in a line with their hands under the mantle like this. They would go to the church, and I'd run and admire them. And after lunch again, they were kneeling in the sitting room. They were reading and then praying.

So I asked Sister one day, "Sister, what do you do? Why are you moving all the time in the church?" Then [she] said, "That is our lifestyle. Our life is full of prayer." So I said, "I would also like to pray like you."[49]

The formation process becomes highly structured and deliberate in postulancy and the first year of the novitiate, where the women receive instruction about the order, its founder and cofounder, and communal life in Christ.[50]

You get up at five o'clock in the morning. The first thing you do, you wash, you go to chapel for meditation. After meditation, you start Lauds. After that, Mass. After Mass, lessons. Sometimes you go to lessons after you go to the field. Midday sharp, run back for prayer. After lunch, go for another lesson until six o'clock [in the evening]. Everybody [to] evening prayer, Vespers. After Vespers, go for dinner [and] come back for night prayer. After night prayer, [we] very strictly observe silence. Then go either for your personal prayer or personal reading until ten o'clock.[51]

In the second year of novitiate, the women go out to live in one of the order's communities in an apostolate serving the people. One Sister comments, "This is, I would say, a pre-test of community life."[52] If the novice passes the pretest, she takes first vows. Though she now becomes a professed Sister, the vocational discernment continues. "So we groom them. Then eventually when they become Sisters, they know their part. And then after becoming a Sister, there's still spiritual growth. So retreats, spiritual courses, like that."[53] All of this extended contact and subsequent similarity with the Little Sisters aim at one primary goal: similarity with Jesus Christ: "We were formed to understand our religious core, Christian core, based on the life of Christ. So the knowledge and the love of Christ are made the foundation during our formation. That is how I understood it. Knowing and living the life of Christ."[54]

It is important to recognize here that the sisters do not disagree with Frazer's contact and similarity account of the workings of what he calls magic; they simply say that it is the work of the Holy Spirit. This is most clearly presented in a brief essay by Sister Delfina Aywelo on the "Spirituality for a Vocation Animator," in the sisters' Golden

Jubilee Celebration publication. The sisters produced the publication in 2000. The war in northern Uganda had been going on for fifteen years, with no indication that it might end soon. Deaths from shrapnel, AIDS, and the vagaries of life in the IDP camps left many corpses unburied. In the words of one Sister, "During the war, there are many people who were killed, and they rotted in the bush."[55] Sister Delfina herself added in an interview with me, "Whenever they start shooting at night and there's a lot of dead people, you could see them in the morning. . . . And sometimes you can even see the leg of people in the tree because of the landmine."[56] And many of the bodies of those still alive were listless, spiritless. Even traditional Acholi religio-cultural practices, tied as many of them are to the localities of clan land, were atrophying in the midst of massive human displacement.

Sister Delfina begins her essay by making an analogy between the situation in northern Uganda and that of Ezekiel:

> Long ago, during biblical times, there was a prophet who found himself one day face-to-face with a dead situation, and was commanded to bring life to it. The story is that of Ezekiel and the dry bones. . . . Our present age is an age that is marked by negative forces. . . . We have become a people of wars, of killing, of crimes of abuse. . . . But the spirit of Yahweh is at work. He is present in the works of the vocation animator, in our young people and in the seemingly dead valleys filled with dry bones.[57]

The role of the vocation animator takes place within the context of the work of animation carried out by the Spirit itself.

> The Spirit is an Animator (with Capital A), while the spirituality we are in search of is the spirituality of the vocation animator (with a small a). This is aiming at centering the vocation animator in the Animator, the Arch-Animator. This is to alert the vocation animator to the presence of the dynamic and transforming force of the Spirit, the Spirit which is at the root of each vocation.[58]

The vocation animator serves as a conduit of the Spirit or animator first of all by being herself an imitable exemplar of the spirit-infused life. In the armed conflict of northern Uganda, youth "see no models of good behavior." The youth "see only insincerity from us grown-ups, when we keep saying one thing and doing just the opposite. . . . They realize that they cannot confide in us, so they confide in themselves, often with fatal results. Thus we are all responsible for the presence of these many deadly situations, 'valleys that are full of bones.'" The animator, therefore, is "most importantly a guiding star." [59] If the vocation animator carries out her role properly, then the Spirit might well come and give new life to the bones in northern Uganda.

So the sisters' accounts sit flush with Frazer's depiction of an "invisible ether"—or in their words, a charism or the Spirit—transmitting through similarity and contact. The sisters' practices, in this sense, constitute a form of magic. In Chapter 2, I described magic as a capacity via symbolic action to transform one reality into another and to have the new reality accepted by the intended audiences. The dis-spirited bodies in northern Uganda, both living and dead, are not carcasses, for instance, but rather "dry bones" that can rise again through animation by the Spirit.

We also saw in Chapter 2, however, how social upheaval—in that case, the upheaval of colonization—can challenge the different competing magics, which then often fail under the various pressures. The British brought the magic of writing in the form of decrees which, in their account, converted Africa into European colonies and protectorates. When the European magic failed to work—that is, the decrees failed to convince the indigenous people of European ownership—the colonizers turned to violence.[60] The locals sometimes responded to violent oppression with violent resistance. The Combonis' magic, for its part, first drew upon the symbol of the Cross to interpret what could otherwise be seen as missionary failure—both in terms of the loss of Comboni lives and the paucity of converts—as the very *precondition* for evangelical success. Later, under the mounting loss of lives and ongoing imperial pressure, the Combonis rewrote salvation history such that the British colonizers became the prime earthly agents of the salvation of the Acholi.

The more recent war in northern Uganda placed the people there under considerable duress and again challenged the operative magics. Like in the period of colonization, displacement undercut those specific location-linked practices centered around chiefdom *jogi*-spirits and ancestral shrines, giving the *ajwaka* spirit medium and her free *jogi*—not tied to any particular locality, and so not hampered by geographical displacement—a virtual monopoly on traditional magic. This had two main effects. The first was a proliferation of false *ajwagi*. The depth of poverty brought on by the war made being a spirit medium—one of the very few money-making practices in the IDP camps— attractive even to those who did not have the calling. The massive displacement of the populace meant that there was little in the way of social controls over who practiced traditional magic and how they did so.[61] The other effect of the war on traditional magic was that it set in motion, in some instances at least, horrendous mutations in the practices of spirit mediumship, of which the case of Joseph Kony is the prime example. Virtually all of the people I met and spoke with in northern Uganda did not doubt that Kony is a powerful medium; they insisted, however, that his powers are "not Acholi"—that is, they are evil, even of Satan. In the words of one Little Sister, "The power of the devil had gone loose."[62] There is evil as well as divine mimesis.

The sisters themselves were not exempt from the stresses of war. It was difficult—often impossible—to have the kind of regularly scheduled communal prayer that constitutes the core structuring practice of their vowed life. In 2013, seven years after the formal end of the war's hostilities in Uganda, the Mother Superior, Susan Clare Ndeezo, made the material-spiritual infrastructure linkage: "The collapse of our infrastructures—as you see in the Motherhouse and maybe in some communities—are a reflection of our inner self that had already disintegrated over time alongside this situation."[63] In light of the evidence we have seen so far and of which we will see more, I would suggest that the sisters' spiritual life, like the buildings (which are still standing, if beginning to crumble), might be in need of some repair and even some foundation work, but has not entirely disintegrated, (Like I said earlier, the sisters are their own harshest critics.) Now that armed conflict has ceased for northern Ugandans, the sisters have tended to that spiritual infrastructure by focusing their first two post-conflict General Chapter meetings—2007 and 2013—on reclamation and renewal of the very practices that I have been describing.[64]

That much said, the stress and disruption of war did have an effect on the sisters' devotional life analogous, at least in part, to that on the practices of traditional Acholi magic: regularly structured communal practice was made difficult, and so there was a turning to less-structured and often more individual forms of prayer. "I was saying the prayer every day—if there was time, eh? Because sometimes you can't because of the schools, because of the shooting, the bombing, and [you] have to care also for the children, especially the young ones. You have to organize for those who are bigger to take care of them: if [we are] running [from attack], they have to carry them."[65] And another: "You cannot settle, you cannot be settled. Everything was just a mess. You want, but you are not in peace."[66]

Given war's disruption of structured communal prayer, a good number of the sisters took part in the more ad hoc gatherings of what is called "charismatic Catholicism," where there is greater emphasis on dramatic cures and healings as the primary means of engagement with God. Similar to the dynamic where disruption of corporate forms of traditional Acholi magic led to a heightening of role of the free *ajwagi*, then, the members of the Little Sisters, under stress of war, turn more to individual spiritual agency. One Sister in particular, who is also a physician, told me of having received the gift of "deliverance." Even here, though, it is important to note that her tools remain the traditional devotional objects like the rosary. More, she insists on manifesting the kind of humility that the sisters identify with Negri and Angioletta, and she cites scripture to make the practice of Jesus her primary point of reference for the shape of her witness:

I have to guide the people of God. And he has prepared me. Because when I was in primary school 7, he even gave me the gift of deliverance. But I never used it until many years later. Mm. The gift of deliverance.

One time one of the biggest, oldest girls among us had demonic attacks. And that was my first time to see demonic attacks, in life, in P7. So the lady was there, beating herself, hurting herself actually. Beating her head on the ground. We didn't understand what was happening. She would talk, "We . . . we . . . we . . ." And we said, "No it is not 'we,' it is you." And we were wondering, who are these "we"? We didn't know it was evil spirits who were talking through her. Then the cook said, "That is Satan, just cast it off. Cast it off." Then we started [saying to the possessed girl], "We are not going [to leave]; we are also created by God. We are not going." Then she started hitting her head on the ground. And then she was pulling out grass from the ground. Hm. Strong grass, she was just tearing them. She really got tormented there. We didn't understand.

And that cook lady said, "Cast it out, cast it out." We said "How?" Then the cook said, "You get any blessed article, the sacramentals, either the rosary, the cross, you put on her, it will go." We were like, does this woman know what she is talking about? Sacrament, rosaries, through them these things go away? What is the relationship? We didn't understand. Then the little one, the youngest, picked a rosary and give me. "Eh, look, they said you should do it."

Then [the possessed girl] screamed my name. Now [the demons] laid down looking at me, "If you provoke us, we shall kill her." They were looking at me, their eyes were poking out, these big eyes poking out. What is this? I got so scared as they shout and she was there screaming my name, so when I held the rosary like this, looking straight at the girl, I see anger and the eyes wanted to come out to shoot me. With fear and trembling I held the rosary. I just held it. I held it [out] like this, trembling. I'm looking at her, I'm looking at it. Then when she screamed again my name, I got scared. Oh, I just close my eyes, I just throw the rosary like this [at the girl/demons].

Then the whole environment was quiet. I said, "Now what has happened to me." It took me a second to open my eyes. Then [she was] sitting. Quietly. And the other pupils were looking at me, looking at her, looking at each other, who were all shocked. None of us have ever seen that before. And I said, eh, is this how powerful the rosary is?

Then the girl asked, "People, what is happening?" We didn't know what to say because we didn't know what was happening by then, were just looking at each other. We couldn't explain. With what language?

[Later], I was in the university. The voice spoke to me, and he said to me, "I have given you this gift of healing and deliverance, but you are not using it." I was like, "Lord, what are you saying? Since when did you give me?" Then, he brought the whole video. I will call it a video. The scenario that took place in [primary] many years back. The whole scene, how it went and how I threw the rosary. I had forgotten totally about that thing. Brought it back, vivid. Then he said, "Yes, that was the moment I gave you the gift of healing, and that insistence was not for nothing." And I said, "Eh, so that was a gift which I was to use." And that is when I started to use it.

And they started bringing people. Then I said, "Oh, Jesus, for me I don't want that behavior. I don't want it. So if you know that this gift is going to make me become proud and misbehave to you, don't give it. Take it away now. But if you know that I will remain docile to you in a gentle, quiet manner, then confirm it, let it remain." Because I told him, "Let them focus on you; I'm just your instrument. Because your hands were nailed on the cross, you need my hands and my mouth now to do things for you. So I don't want the glory to come to me; the glory should come to you." Because I want whatever I do should give glory to God, and the honor should go back to him, not to me. For me I'm just a sinner through and through. I feel I have not grown enough spiritually, to the level that the Lord is educating me in this faith. Yeah, I just want the Lord to use me in a humble manner.

So, the Lord has shown me a lot of things, really. I've seen the person under a deep coma; they come back. They start walking, actively. When I minister, He uses me to pass His healing or deliverance to those people. One patient, with a very long face, a woman looking like in her forties, yet this woman was twenty-two. When we were praying she went into a deep sleep, and I noticed the face was changing and became a round, smooth, and beautiful lady. We left as she got up and started serving, cooking for the husband. And they walked back home.

I've seen a child brought, who was unable even to walk with the parents. But after prayer, the Lord healing him, he got up. He said, "Me, I'm already healed by Jesus." "Are you weak?" "Who told you I am weak? Jesus has healed me, I'm walking back."

I've seen the deliverance of human beings behaving like animals, eating grass. They chew, they swallow the whole thing. After delivery they're okay.

So, he showed me a lot of things.

And that biblical statement he made. "I will stay short in the one, but you will stay longer, you are my disciple, you'll do greater things, hm? You are to go and cast out demons, cure the sick." Jesus is still alive working these miracles with these people. He is doing it, I have no doubts.

So the Lord has taught me a lot. If I was really strong in faith, like other Christians, I think I should have been a holy woman. But I'm still praying for something. I have, I ask him, I want to become holy. Give me that holiness, Lord.[67]

The stresses and surprises of war disrupted the Little Sisters' communal prayer—as we heard, they were having to hide from the displaced people in Padibe, for instance, in order to find time to practice Eucharistic Adoration—to such an extent that they, individually, began to turn more toward personal prayer because that it is what the situation allowed. Some turned to more dramatically charismatic prayer because this is what the situation seemed to demand. And while, as we have seen, the practices that developed in community—the Rosary, the Adoration of the Eucharist—continued to shape and inform their devotional life, the disruption of shared prayer life took its toll.

One of the ways in which the communal stress expressed itself was in some sisters keeping at least part of their incomes for themselves and their immediate families rather than turning the salaries in to the order as part of the communal practice of evangelical poverty in imitation of Jesus and the early post-Resurrection communities. There have been interethnic tensions within the Little Sisters from the start. Bishop Negri founded the order during the Second World War, during much of which he was interned by the British. When they released him in 1942, they refused to allow him to return to Gulu, the center of Comboni missions in the area, but permitted him to settle in what is now part of Arua diocese, where the ethnic Alur live on the west side of the White Nile, separated by the river from the Acholi on the east side. Here, on the west side, then, is where he started the order. Over time, and with the later relocation of the sisters to Gulu, however, the ethnic Acholi became numerically predominant. The Little Sisters' *Chapter Documents* recognize within the community what they term, "tribalism." In a tellingly honest moment underscoring their view that flawed persons can be bearers of charism, their *1989 Chapter Documents* acknowledge that even Mother Angioletta favored one ethnic group over the others—"She did seem to be a factor for division. . . . Europeans usually love and get attached to the people and places of their first mission."[68] After recognizing the positive dimensions of ethnic identification—"Common and sociable life is most valued by Africans because this begins the regeneration and continuity in a clan"—the *1989 Chapter Documents* add that Jesus's "burning love" is for every person "without discrimination." The documents conclude with a dire warning: "Unless we create [a] climate which is against tribalism and segregation, the sisters will go to look for company elsewhere and this will lead to breaking their vows and loss of their vocation."[69]

Some of the sisters who are not Acholi either left the war zone or, at least at first, stayed away from it during the conflict that would become the LRA war. In the words of one member of the Congregation, "After Kony's war [started], a number of Sisters preferred to stay there [at] their homes, [in] their own dioceses. Little by little we lost a sense of belonging to the Congregation. This we should not hide."[70] The Congregation accommodated those who sought to leave. One Sister comments, "[It was] a very trying moment in our lives, because every time guns shoot, every time you hear somebody's killed, and this place is looted, some people abducted. [So we said,] those that feel they can stay, let them stay, but those who are fearful, we take you to other places."[71]

Into this context of war-induced strains on the Congregation came international NGOs with large projects and even larger budgets. The Little Sisters, with their high level of literacy and education—many of them have advanced degrees—and firsthand knowledge of things on the ground, were precisely the kind of staff-persons that the NGOs were looking for, particularly given that many members of the Acholi intelligentsia had left the region. With the communal bonds already weakened by years in a conflict zone, some of the sisters began keeping at least portions of their salaries rather than giving them to the Congregation. "During the war, there were a lot of NGOs," says one Sister, "and many of us got in touch with this and many of us are now very rich missionaries and others very poor. And that's why our Congregation is poor. Because how many built towers, palaces. And yet we don't keep care of the Congregation. And others, they see this one building a palace and others who don't have as much as a good pair of shoes to put on. How did I become a Sister? Because the Congregation helped me to reach the level of education where I am now. . . . [But] each one is working to fill my pocket and develop my family, at least get a car. Even in the community, some people eat rich food [while] others are eating beans, others are going hungry. So the NGOs who've come to help us, we are not clever enough and wise enough to keep to our root, to our vision, you know, to our mission."[72] Others concur: "We lost a sense of what religious life is. We have now become materialistic. And what we get should be for my family, my family, my family. This pulling together has become very weak, very weak. And this is the greatest challenge which the Congregation has now."[73]

The sisters approached the problem head-on in their Chapter meetings. "Our intellectual and professional advancement sometimes lead us to violate the vows of poverty and obedience, e.g. choosing where to work, job seeking, keeping salaries, etc."[74]

Or even more, "Some 'learned' Sisters dominate family council to cover up their mistakes against the vow of Poverty."[75] Disparities in education and certification led, on the part of some, to feelings of intellectual, professional, and even religious superiority—and entitlement. The *Chapter Documents* cite that "some Sisters who earn salaries despise those who do not," and warn of the formation of a "superiority/inferiority complex" and a concomitant "low opinion of certain courses such as catechetical, catering, tailoring, store management, agriculture, etc."[76]

It is important to keep these abuses in perspective. Even with as much time as I spent with the sisters, I did not see much in the way of "towers" and "palaces," though I do not doubt that some sisters sought to build simple homes or purchase vehicles for their families. Here, it is helpful to keep in mind that the *Chapter Documents* consider seemingly simple things like "uncontrolled use of music, telephone, expensive cosmetics and treated hair" as constituting a "luxurious lifestyle."[77] Most often, the pressure to provide for the families was driven by real and dire poverty brought on by years of war, and the *Chapter Documents* themselves highlight this:

> We Chapter members recognize and acknowledge the existence of wrong attitudes about the vow of Poverty because of hardships resulting from prolonged civil war and other societal factors. . . . Observations: The families of many Sisters are needy. War and HIV/AIDS have left many orphans. Many Sisters have been helping their families with money from their salaries. Directives: A Sister will be open to the superior and members of the community about problems in her family. . . . Problems in the family will be evaluated, and if found genuine, necessary and possible assistance will be given. . . . In case the needy person cannot live on his/her own, the community can decide on the best possible assistance to be rendered.[78]

In short, the sisters' magic—their capacity to draw from Jesus's charism the wherewithal to witness to the most vulnerable in the midst of a brutal armed conflict—was under extreme stress, and the flood of NGO money provided an alluring means for self-preservation on the part of some of them. Here, literacy and certification culture turned their charism-infused vocations of education and health care—meant to serve others—on their heads.

What is striking is the sisters' response. They took the issue on directly. "We need a radical change in the way we live the Evangelical Poverty." And while the *Chapter Documents* do make recommendations that require a more rationalized bureaucracy—"Bridging the gap between poor and rich communities will be done by a fair, balanced staffing"—the core of their approach is the reclamation of Jesus's charism through mimetic reenactment of his poverty on the part of every sister. "The Little Sisters of Mary Immaculate of Gulu share in the poverty of Christ, who for their sake became poor, even though he was rich."[79] The sisters are to be "poor in the footsteps of Christ." How they are to be so is worth citing at some length because it makes clear that the sisters responded to the pressures of war and the excesses of being part of literate professional certification culture by appealing to the embodied practice of following and imitating Jesus Christ:

> We are convinced that both our spiritual advancement and our apostolic work depend largely on the witness we give to following Christ the Poor man . . . . In fact, when we consider the lack of goods and comforts which nowadays afflicts our own people and country, and compare it with our own preoccupation not to go without our comforts, certainly we have to ask ourselves whether we are really following Christ as poor Sisters. . . . Too easily, some Sisters make use of what they can get according to their personal choices.
>
> First of all, it is necessary for us all to give a sincere personal witness of Poverty. We are quite aware that we feel deeply our love for our family and clan, as this is a characteristic of our African culture and tradition. However, we should not hesitate in correcting our attitudes according to the new reality brought to us by Christ whom we profess to follow closely. . . . To practice true Poverty, we have to rely on God's providence, share willingly what we have. . . .
>
> Our revised Constitution and Rules place much stress on Poverty lived [also] as a "communitarian witness," that is that the very community, each community, must be poor. It is all too easy for us to develop the mentality that the more we have in our community the better it is. Hence the real danger of accumulating unnecessary means, such as transportation, audio-visual items, enormous quantities of food, etc. . . . Our Religious house is to be always a clear sign of the Church of the poor, and to witness to Christ with continuous prayer, simplicity, sharing and joyous Poverty. In a word: to copy the house and family of Nazareth. . . . This communitarian witness of Poverty, far from discouraging us from doing good to others, even materially, ought to be an incentive to work hard at the service of others. After all, we are spending our very lives in the service of people so that they may know Christ. . . .
>
> Our Congregation was born in moments of great difficulties and distress, in poverty. Our Founder, Bishop Angelo Negri . . . stressed the need for the Sisters to work and to share their small revenues among the various communities. We may consider ourselves as children of Poverty, of sorrow and of work. Let us love this Poverty which will always give us joy and riches in Christ. . . . Let us be poor in the footsteps of Christ.[80]

Sometimes, as we have seen, practicing poverty among the poor was thrust upon the sisters by the displaced persons who flooded to their schools, parishes, and even homes. The force of the sisters' commitment to follow Christ as a "Church of the poor" is even more evident in cases where they went *to* the vulnerable in a practice that was common enough that the sisters have a term for it, "pitching tents":

> One of the things we were always saying was that we should remain present; we should not leave the people alone. And we used to call it "pitching tents." You know, where the people are, we should be there. And where we can open our doors, we

will be there. We said now ourselves and our leaders that they should not move the sisters away. And then what we were trying to say is "Could we not also go there, and be present and make a presence even if this means living [in] tents or shelters?" . . . But the idea was to remain there as much as possible, with the people. Not to leave. Not to come away. And if there was a place, to go and pitch a tent. Then that was what our leaders were doing. They were letting the sisters go back.[81]

The sisters drew on the rich retinue of practices and symbolic resources to infuse their call to pitch tents with those who were suffering. One described it in terms of her following Christ in the Stations of the Cross:

I [would] say the Stations of the Cross, because the cross is the moment of suffering, eh? A suffering that brings joy and salvation. I got this as a devotion because the life that we live is also a life of suffering, a suffering that gives you hope. Like Jesus did. Jesus was tortured. Was going and followed the stations until Calvary. And then he rose again. So I would say the Stations of the Cross. And especially the Third Station, when he falls the first time. In my reflection, I always think Jesus has fallen for the first time not because he was weak, he cannot manage the cross, but because of the weight of sin, of people. So I put myself in that. I don't want to weigh Jesus with a heavy burden in the sense that you don't treat your Sister well in community or you don't help somebody who needs your help. To do this and follow this.

And the suffering of Jesus for me matches very well with the situation people are in. Imagine, you have to walk, you don't sleep in your home [for fear of the LRA], coming to town [to sleep on the storefront porches], or in Lachor [hospital grounds]. We also showed solidarity with people in that situation, sleeping in the camps. We said, "Now, we are sleeping comfortably in a bed, a warm blanket. How are we sharing with the people out there?" So we religious suggested we should also go share with the people in the camps, in the places where they come to sleep. We pray with them, share with them the scriptures, and then we sleep there, and see how it feels. We also carried our [reed sleeping] mat. I said, "Ah, this is the situation our people are in." Because you [as a Sister] cannot remain outside [the region] in fear of the rebel or even the government soldier.

And the suffering there gave me a deep meditation when I put it together with the Cross of Jesus. I was saying, "When Jesus followed the Stations of the Cross, he did not do it in vain, because the Father was with Him . . . and at the end of it all was the Resurrection, which was a great joy."

We look at this situation [in northern Uganda], you know, like being on Good Friday. Everybody is on Good Friday every day. And on Good Friday, Jesus died. This is a period of desperation. If you don't have a strong faith on Good Friday, ah—there was one, of course, [who in Scripture] ran away; there were those [who] say, "I don't know this man."

So I said, "We hope we shall have Easter one day. Because we cannot remain in this Good Friday." And the people remain in this. So our prayer is the prayer of hope—for protection during these times and then that, one day, we shall also experience this peace that other people are having. Because Jesus did not suffer his cross in vain. There is definitely Easter. So we in our suffering [pray] there will one day be Easter celebration. That has been our prayer and message for the people. And that is why I have a good connection of the Cross and the [present] situation.[82]

So strong is the inclination, built up through decades of formation in following Christ, to be with the people who are suffering—again, the Little Sisters speak of their charism as that of Christ's "burning love for the most vulnerable"—that it profoundly shapes their reading of other parts of the tradition. Sister Delfina, for example, in a moment that is either profound interpretation or eisegesis, extrapolates the solidarity message from Ezekiel's dry bones encounter discussed earlier. She writes,

> The ritualistic detail of his being led around the bones is very significant. It is as if Ezekiel must familiarize himself with the situation and must become part and parcel of the scene from which he would rather flee. It is as if to challenge him to the realization that these bones are bones of his brothers and sisters, bones of his sons and daughters. So the way to redeem those bones was for Ezekiel to come closer to them to reflect and to renew his relationship with them.[83]

So while armed conflict and disease outbreaks from Ebola to cholera stressed the spiritual infrastructure that the Combonis handed on to the sisters, the members of the Congregation managed, for the most part and repeatedly in extraordinary ways, to live in a way that witnessed to the charism passed to them through that infrastructure. Most stayed. Most who left returned. In the words quoted earlier, "Because the people are there we said, 'Now we are sent there,' which means the Congregation wants us to die together with the people. So we are not going to leave them." Some sisters who received salaries through NGO-funded organizations sought to divert at least part of the money to themselves or their families (who were themselves often suffering), but the Congregation appealed to them by calling them back to the mimetic practice of following Christ in His poverty. The sisters are aware of their own sins; but rather than weaken the case for the power of charism—of God's *psst* to them through dreams, representational objects, and exemplary persons—the sisters' humanness, their very real frailties, underscores precisely this enabling power without which they would have collapsed both as individuals and as a community.

Both the sisters' humanness and the power of the charism that they embody in their practices are evident in their moments of lamentation, which, without exception in the interviews, they end with thanksgiving. One witness will have to suffice here, that of Sister Josephine, regarding her response to the Ebola outbreak that, on top of the war, saw nearly four hundred cases in Gulu district. It killed thirteen of the health care providers in Lachor Hospital, where Sister Josephine herself worked:

> Yes, yes, yes, I was here [during the 2000 Ebola outbreak]. Ah, too much. I had not [before] experienced what people say, maybe depression. When you just read in

books and then you just say, "This person is depressed," you would not understand. But in 2000 I felt and I experienced that. A very nasty experience. Ebola broke through in October. I remember when we had the first case, eh, when one of our students from the nursing school died. And this student, people and the staff and others, they went to bury her. So, as usual the cultural rituals are that before being buried people view the body. And so this girl also, even from the hospital, is not handled like something dangerous.

A week later, we had another student called Daniel also admitted. Daniel previously, like about five days ago, he was one of the school leaders dealing with what?—entertainment. And he danced very well the *bwola* dance. On the following day he was taken to the hospital. When he was in the hospital, only two days, Daniel died. People still didn't know this was Ebola. I remember we prayed here. As usual, people [were] viewing the body. Others could even touch it with the rosary, that kind of thing. Then Daniel was taken to be buried at their home in Kolongo.

The result came back from South Africa that this was the viral hemorrhagic fever [Ebola]. We were now getting a lot of cases. And immediately now they isolated patients from every ward. Somebody coming with bleeding from any orifice, you have to be what?—isolated. So at the initial state, mm, people are brought and people are dying. Even deep in the village, people were dying. And so they said, "There is a mysterious sickness, let us come [to Lachor Hospital]." People are vomiting blood, people are diarrhating blood, and they don't take long to die. And because these things started at outpatient, the staff not knowing what this thing is like, handling patients as usual, some of the staff also got infected. One of our Sisters was working in that ward of the Ebola. And eh, I remember that was a Sunday. We heard about our Sister who has died. Ah. Was too much.

I became so fearful. And every evening our Sisters who had been working in the ward, they would come. And they would tell you sad news. They would just say, "Oh, today, so-and-so has been admitted. I don't know if this one will survive."

So hearing those things, I became so depressed. Maybe I would be admitted and I will never come back again. I would now die. I will even die when my family—my father, my brothers and sisters, relatives and friends—they will not come to bury me because when you are burying an Ebola patient, the dead, it is very fast, very fast so that the virus what?—doesn't spread.

I don't eat now. It's like, when you go to eat the appetite is not there. Every time you are sad, you are like, like something is in your stomach. I remember that one evening when we sat for prayers, I was with another Sister and we were so fearful. I think now, "But, what can we do? If God wants us to perish, we shall." Two days later, one of our Sisters has the Ebola virus. This is our second Sister now dying of Ebola.

So this day, when Sister died, now I was desperate. And I couldn't take tea. I just went and laid in front of the altar, just prostrated myself. About 30 minutes. I said, "Let me get strength from here. I cannot from food, but let me get strength." In my prayer now, this time, I'm not now quiet, but tears are rolling, and I said, "God, why this suffering? Why all this? Why?" So, even if I say "Why?," at the end of it still I acknowledged that what?—"You are the source of life. You are the one who has the power. Everything lights in your hand."

Then when I got up and eh, one Sister, I remember, Sister Jean says, "So you know what? Dr. Matthew [Lukwiya, an Acholi physician] is addressing all the staff." So when we went, we found Dr. Matthew. He was advising people, "We should not run away, we have to stand, to help our people." I said, "Okay, let me now stay."

[Later,]I met with Dr. Matthew, and he said, "Sister I, I am not feeling well. I have fever and I have to go home. Eh, but I will be okay." So I said, "I hope this is fever, not any other thing." And we work [in the hospital]. The results then came out: he has the Ebola virus. I went up to his place, seeing him so full of what?— tears. But I tried to control myself. I said, "Now doctor, you are already crying." Then he told me, he said, "You see now Josephine, you will never see my tears again. This will be the last one." I said, "We keep on praying." After some few days then, Matthew died. And I felt like . . . I felt like everything has gone.

So basically the Ebola time, for us who have experience, was really a time of depression and sadness. Because at any time we would hear [that] somebody has fallen. Somebody.

There is no appetite, You don't have the gut to eat, and it's like you want to vomit, but even if you want to vomit there is nothing in the stomach. A kind of nausea. You feel undressed also. You, you're not yourself. You can't sit steadily.

At that time my prayer was very meditative. I'm trying to see, "What is this kind of Ebola virus that God has sent for us?" A kind of lamentation. Thinking, "What is it, God, that we have done that this Ebola is coming down to shake us? And, eh, the war?" People were fighting, and then now came this disease which is trying to take us all. I would sit in front of the tabernacle and say, "God, what is it that you are trying to tell us? What is it that you want from us? Why you are sweeping people away?"

And so lamenting, and then meditating.

Still, in that case, "We still trust in You because You are the what?—You are the source of life. You are everything. Even if we are suffering we still trust in You. But now could You save us from this?"

You can imagine, I still have the strength to go out. Just trusting in what?—in the Divine Mercy of God that he will still help us. Just like He rescued the Israelites from slavery in Egypt.

So still I go outside to the people. I still go on, much as I fear. "Let me go and spread your Word." And in that going, it helped me, because [I was] going out also to pass out the message to the people how they should take care of themselves, how they could avoid any form of transmission of the Ebola in case they meet with somebody. So, I remember telling the people what precaution we have to take in case you have this patient. Like, we should not greet each other because these things spread with what?—fluids. The sweat, the urine, the whatever, you can get it. So, I taught the basic knowledge about the transmission of the Ebola.

So, you see, that kind of prayer. You still lament, you still complain to God. And eh, still giving thanks to God that every day you wake up. I still thank God that today we are still alive. "Give us the strength to endure this pain. Give us the strength that we still hold on to You, we still bind together with You, we still receive the blessing that You give us in the day." So, eh?, you complain, and then still you praise him because he's still keeping you alive. When I wake up in the morning I said "Today Lord, today this is yet another day. The sun is bright or it is cold, the wind will blow. Whatever has taken place, or whatever is to be done in the day, we still praise you that you have restored our life."[84]

* * *

We have seen, then, how the Little Sisters' understand their lives as a mode of imitating their founder, Bishop Negri, and ultimately Jesus Christ. Such imitation, a movement toward the exemplar, would be ultimately futile if not for the fact that the exemplar also moves toward the Little Sisters by passing on the Spirit-*psst* of the exemplar to the sisters through objects such as paintings, photos, relics, crucifixes, and pressed wafers. Sometimes, the spirit of the exemplar visits directly through dreams, very occasionally through waking visions. If we are to believe the sisters—that is, if we are to pay attention to and interpret them emically—it is precisely this Spirit-*psst* that gives them the wherewithal to risk their lives on behalf of the most vulnerable even during an armed conflict that is by all accounts horrendous. Still, their witness is fallible—that is to say, human. They are no strangers to narrow individual self-regard and ethnic prejudice. Such shortcomings, I suggest, are testament to the power of the Spirit, without which, all of the sisters without exception testify, their radical witness would be, for them, impossible.

There is much more that I have seen and that they have told me that attests to the power of the Spirit in the sisters, but we need to move on now, because it is important to show how the sisters are right about the Gospel not only with regard to the call to poverty or other specifics, but also—and perhaps most importantly—with regard to how the Gospel itself *works* and how those who claim to be followers of Jesus Christ are to engage the Good News. Paying attention to the Little Sisters requires discussing whether their practices cohere with their sources. For that we need to turn to scripture itself. And if I am right about the sisters, and Catholicism in northern Uganda and South Sudan more generally, in this regard, then perhaps they can serve as bridge cultures for us to understand and live the Gospel more faithfully than we presently do.

Gospel mimesis

Then Jesus summoned his twelve disciples and gave them authority over unclean spirits, to cast them out, and to cure every disease and every sickness. . . . These twelve Jesus sent out with the following instructions . . . "As you go, proclaim the good news, "The kingdom of heaven has come near." Cure the sick, raise the dead, cleans the lepers, cast out demons. You received without payment; give without payment. Take no gold, or silver, or copper in your belts, no bag for your journey, or two tunics, or sandals, or a staff. . . .

"Do not worry about how you are to speak and what you are to say; for what you are to say will be given to you at that time; for it is not you who speak, but the Spirit of your Father speaking through you. . . .

"A disciple is not above the teacher, nor a slave above the master; it is enough for the disciple to be like the teacher, and the slave like the master."

—*The Gospel of Matthew, 10:1, 5a, 7-10a, 19-20, 24-25*

The Little Sisters focus their practices around the imitation of Jesus. Again, "We were formed to understand our religious core, Christian core, based on the life of Christ . . . Knowing and living the life of Christ." From the standpoint of an anthropological approach to doing theology, it is a good place to start. If, as I said in Chapter 1, anthropological theology begins "in the middle of things," and Jesus Christ is its normative content, then an important way into such theology is not through God's *creatio ex nihilo* at the beginning of time working forward, nor via the eschaton at the end of time looking back, but rather in the midst of the biblical account of God becoming human in Jesus of Nazareth. Anthropology's emphasis on particularity highlights the fact that God chose to self-reveal in a definitive way through *this* person at *this* time and in *this* particular culture. From a theological perspective, the failure to take seriously the concrete particularity of Jesus constitutes a de facto methodological denial of the Incarnation. Others have made this point with regard to the importance of attention to the *human* particularity of Jesus for Christian theology.[85] What anthropological theology adds is that the focus is specifically on the concrete Jesus in his *cultural* context—that is, on Jesus *the Nazarene* the Christ. (It is notable that Jesus's followers were first called "the Nazarenes"; see Acts 24:4.)

The pericope above of the commissioning of the disciples—by most accounts an historical occurrence[86]—is itself "in the middle of things" in all three of the synoptic gospels. It is the turning point between Jesus's Galilean ministry and his journey to Jerusalem and death, pivoting incarnation and healing miracles toward crucifixion and resurrection. Though the verb *mimeomai* and noun *mimêtês* do not themselves appear in the gospels, we already have in this passage, in the words of New Testament scholar James Dunn, evidence of "a clear strand of *imitatio Christi* in the New Testament itself."[87] What more is involved, then, in gospel mimesis? What we will find is that the sisters are accurate not only with regard to this or that particular practice—like that of evangelical poverty—of the imitation of Jesus, but also with regard to the practice of mimesis itself as a means of appropriating the gospels. In other words, their *mode* of engaging the gospels is itself *of* the Gospel. Showing how this is the case will lead to the main question of the chapter that follows, that of whether such mimesis can be the center of an academic method.

Frazer's account of magic in terms of contact and similarity is again helpful as an initial lens, this time for interpreting the life and practices of the Jesus community in the gospels. My aim in drawing upon it here is not to enter the debates about the relationship between Jesus and magic in the usual sense, but rather to understand what Michael Taussig calls the "magic of mimesis," that is, the dynamic forces which the agents of mimesis themselves understand to be in play in rendering their actions both intelligible and effective.[88] The New Testament names what Frazer calls the "invisible ether" the "Spirit," or sometimes simply "power" (*dunamis*), and it is in play in instances of both contact and similarity in the gospels. Jesus's comment to the disciples, "It is not you who speak, but the Spirit of your Father speaking through you" (Mt. 10:20), is a recognition and affirmation of the fact that they have had enough contact with him to be sufficiently similar to him to also transmit the Spirit. But I am getting ahead of the story.

Both contact and similarity are evident from the start of Jesus's mission in that John's baptism of him—the water being the conductor of the Spirit—inaugurates his ministry. Interestingly, the relevant interpretive passage, occurring in all three synoptic gospels and so having multiple attestation and therefore significant likelihood of historicity, appears toward the end of Jesus's mission. He is asked by religious figures in the temple—"the chief priests, the scribes, and the elders"—about the source of his claim to *exousia* or "authority" (Mk 11:27-33; cf. also Mt. 21:23-27 and Lk. 20:1-8).[89] He answers by reference to John: "Did the baptism of John come from heaven, or was it of human origin?" This response, with its implication that his authority is "from heaven," is sometimes interpreted to indicate a consciousness on Jesus's part that his authority is unmediated.[90] However, Jesus is referring to his baptism specifically by John—an event of such importance that all of the synoptic gospels testify to it even though it is sometimes seen by biblical scholars to raise difficulties for claims of Jesus's primacy. (As we will see later in this chapter, the early followers of Jesus actually not only had little problem with there being precursors to Jesus, but had need of them to understand who he was.) Jesus is implying in his return question to the religious leaders that his authority must be from heaven—that is, it bears the Spirit-*psst* of God—because it came through contact with water poured by John. He is saying that because he was baptized *by John*, he is—whatever the differences in the shape of their missions might be—*similar to* John in ways that mattered.[91] The Spirit descending as a dove immediately following the baptism confirms the transmission of the charism to Jesus.

Jesus then spreads the power of the Spirit through his own miraculous acts of contact, like that of restoring sight to the blind man of Bethsaida. Notable here is the fact that Jesus's response to the incomplete healing of the first contact is to touch the blind man again:

Some people brought a blind man to him and begged him to touch him. He took the blind man by the hand and led him out of the village; and when he had put saliva on his eyes and laid his hands on him, he asked him, "Can you see anything?" And the man looked up and said, "I can see people, but they look like trees, walking." Then Jesus laid his hands on his eyes again; and he looked intently and his sight was restored, and he saw everything clearly. (Mk 8:22-26)

The most dramatic depiction of the law of contact and the transfer of the Spirit is perhaps Jesus's healing of the hemorrhagic woman. She merely touches "the fringe of his clothes" and the act heals her. Jesus responds, "Someone touched me; for I noticed that power had gone out from me" (Lk. 8:46).[92] Here, Jesus's clothes are already a representational object that can transmit charism.

Of note in both the cases of the blind man and the hemorrhagic woman is that even though Jesus's Spirit, through physical contact, flows into them so as to heal them, neither one is called to imitate him, nor to act with authority. Yet such authoritative imitation is precisely what Jesus calls for from his disciples in the commissioning pericope quoted at the outset of this section. What makes for the difference between the blind man and the hemorrhagic woman on the one hand and the disciples on the other? We can begin to answer this question if we note, as Taussig does, that the law of contact and that of similarity can manifest themselves in combined form, frequently so when eyewitness serves as an ongoing "optical means of contact."[93] The importance of such eyewitness for the early Christian community is perhaps most evident in the account in Acts of the decision process for replacing Judas as one of the twelve disciples. Peter's criterion is that the replacement has to be someone who actively followed the earthly Jesus. No one else has adequate authority to speak on His behalf. "So one of the men who have accompanied us during all the time that the Lord Jesus went in and out among us, beginning from the baptism of John until the day he was taken up from us—one of these must become a witness with us to his resurrection" (Acts 1:21-22).

Jesus frequently calls upon those who would become his disciples to "follow" him (usually *akoloutheo*, but also *deute*; see Mt. 16:24; Lk. 9:23; Mt. 4:19). Conjoining the laws of contact and similarity through eyewitness, then, it is clear that the call to follow Jesus is an invitation to extended contact with—that is witness of—Jesus in a way that facilitates authoritative imitation. Extended contact serves as a conduit for the Spirit to transmit to the witness in a sustained way that enables him or her to imitate the source agent with power and authority. In Taussig's words regarding mimesis generally, extended optical contact brings about a state in which "the representation shares in or acquires the properties of the represented."[94] Recognizing the ancient dynamic of extended contact enabling imitation undercuts the anachronistic separation sometimes made between following Jesus Christ on the one hand and imitating him on the other.[95] Discipleship *facilitates* mimesis.

We see here the pneumatological grounding for a two-tiered ethic in Jesus's teaching: one tier for those who respond with faith to his mission and another for those who go further and follow him.[96] The difference between the two ethical tiers is evident in Jesus's encounter with the rich young man, an exchange that is in all likelihood historical.[97] The rich young man asks, "Good teacher, what must I do to inherit eternal life?" and Jesus responds by quoting most of the second table of the Decalogue. When the rich young man insists that he has consistently followed these teachings, Jesus replies, "You lack one thing; go, sell what you own, and give the money to the poor, and you will have treasure in heaven; then come, follow me" (Mk 10:21[98]). The invitation to follow is a call to imitate. The directive to sell all one has and give the money to the poor leads to a life where the no-longer-rich man travels in the same manner—that is, "like"—Jesus and the disciples as described in the commissioning pericope: "Take no gold, or silver, or copper in your belts, no bag for your journey, or two tunics, or sandals, or a staff" (Mt. 9:9; cf. also Lk. 9:3 and Mk 6:8).

Commentators often note that the call to this way of life is only by invitation—limited mainly to the disciples—but the story of the rich young man indicates that, with persistence, even the wealthy can receive the invitation to follow Jesus (though, importantly, when they make the changes required for such following, they are no longer rich). The call, then, is ultimately open to all, even if we, like the young man, are not likely to respond to it once it is extended. However, it is only through this way of life and the extended contact with the source that a person "shares in or acquires the properties of" Jesus and the Spirit he bears.[99] That is to say, it is only through following Jesus Christ in this way that one legitimately shares in his power and authority (something that has implications for our understanding of church leadership). James Dunn is on point: "*It was only as they shared in his mission that his disciples shared in his authority and charismatic power.* In short, as Jesus did not live for himself but for the kingdom and others, so it had to be with his disciples. . . . Those who gathered around him did so to share in that task, to follow him in his mission, and for no other reason" (emphasis in original).[100]

This understanding of how extended contact with Jesus facilitates the transfer of power and authority in the Spirit illuminates the force of the Resurrection and Pentecost for the apostles. There are debates among biblical scholars regarding the span of time between the Resurrection and Pentecost,[101] but from the perspective of the practice of gospel mimesis, the critical point is that these two events mean that Jesus's death does not foreclose either further contact with or imitation of him, therefore allowing the continuing transferal of his power and authority. The Gospel of Matthew has the resurrected Jesus appear to the women at the tomb, and although his account of the appearance to the disciples is not as elaborate as that in Luke, he ties the disciples' witness of the risen Jesus—"they saw him" (28:17)—tightly to his recommissioning of them in the immediately following verses: "All authority in heaven and earth has been given to me. Go therefore and make disciples of all nations" (28:18-19). Eyewitness, even of the resurrected Jesus, is central in Luke's gospel. Two disciples on the road to Emmaus are the first to see the risen Jesus, "but their eyes were kept from recognizing him" (24:16). When he broke bread with them, however, "their eyes were opened" (24:31). When the two took Jesus to the rest of the disciples, the latter, "thought that they were seeing a ghost," so Jesus urges them, "Look at my hands and feet; see that it is I myself. Touch me and see" (24:37, 39). In Luke's version, the recommissioning does not come until Pentecost, but the pledge of such comes with the resurrection appearance: "I am sending upon you what my Father promised; so stay here in the city until you have been clothed with power from on high" (24:49).

The Book of Acts repeatedly stresses the importance of optical witness on the part of the apostles,[102] and such witness enables their capacity to imitate Jesus and leverages their authority. The apostles imitate Jesus first of all in their performance of wonderworks, most often, like Jesus, through contact with the sufferer—typically the laying on of hands,[103] but also contact through shared cloth (19:11-12, calling to mind Jesus's contact with the hemorrhagic woman, Mt. 9:20-22) and even Peter's shadow (5:15). Mentioned only in Matthew among the gospels (19:13-20), the invocation of Jesus's name as a form of contact, via the apostle, between the Spirit and the sufferer becomes prominent in Acts.[104]

There is one key cluster of mimetic actions that the second, post-Pentecost mission adds to the first for the disciples/apostles. Biblical scholars debate the historicity of Jesus's warnings that following him will inevitably involve suffering and even death on the Cross on the part of the disciples, warnings which Luke and even more so Matthew attach to the first commissioning pericope.[105] However, what cannot be doubted is that the apostles and those who documented their activities viewed the persecution, imprisonments, trials, floggings, and executions of members of the early post-Pentecost community in terms of Jesus's own suffering, death, and ultimate victory over death.[106]

* * *

The confluence between the practices and understandings of the Jesus community on the one hand and the Little Sisters on the other is evident. For both, Jesus is the primary bearer of the Spirit-*psst*. Persons can become like Jesus not only in regard to particular actions, but also as themselves bearers of the Spirit through extended contact with him or with persons who already bear his charism—thus the long formation process for the sisters. The author of Luke-Acts builds his credibility precisely on the claim of a trustworthy provenance of eyewitness, as is evidenced in the prologue to the gospel. It tells us that the events to be recounted "were handed to us by those who from the beginning were eyewitnesses and servants to the word," so that the reader and listener "may know the truth" (1:1-4). And the sisters inform us with regard to their imitation of Bishop Negri, "Our older sisters, they used to teach us, those who have seen him." Disruptions in the chain of eyewitness in the form of the death of the charism-bearing exemplars, however, do not constitute a definitive breakage in part because the charism is already passed on to others and in part because the exemplar and the charism continue in existence through the resurrected body—which can appear through either waking visions or dreams—and representational objects such as clothes, relics, rosaries, wafers, and even the exemplar's invoked name. Such a confluence of practices and understandings between scripture and the Little Sisters suggests that one crucial way for moderns and postmoderns to learn not just this or that teaching of the Gospel, but the way of the Gospel itself—ultimately to inhabit it—is to seek extended contact with the sisters and persons like them. That is what I did. And theology has become the writing out of the encounters along the way.

Pivoting from attention to discernment

Chapters 2 and 3 have been an exercise in what I have been calling "attention," that is, the use of all of the senses to carefully attend to the way of being in the world of an other. The other or others in question are those Acholi Catholics who offered so dramatic a witness to another kind of world during the horrors of the LRA war, a world in which people loved rather than butchered each other. Chapter 2 has provided not only substantive background through description of Acholi life under Comboni evangelization and British rule, but also a sense of what it might be like for someone, like the Combonis, to try to witness under oppressive conditions. This chapter argues that even though the Combonis ultimately cooperated with the evil of empire, the material and spiritual infrastructure that they passed on to the Acholi Catholics provided the latter with a means through which to witness more forthrightly during the LRA war.

The kind of fieldwork necessary to write the previous chapters places the body in the middle of method. Not "the body as 'text,'" but the particular body of the scholar: *this* body—with all of its specific capacities and deficiencies—in *this* setting, encountering *these* persons and *their* bodies. Such centering of embodiment has implications for research. It brings the full array of senses of the scholar into play, not just hearing, stressed by oral historians, but also sight, smell, taste, and touch. Fieldwork therefore requires its own kind of attention—a sensory alertness—that textual investigation, for the sake of its own kind of attention, suppresses. During the weeks when I was taking my doctoral exams, I would sometimes put my morning Cheerios in the refrigerator after breakfast, and put the milk on the shelf in the pantry. The milk spoiled, but I passed the exams with distinction. With fieldwork, lack of sensory attention *is* bad scholarship.

The necessity of sensory attention requires an *askesis*—a training of the attention of the body—for fieldwork. Like training the body for sports, there is both a general "fitness" and a fitness specific to the particular setting. It involves such things as being sufficiently sturdy bodily to withstand the repeated jolts from hardened potholed dirt roads during dry season travel, and drinking enough water not to dehydrate, but not so much that you need a break during a nonstop six-hour bus ride. All this so that you can direct the focus of your attention to the woman who happens to sit next to you as she tells you about her decision to continue to teach in LRA-controlled Pader district when even the government troops fear to go there. Such *askesis* must also be culturally specific. Do I accept this dish of *anyeri*, which the Acholi translate, "giant rat," even though it looks undercooked, or do I risk offending my host who has no chickens to offer and has given me a place to sleep for the next two weeks? Should I, like Sister Mary Clementina, genuflect on both knees?

At the moment of re-presentation of the field encounter, the question is how to carry this body-centric method into writing. This is another point where anthropology, with its "thick description" serves as a good disciplinary partner.[107] Re-presentation that does not attempt to cross-cultural boundaries can remain sparse in detail. In such shared contexts, re-presentation can be metonymic, where certain symbols, phrases, and visual cues stand for and evoke a broad range of experiences in the listener or reader such that much more is presented than what is directly in the performance. *Pars pro toto*— the part stands for the whole. The purpose of the intensity and length—again, up to twelve years—of formation among the Little Sisters is precisely to bring them into a particular context in such a way that that context becomes their metonymic reality. It is what allowed for the continued use and significance of the traditional prayers like the Stages of the Cross, the Adoration of the Eucharist, and the Rosary, even in fragmented form, during the disruption of war. A few minutes here and there of Adoration, and, "Jesus is in me whole, not part of him." Even a small wafer can stand for the whole of Jesus Christ. But the re-presentation of fieldwork as a scholarly method requires more detailed—"thicker"—accounts from the field if readers with no experience of the culture in question are to be able to enter into the scenes.

In specifically *academic* settings, re-presentation tacks back and forth between thick description and more analytic modes of scholarly writing. This is in part because the academy is its own subset of cultures, and, like with any culture, if we want to communicate with it we need to do so in a way that is intelligible to the audience. But the nonlinear re-presentation also aims at verisimilitude with regard to the field encounter. It is not disjuncture for disjuncture's sake or for stylistic panache. Anthropologist C. Nadia Seremetakis makes this point in describing her approach of "montage," which features rupture between the various parts of her essay. "The use of montage here is not simply an aesthetic or arbitrary voice. Sensory and experiential fragmentation is the form in which this sensory history has been stored and dictates the form of its reconstruction."[108] Done well, the rubbing together of more concrete and more abstract modes of discourse also serves as a source of illumination, with each modal moment sparking insight into the other. The back-and-forth—and so nonlinear—movement can, at moments, unsettle or disorient the reader, but the purpose is not disorientation per se. Rather it is, in my case, to unmoor the reader just enough from her present surroundings so that she can more readily enter into the scene and, ultimately, re-present it herself.

All of the material presented in this and the previous chapter is something that could have been written, for the most part, by a more secularly oriented anthropologist, even though my overarching interests, as we will see, are different. This includes the case I made that the Little Sisters' understanding of mimesis fits with that put forward in the gospels. All I did was compare, with the help of the work of turn of the twentieth-century anthropologist James George Frazer and contemporary biblical scholars, the Little Sisters' understanding of mimesis with their primary source texts. Anthropologists regularly do this kind of analysis, whether with Christian or other communities.

But anthropological theology's aims go further. Anthropology traditionally halts with, or does not go much farther than, thick description. That is its task—to render more or less felicitously the lives of others. In fact, as we will see in the next section of the book, there are strong disciplinary pressures against moving beyond thick description, as is evident in the pejorative connotation of the phrase "going native." Still, felicitous rendering of an other's life is a profound and difficult calling.

To the anthropological theologian, however, all the world is an offering from the God who created and redeemed it. All the world is the sacrament of Christ's body and blood. Every face is the face of Christ. Or as Dorothy Day put it, "Those who cannot see the face of Christ in the poor are atheists indeed." Given that every face is the face of Christ, every thick description of that face, that person, that community, is also a calling to the describer: "You too?" The anthropological theologian is, by discipline, haunted by her work. Negri. Sister Esther. The guy at the sugarcane stand. They all whisper Jesus's *psst*.

It is time, then, to pivot from attention to what I have been calling "discernment," that is to say, to the question of what to make of the other's—and the Other's—call to us. The next three chapters take up this moment in the doing of anthropological theology. In Chapter 4, I will ask if mimesis in general and gospel mimesis in particular can constitute an academic method while maintaining the kind of critical distance that is the hallmark of good scholarship. Chapter 5 will provide more specific accounts of the various gaps and obstacles I encountered between the Acholi and myself, gaps that make any kind of imitation seem unlikely. In Chapter 6, I describe what I call "crossings" between Acholi others and me, a jumping of the gaps, however unlikely. Such is the surprise of mimesis.

Notes

1. Interview with Sr. Esther Arach, 12–14, and 38–9.

2. As of 2012, the Little Sisters of Mary Immaculate of Gulu were active in thirteen nursery schools, thirty-three primary schools, and twelve secondary schools. Little Sisters of Mary Immaculate of Gulu, *Immaculate Rays: Celebration of 100 Years of Catholic Faith in Arua Diocese* (Gulu Archdiocese, 2012), p. 29.

3. Interview with Sr. Renalta. This is a pseudonym. In interview passages that refer to abuses by Yoweri Museveni's forces, I use pseudonyms because he is still in power and therefore a threat.

4. Interview with Sr. Perpetua (pseudonym), 8–9. And yet another:

   From the beginning of the war, what I saw there, many people left their home. They came, and stayed, for at first they stayed in the parish. . . . So what the parish did was, eh, in the morning they prepare porridge for the children. The women, they go to look for their food now, because you could not keep children together with women and men [in the field], you could not. So we were now caring for the children, giving them porridge and also lunch. Then, afterward, the women, they come in the evening. Then, eh, in the morning they go back. In the evening they take refuge in the parish. That was the beginning (Interview with Sr. Marie [pseudonym], 24).

5. Interview with Sr. Delfina Aywelo, 34.

6. Interview with Sr. Delfina Aywelo, 7.

7. Ibid.

8. For a listing of the ordinations from 1938 to 2006, see Uma-Owiny Paul Vincent, *Background and Profile of Gulu Archdiocese* (Gulu, Uganda: Catholic Press, 2010), pp. 36–7. Bishop Negri did found an indigenous order of brothers, the Marian Brothers, but they do not have the numbers or impact of the Little Sisters.

9. The catechists most important for Acholi Catholicism are Daudi Okello and Jildo Irwa, who were killed by other Acholi. Precisely why they were killed—for their Christianity or as part of resistance against colonialism or both—is an important question. For one account, see Fr. Mario Marchetti, MCCJ, *Too Long in the Dark: The Story of the Two Martyrs of Paimol and Their Relevance to Uganda Today* (Gulu: Archdiocese of Gulu, 1999).

10. According to Sr. Miriam Kozoa, as of early 2014 there are about 380 Little Sisters living in 60 communities, most, but not all, living in northern Uganda. Interview with Sr. Miriam.

11. See, for instance, China Scherz, *Having People, Having Heart: Charity, Sustainable Development and Problems of Dependence in Central Uganda* (Chicago: University of Chicago Press, 2014); Frederick Klaits, *Death in a Church of Life: Moral Passion during Botswana's Time of AIDS* (Berkeley, Los Angeles, and London: University of California Press, 2010); Fenella Canell, *Power and Intimacy in the Christian Philippines* (Cambridge: Cambridge University Press, 1999); Rebecca J. Lester, *Jesus in Our Wombs: Embodying Modernity in a Mexican Convent* (Berkeley, Los Angeles, and London: University of California Press, 2005); Joel Robbins, *Becoming Sinners: Christianity and Moral Torment in a Papua New Guinea Society* (Berkeley, Los Angeles, and London: University of California Press, 2004); Matthew Engelke, *A Problem of Presence: Beyond Scripture in an African Church* (Berkeley, Los Angeles, and London: University of California Press, 2007); and Matthew Akim Tomlinson, *In God's Image: The Metaculture of Fijian Christianity* (Berkeley, Los Angeles, and London: University of California Press, 2009).

12. It might be tempting to suggest that the key in the turn from cooperation with evil to radical witness was a shift from men (the Combonis) to women (the Little Sisters), but the instances of witness on the part of men, priest and lay, Comboni and Acholi, serve as counterfactuals. I focus on the Little Sisters simply because they are the most readily limned Comboni-to-indigenous development.

13. For an example of the pressures that the Museveni regime placed on Comboni missionaries who pressed for peaceful resolution of the LRA conflict, see Carlos Rodriguez Soto, *Tall Grass: Stories of Suffering and Peace in Northern Uganda* (Kampala: Fountain Publishers, 2009). Also, four Comboni missionaries were killed under the Idi Amin regime. See, Comboni Missionaries, *Supreme Witness: Brief Profiles of Comboni Missionaries Murdered in the Missions* (Leeds: Comboni Missionaries, n.d.), pp. 25–32; at https://www.combonimissionaries.org/index.php/missioneducation/comboni-missionary-martyrs.html.

14. One priest told me of a specific meeting that Museveni held with him and three other priests, during which the president questioned why they remained in northern Uganda during the war and offered them alternatives.

15. I interviewed twenty of the sisters, gathering about thirty hours of material.

16. The Little Sisters of Mary Immaculate of Gulu, *Chapter Documents, 1989* (Gulu: Archdiocese of Gulu, 1989), pp. 26–33. I thank the sisters for allowing me access to these documents.

17. Negri died in 1949, making the jubilee actually fifty-one years since his death, but the event brought together two other events in conjunction—the third millennium and the fiftieth year of the Congregation's founding (which would have been celebrated in 1992 except for the war. The year 2000 marked a lull in the war long enough for the sisters to finally celebrate.

18. Interview with Sr. Esther, 34–5.

19. I refer to Bishop Negri by his last name and Mother Angioletta by her first because this is the custom among the Little Sisters.

20. Interview with Sr. Miriam Kozoa, 1.

21. Fr. Lorenzo Gaiga, *Short Life of Bishop Angelo Negri*, trans. Comboni Missionaries (Gulu: Catholic Press, 1994); Sister Delfina Aywelo p'Layeeting Alertotek, *Reverend Mother Angioletta Dognini: The Great Star for African Women* (Kisubi, Uganda: Marianum Press, 1995). The life of Negri runs 31 pages, while that of Angioletta goes for 59.

22. Interview with Sr. Beatrice Lalam, 1, 9, and 17.

23. Interview with Sr. Delfina Aywelo, 11; Sr. Esther, 10–11; Sr. Josephine Oyella, 20; Sr. Susan Clare, 10.

24. Interview with Sr. Delfina, 12.

25. Interview with Sr. Delfina, 11.

26. Interview with Sr. Delfina, 13.

27. Interview with Sr. Josephine, 21.

28. Interview with Sr. Delfina, 12.

29. Interview with Sr. Mary Clementina Atim, 16–17.

30. *Pianeta* is Italian for chasuble.

31. Interview with Sr. Veronica Achola, 12–13.

32. Interview with Sr. Veronica Achola, 14.

33. Interview with Sr. Delfina, 5–6.

34. Interview with Sr. Esther, 3–4.

35. Interview with Sr. Miriam, 3–4.

36. Donna Tartt, *The Goldfinch* (Back Bay Books/ Little, Brown and Company, 2013), pp. 758, 766, and 770.

37. Interview with Sr. Beatrice, 5.

38. Interview with Sr. Josephine, 63–4.

39. Interview with Sr. Mary Clementina, 15.

40. Interview with Sr. Olga Alur.

41. Little Sisters of Mary Immaculate of Gulu, *Chapter Documents, 2001*, 23; and *The 8th General Chapter Document, 2013* (Gulu: Little Sisters of Mary Immaculate of Gulu, 2013), pp. 5–6.

42. Gaiga, *Short Life of Bishop Angelo Negri*, p. 13.

43. The Little Sisters of Mary Immaculate of Gulu, *Chapter Documents, 1985* (Gulu: Little Sisters of Mary Immaculate of Gulu, 1985), pp. 35–7 and 31.

44. James George Frazer, *The Golden Bough* (Oxford: Oxford University Press, 1998), pp. 26, 37, and 27.

45. For an example of the psychological literature, see Paul Rozin and Carol Nemeroff, "Sympathetic Magical Thinking: The Contagion and Similarity 'Heuristics,'" in *Heuristics and Biases: The Psychology of Intuitive Judgment*, ed. Thomas Gilovich, Dale Griffin, and Daniel Kahneman (Cambridge: Cambridge University Press, 2002), pp. 201–16.

46. Sr. Margaret Aceng, "The Little Sisters of Mary Immaculate and Environment," in Little Sisters of Mary Immaculate of Gulu, *Golden Jubilee Celebrations*, p. 47.

47. Sverker Finnström quotes one Acholi commenting on the flight of elite intelligentsia in the face of armed conflict: "They Lit the Candle, but Then Left for London. Now We are Left Here, and the Bush is on Fire." Finnström, *Living with Bad Surroundings: War, History, and Everyday Moments in Northern Uganda* (Durham and London: Duke University Press, 2008), p. 219.

48. Interview with Sr. Dosoline Lakworo, 2.

49. Interview with Sr. Mary Clementina, 3–4.

50. "In their way of life, the sisters imitate our Lord; His spirit of love without segregation. His zeal of service. And from Our Lady, the sisters imitate her simplicity, humility, spirit

of prayers, etc. . . . From the Founder, the sisters imitate his humility, simplicity, love for all, spirit of prayers and perseverance in the difficult situation, and this is seen in the way the sisters remain strong in their apostolate, especially in war zones." Sister Pauline Silver Acayo, "The Call of the Little Sisters of Mary Immaculate Institute," in Little Sisters of Mary Immaculate of Gulu, *Golden Jubilee Celebrations*, p. 58.

51. Interview with Sr. Martha Acan, 2.

52. Interview with Sr. Josephine, 22.

53. Interview with Sr. Miriam, 2.

54. Interview with Sr. Martha, 2.

55. Interview with Sr. Beatrice, 5–6.

56. Interview with Sr. Delfina, 43 and 18.

57. Sr. Delfina Aywelo, "Spirituality for a Vocation Animator," in Little Sisters of Mary Immaculate of Gulu, *The Golden Jubilee Celebrations: Light in Darkness* (Gulu, 2000), pp. 65–6.

58. Sr. Delfina Aywelo, "Spirituality for a Vocation Animator," in Little Sisters of Mary Immaculate of Gulu, *The Golden Jubilee Celebrations: Light in Darkness* (Gulu, 2000), p. 65.

59. Sr. Delfina Aywelo, "Spirituality for a Vocation Animator," in Little Sisters of Mary Immaculate of Gulu, *The Golden Jubilee Celebrations: Light in Darkness* (Gulu, 2000) pp. 67–9. But even or especially as living exemplar, the vocation animator is to direct others' attention to something or someone else, particularly because of the varied ways in which the Spirit works. "The vocation animator has to be an attentive listener to the spirit, for the spirit has many ways and channels through which he can attain his goals. . . . Instead of this listening being a question of exercising their intellectual capacity in rules that are meant to govern a vocation animator, it is a question of listening to the spirit who is initiating a vocation in the candidates." Ultimately, each vocation animator's own finitude is to serve as a reminder of the primacy of the Spirit. Any given animator "will one day yield her role to others and disappear." The "most important part and the most important moment" in the biblical story is not any action of Ezekiel's, but the action of the Spirit to breathe life into the bones. Cf. 67, and 70–2.

In keeping with the mimetic means of animating others in the Spirit, Sr. Delfina recommends playacting in order to make present the different ways in which the Spirit manifests itself in people. "Stories of God's call can be staged by actors and actresses who can make vivid, almost tangible, what was written thousands of years ago." The playacting is a means for the Gospel to traverse time and space to say *psst* to those in the audience.

60. The given justification for imperial violence is evident in Frazer's own words. In discussing what he considers "the intelligent and thoughtful part of the community," he points out that "we shall find underlying them all a solid stratum of intellectual agreement among the dull, the weak, the ignorant, and the superstitious, who constitute, unfortunately, the vast majority of mankind. . . . It is beneath our feet—and not very far beneath them, and it crops up on the surface . . . wherever the advent of higher civilization has not crushed it under ground." Frazer, *The Golden Bough*, p. 53.

61. The Little Sisters, due to the post–Vatican II call to the indigenization of Catholicism, are much more open to some of the traditional practices than the initial missionaries; however, they are uniformly quite critical of the *ajwagi*, in part because the *ajwaka* remains their primary spiritual competitor, and in part because they are not entirely wrong in their frequent claim that many of the current *ajwagi* are in it just for the money.

62. Interview with Sr. Susan Clare, 7.

63. Interview with Sr. Susan Clare, 10.

64. What the sisters cannot tend to on their own—they do not have the funds—is repair their material infrastructure, the buildings. This will require outside help.

65. Interview with Sr. Esther, 14–15.

66. Interview with Sr. Grace, 27.

67. Interview with Sr. Vincentina Achora.

68. Little Sisters of Mary Immaculate of Gulu, *Chapter Documents, 1989*, p. 29.

69. Ibid., pp. 26 and 32. Also, in 2001, the sisters have to revisit the issue of ethnic rivalry, this time stating specifically that the tension was between "some Alur and some Acholi members" of the congregation. The war exacerbated these tensions. Cf. Little Sisters of Mary Immaculate of Gulu, *Chapter Documents, 2001*, 24.

    One Sister tells of a particularly troubling instance. LRA rebels had seized the compound of the novitiate and the novices first hid in the chapel. The rebels called for them to come out and carry the looted things into the bush. "They said, 'Come on! Some of you come here. Carry the things.' Nobody wants to come out because people feared. And some people think that we who come from this side [of the Nile: Acholiland] should be the ones who go out [because the LRA war is our war]. You know in the novitiate, we are many different tribes and cultures." Sr. Perpetua (pseudonym), 10.

70. Interview with Sr. Martha, 9–10; see also interview with Sr. Delfina 38: "So they, especially those from across the Nile, those from West Nile [and] Nairobi. They decided to pack and go away, that they are going to be killed [if they stay]."

71. Interview with Sr. Beatrice, 2.

72. Interview with Sr. Mary Clementina, 24–5.

73. Interview with Sr. Martha Acan, 10; also interview with Beatrice, 15: "Some other Sisters are really bitter, and some of them feel that they should keep their salaries to themselves, they should help their people."

74. Little Sisters of Mary Immaculate of Gulu, *Chapter Documents, 2007*, p. 11.

75. Ibid., p. 14.

76. Ibid., p. 13; and *Chapter Documents, 2007*, p. 17.

77. Little Sisters of Mary Immaculate of Gulu, *Chapter Documents, 2001*, p. 22.

78. Ibid., pp. 15 and 21.

79. Ibid., pp. 11 and 16.

80. Ibid., pp. 1–9.

81. Interview with Sr. Susan Clare, 4–6.

82. Interview with Sr. Helen Aya, 40–4.

83. Sr. Delfina, "Spirituality for a Vocation Animator," p. 66.

84. Interview with Sr. Josephine.

85. Ernst Kasemann, a leader in the post-Bultmannian "second quest" for the historical Jesus, writes, "To cleave firmly to history is one way of giving expression to the *extra nos* of salvation." Ernst Kasemann, "The Problem of the Historical Jesus" (1954), in Kasemann, *Essays on New Testament Themes* (London, SCM, 1964), p. 33. Taking their cue from Kasemann and similar-minded biblical scholars, theologians from Hans Kung and Edward Schillebeeckx to Jon Sobrino and Elizabeth Johnson have recognized the importance of inquiry into the historical Jesus for theology. James Dunn combines biblical scholarship with theological understanding in his part of the more recent "third quest" for the historical Jesus to keep the concern fresh. Without "the particularities of history," the "humanity of Christ is

likely to be lost again to view within Christianity and swallowed up in an essentially docetic affirmation of his deity." Such a temptation, he says, "still has to be resolutely resisted." See Hans Kung, *On Being a Christian*, trans. E. Quinn (Garden City, NY: Doubleday & Co., 1976; Edward Schillebeeckx, *Jesus: An Experiment in Christology*, trans. H. Hoskins (New York: Seabury Press, 1979), and *Christ: The Experience of Jesus as Lord*, trans. J. Bowden (New York: Seabury, 1980); Jon Sobrino, *Christology at the Crossroads*, trans. J. Drury (Maryknoll, NY: Orbis Books, 1978), and *Jesus the Liberator: A Historical-Theological Reading of Jesus of Nazareth*, trans. Paul Burns and Francis McDonagh (Maryknoll, NY: Orbis Books, 1993); Elizabeth A. Johnson, C.S.J., "The Theological Relevance of the Historical Jesus: A Debate and a Thesis," *The Thomist* 48 (1984), pp. 1–43; Dunn, *Jesus Remembered*, p. 102.

To make the case that the historical Jesus is a necessary source for Christian theology is not to say that it is the only source, as if we can build up all that we can know about Christian faith from what historical criticism and social scientific analysis can reconstruct about who Jesus was. Theologians have described the historical Jesus variously as "starting point" (Kung), "validating ground" (Schillebeeckx), "critical standard" (Sobrino), and "norm" (Walter Kasper). Johnson writes that knowledge of the historical Jesus both "materially informs faith" and serves a "critical function" of helping to validate and rule out various theological claims. Taken together, Johnson argues, these tasks also serve as a hedge against creeping docetism. See Kung, *On Being a Christian*, pp. 540–53; Schillebeeckx, *Jesus*, pp. 41–76; Sobrino, *Christology at the Crossroads*, pp. 1–16; Walter Kasper, *Jesus the Christ*, trans. V. Green (New York: Paulist Press, 1976), p. 35. I am indebted to Johnson for pointing out these identifications. See Johnson, "The Theological Relevance of the Historical Jesus," 10. On Johnson's own view, see pp. 32–3. In her emphasis on the importance of the role of memory, Johnson sounds strikingly like Dunn. In her words, "The reconstructed image of the historical Jesus not only functions today as the equivalent of the memory impression of Jesus in the early Church, but actually is the equivalent of it, i.e. is the means by which significant segments of the present generation of believers remember Jesus who is confessed as the Christ. . . .The Church is never without a memory image of Jesus; this is an essential element passed on in the living tradition. . . . . The Church's memory image is theologically necessary for Christology and, as the quest (for the historical Jesus) has concretely affected the way Jesus is remembered in the Church, the quest and its results have assumed theological pertinence not only for the corrections of the distortions of the tradition (although certainly for that), but also for the constitution of the tradition insofar as it includes remembering." Johnson, "The Theological Relevance of the Historical Jesus," 25 and 28–9.

86. See, for instance, Gerd Theissen and Annette Merz, *The Historical Jesus: A Comprehensive Guide* (Minneapolis: Fortress Press, 1998), pp. 216–17; John Meier, *A Marginal Jew: Rethinking the Historical Jesus, Vol. III: Companions and Competitors* (New Haven and London: Yale University Press, 2001), pp. 154–7. Meier notes (184–5, n. 88) that there is some intense debate over the historicity of the account, with Bultmann being the most skeptical. But then, Bultmann is skeptical of the historicity of most everything in the Gospels.

87. James D. G. Dunn, *Jesus and the Spirit: A Study of the Religious and Charismatic Experience of Jesus and the First Christians as Reflected in the New Testament* (Grand Rapids, MI: William B. Eerdmans Publishing Company, 1997), p. 13. Cf. also p. 363, n. 8. *Mimeomai* does appear in 2 Thess. 3:7 and 9, Heb. 13:7, and 3 Jn 1:11; *mimetes* is in 1 Cor. 4:16 and 11:1, Eph. 5:1, 1 Thess. 1:6 and 2:14, and Heb. 6:12.

88. Michael Taussig, *Mimesis and Alterity: A Particular History of the Senses* (New York and London: Routledge, 1993), p. 48.

I take Morton Smith's argument that Jesus was simply a magician to go well beyond what the evidence supports, but find that Bernd Kollmann's case that magic-like acts were fundamental both in Jesus's ministry and the growth of subsequent Christianity to be convincing. See Morton Smith, *Jesus the Magician* (New York: Harper and Row, 1978); Bernd Kollman, *Jesus und die Christen als Wunderstäter: Studien zu Magie, Medizin und Schamanismus in Antike und Christentu* (Gottingen: Vandenhoeck & Ruprecht, 1996). Frazer is right in indicating that the relationship between religion and magic depends in large part on what constitutes one's understanding of religion. Frazer, *The Golden Bough*, 46. That much said, his claims regarding the evolutionary development from magic to religion, with their attendant description of adherents of magical views as "savage," "ignorant" and "dull-witted," to reflect untenable (and abhorrent) Victorian arrogance.

89. Cf. also, Mt. 21:23-27; Lk. 20:1-8.

90. James Dunn writes, "In his reply, Jesus shows that he took the point by setting in sharp antithesis authority 'from heaven' and authority 'from men.' The implication is clear: Jesus was conscious of a direct and unmediated authority—a transcendent authority which set him above party and (at times) even the law." Dunn, *Jesus and the Spirit*, p. 77.

91. To Elijah and John the Baptist, we can possibly add David as a representative figure in Jesus's role enactments, as evidenced, for instance, in the entry into Jerusalem, the Davidic city (Mk 11:1-10; Mt. 21:1-9). Jesus here may have been enacting the prophecy from Zechariah: "Rejoice greatly, O daughter Zion! / Shout aloud, O daughter Jerusalem! / Lo, your king comes to you; / triumphant and victorious is he, / humble and riding on a donkey" (9:9). Moreover, all three synoptic Gospels have the blind Bartimaeus—which in Mark and Matthew immediately precedes the entry—call Jesus, "Son of David" (Mk 10:47-48; Mt. 20:30-31; Lk. 18:38-39). Luke's gospel inserts only the story of Zacchaeus (19:1-10) and the parable of the pounds (19:11-27) between the healing of Bartimaeus and the entry into Jerusalem.

Earlier in Luke's gospel, Jesus himself asks the disciples soon after their return from mission, "Who do the crowds say that I am?" and they reply like Herod does, that is, with reference to John the Baptist, Elijah, or "one of the ancient prophets." Jesus asks the follow-up, "But who do you say that I am?" and Peter answers, "The Messiah of God" (Lk. 9:18-20; cf. also Mt. 16:13-16; Mk 8:27-29). Christians commentators sometimes take Peter's answer and Jesus's acceptance of it to highlight Jesus's early awareness of his utter uniqueness and freedom from type, but the title—*ho christos tou theou* in the Greek—translates, "God's anointed one," a title that, in the words of one commentator, "typically named a royal Davidic leader who would reconstitute the former political glory of Israel." (Marion Lloyd Swords, comments on Lk. 9:18-20, *The New Oxford Annotated Bible (NRSV)* (Oxford and New York: Oxford University Press, 2001), p. 114 (New Testament). Richard Rohrbaugh even makes the intriguing case that Jesus's questions and Peter's confession—usually read as a later interpolation because (from a modern individualist perspective) Jesus appears to already know who he is apart from consulting others—is actually a pre-Easter instance of Jesus inquiring about his identity by probing outgroup ("Who do the crowds say that I am") and ingroup ("Who do you say that I am?") sensibilities. Richard L. Rohrbaugh, "Ethnocentrism and Historical Questions about Jesus," in *The Social Setting of Jesus and the Gospels*, ed. Wolfgang Stegemann, Bruce J. Malina, and Gerd Theissen (Minneapolis: Fortress Press, 2002), p. 38. Add to the above Jesus's repeated—too often to cite—use of the term "kingdom" to depict the reality he is at once announcing and enacting, and the case for Davidic reference becomes plausible. A good, succinct account of the issues in play in the debate over the historicity of the Davidic references is found in John P. Meier, "From Elijah-like Prophet to Royal Davidic Messiah," in *Jesus: A Colloquium in the Holy Land*, ed. Doris Donnelly (New York and London: Continuum, 2001), pp. 45–83. Regardless of one's judgment regarding Davidic reference, it is clear from the other cases of reference that in first-century Palestine, individual identity is bound up with and largely dependent upon particular social identities.

92. Cf. also Mk 5:30 and Mt. 9:20-22.

93. Taussig, *Mimesis and Alterity*, pp. 55 and 58.

94. Ibid., p. 49. Keeping in mind that for Taussig, as for Hubert and Mauss, what we have is not an exact replica, but "a copy that is not a copy but a 'poorly executed ideogram,'" Taussig writes elsewhere that "the mimetic faculty carries out its honest labour suturing nature to artifice and bringing sensuousness to sense by means of what was once called sympathetic magic, granting the copy the character and power of the original, the representation the power of the represented" (pp. xviii and 17).

95. For a classic statement of the discipleship versus imitation thesis, see Hans von Campenhausen, *Die Idee des Martyriums in der alten Kirche*, second edition (Göttinggen: Vandenhoeck & Ruprecht, 1964), pp. 56–78. For a critique of the Campenhausen interpretation, see Candida Moss, *The Other Christs: Imitating Jesus in Ancient Christian Ideologies of Martyrdom* (Oxford: Oxford University Press, 2010), pp. 20–3.

96. On the two-tiered ethic, see Theissen and Merz, *The Historical Jesus*, pp. 378 and 557. The faith response of persons who do not also follow Jesus is not insignificant. In fact, it is necessary for Jesus's power to work, as is evidenced in his failure in Nazareth (Mk 6:1-6; Mt. 13:54-58). This is one key difference between Jesus's healing mission and magic in the usual anthropological sense: his mission requires a response of faith for it to be effective, while magic, as typically understood from Frazer onward, does not.

97. On the historicity of the rich young man exchange, see Theissen and Merz, *The Historical Jesus*, p. 192.

98. Cf. also Mt. 19:21; Lk. 18:22.

99. There are exceptions, what I would call gospel savants. The one reported incident of this in the Gospels is in Mk 9:38-41 and Lk. 9:49-50. The disciples complain to Jesus that there is someone casting out demons "in your name" a person who "does not follow with us." In other words, they are saying that this man must be a fraud because he does not have the extended contact with Jesus that facilitates the transfer of power and authority. Jesus replies that if the man is truly doing these acts in his name, then he is "not against us," but rather is "for us." We end up, it seems, with five categories of persons in terms of their responses to Jesus's mission: rejection/acceptance/invitation to more/persistence-then-invitation-to-more/savants.

100. Dunn, *Jesus and the Spirit*, pp. 81–2.

101. Ibid., pp. 139–42.

102. Cf. Acts 1:1-9, 21-22; 2:32; 3:15; 4:20; 5:32; 10:39-41; 13:31, 14:17; and 22:15.
    Though Acts is not a history in the modern sense, and its author certainly has specific apologetic interests, it is a mistake to dismiss its accounts entirely as mere fabrications (and to assume that modern historians are without their own interests). Both the broad outline of Acts and many of its details are relatively trustworthy, sufficiently so to point up the evidence that the original twelve apostles (and those who provide accounts of them) understand their authority to imitate Jesus as grounded in their witness of him. For a strong defense of the relative historical trustworthiness of Acts, see James, D. G. Dunn, *Beginning from Jerusalem: Christianity in the Making, Volume 2* (Grand Rapids, MI and Cambridge, UK: William B. Eerdmans Publishing Company, 2009), pp. 68–87.

103. Cf. Acts 3:7; 8:16-19; 9:12-19; and 28:8-9.

104. Cf. Acts 2:21; 2:38; 3:6; 3:16, 4:7-12, 17-18, 30; 5:41; 8:12; 9:34; 10: 43, 48; and 19:14-16.

105. Mt. 10:16-39/Mk 8:31-38/Lk. 9:23-27, 10:3, 12:2-12,14:26-27; 17:22-37; cf. also Mt. 24:9-14/Mk 13:9-13/Lk. 21:12-19; Mt. 5:11-12/Lk. 6:22-23; Mt. 6:13a/Lk. 11:4b.

106. Cf. Acts 4:1-22; 5:17-42; 6:8-8:1; 12:1ff; 16:16-40; 20:27ff; 21:27-26:32.

107. Clifford Geertz, *The Interpretation of Cultures* (New York: basic Books, 1973), pp. 3–31.

108. C. Nadia Seremetakis, "The Memory of the Senses, Part II: Still Acts," in *The Senses Still: Perception and Memory as Material Culture in Modernity*, ed. C. Nadia Seremetakis (Boulder, CO: Westview Press, 1994), p. 23.

PART II
DISCERNMENT

CHAPTER 4
MIMETIC SCHOLARSHIP: ANTHROPOLOGICAL THEOLOGY AS APPRENTICESHIP TO THE OTHER

The man lies in the dirt on his side outside what appears to be his bamboo and mud home. He is covered everywhere with the red-brown dust, even his teeth and—I am not sure why I notice this—inside his ear. His voice is barely audible.

"I am just waiting for my time."

That is enough for Sister Cecilia. She orders me to lift him from under his arms while she takes his legs. We carry him inside. It takes a moment for our eyes to adjust to the darkness. The hardened dirt floor is perhaps eight feet in diameter. Two old and tearing UN food bags stuffed with his belongings hang from the bamboo roof beams. The roof covering is flame-retardant blue plastic, distributed by the United Nations. The plastic is not as breathable as the traditional thatch, however, and makes the inside of the home hotter and more stifling. My nostrils burn and again I cannot see. The man has not been able to make it to the shitting trench.

He tells us his name is Santo and that he is paralyzed from a fall he had some years ago while doing construction. His wife is dead and his son is drunk too much of the time to take care of him. He tells us that he does not have "the sickness"—AIDS—but the men tend not to admit to it in any case, so at this point we cannot trust his answer. Incidence is higher than 30 percent in some camps. I notice a bicycle leaning against the wall, and wonder whether this is from before his fall or whether someone else is already using Santo's home as a storage hut, as if it were vacant.

Sister Cecilia orders a woman outside to bring two wash basins, two wash cloths, some soap, and a jerrycan of water. She gives a boy some coins and sends him to the market to get boiled chicken, rice, and *boo*, a bitter spinach-like green. She turns to me.

"Can you do this?"

I nod. I have been joining her on her rounds of visiting those who are too sick to make it to the infirmary—which itself has no drugs except quinine for malaria—but so far we have just been checking in on people. Most have others to do the care. She clarifies so as to double-check.

"We are going to bathe him."

"Yes."

A girl arrives with the washtubs, soap, and washcloths. Another brings the water. Cecilia pulls two sets of latex gloves from the pocket of her habit and hands one to me. She has known that she would be doing this.

A finger of one of my gloves rips as I am putting it on. Cecilia insists that I take one of hers. I refuse. She insists again.

"I can work with just one. I do not want you to get sick," she says.

We strike a compromise. I take her glove, and she takes my ripped one—which will protect her better than none at all—and puts it on her left hand.

Cecilia carefully pours water from the yellow plastic jerrycan into each of the wash basins. It is twenty-liters-of-pump-water heavy, and she sweats from under the band of her habit headpiece. She is powerfully built, and her body does not bend with the ease that seems to come preternaturally to so many of the Ugandan women.

For the next hour and a half, I follow the pattern of her actions; she with one basin to wash, me with the other to rinse. Head and neck first, including inside his ears. Then chest, shoulders, and arms. He looks like an emaciated Bill Russell. His skin now glistens like polished black onyx.

"You can tell by how his skin shines now that he does not have the sickness," Cecilia observes. "He is only starving."

Santo's paralysis keeps him from even registering to receive UN food, let alone pick it up, and he has no one to do it for him.

We wash his legs, genitals, buttocks—yes, deep into the crack; if there are parasites nesting there, we want them out. We change the water, then wash his feet. His clothes are putrid and infested with lice; we cannot redress him in these. I run to the parish and get a set of mine. When I return, the food is just arriving. We dress him, stay with him while he eats, and tell him that we will return to bathe and feed him again.

We are, I later realize, reenacting in a particular way the Good Samaritan story, with me imitating Cecilia as she imitates the Samaritan. The story fits, too, in that Cecilia is Langi—that is, a member of an ethnic group with a rivalry with the Acholi that extends back to before the arrival of the British. She is, like the Samaritan, an outsider.

I follow Cecilia outside, where she asks a woman to coat the interior of Santo's home with a dirt and cow-dung mixture. It smells for half a day, but gets rid of the lice.

"How much will you pay me?" the woman responds.

I think of Father Olweny's comments about what he calls "the NGO effect" on residents of the camp. "The NGOs, they do not know the people, so when they ask them to do something—even just an interview—they pay them. Now I cannot even call a parish meeting without people expecting to be paid."

Sister Cecilia asks another woman if she will watch over Santo and perhaps share some food with him. She declines, but for a different reason. Santo may be worse off, but he is not the only one who is hungry.

"We do not have enough. We eat only once a day. If we try to feed him, we will starve too."

During the rest of my stay at Pabbo, Cecilia and I return several times to bathe and feed Santo, leaving him with enough food until we can come again. When I leave Pabbo, I give Cecilia enough money for another month of her visits.

"God will intercede," she replies. "You will see. He will bring an end to this war, this suffering. He is patient, but his patience is coming to an end. God will intercede."

In this chapter, I make the case that academic inquiry can, in a way similar to that of the Little Sisters, take the form of gospel mimesis, and that therefore their way of life remains one for us, *as academics*, to consider. The first part of the chapter shows how it is important to understand mimesis in its early oral-gestural context in order to demonstrate how, contrary to text-based understandings, mimesis does not reduce to verbatim copying of fixed models, and thereby does not forfeit the critical distance necessary for academic inquiry. I then turn to a particular kind of anthropology as analogous to ethnography understood as gospel mimesis. It might seem odd that I have chosen anthropology as my main other-than-theological disciplinary partner at this point. After all, at the center of the practice of participant observation, at least in its classic objectivist version, is the counter-mimetic effort to imitate the other while steadfastly refusing to become *like* the other, a practice that from a broadly historical and cross-cultural perspective is strange and perhaps unique to the modern West. More recent anthropology, however, provides an opening for an alternative understanding of ethnography, one where the aim is to become like the other. Paul Stoller, Loïc Wacquant, and Anand Pandian, for instance, all describe ethnography as a form of apprenticeship, and in the second part of this chapter, I explore Stoller's account of his tutelage under Songhay sorcerers in Niger.[1]

In the last part of this chapter, I limn the outlines of what makes gospel mimesis different from even apprenticeship-oriented anthropological approaches: with anthropological theology, we seek not only to become like the other person in front of us, but through that process to become more like Jesus Christ. And cultures that share key characteristics with the culture of first-century Palestine can, in addition to being ends in themselves, serve as interpretive cultural bridges to what it is like and what is required to follow Jesus. Modern and postmodern Western culture carries certain biases that frequently lead to misinterpretation and misappropriation of the Gospel. Life among people of cultures that more resemble that of the ancient Near East can serve as a corrective to such mistakes. I provide the example of the relationship between identity and property in particular to display the point: Western individualism contributes to the neglect and even rejection of the practice of communal property lived out by the first post-Resurrection followers of Jesus; the cultures of northern Uganda are not yet fully overrun by Western biases and so include a more communal sense of identity and, relatedly, the practice of shared property. Examination of their practices discloses how Western Christian resistance to communal property involves a misappropriation of scripture.

Mimetic scholarship and critical distance

It might be objected that mimesis is fine as a personal spiritual practice, but does not qualify as a constitutive part of any *scholarly* method. Imitation of this kind, it might be argued, is the antithesis of the critical distance so important for academic inquiry, and, as such, ought to be avoided. Mimesis does place the body back into method in a way that is absent or obscured by approaches that move only from text to writing. It also calls upon the affect and all of the senses at the point of investigation and seeks in writing to, among other things, re-present the field encounter in a way that evokes the senses of the reader. It would be a mistake, however—one common in more text-centered cultures and subcultures—to not consider this a form of critical knowledge. Both ancient and contemporary sources indicate otherwise.

For instance, as James Dunn argues, oral theologizing is at the root of the gospels. Jewish literacy (in the sense of the ability to read and write) in Palestine at the time of Jesus ran probably between 3 and 10 percent of the population.[2] In its stead, oral performance, argues Dunn, was a communal event of remembering and so knowing that took place in settings of various degrees of formality from prayer[3] to mealtime, to the evening fire.[4] The regularity of the gatherings allowed for repetition of the process, though rarely is the emphasis on rote memorization. What the disciples and early evangelizers were trying to do was perform what Dunn refers to as the "characteristic" Jesus.[5] Members of the audience, particularly elders and other recognized teachers who themselves may be performers on other occasions, would correct the performer if his account was off-character.[6] Over time and retellings, the accounts developed a relatively stable core with controlled variability in the details.[7] Dunn emphasizes, therefore, that the Jesus we have is the Jesus as "remembered" by his listeners, and that that remembering was always already an act of theologizing. The literary paradigm of interpretation, with its emphasis on layers of textual accretion, misses the way in which such oral performance is not a "copy," however redacted, of a previously written text.[8]

Samuel Byrskog is also dissatisfied with modern literary paradigms of biblical interpretation, such that he draws rather from the worldviews and practices of ancient historians from Herodotus to Tacitus to better understand how the gospels work.[9] For such historians, eyewitness to events—what Byrskog calls "autopsy"—is critical for trustworthy knowledge, constituting "a visual means to gather information concerning a certain object" of inquiry. It is not a passive accounting of the external world, but rather an active form of inquiry and interpretation. For the ancients—*contra* modern biases— the observer's involvement in the events does not weigh against the trustworthiness or veracity of the account as long as there is due scrutiny of the observer. In fact, the opposite is the case: observer involvement is "the essential means to a correct understanding of what really had happened."[10] Moreover—and this is where Byrskog (and I with him) goes further than Dunn—when an eyewitness went on to re-present Jesus, his presentation of his account was not only oral, but fully sensual. "Gestures, mimicry, movements, behavior and other paralinguistic means of communication—things that could be seen—interacted with what was communicated by word of mouth. *The deepest continuity with the past was not in memory as such but in mimesis, not in passive remembrance but in imitation*" (emphasis in text).[11]

The original matrix of mimetic re-presentation was oral-gestural. The earliest setting for the word group around *mimeisthai*, according to Hans Koller, was "dance . . . rhythm, musical troops, and storytelling."[12] This is important to bear in mind because of the range of free play that it provides within imitation. Goran Sörbom's careful analysis of the origin and early development of *mimeisthai* in the Greek context shows how mimetic imitation is not a matter of conveying a scene or exemplar with portraiture-like exactitude.[13] Rather, mimesis is a kind of "representational action" that seeks not detailed realism, but the embodied portrayal of the identifying characteristics of another. To imitate in this sense is not to provide a verbatim copy, but instead "to exhibit something vividly and concretely by means of typical or characterizing qualities."[14] Anthropologists from Marcel Mauss to Michael Taussig researching later predominantly oral-gestural cultures insist that "There is nothing resembling a portrait" in imitation (Mauss); rather, what is functioning are "social conventions of classification and representation" responding to and building upon a natural compulsion to imitate (Taussig).[15]

Analyses that focus primarily on textual sources can miss the free play aspect of mimesis. This happens, for instance, in Elizabeth Castelli's *Imitating Paul: A Discourse of Power*. Her analysis of Paul's use of the mimesis word cluster is, in my judgment, spot-on with regard to his utilization of the rhetoric of imitation to construct a set of asymmetrical social relationships in which he is the primary earthly authority over the newly formed Christian communities. I make the case for interpreting Paul in terms of his contestation with other apostles over religious authority in the appendix of this book.[16] However, Castelli takes her analysis further to make claims about mimesis generally. She therefore advances as one of her primary conclusions, "Mimesis is always articulated as a hierarchical relationship whereby the 'copy' is but a derivation of the 'model.'"[17] The critical slippage in Castelli's text that allows her to make such a claim reducing mimesis to exact copying of a fixed model is between the words "similarity" and "sameness" at the beginning of her first chapter:

> The notion of imitation presupposes at least two important and related things: a relationship between at least two elements and, within that relationship, the progressive movement of one of those elements to become similar to or the same as the other. This relationship is asymmetrical, for imitation does not involve both elements moving simultaneously toward similarity, but rather one element being fixed and the other transforming itself or being transformed into an approximation of the first. The favored movement is from difference towards similarity—or ideally and absolutely, toward sameness. Sameness itself becomes a more highly valued quality, and it is a quality which automatically inheres in the model in the mimetic relationship of model-copy.[18]

The term "similarity" then disappears from the remainder of the book. Castelli therefore asserts that mimesis brings with it simultaneously the "erasure of difference" and a "celebration of identity" in a "community of sameness."[19] Such a community is all the more oppressive because, while calling for sameness, it sets up the "model-copy" relationship of authority such that the copy can never achieve sameness with the model. There is "always a nagging difference existing between the eternal model and the mortal copy. The mimetic relationship is motivated by the drive to erase that difference, to create sameness, but there will always be that unbridgeable gap between the model and the copy." Therefore, it "goes virtually without saying that the very practice of imitation dooms one to failure."[20]

If what we have seen in the Little Sisters' accounts of their imitation of Christ is accurate, then outright sameness is not the point. They know that this cannot be achieved. Again, "Now, at this difficult time, I was praying mostly the Divine Mercy. . . . I'm devoted to Divine Mercy because I know that whatever I can do cannot be up to the standard maybe God wants. So, my salvation depends on the mercy of God. I will be saved through the mercy of God, not because of what I am doing." In other words, there is also action from God toward the person, not only from the person toward God. The role of the person, to the extent that she is able, is to act *similar enough* to the exemplar— in this case, God as incarnated in Jesus Christ—so that the Spirit-*psst* might pass to her. According to the Little Sisters, Jesus reaches across the boundaries of time and space *to them*. In fact, their accounts of their childhood callings to vowed life suggest that he makes the primary initial gesture. "Another dream . . . In the midst of the bright light, I saw somebody. Then he took my hand." Most times, the sisters also highlight their active cooperation. "I had dreamt that I was in the chapel, praying. Then the Divine Mercy appeared . . . I went to him and he put a ring on my finger."

Castelli is right that this relationship is asymmetrical; it involves—and there is no point in mincing words here—an act of submission on the part of the imitating or reenacting person. And given that particular mortal exemplars like Bishop Negri and Mother Angioletta are held up for imitation, mimesis has social implications for relationships of power and authority. Those relationships are particularly troubling when the act of submission is not something that is freely given. In light of this, it is significant that a good number of the sisters describe themselves in their youth as free spirits. "I was a rascal sort. I was very playful, very lively."[21] And, "I was a very free child. And I came out of that kind of freedom. A free spirit to the Congregation."[22] In some instances, the sisters' families actively resisted their desire to enter into religious life, such that the women had to exhibit not only a free, but also a strong will at a young age. "Yeah, I told [my parents] I joined, but they didn't want . . . and my brother didn't even want me to go there."[23] Another: "My father was insulted; even my mother and brothers."[24] Two of the sisters I interviewed, though they ultimately received familial support, initially went off to the convent surreptitiously. "So the first time, I sneaked. I came with my bag and I told my mother, 'Mama, I am going to go for school in Kitgum.' I was really going to the convent."[25] Some faced resistance from their spiritual directors within the order itself.

In the novitiate, I think I was misunderstood by my formator, because each and every thing that I do, she remarks [on] it negatively. . . . It is as if God did not call me. So I continued praying, I continued praying. But deep within me, I could hear the voice say, "No, this is my trial, your trial. If you overcome this, you will be a good Sister." Everything I do, she would always detect a mistake. So at last I say, "I'm only forcing my way. I will go back home." But deep within me, there is a voice saying, "No, no, don't make that mistake and go back. You are to be."[26]

I suspect that similar familial and communal tensions and displays of will were present in the early Christian churches as well, particularly given their minority status under the empire. Converting to Christianity at the time was costly, requiring a free and strong will.[27]

It is also worth pointing up once more the fact that the sisters are not uncritical of their mortal exemplars. Again, they are forthright, for instance, about Mother Angioletta's role in exacerbating ethnic tensions within the order: "She did seem to be a factor for division." In this, they recognize that such exemplars need not be, because they cannot be, perfect copies of Jesus Christ in order for them to function as models for the *imitatio Christi*. Here it is also worth mentioning that the outsize character of Paul's own claims to authority—he is "sent from God" (2 Cor. 2:17), and therefore "called to be an apostle, set apart for the gospel of God" (Rom. 1:1)—follow in large part from the fact that his authority is *contested* in the community, as is evidenced in his retort, "Am I not an apostle?" (1 Cor. 9:1). His call to the community—"Be imitators of me" (1 Cor. 11:1)—has the echo, "and not of those other apostles who oppose me." Paul's appeal to the mimesis word cluster is no doubt a rhetorical move to secure communal authority on his part. But to argue from this point to a general thesis about mimesis being not so much about similarity as sameness is, in light of both ancient and present-day evidence, inaccurate.

The root of that inaccuracy, in my judgment, is Castelli's reliance on textual sources at the expense of the oral-gestural matrix of mimesis. "Discourse," for Castelli, refers to "the source texts,"[28] and she takes Plato—who, as Eric Havelock has shown, played a significant part in the shift in ancient Greece toward the predominance of written culture[29]—as her "watershed" figure for mimesis.[30] But, as Castelli herself acknowledges, the first context of mimesis was oral-gestural. And, as we saw in Chapter 2, oral performance involves, according to Walter Ong, "winged words" that are "constantly moving."[31] Writing collects and affixes these words in dictionaries and grammars as if in a pinned collection of dead butterflies. It seems that it is the fixity of words that comes with texts and the focus on them that contributes to Castelli's claim that mimesis involves "one element being fixed and the other transforming itself." In contrast, oral-gestural mimesis, rather than focusing on abstract metaphysical debates about the immutability of God, trains its attention on the *movement* of God *toward* humanity. *God transforms Godself* to become the imitable Jesus of Nazareth. Even if we affirm, with the Nicene Creed, that Jesus Christ is "consubstantial with the Father" and therefore is in a significant sense "born of the Father before all ages," it remains that at a particular point in time and in a particular place, God *becomes* human. Without *this* movement, our imitation of God would indeed be impossible. In the sisters' accounts, God, through Jesus, continues such movement toward humanity on a daily basis.

Though it seeks that contact and similarity that transmit God's *psst* to us, mimesis—sensing, gesticulating, proclaiming, bodily mimesis—does risk interruption and even disruption. The number of people who directly witnessed the acts and words of Jesus the Nazarene—or Negri or Angioletta—was limited, and an unbroken chain of retelling what was witnessed—what Byskorg calls "reoralization" and Dunn terms "second orality"—is difficult to sustain.[32] This is all the more so because mimesis—like the Spirit—resists institutional stability. It at once preserves and creates. It takes place in that space between reality and construction, precedent and the unprecedented. Taussig refers to this space as the "desperate place between the real and the really made-up."[33] Kendall Walton argues that it is where reality and fiction fuse in acts of "make-believe."[34] In Theodor Adorno's words in reference to the practice in Walter Benjamin's work, mimesis is the effort to create an "exact fantasy."[35] The upside is that with mimesis so understood, there are ample resources for critique of any given re-presentation of the characteristic Jesus. There are internal sources: Jesus, as Dunn points out, was himself a performer of the tradition, and said certain things more than once and in different ways. And given that there are multiple witnesses to Jesus's deeds and words, there are also multiple accounts of these actions *from the start*. There are, also what are for the most part, external sources for critique rooted in the fact that there are no pristine cultures; all cultures are, to greater or lesser degree, hybrids. Such hybridity provides social space for critique even on the part of the subaltern.[36] The objectivist myth is that one has to be entirely outside of a situation in order to gain critical perspective; the objectivist conceit is that the studied culture in question has no resources of its own for critique and correction.

Despite the risk of instability, the practice of gospel mimesis is the only continuity with the Good News that we can hope for. There is, in my judgment, enough similarity between the encultured faith of the early Jesus community, on the one hand, and that of the Little Sisters of Mary Immaculate of Gulu, on the other, such that it is worth it to risk extended contact with the Catholicism of northern Uganda and South Sudan as a means—a collective spirit medium, if you will—for mimetically correcting *our* Western academic encultured faith. Such an undertaking—imitating nuns and catechists and such—may seem to be a very unacademic thing to do, pulling as it appears to do in the opposite direction of the effort to maintain "objective" distance, but relatively recent developments in the ethnographic understanding of participant observation—in particular, a turn on the part of some practitioners toward articulating it as a form of apprenticeship—provide a strong analogue to what I have been referring to as the method (and madness) of mimesis. The work of Paul Stoller is a prime example. Rather than make broad statements about the state of theology in the academy to make the case for a theology that draws on anthropology, my approach at this point is one of encountering the work of specific scholars. A mimetic approach asks, "Are there things that they are doing that might be helpful for the way of doing theology that I have just described? Are there ways that I can learn from them, even, in certain respects, be *like* them?" Whatever more generally might be said about theology and the other disciplines in the academy will arise out of both the convergences and the divergences that become evident through such specific engagements. Again, the focus is on embodied particulars.

Anthropological apprenticeship

Djibo picked up the only other chair in my house and placed it next to mine. He knew that I worked in the afternoons and he came to my house to watch me as I typed and to look at my possessions. Sometimes Djibo sat silent and motionless for hours while I typed.

My concentration was soon broken, not by Djibo, but by a rustling in the rafters. It was those damn birds again. I continued to type, but soon I felt something like a large drop of rain splatter on my head.

"Oh shit, those goddam birds have finally done it!" I tentatively touch my hair. "Birdshit! Goddam birds! Goddam country! Goddam village!" I screamed in English as I jumped off my chair and kicked the dirt floor of my house.

Ever since I moved into my house the birds had tested me. I first noticed them a week after my arrival. They had built a small mud nest between the mud-daubed sticks that constituted my ceiling. I did not mind their presence, but I did not like the fact that they had been shitting on my dirt floor . . . . I borrowed from a neighbor a long wooden pole . . . and with it I knocked down the birds' nest. . . . Two weeks later the birds quietly built another nest in my ceiling . . . . I again borrowed the pole and knocked down the second nest . . . . They returned, and so on, until I acknowledged the futility of the battle and surrendered to them. My capitulation: If they shit on my pots and pans, I would clean them; if they shit on my papers, I would wipe them clean.

"Praise be to God," Djibo chanted loudly, raising his hands skyward.

"How can you say that at a time like this!" I snapped.

"I am not laughing at you, Paul. I feel joy in my heart."

"Joy? What joy can there be in this?"

"Yes, joy. I have seen something here today."

"No kidding."

"Yes, I have seen a sign. You see, Paul, I am a *sorko*. My father is a sorko. And my grandfather, and grandfather's grandfather—all have been sorkos."

"What does that have to do with me?" Despite my frustration I was intrigued, for I had heard and read about the powers of the sorko, one of three kinds of Songhay magician-healers.

"Until today, my being a sorko had nothing to do with you," Djibo continued, "but today I have seen a sign. You have been pointed out to me . . . . I want you to come to my compound tomorrow after evening prayer so that we might begin to learn."

"What are you talking about?"

"I am saying that I want you to learn to be a sorko," Djibo said as he cracked his knuckles. "The choice is yours to make. If you choose my path, come to my compound tomorrow."

I had to make a decision. Should I study with Djibo? He had decided that the birds were a sign, but he had not said from whom. I tried to imagine what the great anthropologists would have done. Evans-Pritchard would give me unequivocal advice. Faced with a similar dilemma among the Azande of Central Africa in the 1920s, Evans-Pritchard refused to become personally involved with what he called a witch doctor. Such personal involvement, he reasoned, would compromise his objectivity. Since he still wanted to learn about Zande witchcraft, magic, and sorcery, he sent his cook to study with a witch doctor. Each evening the cook reported to Evans-Pritchard the progress of his apprenticeship.

—Paul Stoller, from *In Sorcery's Shadow*[37]

Stoller did not follow Evans-Pritchard's example. Instead, he undertook the sorcerer's apprenticeship himself. He did so with significant initial hesitation brought on by his training in and ongoing internalization of the predominant disciplinary approach of the time. "My graduate studies sharpened my intellectualist vision and narrowed my sensual horizons. One does fieldwork, I learned, to gather 'data' from informants. One collects these data, brings them 'home' and then, from an objective distance, analyzes them."[38] Stoller worries that, in undertaking his apprenticeship with Djibo, he has "compromised" his objectivity. "Enough. I cannot become more subjectively involved. . . . Djibo had thrust me into a situation in which I could not consider witchcraft dispassionately as a sociocultural process."[39] Such concerns run throughout *In Sorcery's Shadow*, and in publishing the results, Stoller explicitly turns away from naming the work an ethnography, electing instead to call it a "memoir."[40]

Two years after the publication, however, Stoller challenges head-on any strict subjective–objective or affect–intellect separation, and begins calling the work an ethnography.[41] I suspect that timing had much to do with the earlier resistance to naming *In Sorcery's Shadow* an ethnography. The book came out in 1987, just one year after James Clifford and George Marcus's *Writing Culture* and two years after Marcus and Michael Fischer's *Anthropology as Cultural Critique* coalesced the discipline's "interpretive turn," and thus rejection (in theory at least) of objectivist anthropology.[42] Most of *In Sorcery's Shadow* would have already been written, if not in galley proof. More, Stoller was still early in his development as a scholar, and he was aware that the book cut against the inherited conventions of the discipline. "My immediate inclination was to wonder: But what would the members of my dissertation committee think?"[43] What is remarkable, then, is that he, together with Cheryl Oakes, wrote the book—his first—at all. It seems that he was at least inchoately aware of a truth of mimetically based ethnography: bodily practice often—almost always, really—precedes the intellectual wherewithal to articulate more or less adequately what we are doing, but this, of itself, should not inhibit such practice.

Stoller's subsequent full turn to apprenticeship to describe his research leads to his rejection of the classical anthropological participant observation project of imitating the other while steadfastly resisting becoming *like* the other.[44] He calls classical participant observation, "anthropology's most famous oxymoron."[45] Apprenticeship, in contrast, requires careful imitation, with precisely the aspiration to likeness. "These were the Songhay for whom I had searched. They were proud, bound by codes of honor and hospitality, and they were hard. These qualities lured me deeper into the Songhay world, for they were traits that I admired, traits that I wanted to emulate." And elsewhere, "I wanted to be more like them."[46]

Apprenticeship involves practices present but not common, according to Stoller, in anthropology, which in most cases continue to "confront social reality through a disembodied gaze."[47] Apprenticeship first of all necessitates what I earlier referred to as an act of submission, and which Stoller variously calls "humility," "respect," and "open reverence" for the Songhay elders.[48] Such humility "means conceding *our* ignorance and *their* wisdom" (emphases in text).[49] The first task, then, is not so much to analyze the world of the other, but rather, as much as is possible, to allow the world of the other to affect *us*. "Anthropological writers should allow the events of the field—be they extraordinary or mundane—to penetrate them."[50] Such sensory submission places the researcher's body in the midst of investigation as the first "locus of learning."[51] Stoller is adamant that this embodied research "is not primarily textual." Rather, it is "consumed by a world filled with smells, textures, sights, sounds, and tastes." Scholarly work that treats it as a text "strips the body" of its sensuousness.[52] When combined with humility before the wisdom of the locals, such vulnerable sensuousness constitutes "embodied hospitality."[53] Put another way, the practice of fieldwork requires a significant degree of hospitality on the part of the research subjects for the success of the research as we enter their homes and their lives; the *a priori* determination to refuse to become in any significant way vulnerable to and like them in the ethnographic encounter is an in-principle refusal to return that hospitality; it is, at its core, nonreciprocal. And it is, in my judgment, at the heart of oppressive practices often conjoined with participant observation.

The second moment or practice of apprenticeship anthropology—initiation—is actually carried out by one's hosts. This is where, after the anthropologist exhibits due humility, the hosts invite her into the community. When Stoller first arrived in Niger, he peppered the locals with questions, both in oral and questionnaire form. He had not opened up to them, so they felt no compunction about lying in their answers to him. An elder tells him, "Monsieur Paul, you will never learn about us if you go into people's compounds, ask personal questions, and write down the answers. Even if you remain here one year, or two years, and ask us questions in this manner, we would still lie to you. You must learn to sit with people, Monsieur Paul. You must learn to sit and listen."[54] The scene with the birds in his hut enacts cosmologically as well as zoologically Stoller's turn to sitting and listening. At first he tries to organize the hut to his own liking by knocking down the birds' nest. But then he, in his words, "surrenders" to them: "My capitulation: If they shit on my pots and pans, I would clean them; if they shit on my papers, I would wipe them clean." It is only then that the birds mark their acceptance of him by shitting on his head, and Djibo initiates him into the world of sorcery. In keeping with the Songhay worldview, the zoological, the cosmological, and the social align.

Stoller most thoroughly articulates the importance of initiation in his book on Jean Rouch, the French ethnographer and cinematographer. Rouch's life among the Songhay stretches over decades, and it is an indication of Stoller's own initiation when the locals begin to call him "son of Rouch." Yet they would not have initiated Rouch, who filmed numerous possession dances, had not the spirits first invited him in his own version of birds shitting on his head. In fact, the Songhay name him, "the one who follows the spirits."[55] Rouch was deeply aware of his status as an initiate, its implications for what it means to be an "observer," and the obligations that follow:

> Slowly I entered the game, but as soon as certain doors were opened before me, they would close immediately behind me, prohibiting all retreat and cutting all ties with the outside. The observer was completely overwhelmed by what he observed. Was this still a matter of observation? The assurances that I gave these men that nothing would be repeated or published without their agreement enabled me to learn many things, but also limited what could be revealed. It is without doubt that the world of initiation carries with it not only certain conditions of silence, but also a respect, which appeared evident, for those who welcomed me and treated me as a friend. The ethnographer is not a policeman who extorts what one does not want to say or to reveal, and his elementary honesty consists exactly of respecting those he learns to know better, which is to say love better.[56]

Love. Accepting the invitation to participate in the community involves, for better and for worse, what Stoller calls our "implication" and "entanglement" in the lives of our hosts.[57] It is important to keep such entanglement in mind in understanding this moment in anthropological theology that I have been calling "discernment": it does not take place outside of the community to which we have turned our attention, but rather, like that attention, occurs in the middle of things. Stoller finds articulation of this point in the work of Christine Bergé: "Implication is the 'lived among.' It is the exercise of this reality: that there is not a position outside the system, that the anthropological gaze is not a 'gaze upon' but a sort of vibration on a fragile and ultrasensitive antenna."[58] Developing that antenna requires patience.

> "It will take me forever to learn this sorko stuff."
> "What is your hurry?" Djibo asked. "My father studied with his father for forty years. I have been studying with my father and other men for almost twenty years. There are many things I will not learn until my father reveals them to me on his deathbed."
> I was overwhelmed with the undertaking I had accepted. "How can I ever do it?"
> "If you want to learn, you will find a way. With patience and hardness you'll learn."
> "How can I learn [it] all before I have to return to America? I will be leaving in four months."
> "You will have to come back, won't you?"[59]

Stoller returns multiple times over a period of eight years—1976–84—to learn the sorcerer's way, and his writings repeatedly stress the necessity of long-term fieldwork,[60] a lesson he learned by submitting himself to the wisdom of the Songhay.

* * *

You come and steal our knowledge. You steal our culture. You come and talk to us about our knowledge and our culture and then take it all back with you. And we have nothing left.

—Olum, Pabbo IDP Camp

I started out my fieldwork much like Stoller—with formal field interviews in both individual and group settings. I had not yet learned Rouch and Stoller's lesson that, "The ethnographer is not a policeman who extorts what one does not want to say or to reveal." I did not think of myself as extorting or—until confronted by Olum of Pabbo IDP camp—stealing the Acholi's culture from them. Stunned by Olum's bluntness, I changed my approach. I would stroll around the camp until someone would wave me over and engage me in conversation. In doing so, I had stumbled upon what Stoller, in reference to Rouch and by extension himself, refers to as the improvisational *pourquoi pas* (why not) method. I dropped my original research topic—the possibilities and limits of microfinance in IDP camps—to listen to whatever people in the camp wanted to talk about. The Acholi have a phrase for it: *Cito mato yamo* (to go drink the wind). It means to walk about, to meander, to greet whomever you happen to see, and, if asked, to hang out a bit with them. Sometimes people just wanted money. Sometimes I obliged. Other times, they were genuinely intrigued that a white person would voluntarily live in an IDP camp. Reports of my walkabouts would often reach the priest in the parish compound. "I heard you climbed the old water tower today." "Yes." "They say you walk fast for a white man." Improvisational does not mean haphazard, however. Over time, specific relationships emerge and take direction. *Cito mato yamo* is how I met Sister Cecilia.

When I returned to the United States after my first summer in the IDP camps, I went up to Toronto to visit Acholi expatriates there. I was interested in finding out whether and how cultural beliefs and practices held up in the move. (The children of the migrants simply identified as black.) But again, that was not what *they* were interested in talking about. The adults—those who had migrated—wanted to know how things were back "home." So I would tell them about life in the camps, because that is what I knew.

"And you never got sick or hurt?"

"No."

"Mmm. That is something. You must have *tung gwok*."

"*Tung gwok*?" I knew that it translated, strangely, "horn of the dog," but did not know the deeper import of the phrase.

"It means that you are strong and that you are protected. The story is that sometimes a mother dog gives birth to a horned dog in its litter. Usually, she sees that it is strange, and eats it. That is why you never see a dog with horns. But if a person has courage and is fortunate, he can grab one of the horns before she eats the pup. And the horn protects you. You are protected. You went to the camps in the war. You did not get sick or hurt. You must have *tung gwok*. You *are* Tung Gwok."

If a visitor spends enough time in northern Uganda, she is sometimes given an Acholi name. But *Tung Gwok* would be strange even in that context. Still, nods around the living room. A consensus. And just like that—*pourquoi pas?*—I am named. It would not be until seven years later that I would move from sitting and listening to formally interviewing the Little Sisters, however. It takes a long time to learn what constitutes a good question.

* * *

Stoller insists that when the anthropologist moves to re-present what she has learned in the field, she continue to give the senses full play. Anthropological representation should have a "literary vividness" in order to "evoke a world" that "beckons the reader." The aim is to "give our readers or viewers a sense of what it is like to live in other worlds."[61] In practice, most anthropologists leave vivid depiction to informal conversational settings—for instance, between papers at a conference. The conference papers themselves edit out the senses.[62] The consequence is that most anthropological writing, according to Stoller, is of a style that is "as flat, neutral, and sludgy as the prose of the natural sciences."[63] The writer should operate not so much as a detached analyst of the world of the other, but rather as an "intermediary" between worlds.[64] To put the point in Christian theological terms, classical objectivist anthropology seeks to imitate the transcendent deist God who creates ex nihilo and acts at a remove from events while having a totalizing view of them; mimetic anthropology seeks to imitate the incarnate Son, the intermediary between the world of the reader/listener and a world that, for the reader/listener, is as of yet unseen.

Stoller draws on the person of the griot to amplify his point. He recognizes that the traditional griot operates in an oral-gestural context and that professional anthropologists write their words (and that when they speak in public settings, it is usually from a text). Still, he calls upon the anthropologist to incorporate the practice of the griot into her own work as much as possible. "Are there affinities between the quandaries of talking social life and those posed by writing or filming social life? Are there affinities between griots and ethnographers, who usually have the difficult task of representing someone else's social life?"[65] The key to an affirmative answer to these questions is the scholar's recognition that she, like the griot, is an "embodied intermediary."[66] Stylistically, being in the middle of things in this way means that the teller must place himself *in* the tale while at the same time make no claims to offering a totalizing, exhaustive account.[67] Rather, the task is to re-present the culture and its history such that it becomes a *living* tradition, where "the past blends into the present." The aim is for the griot's words and images to "enable the dead to live again."[68]

Bringing cultures to life specifically for academic audiences requires that the ethnographic griot draw upon a mix of genres that, taken together, "tack between the analytical and the sensible."[69] Such movement performs textually the fact that ethnography as an embodied mediating activity involves an instability that necessitates a capacity for living with uncertainties.[70] Still, the attention to irreducible rich detail does not disqualify the work as scholarship, but rather renders such writing, according to Stoller, "*more* rather than less scientific."[71]

The most telling indication that Stoller maintains a critical perspective despite his rejection of objectivist epistemology is the fact that, after eight years of intensive apprenticeship, he discerns that the life of the sorcerer is not his calling. The world of Songhay sorcery is "violent" and "amoral," and Stoller's implication in it creates a deciding unease in him. "When the world of eternal war became 'too much for me,' I renounced the Songhay path of power and, at the suggestion of my teacher, Adamu Jenitongo, opted for the Songhay path of plants—herbalism."[72] "Renounce" is a strong word; it is hard to have more critical distance than that. Both apprenticeship anthropology and anthropological theology of the gospel mimesis sort can constitute forms of fully academic inquiry.

At the time that Stoller is carrying out his initial research for *In Sorcery's Shadow*, there are other ethnographers—Jeanne Favret-Saada, Larry Peters, and Michael Harner, for example—who also recognize their entanglement in the world of their research subjects, and grapple with the issues involved in becoming like the other.[73] More, anthropology's "interpretive turn" creates, in theory and to some extent in practice, a discipline more hospitable to ethnography understood and practiced as apprenticeship. While apprenticeship is nowhere near being the predominant approach in cultural anthropology, it now has enough of a presence—Stoller received the American Anthropological Association's 2002 Robert B. Textor Award for excellence in anthropology—to serve as a disciplinary point of contact with theology understood and practiced as gospel mimesis. If our approach is not to start with general theories about the relationship between theology and the academy—some of that will come in ensuing chapters—but rather first to offer detailed explorations with particular practitioners, then the presence and profile of Stoller and others is sufficient for interdisciplinary appreciation, conversation, and even imitation.

Though both "enable the dead to live again," a key difference between anthropology, even of the apprenticeship sort, and anthropological theology understood and practiced as gospel mimesis is that the latter seeks to enable a particular dead person from a particular culture to live again among us—Jesus the Nazarene the Christ. Our acts of mimesis are efforts to enable specifically His *psst* to pass to the reader-listener. We do this in part through vivid retelling of the Gospel stories. But doing only this can create the impression that the stories are readily inhabitable by persons born 2,000 years later and living in cultures vastly different from that of the ancient Near East. Imitation without mediating cultural analysis can and often does lead us moderns and postmoderns to get the Gospel simply wrong. Here, cultures that have more in common with that of Jesus of Nazareth than does our own can serve as interpretive bridges to the Gospel. Such an approach is not an effort, like that found in earlier anthropology, to seek out somehow "pristine" cultures. There are no pristine cultures, whether in ancient Palestine or in contemporary northern Uganda and South Sudan; again, all cultures are, to greater or lesser degrees, porous hybrids. The idea of bridge cultures is simply that the particular culture in question is *similar enough* to that of ancient Palestine to help serve as a corrective to misreadings we may have of the Gospel message. In other words, imitating exemplar persons in the bridge culture aids us in imitating Jesus the Nazarene the Christ *more specifically*.

One example will have to suffice for now, and to elaborate that, it is best to return to the commissioning pericope, this time the Lukan version, which itself has what to modern and postmodern ears is a strange interruption right in the middle of it.[74] Unpacking that middle section will disclose how a biblical understanding of identity shapes a practice regarding property that, while found in northern Uganda and South Sudan, is foreign to and even disparaged by persons in the modern and contemporary West. In other words, the cultural bridge between the gospels and where we stand is a long one indeed.

Imitating Christ through a bridge culture: Identity and property

> Then Jesus called the twelve together and gave them power and authority over all demons and to cure diseases, and he sent them out to proclaim the kingdom of God and to heal. He said to them, "Take nothing for your journey, no staff, nor bag, nor bread, nor money—not even an extra tunic. Whatever house you enter, stay there, and leave from there. Wherever they do not welcome you, as you are leaving that town, shake the dust off your feet as a testimony against them." They departed and went through the villages, bringing the good news and curing diseases everywhere.
>
> Now Herod the ruler heard about all that had taken place, and he was perplexed, because it was said by some that John had been raised from the dead, by some that Elijah had appeared, and by others that one of the ancient prophets had arisen. Herod said, "John I beheaded; but who is this about whom I hear such things?" And he tried to see him.
>
> On their return, the apostles told Jesus all they had done.
>
> —Lk. 9:1-10a

In between Jesus's sending of the twelve and their return, the gospel of Luke notes Herod's perplexity by reference to John the Baptist. "John I beheaded," Herod insists, "but who is this?" Mark's version tells the Herodias-John the Baptist story even more fully, fifteen verses worth (Mk 6:14-29). These seem to be odd intrusions into the narrative. Why are they there?

In both Lukan and Markan versions, the Baptist story serves, among other things, to raise the question of Jesus's identity.[75] He has just sent out his primary followers to imitate him in healing the sick, casting out demons, and proclaiming the Kingdom of God. Herod's question might also be posed in a more pointed way: "Who does he think he is?" Various formulations of the Herodian query appear elsewhere in the synoptic Gospels. It is in the rejection at Nazareth: "Where did this man get all this? What is this wisdom that has been given to him? What deeds of power are being done by his hands? Is this not the carpenter, the son of Mary and brother of James and Joses and Judas and Simon, and are not his sisters here with us?" The passage adds, "And they took offense at him" (Mk 6:2b-3);[76] in other words, "Who does he think he is?" It is there in his healing (and forgiving) of the paralytic: "Who is this who is speaking blasphemies. Who can forgive sins but God alone?" (Lk. 5:21).[77] Once again, "Who does he think he is?" The challenge to Jesus's identity takes on an added layer in the commissioning pericope because Jesus passes the power (*dunamis*) and authority (*exousia*) that come with his claimed identity on to designated others.

The interruption of the pericope evidences the fact that people in ancient Palestinian culture sought answers to the question of Jesus's identity—and thus his ability to confer power and authority—by reference to previous exemplars in Israel's tradition. Herod is perplexed, "because it was said by some that John had been raised from the dead, by some that Elijah had appeared, and by others that one of the ancient prophets had arisen" (Lk. 9:7b-8; cf. Mk 6:14b-15). Jesus himself fosters this identification with the authority of prior figures both at the beginning and near the end of his ministry. At the beginning, when he is rejected in Nazareth, he replies in Luke's gospel, "But the truth is, there were many widows in Israel in the time of Elijah, when heaven was shut up three years and six months, and there was severe famine over all the land; yet Elijah was sent to none of them except to a widow at Zarephath in Sidon" (Lk. 4:25-26). In other words, Jesus is telling his hometown that he is "like" Elijah. John Meier is correct in concluding the second volume of his *The Marginal Jew* series with the statement, "Jesus the eschatological prophet was acting out the role of the eschatological prophet Elijah."[78] And as we saw in the Chapter 3, near the end of his ministry, Jesus responds to the question from temple leaders regarding his identity and authority by reference to his baptism by John.

Claims in first-century Palestine regarding Jesus's identity and consequent power and authority can only be made, then, by reference to his association and likeness to representative exemplars. Even Jesus's antagonists follow this pattern, countering his followers' claims by arguing that he is not like either Elijah or John, but rather either represents Beelzebul, and "by the ruler of demons he casts out demons" (Mk 3:22)[79] or is simply "Joseph's son" (Lk. 4:22b), that is, without real power or authority. Ancient Near Eastern culture is, in Bruce Malina's words, "nonindividualistic, strongly group-oriented, collectivistic," whereby the "group-embedded, collectivistic personality is one who simply needs another continually in order to know who he or she really is."[80]

It is clear, then, that even though many biblical scholars identify Jesus as a "charismatic," he is not one in the technical Weberian sense of the word indicating a person who draws others simply by the magnetism of his own personality.[81] Weber develops the idea of charismatic authority in large part in response to his diagnosis of modern society as exemplifying an "iron cage": modern bureaucracy has so stifled social innovation that only the amazing individual can break its bonds. He describes the charismatic individual as over *against*—indeed, as "alien to"—received tradition, and as therefore "absolutely unique" and "unprecedented."[82] In first-century Palestine, however, with individual identity tied up with that of the community, those who do not identify Jesus with Elijah or John on the one hand or Beelzebul or simply Joseph's son on the other have only the option of viewing him as mad ("When his family heard it, they went out to restrain him, for people were saying, 'He has gone out of his mind'" Mk 3:21).[83] In first-century Palestine, not to be identified with another representative figure—whether Elijah or

Beelzebul or Joseph—is to be unintelligible. While moderns celebrate autonomy, for the people of Jesus's time, it is the very definition of madness.

Moreover, like Jesus, the early practitioners of the Jesus tradition reach back to the actions of the prophets and John the Baptist as precursors. Indeed, the view that Jesus Christ is the *fulfillment* of prophetic hope is crucial for the new community in making their claims about who Jesus is intelligible to others,[84] and it is a fulfillment that they themselves carry forward in the Spirit through, among other things, their own Elijah-like works of wonder. And, interestingly, they draw their primary post-Pentecost rite of initiation into the community—baptism by water—not from Jesus, who did not practice it, but from John the Baptist, whose act inaugurated Jesus's earthly mission.[85]

What these references to earlier tradition by the first Christians mean from a mimetic standpoint is that even though there is already a shift toward understanding Jesus not just as the Nazarene, but as the Christ—a shift signaled by the frequent acts done in the *name* of Jesus Christ[86]—this is not a move that lifts Jesus Christ *out* of concrete history, but rather one that thrusts him even more deeply *into* the midst of it. To put it another way, the development of the early community into a messianic sect which understood Jesus not as simply the proclaimer of the Good News, but also as the proclaimed Good News himself, did not remove Jesus from the "middle of things," but rather placed him in the middle of *all* things—not just the middle of Galilee, Jerusalem, or even the nation of Israel, but of everything there is. (The fact that there were precursor exemplars—whether Elijah, John, or anyone else—therefore did not undercut Jesus's authority.) And, as testified to in the words of Acts, the Lord whom the apostles name remains very much the concrete "*Jesus* Christ of *Nazareth*" (cf. especially Acts 3:6; 4:10 and 12; and 10:43).[87] The absolute counterpositioning of the Jesus of history over against the Christ of faith, first articulated forcefully for modern biblical interpretation by D. F. Strauss in 1865 and repeatedly underscored by others since, is incapable of grasping the reality of this—for the early Christians—inseparability of person and Spirit.[88]

It is precisely the communal orientation of ancient Palestinian identity, combined with Jesus's shift in what constitutes kinship—"My mother and my brothers are those who hear the word of God and do it" (Lk. 8:21; cf. Mk 3:35; Mt. 12:50)—that makes the call to communal property intelligible to and indeed practicable by the early apostolic community. "Now the whole group of those who believed were of one heart and soul, and no one claimed private ownership of any possessions, but everything they owned was held in common" (Acts 4:32; cf. 2:44). From a mimetic standpoint, the practice of the sharing of goods, however short-lived it may have been (a fact that the author Luke himself acknowledges in Acts 6:1), is best understood as an effort on the part of the early followers of the resurrected Jesus to reinterpret the strictures on property given to the itinerant disciples in the commissioning pericope—"Take nothing for your journey, no staff, nor bag, nor bread, nor money, not even an extra tunic" (Lk. 9:3)[89]—for circumstances in which not every person seeking to imitate Jesus was itinerant. What is noteworthy in the biblical accounts is how tightly the two relevant passages identify the economic practice to be the result and expression of God's power and authority in the early followers—that is, as a piece of the overall mimetic reenactment of Jesus Christ.

The first passage links the wonderworking of the apostles to the economic practice recommended by Jesus to the rich young man—sell all your possessions and give the proceeds to the poor:

> Awe came upon everyone, because many wonders and signs were being done by the apostles. All who believed were together and had all things in common; they would sell their possessions and goods and distribute the proceeds to all, as any had need. Day by day, as they spent much time together in the temple, they broke bread at home and ate their food with glad and generous hearts, praising God and having goodwill of all the people. And day by day the Lord added to their number those who were being saved. (Acts 2:43-47)

The second passage describing the early economic practices interweaves them with the fact of witness of and testimony to Jesus, wrapping the economic practices around the witness and testimony. After informing us that the "whole group" was "of one heart and soul" and therefore held all of their property "in common" (Acts 4:32), the passage immediately goes on to state, "With great power the apostles gave their testimony to the resurrection of the Lord Jesus, and great grace was upon them all" (Acts 4:33). And the evidence for such grace? It immediately follows: "There was not a needy person among them, for as many as owned lands or houses sold them and brought the proceeds of what was sold. They laid it at the apostles' feet, and it was distributed to each as any had need" (Acts 4:34-35).

Yet one form of the imitation of Jesus often dismissed as unhistorical or set aside as not finally relevant by modern Western biblical commentators—even Dunn—is the sharing of goods among believers.[90] It is as if the commentators have preemptively decided, "Well, the Gospel can't mean *that*." But it can, and does. Why the resistance to this teaching and practice? I suggest that it is because such a practice remains largely unintelligible to a culture that has a more atomized understanding of identity. Evidence that this is the case comes through examination of cultures where a communal orientation of identity is stronger.

Traditional Acholi culture shares, again to use Malina's words, the "nonindividualistic, strongly group-oriented, collectivistic" orientation characteristic of ancient Palestine. In traditional Acholi culture, persons do not receive a last name because they already have a clan identity. In the words of one elder whom I interviewed, "For the Acholi, once you have given birth the child is for the clan. It is not yours. So anything was done to help the child to grow up in the clan. And if this child misbehaves, the whole clan will take care of that. Orphans are not taken to the orphanage. The orphans are cared for in the [extended] family. You see?"[91]

The communal orientation in traditional Acholi culture manifests itself economically in the fact of clan—that is, shared—land. One clan elder put it to me this way:

> Supposing we come back [to our clan land from the camps after the war is over] and one of us begins saying that this land belongs to his grandparents alone. How

would it sound? It would not sound properly because the whole of the Acholi have been staying there. So the land that has been left behind there was not one man's land. That's how ancestral land is. It is not one man's property. You as a given tribe, you dig on that land together and the clan members eat together.[92]

By far and away, most Acholi in northern Uganda and South Sudan are small-scale farmers, and land is the primary source of whatever propertied wealth they have. In most instances, such land has been held in what the Ugandan constitution formally recognizes as "customary" ownership. That is to say, ownership is not conferred through individual written title, but rather through oral-based clan authority. The controlling idea even for land on which an individual family settles is that it ultimately serves the common good of the clan. Tellingly, when I have asked where they are from, individual Acholi have most often responded with reference to their ancestral clan land and not to wherever they happened to have grown up, even if they themselves have never lived on the clan land. One important study describes the understanding of clan land in helpful detail:

The land which a family owns is not considered as being totally "theirs": it is their heritage and the future heritage of their children. Since they see that a family exists only as a part of a wider community, so its land is held within the wider structure of a community (clan) and as clan's land. Land is the fundamental productive asset, without which one cannot survive, and so one's social obligations and claims are intimately connected to claims and rights over land. These obligations extend to the next generation: land must therefore be protected for them and if anyone who leaves the village and fails to survive in the urban economy, the customary land is a safety net, because they can always return and be allocated a plot. Land is also the link with people's heritage—quite literally, since it is on the family land that one is buried.[93]

Hunting and grazing lands are held by and serve the clan as a whole. They are best utilized when multiple families access them whole rather than as divided up into smaller bits. In short, the communal orientation of the Acholi people manifests itself in the form of sharing the fundamental source of wealth, in this case land.

Like Jesus does in the gospels, the Little Sisters of Mary Immaculate draw upon the traditional communal orientation of their inherited cultures and then shift the locus of primary kinship loyalty. One's "mother" and "sisters" are first of all, again in Jesus's words, "those who hear the word of God and do it." The shift in kinship is evident in the fact that the sisters take on a new name when they join the order. Yet I suggest that it is the initial communal orientation, inherited from Acholi and contiguous cultures in northern Uganda and South Sudan, that serves to make the subsequent vow of poverty and the sharing of wealth it involves intelligible to potential postulants. This is not to say that the practice of sharing property is easy for them; all three communities—the early Christians, the Acholi, and the Little Sisters—struggle with it. But it is precisely the fact of that struggle that points to the hold that the practice has on the communities.

With regard to the basic communal orientation for identity, then—and despite the tensions between ongoing traditional familial demands and the sisters' vow of poverty— the two communities are more alike than not. When years of war created stresses on and in the identity of the Congregation, their first response was to delve more deeply into the lives not of their individual selves, but of exemplar people, Bishop Negri and Mother Angioletta, because only retrieving these two would inform the sisters who they themselves were. Given the orientation toward communal belonging in both traditional Acholi culture and among the Little Sisters, the move from shared "customary" land ownership to shared property in the vow of poverty is bridgeable.

For centuries, Western Christianity responded to the economic implications of the Gospel by segregating yet retaining the practice of communal property. It did this through the formation of religious orders, which in proto form as early as Pachomius in the fourth century reclaimed the practice of shared property dropped by the rest of professed Christians. Cenobitic monasticism and later other religious orders gained further social approbation of their practice as constituting a way of life that embodies the Gospel more fully than that of other Christians. To put it in mimetic terms, the predominant view was that vowed religious life reenacted the community of Jesus more faithfully.

Vatican II's opening of the Catholic Church to the "modern world" included *Lumen Gentium*'s "universal call to holiness," which sought to overcome, at least in part, the religious/lay spiritual hierarchy.[94] However, consistent with the modern world with its neoliberal individualistic economics, such broadening of the call to holiness has not involved a corresponding extension of the communal sharing of property to the whole of the Catholic Church. In fact, the wealth gap both in the world and in the United States is at record levels and continues to grow.[95] In the meantime, the number of vowed religious—those who heretofore were the exemplars of shared property—has declined dramatically in the developed world. In the period between the Second Vatican Council and 2014, the number of people in formal religious vocations has decreased in the United States by almost 70 percent—from 215,000 to 66,000—even while the absolute number of Catholics in the United States has grown over the same period from 48.5 million to 76.7 million.[96] Such data, coupled with that on the wealth gap, indicates that a way of life that involves communal property makes sense to fewer and fewer people in the developed world.

It is therefore telling that religious vocations are on the increase in the countries of Africa (up 18.5 percent between 2001 and 2013, considerably outpacing even the 4.3 percent overall growth of the Catholic Church on the continent[97]), suggesting, among other things, that there the sharing of property remains intelligible and even desirable. Yes, the reasons for joining or not joining religious life are complex, and I mean my argument here to be only suggestive, but the basic lineaments are clear: in the modern/ postmodern world, individualism with regard to identity leads to the downplaying and even rejection of the Gospel practice of communal property. Reading scripture through the lens of cultures that as of yet have not been fully overrun by individualistic biases can help lead us back to the Gospel.

A fragile convergence

In this chapter, as a first step in the moment of "discernment" in anthropological theology, I have shown how gospel mimesis of the sort practiced by the Little Sisters can also constitute a mode of academic inquiry. If we understand mimesis in terms of its early oral-gestural context, then it becomes clear that imitation need not collapse into the attempted exact copying of fixed models. More, the "interpretive turn" in cultural anthropology has fostered a strong disciplinary analogue to gospel mimesis in the practice of ethnography as apprenticeship. Those who do practice ethnography in this way remain in the minority, but their presence in terms of both numbers and stature means that interdisciplinary engagement is possible. The main difference between gospel mimesis and anthropology as apprenticeship is that the former, in addition to its other aims, carries out ethnography in order to better follow and imitate Jesus the Nazarene the Christ. Cultures that have key elements in common with that of ancient Palestine can also show us more specifically how to imitate Christ and his early community of followers. I have drawn upon the instance of communal identity and property to show how the Acholi can provide a bridge culture to that of the early followers of Jesus.

The conditions for ethnography so considered, however, are fragile. In the case of northern Uganda, the NGO precedent of paying people to attend meetings has made it more difficult to gather clans or congregations together. Years of displacement and parentless existence has left many youths with little clan attachment, with some not knowing at all to which clan they belong, creating a crisis of identity. My Acholi name, *Tung Gwok*, has served as a kind of working index for me of the impact of war and displacement on culture: older Acholi know its background meaning; younger Acholi most often do not. Knowledge of the story of *tung gwok* is normally passed on when the extended family gathers around *wang oo*, the evening fire. But during the war, the fire signaled to the LRA that people were still outside, and would bring an attack. People ceased the practice. In the meantime, radio advertising has been quite willing to resolve the youths' identity crisis: commercials for beer appeal to listeners as consumers by telling them, "It's all about you."

Still, for the Catholic Church in sub-Saharan Africa, the Second Vatican Council's call to open up to the world has meant opening up not only to the modern world, but also to the worlds of indigenous cultures. And for the sisters, this has meant the affirmation of the communal orientation among indigenous peoples. Again, even when addressing the divisiveness of ethnic identification within the Congregation, the sisters' Chapter Documents affirm, "Common and sociable life is most valued by Africans because this begins the regeneration and continuity in a clan." Consistent with the affirmation, found both in Acholi culture and in the gospels, of the fundamental continuity between the community of this life and that of the next, one of the sisters, whom I quoted in Chapter 1, makes the comparison between the ancestors encountered in rites around the *abila*, or ancestral shrine, and the Christian communion of saints: "And then, there is this ancestral shrine, mm? And I think this also could be connected with our Christianity because we believe in the saints. The saints are our ancestors."[98]

Another Sister concurs:

We believe in the life after, so we feel that our ancestors who have died they still live. And where we can find them is in the shrine. Our tradition believes that in the shrine [is] where we can have our ancestor, because the shrine is always put in the middle of the what?—of the home. Of the compound. So [the ancestor] is the overseer. Our ancestors, they are still living with us. So we go and consult them there. Thinking that they are still are living beings, even if they are away from us. They still oversee the family. That can fit with Christianity. Because as we go to the altar of the Lord and we talk, our shrine is somehow an altar whereby we go and consult our ancestors for help, for blessing. Yeah.[99]

As long as such cultural convergences between Acholi culture and that of the ancient Near East continue, they can, I suggest, provide an interpretive bridge for the rest of us to the Gospel. We have seen how this is the case with property.

The idea, let alone the practice, of common property is alien and even anathema to the capitalist West. This is why so many biblical scholars read the practice among the early followers of Jesus Christ to be not of much contemporary import. It is simply too strange. Imitation of exemplars of cultures that can form bridges to the practices of Jesus and his followers presents the anthropological theologian with gaps that appear to be unbridgeable. If we are not to romanticize the practice of mimesis, we need in our discernment to attend to those gaps. I do so in the next chapter.

Notes

1. See Paul Stoller and Cheryl Olkes, *In Sorcery's Shadow: A Memoir of Apprenticeship among the Songhay of Niger* (Chicago and London: The University of Chicago Press, 1987); Loïc Wacquant, *Body and Soul: Notebooks of an Apprentice Boxer* (Oxford and New York: Oxford University Press, 2006); and Anand Pandian, "Ethnography, Devotion and the Ethics of Wonder." Paper delivered for "Ethnography, Religion, and Ethics: The 4th Annual Workshop in Applied Ethics" (Boston, Northeastern University, October 2014).

2. The vast majority of people, even more so away from Jerusalem and the Temple, learned of and engaged in the tradition of Israel through hearing and retelling in village assemblies or *synagogai*. Synagogues were private rooms opened to the public so that people could gather to hear and discuss—or, more precisely, to perform and witness—the tradition. See Gerd Thiessen and Annette Merz, *The Historical Jesus*, p. 167.

    Scholars of the historical Jesus often ask whether he could read and write, but the question is largely misplaced; the relevant literacy during his time regarded not whether one could read or write, but whether one knew the tradition. Jesus knew Israel's traditions well enough such that he could imitate—that is, re-present—its main figures through conventions in such a way that they were recognizable.

    On literacy rates, see, for instance, Catherine Hezser, *Jewish Literacy in Roman Palestine* (Tubingen: Mohr Siebaeck, 2001; Meir Bar-Ilan, "Illiteracy in the Land of Israel in the First Centuries CE," in *Essays in the Social Scientific Study of Judaism and Jewish Society*, ed. Simcha Fishbane and Stuart Schoenfeld (Hoboken, NJ: Ktav, 1992); and William V. Harris, *Ancient Literacy* (Cambridge, MA: Harvard University Press, 1989); Susan Niditch, *Oral and Written Word* (Louisville: Westminster/John Knox, 1996); and Mary Beard, ed., *Literacy in the Roman World* (Ann Arbor: Journal of Roman Archeology, 1991).

3. Dunn, *Jesus Remembered*, pp. 227–8.

4. Dunn cites from Kenneth Bailey the example of orality in Middle Eastern culture, which centers around the evening fire called *haflat samar,* meaning, "the social gathering to preserve" the traditions. Dunn, *New Perspective on Jesus*, pp. 45–6.

5. James D. G. Dunn, *A New Perspective on Jesus* (Chapter 3: "The Characteristic Jesus"), pp. 57–78. Dunn draws (and develops) his emphasis on the "characteristic" Jesus from Leander E. Keck, *A Future for the Historical Jesus* (Nashville: Abingdon, 1971), p. 33. Other scholars who develop the idea of orality/aurality include: Richard A. Horsely, *Jesus in Context: Power, People, & Performance* (Minneapolis: Fortress Press, 2008); Richard A. Horsley, Jonathan A. Draper, and John Miles Foley, eds., *Performing the Gospel: Orality, Memory, and Mark* (Minneapolis: Augsburg Fortress, 2006); Richard A. Horsley and Jonathan A. Draper, *Whoever Hears You Hears Me: Prophets, Performance, and Tradition in Q* (Harrisburg: Trinity, 1999); Werner Kelber, *The Oral and Written Gospel* (Philadelphia: Fortress Press, 1983); Alan Kirk and Tom Thatcher, *Memory, Tradition, and Text: Uses of the Past in Early Christianity*, Semeia Studies 52 (Atlanta: Society of Biblical Literature, 2005); L. H. Silberman, ed., *Orality, Aurality and Biblical Narrative, Semeia* 39 (Atlanta: Scholars Press, 1987); W. O. Walker, ed., *The Relationships among the Gospels* (San Antonio: Trinity University, 1978), pp. 31–122; Paul J. Achetmeier, "Omne Verbum Sonat: The New Testament and the Oral Environment of Late Western Antiquity," *Journal of Biblical Literature* 109 (1990): 3–27; Pieter J. J. Botha, "Greco-Roman Literacy as Setting for New Testament Writings," *Neotestamentica* 26 (1992): 742–59; Pieter J. J. Botha, "Mark's Story as Oral Traditional Literature: Rethinking the Transmission of Some Traditions about Jesus," *Hervormde Teologiese Studies* 47 (1991): 304–34; Joanna Dewey, "The Survival of Mark's Gospel: A Good Story," *Journal of Biblical Literature* 123 (2004): 495–507; Joanna Dewey, ed., *Orality and Textuality in Early Christian Literature, Semeia* 65 (Atlanta: Scholars Press, 1995); Joanna Dewey, "The Gospel of Mark as Oral-Aural Event: Implications for Interpretation," in *The New Literary Criticism and the New Testament*, ed. Elizabeth Struthers Malbon and Edgar V. McKnight (JSNTSup 19; Sheffield: Sheffield Academic, 1994): 148–57; Joanna Dewey, "Mark as Aural Narrative: Structures as Clues to Understanding," *Sewanee Theological Review* 36 (1992): 45–56; Joanna Dewey, "Oral Methods of Structuring Narrative in Mark," *Interpretation* 53 (1989): 32–44; Joanna Dewey, David Rhoads, and Donald Michie, *Mark as Story: An Introduction to the Narrative of a Gospel*; Walter J. Ong, S. J. *Interfaces of the Word* (Ithaca, NY: Cornell University Press, 1977), and Joanna Dewey, *Orality and Literacy* (New York: Routledge, 1982); Birger Gerhardsson, *Memory and Manuscript: Oral Tradition and Written Transmission in Rabbinic Judaism and Early Christianity* with *Tradition and Transmission in Early Christianity* (Grand Rapids, MI: Eerdmans/Livonia Michigan: Dove Booksellers, 1998).

6. On the importance of correction by the community and the role of elders and teachers in the oral traditioning process, see Dunn, *Jesus Remembered*, pp. 224, 240–1; *New Perspective on Jesus*, pp. 49–50.

7. This is why the writers of Luke and Matthew, for instance, both (according to the literary paradigm) presumably drawing from the same Q source, can provide accounts of a Jesus story that are virtually word for word in some sentences and yet offer strikingly different details in other parts of the same passage.

8. Dunn still has confidence, as I do, in the historicity of many of the Gospel accounts. This is not an over-certitude that every jot and tittle in the Gospels is just as Jesus said or did it.

For Dunn, the focus on the oral nature of the early tradition raises the point that the fact of even a pre-Easter faith—and thus theologizing—of some kind does not, of itself, undercut the trustworthiness of memory. On my part, it backs the judgment that there is enough material carried into the synoptic Gospels to provide a reasonably accurate account of the characteristic Jesus such that it can serve as the basis for further mimetic depiction of him and his mission. Cf. Dunn, *Jesus* Remembered, pp. 102–5.

In reconstructing the historical Jesus, Dunn's emphasis, and mine also, is on the synoptic Gospels. Dunn does not, however, entirely discount John's Gospel. For instance, he holds to the view that Jesus's ministry likely took place over a period of three years, in accordance with the Fourth Gospel, rather than the roughly one year depicted in the synoptics. For an argument that John's Gospel is more historically reliable than is generally credited, see Francis J. Maloney, SDB, "The Fourth Gospel and the Jesus of History," *New Testament Studies* 46 (2000): 42–58.

9. Byrskog, *Story as* History, p. 45. Dunn criticizes Byrskog because the latter does not provide a theory for transmission other than reliance of the evangelists on the testimony of eyewitnesses. Byrskog therefore has to argue for direct linkages between, for instance, Peter and the author of Mark. Dunn, *Jesus Remembered*, pp. 198–9, n. 138. For another of their exchanges, see Byrskog, "A New Perspective on the Jesus Tradition: Reflections on James D. G. Dunn's *Jesus Remembered*," *Journal for the Study of the New Testament* 26, no. 4 (2004): 459–71; and Dunn, "On History, Memory and Eyewitness: In Response to Bengt Holmberg and Samuel Byrskog," *Journal for the Study of the New Testament* 26, no. 4 (2004): 473–87.

Whatever their differences, my interest in retrieving Byrskog is in using his recognition of the importance of autopsy to augment Dunn's account of oral tradition so that seeing as well as hearing figures adequately into the account of the development of the Jesus tradition. The importance of sight is not only that of taking into account a broader array of the senses, however, but also in recognizing that transmitting the tradition is not just a matter of reiterating it, but of reenacting it. Byrskog's emphasis on sight therefore leads to a corresponding stress on *mimesis* as a central means for carrying on the Jesus tradition.

10. Byrskog, *Story as History*, pp. 48 and 154. Cf. also pp. 145–57, 162, 166, and 301–2. Moreover, an author's specifically theological interest does not rule out, as Dennis Nineham would have it, historical interest. Dennis Nineham, "Eye-Witness Testimony and the Gospel Tradition, I," *Journal of Theological Studies* 9 (1958): 13–25; Nineham, "Eye-Witness Testimony and the Gospel Tradition, II," *Journal of Theological Studies* 9 (1958): 243–52; and Nineham, "Eye-Witness Testimony and the Gospel Tradition, III," *Journal of Theological Studies* 11 (1960): 253–64. See Byrskog, *Story as History*, pp. 274–5.

11. Byrskog, *Story as History*, p. 107; see also p. 301. It is worth noting that the dynamic of extended contact with an exemplar

12. Hans Koller, *Die Mimesis in der Antike: Nachahmung, Dartstellung, Ausdruck* (Bern: Dissertationes Bernenses), ser. 1, fasc. 5, p. 119.

13. Goran Sörbom, *Mimesis and Art: Studies in the Origin and Early Development of an Aesthetic Vocabulary* (Stockholm: Svenska Bokforlaget, 1966), p. 39, note 49. Sörbom adds "reenacting" to Liddell-Scott's translations of *mimeisthai* as denoting the activity of "imitating, representing, portraying."

14. Goran Sörbom, *Mimesis and Art: Studies in the Origin and Early Development of an Aesthetic Vocabulary*, 38. See also 39, where Sörbom writes that to imitate is "to represent something vividly and concretely by means of qualities that are similar to qualities in other phenomena."

15. Marcel Mauss and Henri Hubert, *A General Theory of Magic*, trans. R. Brain (New York: Norton, 1972), p. 68; Michael Taussig, *Mimesis and Alterity*, p. 52. Taussig elsewhere describes the "mimetic faculty" as "the nature that culture uses to create second nature" (p. xiii).

16. We both make clear that a reading in terms of power is not the only reading of Paul. Elizabeth A. Castelli, *Imitating Paul: A Discourse of Power* (Louisville: Westminster/John Knox, 1991), p. 121.

17. Paul. Castelli, *Imitating Paul: A Discourse of Power*, p.16.

18. Ibid., p. 21.

19. Ibid., pp. 119, 22, and 113. See also pp. 57, 70, 86, 89, 99, 103, and 120.

20. Paul. Castelli, *Imitating Paul: A Discourse of Power*, pp. 68 and 13. See also 22 and 75.

21. Interview with Sr. Martha, 1.

22. Interview with Sr. Susan Clare, 1.

23. Interview with Sr. Grace, 15.

24. Interview with Sr. Mary Clementina, 5.

25. Interview with Sr. Mary Clementina, 5–6.

26. Interview with Sr. Rosalba, 3.

27. It is important to note here that Christians at the time of Paul usually converted as households, following the head of the household. Women, children, and slaves did not have much, if any, say in the matter.

28. Castelli, *Imitating Paul*, p. 15. See also p. 18, where she describes her project as one of "experimenting with another way of reading the text."

29. Eric Havelock, *Preface to Plato* (Cambridge, MA and London: The Belknap Press of Harvard University Press, 1963).

30. Castelli, *Imitating Paul*, p. 67.

31. Walter Ong, *Orality and Literacy* (London and New York: Routledge, 2002), p. 76.

32. Byrskog, *Story as History*, pp. 92, 99, 111, 160; on "second orality," see Dunn, *Jesus Remembered*, pp. 200–9, 217–18, and p. 250; *A New Perspective on Jesus*, pp. 47, 51, 94, and 110. Ancient historians suspected the written text in part because it could serve to undermine the practice of memory.

33. Taussig, *Mimesis and Alterity*, xvii; Taussig says elsewhere that mimesis occurs in a place that is always "sliding between photographic fidelity and fantasy, between iconicity and arbitrariness, wholeness and fragmentation" (17).

34. Kendall L Walton, *Mimesis as Make-Believe: On the Foundations of the Representational Arts* (Cambridge, MA: Harvard University Press, 1993).

35. T. W. Adorno, "A Portrait of Walter Benjamin," *Prisms*, trans. Samuel and Sherry Weber (Cambridge, MA: MIT Press, 1981), p. 233.

36. I am aware of the postcolonial debate over the term "hybridity" and its relative valuation. My use of it here is simply to signal a point made by Marwan Kraidy that "traces of other cultures exist in every culture." Kraidy makes the point as a response to recent globalization, but I would extend it to much earlier periods of cultural interaction. Marwan Kraidy, *Hybridity: The Cultural Logic of Globalization* (Philadelphia: Temple University Press, 2005). For the case for hybridity having much earlier instantiations, see Philipp Wolfgang Stockhammer, ed., *Conceptualizing Cultural Hybridization: A Transdisciplinary Approach* (London and New York: Springer Heidelberg Dordrecht, 2012). For postcolonial analysis of hybridity, see, for instance, Homi Bhabha, *The Location of Culture* (London: Routledge, 1994).

37. Stoller and Olkes, *In Sorcery's Shadow*, pp. 22–5.

38. Stoller, *The Taste of Ethnographic Things* (Philadelphia: University of Pennsylvania Press, 1989), p. 4.

39. Stoller, *The Taste of Ethnographic Things*, pp. 51, 57–8.

40. Ibid., p. xii: "This book is not a standard ethnography; it is a memoir."

41. Stoller, *The Taste of Ethnographic Things*, pp. 5, 38, 50, and 155; Paul Stoller, *Sensuous Scholarship* (Philadelphia: University of Pennsylvania Press, 1997), pp. xi–xii.

42. James Clifford and George E. Marcus, *Writing Culture: The Poetics and Politics of Ethnography* (Berkeley and Los Angeles: University of California Press, 1986); George E. Marcus and Michael M. J. Fischer, *Anthropology as Cultural Critique: An Experimental Moment in the Human Sciences* (Chicago: The University of Chicago Press, 1986).

43. Stoller, *The Taste of Ethnographic Things*, p. 41.

44. For references to anthropology in terms of apprenticeship, see, for instance, Stoller, *The Cinematic Griot: The Ethnography of Jean Rouch* (Chicago: The University of Chicago Press, 1992), pp. 19, 24, 214–15, and 219 ff.

45. Stoller, *The Taste of Ethnographic Things*, p. 155; and Stoller, *The Cinematic Griot: The Ethnography of Jean Rouch*, p. 214.

46. Stoller and Olkes, *In Sorcery's Shadow*, pp. 46 and 11. See also p. 153.

47. Stoller, *Sensuous Scholarship*, p. 22.

48. Stoller, *The Taste of Ethnographic Things*, pp. 5 and 56; Paul Stoller, *The Cinematic Griot*, pp. 214–15 and 83.

49. Stoller, *The Cinematic Griot*, p. 172.

50. Stoller, *The Taste of Ethnographic Things*, pp. 54; see also 39.

51. Stoller, *Sensuous Scholarship*, pp. 22.

52. Stoller, *The Cinematic Griot*, pp. 85 and xiv.

53. Ibid., p. xviii.

54. Stoller and Olkes, *In Sorcery's Shadow*, p. 11.

55. Stoller, *The Cinematic Griot*, pp. 171 and 167.

56. Jean Roche, *La religion et la magie Songhay*, 2nd edition, corrected and expanded (Brussels: Université de Bruxelles, 1989 [1960]), p. 17; quoted in Stoller, *The Cinematic Griot*, p. 84.

57. Stoller, *The Cinematic Griot*, pp. 47, 172, and 214.

58. Christine Bergé, "De l'autre côté du miroir," unpublished manuscript, n.d., 6; quoted in Stoller, *Sensuous Scholarship*, p. 33.

59. Stoller and Olkes, *In Sorcery's Shadow*, pp. 37–8. For other references to the need for patience, see ibid., pp. 13, 31–2, 51–, 53, 55, 58, 71, and 90.

60. Stoller, *The Taste of Ethnographic Things*, pp. 6–7, 10–11, and 56–7; Stoller, *The Cinematic Griot*, pp. 18, 19, 21, 23, 213, 219, and 220; Stoller, *Sensuous Scholarship*, p. 26.

61. Stoller, *The Taste of Ethnographic Things*, pp. 29, 31, 54, and 156.

62. Ibid., p. 39 and 155; see also Stoller and Olkes, *In Sorcery's Shadow*, p. ix.

63. Stoller, *The Taste of Ethnographic Things*, pp. 29–30 and 51. See also pp. 8, 26–7, 50, and 135–8; Stoller, *Sensuous Scholarship*, pp. 34–6; and Stoller, *The Cinematic Griot*, p. 203.

64. Stoller, *The Taste of Ethnographic Things*, pp. 54 and 56.

65. Stoller, *Sensuous Scholarship*, p. 29.

66. Ibid., p. 32.

67. Stoller critiques third-person ethnography in *The Taste of Ethnographic Things*, pp. 3–5, 28, 32, 40ff, and 49.

68. Stoller, *The Cinematic Griot*, 47; and *Sensuous Scholarship*, pp. 27 and 32. See also, *The Cinematic Griot*, pp. xvi, 48, 50, 94 and 221.

69. Stoller, *Sensuous Scholarship*, p. xv. For the call to mixed genres, see also pp. 39, 40 and 47; and Stoller, *The Taste of Ethnographic Things*, pp. 32, 142, and 153; and *The Cinematic Griot*, pp. 208–9 and 217.

70. Stoller, *The Taste of Ethnographic Things*, pp. 144–5; and Stoller, *The Cinematic Griot*, pp. 212–13.

71. Stoller, *The Taste of Ethnographic Things*, p. 9; see also p. 138.

72. Stoller, *Sensuous Scholarship*, p. 36. On the violently amoral world of Songhay sorcery, see also pp. 12–13; and Stoller and Olkes, *In Sorcery's Shadow*, pp. 109–19, 204–5, 221–2, and 225–9; Stoller, *The Taste of Ethnographic Things*, p. 119; and *The Cinematic Griot*, pp. 113–17.

73. Jeanne Favret-Saada, *Deadly Words: Witchcraft in the Bocage* (London: Cambridge University Press, [1977] 1980); Larry Peters, *Ecstasy and Healing in Nepal* (Malibu: Udena Publications, 1981); Michael Harner, *The Way of the Shaman* (New York: Harper and Row, 1980).

74. Though the Lukan version (9:1-10a) does not have the "like the teacher" phrase found in Matthew, Dale Allison comments that it involves, "an implicit call to imitate Jesus." Dale C. Allison, Jr., "Matthew," in John Barton and John Muddliman, eds., *The Oxford Bible Commentary* (Oxford: Oxford University Press, 2001), p. 858.

75. In Mark, the question of Jesus's identity does not split the commissioning pericope, but comes immediately after it.

76. Cf. also, Mt. 13:54b-57a; Lk. 16:22b.

77. Cf. also Mk 2: 7; Mt. 9:3.

78. John P. Meier, *A Marginal Jew: Rethinking the Historical Jesus, Vol II: Mentor, Message, and Miracles* (New York: Doubleday, 1994), p. 1045.

79. Cf. also, Mt. 12:24; Lk. 11:15.

80. Bruce J. Malina, *The New Testament World: Insights from Cultural Anthropology*, 3rd edition (Louisville Kentucky: Westminster/John Knox Press, 2001), pp. 60 and 62. Malina is a member of the "Context Group," a collective of scholars who take social scientific, including anthropological, approaches to Scripture, and emphasize this point regarding Jesus's communal identity more than most scholars. I am not going to enter into the debate her about whether anthropology is a social science or a more broadly hermeneutical discipline or some combination of the two. For now, it is only necessary to point out that the Context Group identifies itself as taking social scientific approaches to the New Testament, and includes anthropology under this description. See www.contextgroup.org.

81. Biblical scholars who identify Jesus as a charismatic include, for instance, John G. Gager, *Kingdom and Community: The Social World of Early Christianity* (Englewood Cliffs: Prentice-Hall, 1975); John H. Schutz, "Charisma and Social Reality in Primitive Christianity," *Journal of Religion* 54 (1974): 51–70; James D. G. Dunn, *Jesus and the Spirit: A Study of the Religious and Charismatic Experience of Jesus and the First Christians as Reflected in the New Testament* (Grand rapids, MI: William B. Eeerdmans Publishing Company, 1997); Gerd Theissen and Annette Merz, *The Historical Jesus: A Comprehensive Guide* (Minneapolis: Fortress Press, 1998), Chapter 8, "Jesus as a Charismatic: Jesus and His Social Relationships," especially

pp. 190–1. For a critique of the identification of Jesus as a charismatic, see Bruce J. Malina, "Jesus as Charismatic Leader?," *Biblical Theology Bulletin* 14, no. 2 (1984): 55–62. In my judgment, given the pervasiveness of Weber's understanding of charisma in the social sciences, the onus is on the interpreter who wishes to use the term with regard to Jesus as to how he or she means it in distinction from the Weberian usage. One way to do this is to provide at least a glimpse of the historical usages of the term. For a helpful historical overview, see John Potts, *A History of Charisma* (New York: Palgrave Macmillan, 2009). A more polemical account can be found in Philip Rieff, *Charisma: The Gift of Grace, and How It Has Been Taken Away from Us* (New York: Vintage, 2008).

82. Weber, *Economy and Society*, vol. II (Berkeley, Los Angeles, and London: University of California Press, 1978), pp. 1115 and 1117.

83. It is important to distinguish the view that Jesus was mad from the one that he was possessed by Beelzebul (Mk 3:19-22; Mt. 12:24; Lk. 11:14-15). The charge that he "has Beelzebul" is a recognition that he has power—"and by the ruler of demons he casts out demons"—but does not have the religious authority—the Spirit—to exercise such power. The claim of madness is that he cannot be associated with anyone. It is a modern preconception that possession (even by the devil) is equivalent to madness.

84. Cf. Dunn, *Beginning from Jerusalem*, pp. 165–6.

85. I am aware of Jn 3:22: "After this Jesus went into the Judean countryside, and he spent some time with them and baptized." This line must be read in light of the clarifying Jn 4:1-3: "Now when Jesus learned that the Pharisees had heard, 'Jesus is making and baptizing more disciples than John'—although it was not Jesus himself but his disciples who baptized— he left Judea and started back to Galilee." Here, the author of John goes out of his way to indicate that Jesus did not baptize. As we have seen, the fact that the disciples appropriate the practice from someone other than Jesus does not, for them, threaten Jesus's authority. John Meier's argument that Jesus practiced baptism is a strained one. Here, Dunn is on firmer ground when he argues that the early post-Pentecost community took the practice over from John the Baptist. See Dunn, *Beginning from Jerusalem*, pp. 185–9.

86. Cf. Acts 2:21, 38; 3:6, 16; 4:7-12, 17-18, 30; 5:40-41; 8:12; 9:34; 10:43, 48; 19:14-16.

87. See also Acts 2:38; 3:16; 4:17-18, 30; 5:40-41; 8:12; 9:34; 10:48; and 19:14-16.

88. Beginning with D. F. Strauss, this shift has often been articulated in terms of the movement from the "Jesus of history" to the "Christ of faith," but this way of phrasing the matter rules out the possibility—lived out by the earliest post-Pentecost community—that the two may be viewed as inextricably intertwined. D. F. Strauss, *Der Christus des Glaubens und der Jesus der Gischichte* (Berlin: Duncker, 1865). Dunn writes about the shift in terms of one "from believing *in response to* Jesus to believing *in* Jesus." Dunn, *Beginning from Jerusalem*, p. 10.

89. Cf. also Mt. 10:1-11:1; Mk 6:7-30; and Lk. 10:1-20.

90. For commentators who dismiss the practice of sharing goods outright as simply a Lukan creation, see F. C. Baur, *Paul: The Apostle of Jesus Christ*, vol I (London: Williams and Norgate, 1873), p. 32; Ernst Haenchen, *The Acts of the Apostles: A Commentary* (Louisville, KY: Westminster John Knox Press, 1971), pp. 193–6, 232–5. For an account that suppresses its importance, see Dunn, *Jesus and the Spirit*, 16, and *Beginning from Jerusalem*, pp. 181–4.

91. Interview with Sr. Mary Clementina, 25.

92. Interview with clan elder.

93. Judy Adoko and Simon Levine, *Land Matters in Displacement: The Importance of Land Rights in Acholiland and What Threatens Them* (Kampala: Civil Society Organizations for Peace in Northern Uganda (CSOPNU) and Land and Equity Movement in Uganda (LEMU), 2004):

5; available at http://www.land-in-uganda.org/assets/LEMU-Land%20Matters%20in%20 Displacement.pdf.

94. See the Second Vatican Council, *Lumen Gentium*, Chapter V, pars. 39–42. It is the council's *Gaudium et Spes* that addresses the church specifically "in the modern world."

95. See OECD, *In it Together: Why Less Inequality Benefits All* (Paris: OECD Publishing, 2015), at http://www.keepeek.com/Digital-Asset-Management/oecd/employment/in-it-together-why-less-inequality-benefits-all_9789264235120-en#page3; and Richard Fry and Rakesh Kochhar, "America's wealth gap between middle-income and upper-income families is widest on record," at http://www.pewresearch.org/fact-tank/2014/12/17/wealth-gap-upper-middle-income/.

96. CARA Religious Life Research, at http://cara.georgetown.edu/CARAServices/rellife. html; and Michael Lipka, "The number of Catholics is growing, so why are there fewer parishes?" *Pew Research Center* (November 6, 2014), at http://www.pewresearch.org/fact-tank/2014/11/06/the-number-of-u-s-catholics-has-grown-so-why-are-there-fewer-parishes/.

97. Carol Glatz, "Church Is Growing Worldwide, Especially in Asia, Africa, Vatican says," *Catholic Review* (May 13, 2013), at http://www.catholicreview.org/article/faith/vocations/church-is-growing-worldwide-especially-in-asia-africa-vatican-says.

98. Interview with Sr. Ventorina Achora, 21.

99. Interview with Sr. Rosalba Akello, 12.

CHAPTER 5
GAPS: THE LIMITS OF MIMESIS

"Do you think it will bother him more for a white man or for a woman to wash his genitals?"

"It does not matter to him. He is dirty and he is hungry. He just wants a bath and food."

Sister Cecilia and I are bathing Santo again. The dirt has colored him a light red-brown since our last visit. His skin is normally that shade of black that is so dark it seems purple, like a starling. His son, Komakec, is off again somewhere partaking in the early morning routine of many of the men at Pabbo IDP camp of drinking the gin-like home-distilled *arege* from Coke bottles or plastic baggies. Komakec's wife says that there is no way in hell that she is going to take care of two men.

Now I am bent over Santo in his shelter. I pause after rinsing his chest and stomach. I drop my washcloth in the red plastic basin we brought with us and wring it out, then dip it in the cleaner water of the blue one. I look over to Sister Cecilia and ask her my question. I am asking her, I later realize, whether there really is or can be a situation, however fleeting, where there is "no longer Jew or Greek, there is no longer slave or free, there is no longer male or female." Or is Frantz Fanon right in *Black Skin White Masks*? "You come too late, much too late. There will always be a world—a white world—between you and us."[1]

* * *

Mimesis stakes its claim on the possibility that one person can in fact become in nontrivial ways like another. That claim has been drawn upon for the colonial purpose of making others more like white Europeans, with oppressive and frequently fatal results. And despite the mid-twentieth-century move to political independence on the part of African nations, the inheritance of past practices, given new force by more recent patterns of neocolonialism, continues to shape social and cultural interaction. How, then, can Western ethnographers engage the other in places like sub-Saharan Africa in ways that do not simply reinforce the status quo? This is one kind of question that mimetic scholarship needs to take up in this, the "discernment" stage in the doing of anthropological theology. We need to attend to the economic, cultural, racial, and even theological gaps between self and other—and the power relationships that these gaps point toward—if we are to avoid putting forward a romanticized account of mimesis.

In this chapter, I limn the gaps that have marked my effort to live among and follow—to apprentice myself to—people of northern Uganda and South Sudan like Sister Cecilia in Pabbo IDP camp. In the first part of the chapter, I present these gaps as I have encountered them in light of economic, racial, and theological concerns made clear to me by the people themselves in the encounters. In most exchanges, Acholi did not want me to become like them, but rather to use my difference—my economic and cultural power relative to them—to their advantage. I then, in the second part, display how theology can be used to downplay and even blot out the differences between researcher and local, and this for the worse. Interestingly, I use the case of a qualitative sociologist, Loïc Wacquant, to display this problem. Wacquant, despite his sociological pedigree, uses religiously oriented language to erase the differences between him and the African American Southside Chicago boxers he is researching. Social scientists are right to worry about this kind of religious reasoning. While mimesis does not—*pace* Elizabeth Castelli—necessarily involve a quest for sameness (as distinct from likeness), the temptation to seek sameness remains strong, and this is especially the case in theological modes of ethnography where claims of transcendence can lead the quest for likeness to ignore the reality of steadfast cultural, social, and economic differences. In the third part of this chapter, I set out how the social sciences have worked to maintain the gap between self and other in the field, first through the practice of "ethical neutrality" in the name of science on the part of early researchers, and then through the effort of reflexive self-neutralization for the sake of egalitarianism by more recent scholars. Still, theology does have resources for a suitably chastened mimesis that adequately recognizes difference, and I end this chapter that one such resource is the claim that Jesus Christ, the ultimate Other, is finally inimitable.

Whiteness made visible: The gap in Acholiland

"Munno. Bin kany."

White man. Come here.

The man selling sundry items by the roadside wants my attention. It is an easy enough moniker to work. Munno: white man or, more precisely, European. I am one of only two whites living in the camp of over 65,000 people, the other being an Irish nun who has been here for years and who few people like because, as Olweny says, "She is mean."

"Pe atye munno," I reply. "Atye Acholi matar."

I am not a European. I am a white Acholi.

It is good enough for a laugh from the women selling roasted corn for three cents an ear. The man is doubly caught off guard, by the joke and by the fact that I speak some Acholi. Few whites get out of their Land Cruisers—a generic term, like Kleenex, that the Acholi use for all SUVs—for more than the couple hours it takes to deliver foodstuffs, and are never the ones lifting the bags. Fewer still attempt to learn the language. The emergency relief director for Catholic Relief Services—a white Californian—has been in northern Uganda for ten months, and does not know a word of the language. She is not apologetic about the fact.

"Icito kwene?"

Where are you going?

He is curious now.

"Ka cuk."

To the market.

A child walks out from behind a tin-roofed building and sees me.

"Munno. Munno. Munno."

It is less a greeting to me than a signal to other children that a white man is in the area if they want to come have a look. He is saying the word like it is a flashing light—each utterance a staccato bark, with the effect of punctuating the pauses in between.

"Munno. Munno. Munno."

Soon eight or nine children fall in behind me as I walk the main road of the camp. When I turn and check a minute or two later, there are over twenty. The word now becomes a chant, even a taunt, with the first syllable drawn out and inflected downwards; the second syllable—clipped and accented—shooting up.

"Muuuu-no. Muuuu-no."

* * *

Practitioners of critical race theory and white studies often claim that a chief characteristic of whiteness is that it is invisible to those who are white. An abridged version of Peggy MacIntosh's "White Privilege: Unpacking the Invisible Knapsack" is ubiquitous on websites and in edited volumes addressing whiteness, and her view is standard in the literature. "I have come to see white privilege as an invisible package of unearned assets that I can count on cashing in each day, but about which I was 'meant' to remain oblivious. White privilege is like an invisible weightless knapsack of special provisions, maps, passports, codebooks, visas, clothes, tools, and blank checks."[2] James Baldwin articulates this view earlier when he writes, "Being white means never having to think about it."[3]

However, virtually all critical race theory and whiteness studies focus on the situation in the United States. Articles that address whiteness in a global context tend to merely extend, rather than challenge, the claim of invisibility because they attend to the attitudes and statements of Americans who, even by American standards, are in situations of enormous power, for instance, governmental and pharmaceutical representatives.[4] Correspondingly, and oddly, postcolonial studies after Fanon has largely ignored race.[5] Alfred Lopez, in a volume intended to address this lacuna, suggests that this may be because of a "simple conflation." In his words, "whiteness in this context may be so closely associated with colonial domination that no further distinction seems necessary or desirable."[6] Whatever the reason, critical race theory, white studies, and postcolonial studies have, for the most part, failed to address adequately how whiteness operates in the global context.[7] The irony is that the simple and perhaps simplistic projection of a conception of whiteness onto the global context—whether from the American context or the perspective of colonial studies—has made on-the-ground whiteness invisible to the theorists of whiteness themselves.

However, for the white anthropologist in certain contexts, his whiteness brings a quite visible complication—I am not saying impediment—to the participant observer methodology. In my research in northern Uganda and South Sudan, I have found that I, as a white male, enter into a field of already-set expectations as to my behavior. My task has not been that of making the invisible visible to myself and other whites, but to make what is already visible intelligible. If we are to use a pair of ocular metaphors, then, it is not that of invisibility versus visibility, but of myopia versus focus.

* * *

"Will you remember us?"

It is two weeks before I will be leaving Pabbo, so Justin's question at first seems odd to me. Then I figure that he has seen other whites go and not return, not keep up contact. They may not have told the whites back in America what they have seen and witnessed in northern Uganda. Maybe what he is asking me is less that I stay in contact than that I testify in the United States to what is going on here.

Justin is a catechist. In a continent where there are eight thousand people for every priest, lay persons are of necessity prime evangelists. Justin wears a dark ballcap and a climate-bleached t-shirt that says, "Angelo Negri: Light in Darkness" around a faded likeness of the bishop. The LRA has killed seventy-five catechists in the war. I met the widow of one earlier this week. When she tried to resist the rebels, they set her hands on fire. There is a lot to remember and a lot to tell.

"Yes. I will remember you. And I hope to come back next year."

"Because we catechists have it very difficult."

I nod. Yes. Yes. We are standing under a mango tree just outside the parish compound, on top of, I am later told, a mass grave of Acholi killed by the government army, the UPDF. Although the mangos are not ripe yet, only those at the very top of the tree remain. Hungry children have knocked the rest off with sticks and eaten them green and hard.

"We earn only seven thousand eight hundred for six months. That is not very much, is it?"

I hesitate, startled by what seems to be a new line of questioning. I do the computation anyway. It is about four U.S. dollars.

"No."

The conversation—or, more accurately, my perception of it—begins to shift.

"Can you find me a friend in America?" he asks.

His reaction prompts recollections from my first trip to Uganda. An assertive young man extended a pad and pen toward me as I walked to Mass in Kyarusozi in western Uganda and asked to exchange addresses. "I have always wanted a friend in America." His letter arrived two months later with a request to sponsor his schooling. Conversation decoded: In discourse between blacks and whites in Uganda, to "remember" is to fund-raise, to "befriend" is to become a benefactor, and to be white is to be constantly reminded that you are the promise of both.

I look up at the mango tree and then at Justin.

"I'll see what I can do."

* * *

Anthropological and other disciplinary study of patronage systems has seen two sea changes in analysis. Research coming out of the 1960s and earlier tends to view the patron-client relationships, however asymmetrical, as mutually beneficial. The client develops a personal relationship with the patron in order to gain political and economic access, while offering service to the patron. The relationship is often unofficial, but is no less formal for being so.[8] The 1970s bring Marxist analysis to the idea of patronage, with the argument that the determinant is class domination. Appeals to the personal nature of the relationship and to its complementarity simply mask its fundamental unjustifiability.[9] In the 1990s, some authors begin to argue that what is often pejoratively called "corruption" is not the result of a failed set of relationships, but rather the well functioning of what is merely a different kind of system than that of the modern West. While not as uncritical of patronage systems as the earliest research, neither do these studies view patronage systems as necessarily dysfunctional.[10]

The white theologian *cum* anthropologist in Uganda steps off the plane and into a field of interwoven patronage relationships. How he is to understand, assess, and respond to these relationships depends in large part on his previously held empirical assumptions and normative judgments about patronage. Do patronage systems arise only when states fail and unofficial alternative sources of power fill the void? Or are they alternative forms of political, economic, and cultural relationship that can also be legitimate? To shift from the language of anthropology and political science to ethics: Is patronization intrinsically evil? Can one weigh consequences in assessing an act of patronage? Do the evil consequences always outweigh the good ones? More theologically: Can two Christians relate as patron and client? Or do we add, "There is no longer patron or client," to Gal. 3:28?

* * *

"I need your help. God has sent you to me."

Orach Otim is a large man[11]—six-two or so, perhaps two hundred ten pounds. Oddly, he looks like he once was larger, though never fat. It is in his face. He looks like Magic Johnson—same large eyes and expressive mouth—but a version of the man who has lost his effervescence and is shot through with sorrow. He was the elected leader of Pabbo when it first became a camp, but his outspokenness got him arrested by the UPDF. Now we are meeting clandestinely in the back room of a store. I give the gawkers at the door some change so that they will go away.

Even shrunken, Orach has a way of taking up the whole of the couch across from me. He leans forward across the coffee table between us and spreads his hands over the papers he has laid out there. I sit on the front edge of my chair to examine them.

"I have kept careful documentation. I have kept a diary for ten years. Everything is there. Names. Dates. You know about the mass grave under the mango tree by the parish compound. I know the commander who did this. I can give you the names of people in the ground."

"What do you want me to do?"

"I want you to be my Charlie Wilson."

"Who is Charlie Wilson?"

"The man who campaigned in the United States on behalf of the *mujahideen* in Afghanistan. He got Congress to recognize what was going on there. To give support."

"But I am not a lobbyist. I do not know how to go about lobbying Congress. I am an academic. I write things. Articles."

"Look at me. I cannot even make love to my wife. They tied a cord around my testicles and forced me to jump off of a box."

I flinch. I am sure he sees it.

"They kept me in a room with two inches of water for eight days. I had no way to relieve myself except in a bucket in a corner, and they never emptied it. It overflowed. You know it overflowed. There was no way for me to lie down to sleep. Eight days. When my wife first came to the prison, they just said, 'We do not know where he is.'"[12]

Orach is now out on bail after a second arrest and imprisonment on charges of treason. He goes for a hearing to extend his bail next week. If the judge does not extend the bail, Orach goes back in prison. We think—hope, really—that this will not happen, that the purpose of bail is simply to pose the threat of reincarceration, and so keep Orach quiet.

"What do you want me to do?"

"You need to tell them what is going on here. I need a partner to collaborate with me to help get the story out. I need a computer and training how to use it. I need money to support me because I have no job. There are no jobs for me here. I can put all this information on a disk. And I need internet. You can use the information. I need you to tell the people in the United States what is going on."

Orach sits back as a signal that he has completed his appeal. I continue examining the papers on the table to avoid looking at him.

I know the meaning of the word "partner" and its analogues in this context now. Earlier in the week, I met a man while in Gulu buying supplies. He heard me speaking Acholi to the woman in the shop, and turned to me. After initial greetings, he said, in English, "So, we can join together and collaborate on a project to help the elderly in Gulu. There are many elderly in Gulu who need help. It is easy to get money in the United States, yes? We can collaborate."

My attention turns back to Orach. I think first of the more immediate risks, and look up.

"If I write about you, won't the UPDF be angry and come after you?"

He sits forward again, plants his elbows on knees and clasps his hands—the only things that keep him from leaning even further across the table to touch foreheads. As it is, we are inches apart.

"All I have is the truth. They have taken everything else. They can do nothing to me that they have not already done. I am not afraid of death. They have already taken my life. My only hope is in the truth."

Orach and I say our parting words, and agree to continue the conversation. I exit the door and see that the gawkers have returned. The leader among them holds a knotted baggie of *arege*, like a child with a goldfish bag—same beaming sense of chosenness in a missing-tooth smile—only without the goldfish.

Back in the parish compound, the questions flicker in time with the paraffin lamp on my desk: Is altruistic patronage bad *tout court*? Is there such a thing as patronage on behalf of justice? What would it look like?

* * *

One of the critiques of whiteness studies is that it does not take into adequate account the socioeconomic basis of racism, and the fact that in a class society, even those who are white-skinned may be considered "white-skinned negroes."[13] In the northern Ugandan context, the transferability of race manifests itself in one key way: there are some people who are more black—read, "backward," poor, lower in the strata of the patronage system—than other black Africans. The Acholi are not only on the whole darker-skinned than most southern Ugandans, they are also often described as less modern and more "backward" by others in the country. In part, this is a result of the colonialization process, where the British made Kampala, in the south, the administrative center of Uganda, and sought out the Acholi for the soldier-warrior class.[14] Some of the Acholi, in attempting to modernize, further this view themselves. This is the nub of Okot p'Bitek's poem, *Song of Lawino*, which is a wife's lament of her changed husband. *Lawino* is the most widely read Acholi literary work.

My husband pours scorn
On Black People,
He behaves like a hen
That eats its own eggs
A hen that should be imprisoned
  under a basket . . .
He says Black People are
  primitive

And their ways are utterly
    harmful,
Their dances are mortal sins
They are ignorant, poor and diseased!

Ocol says he is a modern man,
A progressive and civilized man,
He says he has read extensively
    and widely
And he can no longer live with
a thing like me . . . [15]

Ocol does not dispute Lawino's account. In the correlative poem, *Song of Ocol*, he says,

You Pigmy men
Skinning the elephant
With rusty knives,
I see your children
Happy, dancing,
Swinging from branch to
    branch
Like naked hairless
Black Apes.[16]

And elsewhere:

What is Africa
to me?

Blackness,
Deep, deep fathomless
Darkness;

Africa
Idle giant
Basking in the sun,
Sleeping, snoring,
Twitching in dreams;

Diseased with a chronic illness,
Choking with black ignorance,
Chained to the rock
Of poverty . . .

Stuck in the stagnant mud
Of superstitions,
Frightened by the spirits
Of the bush, the stream,
The rock,
Scared of corpses . . .

Mother, mother,
Why,
Why was I born
Black?[17]

That the realities described are not simply in the mind of a poet who died in 1982 is evident in statements Ugandan president Yoweri Museveni made on a trip to Gulu on the occasion of the installation of the new auxiliary bishop of the Archdiocese of Gulu, Sabino Odoki Ocan, on October 22, 2006: "We shall transform the people in the north from material and spiritual backwardness to modernity."[18]

If some blacks are more "black" than others, a select few are more "white." This, too, is Lawino's complaint:

And they dress up like white
        men,
As if they are in the white
        man's country.
At the height of the hot season
The progressive and civilized
        ones
Put on blanket suits
And woolen socks from Europe,
Long under-pants
And woolen vests,
White shirts;
They wear neck-ties from Europe.[19]

However, it is Ocol who articulates the core of what it means to be "white" in Africa, and his words—published by p'Bitek in 1966, soon after Uganda's independence and well before the presidencies of Amin and Museveni—are prescient, pointing to what will befall Orach Otim of Pabbo:

We have property

And wealth,
We are in power;

Trespassers must be jailed
For life,
Thieves and robbers
Must be hanged,
Disloyal elements
Must be detained without
     trial . . . [20]

Given the apparent transferability of race in a patronage culture, is it possible to close the gap and become a white *cum* "black" person allied in solidarity with the black *cum* "deep, deep fathomless darkness" black against the black *cum* "white" and the white? If race is transferable such that black can become "white" and black can be made even more "black," what are the possibilities and limits of whites becoming "black" as a way to subvert patronage? If I place my gifts, skills, and advantages at Orach Otim's disposal to serve his ends over against Museveni and the US government that continues to back him, can I, as some whiteness studies texts suggest, "disrupt whiteness from within" and "dismantle privilege"?[21]

I am encouraged by the lack of historical stability of the Acholi word, *munno*. Originally, the word meant all people other than blacks. Blackness was the norm. *Munno* meant nonblack. The word for white people was *otara*, coming from the word *tar* or "white." *Tar* was and is a positive term. For instance, *lak tar* means "white teeth," and is an indication of happiness (one is smiling) and strength (one has good teeth with which to chew food). The Acholi first applied *munno* to the Arab traders and slavers who came south into Acholiland.[22] British explorers did not arrive until 1862. King Mutesa I of Buganda in southern Uganda welcomed them as sources of protection against the slave traders, and, in 1894, Britain did make Uganda a protectorate. When the explorers and missionaries reached northern Uganda, the Acholi began to distinguish between Arabic and European people, first calling the Arabs *munno abac abac* ("neither black nor white") and the British *munno ingelesa* ("English white"). Still later, when the Roman Catholic Comboni missionaries came, the Acholi called them a third name, *munno hartung*, and realized that the latter were not interested in political rule in the same way.

Being Roman Catholic, then, might help close the black–white divide in Acholiland. Except for a few chiefs and men whom they made chiefs, the Anglican British bothered little to evangelize the Acholi. Their focus was on the kingdom of Buganda to the south. As a result, while a third of Uganda is Roman Catholic, close to three-quarters of the people in the north are. In the hierarchy that is Uganda, Catholics are at the bottom. It helps, then, that the Catholic community is my main entry into northern Uganda. Nuns of the Little Sisters of Mary Immaculate of Gulu introduce me to the Comboni missionaries, the director of the Catechist Training Center, and the priest in Pabbo, all of whom put me up during my research. When I want to venture further out in the bush and live in Lokung IDP camp, the director of the Catechist Training Center talks to the priest of Padibe parish who relays word to the catechists in Lokung that I am coming. Many in the north view Catholics as particularly dedicated Acholi, as those who stayed committed to the north throughout the war. In the twenty years of the war, the percentage of people in the north who are Roman Catholic increased due to the fact that large numbers of others left. To be Catholic and to be in the north, then, is to be in solidarity with the Acholi, the black of the black.

How far can a white man press his Catholicism to become "black"? Noel Ignatiev's provocative book, *How the Irish Became White*, argues that the Irish in the United States were once religiously, culturally and socioeconomically equivalent—or at least strongly analogous—to being "black."[23] The book is now a staple in white studies. If it is correct, then it carries with it an interesting possible corollary: perhaps a white person can reverse the process and become, once again, "black."

* * *

Gulu town is the urban center of northern Uganda. With a population of less than 40,000 before the war, it now has over 150,000 people due to migration during the conflict. If one is upper-middle class, one moves one's family to Gulu; if one is rich, one moves to Kampala or even London. There are whites too—many of them—and here they get out of their cars: NGO field directors, war researchers, and adventure travelers in shorts—considered indiscreet in Acholiland unless one is a child or on a soccer field—and sporting rolled bandana headbands knotted in the back.

Mega FM radio has been announcing the traditional Acholi culture night for over a week. Even the people in the camps are talking about it, though they cannot afford to go. Tickets are three thousand Uganda schillings for locals, ten thousand for others (read, *munni*). The event is at the Acholi Inn, the hotel of choice for senior UN representatives and high-ranking rebel officers who have surrendered and are now under government protection. They are subsidizing the UPDF commander who owns the hotel.

The crowd assembles early. The women attending sport technicolor *agomo*—dresses with puffed-out sleeves—and wear their hair long and straightened, a sign to others that their houses have running water. In the camps, the women shave their heads regularly, and do not let it grow longer than a quarter inch away from the scalp so as to avoid lice.[24] Long, straight hair conveys distance from pestilence, from "darkness." I am reminded of Lawino's words: "They cook their hair / With hot irons / And pull it hard / So that it may grow long . . . / They fry their hair in boiling oil / As if it were locusts, / And the hair sizzles / It cries in sharp pain / As it is pulled and stretched . . . / It lies lifeless / Like the sad and dying banana leaves / On a hot and windless afternoon."[25] The men in the audience at Acholi culture night wear button shirts and pressed trousers, if not coats and ties. It is the whites who dress down. They are, without exception, in t-shirts and with uncombed hair. Playing Africa.

Three Acholi with video cameras go up on stage for closer shots of the dancers. In the next set, I follow suit. The performer is Ajere, a singer-songwriter who plays the *nanga*, a flatboard string instrument with no neck that backs the Acholi version of the blues. He is special. This video is not for research; it is for me. Though I arrived early and got a first-row seat, the other videographers obstruct my view. I go up on stage in front of the side seats, but lie down on my side so as not to bother those who are seated there. Still, one of the women complains, saying something about the presumption of the *munno*. I do not catch everything, but turn and respond to her remarks anyway in a formal manner.

"An pe aloko leb Acholi maber," I myself do not speak Acholi well.

Again, the surprise of a *munno* speaking Acholi brings laughter. It seems that, for a moment, the boundaries dissolve.

No one is fooled, however. Despite everyone's effort at racial cross-dressing, no one challenges the fact that whites are charged more than three times the Acholi rate for the event. A cartoon in the Ugandan newspaper, *New Vision,* earlier that week depicts two black Ugandans watching a white man in t-shirt, shorts, and backpack. One says to the other, "Boy, that *muzungu* is really stinking." The other responds, "Yeah, stinking rich!"

* * *

There are first of all, then, economic limits to the pliability of race in Uganda. Although Museveni may be atop the patronage pyramid in Uganda, the fact remains that during the time of my fieldwork between 30 percent and 50 percent of the Ugandan government's budget had been from foreign aid.[26] There is little argument that Museveni is using the money for his own end of maintaining power. Foreign aid decreases the accountability he has to those within his own country and supports his patronage network within it. While such aid has been used to fund national primary education and other reforms, for instance, one study has shown that only 13 percent of Uganda's education budget reaches the schools. The rest is "captured by local officials and politicians."[27] The fact of corruption stirs debate over whether foreign aid as a whole is good or bad for the poor in Africa, whether it is reformable so that it can serve the poor or is beyond repair.[28] Still, it remains that as foreign aid exists now, it forms the economic backbone of an international system of patronage in which whites are at the apex.[29] Under this system, Museveni has to make Uganda at least *look* democratic to the whites. The language of freedom is the mask of international patronage, with elections the main marker of progress. In 2005–6, Museveni's failure to end the war in the North, combined with his alteration of the Ugandan constitution to allow him to run for a third term as president in a campaign in which he jailed his main opponent, led several countries to withhold portions of their donations. That the US government did not follow suit but rather increased its aid is less evidence that it was being used and so was not in control than that it is more concerned about Uganda as a post-9/11 East African ally than about human rights.

At once side-by-side and integrated with the intergovernmental patronage system is that which functions through nongovernmental organizations (NGOs). Some donors give money directly to NGOs through commercial banks, and do not go through Uganda's central bank. Other NGOs receive their funding not from governments at all, but from charitable donations and foundation grants. In Uganda, this has the effect of increasing the amount of money that government officials can skim because the administration can direct much of the NGO efforts to aid the north, allowing the officials in Kampala in the South to keep more of the foreign assistance that comes from states for themselves. And, often, even the aid monies intended for northern Uganda never get there. In 2012, for instance, $12.7 million in development assistance for the north disappeared in the Ugandan prime minister's office.[30]

On the ground in the north, the presence of NGOs means that even those people bypassed by the system that has Museveni's government and ethnic group at the center get pulled into the dynamics of patronage. The literature on development is replete with analyses—some more polemical than others—of the ways in which humanitarian and development aid increases dependence.[31] The impact in northern Uganda, felt first in the IDP camps during the conflict and now spread to the whole post-conflict region, is most evident in the way that money exchange has displaced other forms of relationship. As we heard in Chapter 4, when Sister Cecilia asked Santo's neighbor to rub the floor of his dwelling with a cow-dung mixture so as to rid it of lice, the woman responded, "How much will you pay me?," and I was reminded of Father Charles Olweny's ongoing complaint of the "NGO effect": "They do not know the people. They have no other way to relate to them. So when they meet with them, they pay them money. Now when I want to gather the people in my parish, they all expect to be paid."

Though I have made efforts at solidarity—living in the camps, using public transportation that often has amounted to the back of a pick-up truck, and speaking, however remedially, the language—by far, most Acholi with whom I have come into contact have viewed me—my whiteness—through the lens of the patronage system structured by international and nongovernmental aid. They watch, study, and assess me even more closely than I them. I am always also the ethnograph*ee*. Their study yields a variety of approaches. Sometimes they are direct—"I need money for drugs." At other times they are indirect, and engage in a kind of trolling for schillings—"I have not been feeling well. I have pain in all of my joints." Still other times, they misdirect—"Please, come into my house for some tea." Then, when we enter, "and these are the five orphans I have been taking care of." Their requests may be for material goods or for me to speak on their behalf. They do not want me to "disrupt" the system, let alone "dismantle" it. They want me to be a good patron.

* * *

"It is not enough."

"What?"

"You are stranding me."

Okec James[32] sits across from me in the dining room of the Catechist Training Center. It is well after mealtime, so we are alone. At sixteen years old, he is the male head of a family of at least six—there may be more. He wears a white t-shirt and blue basketball warm-up pants with stars going down the sides. They are too long for him and drag when he walks. I tell him that this is in style in the United States, and he smiles.

Okec's father died last year, probably of AIDS. We know this because his mother is in the hospital in Kitgum town for treatment. I have been to two funerals so far while in northern Uganda; both people died of AIDS. When the men die of AIDS, they do so in silence.

The rebels abducted and killed Okec's older brother when he was riding his bicycle home for school holiday. He was in S6—the equivalent of a senior in high school—and on the cusp of obtaining the virtually impossible in northern Uganda: a diploma in the camps.

The Training Center must seem the equivalent of a resort and spa to Okec. It has running water and—at least most of the time—electricity. He will have his own room tonight with an off-the-ground bed. But that is not why he came. The smile from my sartorial comment does not last long, and shifts into a frown. He has made the journey from Lokung IDP camp, where I had been staying, to request—no, demand—his school fees for the next year.

His visit seems presumptuous only to the uninitiated. When I first met Okec, a friend of the family I lived with in Lokung, I gave him a soccer ball. I had fit a dozen deflated used balls and a couple of pumps in a duffel to bring over with me. I gave Okec the last of the balls. To me it was simply a gift. To him it was the beginning of a relationship. The next day he brought over a couple of his friends and made an indirect request, where description of the situation is understood as proposal. "These are my friends Beatrice and Joseph. They are in P7. Next year they will be going to S1 and will have to pay fees." For Okec, the soccer ball signified a familiarity that sanctioned his serving as a broker between his friends and me. Later, Okec would write and direct morality plays that the Christian youth group would perform for my benefit.

Now he is making his own case.

"You are stranding me."

"You asked for 160,000 for school next year. I said that I would give it to you."

"I need to pick up my mother at the hospital and take her home. We need to get home."

A good patron anticipates the needs of his client. Of course Okec needs to get home. He literally has spent his last schilling getting to the Training Center.

"I could not even afford to pay the boda-boda that brought me here. You left me at the mission."

Okec had taken "taxis"—ridden in the back of trucks—to Gulu. He called when he reached Kitgum, about halfway between Lokung camp and Gulu. "I am coming to get you. Don't leave. I didn't have a chance to say good-bye." He spent his remaining schillings on a phone call from Gulu. "Where are you?" I told him, and he hung up before I could give directions. Instead of going to the Catechist Training Center, he went to a mission a couple miles down the road. I did not know where he was and could not reach him. Finally, he talked to a nun who knows me and made his way to the Training Center. No matter what explanation I try to give him, he considers the fault mine. "You left me at the mission." The words make me recall his earlier comment coming out of the chapel in Lokung after service one Sunday. He had been working for the International Refugee Council, but, in his account, they let him go when they discovered that he did not have a high school degree. "They abandoned me."

Now the charge is leveled at me, both for not knowing that he got dropped off at the wrong place and for not foreseeing that he needed money for his and his mother's return to Lokung. Strand. Leave. Abandon. These words, too, are part of the patronage system lexicon.

* * *

Omniscience, omnipresence, and omnipotence. These are the traits Christians traditionally assign to God. Most of the Acholi I met in the camps assigned them to me. Ojara, my host in Lokung camp, tries to explain. "White people bring all these things. This technology. And they work. Like magic. You are like gods. Even educated Acholi do not see that whites also have weaknesses and make mistakes, just like Acholi." Yet even Ojara is surprised when I tell him that I do not have enough money to cover both the medical costs and the care of orphans that the woman he has brought to me requests. Ojara's hospitality during my stay at Lokung carries with it his role as patronage broker. In the afternoons, when I sit outside of my quarters and write, he regularly brings me potential clients. After the woman unfolds her story, I hand Ojara 20,000 schillings.

> "This will cover transportation to Kitgum hospital, where she will receive care."
> He begins to hand it to her, but then looks back at me in surprise.
> "What about the orphans?"
> "I do not have enough for them."
> I had just come from my daily walk around the camp, toward the end of which I had thirty or so children following me. "Munno. Munno." A man chides, "Why don't you give them all something." I respond, "There are 22,000 people in Lokung. I cannot give them all something."
> Ojara keeps his eyes on me for a moment—shock, disappointment—and then turns to hand the money to the woman. My failure is his too, just as my presence increased his stature in the community.

* * *

Beatrice Oryema, a traditional Acholi spirit medium, agrees to call upon her *jogi* to speak to me. The session takes over an hour of incantation and response. She is sweating, but is refreshed rather than spent. She sends her daughter, Aber Auma, who is also an *ajwaka*, out to get me a bottle of *arege*, and the exchange begins.[33] I pay her ten thousand Ugandan schillings for her time. Aber returns with the drink to complete the deal, but first adds her own request to the bargain.

"Take my daughter, Beatrice's granddaughter, with you back to America."

All of the portrayals of Jesus and Mary that I have seen in the north thus far—in murals, statues—are of white people. White people on the cross. White people ascending into heaven. Iconic theology underwrites the economic system. P'Bitek provides an account of an Acholi's conversion to Christianity as his being "taken" by "the white man."[34] Now Beatrice and Aber are entreating me to take their granddaughter/daughter.

I assume that the girl must be an infant, one too many mouths to feed, but I am wrong.

"She is a good girl. Fourteen and in P7. Please."

I do not wish to offend her, so I reply that I will need to check with my wife. In the patronage world, equivocation is a polite way of saying no. Over the next several days, Aber's proposal stays with me and is repeated unbidden by others.

"Bring me to America with you. I can live with you."

They want to be "taken by the white man" too.

That Thursday, Aber performs her own incantations for me, after which she comments,

"It will be a long time before this war ends. After that there will be a second war, a war among tribes. It too will go on for a long time."

I assume she is functioning as a seeress and that one of her *jogi* has informed her of this future in a dream. However, when I ask her how she knows these things, she answers sociologically.

"All the kids know is fighting. The movies they watch are all fighting movies. Chuck Norris. Van Damm."

She is right. Enterprising Acholi bring generators to the larger camps and show action movies. I watch *Rambo: First Blood, Part II* for the first time in the parish mission in Padibe. One of the most frequent poses I get from young boys wanting their picture taken is that of a kung fu fighter in a preparation-to-fight stance—slightly crouched, arms bent, forearms up at different angles, hands straight and ready to strike.

Aber finishes, "And when they play, all they play is war. They pick up long sticks and one says, 'I will be LRA and you be UPDF.' All they know is war."

Aber simply wants her daughter out of extreme poverty and violence. If the white person is God, then the United States is God's kingdom, the city on the hill.

* * *

"Do you want to learn to speak Acholi?"

The young man catches up to me after I finish talking to an elder in the market in my broken Acholi and am heading home. He is about Okec James' age, but is shorter and with ragged clothes.

"I already have a teacher."

We walk in silence for a minute or two.

"So you want to learn to speak Acholi?"

Again, "I have a teacher."

"Oh."

More minutes of silence.

"Do you know how someone like me can get a friend in America?"

"No."

"No? You have no friends?"

The bargaining has begun in earnest. I try equivocation.

"I have my family."

"Only your family? That is it? No friends?"

It is not working. It is time for me to be direct.

"What you mean by friend and what I mean by friend are two different things. You mean someone who can pay your school fees."

He nods without any obvious embarrassment. He is not dissuaded.

"How about a friend just to write back and forth? Like in school?"

"I do not know."

"You were not in school?"

"That was a long time ago. I am older than I look."

We walk in silence some more. Peasant farmers pass by in the opposite direction and he teaches me the Acholi words for ax and hoe. A group of children begin following us, shouting, "Cala! Cala!" My picture! My picture! I tell them, "Camera pe"—No camera—and they leave. The young man says to me, "It is a big thing for them to get a picture taken by a white man. They run and tell the others."

My shooing away of the children seems to make him realize that I am not going to be a good source of money. He turns curious.

"Are there many blacks in America?"

"Yes, about thirteen percent of the people; so there are more than forty million blacks in America."

"Really?"

"Yes."

"I thought that you had laws where blacks could not live there."

"No. There are about forty million blacks. About fifty years ago there were laws passed where if you had a restaurant you had to serve everyone, and if there is a bathroom, anyone can go there. But there is still prejudice. There are many places where there are almost no blacks, but other places in America where there are many blacks."

"So there are blacks there. I did not know that."

His lack of empirical knowledge is as common as the interpretation that the United States is an exclusive place. Many Acholi tell me that they did not know that English is the primary language. They thought it was Latin, assuming a link between contemporary American prevalence and historical Roman Catholic mission. It makes sense that the gods must be related. Educated Acholi living in Kampala—one a school teacher and the other a receptionist at a hotel—come to Pabbo for their father's funeral and are surprised when I tell them that a foreigner who marries any U.S. citizen can also become a citizen. They think the requisite is that one marry a *white* U.S. citizen. They are only too aware that only few are chosen for the promise that is America. Those chosen, in turn, are miserly with their fortune. The most frequently spoken perception during my research is that United States law forbids couples to have more than a certain number of children. The assumed number varies—anywhere between two and five—but the idea is the same: Americans do not even let the souls of their own potential children in.

We reach the parish and the young man turns to head back to where he first spotted me.

"It is a shame that you do not have your camera. They run and tell their friends that a white man has taken their picture."

If they cannot go to America in person, the children reason, maybe they can through their image.

* * *

Displeasure at whites and their construal as being in some way divine comes in a number of forms. One is the disappointment when the white person's resources are found not to be endless, and so he is found to be a not very good god. We are then gods who, in Okec James's words, "abandon" the Acholi. We are occasions for lament. At other times, continuous disappointment leads to the realization that whites are not gods at all, and that our representation of ourselves as such—suffering more on the Cross for having come to such a hellish place and ascending to heaven for having suffered—is a sham that inflicts severe damage on and even destroys Acholi culture. We have pressed our economic advantage such that the Acholi, according to poet Christine Oryema-Lalobo, have no choice but to, "eat from charity / handed out / by the white man / in deep silence."[35] This is why an earlier poet, Omal Lakana, wrote: "Adok Too / Adok Too / Kono apoto i wi munu" (If I could become Death / If I could become Death / I would fall on the white man).[36] Lakana became so well known by this poem that he came to be called Adok Too. He was jailed in 1938 by the British for being too vocal in opposition to their presence in Uganda.

The occasions when I experienced the most forceful rejection and disdain for being an outsider occurred precisely at those moments when I was invited to become more of an insider, more Acholi:

This is the third night that the drums are playing—joyously rumbling and shouting, really—somewhere off the south edge of Magwi, South Sudan. This long and this loud, it has to be either a wedding or a funeral.

I take a walk each evening before dark. I am expected to be back in the compound before the stars come out because even though the SPLA government army has arrived to protect the people from the rebel LRA, this has made the town little safer. The diocesan clinic has been closed for four days because SPLA soldiers abducted and beat two health care workers when the latter refused the order to hand over one of their patients.

But the sky is still streaked with pink, and Father Joseph Otto commented that the drums are a sign of peace: even though the LRA looted as recently as last month, the people feel that they can dance all night—and they do. Last night's celebration tapered off only at eight o'clock this morning.

So I leave the road and take a path toward the sound. It is a funeral. By the time I get to the gathering, the drums have stopped, and two men clutching long sharpened sticks as spears take turns moving—run, stop, hop, skip, run—across a cleared area in front of the crowd, narrating and reenacting the dead man's life in a call-and-response with each other. The crowd—not merely an audience—often interrupts with ululations and laughter. They honor the deceased so that he returns as a benevolent ancestor rather than as *cen*, an unsettled or even vengeful spirit.

I stand at a respectful distance of about thirty meters, still on the path as if a passerby. Two men, drinking on the occasion or perhaps just drinking, come to tell me that this is a "second grieving." The Acholi have two funerals for the dead, one within three days of the death and one later, for when all the family, relatives, and clan members can gather. The two men cannot agree on how long ago the man died. One says four years, the other eight. Either way, the decades-long overlapping wars in South Sudan and northern Uganda have made the gathering impossible until now. All the more reason to celebrate. When a person has lived a long life and died of natural causes, the Acholi, after due grieving, dance to start up life again. In the early morning, men and women break off in pairs to make love to ensure that this new life will be more enduring. I find myself thinking, *I want a funeral where people dance.*

The drums start up again—three of them, one large, about three feet tall, and two smaller ones, goat skin pulled tight around hollowed wood and thumped by young men with no shirts. *Boom-'-ba-boom-boom, boom-'-ba-boom-boom* overlaid with *thakata-thakata-'-thak-thak, thakata-thakata-'-thak-thak.* This is a remote village; some of the women do not wear shirts either. Some have their infants wrapped to their backs with bolts of cloth. People, maybe thirty of them, dance in a circle around the drums—*shuffle-step-shuffle-shuffle-stomp, shuffle-step-shuffle-shuffle-stomp*—the two previous nights' dancing having thudded the grass into a ring of dry dirt. Dust rises and meets with a sky no longer streaked, but still orange, creating a haze where people come into focus only up close, silhouettes exploding into color.

They invite—no, urge—me to dance. I do. Most Americans stop dancing once they are past young adulthood. Here, if you are alive, you dance. A *mego*—an old woman, toothless and with the help of a walking stick—shimmies.

I shuffle when I am supposed to stomp, and step when I am supposed to shuffle, but the other dancers are forgiving. They smear my head with a double handful of ashes, designating me a lead dancer—*shuffle-step-shuffle-shuffle*-wait, what is next? They hand me a red plastic pitcher full of *kwete*, the local mash brew, to take a swig and pass on. "You honor us by coming, so we honor you." Unlike *arege*, *kwete* is low in alcohol. It is not intended to get you drunk, but to make you light. I think of it as a performance-enhancing drug for the rhythmically impaired. It seems to work. *Shuffle-step-shuffle-shuffle-stomp. Shuffle-step-shuffle-shuffle-stomp.* I get it, and soon I can join in the call-and-response.

At some point, someone asks me. "Don't you have a camera?" All white people have cameras. The question pulls me out of the dance.

"In the compound."

"Is it far?"

"No"

"You can take some pictures."

"A good idea," I think. I use photos and video when I am back home to help me recollect—and, in this way, re-collect—the field when I write.

There is only a little light. I run back to the compound. Father Joseph Otto and Robert, my Ugandan Acholi traveling companion, are there and look at me—sweat pressing through ash—with at first troubled but then bemused eyes. Robert and I return to the celebration, with photo and video cameras. The people are still dancing, but everything changes. I cannot dance and document at the same time. Some of the women cover up, recoiling under the flash of the camera's artificial light. I am given more *kwete*, but am just watching now. A spectator. A couple of the young men sidle up and ask me questions about the camera, though I cannot hear them above the drumming and singing. They back away into the fringe of the surrounding woods. Soon, two elders whom I had interviewed earlier in the day come up and warn Robert and me, "You better leave. We think those young men are planning to beat you."

And, like that, I am again reminded that I am an outsider.

The theological temptation to sameness

My work in northern Uganda and South Sudan, then, affirms due consideration of the gaps between self and other is important for those who understand and practice ethnography as a form of apprenticeship. This is because the premium placed on becoming *like* the other can lead to mistakenly thinking that we can become the *same* as the other. While mimesis does not *necessarily* involve a quest for sameness, a temptation to seek a sameness that erases differences often remains. And it is a temptation that is perhaps strongest in theologically interpreted contexts, as is evident, interestingly, in sociologist Loïc Wacquant's *Body & Soul: Notebooks of an Apprentice Boxer*.

As the book's subtitle indicates, Wacquant understands and practices ethnography as a mode of apprenticeship,[37] and his work has drawn comparison to that of Paul Stoller.[38] Like Stoller, he places the researcher's body in the middle of inquiry as the medium for perception and knowledge.[39] "Pugilistic knowledge" in particular is "transmitted by mimeticism."[40] To convey this knowledge in writing to his academic audience, Wacquant, again like Stoller, draws upon a mix of genres, some more analytic, others more sensual and vivid, with the aim of drawing the reader into the scene:[41]

> I slip on my red training gloves and climb into the ring. I'm all alone at first and it's a little intimidating to shadowbox in front of all the old-timers and the matchmaker Jack Cowen, who are watching me from the foot of the ring. I concentrate on throwing my jab well, on doubling up on it, on following it up with left hooks while keeping my feet firmly on the mat and turning my torso correctly. In the second round, Smithie (in a blue tank top and shorts, his hands wrapped in red, a white bandana around his forehead) climbs into the ring, and I can observe him up close and imitate his moves. He's like a boxing machine: bent forward slightly from the waist, his hands set out like a fan in front of his face, his gestures are short, precise, restrained, and so well coordinated they seem almost mechanical. He is streaming with sweat and his face looks serious to the point of sullenness; every gesture rips a Homeric grimace from him. I follow him like a living model: when he doubles up his jab, I double mine up; when he bends his legs to deliver a series of short uppercuts by slipping under the guard of his imaginary opponent, I do likewise. . . . And now Cliff also slips through the ropes and joins us. I love his short, low jab and try to imitate it. . . . *"Time out!"* We catch our breath.[42]

Such sensory quality leads Stoller in a review to comment, "*Body and Soul* is ethnography at its best,"[43] and in many respects this is accurate. Wacquant practices a disciplined physical, psychological, and even spiritual openness to the world of the boxing gym, and he frequently renders that world with refreshing immediacy.

However, the typically irenic Stoller also warns, "How disappointing it is for ethnographers to admit, and in my case it was a grudging admission, that the relationships they develop in the field, while close, are, in fact, not usually as special as they might think. This casts a provocative shadow over Loïc Wacquant's brilliantly rendered ethnography."[44] Other reviewers are not so kind. The Woodlawn Boys Club where Wacquant, a white Frenchman studying at the University of Chicago, boxes is in the heavily African American and economically marginalized South Side of Chicago. Judith Farquhar writes, "'Busy Louie' [Wacquant's *nomme de guerre*] had a very different starting point than, e.g., Curtis or Butch [two locals], and came to be embodied as a boxer in a way that was really quite different from theirs. For all his incorporation of the boxer's disciplined life, Wacquant's different trajectory makes a very big difference that, rather than being analyzed, tends to lurk outside the narrative of *Body and Soul*." Wacquant, therefore, is guilty of "conflating Busy Louie's body with those of his gym mates."[45]

The evidence supports Farquhar's (and others') reading. Though Wacquant provides a brief sketch of the racially manifested economic realities of the neighborhood around the boxing gym early on in the book, such analysis all but disappears in what follows. This development could perhaps be attributed simply to a genre shift to the kind of sense-filled first-person narratives found in apprenticeship ethnography except for the explicit statements that Wacquant makes along the way. Though he is the only white boxer in the gym, he is able to "blend in," he claims, because the sport of boxing is "egalitarian" and "colorblind," and because he is not like other whites in the United States: he is French, and African Americans have a good history with the French. Besides, he avers, he does not share "the *hexis* of the average white American." Such exculpatory reasoning leads Wacquant to claim in regards to the Woodlawn boxers after his one (and only) formal bout, "I am fully one of them."[46]

This "conflating," to use Farquhar's term, of self and other happens in *Body & Soul* despite the fact that racial themes recur in the first-person narratives: one boxer refuses to wait outside the white-neighborhood apartment of Wacquant, even after the latter's repeated insistence, because he knows he will be picked up by the police "for nuthin"; another club member wonders aloud before a match featuring a boxer from the suburbs, "How they get all those white guys to come out all the way to d'South Side like that?"; one says to another before the latter climbs into the ring, "Don't forget you're from Woodlawn, nigger!"; when Wacquant arranges for a French boxing team to come to the United States, he does not trust, despite their non-American status, that they will get a racial pass from the neighborhood, similar to Woodlawn, in which they will be staying: he has the doors to their quarters, "chained and padlocked *from the outside* so as to prevent any of them from risking going out into the neighborhood at night" (emphasis in original).[47] Again, it might be possible to make the case that this *is* how to raise the issue of race in narrative form, except for the fact that Wacquant claims in reference to the Woodlawn boxers to be "fully one of them." Despite his insistence that being French makes a difference and that he does not share the typical American *hexis*, then, Wacquant appears at key moments in *Body & Soul* to be carrying the quintessential white American invisible knapsack. How does this happen? My reading is that it takes place through his "theology" of boxing.

To deepen his account of what is involved in pugilistic mimesis, Wacquant draws on religious language. The boxing gym is a "sanctuary," where the "novice" undergoes an "initiation" that introduces him to a "catechism" consisting of "monastic penance" and "rituals of mortification."[48] Photos and posters on the walls form a "profane iconography" that functions much like the photos and paintings of Bishop Negri and Mother Angioletta do for the Little Sisters:

> In both layout and adornment, the gym constitutes something of a temple of the pugilistic cult by the presence on its walls of the major fighters, past and present, to whom the budding boxers from ghetto gyms devote a selective but tenacious adoration. Indeed, the champions demonstrate *in vivo* the highest virtues of the profession (courage, strength, skill, tenacity, intelligence, ferocity) and incarnate the various forms of pugilistic excellence. They may moreover intervene directly into the life of the most modest apprentice pug, as attested by the photograph of Mike Tyson flanked by DeeDee [the gym's coach] and Curtis [the gym's star boxer] prominently displayed on the main wall of the back room, which reflects a speck

of the symbolic capital of the star from the ghetto of Brooklyn on them. . . . The idea is thereby given of a great pugilistic "chain of being": that there would exist a continuity from the anonymous footsoldier of the most modest club to the global star.[49]

Though Wacquant briefly states that the "continuous and gradual 'ladder of mobility'" whispered by the posters and photos is an "illusion," he elsewhere views himself as part of the very chain of being that they convey. He finds it significant enough to write that former world champion Joe Louis "used to do his daily roadwork in the same Washington Park where I go running every morning." He also indicates that former champs Sonny Liston and Cassius Clay both "honed their skills" at the same tournament he is to enter.[50]

Describing the Woodlawn Boys Club as a sanctuary not only allows Wacquant to segment off his account of the activity that takes place within it from the environs outside, but also contributes to his failure to take up adequately how those environs continue to exhibit force *inside* the gym. More, the intensity of the workouts, which he describes as an "ascesis," leads to a form of pugilistic rapture that he at several points calls "intoxication," which is not so much a lifting out of the body but a profound inhabiting of it in such a way that it *appears* to lift one out of social context.[51] The posters and photos on the wall further the impression for club members that boxing is indeed a means through which they can leave their present social location. Segmentation, intoxication, and iconography combine in this theology of the "sweet science." And it leads Wacquant to overstate the degree to which he can inhabit, without remainder, the world of the gym. Such is the pull of boxing's chain of being that before he leaves for Harvard, Wacquant briefly considers quitting the academic life: "I'm at the point where I tell myself that I'd gladly give up my studies and my research and all the rest to be able to stay here and box, to remain 'one of the boys.'"[52] What his pugilistic theology obscures for him here is that even if he were to leave academia and stay at the gym, he would remain different in the significant sense that this for him would be a choice in a way that it is not for those from the local neighborhood who take up boxing. In this sense, he can never be "one of the boys." In a similar way, what most marked me off from most Acholi, particularly when the LRA conflict centered in northern Uganda, was that, within certain limits, I could come and go as I saw fit. I read *Body & Soul* as both an exemplar of apprentice ethnography with its vivid depictions and an object lesson on the liabilities of theological ethnography regarding the temptation to seek too-thorough a transcendence of finitude. If even a protégé of Bourdieu like Wacquant can succumb to (ultimately) theologically driven, socially decontextualized representation, then we are all vulnerable to the same syndrome.

For this and other reasons, social science itself has worked to carefully maintain the boundary between the researcher and the researched. While the exact driving force of these efforts has shifted—from the search for neutrality in "objective" investigation to the quest for what might be called self-neutralization due to a concern about the undue exercise of power—the long-standing consensus is that self–other boundary crossing is a bad idea. If anthropological theology is to draw from the social sciences, it needs to engage this history, and that is what I do in the next section of this chapter.

Maintaining the gap: From "ethical neutrality" to ethical neutralization

It is July, the month that the Acholi call *Odunge*, "severe starvation," because the food in the bins is gone and the crops in the field are not ready for harvest. Expected seasonal rains have not come, so the subsistence farmers cannot plant *sim sim* (sesame) as they usually do this time of year. The seeds will not germinate in dry soil. The World Food Program trucks have not arrived yet this month, and the people of Lokung IDP camp do not know when they will. The WFP does not announce drop-off dates for fear that the LRA will set up an ambush. When the trucks do come, men often sell their foodshares to buy *arege* liquor, setting off camp-wide marital disputes. A woman comes by my hut to ask me for money by lifting her shirt and showing me her shriveled stomach and breasts. *Amiro otoo*, she says. "I want to die." Residents of the camp cannot garden more than a mile out without undue risk of abduction, mutilation, or death at the hands of the LRA. Last year, eight women went further out to gather water during dry season. Members of the LRA tracked them, chose three, cut off their lips and ears, stripped all of them, and sent them back to the camp as a warning.

"We are cursed," Ojara, my host, tells me. We are seated outside his family's sleeping hut that he has given over to me for the duration of my stay. In this version of Acholi hospitality, the family sleeps on the soot-sprinkled floor of the cooking hut.

Ojara continues. "In three days in January 1997, the LRA killed 550 Acholi in Lokung sub-county. They did not use guns at first, but clubs and *pangas*. I lost a sister and her husband and nine children. They cut people up. Lips, the penises of men, the breasts of women. Then the army bombed Lokung to attack the rebels and 417 more people died."

"The Acholi people are cursed in a number of ways. First, Kony comes from a family of devil worshippers. The father went away and got lost. The woman also went away. When she came back, she was pregnant with Kony. Later the man came back. Kony was born and they became devil worshippers. He was strange from the beginning. Acting crazy and making himself disappear in front of people's eyes. He was a spirit diviner before he was a soldier. This is the first Acholi secret, that Kony is a devil worshipper."

"The second secret is that the Acholi leaders put a curse on the Acholi people. There was a soldier who killed a child. They searched for the man. He was already cursed, so they put a curse on the whole people. They buried the child, and side-by-side with its grave they dug another and put some *sim sim* in it, and said that when the *sim sim* rots, the curse will end. So the Acholi leaders put a curse on the people. The *sim sim* has not rotted. That is the second Acholi secret.

"The third secret is that the people are misled. The religious leaders say all religion is one because God is one. But we worship Jesus Christ." Ojara, a charismatic Catholic, points to the Bible in his hand. "We read it here."

"But they say, 'Let's get together and pray.' The Catholic, the Anglican and the Muslim. But this is the devil's work. There is one God, and the way is through Jesus Christ, who founded his church and built his church on the apostles. This is why their peace effort failed. It was bound to fail. The devil was misleading the Acholi religious leaders. The curse can only be lifted through prayer to the Sacred Heart of Jesus. The Muslim does not even think that the savior has come. They are still waiting for the savior. And the other Christians, they do not believe that communion is really a sacrament, the real body and blood of Christ. So it was bound to fail."

Ojara's claim that the ARLPI is the work of the devil startles me. I see it as the reverse, that one of the very few graces of the war is that it has brought previously mutually distrusting religious groups together to work on behalf of peace. I try to choose my words carefully, not wanting to be or appear to be ungrateful for his hospitality.

"I do not see the devil in the work of the Acholi religious leaders. I think that it is possible to cooperate with people with whom you disagree in order to achieve practical things. I know that diverting attention from God is a genuine danger. But I think that what ARLPI is trying to do is to cooperate in order to bring peace. When I was in Gulu last year, I interviewed the Sheik. I think that you can cooperate on a practical level while still keeping your eyes on God."

I give the example of my work on abortion, with its emphasis on pro-life/pro-choice cooperation to reduce the incidence of abortion.

"Some people in the pro-life community are suspicious of me because of this work, but I think that this is where the Gospel takes us. That is how I see the work of ARLPI, not as the work of the devil."

Ojara nods tightly with pursed lips. "But there are some others."

"Like who?"

"Do you have to talk to the *ajwaka*? Does your research require you to talk to the witch doctor?"

* * *

On classic and even some more recent accounts of proper research protocol, I overstepped my boundaries—the gaps constructed between self and other in the name of science—when I openly disagreed with Ojara. The classic objection proceeds from a strict fact/value separation, and it finds articulation in one of Max Weber's earliest essays, "The Meaning of 'Ethical Neutrality' in Sociology and Economics." In Weber's words, "What is really at issue is the intrinsically simple demand that the investigator and teacher should keep unconditionally separate the establishment of empirical facts . . . and *his* own practical evaluations, i.e., his evaluations of these facts as satisfactory or unsatisfactory" (emphasis in original).[53] According to Weber, value statements are unadjudicatable and therefore necessarily involve conflict between the parties that hold them. "It is really a question not only of alternatives between values but of an irreconcilable death-struggle, like that between 'God' and the 'Devil.' Between these, neither relativization nor compromise is possible."[54]

Examining Weber's account is important not only for historical purposes, but also because there are not a few practitioners in the social sciences who still, even if tacitly, operate within its parameters. Most, but not all, such practitioners are quantitatively oriented, and most often they do not explicitly base themselves on Weberian epistemology so much as they assume the fact/value split in a way that displays a decided lack of interest in epistemological questions altogether.[55] Like Weber, they assume that once they select and set up their project, they can succeed in eliminating bias. Unlike Weber, they do not couple their applied projects with careful epistemological analysis.

In the background of the fact/value separation is another separation that goes back at least as far as Francis Bacon and which is critical to the conceptualization of what constitutes science, a separation of material and efficient causality from the broader context of formal and final causality found in Aristotle and Medieval theology. Bacon writes of a "just division of philosophy and the sciences": "Let the investigation of forms, which are . . . eternal and immutable, constitute Metaphysics; and let the investigation of the efficient cause, and of matter . . . constitute Physics."[56] Formal and final causality allow the investigator to interpret "empirical" facts as existing within a more comprehensive— and normative—teleological trajectory. Facts are then not simply facts, but have normative intention and content built into them. That Weber rejects formal and final causality in what he regards as scientific investigation is clear from his methodological writings: "Those who view the painstaking labor of [materially and efficiently] causally understanding historical reality as of secondary importance can disregard it, but it is impossible to supplant it by any type of 'teleology.'"[57]

It is important to recognize here that Weber is not saying that value claims cannot be objectively true, only that they cannot be decided upon rationally and therefore cannot be adjudicated by science.[58] In fact, he is insistent that the starting point of any research project is a value judgment about what is worth investigative attention;[59] value judgments even go into the construction of the initial conceptual scheme of inquiry.[60] Social science as a set of disciplines, according to Weber, itself arose in response to a specific problem that investigators believed merited special attention, the problem of scarcity.[61] It would seem, then, that he would have no difficulty with my observation that his fact/value separation is the product of social science's effort to establish itself as a legitimate set of disciplines in the university setting; he would simply respond that that does not make the fact/value separation untrue. Even more encompassing for Weber, science relies on a "belief in the value of scientific truth," which in turn is "the product of certain cultures and is not a product of man's original nature."[62] In other words, affirmation of the truth value of science is a kind of faith claim. But once the scientific project is up and running, specific value claims have no place, and the results ought to be intelligible to anyone, even to those whom Weber identifies as the ultimate "other": "It has been and remains true that a systematically correct scientific proof in the social sciences, if it is to achieve its purpose, must be acknowledged as correct even by a Chinese."[63]

It is clear that Weber places theological claims and even theological depictions together with value judgments as being unadjudicatable and therefore as simply a matter of choice. He argues that entering value judgments into an investigation—once the belief in the value of scientific truth, the valorization of the problem of scarcity, and the acceptance of the initial investigative constructs are all in place—turns the academy "into a theological seminary—except that it does not have the latter's religious authority."[64] Values are a matter of choice, but "to *judge* the *validity* of such values is a matter of *faith*." Weber elaborates, "Only positive religions—or more precisely expressed: dogmatically bound *sects*—are able to confer on the content of *cultural values* the status of unconditionally valid *ethical* imperatives" (emphases in original).[65] On this account, religious authority is no different than political authority in its being characterized simply by power and domination. Such power and domination pertain, "regardless of the basis on which this probability rests," whether religious or political.[66] Social science skittishness about researchers introducing theological perspectives and terms into the investigative process stems largely from a concern that such introductions manifest an irrational—that is, nonscientific—extension of power and domination by "dogmatically bound sects" into the academic realm. Weber's wager in making the case for ethical neutrality is that while authority in politics and religion is an extension of the power to get others to accept one's own value judgments, authority in the academy can stem from the rules of investigative procedure. There is bias in such things as the selection of research topic, to be sure, but protocols proper to social science—which Weber is careful to distinguish from those of natural science[67]—can limit and even transcend whatever initial biases structure the investigation.

Though the Weberian fact/value split and the claim of ethical neutrality die hard, it does not take long for many scholars to recognize that the academy is also an arena of conflict over value judgments that project power. At first, this recognition involves a wariness about investigators projecting their own "Western" value judgments onto their research subjects, thereby committing acts of violence. While confidence in the capacity of science to delimit the exercise of investigative power diminishes in many quarters of the academy—many anthropologists reject the label of science altogether[68]—the view that value claims are unadjudicatable remains, making the assertion of power all the more a concern.

A case in point: In *Anthropology as Cultural Critique*, George Marcus and Michael Fischer argue that there is no simple realism and that all anthropological investigation involves interpretation. However, in the book's conclusion, they break from their narrative—"We end with a word about the moral or ethical dimension"—to make the point that anthropology ought not to be involved in the "assertion of values."[69] To "assert values" is to risk being oppressive. Rather, anthropology should simply be about "the empirical exploration" of the conditions for the articulation of values. In other words, after a full book detailing how there are no simple "facts," Marcus and Fischer end with a coda restating the fact ("empirical")/value split in order to avoid appearing moralistic and therefore oppressive. As mentioned in Chapter 4, Marcus and Fischer's book is significant in that it is frequently cited, together with Marcus and James Clifford's *Writing Culture*, as a classic text of the 1980s that brings together and projects into the future cultural anthropology's hermeneutical turn.

What Marcus and Fischer are wanting, in a discipline that has largely rejected the idea of value neutrality, is some mechanism for value *neutralization*. If early researchers insist on the gap between self and other in the name of science, later scholars do so for the sake of moral nonimposition, if not egalitarianism. What can serve as at least a partial check on the projection of investigative power? The answer that the social sciences have developed in a variety of ways and across a wide range of disciplines but given one label is "reflexivity." Reflexivity is one of those protean terms that find usages with differing emphases, such that a literature has developed around the attempt to trace its genealogy and implementations.[70] In the context of such pluriform usage, any effort to offer a definition is liable to distort, but I would like to quote psychologist Desley Hennessy in order to provide a starting point: "Reflexivity might be considered the attribute of a theory that allows it to be applied to itself."[71] Others expand the definition to include the application of the theory not just to the theory but to the theorist and the theorist's social context, what social scientists refer to as the researcher's "positionality." Making clear our positionality requires in our accounts of both the research and its findings an overt layering up of both the theoretical and lived assumptions that make the practice of research possible. The wager of the practice of reflexivity is that if we turn our theories back on ourselves, then this can serve to neutralize the extension of power that comes with our study of others.

Again, on this read, there is a *moral* impetus to the advancement of the concept and practice of reflexivity, a kind of reverse Golden Rule: "Do unto yourself as you would do unto others." Sociologist Lorraine Nencel writes of the moral aim of the practice in a way that underscores the emphasis on difference—the gap between self and other—and therefore the rejection of any attempt at mimesis: "Reflexivity in this context has a corrective function. It ensures research relationships that are egalitarian, non-authoritative and intersubjective. Through self-reflexivity, the researcher enables a research relationship to develop that recognizes difference and the (im)possibilities this creates. In this sense, reflexivity is used to correct previous ethnocentric and naïve representations of the research relationship."[72] I doubt that reflexivity *ensures* egalitarian research relationships, but it can disclose the power differentials in the field, as is evident in my encounters in the IDP camps. In the process, reflexivity, so understood, abandons intercultural mimesis, either of the they-become-like-us or we-become-like-them variety. To use Nencel's words, the "difference" disclosed by self-reflexivity creates "(im) possibilities." It is enough of an achievement to just let the differences stand, perhaps also to underscore them. White researchers in places like northern Uganda might be, as Fanon says, "much too late" for there to be any cultural boundary crossing.

Theological Resources for Difference (and more)

Despite errors like those committed by Wacquant, theology does offer resources to counteract the temptation to sameness, not least because there is a theological analogue to the social reality of the gap between self and other: as much as we might engage in acts of *imitatio Christi*, there is but one Jesus Christ. I think of the gap between self and Christ in terms of a virtue theory twist on the traditional accounts of the "uses of the law." Now we have the "first use" of the exemplar: however much we may try to imitate Him, the attempt to follow Christ in the particularities of face-to-face encounters with others throws us back on the fact that we are not Christ. I cannot do a modern-day loaves and fishes and ensure that all of the people in Pabbo and Lokung camps have enough food. I cannot make Santo get up and walk. I cannot make the war end. Whatever we do, being in the field forces upon us the fact that, as Okec James told me and as I have been repeatedly reminded by the realities of northern Uganda and South Sudan since, "It is not enough."

Some theologians might charge that, because of Christ's uniqueness, the effort to imitate Him is itself wrongheaded, indeed presumptuous, and therefore problematic from a theological and not simply a practical standpoint. There is overlap between such theologians and those social scientists who absolutize difference and warn against any attempt at mimesis. I suggest, however, that it is precisely in the effort to imitate that the gap between self and other—and self and Other—becomes most evident to us. It seems to me that the presumption is on the part of the theological critic of mimesis: a presupposition that we can take on the identifier of Christian and, more, the communal authority of being a Christian *theologian*, while *a priori* exempting ourselves from the social consequences that are often concomitant with following Christ—marginalization, harassment, and sometimes death. Christ suffers, while we predetermine that we don't have to risk that. But James Dunn is right: "It was only as they shared in his mission that his disciples shared in his authority."[73] And theologians, whatever else we say—in fact as the basis for whatever else we say—claim to be authorities of a particular kind in the Christian community.

And, if the Little Sisters are right, theologians and others who reject mimesis on account of the fact that we cannot adequately image Christ miss the most important part of the dynamic: Christ the Other also moves toward us. Perhaps the best way to unpack further how this is the case is to turn to cultural *crossings* that have occurred in the field and, like I did in delineating the self/other *gap*, move from such crossings to their theological analogues. Adequate account of the discernment stage of the process of mimesis must take such crossings into account as well as the gaps. Acholi repeatedly moved across the cultural gap toward me, from countenancing my bungling of their language to offering extended hospitality in their modest homes. If there were times—like at the funeral dance in Magwi—when they threatened me just when it seemed I was an insider, there were also critical times when they took me, an outsider, in when the threat to me was greatest. These and other crossings are the focus of Chapter 6.

Notes

1. Frantz Fanon, *Black Skin White Masks*, trans. Richard Philcox (New York: Grove Press, [1952] 2008), p. 101.

2. Peggy MacIntosh, "White Privilege: Unpacking the Invisible Knapsack," *Independent School* 49, no. 2 (Winter 1990), pp. 31–5.

3. Quoted in Tim Wise, "Membership Has Its Privileges" (2006) at http://www. rethinkingschools.org/archive/16_04/Memb164.shtml.

4. See, for instance, Kendall Clark, "The Global Privileges of Whiteness," at http://monkeyfist. com/articles.

5. An exception would be the work of Homi K. Bhabha. See Bhabha, *The Location of Culture* (London: Routlege, 1994).

6. Alfred J. López, "Introduction: Whiteness after Empire," in *Postcolonial Whiteness: A Critical Reader on Race and Empire*, ed. Alfred J. López (Albany and New York: State University of New York Press, 2005), p. 3.

7. There have been some recent attempts to retrieve Fanon in ways that redirect postcolonial studies to pay specific attention to matters of race. Paul Gilroy, particularly in his later work, analyzes historical and current racial categories on behalf of a more general humanism, but knows that any reconstruction of racial categories will only come through such careful analysis. His use of Fanon is often implicit or indirect. Anthony Alessandrini brings Fanon front and center. See Paul Gilroy, *Postcolonial Melancholia* (New York, Chicester, and West Sussex, 2005); and Gilroy, *Against Race: Imagining Political Culture Beyond the Color Line* (Cambridge, MA: Belknap Press, 2002). For his earlier work, which is more directed toward reconstructing blackness than making the case for a wider humanism, see Gilroy, *The Black Atlantic: Modernity and Double-Consciousness* (Cambridge, MA: Harvard University Press, 1993). Alessandrini analyzes Gilroy's use of Fanon in Anthony C. Alessandrini, *Frantz Fanon and the Future of Cultural Politics* (Lanham: Lexington Books, 2014). Both Gilroy and Alessandrini can be read in terms of a larger recent effort to wrest postcolonial studies from the predominant poststructuralism, as is found in Neil Lazarus, *The Postcolonial Unconscious* (Cambridge, UK: Cambridge University Press, 2011).

8. Here I am distinguishing the anthropological study of patronage in various cultures from the narrower understanding of political patronage in the United States, where the winner of democratic elections has the right to make political appointments.

9. See, for example, Michael Gilsenan, "Against Patron-Client Relations," in *Patrons and Clients in Mediterranean Societies*, ed. Ernest Gellner and John Waterbury (London: Duckworth, 1977), p. 167ff.

10. See, for instance, Patrick Chabal and Jean-Pascal Daloz, *Africa Works: Disorder as Political Instrument* (Bloomington: Indiana University Press, 1999); William Reno, *Warlord Politics and African States* (Boulder, CO: Lynne Rienner Publishers, 1999); Akhil Gupta, "Blurred Boundaries: The Discourse of Corruption," *Ethnologist* 22, no. 2 (1995), pp. 375–402; and Jon P. Mitchell, "Patrons and Clients," in *Encyclopedia of Social and Cultural Anthropology*, ed. Alan Barnard and Jonathan Spencer (London and New York: Routledge, 2002). For a more recent argument that patron-client relationships can be positive, see China Scherz, *Having People, Having Heart: Charity, Sustainable Development and Problems of Dependence in Central Uganda* (Chicago: University of Chicago Press, 2014).

11. At his specific request, I am using Orach Otim's own name. His reasoning is that the government authorities already know about him and have already tortured him because of his activities; the best way to protect him, then, is to use his name, so that the government

knows that others know of his situation and are watching after him. This is one case where, for me, the subject's agency trumps the standard (and often necessary) paternalism of the practice of keeping the subjects anonymous. In my consent forms, approved by the University of Notre Dame's IRB, I allow research subjects to choose whether to remain anonymous or not.

12. So far, I have verified Orach's story with two others. For more on the human rights abuses of the Ugandan military, see, Human Rights Watch, *Uprooted and Forgotten: Impunity and Human Rights Abuses in Northern Uganda* (2005), available at www.hrw.org.

13. See Noel Ignatiev, *How the Irish Became White* (New York and London: Routledge, 1996). In the latest edition of his book, George Lipsitz takes into account and incorporates this criticism of earlier editions. See George Lipsitz, *The Possessive Investment of Whiteness: How White People Benefit from Identity Politics* (Philadelphia: Temple University Press, 2006).

14. See Samwiri Rubaraza Karugire, *A Political History of Uganda* (Nairobi and London: Heinemann Educational Books, 1980); Mahmood Mamdani, *Politics and Class Formation in Uganda* (New York: Monthly Review Press, 1976); Mahmood Mamdani, *Imperialism and Fascism in Uganda* (Nairobi and London: Heinemann Educational Books, 1983); and Thomas Ofcansky, *Uganda: Tarnished Pearl of Africa* (Boulder, CO and Oxford: Westview Press, 1996).

15. Okot p'Bitek, *Song of Lawino & Song of Ocol* (Oxford: Heinemann Publishers, 1984), pp. 35–6.

16. P'Bitek, *Song of Lawino & Song of Ocol*, p. 145.

17. Ibid., pp. 125–6.

18. Chris Ocowun, "Museveni Hails Gulu Archbishop Odama," *New Vision* (October 22, 2006), p. 1.

19. P'Bitek, *Song of Lawino & Song of Ocol*, p. 45.

20. Ibid., p. 142.

21. See Jennifer Harvey, Karin Case, and Robin Howley Gorsline, eds., *Disrupting White Supremacy from Within: White People on What We Need to Do* (Cleveland: Pilgrim Press, 2004); Mary Hobgood, *Dismantling Privilege: An Ethics of Accountability* (Cleveland: Pilgrim Press, 2004).

22. Alexander Odonga, *Lwo-English Dictionary* (Kampala: Fountain Publishers, 2005), p. 157.

23. Ignatiev, *How the Irish Became White*.

24. Also, though the *agomo* are taken as "African," a couple generations ago, the Acholi of both sexes in the far north wore nothing until puberty and then wore only loincloths. There is no small bit of irony, then, in the debate in Uganda concerning mini-skirts. The case is argued that the miniskirt is too modern, and that "African" dress is more modest; yet it was the European Christian missionaries, not the Africans, who first made the case that nudity and loincloths were immodest. The *agomo* continue to be the dresses whites buy in the markets of Gulu and Kampala when want to buy "African" clothes.

25. P'Bitek, *Song of Lawino & Song of Ocol*, p. 54.

26. Thomas Ayodele, Franklin Cudjoe, Temba A. Nolutshungu, and Charles K. Sunwabe, "African Perspectives on Aid: Foreign Assistance Will Not Pull Africa Out of Poverty," *Economic Development* 2 (September 15, 2005), at http://www.cato.org/pubs/edb/edb2.html; and Andrew Mwenda, "Foreign Aid and the Weakening of Democratic Accountability," *Foreign Policy Briefing* (July 22, 2006) at http://www/cato.org.

27. Ritva Reinikka and Jokob Svensson, "Local Capture: Evidence from a Central Government Transfer Program in Uganda," *Quarterly Journal of Economics* 119, no. 2 (2004), p. 679.

28. Ayodele, et al. and Mwenda are against foreign aid. For the view that rightly structured aid is still helpful, see David Beckman, "Debunking Myths about Foreign Aid," *The Christian Century* (August 1–8, 2001): 26–8.

29. Whites being at the patronage apex has been changing with the ascension of China as a donor and investor in Africa. See John Burnett, "China is besting the U.S. in Africa," *U.S. News and World Report* (March 24, 2015), at http://www.usnews.com/opinion/economic-intelligence/2015/03/24/china-beating-us-in-race-to-invest-in-africa. Still, whites predominate if we take into account countries other than the United States as well, particularly those in Europe. Also, whites continue to dominate the highest levels of the World Bank and the International Monetary Fund.

30. See Human Rights Watch, *"Letting the Big Fish Swim": Failures to Prosecute High-Level Corruption in Uganda* (October 21, 2013), at https://www.hrw.org/report/2013/10/21/letting-big-fish-swim/failures-prosecute-high-level-corruption-uganda.

31. See, for instance, Deborah Eade, *Development and Patronage* (London: Oxfam Publishing, 1997); Ian Smillie, *Patronage or Partnership? Local Capacity Building in Humanitarian Crises* (Bloomfield, CT: Kumarian Press, 2001); Monica Kathina Juma and Astri Surhke, *Eroding Local Capacity: International Humanitarian Action in Africa* (Uppsula: Nordic Africa Institute, 2003); Michael Maren, *The Road to Hell: The Ravaging Effects of Foreign Aid and International Charity* (New York: The Free Press, 2002); Alex de Waal, *Famine Crimes: Politics & the Disaster Relief Industry in Africa* (Bloomington: Indiana University Press, 1998); Fiona Terry, *Condemned to Repeat? The Paradox of Humanitarian Action* (Ithaca: Cornell University Press, 2002); David Rieff, *A Bed for the Night: Humanitarianism in Crisis* (New York: Simon and Schuster, 2003); and Treje Tvedt, *Angels of Mercy or Development Diplomats? NGOs and Foreign Aid* (Lawrenceville, NJ: Africa World Press, 1998).

32. The name is a pseudonym.

33. Both names in this scene are pseudonyms.

34. Okot p'Bitek, *Religion of the Central Luo* (Nairobi, Kampala, and Dar Es Salaam: East African Literature Bureau, 1971), pp. 95–6.

35. Sverker Finnstrom, *Living with Bad Surroundings: War and Existential Uncertainty in Acholiland, Northern Uganda* (Uppsala: Department of Cultural Anthropology and Ethnology, 2003), p. 192.

36. Okot p'Bitek, *Horn of My Love* (Nairobi: Heinemann Kenya Ltd., 1974), p. 13.

37. Loïc Wacquant, *Body & Soul: Notebooks of an Apprentice Boxer* (Oxford and New York: Oxford University Press, 2004), pp. 7, 10, 11, 15, 16, 40, 71, 100, 113, 117, 125, and 126.

38. See Steve G. Hoffman and Gary Alan Fine, "The Scholar's Body: Mixing It Up with Loïc Wacquant," *Qualitative Sociology* 28, no. 2 (Summer 2005), p. 154.

39. Wacquant, *Body & Soul*, pp. vii, viii, 7, 16, 58ff, 69, 91, 95–102, 107, 126, n. 115 and 116, 127–30, and 141–9.

40. Wacquant, *Body & Soul*, p. 117. See also pp. 7, 100, 102, and 118–20.

41. Wacquant, *Body & Soul*, p. xii.

42. Ibid., p. 118.

43. Paul Stoller, "The Presence of the Ethnographic Present: Some Brief Comments on Loïc Wacquant's *Body and Soul*," *Qualitative Sociology* 28, no. 2 (Summer 2005), p. 198.

44. Stoller, "The Presence of the Ethnographic Present: Some Brief Comments on Loïc Wacquant's *Body and Soul*," p. 198.

45. Judith Farquhar, "Whose Bodies?" *Qualitative Sociology* 28, no. 2 (Summer 2005), pp. 193–4. For similar critiques of *Body & Soul*, see Steve G. Hoffman and Gary Alan Fine, "The Scholar's Body: Mixing It Up with Loïc Wacquant," *Qualitative Sociology* 28, no. 2 (Summer 2005), pp. 151–7 ; Robert Zussman, "The Black Frenchman," *Qualitative Sociology* 28, no. 2 (Summer 2005), pp. 201–6; Patrick M. Krueger and Jarron M. SaintOnge, "Boxing It Out: A Conversation about *Body and Soul*," *Qualitative Sociology* 28, no. 2 (Summer 2005), pp. 185–9; Reuben A. Buford May, "Shadowboxing: A Review of Loïc Wacquant's *Body & Soul*," *Symbolic Interaction* 28, no. 3 (Summer 2005), pp. 429–31; Douglas Hartmann, "Review of *Body and Soul: Notebooks of an Apprentice Boxer*," *Social Forces* 84, no. 1 (September 2005), pp. 603–5; and Gary Alan Fine, "Review of *Body and Soul: Notebooks of an Apprentice Boxer*," *Journal of Sociology*. 110, no. 2 (September 2004), pp. 505–7.

46. Wacquant, *Body & Soul*, pp. 5, 53, 10, and 255.

47. Ibid., pp. 178, 188, 248, and 191, n. 23.

48. On the gym being a "sanctuary," see Wacquant, *Body & Soul*, pp. 14 and 238; for "temple" and "cult," see p. 31; for "novice," "novitiate," and "initiation," see pp. vii, 3, 7, 11, 15–16, 58, 71, 102, and 120; for "catechism," see p. 192, n. 24; for "monastic," see pp. 15, 60, 67, and 235; for "ritual of mortification," see p. 236. For other religious references to describe boxing, see pp. 6, 71, 100, 101, 108, 147, and 235.

49. Wacquant, *Body & Soul*, pp. 35–6.

50. Ibid., pp. 36, 236, and 235.

51. Ibid., pp. 4, 71, 116, and 206.

52. Ibid., p. 4, note 3.

53. Max Weber, "The Meaning of 'Ethical Neutrality' in Sociology and Economics," in *Max Weber on The Methodology of the Social Sciences*, ed. Edward A. Shils and Henry A. Finch (Glencoe, IL: The Free Press, 1949), p. 11.

54. Weber, "The Meaning of 'Ethical Neutrality' in Sociology and Economics," pp. 17–18. See also pp. 19, 26–7, and 36. See also Weber, "'Objectivity' in Social Science and Social Policy," pp. 57 and 105.

55. When I asked sociologist Christian Smith how his broad, philosophically inflected work on human nature and epistemology is received by other sociologists, he replied that most ignored it as not the kind of thing that they do. For a recent example of his work, see Christian Smith, *To Flourish or Destruct: A Personalist Theory of Human Goods, Motivations, Failure, and Evil* (Chicago: University of Chicago Press, 2015).

56. Francis Bacon, *The New Organon* (Cambridge, UK and New York: Cambridge University Press, 2000), Book II, Aphorism 9.

57. Weber, "'Objectivity' in Social Science and Social Policy," p. 83; see also Weber, "The Meaning of 'Ethical Neutrality' in Sociology and Economics," p. 4.

58. Weber, "The Meaning of 'Ethical Neutrality in Sociology and Economics,'" pp. 12–14, 17–18, 22–3, and 28.

59. Weber, "The Meaning of 'Ethical Neutrality in Sociology and Economics,'" pp. 11, 21–2; Weber, "'Objectivity' in Social Science and Social Policy," pp. 82, 84, 107.

60. Weber, "'Objectivity' in Social Science and Social Policy," p. 84.

61. Ibid., pp. 64–8.

62. Ibid., p. 110.

63. Ibid., p. 58.

64. Weber, "The Meaning of 'Ethical Neutrality' in Sociology and Economics," p. 7.

65. Weber, "'Objectivity' in Social Science and Social Policy," pp. 55 and 57.

66. Max Weber, *Economy and Society: An Outline of Interpretive Sociology*, ed. Guenther Roth and Claus Wittich (Berkeley, Los Angeles, and London: University of California Press, 1978), p. 53. Weber defines power and domination as "the probability that one actor within a social relationship will be in a position to carry out his own will despite resistance" (power), and "the probability that a command with a specific content will be obeyed by a given group of persons" (domination).

67. Weber, "'Objectivity' in Social Science and Social Policy," pp. 80–8, and 92–3.

68. See Nicholas Wade, "Anthropology a Science? Statement Deepens a Rift," *The New York Times* (December 9, 2010), at http://www.nytimes.com/2010/12/10/science/10anthro pology.html.

69. George E. Marcus and Michael M. J. Fischer, *Anthropology as Cultural Critique* (Chicago and London: University of Chicago Press, 1986), p. 167.

70. See, for instance, Ray Holland, "Reflexivity," *Human Relations* 52 (1999), pp. 463–84; Philip Carl Salzman, "On Reflexivity," *American Anthropologist*, New Series 104, no. 3 (September 2002), pp. 805–13; Russell Walsh, "The Methods of Reflexivity," *The Humanistic Psychologist* 31/, no. 4 (2003), pp. 51–66; Lorraine Nencel, "Situating Reflexivity: Voices, Positionalities and Representations in Feminist Ethnographic Texts," *Women's Studies International Forum* (2013), http://dx.doi.org/10.1016/j.wsif.2013.07.018.

71. Desley Hennessy, "Reflexivity: What in the 'GAK' Is That?" in *Reflections in Personal Construct Theory*, ed. Richard J. Butler (West Sussex, Oxford, and Malden, MA: Wiley-Blackwell, 2009), p. 222.

72. Nencel, "Situating Reflexivity," p. 3.

73. James D. G. Dunn, *Jesus and the Spirit: A Study of the Religious and Charismatic Experience of Jesus and the First Christians as Reflected in the New Testament* (Grand Rapids, MI: William B. Eerdmans Publishing Company, 1975), pp. 81–2.

CHAPTER 6
CROSSINGS: THE SURPRISE OF MIMESIS

These Yamaha 175s aren't bad. Bigger would be a bit better though. 200. 250 maybe. Faster on the good roads. More weight better in the mud. But these aren't bad. Better than the 125s.

Acholibur should be coming up soon. Turn off there to Gulu. I'm ready to be back. Good stay in Madi Opei. Agoro. I like the catechists in Agoro.

Bicyclist ahead. Pothole. There. Good groove around it. She's coming *this* way. No. *My* side of the road. No time. Gravel. Air. Roll when you hit. *Unghh.* Roll! *Arunnhh-ahhh!* Fucking pack. *Aaawwwahhh!* I can't *see!*

Painpainpainpainpainpain. All. Pain. *Aaawwwahhh!*

Paralyzed?

Don't pass out. Don't pass out. Whatever you do, don't pass out.

Get the pack off. Good. My arms move. Not a quadriplegic. Goodgoodgood. Top buckle. There. Bottom buckle. Okay. Slide strap. Slide other strap. Good.

Legs? *Aaawwwahh!*

My voice. That's *my* voice. Have I been saying everything? Legs. Check again— *aahh-aahhwuahhahh!* But they moved. They moved. Goodgoodgood. Try again. *Oh-oh-oh-oh-oh.* Yes. They moved. Not paralyzed. But pain. Keep talking. Keep talking. Don't go under.

Get your helmet off. Chin strap. Good. Slide past the ears. Good. There are people here? Already? Five? Ten? But they are just standing. How is the woman? How. Is. The. Woman? *Dako tye nining?*

No answer. They are not here to help.

Do you have anyone you can call?

A voice in my head, but it isn't mine.

Do you have someone you can call? Do you have a cell phone?

Joseph Okumu. Father Joseph Okumu. Here.

He has a cell phone? A different voice. A woman.

Man: Who do you want us to call?

Okumu Joseph. Look under Okumu Joseph. *Araugh-ahh!*

Woman: I know him.

Man: I can't find it.

Woman: Look under Okumu Joseph.

Man: Father Joseph Okumu? Yes, this is Kenneth Okot. We are with your friend here. What is your name?

Todd.

What?

Todd. Tung Gwok.

We are with you friend here. Todd. He has had a motorcycle accident. We are going to take him to Kitgum Hospital. St. Joseph's? Okay. We will take him to St. Joseph's Hospital in Kitgum. Can you meet us there? You are in Gulu?

Woman: Yes, he is at the Catechist Training Center there. I know him.

Man: Okay. You can come? Okay. We will take him to St. Joseph's Hospital Kitgum. Bye. We are taking you to the hospital.

No. I am okay. I just need to recover a bit.

No. You need to get to a hospital.

Just give me a second.

Help him up.

Two other men.

I just need a second. I don't want to go to the hospital.

You can't ride the motorcycle like you are.

Okay. Okay. How is the woman?

Fine. She ran off shouting she was on the side of the road.

No she wasn't. She was in the road. Wrong side of the road. She's okay?

Yes. She's drunk. She's fine. Help him up.

She's drunk?

When she hit you.

The two men again. An arm around each. Like at football games. Stretcher: bad. Hobble off even with the aid of others: good. No applause from the fans here, though.

Hah! Humor! Good sign they say. Not sure. My second grade report card teacher's comment: "Thinks he's funny." And the people. I can see them better now. They are just staring. Waiting?

Man: You can get in the vehicle. We have your bag in the back. Did you just have this yellow one?

No. A backpack. A red backpack too.

A moment.

Man: Boy, come here. Okay, we have your red bag. A boy was taking it.

You mean that the people were standing around just waiting to take my things?

Yes. There was a man in Gulu district who had an accident, and they took everything. Even his clothes. They just left him lying there.

They were just waiting for me to pass out or die so that they could take the rest of my things?

No answer. Good. Maybe I did not say it out loud.

Thank you. Thank you for getting me.

Let's go to the hospital.

Man on my left: Can you get in the car?

I think so. Ow-ow-ow-ow-*ow*. Where is God the opiate when you need Him? No laughter. Thinks he's funny.

Woman sitting on other side in back. You can lie down here, she says, put your head on the pack.

Ow-ow-ow. Can't. This is more comfortable. Hands and knees on seat. Pressure off back. Face pressed into the pack. *Apwoyo wukonya. Rubanga konyi.* Thank you for helping me. God bless you. I think they hear me.

My motorcycle?

Man: One of the others is driving it up to Kitgum. It will be there for you when you are ready.

Apwoyo wukonya. Rubanga konyi. All the way to Kitgum.

Over potholes. Many, many potholes.

We stop.

Doors open. Lights go on. The two men appear again.

We are here. Can you climb out?

We are here?

Can you climb out?

Arms under mine, then shoulders under my arms.

Third man lifts my legs.

Down gently—*aruaww-ow-ow!*—on the cart.

Man: Which bags are your valuables in?

Both.

Both?

Yes

Do you want them left in the hospital or do you want us to take them where they will be safe?

You take them.

Woman: Is there someone in Kitgum that you know who we can leave them with?

Bishop Ochola.

Man: Bishop Ochola?

Woman: I know where he lives.

Man: Okay. We are taking your bags and your motorcycle to Bishop Ochola's. They will be there. Father Joseph is on the way from Gulu. He will be here soon. How are you feeling?

Okay. Okay. Your contacts.

Our contacts?

Yes, I need your contacts.

That is not the most important thing. The most important thing is your health. But here. I am putting our contacts in your back pocket.

Rubanga konyi.

* * *

If I, in following Cecilia, imitated the Good Samaritan in relation to Santo in Pabbo, then with the motorcycle accident I am literally the injured man on the side of the road. It is not quite the reciprocity I intended, but a more profound kind, one not engineered by me, however reflexive my scholarship might be, and discernment must take this into account. When they first stop, my rescuers do not know that I am white, they only know that I am injured or dead. They violate NGO protocol—something for which they could receive a reprimand or even lose their jobs—by stopping at all. Part of the protocol is simply a product of Western bureaucratization: no one is to ride in agency vehicles without completing information and disclaimer forms first. Part of it is due to the danger of stopping on the road at all.[1]

Like in the Gospel story, those who come to my aid do not end there, but work to assure the continued good care of the wounded. The biblical Samaritan gives two days' wages to the innkeeper and lets him know that he will be back to check up on how the wounded man is doing. My Samaritans make sure that my belongings remain safe even after they deliver me to the hospital. Later that evening, after I receive a painkiller shot and am resting in a hospital bed, I receive a text message from Kenneth—I learn his name from the card he gave me—telling me that they could not find anyone at Bishop Ochola's place, so they have the bags with them at Boma, a Kitgum hotel, and will wait until Father Joe picks them up from them. Three days later, Kenneth sends me another text message—knowing a phone call might awaken me from needed sleep—asking how I am. When I call him, he asks, "Can you walk? Yes? Oh Wonderful. We were so afraid that you wouldn't be able to walk."

What would have happened had they not stopped? Best case scenario: I manage to maintain consciousness and crawl to the motorcycle. The red backpack, which I had set next to me, is long gone with the boy who has taken it. It has three thousand dollars' worth of technical gear: a digital SLR camera with a new memory card, two lenses, and a video camera. There is about fifty dollars in Ugandan schillings in the lid pocket. In other words, the loss is only financial. What is more important to me at the time is in the yellow bag strapped to the rack of the motorcycle. My travel doctor and I planned for the possibility of a moment such as this and I have on hand a powerful painkiller—oxycodone. I take one pill. If that is insufficient to cut the pain, I take another. I call Father Joe and wait. I sit next to my belongings, protecting them, far less likely to succumb to the pain. This is the best case.

Another scenario: The pain is too much and I lose consciousness, or simply go into a state of defenseless shock. I awaken and, like the man in the accident in Gulu district, am naked. If I am fortunate, I am otherwise unharmed. My cell phone, in my pants, is gone. I cannot call anyone. I cannot walk on my own yet. It is late afternoon Sunday, and not much chance of another vehicle passing by. I must crawl to the nearest trading center, Acholibur, calling, "*Konya! Koma lit!*" (Help me! I am hurt!) to whomever passes. I think it is only a couple kilometers to Acholibur. Maybe, if I don't go under, I can get there before dark. With nothing left to have robbed, I think I can get there, and I am fairly certain someone there will call Father Joe for me.

I have never felt so vulnerable. I have been in situations of potential and real danger, but always with the sense that I could *do* something—flee, hide, strike back—if something arose, even if my effort would fail. Now, I could do almost nothing. Even if I did not pass out or die, people could take all of my things, and all I could do was watch.

Sometimes the other crosses the gap to us. It is not all on us, we self-sufficient, autonomous selves. Most such crossings that I experienced were of what we would call the mundane type, though they were often enough remarkable: peasant farmers slaughtering their only chicken so that they could welcome me with the hospitality that they thought was my due, travelers on the back of a produce-packed lorry finding just enough room for me to sit atop a bag of charcoal so that I do not have to wait until the next day to travel. In each case, a recognition-even-in-otherness extended itself from them to me, all acts of hospitality.

In Acholi cosmology, such crossings are not limited to the mundane world. Nearly all of the Acholi I have met in northern Uganda and South Sudan—I cannot remember an exception—live in a spirit-infused world. They offer meals to their ancestors, and consult the *ajwaka* to call upon her spirits to intervene on their behalf. It is this kind of crossing that an American scholar is likely to have the most difficulty with. The academy is, in Weber's words, a "disenchanted" place. It is in this regard, then, that we need most to attend to in this moment in anthropological theology that I have been calling "discernment." We are discerning whether we can inhabit, really, the world that has been offered to us by those with whom we have been living, and so take on features of that world in a way that goes well beyond mere external copying.

In this chapter, then, I draw on my experience of a visitation to me of the spirit of a murdered two-year-old Acholi girl to suggest how the practice of apprentice or mimetic ethnography can, with the aid of the spirit-*psst* of the other crossing over, fundamentally alter—reverse, really—key aspects of the assumed worldview of the scholar. In the first part of the chapter, I describe the visitation and its immediate effects. Other anthropologists have had similar experiences, and in the second part of this chapter, I provide an account both of those experiences and of anthropology's resistance to registering the experiences in indigenous terms. There are deep epistemological and professional blockages to acknowledging, in emic terms, "This is what happened." I suggest that such spirit-crossings are, among other things, a kind of stinging mercy or loving vengeance on the part of the other toward the modern/postmodern scholar for prior colonial impositions.

Given that, even with such crossings, I am in crucial ways still very much a Western scholar, it is important to try to relate the world that has visited me in the girl's spirit to the world I continue to inhabit most months of the year. In the third part of this chapter, then, I bring traditional Acholi and modern therapeutic discourses, both incomplete and open-ended, into conversation with each other. Recognition of such incompleteness or underdetermination of discourses creates room, I suggest, for theological language to enter into the conversation in Western intellectual settings that otherwise have tended to manifest a totalizing secular discourse.

Spirit visitations are common both in northern Uganda and the ancient Near East, so I then return in this chapter's fourth part to the theme, initiated in Chapter 4, of cultures that can bridge our own world with that of Jesus Christ. Here, I work out the implications of spirit-crossings for understanding the relationship between justice and forgiveness. Biblical scholars debate, quite intensely, whether Jesus's mission was primarily one of justice for the poor in the here and now or one of forgiveness of the wicked against the horizon of a world yet to come. The difficulty of either reading is that the New Testament has Jesus articulating and living his missions to both the poor and the wicked. The root problem with both sides of contemporary debate among scholars is that they presuppose an uninterrupted linear view of time; Jesus therefore either has to be for justice for the poor in this world or for forgiveness of the wicked in light of the Kingdom to come. A cosmology that includes spirit visitation, however, allows for the disruption of linear time, and it is just this cosmology that Jesus presupposes in his twin missions to the poor and the wicked. To get Jesus right ethically, then, we have to get him right cosmologically, and we can learn from the Acholi in this regard. Surveys of Acholi show that the majority want both justice and forgiveness with regard to perpetrators from the LRA conflict. I draw upon the Acholi reconciliation ritual of *mato oput* to show how a practice that involves spirit intercession works to combine justice and forgiveness. I then close by making the case for a spirit-interrupted "magical Christianity" that, precisely *because of* its openness to spirit intervention, is present to both the poor and the wicked. That is a lot to consider, a lot to discern. Mimesis can bring responses from the other that go well beyond what we anticipate.

Laker's *Psst*

Two year-old Laker (*Lăkā*) presses against my lower left leg, only she is now a spirit. The odd thing is, I never knew her in "real" life. She is already dead when Father Vincentio Olim shows me four-megapixel pictures of her on his computer: lying on her back in a creek bed, her face cut off and the entirety of what is left in its place so completely covered with flies that it looks as if she is wearing a fencing mask. Multiple photos: pan-views of the scene; close-ups of what was her face; this angle, then that.

"Six devil worshippers did this. They brought it up from Kampala. We never had this sort of thing before."

In a social context with eroded traditional mechanisms and without modern juridical structures, Father Vincentio has served as both pathologist and lead crime investigator. The digital photographs are his Exhibit A.

"The mother was visiting another woman and brought her girl, who was playing with the other children. The mother had to go back to her hut for something, and the woman agreed that the child could stay until she got back. When she returned, the child was gone. 'Where is my child?' she said. And the woman answered, 'She left.' People looked everywhere. They couldn't find her. They surrounded the woman's home and threatened to kill her. The local police tried to intervene but shot three people."

Father Vincentio dispersed the crowd and questioned the woman.

"A witch doctor told her to do it. That it would bring her good fortune."

In Acholi tradition, a person who dies of untoward causes comes back as *cen*, an unsettled spirit. Father Vincentio is right: child sacrifice is unheard of in traditional Acholi culture. It is a perversion. The woman who killed the child is in prison awaiting trial.

I push down on the table to get up from the chair next to Father Vincentio because my legs do not seem to be able to get me up on their own. I try walking to the door to outside as he continues his account.

"The Anglican priest did the burial ceremony in the father's compound. They thought things were done and set right. Twice, however, when women put their grains to dry in the compound, wind came up and blew only the grain of the mother away. If this is true, we will call together a prayer ceremony to drive the evil spirit away."

But she has come to me, now back in the United States, while I am lying in my bed.

* * *

It appears that the Little Sisters are right: pictures can transmit spirits. Something—some*one*—crossed the gap that race, economics, and culture placed between the Acholi and me, and she came from elsewhere. None of my efforts at *imitatio Acholi*, of themselves, seemed to cause this. I met and talked with spirit-mediums, but I followed the nuns and catechists. Wouldn't, then, Bishop Negri or Mother Angioletta or maybe even Jesus Christ appear to me? Why this disfigured toddler? Why a visitation at all? A modern might explain that the appearance of Laker was a willful, if subconscious, psychological projection—a result of one too many interviews with *ajwagi*. The feel of Laker pressing up against my lower leg, however, was as phenomenologically vivid as my keyboard is to me now, in fact much more so. If the gap between self and other can or should not be bridged from our side, maybe it can be transgressed from the other. Ethnographic method, it would seem, allows us to hang out taking field notes until, possibly, the other upends our construal of her world and ours.

And, in my case, it has been an overturning, though in an odd way. At the time that Laker appeared to me, I took her presence matter-of-factly. Parents, aunts, and uncles of young children are familiar with the sensation of the hug around the upper calf/knee area by a small child standing next to you. That is what this was. My surprise at her presence and at my immediate response to it came only later. It seemed strange only in retrospect, and only intellectually. This can't *be*, I thought. Discernment regarding another culture can't involve *this*. But the givenness of the experience has been stubborn. It refuses to be explained away, and has forced a retracing and reconsideration of the deeply embedded presuppositions of modern and postmodern intellectual culture. In other words, what has to be explained is the culture that is used to doing the explaining.

Laker's visitation has led me to realize that my most fundamental difference with Ojara regarding the Acholi religious leaders was not over whether the devil per se was working in them—though I disagreed, and still do, with that as well—but had to do with his construal that populates the world with intervening spirits at all. And I have been moved from one who, in that overly circumscribed way of much academic thinking, was not closed, intellectually, to the possibility of spirits interacting with humans to one who has experienced just such a possibility. This has required me to reassess—that is, to re-discern—what I think on a wide array of other things; for instance, that rather than what has been called "magical thinking" being a lack of critical rationality, I have had to reconsider whether critical rationality in many of its modern and postmodern forms is an obstruction to magical thinking. In other words, my *pistological* conversion (*pistis* meaning "faith") has required a radical reworking of other things that I know, involving an *epistemological* conversion.[2] To be sure, I was trained in divinity schools—again, something that Weber would hold excludes me from the proper university—but they were the Harvard and University of Chicago divinity schools. We worked with concepts—at most, perhaps, grace in some general prevenient way—not beckoned spirits. The working presupposition was that Christianity could be reasonable in a way that was acceptable to the academy on the academy's already given terms. Now it is clear that the idea that God became human, died, and resurrected is a fantastic (in both senses of the word) *event*. And this, in turn, has allowed me to view other accounts of the world—invisible hands and dialectical marches both—as they are, also strange.

How, then, to interpret this strangeness? Most straightforwardly, as interpreted by the Acholi to whom I told of this experience, Laker came to me because I showed compassion toward her when I saw the pictures, and, given her mother's own depressed state, she was lonely. More broadly, in the context of the history of the encroachment of Western ideas and institutions in the form of the practice of anthropology, Laker's unbidden (as far as I could tell) visitation can perhaps be seen as the instigation of a kind of reversal in the direction of influence, a kind of loving vengeance on the scholar. Perhaps, given the kind of reversals involved, the theological categories of conversion and mercy can apply even to anthropologists.[3]

Reversal: The mercy of the other

The anthropology of conversion has developed rapidly in the last thirty years or so, and it has done so in a variety of field contexts and with a wide array of emphases.[4] Here, I would like to add to the complex of interpretations by suggesting that one overlooked instance of conversion—that of the anthropologist from modern/postmodern over to magical worlds—might be understood in terms of a reversal instigated by the other, and this in three ways: the epistemic, the political, and the cosmological. Epistemic reversal occurs through challenges to the objectifying gaze of ethnography in both its modern realist and postmodern interpretive forms. It upends the conceit (in both senses of the term) of participant observation that we can imitate the other without being affected ourselves;

it is a counter to our ingratitude for the hospitality of the subaltern, their offering of their world to us.[5] This aspect of reversal, then, is perhaps most evident precisely when anthropologists resist it.[6] Even Paul Stoller, in the earlier stages of his apprenticeship, protests after he has a vision of a river demon, "This sorcery and philosophy I had been learning had to be an illusion, certainly not something one might reduce to tangible data, to facts. I realized at that moment that I must not relinquish my role as objective observer, no matter how involved I might become in the Songhay world of magic. I must not forget, I told myself, that I am an anthropologist, a scientist of the human social condition."[7]

Stoller's reference to his "role" as an objective observer points to the fact that epistemic reality is also a social, even political reality. Since the Talal Asad-edited 1973 volume, *Anthropology and the Colonial Encounter*, many and perhaps most anthropologists have had a heightened awareness of how the objectivist gaze of ethnographic realism has been part and parcel of colonial imperialism.[8] The other-instigated reversal of our ways of knowing are therefore also acts against the ways of organizing social life that anthropologists have relied upon to do their work. This is perhaps most evident when such conversion appears as a threat to the researcher's professional standing.

Anthropologist Katherine Ewing writes of a visitation from a Sufi saint that she receives in a dream and her struggles to reconcile her commitment to professional anthropology with the stark realness of her experience (Interestingly, hers also is an experience involving touch: "In the dream I had the clear sensation of something touching my thumb, which startled me awake. . . . I was haunted by the odd sensation of the touch."[9]). Ewing writes that "the idea of 'going native' is one of the few taboos remaining within anthropology."[10] The phrasing of the term, "going native," like the claim that "religion is okay for those who need it," bears its own condemnation. Others have also commented on anthropology and its practitioners' resistance to internalizing— accepting into the discipline—emic explanations of events.[11] What Ewing adds is that even anthropology that makes the postmodern hermeneutical turn rejects the idea of the researcher accepting emic explanations as her own. In fact, it is precisely the postmodern premium placed on the otherness of the research subject that serves as the key obstacle. Ewing is unstinting in her critique:

> Those of an interpretive bent are far more comfortable embracing the idea of "difference," an epistemological abyss between the interpretive world of anthropologist and informant, than seriously entertaining the possibility of entering or believing in the world of the people they meet during fieldwork. . . . I argue, in contrast, that the experience of the abyss between the interpretive world of the anthropologist and the people he or she gets to know stems largely from the taboo against going native. It results from a refusal to acknowledge that the subjects of one's research might actually know something about the human condition that is valid for the anthropologist: it is a refusal to believe. This refusal constitutes a hegemonic act, an implicit insistence that the relationship between the anthropologist and "informant" be shaped by the parameters of Western discourse.[12]

In other words, like Weber before them and the impetus for him to make the fact/value separation in large part in order to establish sociology's disciplinary validity as a science, most among even those anthropologists who have taken the hermeneutical turn resist the internalization of emic explanations of events in large part because such a move—such vulnerability—threatens, or appears to threaten, their claim to a place in the academy.

The concern about losing one's place in the academy is probably most clearly stated by Tanya Luhrmann. While researching witchcraft in contemporary England, Luhrmann had experiences that she labels "magical," seemingly causing her watch to stop in one case and a battery to melt in another. She also, one morning, had a vision of six druids, and writes of what she learned from it: "It taught me experientially what I learned intellectually: that when people said that they 'saw' Christ, or the Goddess, they were not necessarily speaking metaphorically." She adds of her participation in various rituals that it was "as if I felt the power but was too raw to handle it with skill. . . . Perhaps there is something like a spiritual capacity which, like the capacity to swim or draw, all people possess to some degree but which few of them exercise and train."[13] At first, Luhrmann does not seem to view the magical and, in her words, "common sense" explanations to be necessarily at odds: "The spirituality, the dreams, the intense mental imagery enriched my world." However, she backtracks because of the taboo against going native and the observer objectivism that epistemologically underwrites such a prohibition. She then shifts to set up emic and etic explanations as mutually exclusive:

> The only reason I continued to think of myself as an anthropologist, rather than as a witch, was that I had a strong disincentive against asserting that rituals had an effect upon the natural world. The anthropologist is meant to become involved, but not native. The very purpose of my involvement—to write an observer's text— would have been undermined by my assent to the truth of magical ideas. . . . Most ethnographers do not admit to a fearful belief in their ethnographic subject's ideas about witchcraft and so forth; fewer claim that such belief is essential to the project. I stood to gain nothing by belief except power which I was told that I could exercise unconsciously even if I made no explicit acceptance, but *I stood to lose credibility and career by adherence.* (emphasis added) [14]

With ethnographers less forthcoming about institutional vulnerability than Luhrmann, such resistance to emic explanation of events gets articulated in terms of the need to maintain "critical distance." However, Ewing has it exactly right: to assume that critical distance comes only from within the academy is to presuppose that the cultures of the research subjects have no resources of their own for critical reflection. I would add that that resistance is itself an indication of a lack of critical distance on one's own constructs. Once again, this time in postmodern hands, the other becomes, despite protests to the contrary, the exoticized "primitive," with all of the hegemonic connotations that that term implies.

Reflexivity—our application of our theories to ourselves—is not sufficient to arrive at non-oppressive interpretation of the subjects of our research. The problem with research that ends with reflexivity is that it disallows crossings in either direction. Reflexivity is still and always *our* theory that we apply to ourselves—it is, in Lorraine Nencel's phrasing, still *self*-reflexivity. The result is investigative practices that are in fact doubly troubling because they reinforce the hegemony of certain academic constructs while convincing the investigator that he is undoing precisely those practices. In feminist scholar Wanda Pillow's words, self-reflexive practices "perpetuate colonial practices while at the same time attempting to mask this power over the subject."[15] Pillow and others try to offset this problem by representing the research subject as a postmodern fractured and unstable and therefore irreducible subject, but as Nencel notes, "their post-foundational, messy dialogical subjects do not escape from being ontologically predefined."[16] The researcher has simply replaced the projected modern subject with the projected postmodern subject.

Ultimately, the other-instigated reversal is cosmological. Ewing argues that most anthropology, modern and postmodern alike, is operatively atheist. In her words, interpretive and reflexive ethical neutralization develops, "in reaction to the reductive atheism of earlier, especially Durkheimian, social science, but it remains an atheism nonetheless. While espousing cultural relativism, the anthropological community has maintained a barrier to belief."[17] Ewing is not alone in her critique. Charles Stewart, Henri Gooren, and Claude Stipe, among other anthropologists, have made the charge as well.[18] Though there are debates about how thoroughly the disenchanted secularism of the "modern" world pervades contemporary society even in the West,[19] there seems to be little disagreement that, with some exceptions,[20] it rules most of academic anthropology. In Stewart's words, "We study the sociocultural construction of miracles, while distancing ourselves from a belief in them."[21] It is no wonder, then, that often when anthropologists experience trans-normal phenomena, we resist understanding them as such.

Among the possible interpretations of the other-instigated reversal of our beliefs, an emic-indebted one might be that spirits, either of their own accord or sent by someone else, are acting to set right a wrong. Acholi have told me of how the socially and politically powerless turn to the *ajwaka* spirit medium as a last (and sometimes first) recourse against those in power who have wronged them.[22] If anthropologists generally agree that the early progenitors of our discipline were complicit in imperial oppression, then among the emic-indebted interpretations that we would have to include in our layering up of possible accounts is that the visitations experienced by and disrupting contemporary anthropologists is our politico-cosmological comeuppance wrought by spirits, an act that strings us up between our desire to belong to our discipline on the one hand and our commitment to report openly what happens in the field on the other.

To interpret the conversions of anthropologists as instigated by the other—that of the subaltern, both human and spirit—places the initiative outside the anthropologist. Such an interpretation might seem academically irresponsible on the part of the anthropologist, but here is where we must be attendant to the layers that are often hidden in modern (and postmodern) interpretations themselves. Talal Asad, whose *Formations of the Secular* goes a long way in stripping bare those layers,[23] cautions, in an essay titled, "Comments on Conversion," against too quick a judgment that converts' reports of being acted upon by an "other" are irrational and thereby irresponsible. Though he is here specifically referring to conversion to Christianity, his criticism applies to our understanding of conversion generally, even that of the anthropologist to magical thinking, whether Christian or otherwise.

> Why does it seem so important to us to insist that the converted are "agents?" Why do we discount the convert's claim that he or she has been "made into" a Christian?
>
> One aspect of "agency," of course, is the old Protestant doctrine of individual responsibility. Individuals are agents because they are responsible for their own souls. . . . The secular concept of agency is also connected to the spirit of capitalism. It invokes the mutually dependent figures of the entrepreneur and the consumer, or, more abstractly, the functions of initiating and choosing. Liberalism has worked these figures into its individualist theories of politics and morality. . . . Modern definitions of agency typically operate to render a world of "accidents" into a world of moral and legal responsibility. . . . The paradigmatic agent is the human individual.
>
> Too often, the assumptions we bring with us when talking about the conversion of people in another epoch or another society are the ideological assumptions in and about our modern condition. Conversion is regarded by moderns as an "irrational" event or process, but resort to the idea of agency renders it "rational" and "freely chosen." . . . The doctrine of action has become essential to our recognition of other people's humanity. Suffering, we think, does not serve to mark humans off from other animals. And that distinction is crucial for those who want to justify conversions to modernity.[24]

From a Christian theological standpoint, it is possible to interpret the dramatic epistemological, political, and cosmological reversal effected by spirit-crossings as a form of mercy. Call to mind again Sister Esther's words from Chapter 3:

> Now, at this difficult time, I was praying mostly the Divine Mercy. . . . I'm devoted to Divine Mercy because I know that whatever I can do cannot be up to the standard maybe God wants. So, my salvation depends on the mercy of God. I will be saved through the mercy of God, not because of what I am doing.

She imitates Jesus Christ, but knows that the pivotal event is when Christ moves toward her. Mercy is the other crossing the gap when even our best efforts at imitation ultimately fail, as they always will.

In the ethnographic context, spirit-crossings—or to use the common term in postmodern writing, "transgressions"—now understood as a kind of mercy, involves, instead of violence as a response to our violence, a re-offering on the part of the subaltern of that hospitality without which our life with them would be impossible, only this time it is offered through that which is most intimate in the host culture and which the disenchanted world most denies, the whisper of *psst*. What was a threat to professional standing is now gift.

The Gospels are replete with stories of reversals—the prodigal son (Lk. 15:11-32) and the great banquet (Lk. 14:15-24; Mt. 22:1-10) among them. The Sermon on the Plain tells us that the poor will know the Kingdom of God, the hungry will be filled, and the excluded will leap for joy; that the rich, if we do not alter our practices, will get no further consolation, go hungry, and mourn and weep (Lk. 6:20-26; cf. Mt. 5:3-12). Is it so incredible to see the visitations of spirits upon anthropologists and theologians *cum* anthropologists, with all the epistemological, political, and cosmological upending of our symbolic capital involved, as enacting just this kind of reversal? They are saying to us, "You have not yet really shaken off Frazer's hierarchical evolutionary ranking of cultures from magic ('backward') to religion (more acceptable) to science ('civilized'). Here is your chance. Start over again. Reconsider."

Relating worlds?

Because, even with the experience of spirit-crossings, we never become the other, we are left with the task—not always possible—of relating at least some aspects of the two worlds to each other—in my case, those of rural Acholiland and American academia. My own effort in this regard involves the rejection of "Ockham's razor." Also called the principle of succinctness, economy, or parsimony (*lex parsimoniae*), William of Ockham's "razor" in logic states that preference is for those explanations with the fewest assumptions, and it forms, in my judgment, the basis of interpretive reductionism, scientific and otherwise. I call it the "fallacy of singular causal explanation." More succinct is not always better or even to be prima facie preferred in interpretation and explanation. Sometimes we can nicely dovetail the emic and etic explanations, sometimes we cannot; either way, recognizing Ockham's razor as a fallacy provides a modern/postmodern Western way of non-resistance to emic representation. Sometimes it is better to pile up assumptions of causality rather than try to reduce them to one, such as in the case of Laker's visitation.

When I arrived back home after seeing the photos of Laker, I was edgy and unable to sleep. I spoke with both a psychiatrist and a psychologist. The first told me that I had post-traumatic stress disorder—the photos (and everything else one sees in a conflict zone) were that disruptive of my psyche—and suggested that I undergo something called EMDR: Eye Movement Desensitization and Reprocessing therapy. In EMDR, the therapist leads the client in recalling the traumatic event while guiding the client to move her eyes back and forth. Something about the eye movement—just what it is exactly is debated—allows the disruptive experience to be lifted out of the initial context and reintegrated in the client's psyche in a way that is not traumatizing.[25] The client, eyes moving, recalls the event for a given span of time—say, a minute—and then, on cue from the therapist, brings to mind a safe and comforting image; for me it was the time my wife and I slow-danced in the aisle of our local supermarket to Bruce Springsteen's "Tougher Than the Rest" coming over the speakers. I can say that EMDR worked for me. Several sessions, and I began to sleep well again.

But that is not the end of it. I feel better, but continue to bring the slow-dance scene to mind when I go to bed to aid the transition to sleep. And, one night, Laker appears pressing in on my leg, not in the scene in my head, but in the bed, next to me. It is not a visual presence, but neither is it a vague feeling of something or other happening. It is her, clutching me. She wants, somehow, to be in the scene, in the mix with my wife and me. I do not know what to do, so I simply let her hang on to my leg in the bed, and I fall asleep, just as if it was one of my own daughters at that age asking to be in the bed because she is scared.

When I tell the psychologist of the visitation, he says, gently, that whether the visitation is real or not does not matter, what matters is my experience. What he misses is the fact that what *makes* it matter is precisely my experience of it as real. To the question of whether it is possible that it is not real, I answer that it is possible in the same way that it is possible that my keyboard is not real, but rather a projection, in an update of Berkeleyan idealism, of my psyche; that is to say, it is interesting as a kind of philosophical question—such as when Hilary Putnam asks if it could be true that we are all actually just brains in a vat sensing a world that is not really there[26]—but given, like with my keyboard, the phenomenological thereness of the experience, it is something that would seem to me, once it has occurred, to be rather silly to deny.

So what happened? I do not reject psychological insights about events. The psychiatrist has an explanation for the trauma. During the first week of that trip to Uganda, one of my daughters back at home had an asthma attack severe enough that one of the local hospitals could not handle the case, and transferred her to another hospital. My wife called me to give me an update. My daughter's condition was touch and go. We talked about whether I should come home. My wife said, "I thought about it, but figured, no, because, either way, it would be over by the time you got here." *Either way*: that is to say, whether my daughter died or was back in school as if nothing happened; severe asthma attacks indeed attack and, possibly, leave that quickly. The psychiatrist says that, subconsciously, I have put my daughter's face on the missing face of Laker.

But why, precisely, the visitation? An emic explanation—that is, one at home in Laker's rural Acholi culture—is that my initial response at seeing the pictures—the ones that so unsettle me that I can barely walk—is a response to her troubled spirit, a spirit who is, among other things, seeking comfort. And the EMDR sessions, as successful as they are in reducing my trauma, also, through conscious recollection of the photos, repeatedly call her to me such that, once I am comfortable enough with the thought of her, she in fact comes. In short, my structured recollection of Laker in EMDR served *both* to heal me psychologically *and* to call her spirit to me.

I return to Uganda five months later and bring up the subject of Laker's visitation with an elder, one who is also Western educated. He says, "Of course she came to you [given that I had been calling her]. Of course she troubled you. This is why the Acholi have only the female relatives—the mother, the grandmother—go up to the grave when she is buried. That is for them to do." I must tell her to go away. As long as she is attached to me, she cannot go to where she needs to be. When I return to Madi Opei, Laker's village, she comes near me during Mass, but I tell her that she must go, and she does.

* * *

Beyond the specific case of interpreting Laker's visitation, the broader recognition of the limitations of all conceptual construals and the need of layering up assumptions in rejection of any preference for singular explanation have important implications for theological interpretation in the academy. First and foremost, it means that there need be no special pleading for theological reasoning to enter into academic conversation; all construals have, to use a sociological term, their functional equivalents to theological interpretations and claims—like neoliberal economics' postulate of the rational actor and the free market or the various accounts of historical materialism or Foucaultian accounts of the will to power. Again, to the objection that theism or spirit-belief is different in kind, that it is neither ethically neutral nor has the reflexive capacity of ethical neutralization, Ewing argues that such an objection, whether modern or postmodern in its influences, masks a refusal to believe and thus constitutes a fundamental ontological atheism. Here I would part slightly with Ewing and side with Weber that "scientific" investigation involves its own faith claims, its own institutionally enforced dogmas. What appears as non-belief is here belief in something else. But the remainder of what Ewing says is quite accurate:

> The act of entertaining this possibility [of belief in emic claims] is not the same as the paradoxical and ultimately impossible, or at least paternalistic, effort to give 'voice' to one's informant; it is the *far more radical concession* of acknowledging that the person one is talking to might actually know something about the human condition and the encompassing 'reality' that is valid for the anthropologist (emphasis added).[27]

That theology need not make any special pleading to enter into academic argument is not to say that there is no price to pay for admission. The incompleteness of all construals means that theological accounts, too, have their limits. There are, of course, extended theological traditions about the limits of language to express God's fullness, and of the consequent need for multiple names for God; in other words, a piling up of assumption after assumption. But I mean something more here, and that is that God or spirit language itself is not always appropriate. Sometimes not just psychoanalytically, but also theologically, a cigar is just a cigar, and what one is experiencing with one's lower leg while one lies in bed is just restless leg syndrome. Yes, God is everywhere and in everything, but Weber is right: teleology, whether theological or otherwise, cannot replace the "painstaking labor of [materially and efficiently] causally understanding historical reality."

* * *

Ojara the catechist has told me to join him in an exorcism. "There is a man who has the devil in him." It is after eucharistic service, and the chapel has emptied out except for eight or nine of us and the possessed man. I recognize him as the man who entered the chapel in the middle of the service and sat on the rise in front of the altar. The children sitting on the floor up front scooted away. At first I thought he was blind, but then realized he was more accurately near-catatonic.

Ojara proceeds to gather us around the man, who is about my height, five-foot-eight, and perhaps 120 pounds. He wears a torn multicolor blue print shirt with palm trees and red and white sailboats. He is barefoot, and his nails, ragged, extend well beyond the ends of his toes. His eyes do not appear to register anything, so to say that they stare straight ahead is to say too much.

We sing, gently and seated, at first, Ojara next to him. After about an hour, the group stands and moves closer. Some continue to sing, some pray. Louder. Ululations punctuate the drone. Another hour. Ojara is sweating now, and loud-whispers something in the man's ears. He calls us to a laying on of hands.

The man finally speaks. *En tye ka wang.* He is burning me.

Opira replies, *Meno tye Tipu Maleng ni tye ka wang ryem Sitan.* That is the Holy Spirit burning away Satan.

We finish and the man exits the chapel, looking, to me, no different than before.

Ojara whispers to me, "Five months ago he simply walked off into the bush. He was just in the bush all that time, living on nothing. All that time, no one saw him. We all thought he had died."

"Was he okay when he left?" I ask.

"The devil was in him. The devil told him to go into the bush."

"Did he drink a lot before?"

Bad batches of *arege* circulated all over Uganda in the previous months. Seventy people died from it; many others went blind.

"Yes, he drank a lot."

"Do you think that he may have had some of that bad *arege*?"

"Yes, maybe."

* * *

It is possible that the man had the devil in him and that Ojara exorcized it, but the lack of any palpable change suggests that, no, the man has simply corroded his brain with bad liquor (It is worth noting that even biblical—that is, faith-oriented—accounts of the casting out of demons typically depict observable changes in the subject of the exorcism.). The price of admission to the academy is that theologians, like everyone else, must pay close attention to the mundane, and that means accountable appropriation of the investigative tools of social science. Ethnography, I tell my students, is more than hanging out; it is, as one anthropologist, only half-jokingly, told me, "deep hanging out." In other words, the social sciences are bearers of rich traditions of reflection about the world, and theologians, if we want to engage in conversation in the academy, need to undertake Weber's "painful labor" of learning these traditions and engaging their practitioners. Of course, the reverse is true as well. If social scientists wish to study religious communities, they must learn the traditions and texts of those communities. An ethnographer who researches evangelical Christians once told me that he did not have to read Jonathan Edwards or George Whitefield to understand the studied communities, in his words, "as they really are." That is bad science, even on Weberian grounds: ideas matter, even when—perhaps especially when—they persist only in the form of unspoken remnants of earlier stages of the tradition.[28]

* * *

By now it is evident that I have already moved in the last three chapters from "discernment" regarding the culture of the Acholi well toward the next moment in anthropological theology, that of "commitment" to the people researched and their culture. It is not, as we have seen, a commitment without remainder, but the Acholi have formed me in ways that I have not anticipated, particularly as regards spirit-crossings. It is in light of the reality of such crossings that yet another area becomes evident in which Acholi culture can be a bridge for anthropological theologians to a better understanding of what it means to follow Jesus the Nazarene the Christ. In Chapter 4, I showed how Acholi understandings of communal identity illuminate the practice of communal property in Acts. Now, I will draw upon what we have seen regarding Acholi belief regarding spirit-crossings to clarify the relationship between justice and forgiveness in Jesus's teachings and actions. I suggest that cultural recognition of these crossings, such as is the case in Acholiland and the ancient Near East, creates a cosmological interpretive context that allows for the integration of justice and forgiveness. In other words, in order to get Jesus right normatively (on justice and forgiveness), we have to get him right cosmologically (on the intervention of spirits). That moderns struggle with relating justice and forgiveness is evident in debates within biblical studies. Detailing these debates will help show how a particular cosmology—and with it a particular understanding of space and time—is necessary to understand and practice Jesus's ethics.

Bridge cultures, II: spirit-crossings, justice, and forgiveness

The Toronto Sheraton Centre Hotel's forty-three floors of off-white sandstone exterior are courteously smooth, and yet shoot up as if by seismic accident. The main lobby is dark-paneled and judiciously populated with rust and limestone-colored wing-backed chairs and the occasional bookshelf to make it look like someone's den or library. Soft-light lamps abut couches with throw-pillows. Escalators take you up to a second floor outdoor garden. There, smoothed red-brick walkways with slat-board bridges cross what seems to be a creek—a creek?—that leads to a waterfall that descends down into the lobby. Accommodating curved-back wood and wrought iron benches by the waterway offer themselves to the weary.

Back inside in the foyer of the Dominion Ballroom, there is sconce lighting and a row of chandeliers. Refreshments have been set out on a white-linen-covered table. In the Ballroom itself, where the plenary takes place, there are eight more chandeliers. Gold fabric curtains and bunting are marked off by potted plants of some broad-leaf variety. This is the site of the annual meeting of the Catholic Theological Society of America.

John Meier speaks from the Ballroom podium during the plenary. "I had to ask myself: What concrete example in the field of theology today best exemplifies the promises and pitfalls of using the scriptures as a source of theological reflection?'"

He chooses liberation theology, he says, because it has "brought a breath of fresh air" to the discipline. Moreover, it "represents a fierce drive" to make academic theology accountable, in Meier's words, to "the lived Christianity of a suffering people." He warns, "It is all too easy for armchair exegetes in the safety of the United States or Canada to criticize Latin American authors who daily risk their lives by writing with a relevance that could be deadly to themselves."

Then the talk takes a critical—in both senses of the word—turn.

"If, to support one's argument, one chooses to play the academic game, then one has to be willing to be judged by the rules of that game."

Meier analyzes the work of Jon Sobrino: it is lacking in academic rigor, he says, and therefore seriousness in its appeal to the historical Jesus.

"At times, the historical Jesus seems to be Jesus insofar as he fits into Sobrino's program of liberation theology. For all the talk of a new approach, we are not all that far from the proof-text use of scripture in the old Catholic manuals of dogmatic theology."

The talk turns from method to substance. Meier criticizes Sobrino's emphasis on the "option for the poor." Closer examination of scripture, Meier says, reveals that what is really at stake is that Jesus forgives sinners. "There is no proof that Jesus' concern for economically poor or uneducated people caused a major scandal or persecution, or was the major reason for his execution. Matters may have been different with his free offer of forgiveness to public sinners," including "economic oppressors."

He goes on, "The damaging charge against [Jesus] was not that he associated with the poor, but that he associated with the wicked. It is a mistake to think that the Pharisees were upset because Jesus ministered to the ordinarily pious common people and the economically impoverished."

In closing, Meier comments that he is not opposed to liberation theology. Rather, he says, "I would like to aid it by fraternal correction."[29]

* * *

Given the near-palatial setting of Meier's talk, it might be tempting to summarily dismiss it as simply a diatribe masked by footnotes, with the references to liberation theologians' willingness to "daily risk their lives" in order to be accountable to "the lived Christianity of a suffering people" at the beginning and his claim of offering mere "fraternal correction" at the end forming a disingenuous *inclusio* around the real message. However, it is important, like Meier urges us, to look more closely at the scriptural evidence.

Jesus's deeds and words do convey a foregrounded message of forgiveness of the wicked. Concerning his deeds, Mathew and Luke depict, without rebuttal, Pharisees and scribes—"this generation"—criticizing Jesus for welcoming, befriending, and eating with sinners (Mt. 11:16-19; Lk. 15:2). With regard to his words, all three synoptic gospels witness to Jesus's proclamation, "I have come to call not the righteous but sinners" (Mk 2:17; Mt. 9:13b; Lk. 5:32). The Sermon on the Mount/Plain in Matthew and Luke admonishes us to love our enemies (Mt. 5:43-48; Lk. 6:27-36), and to forgive the debts or sins of others (Mt. 6:12; Lk. 11:4). Luke follows the call to love our enemies immediately with the specific command not to judge or condemn, but to forgive (Lk. 6:37). And Jesus's words on forgiveness extend to the parables. Both Matthew (18:12-14) and Luke (15:1-6) tell the parable of the lost sheep, and Luke, once again, spells out its implications: "There will be more joy in heaven over one sinner who repents than over ninety-nine righteous persons who need no repentance" (15:7).[30] Luke takes the message of forgiveness all the way to the Cross: "Father, forgive them; for they know not what they are doing" (23:34).[31]

Meier has a point, then, and a crucial one at that, regarding what may fairly be called Jesus's "option for the wicked," a point which Sobrino, at least, reads out of the Gospel. The latter's liberation theology so reads scripture in terms of justice as a response to the oppressor/oppressed dynamic that it leaves little room for forgiveness of the wicked. The task of mercy here is not foremost to forgive the oppressors, who, according to Sobrino, are the "sinners par excellence," but rather, again in Sobrino's words, to "take the crucified people from the cross." Yes, God is "essentially inclined to forgiveness," Sobrino says, but there are differences between kinds of sinners, and the "presence of the greater sin" lies with "the oppressor."[32]

We should not let Meier off the hook, however. He works hard to minimize any option for the poor in the gospels. I already cited in an earlier chapter Jesus's blessings on the poor and woes to the rich and the former's centrality to Jesus's mission such that they feature, for instance, in the Sermon on the Plain: "Blessed are the poor" (Lk. 6:20-26; cf. also Mt. 5:3-12). Most of Meier's references in his five-tome work, *A Marginal Jew*, to a mission to the poor, however, are only in passing.[33] The case against any "option for the poor" becomes explicit when he argues that, because the poor were so many at the time, the claim that Jesus went *specifically* to the poor is all but empty of import. When Meier mentions that "Jesus reached out to Jews of all stripes, the respectable and (especially) the sinful, the rich and (especially) the poor," he adds the important qualifier that, "to say that Jesus was concerned about the poor does not in the end say very much. About 90 percent of Galilean Jews would probably have qualified as 'poor' in some sense of the word."[34] Meier may mention some kind of preference for the poor in passing, but then immediately undoes it in his analysis.

Why the bifurcation of Jesus's mission, with Meier going one way and Sobrino the other? Why can Jesus not have special missions to both the poor and the wicked? The impediment, I suggest, is a modern sense of time and space that places justice on behalf of the poor in the present world and interprets forgiveness of the wicked as an act in anticipation of another world, one that has yet to come. This is all the more evident in the purer examples of what we might call the liberationist and dispensationist ideal types of historical Jesus interpretation.[35]

Richard Horsley is closer to the ideal type of the liberationist than is Sobrino. Like liberationists generally, he wants to offer a "people's history" of the gospels, a view from below, and foregrounds the oppressor/oppressed axis of interpretation. "The dominant reality in the political-economic-religious structure was the fundamentally conflictual divide between imperial rulers and their Herodian and high priestly clients whose wealth and power derived from the tribute, taxes, and tithes they extracted, on the one hand, and the village producers they ruled and taxed, on the other."[36] What makes Horsley a purer instance of a liberationist ideal type than Sobrino is his outright rejection of any future, otherworldly references in Jesus's teaching and mission. Claims in the gospels of a Kingdom of God coming in the future functioned simply as, in Horsley's intended-to-be-pejorative words, a kind of "magic charm" that some peasants believed was "capable, by itself, of transforming the world." This constituted a "mystification of the imperial situation." Any otherworldly cosmic struggle between God and Satan "was simply a symbolization of the violent social-political-religious conflict in which the people were caught individually and collectively." Expectations of a Messiah in the gospels are merely a "Christian scholarly projection."[37] It is not surprising, then, that Horsley doubts the historicity of Jesus's forgiveness of the wicked.[38]

E. P. Sanders is a purer instance of the dispensationist type than is Meier.[39] He stresses that Jesus was not the leader of a social movement, but a theologian, and necessarily so. Jesus viewed his mission as introducing the climax of *salvation* history, which takes precedence over any political history with which it overlaps. The primary conflict, then, is not between the Galilean peasants on the one hand and imperial and local oppressors on the other, but between the theological sources of good and evil, God and Satan. This is why "the gospels put at the outset a major conflict with the chief of the powers of evil, Satan himself." In such a setting, a reading of the gospels that presses the fact that religion is embedded in politics to the point of reducing the former to the latter is untenable. "Now we see that we cannot pare the gospel material down to the non-theological core, and then proclaim that we have found Jesus, since Jesus himself was a theologian."[40] Sanders writes that if "Jesus expected *God* to change history in a decisive way in the immediate future, it seems unlikely that he was a social reformer" (emphasis in original).[41] Yes, Sanders concedes, Jesus preached the Kingdom of God, and the concept of "kingdom" is a political one, but, he then claims, it "refers only to supernatural society." To the extent that it is here and now, it can only be, in his words, "invisible."[42] Despite Sanders's emphasis that Jesus was a theological figure, his is a God who is not here, not yet. At this point, he sounds much like Meier, who writes, "The definitive arrival of God's kingly rule was imminent; calls for social and political reform, launched—and often botched—by human beings, were thus beside the point."[43]

What makes Sanders a purer example of the dispensationist ideal type than Meier is the degree to which he presses the point that Jesus offers forgiveness to sinners *without the need of their repentance*.[44] For instance, when taking up the story of Zacchaeus, the tax collector who promises to give half of his wealth to the poor and to repay fourfold those whom he has cheated, Sanders argues that it is an anomalous case, and that, besides, Jesus does not ask or require him to do all this.[45] He concludes, "Jesus was not a preacher of repentance: he was not primarily a reformer, and in his association with tax collectors and sinners he was not trying to persuade them to do as Zacchaeus did."[46]

Something is off about both the Sobrino-Horsley and Meier-Sanders reads of scripture. The scriptural texts evidence that Jesus clearly has a preferential option for the poor *and* for those deemed particularly wicked.[47] If we are to imitate *this* Jesus Christ, then we need to discern how he joins the two missions into a single one in announcing the Kingdom of God. For the one point on which Sobrino and Meier agree is that the poor and the wicked are not the same people; Sobrino and Meier's shared mistake is that they trade one off for the other. But in order to understand how Jesus joins the two missions, it is helpful, first, to delineate how they become rendered as separate in the modern era, and for this, Weber's concept of rationalization is illuminating.

* * *

It has often been argued that "rationalization" is the core concept in Weber's analysis of the modern era.[48] In many cases—and this happens to be one of them—core concepts of key thinkers are maddeningly elusive to summarize. Weber applies it in many ways to a wide range of social spheres. However, in most instances, he is referring to the rise and spread of instrumental means-end reasoning. As instrumental reasoning, once one's desired end, whatever it may be, is chosen, the highest value is given to the predictable calculability of the means. Weber takes an earlier argument offered by Werner Sombart that calculability is the defining characteristic of the capitalist economy and applies it to all social spheres—for Weber, the value of predictable calculability is definitive of modernity as such.[49]

The desirability of predictable calculability has led to the division of time and space into discrete and uninterrupted units. Although, as Weber makes clear in *The Protestant Ethic and the Spirit of Capitalism*, full-blown rationalization of religion did not come about until the Reformation, the book also highlights medieval precursors. He argues that the cloistered monk, with his ascetic life rationally—that is, instrumentally—ordered to achieve the end of salvation, was "the first human being" in the medieval West "to live according to a time schedule."[50] Later Weber scholars will push the case even further and argue that the medieval cloister, with its methodical time regimentation, efficient labor, and technological advances was a nascent capitalist factory.[51] Even scholars who do not accept the full force of this latter interpretation of the rationalization of monastic life note the very Calvinist-sounding statement in Benedict's Rule, "idleness is the enemy of the soul."[52] While the full-fledged division of labor, and thus the compartmentalization of not only time, but also space into discrete units, does not come until later, it does come, and with it the eclipse of any cosmology or theology that allows a blurring or, worse, rupturing of the discrete units of three-dimensional space and strict linear time.

The cosmological and theological implications of this compartmentalization of space and time did not go unnoticed by Weber. In fact, he noticed it even more as his thinking developed, such that in his revised version of *The Protestant Ethic* he introduces the concept of disenchantment, and he develops it further in later essays. The modern world is such that, in Weber's words, "there are no mysterious incalculable forces that come into play, but rather . . . one can, in principle, master all things by calculation. This means that the world is disenchanted." The entire world has been "transformed into a causal mechanism."[53] Theologically, disenchantment is characterized by a remote God, one who does not interfere with our parsed time and space—and it is not incidental that the two theologians most influenced by Weber and his colleague Ernst Troeltsch—that is, H. Richard Niebuhr and James Gustafson—would write of "radical monotheism" in Niebuhr's case and claim that "Jesus is not God" in Gustafson's.[54] This is a God who, in the end, will not bend down through the universe even for the Incarnation.

The use of methods of calculability in the modern search for the historical Jesus grew out of the disenchanted world that Weber describes, such that even scholars with other theological commitments are profoundly shaped by it. The result is a Jesus whose sense of time and space is parsed into discrete, uninterrupted (because uninterruptable) units: Jesus either is a reformer who calls for social change in the here and now *or* he is an "eschatological prophet" who points toward a future, if immanent, world that, at present, is elsewhere. To affirm both would constitute a contradiction, a violation of the laws of time and space. The consequence on the normative level is another parsing: Jesus is either for justice for the poor (in the here and now) or for forgiveness of sinners (in the hopes for a world that is not here, but is yet to come). This compartmentalization of the ethics of Jesus is precisely what comes to the fore in both Meier's plenary address and Sobrino's liberation theology.

* * *

The Acholi practice of communion with and even possession by spirits cuts across the modern strict demarcations of time and space that separate God acting here and now from God acting in a different place and time. It is not that the Acholi do not have a sense of linear time, but that spirits can interrupt time; past, present, and future can and do cross-cut. Again, spirits—*jogi*—of the dead interact with the people who remain on earth. The dead are buried in family compounds where they can continue to dwell where they always have. When a person dies from unnatural means or is not given a proper burial, he returns as *cen*, a restless spirit. The *ajwaka* or spirit medium regularly confers with her *jogi*—often the spirits of people long dead or even not-yet-born and geographically and thus spatially distant from the medium. When necessary, the *jogi* speak and act quite literally in and through her. Similar practices run throughout much of sub-Saharan Africa.[55]

With such openness to spirited interruption of space and time, it is not surprising that most Acholi see no zero-sum trade-off between justice and forgiveness. Studies of Acholi attitudes toward the LRA conflict show that the majority want both justice for the oppressed and forgiveness of the wicked, and see little contradiction between the two desires.[56] This is not a matter of inconsistent thinking, but rather reflects a particular cosmology. The Acholi enact this cosmology in a particularly focused way in the practice of *mato oput*, a mix of trial, negotiation, repentance, reparation, ritual, and banquet that joins justice for the wronged and forgiveness for wrongdoers.

Acholi typically practice *mato oput* when there has been a murder. Elders gather members of the two clans—that of the killer and that of the victim—and determine what transpired. Most often, *cen*, the wronged spirit of the victim back from the past and now ever-present, haunts the perpetrator, and drives him to confess ahead of time. The clan of the killer pays remuneration to the clan of the victim, typically an agreed upon number of livestock (thus the justice aspect to the practice). A lamb is slaughtered and there is a feast. At the center of the process is the ritual—no less literal for being so—of drinking the mashed and liquefied root of the *oput* tree, which tastes very bitter. *Mato oput* translates, "drinking of the bitter root." The killer and a clan member representing—that is, reenacting the spirit of—the victim kneel facing each other with their hands behind their backs and drink simultaneously from an *oput*-filled calabash. Often, their foreheads touch.[57] They literally and figuratively swallow the bitterness. All Acholi gather—the dead, the living, and the not-yet-born—in a justice that forgives and a forgiveness that is just.[58] The role of the spirits is particularly important when, as is often the case in northern Uganda, the aggrieved and the guilty are what are called "intimate enemies," people who know each other well and have deep social ties.[59] In otherwise intractable life situations, the intervention—that is, the interruption of normal space and time—by the not-currently living is often necessary to effect reconciliation among the living, to help call to mind and bring to reality a different time and space than the present conflictual one. Without *mato oput*, *cen* will continue to haunt not only the individual perpetrator, but the other members of his clan as well.

Mato oput is not a panacea. It has limits. It was not originally intended for addressing the kind of mass killings that have occurred in the LRA conflict. More, the ritual requires the presence of some wealth to fund the gathering and the feast, and the Acholi lost most of their material capital—98 percent of their cattle (the traditional banking system)—due to theft during the conflict. Also, years in the IDP camps have brought cultural erosion—there is an entire generation of Acholi that has not experienced *mato oput*. And, as indicated in the previous chapter, modern individualism has made major incursions through media like radio ads that tout a consumerist mentality and way of life.[60]

Still, the practice of *mato oput* has made a comeback, evidencing the perdurability of the spirit-infused cosmology. In fact, the breadth of the disruption of the conflict has led to the expansion of the applicability of the ritual. Acholi with whom I have spoken see little problem not only with retrieving the practice, but also with extending it to include the possibility of reconciliation with people who have committed crimes—rape, incest, and cannibalism—previously considered unforgivable. People who have committed such crimes are traditionally called *obibi*—literally, "ogres"—to connote their nonhuman status. The category of *obibi* would rule many former LRA out of participation in *mato oput* because they have abducted and used girls as sex slaves and commanded abductees to eat human flesh. However, advocates of *mato oput* also stress the need, in this situation, to extend the ritual to people previously considered *obibi*. As Acholi elder and Retired Anglican Bishop MacLeod Baker Ochola told me,

> First of all, you need to know that what is happening has no comparison in our past history. Nothing like this ever happened to us. Nothing. These are new phenomena

that are happening now. . . . A lot of bad things have happened. Some people have even maybe eaten human meat. You know? They've become cannibals.

Now can *mato oput* really help in all this? I say yes.[61]

* * *

If we read scripture in terms of a cosmology like that articulated and practiced in traditional Acholi culture, then we need not suppress the moral implications of the workings of spirits and the Spirit in the gospels. Biblical scholar John Pilch describes Jesus's cosmology as a "densely populated spirit world with ready interference of those spirits in human life,"[62] and charges that most historical-critical method, with its modern presuppositions with regard to spirits, space, and time, is "neither sufficiently historical nor critical."[63] Pilch examines Jesus's baptism, the testing in the desert, the walking on the sea, the transfiguration, and the resurrection experiences, and finds in each case a "real experience of a real event in alternate reality."[64] The only point that I would add is that such experiences for ancient Mediterraneans as well as for others who have them are not so much of an "alternate" reality—that is still modern language talking—but rather is an integrated part of reality taken as a whole. This is what Paul Stoller means when he talks of the "fusion of the worlds" that takes place in Songhay witchcraft: engagement with and possession by spirits overcomes the modern unbridgeable bifurcation between the here and the there, the present and the past or future, the physical and the trans-physical worlds.[65] It is precisely this fusion that allows Jesus the Nazarene to understand his missions to the poor and wicked as not a contradiction between the here/now and the there/future. Like we saw in Chapter 4, Jesus's own authority to theologize came from his ability to make God present through his reenactment of key figures—particularly Elijah, but also Moses and David—from Israel's past. He re-presented these figures through a mission that turned its attention particularly to the poor and the wicked in acts of healing and parables announcing the Kingdom of God. These acts and words crossed the boundaries—already permeable in the ancient Near East—between human and divine, between past, present, and future, and, as a result, between the wicked and the poor and the good news. If we read scripture through the cosmology of rural northern Uganda and South Sudan, we do not need to suppress this component of the Gospel, which, I will now argue further, is critical if we are to follow Jesus the Nazarene the Christ.

Pivoting from discernment to commitment:
The case for magical christianity

Again, by now it is clear that the Acholi people have profoundly impacted me and my understanding of what it means to be a person in the world, so it would not be out of place to close this chapter by pivoting from *discernment of* their culture to *commitment to* the people who constitute it, at least to the point of making a case for the worldview that they hold, one that early anthropologists disdained as "magical thinking," and that even present-day academics tend to fight off rather than take on as their own. Here, as elsewhere, it is helpful to begin with Weber.

Weber identifies modern religion as not just a move toward rationalization, but also a move away from what he considers magic. (Some translators prefer to render *Entzauberung*—usually translated as "disenchantment"—as "demagification.")[66] Cosmologically, while religion worships the one God, magic appeals to a variety of lesser spirits in attempts to manipulate them for human benefit. Ethically, religion is systematically ascetic while magic is lax: "Wherever the attachment to purely magical or ritualistic views have been broken by prophets or reformers, there has hence been a tendency for artisans, craftsmen and petty-bourgeois to incline towards a rationalistic ethical and religious view of life." And elsewhere, "Wherever the Eucharist was most completely stripped of its magical character . . . e.g. in Puritanism, communion nevertheless exerted an ethical effect, in some cases precisely because of the absence of magical and confessional controls." At times, Weber reads as if all sacraments are problematic, such as when he refers to "purely magical sacraments." The problem with such sacraments is that they let the believer off the hook by substituting incantation and ritual for moral reform. "Every type of actual dispensation of grace by a person, regardless of whether his authority derives from personal charismatic gifts or his official status within an institution, has the net effect of weakening the demands of morality upon the individual, just as does ritualism."[67] Though Weber claims to be providing merely a descriptive account of how rationalized modern society came into being, it is difficult to take him at his word—or rather, other words of his seem to contradict the claim. Sacramentality, for Weber, is the enemy of ethics. Even the Incarnation "*stands in the way* of a strict monotheism" (emphasis added).[68]

Weber writes that in the effort to win and hold converts, priests had "to compromise with the traditional views of the laity in formulating patterns of doctrine and behavior." Such compromise meant that priests were unable to release "the faith of the masses from its *bondage* to traditions based upon magic" (emphasis added).[69] The Weber-informed historian, Lutz Kaelber argues similarly that miracles and sacraments are a priestly "concession" to the laity.[70] Keith Thomas adds, "The claim to supernatural power was an essential element in the Anglo-Saxon Church's fight against paganism. . . . The medieval church found itself *saddled with the tradition* that the working of miracles was the most efficacious means of demonstrating its monopoly on the truth" (emphasis added).[71] Such a tradition, claims Thomas, is "now all rightly disdained by intelligent persons."[72]

If I am right, however, it is precisely "magical" Christianity, perhaps uniquely so, that can keep the faith true to Jesus the Nazarene the Christ. If the gospels are even roughly accurate depictions of who Jesus was, then it is precisely through such miracles—particularly the physical healings effected through touch as well as word—that Jesus the Nazarene leveraged his authority, especially early on in his ministry. And the opposition between magic and ethics is a false one, indebted to Weber's identification of ethics with a particular understanding of strict ascesis. Jesus the Nazarene was not an ascetic in the manner of John the Baptist. In fact, he was accused by his critics, probably not all that inaccurately, of being an at least sometime winer and diner. His disciplines—the itinerancy, the rules for what to take on the road—were, like his suffering and death on the Cross, not ends in themselves, but practices in service to his mission. Yet that mission is deeply ethically oriented: solidarity with the poor; forgiveness of the wicked.

The building of shrines, prayers to intercessory agents, the use of relics—these are all practices that Weberians identify with bondage. I interpret the practices to be part of a theological cosmology that breaks down the boundaries between the here and the there, the present and the future, ourselves and God's Spirit—a cosmology that facilitates our reenactment of Jesus Christ. Kaelber indicates that in the later Middle Ages, Adoration of the Eucharist began to take precedence over the use of relics as a source of, in his words, "supernatural power."[73] I have already shown in Chapter 4 how Eucharistic Adoration—and the cosmology it presupposes—is central to the devotional life and witness of the Little Sisters of Mary Immaculate of Gulu. Perhaps it will be helpful here to turn to another witness, John Baptist Odama, Archbishop of Gulu, and how his devotion to the Eucharist feeds his own twin missions—*moral* missions—to the poor and the wicked. He is an exemplar of the fact that sacramental devotion does not contravene a profoundly ethical life.

* * *

Archbishop John Baptist Odama has offended everyone: the LRA rebels have threatened to kill him, and the Ugandan government has labeled him a rebel collaborator. His outward appearance gives no indication as to why this is. He is dressed in the only outer clothes I have ever seen him wear—a white episcopal cassock with red piping and buttons; a two-inch silver cross pendant that hangs down by his abdomen—and I have met with him many times in my trips to northern Uganda. Born into an ethnic Luo community that has deep cultural and linguistic affinities with the Acholi, he is short, bald, and very black. He chuckle-giggles often. His voice and comportment are light, with an absence of sudden gesture. Nothing betrays the things he has seen or endured.

Archbishop Odama is a man of symbolic acts that are not simply symbolic. He has offered, in a modified reenactment of the Barabbas scene, to go to jail in place of rebel leader Joseph Kony if that would stop the conflict. He is serious in his offer. This is the real body and blood. When the government insisted that it provide security forces for him after the LRA threatened to kill him, he replied, "No, my security is linked with the people. If they are secure, I will be secure. If they are not secure, my isolated security will not mean much. So, please, protect the people. I will be okay."

After having known the Archbishop for five years, I have asked to interview him formally, because the interviews by journalists have inquired only about his political role. They have not, for instance, asked about his devotional life—one in which he goes for Eucharistic Adoration for twelve hours every Thursday, missing both breakfast and lunch. They do not reveal that he talks to Jesus, person to person, through the Holy Spirit. They have provided no openings for him to give *his* account of the world. He tells me, "Especially when I'm before the Blessed Sacrament, words of the Bible come spontaneously. Yeah, they come spontaneously. 'Be not afraid. I am with you.' Then, 'Abide in me as I abide in you.' These words come when I'm there before the Blessed Sacrament. They come in and they kind of reinforce, yes they reinforce, my faith and also my commitment and outlook on the real life. I've ever been hopeful, always—even in the most desperate situations, I tell people, 'Don't lose hope. Don't lose hope. Let us keep going. The Lord is there.'"

We are talking in the Archbishop's residence. It was built by the Comboni missionaries when they administered the archdiocese after evangelizing the region, so it is better appointed than most structures in the area, but that is a relative comparison. The brick walls are thinly plastered over and painted flat white. The couch on which he sits has a simple-cut external wood frame with purple velour- (not velvet-) covered seat cushions accented with white doilies. The relative comfort can give a misleading sense of safety. In Gulu, many night commuters sleep on the tin-visored porches surrounding the bus park. In June 2003, Archbishop Odama and other members of the ARLPI slept four nights there. Unlike in Meier's account of Jesus, the Archbishop makes no argument to the effect that because there are so many poor he has no special mission to them. From our interview:

TDW: *You have done some things where it very much appears [that] the Lord is indeed abiding in you. For instance, when you slept in the bus park. . . . Can you say a little bit about that?*

JBO: We wanted to raise something which was challenging to us, as the group of Acholi religious leaders. We said, "What can we do?" They said, "Archbishop, are you ready, really, to go and sleep in the street there with the children?" I said, "We go." And, that really came just spontaneously and with very strong force. Very strong force and conviction, immediately.

So, this visit to the Eucharist, for me, it gave me a lot of courage and a lot of determination. Really, to be honest, it was a kind of motivation, also—what really motivated me. So, going there to sleep on the street was something very . . . for me, it was just a very simple thing. The first thing I went with was a paper, you know, a piece of paper to put as a mat, down, and then a piece of blanket. One blanket.

When the children saw me lie down, now, like them . . . that thing, I saw it struck them. Because, I don't know what was deep inside them, what they were thinking, but, seeing me lie down in public like them, and on a *[chuckle]* you know, just on a mat. They were just, they were stuck; they were stuck. But, later, they began to *see*, because we went there four times, you know. They began to see it was something of our concern for them. And, they began to call us, you know, colleagues. Colleagues, yes. They began to call us colleagues. And, therefore, we felt very close to them, and also they felt close to us. That, to me, was very, very . . .

Then, the other thing which I felt also the Adoration helped me to see more . . . I was beginning to feel now, more and more, in a relation with people—with any group. Compassion and sympathy for the people's conditions began to grow more and more in me. More and more in me. And, even to the extent that I didn't bother about my security.

So, in a way, this devotion of life, I don't know how many fruits, I cannot count them [chuckle], even the ones growing in the bush.

The Archbishop's reference to "the ones growing in the bush," namely, the rebels, prompts me to shift the direction of the interview. He has been involved in multiple negotiations—by his count, at least twelve—with top LRA rebel commanders in the bush country. These are not just your ordinary sinners. These are, as Sobrino would say, "sinners par excellence." Yet, unlike Sobrino, Odama's witness is to these ones "in the bush," as well as to those whom they victimize. To use Sobrino's phrase, the ones in the bush also need to be "taken down from the cross." I press on with the interview:

TDW: *Let's talk a little bit about* [the ones in the bush] *because, one of the things that seems a little, I won't say quite unique, but unusual about your witness is, not only that you're willing to go out to the bush, but that you are willing to, well, to put it Biblically, 'forgive the wicked.' In one of the things you wrote, you quote Ezekiel on that.*

JBO: Yes, yes, yes. You have correctly touched on those key quotations. The text of Ezekial, where the Lord says, "I don't take pleasure in the death of the wicked, but, rather, in the conversion of the wicked." That text struck me several times. And, I repeated it to myself many, many times. I was even telling this to the seminarians this morning. I said, "Look, to be honest, Jesus could have asked his father to send the angels, to wipe all those who killed him, I mean, who fixed him on the cross. But, now, you hear what he says. He says fundamental points. One, he says, 'You, God, you are our common father. My father, and the father to these others.' Two, he says, 'Forgive them. Don't do the wrong they did to me back to them. No, no, no, no. Forgive them.' He added, 'Because they don't know what they are doing.'"

It has struck me often, those who have done a lot of evil, when they are faced with the grace of God, they are faced with the touch of the love of God. Despite the evil they have done, they have not been killed by God. God allows them to live on. In reality, what God is showing is that, the sinner, in his or her condition, is helpless. I've said this even about those of Kony. . . . But, now, [Kony's] problem is, "If this is what I have done, can I be accepted by anybody?" This is where his situation of being stuck is. "Who can accept me after having done all this? Who can take me back to my status of being a human person, a child of God? Who can do it?" And, I discovered this, the way of looking at [Kony], and the way of talking to him, and the way, when we are together with the others, very often he recognizes my presence immediately. And, he kind of focuses on me in the way of saying, "Can you do something to change my condition?" This is a kind of feeling I draw from him, and also from the others.

So, if this is true, the heart of God is truly deeper than what we are saying, because what does God get stuck on? God's love is beyond the sin. His love cannot be prevented by sin, no. He loves the sinner as he or she is. What he desires for the sinner is: "I love you so much, can you respond to me? Can you respond?"

It seems clear, then, that Archbishop Odama's veneration of the Host not only does not "stand in the way" of a moral life, as Weber and his intellectual descendants would have it, but rather—along with the other of his devotional practices—gives impetus to steadfast love for the poor and the wicked, a love that seeks justice in solidarity with the former and offers forgiveness to the latter.

* * *

Archbishop Odama's witness tells me that there is much more that I need to do in response to the world of the people of northern Uganda and South Sudan. The spirit-infused cosmology exhibited there does not take place in a political and economic vacuum. What has made Odama's and others' witness so remarkable is that they carried it out in the context of a prolonged armed conflict, and therefore brought with it attendant risks. In Chapter 5, I said that it was presumptuous to take on the identifier of Christian while exempting ourselves from the social consequences that are often concomitant with following Christ—marginalization, harassment, sometimes death. Over the course of my research in northern Uganda and South Sudan, many Acholi told me things that cut against the received narrative of the war, a narrative in which the Acholi are the sole cause of the conflict and its brutality. American geopolitical interests, which continue to rely on the good graces of Ugandan president Yoweri Museveni in order to have a presence in East Africa, align with and perpetuate the received narrative.

Given what people in the IDP camps told me, I found myself in a situation much like that of the early Comboni missionaries that I described in the second chapter: I could remain silent regarding what I knew and be guilty of cooperating with evil, or I could write as implored by Orach Otim—he who was hung by his testicles—and many others and risk being barred from re-entry into Uganda, making me unable to finish my research. Following the terminology that I have been using to structure this book, it was time in the process of mimesis to move from discernment *about* Acholi culture to commitment *to* the people who give that culture life. That commitment manifested itself in writing, and the result, with updating, is the substance of the next chapter. Its tone is intentionally prosecutorial: I bring the United Nations Convention on the Prevention and Punishment of Genocide to bear on Museveni and his forces. If the US government and the International Criminal Court will not take Museveni to task for his treatment of the people in north Uganda, others who claim any sort of knowledge of and allegiance to the Acholi have to at least try to do so.

Notes

1. Martin Luther King's exegesis is the only one that I have read of the Good Samaritan story that points out that one of the reasons the others did not stop is because of the danger of doing so:

   Now you know we use our imagination a great deal to try to determine why the priest and the Levite didn't stop. At times we say they were busy going to church meetings—an ecclesiastical gathering—and they had to get down to Jerusalem so they wouldn't be late for their meeting. At other times we would speculate that there was a religious law that "One who was engaged in religious ceremonials was not to touch a human body twenty-four hours before the ceremony."

But I'm going to tell you what my imagination tells me. It's possible that these men were afraid. You see, the Jericho road is a dangerous road. . . . In the days of Jesus it came to be known as "Bloody Pass." And you know it's possible that the priest and the Levite looked over that man on the ground and wondered if the robbers were still around. Or it's possible that they felt that the man on the ground was merely faking. And he was acting like he was robbed and hurt, in order to seize them over there, lure them there for quick and easy seizure. And the first question the Levite asked was, "If I stop to help this man, what will happen to me?" But then the Good Samaritan came by. And he reversed the question: "If I do not stop to help this man, what will happen to him?"

In the face of the violence he is sure that he will encounter, King seeks to embody the Samaritan, and calls his listeners to do so as well. He tells them to ask what would happen to the Memphis sanitation workers, who lack basic necessities, if he and his audience do not stop to help. That he is not ignorant of the implications is evident in the fact that he then relates the story of his being stabbed at a book signing several years earlier, and he wants to convey that there may well be similar dangers for him and his followers. As an outspoken politically active black man in the 1960s, his social location makes the risks clear to him. The day after his Memphis speech, King is shot. Martin Luther King, Jr., "I See the Promised Land," in Martin Luther King, Jr., *A Testament of Hope: The Essential Writings and Speeches of Martin Luther King, Jr.*, ed. James M. Washington (San Francisco: HarperSanFrancisco, 1990), pp. 279–82.

2. I draw the term *pistology* from H. Richard Niebuhr, *Faith on Earth: An Inquiry into the Structure of Human Faith*, ed. Richard R. Niebhur (New Haven: Yale University Press, 1991), pp. 63–4.

3. It would be wrong of me not to add that it appears that Ojara, my catechist host who told me that the cooperation between Acholi religious leaders is "of the devil," has had something of a conversion himself. I do not know what brought it about, but I am happy for it. When I saw him in 2010, the LRA had left Uganda and most of the people had moved from the camps. Ojara had been reading the creation accounts in the Book of Genesis and offered me his interpretation:

> "It is seeing God in all. If you love your lips, you love their lips. If you love your leg, you love their leg. Even the Muslim."
> "The Muslim?"
> "Even the Muslim. . . . Even the rebels."

4. For an overview of the development of the anthropology of conversion, see Henri Gooren, "Anthropology of Religious Conversion," in *The Oxford Handbook of Religious Conversion*, ed. Lewis R. Rambo and Charles E. Farhadian (Oxford and New York: Oxford University Press, 2014), pp. 84–116.

5. I am aware of the literature both on "home" anthropology, that is, studying one's own culture, and on "studying up," that is, studying elites. The vast majority of cultural anthropology still focuses on the culture of the "other," typically a culture with less power than our own.

6. It is important to emphasize that a willing e/pistemic vulnerability does not necessarily bring conversion—again, it is not a gap that we can cross of our own accord. It is entirely possible that even when an ethnographer practices such vulnerability, the studied culture, or a particular aspect of that culture, just does not "take," and this for any number of reasons.

It could be that the need to publish results cuts short the time necessary for sufficiently profound participation. Although a year or two can seem a long time to observe, it is nowhere close to a lifetime. A Songhay possession priest told Paul Stoller after the latter had been studying the culture for ten years and participated in more than seventy-five possession dances, "I could tell you so much about our way, but you would not hear me because you are not ready to learn these things." See Paul Stoller, "Beatitudes, Beasts, and the Anthropological Burden: Three Studies of Shamanism, Trance, and Possession," *Medical Anthropology Newsletter*13, no. 4 (August 1982), p. 1.

It also could be that the researcher is not the kind of person to whom certain kinds of things are revealed; even in the host culture, there are specialists for different kinds of activities. Often, the host culture looks upon these latter people as having received a call to that specialist role from something or someone external to themselves. Such a call is not something a person can simply will in order for it to take place. The Acholi speak frequently of false *ajwagi* who are in it for the income and do not have any true calling. More, receiving a call of a particular kind is not in itself something for which someone can take any sort of credit or claim a kind of superiority; beyond the initial practiced vulnerability, there is merit or blame, if there is to be any at all, only in how the person *responds* to the call. Further, it is possible to convert to some parts of a culture and not others. This is particularly worth noting because the researched cultures are already hybrids. For instance, Ojara, my host, is a Christian of a sort who incorporates traditional Acholi patterns of interaction with spirits. And certain aspects of a culture may be justifiably objectionable and therefore resisted, such that there is a selection process even for those who receive and respond to a call to a specific kind of emic interpretation.

7. Stoller and Olkes, *In Sorcery's Shadow*, 100. For Stoller's resistance to his trans-normal experiences and insistence on an "objective" standpoint, see also pp. ix–x, 24–7, 31, 38, 50–1, 58, 75, 110–13, 118–19, 123–4, and 199.

8. Talal Asad, ed., *Anthropology and the Colonial Encounter* (Ithaca and New York: Ithaca Press, 1973).

9. Katherine P. Ewing, "Dreams of a Saint: Anthropological Atheism and the Temptation to Believe," *American Anthropologist* 96, no. 3 (1994), p. 574.

10. Ewing, "Dreams of a Saint: Anthropological Atheism and the Temptation to Believe," p. 571. For other writing on the taboo against "going native," see Paul Stoller, "Eye, Mind and Word in Anthropology," *L'Homme* 24, nos. 3–4 (July–December, 1984), pp. 91–114; and Stoller, "Beatitudes, Beasts, and Anthropological Burdens," pp. 1–2, 6–10.

11. Edith Turner, "The Reality of Spirits," *ReVision* 15, no. 1 (Summer 1992). See also Edith Turner, *Experiencing Ritual: A New Interpretation of African Healing* (Philadelphia: University of Pennsylvania Press, 1992).

12. Ewing, "Dreams of a Saint," p. 571.

13. See T. M. Luhrmann, *Persuasion of the Witch's Craft: Ritual Magic in Contemporary England* (Cambridge, MA: Harvard University Press, 1989), pp. 318–21. What Ewing would call Luhrmann's "resistance" to emic explanation has engendered somewhat of a backlash against Luhrmann in the reviews on amazon.com, where most reviewers interpret her as being dismissive of emic interpretations: http://www.amazon.com/Persuasions-Witchs-Craft-Contemporary-England/dp/0674663241/ref=sr_1_1?s=books&ie=UTF8&qid=1383501091&sr=1-1&keywords=persuasions+of+the+witch%27s+craft (retrieved November 3, 2013). Luhrmann herself is more open in her later work. See T. M. Luhrmann, *When God Talks Back: Understanding the American Evangelical Relationship With God* (New York: Vintage Books, 2012).

For an account of anthropological involvement in witchcraft that does not back off emic interpretation because of disciplinary taboo, see Jeanne Favret-Saada, *Deadly Words: Witchcraft in the Brocage* (Cambridge, UK and New York: Cambridge University Press, 1981).

I am indebted to China Scherz for pointing me to both the Luhrmann and Favret-Saada works.

14. Luhrmann, *Persuasion of the Witch's Craft*, pp. 318–21.

15. Wanda Pillow, "Confession, Catharsis, or Cure?: Rethinking the Uses of Reflexivity as Methodological Power in Qualitative Research," *Qualitative Studies in Education* 16, no. 2 (2003), p. 185. For the limitations of self-reflexivity as a practice, see also Richa Nagar, "Collaboration across Borders: Moving Beyond Positionality," *Singapore Journal of Tropical Geography* 24, no. 3 (2003), pp. 356–72; and Patti Lathar, "Postbook: Working the Ruins of Feminist Ethnography," *Signs* 27, no. 1 (2001), pp. 199–227.

16. Nencel, "Situating Reflexivity," p. 4.

17. Ewing, "Dreams of a Saint," p. 572.

18. Charles Stewart, "Secularism as an Impediment to Anthropological Research," *Social Anthropology* 9, no. 3 (2001), pp. 323–8; Henri Gooren, "Anthropology of Religious Conversion," in *The Oxford Handbook of Religious Conversion*, ed. Lewis R. Rambo and Charles E. Farhadian (Oxford and New York: Oxford University Press, 2014), p. 111, note 144; Claude E. Stipe, "Anthropologists versus Missionaries: The Influence of Presuppositions," *Current Anthropology* 21, no. 2 (1980), pp. 165–79.

19. See, for instance, Joshua Landy and Michael Saler, eds., *The Re-enchantment of the World: Secular Magic in a Rational Age* (Stanford, CA: Standford University Press, 2009).

20. See, for instance, Eloise Meneses, Lindy Backues, David Bronkema, Eric Flett, and Benjamin L. Hartley, "Engaging the Religiously Committed Other: Anthropologists and Theologians in Dialogue," *Current Anthropology* 55, no. 1 (February 2014), pp. 82–104. See also Joel Robbins, "Social Thought and Commentary: Anthropology and Theology: An Awkward Relationship?" *Anthropological Quarterly* 79, no. 2 (Spring 2006), pp. 285–94.

21. Stewart, "Secularism as an Impediment to Anthropological Research," p. 327.

22. Okot P'Bitek writes with regard to the *ajwagi*, "In a significant way, their office operated as a powerful social control factor. They could always be hired by a man who had been wronged by someone stronger than him." Okot P'Bitek, *Religion of the Central Luo* (Nairobi, Kampala, and Dar Es Salaam: East African Literature Bureau, 1971), p. 143.

23. Talal Asad, *Formations of the Secular: Christianity, Islam, and Modernity* (Stanford, CA: Stanford University Press, 2003).

24. Talal Asad, "Comments on Conversion," in *Conversions to Modernities: The Globalization of Christianity*, ed. Peter Van der Veer (New York and London: Routledge, 1996), pp. 271–2.

25. Francine Shapiro and Deany Laliotis, "EMDR and the Adaptive Information Processing Model: Integrative Treatment and Case Conceptualization," *Clinical Social Work Journal* 39, no. 2 (October 12, 2010), pp. 191–200; Ulrike Feske, "Eye Movement Desensitization and Reprocessing Treatment for Posttraumatic Stress Disorder," *Clinical Psychology: Science and Practice* 5, no. 2 (1998), p. 171.

26. Hilary Putnam, ed., "Brains in a Vat," in *Reason, Truth, and History* (Cambridge and New York: Cambridge University Press, 1981), pp. 1–21.

27. Ewing, "Dreams of a Saint," p. 572.

28. One benefit for ethnographers of the rejection of Okham's razor and rather of layering up descriptions (even theological ones) is that, once we set aside modern singular causality/agency, we can realize that to affirm the idea of being acted upon by an other is not to deny our own agency altogether. We see such "nonetheless" agency perhaps most in peoples who have been subjugated by colonial or other forces. Such people may exercise, as Saba Mahmood has pointed out in critique of modern understandings of agency, "restricted" agency, but it is agency nonetheless. See Saba Mahmood, *The Politics of Piety: The Islamic Revival and the Feminist Subject* (Princeton, NJ: Princeton University Press, 2005).

In the case of the Acholi, particularly in the far rural areas of northern Uganda and South Sudan where, even now, visits by priests are infrequent, the melding of Tridentine Christianity and traditional Acholi practices of spirit intervention has wrought, quite apart from the renewal of Vatican II or the advent of Pentecostal religion in the region, a charismatic Catholicism that mirrors—that is, imitates—traditional Acholi culture even as it, at least on the surface, opposes the latter, as is evident in this scene:

> In the mural behind the altar of the chapel in Lokung IDP camp, the Holy Mother floats in Marian blue with arms outstretched. She appears to be painted pinkish-Caucasian, but with there being no electricity and therefore no lighting in the building, it is hard to tell. As one walks from the entrance toward the front of the church, her features become clearer. She is white, more or less, but her hair is black, her brow is heavy, her nose is wide, and her lips are thick. The mural is not a request for patronage, but a protest and a sign of hope from whoever painted it: perhaps even Acholi can ascend into heaven.
>
> Outside, Aber Christine walks across the thatch-broom swept chapel courtyard area singing, *Woro obed malo bot Rubanga, wa i lobo kuc obed bot jo cwinygi ber.* Glory to God in the highest, and on earth peace to people of good will. Word-for-word from the Mass. She comes upon a simply dressed young man and reads to him from the Gospel. *Tomaso owacce ni, "Rwot, pe wangeyo ka ma icito iye, wun wungeyo yone." Yesu ogamo ni, "An aye yo, ada ki kwo. Ngat mop e bino bot Won, do kono ki bota keken"*—"Thomas said to him, 'Lord, we do not know where you are going. How can we know the way?' Jesus said to him, 'I am the way, and the truth, and the life. No one comes to the Father except through me.'"
>
> Christine begins to preach, but the man cannot hear the Gospel because he holds herbs from the *ajwaka* in his hand. Three demons take him by the arms, fly him away, and cast him to the ground, the herbs useless in protecting him.
>
> It is the last full day of my first extended stay in Lokung IDP camp. I am scheduled to leave after chapel service tomorrow. The Catholic community here does not want me to go until they can show me—dramatize—who they are, so they have set aside the afternoon to perform Christian morality plays. Christine is a *mego*, a woman elder, the demons three youths. One wears a USAID gunny sack used for World Food Program grain distribution turned inside out, cut holes for head and arms. Another has wrapped and tied a torn cloth, sash style, over his shoulder. The third has several woven-grass garland hoops draped on his arms. All have tied strips of cloth around their heads bandana-style, with shrub branches stuck into them. They have smeared their faces and arms with orange-brown mud paint and the white ash from charcoal fire. They *look* like demons.
>
> Christine approaches a woman in a blue t-shirt and preaches. *Wamyero lego matek.* We must pray hard. But the woman, too, holds the *ajwaka*'s herbs, and the demons swarm her, tug on her shirt and hair, then sweep her away and throw her down.
>
> A woman in a red gingham shirt and yellow flower-print skirt crosses the courtyard, and Christine preaches again. This time the woman holds no herbs, and when the demons fly in, she turns with Christine to speak the Word of God to them, and the formality and the rubrics of the Mass recede. *Jesu ony maci. Jesu ony maci*, they shout. Jesus, pour out your fire. Suddenly, an angel—the youth leader, Okec James, in a clean and pressed white

dress shirt, with arms outstretched—materializes in front of the women and faces down the demons. A presence without words. The demons wither and collapse as if into the ground. Their previous two victims rise up. Christine and the resurrected break out into call-and-response song with the crowd,

Wan wanyono sitan, bin baa.	We crushed Satan, please come.
Wanyono en.	We crushed him.
Bin ba wanyono sitan.	Please come, we crushed Satan.
Bin ba wanyono en.	Please come, we crushed him.
Bin ba wayilo yesu.	Please come, we raise Jesus.
Bin baa Wayilo en.	Please come, we raise him.

29. John P. Meier, "The Bible as a Source for Theology," in The Catholic Theological Society of America, *Proceedings of the Forty-Third Annual Convention* 43 (Louisville and Chicago: The Catholic Theological Society of America, 1988), pp. 1–14.

30. Luke then proceeds to recount the parables of the lost coin and the prodigal son to similar effect (15: 8-32). Matthew instead provides detailed, almost legalistic procedures for forgiveness, but then undoes any punitive legalism with Peter's follow-up question—"Lord, if another member of the church sins against me, how often should I forgive?"—and Jesus's answer—"Not seven times, but, I tell you, seventy times seven times" (Mt. 18: 21-22; some sources have "seventy-seven times")—in other words, there is no statute of limitations on the call to forgiveness. Earlier in the gospel, Matthew even reverses the salvific places of the plaintiff and the defendant: "For I have come to call not the righteous, but sinners" (9:13b).

31. There is also one pericope that combines forgiveness in deed and word in a forceful way, and that is the healing of the paralytic, which appears in all three synoptic Gospels (Mt. 9:1-8; Mk 2:1-12; Lk. 5:17-26). Jesus was in a house in Capernaum, and, because of the crowds, some men could not get a paralytic in to see him. They manage to remove part of the roof so as to lower the man down into the room where Jesus is teaching. All three synoptics have Jesus noting the faith of the man's friends, and, as a result, forgiving the sins of the man. The scribes (Luke adds Pharisees) question Jesus's authority to forgive sins and charge him with blasphemy. He then tells the paralytic to get up and walk. The paralytic's ability in doing so is taken by the crowd as evidence of Jesus's authority from God to forgive sins.

32. Jon Sobrino, *The Principle of Mercy: Taking the Crucified People from the Cross* (Maryknoll, NY: Orbis Books, 1994), especially pp. 87–90.

33. See, for instance, John P. Meier, *A Marginal Jew: Rethinking the Historical Jesus, Vol. II: Mentor, Message, and Miracles* (New Haven and London: Yale University Press, 1994), pp. 127, 134, 154, 169, 176, 202 n. 102, 400. 401. 436, 1042, 1043; Meier, *A Marginal Jew: Rethinking the Historical Jesus, Vol. IV: Law and Love* (New Haven and London: Yale University Press, 2009), p. 481. Interestingly, although Meier at points indicates a special mission to those considered truly wicked, over the course of *A Marginal Jew*, he shifts his focus: he stresses less Jesus's positive mission to the wicked than the *absence* of a meaningful mission to the poor. Sinners here are those who "intentionally rejected the commandments of the God of Israel." They are "Jews who, for all practical purposes, had thumbed their noses at the covenant and the commandments of God." Meier, *A Marginal Jew*, Vol. II, p. 149.

34. Meier, *A Marginal Jew*, Vol. II, pp. 1042 and 1048, n. 2. See also Meier, *A Marginal Jew: Rethinking the Historical Jesus, Vol. III: Companions and Competitors* (New Haven and London: Yale University Press, 2001), pp. 246 and 620. Meier's repetition of this argument indicates that it is not simply an anomaly occurring in one passage.

35. Types are conceptual constructs used to examine complex empirical phenomena, and the various accounts of the historical Jesus both assess and themselves constitute such empirical information. For Weber's writings on ideal types, see Max Weber, *Essays in the Methodology of the Social* Sciences (1949), pp. 89–105; and Max Weber, *Economy and Society*, ed. Guenther Roth and Claus Wittich (Berkeley, Los Angeles, and London: [1922] 1978), pp. 387–98. Weber was careful to distinguish ideal types from average types. While the latter constitutes a category that analytically stays relatively close to the empirical data, the former abstracts from and even exaggerates certain features of the data in order to form a conceptual construct that can then provide analytical clarity when looking at the data. In Weber's words, an ideal type is an "analytical accentuation (*Steigerung*) of certain elements of reality." Weber, *Essays in the Methodology of the Social Sciences*, p. 90.

    The dispensationist ideal type used here is not to be confused with the historical movement of "dispensation*alist*" theology.

36. Richard A. Horsley, *Jesus in Context: Power, People, and Performance* (Minneapolis: Fortress Press, 2008), p. 128. See also pp. 3, 11, 225 and 227.

37. Horsley, *Jesus in Context: Power, People, and Performance,* p. 222, citing James C. Scott, "Protest and Profanation: Agrarian Revolt and the Little Tradition," *Theory and Society* 4 (1977), p. 220; Richard A. Horsley, *Jesus and the Spiral of Violence: Popular Jewish Resistance in Roman Palestine* (San Francisco: Harper and Row, 1987), pp. 186–7; and Horsley, *Jesus in Context*, pp. 158–60.

38. Horsley, *Jesus and the Spiral of Violence*, pp. 213–18.

39. Sanders returns repeatedly to the point that Jesus was in fact not a moral or social reformer—there is no special social mission to the poor—and Meier follows him on this point. See, for instance, Sanders, pp. 178–9, 183, 188, 230, 236, 255, 257, and 260–1. Meier explicitly cites Sanders over against Richard Horsley. See Meier, *A Marginal Jew*, Vol. II, pp. 644–5, nn. 37 and 38.

40. Sanders, *The Figure of the Historical Jesus*, pp. 115 and 97.

41. Ibid., p. 178. In much of his writing, Sanders appears to have Horsley and similar writers in mind, and at one point mentions Horsley explicitly as one who reduces Jesus to a social reformer who "did not expect God to do anything dramatic or miraculous in the future." (176).

42. Sanders, *The Figure of the Historical Jesus*, pp. 178 and 170–1.

43. Meier, *A Marginal Jew*, Vol. II, p. 332.

44. Against Sanders, Meier stresses that repentance, of a certain sort anyway, is necessary. Meier writes, "It may be that Jesus reformulated repentance in terms of accepting his message and himself." (Meier, *A Marginal Jew*, II, p. 485, n. 152, and p. 212, n. 154). Meier argues that the historical Jesus did not reject the Temple, such rejection being "on the level of Mark's redactional composition and theology." Meier, *A Marginal Jew*, IV, p. 496. Meier, much more than Sanders, stresses that Jesus was a prophet who upheld the law. This Jesus, in the end, really has no special option for any group. Jesus, according to Meier, is above all an "inclusive prophet" who "addresses himself to the *whole* people of Israel. . . . *All* Israel is the focus of this mission of the Elijah-like prophet of the end time" (Meier, *A Marginal Jew*, Vol. III, p. 628 and pp. 152–3, emphases in original). Therefore, in the end, there is not much of a particular mission to the wicked either in Meier, and this works to undo any plausibility to his portrayal of Jesus.

    The problem is that in undercutting any option for the poor and moving away from Sanders's option for the wicked to a generalized mission to all sinners regardless how venial their sins, Meier strips the account of the only things that, even in Sanders's judgment, can conceivably have led to Jesus being executed. Sanders tops his argument for the lack of call for repentance on the part of Jesus by making the case that it is the only possible answer to the core question in interpreting who Jesus was: What stirred the ire of the religious leaders such that they wanted to have him killed? If Jesus offered forgiveness upon repentance, this would not have made religious leaders angry; on the contrary, they would have celebrated the return of the former sinners to righteous life. No, it had to be that Jesus offered forgiveness without repentance. This is the only possible explanation for the recommendation that he be executed. (Sanders, *The Historical Figure of Jesus*, pp. 235–6). Take this away, as Meier has done, and we have a Jesus whom no one would kill. Meier lists "the criterion of rejection and execution" as one of the five primary criteria for ascertaining what is historical in the Gospels, and, after almost three thousand pages, his account of Jesus fails.

45. To support his case that there was no gospel call to repentance, Sanders counts the number of times that the terms "repent" and "repentance" appear in Jesus's preaching, and finds the occurrences rare. But see Mt. 4:17: "From that time [of John the Baptist's arrest] Jesus began to proclaim, 'Repent, for the kingdom of heaven has come near'" (cf. also Mt. 9:13). The phrasing indicates that this instance is not the only time Jesus preached repentance. The author of Luke has Jesus indeed preaching repentance quite forcefully. When Pharisees and scribes complain that he is drinking and dining with tax collectors and sinners, Jesus replies, "Those who are well have no need of a physician, but those who are sick; I have come to call not the righteous but sinners to repentance" (Lk. 5:31-32; cf. also Mt. 9:13). The theme of repentance also figures centrally in the parables of the lost sheep and lost coin (Lk. 15:7 and 10). Mk 6:12 has Jesus passing on the message of repentance to his disciples to preach. Acts testifies to the disciples preaching just that (2:38, 3:19, 5:31, 11:18, 17:30, 20:21, and 26:20). What we have, then, is multiple attestation of the call to repentance at key junctures of Jesus's ministry and that of the disciples and apostles. Sanders's thesis that there is not a call to repentance does not stand up to scrutiny.

     The question is rather to what kind of life is Jesus calling people *to* in his message of repentance, and it is this, together with his mission to the poor and actions in the temple, that gets him killed.

46. Sanders, *The Historical Figure of Jesus*, p. 230.

47. This is not to say that Jesus would not accept persons other than the poor and the wicked if they approached him, as is evident in the case of the "Rich Young Man." It remains, however, that 1) there is a theologically specific and special mission to marginalized, both the poor and the wicked, and 2) practically speaking, those who are not so marginalized tend to turn away from or attack the message (and messenger) of the kingdom of God when they hear it.

48. Karl Mannheim writes, "Max Weber's whole work is in the last analysis directed toward the problem: 'Which social factors have brought about the rationalization characteristic of Western civilization?'" Karl Mannheim, *Man and Society in an Age of Reconstruction* (New York: Harcourt, Brace & World, [1940] 1967), p. 52.

49. On this point, see Lutz Kaelber, *Schools of Asceticism: Ideology and Organization in Medieval Religious Communities* (University Park, PA: The Pennsylvania State University Press, 1998), p. 14.

50. Max Weber, *The Protestant Ethic and the Spirit of Capitalism* (New York and London: Penguin Classics, 2002), p. 78, n. 11.

51. See, for instance, Eviatar Zerubavel, "The Benedictine Ethic and the Modern Spirit of Scheduling: On Schedules and Social Organization," *Sociological Inquiry* 50 (1980),

pp. 157–69; Lewis Mumford, *The Myth of the Machine* (New York: Harcourt Brace Jovanovich, 1967); and Randall Collins, *Weberian Sociological Theory* (Cambridge: Cambridge University Press, 1986).

52. Kaelber, *Schools of Asceticism*, p. 64.

53. Max Weber, *From Max Weber: Essays in Sociology*, ed. H. H. Gerth and C. Wright Mills (Oxford: Oxford University Press), pp. 139 and 350.

54. H. Richard Niebuhr, *Radical Monotheism and Western Culture* (Louisville, KY: Westminster John Knox Press, 1993); and James M Gustafson, "The Sectarian Temptation: Reflections on Theology, the Church, and the University," *Proceedings of the Fortieth Annual Convention: The Catholic Theological Society of America* 40 (1985), p. 93.

55. See, for instance, Peter Geschiere, *The Modernity of Witchcraft: Politics and the Occult in Post-Colonial Africa* (Charlottesville and London: The University Press of Virginia, 1997), and Bettina E. Schmidt and Lucy Huskinson, eds., *Spirit Possession and Trance: New Interdisciplinary Perspectives* (London and New York: Continuum, 2010).

56. For Acholi attitudes toward various paths of resolution to the conflict, see International Center for Transitional Justice (ICTJ) & Human Rights Center (HRC) at the University of California, Berkeley, and the Makerere University Institute of Public Health, *Forgotten Voices: A Population-Based Survey on Attitudes about Peace and Justice in Northern Uganda* (Berkeley, July 2005); HRC, ICTJ, and Payson Center for International Development, Tulane University, *When the War Ends: A Population-Based Survey on Attitudes about Peace, Justice, and Social Reconstruction in Northern Uganda* (December 2007)—access both at www.ictj. org.; and Office of the High Commissioner for Human Rights (UNOHCHR), *Making Peace Our Own: Victims' Perceptions of Accountability, Reconciliation and Transitional Justice in Northern Uganda* (UN, 2007).

57. For an excellent treatment of the ceremonies discussed here, see Thomas Harlacher, et al., *Traditional Ways of Coping in Acholi: Cultural Provisions for Reconciliation and Healing from War* (Kampala: Caritas Gulu Archdiocese, 2006), pp. 74–90.

58. The importance of future generations—those as yet not born—is evident in Acholi attitudes toward land. "The land which a family owns is not considered as being totally 'theirs': it is their heritage and the future heritage of their children. Since they see that a family exists only as a part of a wider community, so its land is held within the wider structure of a community (clan) and as clan's land. Land is the fundamental productive asset, without which one cannot survive, and so one's social obligations and claims are intimately connected to claims and rights over land. These obligations extend to the next generation: land must therefore be protected for them and if anyone who leaves the village and fails to survive in the urban economy, the customary land is a safety net, because they can always return and be allocated a plot. Land is also the link with people's heritage—quite literally, since it is on the family land that one is buried." See Judy Adoko and Simon Levine, *Land Matters in Displacement: The Importance of Land Rights in Acholiland and What Threatens Them* (Kampala: Civil Society Organizations for Peace in Northern Uganda (CSOPNU) and Land and Equity Movement in Uganda (LEMU), 2004): 5; available at http://www.land-in-uganda.org/assets/ LEMU-Land%20Matters%20in%20Displacement.pdf.

59. On this point, see Erin Baines, "Spirits and Social Reconstruction After Mass Violence: Rethinking Transitional Justice," *African Affairs* 109, no. 436 (2010), pp. 409–30.

60. For a study that recognizes both the potential and the limits of *mato oput* and other traditional practices, see Liu Intitute for Global Issues, Gulu District NGO Forum, and Ker Kwaro Acholi, *Roco Wat I Acoli: Restoring Relationships in Acholiland: Traditional Approaches*

to Justice and Reintegration (September 2005), at http://www.ligi.ubc.ca/?p2=modules/liu/ publications/view.jsp&id=16. For an attempt to debunk the usefulness of such practices, see Tim Allen, *Trial Justice: The International Criminal Court and the Lord's Resistance Army* (London and New York: Zed Books in association with International African Institute, 2006).

61. This interviewee was also very clear that abductees forced to have sex with other abductees or to eat people are not required to go through *mato oput* for reconciliation. "Because children who are abducted by force, they will be cleansed [in a different ritual]. Okay? But, people who force them to do that one, they have to reconcile. This is the *mato oput*. You know, the Luo people are very clear on these things—very, very, very clear. We don't enter *mato oput* if I have not done anything bad. If you are forced to do something, that is a different matter. You are treated as a victim. But if you have done it, like abduction of children—that is a crime—so, you can *mato oput* with the population. Eh, treating anybody as sex slaves, that will now require because you have played sex in the bush. It will need cleansing and *mato oput*." Abductees who were forced to commit atrocities would participate in *nyono tong gweno*, or "the stepping on the egg," another Acholi practice. See Harlacher, et al., *Traditional Ways of Coping in Acholi*.

62. John J. Pilch, *Flights of the Soul: Visions, Heavenly Journeys, and Peak Experiences in the Biblical World* (Grand Rapids, MI and Cambridge, UK: William B. Eerdmans Publishing Company, 2011), p. 134.

Roman Catholic Christianity can learn from the Acholi practice of *mato oput* about socially structuring justice, forgiveness and reconciliation. The split between "external" and "internal" fora for confession in Western Christianity begins to take place in the latter part of the twelfth century (See Joseph Goering, "The Internal Forum and the Literature of Penance and Confession," *Traditio* 59 (2004), pp. 175–227). "External" fora consist of public ecclesial courts and "internal" fora refer to individual lay penance before a priest. It is canon six of the Council of Trent's penitential canons that, by claiming it has always been this way and therefore always must be, drives personal confession in the Catholic Church literally into the closet: "If anyone denies that sacramental confession was instituted by divine law or is necessary to salvation; or says that the manner of confessing secretly to a priest alone, which the Catholic Church has always observed from the beginning and still observes, is at variance with the institution and command of Christ and is a human contrivance, let him be anathema." (*Si quis negaverit, confessionem sacramentalem vel institutam vel ad salutem necessariam esse jure divino; aut dixerit, modum secrete, confitendi soli sacerdoti, quem Ecclesia catholica ab initio semper observavit et observat, alienum esse ab institutione et mandato Christi, et inventum esse humanum: A.S.* See H. J. Schroeder, *Canons and Decrees of the Council of Trent* (St. Louis: B. Herder, 1941), p. 102 ff.) The fact of the matter is that there are periods, particularly early on in its history, in which the Church *has* practiced more expressly communally situated confession, penance, reparations, and reconciliation. Yes, the Council, in part in response to the Protestant Reformation, accented individual private confession with a priest as a way to tie the average layperson more tightly into the structure of the Catholic *Church*. However, its structured insistence that the penitent speak secretly to the priest as if alone and directly to God has had the ironic effect of establishing within Catholicism a laboratory for the very individualism of which Catholics have sometimes charged Protestant faiths. The present upshot is that in the aftermath of widespread violence there is a void in what the Catholic Church can offer in terms of structured practices that bring together victim and perpetrator in a communal context in a spirit of reconciliation. (I am not arguing that the Catholic Church should do away with private confession, which has its own place in the life of the community, only that we should supplement it by developing liturgical or para-liturgical practices that can respond to the more expressly *communal* need for penance, reparations, and reconciliation after widespread violence.)

The upside of the undeniable healing dynamic of *mato oput* and other reconciling practices such as *nyono tong gweno* ("stepping on the egg") is that they have had the effect of opening up Christian leaders in northern Uganda more fully to the strengths of indigenous cultural practices. It would prove even better if they and we could draw on those practices to improve our own in the Catholic Church.

63. Pilch goes on to argue, "Historical-critical biblical scholars concerned with determining factual, historical events in Jesus' life never attend to his *Mediterranean culture's consensus reality*, which is quite different from *Western culture's consensus reality*" (emphasis in original)." The ancient Mediterranean cultural consensus is one that involves spirit-crossings, experiences that "are usually dismissed by [our] contemporaries as unscientific and uncritical." John J. Pilch, "Altered States of Consciousness in the Synoptics," in *The Social Setting of Jesus and the Gospels*, ed. Wolfgang Stegemann, Bruce J. Malina, and Gerd Theissen (Minneapolis: Fortress, 2002), pp. 103, 112, and 105.

64. Pilch, "Altered States of Consciousness in the Synoptics," p. 110; cf. 112. Interestingly, Meier insists on the reality of Jesus's miracles and thus the crossing of transcendent/imminent boundaries, but the modern understanding of discrete time and space which he inherits from the presuppositions of historical-critical method does not allow him to affirm in any forceful way a mission to both the poor and the wicked. Again, in the end, he undoes both missions (cf. note 44 above.).

65. Paul Stoller, *Fusion of the Worlds: An Ethnography of Possession among the Songhay of Niger* (Chicago and London: The University of Chicago Press, 1989).

66. See, for instance, S. N. Eisenstadt, "Introduction: Charisma and Institution Building: Max Weber and Modern Sociology," in *On Charisma and Institution Building*, ed. Max Weber (Chicago: University of Chicago Press, 1968), pp. ix–lvi; Stephen Kalberg, "The Search for Thematic Orientations in a Fragmented Oeuvre: The Discussion of Max Weber in Recent German Sociological Literature," *Sociology* 13 (1979), pp. 127–39; and Stephen Kalberg, "Max Weber's Types of Rationality: Cornerstones for the Analysis of Rationalization Processes in History," *American Journal of Sociology* 85 (1980), pp. 1145–79.

67. Weber, *Economy and Society*, pp. 484, 532, 560, and 561.

68. Ibid., pp. 415. See also pp. 467 and 506.

69. Quoted in Kaelber, *Schools of Asceticism*, p. 105.

70. Kaelber, *Schools of Asceticism*, p. 105.

71. Ibid.

72. Keith Thomas, *Religion and the Decline of Magic: Studies in Popular Beliefs in Sixteenth and Seventeenth Century England* (New York: Oxford University Press, 1971), p. ix.

73. Kaelber, *Schools of Asceticism*, p. 110.

PART III
COMMITMENT

CHAPTER 7
RISK: NAMING GENOCIDE

I have seen a few things that I will never forget in my life—atrocious acts of killing that I have seen in my home among my Acholi people. I will not forget this. I would see how people were arrested, and how people were tortured and eventually killed. I have seen so many young people arrested, for no reason, and taken away. . . . I have seen young people arrested in my area and put underground where a big hole had been dug by the military. And there, they suffered underground, and they [the military] would make bread and throw it to these people who were suffering in the ground, like little rats. I have also seen many of these young people who were thrown in the ground, in a pit, being killed by shooting, being killed by beating. Many people died in this way. They died from many causes—either you suffocated or you were beaten to death or you were shot and left dead in the pit.

One other thing that I will not forget that the military has done in this area is taking away all the possessions from people—the cattle—taking away from people whatever they had in their food store—the rice, maize, groundnuts—all foodstuffs, taking them away. The military would come and defecate in our pots where we had clean water, and they would expect you to drink this when you come, thirsty, back into your house.

—Interview with Acholi mego *(female elder)*

Years after taking me along on her rounds to the sick in Pabbo IDP camp, Sister Cecilia told me of her intent for me, a specific way in which, given my positionality, I can help her in her own work: "Eh, I asked you that if you would come over around to visit the people. I wanted you to see the sorrow of people. So that you also . . . you can pray for them. Because you cannot pray for something which you do not know. Aha. Because your work was also. . . . If you say something to the, eh, to the leaders, they can also hear. Aya, if you say something, they can also hear. So you saw it, and you see how they were suffering. Mm. Some they were naked. You see? It is not a good life, an easy life. A very difficult life that time for them. That was my aim: taking you around so that you pray, and you can also talk to the leaders."[1]

Ocena Charles placed a folder of documents in my lap and requested that I publish them. Orach Otim insisted, as we heard in Chapter 5, "I have kept careful documentation. I have kept a diary for ten years. Everything is there. Names. Dates. You know about the mass grave under the mango tree by the parish compound. I know the commander who did this. I can give you the names of people in the ground. I want you to be my Charlie Wilson, the man who campaigned in the United States on behalf of the *mujahideen* in

Afghanistan. He got Congress to recognize what was going on there." When I protested that I am simply an academic, he retorted, "Look at me. I cannot even make love to my wife. They tied a cord around my testicles and forced me to jump off of a box. . . . All I have is the truth. They have taken everything else. . . . My only hope is in the truth."

I discussed in Chapter 1 Olum of Pabbo's "J'accuse!"—"You come and talk to us about our knowledge and our culture and then take it all back with you. . . . What are you going to do for us?" and how in response I cofounded PeaceHarvest, an NGO that combined agricultural training and peacebuilding in northern Uganda and South Sudan. But Sister Cecilia, Orach, and dozens of others were asking for something more and different. These northern Ugandans were asking me not only to do what I could to help them materially, but also to serve them epistemically, that is, to play a role in altering what the world knows about their lives, to use whatever access and capability I might have to speak and write of things that they think the world outside of northern Uganda ought to know, but either does not know or ignores. They were asking me to be a scribe, one different than those that the people of northern Uganda experienced in the first "scramble for Africa," documenters who, in the words of the missionary, Joseph Pasquale Crazzolara, "wrote on their registers the names of the balky ones," so as to report them to the British colonizers for imprisonment.[2]

In asking me to serve as a scribe—*their* scribe—these Acholi were requesting that I commit to their world in a particular way that needs underscoring. They were asking that I situate myself sufficiently within their world to learn of it in a way that approximates their own account of things—"Because you cannot pray for something which you do not know"—but then to steadfastly maintain my position *outside* of their community, and all the advantages that that brings, in order to do what I can on their behalf—"If you say something to the, eh, to the leaders, they can also hear. Aya, if you say something, they can also hear." We saw in Chapter 5 how most Acholi, when they sought material aid from me, did not want me to dismantle my whiteness, but rather to use it in their particular favor. As with material help, so with epistemic aid. Here we see regarding the prospect of "going native" without remainder in the moment of commitment in anthropological theology that not only is it impossible, but attempting to do so is not, from the perspective of the locals, even desirable. Rather they are telling me that I am most inside their community—within its worldview and in alignment with its desires—when I remain also firmly outside the community. Learn the language, dance the dances, witness the devastation, the message is, but do not try to abandon what is most useful to us of your capacities.

And exercising those capacities is not without its own pressures. We saw in the second chapter how the early Catholic missionaries to the region were at first willing, quite literally, to lay down their lives for the Africans that they encountered, and among the risks they took was that of speaking plainly about the abuses of the colonialists. We also saw how, over time and as their efforts aligned more with the aims of the British, the Comboni missionaries found it more "prudent to keep quiet."[3] They were finding it increasingly difficult, once they attached their mission to that of an entity—the British Empire—that sought to expand itself, to exercise the kind of willingness to sacrifice themselves that marked their earlier mission encounters. In the end, I argued, these later

Combonis cooperated with evil: they used their power of the pen to inscribe the British as outsize heroes. Today, President Yoweri Museveni is hailed by Western powers as one of the "new breed of African leaders" directing their countries out of want and misery. I, like the Combonis, am attached to entities that seek to expand themselves—both the US government, which particularly since 9/11 has extended to effect "securitization" in sub-Saharan Africa,[4] and the University of Notre Dame itself, which, as part of its own internationalization trend, has multiple programs and project sites in Uganda for researchers and students, both graduate and undergraduate.

The risks entailed in exposing and discussing the atrocities of Museveni's forces were real, and ranged, in my case, from expulsion or denied re-entry—and thus the inability to finish the research upon which academic reputation depends and most of which the university paid for—to detention and, though less likely, injury or death. Yet, was I, given what I have been told by Acholi, to meet the exonerating claims of Museveni being a "new breed" of leader with silence? Wouldn't this, once again, be cooperation with evil? A sentence from Proust's *A la recherche du temps perdu* haunted: "In my cowardice I became at once a man, and did what all we grown men do when face to face with suffering and injustice: I preferred not to see them."[5] More, life among Acholi Catholics, as I have tried to describe it in this book, brought a shift in focus regarding the multiple requests for me to publish about Museveni's abuses; they were not so much about risk with possible negative consequences for me, but were a *gift*, the offering of an opportunity to imitate, even if unevenly and for only a short time, the Little Sisters' practice of "knowing and living the life of Christ."[6] Was I going to take up that invitation and commit, as much as I was able, to their world of witness?

I should make plain that, other than as a parent, self-abnegating love is not a usual part of my own daily practice. When I received the job offer from Notre Dame over the phone in my Chicago apartment in December of 1990—I remember where I was standing, the kitchen—I did not need any time to consider it. I accepted, almost without thinking, because the things that drew me to the university were things that I had already internalized and were part of my *habitus*: Notre Dame, as its College of Arts and Letters website itself informs us even now, is the "preeminent Catholic university in the world."[7] We can debate the accuracy of this claim, but what is clear to me, even more so in retrospect, is that when I received the phone call, I sought to embody, whatever else I may have desired, what philosopher John Casey calls "pagan" (as distinct from Christian) virtue. The former, according to Casey, seeks "greatness of achievement" with "proper pride" and "fulfilled in a public sphere"; the latter, "humility and self-denial." I am not berating myself here, only trying to be accurate. Casey, at least in my case, has it right: "When we think most rigorously and realistically" about ourselves, "we are 'pagans' in ethics, but . . . our Christian inheritance only allows a fitful sincerity about this."[8]

But the stories from the camps kept coming, so in response to the requests I received to, as Sister Cecilia put it, "say something to the leaders," I published a peer-reviewed article in December 2010 arguing that that the soul- and culture- as well as life-destroying tactics of Museveni's forces toward the Acholi—rape, forced sex between family members, repeated defecation in food pots and the water supply—created an apocalyptic-hued atmosphere—the world as the Acholi knew it seemed with all plausibility to be meeting a cruel and violent end—that made spirit-medium-led defenses appear to be the only viable response. In other words, not only the killings, but the perversions of Museveni's National Resistance Army (NRA)—actions which taken together I argued qualified as genocide—presaged and created the conditions for the grotesque actions of Joseph Kony's LRA. In keeping with the request from northern Ugandans to have whatever I write be for them, I published the article in an online journal so that they could access it. It was picked up by an opposition leader during a presidential campaign and made the front page of the national press in Uganda.

In what follows, I first provide an overview of the dominant account of the LRA conflict in northern Uganda. Doing so will help make clear what is at stake in making public charges regarding atrocities carried out by Museveni's forces. The dominant account is one of a lone madman, Joseph Kony, who through violence and cult-like manipulation has wreaked terror in the region. Museveni himself has played a major role in shaping this narrative, one which is then picked up by the International Criminal Court (ICC) and the US government for their own purposes. These are people and organizations that have not taken the time—they do not have the desire—to adequately understand the world of the Acholi.

I should say at the outset that I find Kony and his actions to be not merely wrong, but deeply evil, even demonic. It is quite another thing, however, to say that those actions are fully explanatory of the suffering of the people of northern Uganda leading up to and during the LRA conflict. After laying out the dominant account as it is articulated by Museveni, the ICC, the US government, and the nonprofit group, Invisible Children, I set out a corrective account, one which highlights the fact that the life- and culture-destroying tactics of Museveni's NRA created a social context in which spirit-medium-led resistance seemed to the Acholi to be the only possible defense. This is what my beseechers asked that I convey: their very world and everything in it was being purposely and systematically crushed. In the last part of the chapter, I set out the circumstances—the responses from both the Ugandan government and friends—that kept me from trying to reenter Uganda for three years. Though it delayed the completion of this book, it was far less risk than that taken on by many Acholi.

The dominant narrative of the conflict in Northern Uganda

Nine and a half minutes into the video, *Kony 2012*, the camera focuses on a towheaded pre-school boy seated at a table for a line of questioning. The boy is the son of Jason Russell, the film's maker and a cofounder of the nonprofit advocacy organization, Invisible Children.

"What do I do for a job?"

"You stop the bad guys from being mean."

"Who are the bad guys?"

"Um, Star Wars people?"

"Can I tell you the bad guy's name?"

"Yeah."

Russell puts a photo on the table between him and his son.

"This is a guy, Joseph Kony."

"He's the bad guy?"

"Yeah."

Russell then puts a photo of a night commuter whom he has befriended and brought for visits to the United States on the table.

"Who is this?"

"Jacob."

"Joseph Kony. He has, um, an army, okay? And what he does is he takes children from their parents. And he gives them guns to shoot. And he makes them shoot and kill other people. He forces them to do bad things. What do you think about that?"

"Sad."

The video then turns to the ICC's first Prosecutor, Luis Moreno Ocampo, and interpolates his testimony with that of Russell's son:

Ocampo: "We need a plan how to arrest Kony."
(Cut to Russell and son)
Russell: "So what do you think we should do about it?"
Son: "We should stop him."
(Cut to Ocampo)
Ocampo: "The criminal here is Kony. Stop him and then solve other problems."
(Cut to Russell and Son)
Russell: "We should stop who?"
Son, pointing to the picture of Kony: "Him."[9]

In their pre-African adventure filming of themselves, the soon-to-be founders of Invisible Children acknowledge in their opening 2003 video, *Invisible Children: The Rough Cut*, "We are naïve kids," and in their post-trip voiceover admit, "None of us knew what we were doing." They initially embarked for Sudan, but they found the heat in the Nuba Mountains to be insufferable. "This was not the adventure we had expected." They came to Sudan, in their own words, "to explore and conquer," but declared themselves "disappointed" in what they found and, bored, proceeded *Jackass*-style to blow up a termite hill and use fire to force a snake from its den, whereupon they chop it up with a hatchet.[10] Under the inaccurate claim that "most of the southern Sudanese fled the country to live as refugees in northern Uganda" anyway, Jason Russell and his colleagues headed south to Uganda.[11] There they stumbled upon the phenomenon of the "night commuters," the children who came into and slept in the towns at night to avoid abduction by the LRA. The filmmakers declare, "We found our story."[12] Nine years and multiple trips to northern Uganda later, and so presumably no longer naïve, they stick to their monocausal explanation of events in the *Kony 2012* video: "Our only purpose is to stop the rebel group, the LRA, and its leader Josephy Kony." The madman Kony is the cause of it all, and the only answer is to root him out like the snake from its den.[13]

Russell and his colleagues present their interpretation as if it is new, but it has an extended history, reaching back to the first encounters between whites and the Acholi. The colonial British, finding Acholi polity to be decentralized, described the people as "brutish" and ungovernable, suitable only for warfighting. The unruly, "warlike" Acholi continued to be disproportionately represented in the military until the ascendency of Museveni, who made the case that the northerners were in fact too violent to serve even there. Museveni has blamed—and continues to do so—the entirety of the excess of the 1980–5 bush war that brought him to power on the Acholi. His 1996 campaign poster makes this clear (Figure 7.1). The photo is of the skulls of people killed in the bush war, where Museveni's forces fought a largely Acholi military. The caption: "**DON'T FORGET THE PAST:** Over one million Ugandans, our brothers, sisters, family and friends lost their lives; **YOUR VOTE COULD BRING IT BACK:** In 10 years under Museveni, peace and development has come to our country. Let's keep it."[14] The poster continues on to tell the viewer that a vote for Museveni is a vote for peace, unity, democracy, and modernization, as opposed to the Acholi, who Museveni elsewhere claims are marked by, "material and spiritual backwardness."[15]

The Kony as madman account as adequate explanation for what has ailed northern Uganda follows from the historical depiction of the Acholi as "primitive" and "backward": it makes full sense in such an account that such a man would arise out of such a people, and this despite the Invisible Children founders' seeming depiction of the night commuters as innocents. Again, the filmmakers came "to explore and conquer." Why would someone who is not in need of reform need conquering? The colonial narrative is hidden when the word "save" and its analogues are substituted for "conquer": the people need rescuing from themselves. This latter aspect of the narrative illuminates why Invisible Children views the primary means to address the difficulties in northern Uganda to be US-backed military intervention and ICC-adjudicated prosecution. That *Kony 2012* heavily features the ICC's Ocampo is not incidental.

The ICC's own skewed application of justice has been evident from the start. It began its investigation of the crimes of the LRA at the request of Museveni himself in 2003—the same year that the founders of Invisible Children first visited northern Uganda—and in 2004 Ocampo, then prosecutor for the ICC, announced the investigation of LRA leaders at a joint press conference *with Museveni by his side*. There is little debate among unbiased observers that Museveni's forces—first the NRA and then its later embodiment as the UPDF—have, at minimum, committed war crimes and crimes against humanity in northern Uganda, yet, despite promises to investigate, the ICC has announced no prosecutorial cases, thus manifesting an asymmetrical application of justice. It circumvents its own powers of prosecution in two ways: first, it argues that the worst crimes committed by Museveni's forces occurred before the ICC was constituted in 2002; second, it refuses to view the government's forced displacement of over a million people into squalid IDP camps where tens and even hundreds of thousands unceremoniously died due to a lack of basic necessities as a crime. Human Rights Watch writes, "In light of abuses by government personnel and a failure of the government to protect its citizens in the north, it is not surprising that Uganda's referral to the ICC of the situation in 2003

Figure 7.1 Museveni campaign poster.

struck many as nothing more than a ploy to strengthen its hand in a rebellion it had been unable to end over nearly two decades."[16]

In December 2013, when the ICC later initiated a case investigating Musveni's political ally in Kenya, Uhuru Kenyatta, the Uganda president accused the ICC of having the "arrogance of the colonialist" and not respecting the sovereignty of African nations. In December 2014, Museveni went further and called for the African Union states to withdraw from the ICC: "I will bring a motion to the African Union's next session. I want all of us to get out of that court of the West. Let them (Westerners) stay with their court"[17] In January 2016, Kenyatta formally proposed and Museveni supported such a withdrawal.[18] However, when the Ugandan government had Dominic Ongwen, a former LRA commander, in custody in January 2015, it handed him over to be prosecuted by the ICC at The Hague.[19] The ostensive reason given for handing Ongwen over is that the LRA had become an international problem,[20] but the heading of the ICC's own arrest warrant for Ongwen is "Situation in Uganda," and the warrant itself states that it refers to "all of the crimes alleged against **DOMINIC ONGWEN** . . . within the context of the situation in Uganda."[21] Museveni is using the ICC for his own ends—cooperating when it serves his interests, excoriating when it does not—rather than the other way around. Thus far, the ICC is cooperating with Museveni by not mounting any serious investigation into his crimes.[22] In fact, in March 2017, the president of the ICC, Silvia Fernández de Gurmendi, met with Museveni, cited his role in bringing forward the Kony case, and, perhaps worried about the prospect of Museveni's withdrawal of Uganda from the Court, summarized, "Uganda's cooperation and support for the Court's operations is and will remain crucial for the implementation of the Court's mandate."[23] No investigation of Museveni is forthcoming.

The US government constructs an account of northern Uganda that complements those of Invisible Children and the ICC. It claims, at least on the surface, that Museveni is one of what has been called the "new breed of African leaders." Such leaders embrace the economic protocols of international financial institutions like the World Bank and the International Monetary Fund and, even if only superficially, make some democratic reforms.[24] This has allowed leaders in the West to overlook the continued anti-democratic tendencies in Uganda. In Africanist Joseph Oloka-Onyango's words, "All the new-breed leaders have seen significantly increased aid-flows to their countries, accompanied by much praise for their economic management skills. They have been lauded for the dexterity with which they have handled the often painful prescriptions that outsiders have made to effect such transformations. In particular, Uganda's adoption of free-market reforms encompassing economic liberalization, privatization, and the reform of public enterprise has earned accolades from many in the West. Long favored by Western powers, Museveni thus gets away with actions that would not be tolerated were they to be committed by an old-breed leader."[25] Here, the foreign aid and the anti-democratic practices reinforce each other: the former makes local political dependence on open processes less necessary and even undesirable. Aid to Uganda has constituted as much as 50 percent of its national budget, and now stands at around 30 percent.

Post-9/11 reality has only reinforced the dynamic. Uganda is strategically located in the "war on terror." With radical Islam-influenced Sudan and warring South Sudan to the north, chaotic DRC and rebuilding Rwanda to the west, and unstable Kenya to the east, there are few other places for the United States to anchor itself in Central and East Africa, and the United States has carried out repeated military trainings in Uganda.[26] Museveni has indebted the United States even more deeply to Uganda by sending the largest contingent—over 6,000 troops—to fight the war on terror in Somalia on behalf of the United States. The United States' "Black Hawk Down" experience there in 1993 has made it wary of committing its own troops—part of a larger US trend in using proxy armies[27]—and Uganda above all other countries in East and Central Africa has filled the gap. In June 2011, the Pentagon authorized $45 million for support to the Ugandan and Burundian contingents fighting in proxy for the United States in Somalia. President Trump only ratcheted up the US stake in Somalia by issuing a presidential directive in 2017 officially declaring it a war zone.[28] Such a declaration clears the way for US drone and other airstrikes in Somalia, requiring Ugandan boots on the ground all the more. As of April 2018, Ugandan troops are still losing their lives in the conflict, making the United States all the more indebted to Museveni.[29]

The United States is loathe, therefore, to criticize the Ugandan government and even less inclined to take action. When Museveni had political opponent Kizza Besigye imprisoned during the 2006 campaign, some countries withheld aid to Uganda;[30] the United States not only continued, but increased aid at the time. During and immediately after the campaign for the 2016 election, police arrested and detained Besigye multiple times, a period during which, as Human Rights Watch argued, "freedom of expression and association" were "under serious threat" from the government.[31] Such actions brought only a brief critical statement from a deputy spokesperson from the US Department of State and a vague finger-wagging private phone call from then US Secretary of State John Kerry to Museveni.[32] There are no indications that there will be any suspension of the annual $750 million in aid to the government of Uganda.

Regional competition with China and Russia, which both overlook Museveni's rights violations, likely means that no concrete action by the United States is forthcoming.[33] In 2012, $12.7 million of aid intended to go to the poorest parts of Uganda—Acholiland and its eastern neighbor, Karamoja—went missing in the office of the Ugandan prime minister. The European Union, the United Kingdom, Germany, Denmark, Ireland, and Norway all suspended aid. The United States did not, even though as early as 2010, Jerry Lanier, the US ambassador to Uganda sent a cable—made public through WikiLeaks—to Washington under the title, "Uganda's All You Can Eat Corruption Buffet."[34] Instead, the United States increased aid for the pursuit of Joseph Kony.[35]

In recognition of the special US-Uganda relationship, in June 2011—the same month as it committed moneys to the Somalia effort—the Senate Armed Services Committee directed $35 million for the Ugandan military and other regional forces to fight the LRA in the latter's regional holdouts in the DRC, South Sudan, and the Central African Republic.[36] In March 2014, President Obama announced that the United States would be sending an additional Osprey CV-22 and refueling aircraft along with an additional 150 armed personnel (including members of Air Force Special Operations) to fly and maintain the planes.[37] The US-Uganda mission to seek and take out Kony officially ended in late April 2017, when the two countries began withdrawing their troops from the Central African Republic, where it was thought Kony was hiding out.[38]

Though the US-Uganda search for Kony has ended, the close relationship between the two countries remains. President Trump has a positive predilection toward strongmen rulers, and is most often silent in the face of their abuses.[39] Museveni clearly counts as a strongman. Through a combination of patronage and intimidation, he had the Ugandan Parliament suspend presidential term limits in 2005 and end the age limit in late 2017—effectively making Museveni president for life—even though 75 percent of the people of Uganda opposed the changes.[40] The Uganda Law Society has petitioned to have the new law nullified, but optimism for reversal is low because what are commonly called "cadre judges" stock the courts.[41] Museveni, in turn, has a very positive assessment of the US president. When other African leaders protested vociferously after Trump called their nations "shithole countries," Museveni doubled down on his relationship with the United Sates and declared, "I love Trump."[42]

The narrative of the conflict in northern Uganda that highlights the atrocities of Joseph Kony and the LRA while glossing over the actions of Museveni's forces is a narrative that the founders of Invisible Children stepped into rather than invented. This is a significant part of why *Kony 2012* garnered, according to YouTube, almost 100 million viewers and raised $32 million.[43] Adam Branch, an American researcher who studied the conflict in northern Uganda for over a decade, articulated most clearly the context and real, on-the-ground impact of the Kony 2012 campaign:

> It is an excuse that the US government has gladly adopted in order to help justify the expansion of their military presence in central Africa. Invisible Children are "useful idiots," being used by those in the US government who seek to militarise Africa, to send more and more weapons and military aid, and to bolster the power of states who are US allies. The hunt for Joseph Kony is the perfect excuse for this strategy—how often does the US government find millions of young Americans pleading that they intervene militarily in a place rich in oil and other resources? . . . In northern Uganda, people's lives will be left untouched by this campaign, even if it were to achieve its stated objectives. This is not because all the problems have been resolved in the years since open fighting ended, but because the very serious problems people face today have little to do with Kony.[44]

When the *Kony 2012* film was shown in Lira, one of the districts most impacted by the presence of the LRA, members of the audience threw rocks at the screen.[45]

Clearly, if our account is to be adequate to the experience of the people of northern Uganda, we will need a narrative other than the one provided by the ICC, the US government, and Invisible Children.[46] Such a narrative would have to take into account not only the abuses of the Museveni regime, but how those abuses in the mid-1980s played a role in the rise of Joseph Kony and the LRA. This is the story that the northern Ugandans who urged me to write wanted me to tell and that I did articulate in the 2010 article. In what follows, I provide a brief version of that account. The quotations in the text boxes are from over 350 hours of interviews I gathered from the Acholi. They represent only a fraction of the gathered testimony that reported abuses by Museveni's forces and government, but offer, I hope, enough insight into what was going on to correct the dominant narrative. I should add that the interviews did not ask anything specifically about Museveni and his forces. Most of the statements regarding them arose when people were asked, "What things will you never forget about the war?" In making the case that the actions of Museveni and his forces qualify as genocide, I follow the strict legal definition of the term as given in the UN Convention on the Prevention and Punishment of Genocide rather than the advocacy-driven understanding, for reasons that will become clear. This will help highlight what was at stake in publishing the information and argument.

A corrective narrative in brief[47]

The Convention defines genocide as any of the following acts committed with the intent to destroy, in whole or in part, a national, ethnical, racial, or religious group, as such: killing members of this group; causing serious bodily or mentally harm to members of the group; deliberately inflicting on the group conditions of life, calculated to bring about its physical destruction in whole or in part; imposing measures intended to prevent births within the group; forcibly transferring children of the group to another group.

> —*Article 2 of the United Nations 1948 Convention on the Prevention and Punishment of the Crime of Genocide, which is restated in Article 6 of the Rome Statute of the International Criminal Court*[48]

When the results of the 1980 Ugandan presidential election showed Milton Obote to be the victor, Museveni charged fraud and formed the rebel NRA. Five years of bush war followed, with multiple groups fighting to overthrow Obote. Two Acholi leaders, Tito Lutwa Okello and his brother Bazilio Olara-Okello, succeeded in 1985. After the coup, Tito Okello tried to unify the country by extending offers of peace to the remaining rebel groups. The efforts led to the Nairobi Agreement between the Tito Okello government and the NRA in December 2005.[49] Museveni, however, used the time granted by the agreement to build up his own army, and a month later he seized the capitol. The remnants of Okello's forces retreated into northern Uganda and what is now South Sudan. Musveni's army followed, taking vengeance on the civilian population. Again: *I have also seen many of these young people who were thrown in the ground, in a pit, being killed by shooting, being killed by beating. Many people died in this way. They died from many causes—either you suffocated or you were beaten to death or you were shot and left dead in the pit.*

At first, the Acholi did not resist. Political scientist Adam Branch makes the case that this was an instance of "a counterinsurgency without an insurgency."[50] My conversations with the people of northern Uganda who were there at the time of the NRA's actions support Branch's analysis. One elder from Madi Opei told me the following:

> When the NRA came, the people went into the cave that runs the full length of Got Latoolim [the mountain in between Madi Opei and Agoro]. It is a big cave, so everyone who wanted could fit there. They took supplies and some of them had guns so they could stay there a long time and protect themselves.
>
> They stayed there for two months. The NRA could not get them out. They had food, defense. So the NRA sent some Acholi who were NRA to talk them out, and after two months they came.
>
> At first they were treated okay. But then a second detachment of NRA came and started treating them badly. Beating them. Raping. People "disappearing." I tell you, if it were not for that bad treatment, there would not have been any rebellion. The former [Okello soldiers] would have just diffused back into the community and that is it. When those in Sudan heard how the people in northern Uganda were treated, then they started planning [for insurgency].

When a resistance group finally did form, it did so through response to violence initiated by Museveni's NRA. Remnants of Tito Okello's forces began resisting in a loose, unstructured way, in groups that locals refer to as the *cilil* (pronounced "che-leel"). But ragtag responses to the structured violence unleashed by the NRA on Acholi seemed inadequate. It felt to the Acholi that they were in the process of being wiped out. More, the NRA soldiers indicated through various symbolic acts—they came up too often in my interviews to be random—that far more was at stake than simply pacifying a people. From another interview: "Defecating in the flour, maize flour, that would be used for

---

"What happened in the war that lasted 20 years. . . . The [Museveni] government came and gave people ten days and said that within those ten days if you are a fighter, if you have been in the past government, you are going to be given amnesty for ten days. . . . Now with only ten days given, we might decide to take these arms back, but then get arrested by the government. Other people started running, going to the Sudan and others going to their hiding places. After the ten days, the government resorted to arresting people. . . . When they come across you, they would arrest you. And upon that arrest, where you will be taken is not known to anyone. . . . The government started bringing the issue. Whenever they move in the villages, they would arrest people and start raping women, and burning houses and cattle. They would kill them all. Sometimes you would find the head of a cow that has been slaughtered, the mouth has been defecated into. . . . People started seeing that this is not good. The youth who were still young started running after their brothers who still had their arms and started staying in the bush. This type of army was called *cilil*. . . . The government continued doing bad things, entirely bad things, killing people in the villages. And after that came another type of rebels; they were called group of the Holy Spirit."

---

mingling bread by the Acholi. They would defecate in all of the water pots . . . or if they killed an animal, a cow, they would open its mouth and defecate in it. Or even in the oven where the Acholi would be cooking. Burning granaries, food stores, and houses of people. And also taking women with them. A woman would be taken from a man, and if you are unfortunate at night, and they find you with your wife in the house, you are laid, the man is laid face up, then the woman is laid on top of you. They have sex with your wife on top of you there. In other cases, you as a man, they would have sex with you.[51] And if they are too lazy to have sex themselves, they would just force you as the father to have sex with your own daughter, to have sex with your children. These are the bad things that were happening, that the soldiers, these soldiers were doing." Museveni's soldiers aimed not just to kill people, but to upend the entire spiritual, cultural, and moral universe of the Acholi. Such apocalyptic circumstances required a different kind of leader for any resistance that might arise. Alice Lawkena, a spirit medium, fulfilled that role. Her Holy Spirit Movement, which launched the first major insurgency, was initially—before NRA atrocities—a non-violent, gender-equal religious movement. The extent and deliberate symbolism of the NRA's atrocities changed all that. Lakwena and her followers absorbed the *cilil* and transformed in the process into a group whose fighters believed themselves to be protected by her anointing and that the rocks they threw would turn midair into grenades. They drove the NRA back to within seventy kilometers of the capital.

The Holy Spirit Movement ultimately met with defeat, however, and the LRA formed in the crucible of further social and cultural loss. The continuity in the minds of the Acholi between the Holy Spirit Movement and the LRA is such that still today they often refer

---

"The second war that came was when Kony started fighting with the government. During that time, Kony was not abducting anybody. People were even living with Kony without any problems. He would come and cook his food within the villages. And if you were willing to go and help him, you would go on your own."

"The RDC [Resident District Commissioner] called Ocaya came and started writing our names—that everyone should go and get a *panga* [machete]. He started registering all the people. . . . If you didn't come along, your colleagues who were already there would arrest you and beat you severely. I personally was beaten and suffered that pain for almost six months. They would put your face in the water and send you to do hard labor so that next time you would go and fight Kony using *pangas*. After that, Kony changed his mind toward the Acholi, he started cutting off their hands, chopping off their ears and also cutting their lips. Cutting of the lips did not come from the mind of Kony alone. It was from using our mouth to talk about him and the ears that we use for hearing and the hands with which we are holding *pangas* against him."

"I ran all the way to Masaka [450 kilometers south of Gulu]. They had started forcing all the people to become soldiers to fight against those who were in the bush. . . . That time of the militia was when I ran and hid in Masaka."

to the latter as "the Lakwena," after Alice Lawkena, the Holy Spirit Movement's foundress. At first, the LRA had the backing of local Acholi. One elder told me, "Most people of the Acholi received Kony as their helper"—in fact, "kony" means "to help" or "to bless"—"but later on the problems brought by this war remained as trouble for the Acholi." Government officials conscripted locals to arm themselves to fight the LRA, which had the effect of turning the LRA against the Acholi. The man who referred to Kony as a helper continued his interview by singing a song that told, in its own words, about the change in Kony:

> I used to say it was good.
> I used to say it was
> a leopard of Anyaga.
> The one who has ruined the situation
> has done it.
> This child has spoiled our family life.
> I used to say it was good.
> This leopard belonged to Anyaga.
> This child has spoiled our family life.
> I used to say it was good.
> I said it was the leopard of the Anyaga.
> I used to say it was good.

The best early chance of a peaceful resolution to the conflict came in 1994, when Kony called for comprehensive peace talks with the government involving leaders of the Acholi people and members of the political wing of the LRA—essentially the same arrangement as later took place in the 2006–8 peace talks held in Juba, South Sudan. Kony said that arranging for such talks would take six months (which it did in the case of the Juba talks). When Museveni heard the request, he gave an ultimatum: the LRA forces were to surrender themselves and all weapons in seven days or the "talks" were off. When they refused to surrender their weapons on such short notice, Museveni attacked the site where the LRA leadership was gathered. One need not be naïve about the LRA to recognize that Museveni sabotaged the 1994 negotiations just when they were getting serious.[52] Museveni summarized his approach to peacebuilding in a conversation with Jan Egeland, then the UN Undersecretary-General for Humanitarian Affairs, at the beginning of the 2006 Juba Peace talks:

Museveni: "You were just wasting your time in the bush with [the leaders of the LRA]."

Egeland: "No, I think it was useful to meet them. It was good for peace and therefore to your benefit."

Museveni: "No, those talks were not to our benefit. Let me be categorical—there will only be a military solution to this problem."[53]

In the interim between the 1994 and 2006 peace efforts, Museveni forcibly displaced the people of northern Uganda into squalid, under-protected camps. The decision to displace the people into camps—first made on September 27, 1996, and later broadened in 2002 and 2004—was by fiat. When Acholi MPs found out about the plan, they protested; Museveni then promised to re-consult with the military and to get back to the MPs in two weeks. He never did. It is noteworthy that it was his brother, General Salim Saleh, who gave the reason for Museveni's not doing so, pointing up the tight relationship between Museveni and Saleh: no consulting took place because Museveni and Saleh, "suspected bureaucracy and politicking over the issue." That is to say, they were concerned about resistance to and perhaps defeat of their plan of forced displacement should the issue go to Parliament.[54] When individual people refused to move to the camps, the soldiers beat them; when whole villages refused, the UPDF—the new instantiation of Museveni's earlier NRA—often used attack helicopters against the inhabitants. A report from the ARLPI is worth quoting at length.

> In every camp we visited in Gulu, people told us invariably that they were forced. In some cases people remember that soldiers gave them a seven-day deadline (Opit) or only three days (Awac), threatening to treat those who resisted as rebels. In most cases, however, it would appear that soldiers just stormed villages—often at dawn—without any previous warning. They told people to move immediately without giving them much time to collect their belongings. People were often beaten to force them out of their compounds. Much of the property left behind was looted by both rebels and soldiers. A number of people who ventured to go back to their former homes soon after found them burnt down. Men told us that they were harassed and even shot at, and women raped. . . . In Pabbo, Opit, Anaka, Cwero and Unyama we met a good number of people who had direct experience of having had their villages shelled. We were told that big guns of the BM21 6 barrel type were used to fire at villages where people refused to move. . . . Aerial bombardments were used—we were told—in places like Kaloguro village, in Pabbo, Awach, KocGoma, Amuru and Anaka. This first wave of

---

"The government entered into villages to rob people, burning houses and granaries. All the people they would find would just be killed. [The government said] that people should all go stay in the camps or go to town."

---

forced displacement occurred at a time of the year which normally marks the beginning of the harvesting season. Given the fact that in most cases people were not given time to collect any foodstuff, their crops remained in the fields or in the granaries. In Pabbo and Opit people told us that there were cases of Army helicopters being used to collect foodstuff from abandoned villages. Force was also used by the UPDF some months after the camps were started, in order to compel back into the camps those who had gone home to tend their fields. We heard this complaint in every camp we visited in Gulu and in some in Kitgum.[55]

The frequent justification offered by government officials for the forced displacement of the Acholi people is that it was to protect the latter. In fact, the name officials often gave the camps was "protected villages." However, such justifications do not stand up to empirical scrutiny for the straightforward fact that the government did not adequately protect the camps, even when it had the military capacity to do so.[56] Instead, the camps served as LRA magnets, and most of the worst massacres occurred there. People I interviewed confirmed this experience of being left vulnerable: "The government soldiers who were protecting us were few. Many times when these people [the LRA] came, they [the government soldiers] ran away. They could not protect the people in the camp, and the rebels would abduct people at will. The rebels would burn houses at will. The rebels would do whatever they wanted at will."

"The government soldiers were there, but they were few in number, and they all ran away on that day when the rebels came to Alero IDP camp. All the government soldiers took off together with the civilians. They ran together, the same speed."

While failing to protect the people of northern Uganda, Museveni had thousands of troops in the DRC committing, according to a 2010 UN report, war crimes and crimes against humanity, including a "campaign of ethnic cleansing," on the way to plundering natural resources.[57] The UN publication is a "mapping report" of the worst atrocities committed in the DRC between 1993 and 2003, and verified a 2002 UN report and a 2005 International Court of Justice (ICJ) report that documented the plunder (specifically naming Museveni's brother, Salim Saleh). The ICJ report ordered Uganda to pay the DRC $10 billion in restitution (yet to be paid), while also citing the Ugandan military with killings, torture, and other atrocities committed against Congolese citizens.[58] Included among the 2010 UN mapping report findings are multiple instances where the UPDF, or Congolese rebel factions operating with the support of the UPDF, committed acts which the UN report argues fit the legal definition of war crimes and crimes against humanity. An earlier draft of the report applied the term "genocide," but the UN withdrew it when the government of Rwanda, also involved in the DRC, protested. The UN report split the difference by explaining that it could not officially determine whether genocide had taken place because the office that drafted it was not a juridical body, but that such a body should launch just such an investigation.[59]

For comparison with the actions of Museveni's forces in northern Uganda, one paragraph in particular stands out. The mapping the report states:

> UPDF soldiers instituted a reign of terror for several years with complete impunity. They carried out summary executions of civilians, arbitrarily detained large numbers of people and subjected them to torture and various other cruel, inhuman or degrading treatments. They also introduced a particularly cruel form of detention, putting detainees in holes dug two or three metres deep into the ground, where they were forced to live exposed to bad weather, with no sanitation and on muddy ground.[60]

What we now know from my interview quoted at the onset of this chapter is that Museveni's forces developed and perfected the "pit" technique a decade earlier in northern Uganda against the Acholi: "I have seen, also, young people arrested in my area, and put underground where a big hole had been dug by the military. And there, they suffered underground . . . like little rats. I have also seen many of these young people who were thrown in the ground, in a pit, being killed by shooting, being killed by beating." Such testimonies are important not only morally for the facts they report, but legally as well, because they establish that the NRA/UPDF had no intent to "protect" the Acholi, and that the idea that the NRA/UPDF—the same forces that shit in their pots and executed their children—had a sudden change of heart the moment they used armed force to drive the Acholi into the IDP camps does not stand any test of reason. What, then, was the primary motivation for the forced displacement? There is ample evidence that the parallel with Museveni/Saleh's actions in DRC holds here as well: the plunder of natural resources, in this case land.

Early on in the conflict in northern Uganda—April 5, 1988—Salim Saleh conducted a flyover of the region and commented on the record to reporters who were present, "What do you think of this unpopulated place? Couldn't it be utilized for growing food, cash crops and ranching to improve our economy, being such a fertile area?"[61] Well over a million Acholi—farming—lived below. The cultivation of land is the primary source of wealth-generating production, and thus livelihood, in northern Uganda. The vast majority of Acholi are rural-dwelling small-scale farmers. They often supplement their diet with game procured through hunting.[62] The land available for these activities is, for the far greater part, held in customary ownership. That is to say, ownership, even when it is individual ownership, is not conferred via government-authorized written title, but rather through oral mechanisms of clan authority. Even when an individual—or more precisely, an individual family—holds claim to a parcel of land, the controlling idea is that it is held ultimately for the common good of the clan.[63] Hunting lands (*tim*) and grazing lands (*olet*) are held in trust by the clan as a whole. *These are not empty lands*; rather their purposes are best stewarded through allowing multiple families to make use of them whole rather than as divided up into smaller parcels. The fact that ownership is largely orally based and dependent upon the memories of the persons involved makes customary ownership, particularly but not solely of the hunting and grazing lands, vulnerable in crisis situations such as the twenty-year conflict in northern Uganda.

"Supposing we come back [to our clan land from the camps after the war is over] and one of us begins saying that this land belongs to his grandparents alone. How would it sound? It would not sound properly because the whole of the Acholi have been staying there. So the land that has been left behind there was not one man's land. That's how ancestral land is. It is not one man's property. You as a given tribe, you dig on that land together and the clan members eat together."

When Museveni forced the Acholi off their land, Saleh did not hesitate to move in. The ARLPI reported, "Soon after the forced removals of people from the countryside [in 1996], Maj. Gen. Salim Saleh started some kind of commercial farming business in Kilak country."[64] A later land study describes a 1998 project "initiated by a senior army officer" to give loans to farmers to implement mechanized farming on 250 acres of land in Amuru district in northern Uganda. The hitch is that the actual landowner never gave consent for this project. The officer? Salim Saleh. The report goes on to describe a 1999 proposal by "a company for turning Northern Uganda into the breadbasket of central Africa." The company's proposal itself claims, in words that echo Saleh's during his flyover, that there are "vast, highly fertile lands . . . available for large scale grain production."[65] The company? Divinity Union Ltd., owned by Salim Saleh.[66] Undeterred by criticism from Acholi religious leaders and other advocates on behalf of Acholi land rights, Saleh and Divinity Union proposed a "Security and Production Programme" (SPP) in 2003. The Production Programme's plan was for all Acholi customary land "that is not tilled, being grazed on or privately registered" to be turned into militarized working farms, with local youth recruited and trained by the government to protect the fields. Though the SPP literature nods toward consultation with local traditional chiefs regarding the land, it states that the Production Programme is really a "government Project Implementation Unit" to be run by the central administration offices, including the Ministry of Defense. Neocolonial rulers consult local leaders no more than traditional colonial rulers did. Ostensibly proposed as a way to reduce population dependence on food aid during the war, SPP, if implemented, would have placed all Acholi customary land not being actively tilled under government control and have Acholi work the land not as landowners, but as low-wage laborers or quasi-serfs. The plan was not carried out in the end in part because of resistance to it and in part because the conflict moved out of northern Uganda before it could be implemented (though Museveni and Saleh have since pursued other avenues to take Acholi land[67]). Still, the intent is clear. Just how militarized and controlled the farms would have been is evident from pictographs from the SPP's own literature: (Figure 7.2).[68]

In short, Museveni and Saleh unilaterally declared that it was necessary to forcibly displace the Acholi people—that is, to use the military and armed attacks to move them off of their own land against their will—for the Acholi's own "protection." Museveni, through the UPDF, failed to provide that protection. However, Saleh still found there

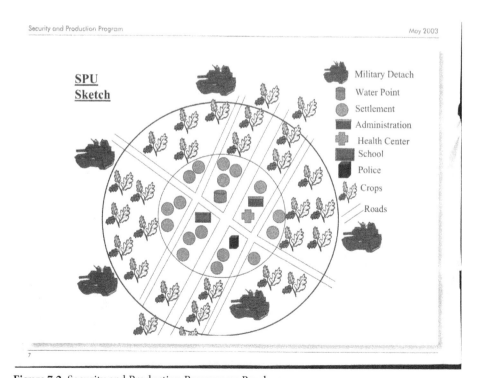

Figure 7.2 Security and Production Programme Brochure.

to be enough military wherewithal to protect the proposed government SPP farms on land formerly held by the Acholi and upon which the Acholi were to serve as serf-like laborers. The evidence indicates that the motivation and goal of the camps was takeover of the land, not the protection of the people.

In the DRC, Museveni, according to the 2010 UN mapping report, "created and supported" a rebel group to disrupt areas of the country where he wanted to take natural resources.[69] In northern Uganda, his "counterinsurgency without an insurgency" that ultimately generated the LRA served that purpose. Only four days prior to Saleh's April 1988 flyover of northern Uganda, Joseph Kony was just a local spirit medium who had taken his eleven followers, with no guns, outside of his home village of Odek for the first time. Kony soon—only days later—met up with some remnants of Tito Okello's soldiers, who became followers after he told them that Museveni was intent, as one documenter put it, "on slaughtering all the Acholi."[70] The actions of Museveni's army up until that time—the rapes, the murders, the defecations—gave the claim all the credibility it needed. Kony and his newly recruited soldiers then attacked Museveni's troops in Gulu, who, at the time, fled, and Museveni had a rebel group at hand to disrupt the north. The process was not as planned-out as that in the DRC, which came later. Instead, we see that *northern Uganda was the training ground for what the UN calls the UPDF's "ethnic cleansing" in the DRC.* In both cases, Museveni and Saleh used "rebel" activity as a pretext for plunder.

In the interim between the 1994 and 2006 peace efforts, Acholi were dying by the tens of thousands in the camps. As cited in Chapter 1, the WHO carried out a study of the conditions in the IDP camps in northern Uganda. It is the most extensive study of camp conditions, covering all of the districts of northern Uganda. Given the late date of the study relative to the war—2005—the findings are on the conservative side. The camps at that time were in far better condition than in earlier stages of the conflict, when they were less organized and international organizations like the UN World Food Program were not yet delivering food aid. Unbiased, extensive, and conservative, the report, after

---

"There are a great number of people in one place [in the camps]. . . . And because of lack of land, a small piece of land would be used to put latrines very close to your house, and you find that all the dirts that come from the latrine would come back into your house. . . . There were a number of diseases, and people most of the time would hear that so-and-so has died."

"When you go to the camps, you'd find there are many people. There are blind people, others who have become disabled by land mines. And there are some people who are very old and weak. And also, some people who are suffering from leprosy, and all their hands are off. Then you find . . . people who are suffering from HIV/AIDS."

"During the time that we were in the camp, what was happening was death. Diseases were killing young children."

"We even felt that if we could die, it would be better."

"For us now, we were defeated because the government collected us like cattle and then we were just poured there [in the camps]. We were not working. We were not employed. We had no power whatsoever. We were just asking for their mercy. . . . What is now finishing us is hunger."

careful analysis of the situation on the ground in the IDP camps in comparison with "non-crisis" levels in the northern districts of Kitgum, Pader, and Gulu where the Acholi people predominate, found that there were almost 1,000 *excess* deaths per week due to malaria, AIDS, malnutrition, diarrhea, violence, and other causes. In other words, 52,000 Acholi were dying per year from camp conditions. About 90 percent of the population in these districts—about 1.2 million people—lived in camps at the time of the report.[71] It is also important to highlight the fact that the study is of the conditions and deaths that occurred well *after* the formation of the ICC. In other words, this is legitimate evidence for the ICC to take into account in its assessment of Museveni's actions. The ICC refuses to do so.

The 2010 UN mapping report of the DRC follows previous decisions—particularly those of the International Criminal Tribunal for the former Yugoslavia (ICTY), a precursor of the ICC—in distinguishing between genocidal intent and whatever other motivations the perpetrators might have. What this means is that the presence of other motivations in conjunction with the genocidal intent does not offset that latter intent in a court of law. The mapping report is clear:

> Intention is not synonymous with motivation. The personal motive of the perpetrator of genocide, for example, may be the prospect of personal economic benefit, political advantages or a particular form of power. The existence of a personal motive does not mean that the perpetrator may not also have the specific intention of committing genocide.[72]

The import of the distinction between motive and intent is that Museveni and Saleh's avariciousness regarding gold, diamonds, and land does not nullify their intent to commit genocide. More, the report notes that Article 3 of the Convention states that the "conspiracy to commit genocide," the "attempt to commit genocide" and the "complicity in genocide" are all also considered acts of genocide punishable under the Convention.[73] What this means is that neither Museveni nor Saleh need to have had a gun in their hands to be guilty of genocide.

The UN report is also helpful in that it again draws on ICTY precedent, and thus case law, to detail the seven factors that international courts use to determine if genocidal intention is present. Detailing how these factors are present in the Museveni case shows that he indeed had, in legal terms, genocidal intent. The first such factor is *the existence of a genocidal plan or policy and the recurrence of destructive and discriminatory acts.* There have been two kinds public statement made by Museveni that give at least indirect evidence of a genocidal plan or policy. The first is where Museveni dehumanizes the Acholi, referring to them as "backward," "primitive," and even as insects. As cited in the first chapter, as early as 1987, in reference to the fight with the Holy Spirit Movement— the Acholi precursor to Kony's LRA—Museveni claimed, "This is a conflict between modernity and primitivity."[74] As late as 2006, just a month before the ceasefire with the LRA, Museveni declared, "We shall transform the people in the north from material and spiritual backwardness to modernity."[75] Thus from the beginning of the conflict up to the ceasefire agreement, Museveni drew upon the colonial lexicon of backward/primitive versus civilized/modern to frame the situation.[76]

Reference to the Acholi as primitive as opposed to civilized is another way of saying that they are less than human. In two public statements in particular, Museveni made this clear. In his first address to Acholi elders in a gathering at the Acholi Inn, a hotel in Gulu, in 1986, participants report him as saying in reference to the Acholi people, "We will put them in a calabash like *nsenene* (grasshoppers) and let them bite themselves to death. In this way we will rid Uganda of *gasiya* (nuisance) once and for all." He is reported also to have made similar statements referring to the Acholi as grasshoppers—that is, as disposable insects—in addresses at Kaunda Grounds in Gulu in 1987 and 1988. Museveni's head of the Army Political School in Entebbe, Kajabagu Ku-Rusoke, has been even more direct. In a statement to the Uganda Human Rights Commission in August 1987, Ku-Rusoke said, "We don't count those who oppose us as people."[77] And again, Saleh's description of the north as "unpopulated" and thus ready for exploitation, despite the million-plus people there, elaborates in a pragmatic way the underlying viewpoint: the Acholi are not people. Gregory Stanton, the president of Genocide Watch, states that such dehumanization, "overcomes the normal human revulsion to murder."[78] Other empirical studies indicate that where there is verbal dehumanization, there is also a policy to kill.[79] If there is question about the function of dehumanizing language in Museveni's case, reference can be made to a second type of public statement that he has made, where he makes a direct, if unspecified, reference to policy. He is reported as having said twice, once to the East African Law Society, "As Hitler did to bring Germany together, we should also do it here. Hitler was a smart guy."[80]

The question that arises is whether the deaths of the Acholi living under the IDP camp policy of Museveni are the result, in the words of the UN mapping report, of "destructive and discriminatory acts" on his part. Here it is important to distinguish between the formal legal meaning of genocide and that which is often present in the popular imagination and even among advocates against genocide. The popular image of genocide is that which is depicted in movies such as *Hotel Rwanda*, where screaming young men in multi-colored fright wigs beat their machetes in unison against the sides of trucks and commence a bloody attack. The slow but sure deaths from malnutrition, dysentery, and other such causes that occur in the IDP camps do not make for Hollywood material.

Even some anti-genocide advocates contribute to misleading understandings of the phenomenon. Gregory Stanton—again, he is the president of Genocide Watch—has written that the segregation of a specific group into ghettos or concentration camps is only a "preparation" for the acts of mass killing "legally called 'genocide.'" Stanton calls the latter stage "extermination," which focuses on killing by armed forces or militias.[81] However, this is a misunderstanding of the legal definition and understanding of genocide, a misunderstanding perhaps rooted in the model of the Nazi use of ghettos to segment off the Jews *before* exterminating them in the separate concentration camps. A better example for the case in northern Uganda is the Holodomor—Stalin's genocide through the destruction of the livelihoods of Soviet Ukrainians in 1932–3.[82]

In light of this latter context it is clear that what happened to the Acholi was not a mere "side-effect" of war, but part of a patterned plan of action that has historical precedent. International law also makes this clear. Again, the Convention on Genocide includes "deliberately inflicting on the group *conditions of life*, calculated to bring about its physical destruction in whole or in part," as an act of genocide (emphasis added). Again, Museveni placed *not enough* soldiers in northern Uganda to protect the Acholi from the LRA but *just enough* to keep them *away* from their gardens and livelihoods in the villages and *forcibly in* the camps where they died. Therefore, there is strong evidence not only of "the existence of a genocidal plan or policy," but also of the "recurrence" over the course of at least a decade of "destructive and discriminatory" acts against the Acholi—in this case in the camps—on the part of Yoweri Museveni.

The second factor indicating genocidal intent is what the UN mapping report terms *the general context*. There are a number of ways to frame the general context in the case of Uganda depending on how general one wants to get. Most broadly, it is possible to view the context as one of the tight relationship between colonialism and the rise of modern genocide. In *"Exterminate All the Brutes,"* Sven Lindqvist follows Hannah Arendt to

---

"In the camp, people were finding difficulties finding where to dig, cultivate, because people were already collected, squeezed in one place. Yet there was no food, so the distribution of food and blankets and other things [by the UN World Food Program], would not satisfy the needs of the people, because the food that was being given was inadequate; indeed so much so that it could not take care of the crowd."

---

make the argument that the genocides on the part of fascist and totalitarian regimes in the mid-twentieth century, including the Nazi genocide of the Jews, are not unique circumstances, but rather constitute the continuation of a colonial mindset that developed most vigorously in the exploration and subsequent occupation of sub-Saharan Africa in the late nineteenth and early twentieth century. The book is an extended reflection on its title, which comes from the last sentence of Joseph Conrad's *Heart of Darkness*. Lindqvist states his conclusion early: "The core of European thought? Yes, there is one sentence ["Exterminate all the brutes"], a short simple sentence, only a few words, summing up the history of our continent. . . . It simply tells the truth we prefer to forget."[83]

Lindqvist makes clear that the colonial justification for the right to mass killing is grounded in the unilinear view of social and cultural evolution.[84] The colonial powers mapped the differences between sub-Saharan cultures and their own onto a worldview that had humanity evolving through pre-specified stages. Given the assumption that European culture was at the most advanced stage, the colonizers identified the cultures of Africa as belonging to earlier stages. This evolutionary scheme is what gives rise to the distinctions between barbaric and civilized, primitive and modern. Of importance here is that although the colonizers often turned to rougher, more blatant terms—"brutes," "animals," "insects," and the like—to refer to Africans, such appeals were and are not always necessary to leverage the act of genocide.

The British dominated Uganda through "indirect" rule, that is, by designating one indigenous group to rule over the rest on behalf of the empire. Indirect rule, coupled with the British quest for bureaucratic order, hardened and reified ethnic differences by setting African over against African.[85] A form of indirect rule continues today. As stated earlier, during the period of my fieldwork, President Museveni's NRM government received between 30 and 50 percent of its budget from foreign aid in a way that reinforced his more than thirty-year presidency and lack of democratic accountability.[86] What is taking place in Uganda today is de facto indirect rule by the donor nations. They get a president who meets their strategic interests and he—with no age or term limits—gets to rule in perpetuity. In the meantime, Museveni thinks of northern Uganda (and the DRC) in much the same way that colonialists thought of African countries: as a source of personal economic gain through plunder.[87] This is the "general context" within which to understand Museveni's public use of the terms "primitive" and "backward" to refer to the Acholi over against his depiction of "modern" and "civilized" societies, and his referring to the Acholi as "insects": the language leverages his avarice.

"The Acholi have been understood in a bad way, especially by the first whites who came here. They understood the Acholi to be the roughest people, who use force and crudeness. And that is why they have said, 'Since you are a very crude people, the best work you can do is the work of crudeness.' And that thing grew and now Acholi are taken everywhere as people who are very crude, and yet not all are like that."

According to the UN mapping report, the third factor indicating the intent to commit genocide is *the perpetuation of other reprehensible acts systematically directed against the same group*. Here, it is first of all important to note that the cases of crimes against humanity, war crimes, and even participation, again, in what the UN report calls "a campaign of ethnic cleansing" in the DRC on the part of the UPDF indicates that the (putative) relative decline of these kinds of overt and more readily documented atrocities on the part of the NRM/UPDF in Uganda post-2002 was *not* due to an increase in professionalism, as is sometimes claimed. In fact, May 2017 reports of UPDF abuses in the Central African Republic, "including rape, sexual slavery, and the exploitation of young girls," while ostensibly chasing Joseph Kony indicates that old patterns continue.[88] Any seeming decline in abuses by the UPDF in northern Uganda was due to the fact that the combination of horrid camp conditions and the continued presence of the LRA in Uganda was sufficient to serve Museveni and Saleh's aim of land acquisition. In fact, the efficiency of the displacement method in meeting this goal actually *freed up* military personnel for the exploitation of resources in the DRC. It is not incidental that the initiation of forced displacement in northern Uganda and the commitment of Ugandan troops to the DRC to plunder occurred in the *same year*, 1996.

The fourth factor indicating genocidal intent is *the scale and number of atrocities committed*. Again, according to the WHO, there were 52,000 excess deaths in the camps in 2005, the *tenth* year since Museveni's military-enforced mandate that all people in northern Uganda move to the camps. In the earlier years, there were fewer people in the camps, but the conditions were far worse. For instance, the WHO reports that Pader, one of the three districts, "was almost entirely inaccessible due to insecurity for much of 2001 through 2003."[89] Estimates of the number of people Idi Amin killed during his seven year reign range from 100,000 to 500,000. Even conservative extrapolation from the WHO study indicates that the number of Acholi deaths due to the forced displacement by Museveni, Saleh, and the NRM/UPDF clearly surpasses 100,000, and is perhaps closer to 300,000, *the same number of deaths often attributed to Amin's regime*. In either case—whether macheted by Amin's soldiers or taken out by malnutrition and disease in Museveni's camps—the people are just as dead. Once we bring ourselves around to the fact, as the Convention on Genocide clearly insists, that planned deaths via starvation, malnutrition and similar causes—again, a policy of not enough soldiers to protect the camps, but enough soldiers to keep the people there and away from their gardens and livelihoods—count every bit as much as atrocities as deaths by gun or machete, then it is not difficult to understand why the mass forced displacement of the Acholi constitutes genocide on the part of Museveni and his cohort.

The fifth indicator of genocidal intent is *the fact of targeting certain victims systematically because of their membership of a particular group*. Here, it is significant that the Acholi were chronologically the first and always numerically by far the most in the IDP camps. Forced displacement by the NRM/UPDF was practiced *only in Acholi districts*, even though other districts—for instance, Lira and Soroti—came under heavy LRA attack.[90] These facts fit with Museveni's history of singling out the Acholi people.

The sixth factor named by the UN mapping report is *the fact that the victims had been massacred with no regard for their age and gender*. Again, once we get used to the fact that "massacres" can take place, in the words of the Convention on Genocide, by "deliberately inflicting on the group conditions of life, calculated to bring about its physical destruction in whole or in part," then the criterion that there is no regard for age or gender is not problematic for a determination of genocide. In fact, those who suffer most in camp conditions are the very young and the very old because their immune systems are weak and their general strength is low.[91]

The seventh and final factor that the UN names as indicating genocidal intent is *the consistent and methodical manner in which acts were committed*. At the time of the WHO study, 1.2 million people, around 90 percent of the population of the districts in Acholiland, lived in 121 camps. The rest of the Acholi moved to the towns. After the initial forced displacement in 1996, the NRM/UPDF *repeated* the measure for all remaining people in the villages in 2002 and again in 2004 (*after* the signing of the Rome Statute and the founding of the ICC). Anyone found outside the camps was deemed a rebel. There is no question, then, that the operation was both consistent and methodical.

It is clear from the evidence above, then, that not only the actions, but the specific intent—what international law calls the *dolus specialis*—of Museveni, Saleh, and the NRM/UPDF's policies and activities toward the Acholi, policies and activities that continued well after 2002, constitutes genocide in the strict legal sense. Given the disregard for human life exhibited by these parties toward Congolese citizens as highlighted in the 2010 UN mapping report, such genocidal intent and activity toward the Acholi ought not come as much of a surprise. My interviews with IDP camp residents as quoted above show that that disregard was in fact the norm. The portrayal of the IDP camps as "protected villages" is simply not credible: the requisite ideational and psychological reversal on the part of Museveni, Saleh, and the troops from attacking people they considered to be less than human to protecting those same people under dangerous circumstances as if they were their own is too fantastic to be believable.[92]

This is the message that the Acholi who approached me wanted to get out. *This* is the world that *they* inhabited. *This* is what Sister Cecilia wanted me to report when she requested that I "talk to the leaders"; what Orach, he who was hung by his testicles, insisted that I make more widely known: "I want you to be my Charlie Wilson." They and people like them offered me the hospitality—food, shelter, relationships— without which fieldwork and life itself is impossible. They allowed me into their world (as much as this is possible). I owed them. I owed them profoundly. And their own witness put me to shame. What kind of person would I be if I tucked away in silence all of *this* so that I could continue on with my prescribed research? *This* is why, despite the real risk of not being allowed back into Uganda to finish that research, I published the article.

Otunnu Unleashes Dossier on Alleged Acholi Genocide

On January 4, 2011, about ten days after its publication, Olara Otunnu, an opposition candidate for the presidency of Uganda, called a press conference where he highlighted my article. The next day, a Ugandan national newspaper, *The Daily Monitor*, featured the press conference.[93] Later, on the morning of the newspaper coverage, I received an email from someone identifying himself as a "concerned Ugandan," asking me about the article and its documentation. Curious, I googled the name, and found out that its author, Simon Kuteesa, was the Commissioner for Media Crimes at the Crime Investigations and Intelligence Directorate in Uganda. I did not reply. Friends warned me to stay out of country for a while, for my own safety. I waited three years. In December 2013, I returned to Uganda without incident to complete the research necessary for this book. Whether I was allowed in because I was deemed to be no longer a threat or because the government did not have the technology to track my re-entrance remains unclear.

Publication of the article did and did not make a difference. It did not make a difference in the sense that Museveni is still in office and remains uncharged for his crimes. It did make a difference in that people in northern Uganda appreciated my effort to articulate in a public forum what they had told me of their experience. An Acholi woman, when introduced to me three years after the publication, said simply, "Oh, you are the one who wrote the article." A Notre Dame colleague, upon returning from his first research trip in northern Uganda, told me, "You've cut a wide swath there." During my last trip, several people stopped to thank me, with one priest telling me that he has gone over the article several times.

It is important to understand just what my contribution, such as it is, is here. It is not that I gave "voice" to what the Acholi themselves have been unable to articulate. Acholi are perfectly capable of articulating what has gone on. Olara Otunnu, the 2011 opposition candidate, had already been speaking and writing about the genocide of the Acholi.[94] What I added other than my specific version of the argument was my positionality as a white American scholar to the conversation. And, again, this is what the Acholi who requested that I write wanted me to do: to live in their world long enough to get a good sense of it, and then to use my capacities gained from living *outside* of that world to convey what I saw.

Philosopher Amanda Fricker writes of what she calls "epistemic injustice," that is, the systematic marginalization of the perspectives of certain categories of persons. Again, the dominant narrative—crafted by Museveni and echoed by both international and American national governmental bodies—about the conflict in northern Uganda is that the "backward" (to use Museveni's term) Acholi gave birth to the madman Kony, and that this is the sole source of all Acholi suffering. This narrative leads to the rest of the world having what Fricker calls a "low credibility judgment" regarding Acholi testimony about Museveni's abuses. The effort of persons like me is to try in whatever way we can to get these governmental bodies to "revise upward," to use Fricker's phrase, their credibility judgment regarding the Acholi, and in this way to help "neutralize the impact of structural identity prejudice."[95] Maybe if I, a white Western scholar, "talk to the leaders," to again use Sister Cecilia's words, they will listen.[96]

So far, anyway, they have not. The global narrative is structured such that Maximino's testimony, given in Chapter 1, that Museveni's forces hacked to death the young men in Koc Laminatoo—"Eighteen young people, who were in my neighborhood, were picked by the NRA rebels of Yoweri Museveni. . . . Their heads all beaten with heavy logs"—does not count as worth "the leaders'" while. The low credibility judgment is such that Acholi witness is still dismissed, even in such direct a testimony, as somehow being deceived about what is really going on. I tried and failed to change that.

Pivoting from commitment to return

In the last movement of anthropological theology, the researcher takes what she has learned from inhabiting—as much as this is possible—the world of the other and shares it—as much as *this* is possible—with her home community. This, too, is not as straightforward as the language of "pivoting from commitment to return" might seem to imply. This is in large part because if she has truly inhabited the world of the other to any significant degree, she will be changed, and perhaps changed in ways that do not sit flush with her home community. In other words, if going native without remainder is an impossibility, so is going home without remainder when one has made elsewhere home for a while. I sometimes tell Acholi, *Kumalo me Uganda tye ganga me aryoo*. Northern Uganda is my second home. And so it is. The practice of ethnography as I think of and, I hope, embody it is not simply that of inhabiting, for a while, the world of an other, but that of the movement *between* worlds. Most ethnographic accounts end before the attempted return home, and therefore, in my judgment, prematurely. Writing the return is important if ethnography is to get beyond the objectifying gaze on the other to instead be "in the middle of things." What this means is that returning to one's first home can be difficult.

Publication of the article charging Museveni with genocide severely strained some important friendships of mine at Notre Dame. One colleague—saying that he represented not only himself but the concern and opinion of others as well—insisted that I withdraw from public debate on the issue of the Ugandan government's actions and, barring that, that I do not identify myself with the University in anything I write on the matter. The argument was that I had put other University and associated programs and projects at risk. My counter-argument, other than that the risk to these projects and programs was minimal, was that silence on government human rights violations is frequently the unexamined cost of doing business in countries with oppressive regimes, and that that cost needs to be examined in our practical discernments.[97] Another colleague, who backed the first in the insistence that I withdraw from public debate, told me afterward that their differences with me were simply ones of prudential judgment on the concrete particulars of this case, not of basic principles or deeply held beliefs. At first I thought that this was correct. However, subsequent actions by the university in Uganda and elsewhere prompted me to re-examine this claim.

I must say that given my own claim that Christian ethics is about following exemplars and that I offer my efforts as an example, however flawed, *ad hominem* arguments in response regarding *my* actions, appropriately socially situated, are fair game, of the sort, "He claimed that following Christ is about x and y, but he did z in those circumstances, so he really did not live up to following Christ." This is a built-in part of any attempt at *imitatio Christi*. There is no doubt in my mind that many others in the same circumstances could have done much more and much better.

It is also important to be as clear-eyed as possible about the various levels on which one's motives can run. War photojournalist Peter van Agtmael, who has worked in Iraq and Afghanistan as well as in IDP camps in northern Uganda, gives a sobering reminder that we ought not to get too morally excited about our own actions:

Why go to war? I had strong beliefs. I believed that journalism, however flawed, was one of the key checks against corruption and power-mongering. I found photography when I was 19, and soon there was a feeling of completion that had never been there. It sensitized me. It crystallized a hatred of cruelty, while giving me a reverence that every moment was of potential beauty and consequence.

These were my stated reasons, to family and friends troubled and curious about my decision. It was the truth, but a limited one. Stewing under the surface was an uncomfortable secret that I kept even from myself. I had a deep and hungry fascination to experience war. I still can't explain it. I'd felt it in me from my earliest memories. I was ashamed of the darkness it revealed.

I coveted the idea of being brave. I felt as if I were someone else and needed to do certain things to inhabit that skin. I've tried to find a cause for these instincts for years, but nothing has stuck. I now no longer think that consciousness can really correct primal excesses. Not enough, anyhow.[98]

I am unsure to what degree the reasons that I have given for my actions—the effort to imitate the Little Sisters in imitating Christ—were operative when I carried them out during and after the article charging Museveni with genocide, and to what degree I am constructing them in retrospect. Like Agtmael, my sense is that my constructed version of the past is "the truth, but a limited one." Like him, I cannot explain my fuller motivations adequately. I have always been morally earnest—my senior photo in my high school yearbook bears the motto, "To see the world in one PEACE" next to it, and my older brother stood up and said at my wedding rehearsal dinner that he knew years ago that I would go into theology because when we played with our toy soldiers in the backyard sandbox while growing up, I would always bury the dead (it was funny because it was true enough).

At some point, it became serious, and my version of Agtmael's "skin" that he needs to inhabit is a sense, a subliminal pulse of some kind—most times just at the edges of awareness, other times more demanding—that the only life worth living is one that might be lost. The narrator in Denis Johnson's *Resuscitation of a Hanged Man* brings it to our attention: "On the other hand—would God ask for anything sane? Did He come to Elijah and say, Go, secure a respectable position and wear out your days in the chores of it? Did His strange monstrous finger guide a person toward the round of events that wears us down and evens us out until even the meanest is presentable, if wrinkled and feeble? Or did it point straight to an earthquake and say, don't you dare come back until you've died."[99] Most times, it remains unarticulated. I do not construct it or bring it about, at least not consciously so; it chases me, always a little faster than the pace I am keeping. There is certainly no credit and perhaps little blame to be taken for this hound of heaven or hellhound (I am unsure which it is; it has been both creative and destructive). It is simply there. And if I do not give it its due, ease up and let it overtake me from time to time, I lose my bearings altogether. While it is a mistake to reduce reason-giving to psychological biography, it is also a mistake to not at least gesture in the direction of the latter as a way of saying, "I am not telling you everything. I do not tell myself everything."

At its best, the practice of going out to do fieldwork and then returning to our initial community in anthropological theology creates a space-between-places that can open up the possibility of imagining, even if "through a glass darkly," Gospel alternatives to the way things presently are. Precisely because she moves between two worlds with all of the relationships, assumptions, and practices involved, an ethnographer's return to her first home is not always an easy one, as we will see in the Chapter 8. Still, it is important for the anthropological theologian to share with her home community what she learned from the people she met in the field, and I will try to do this as well.

Notes

1. Interview with Sister Cecilia.

2. Mario Cisternino, *Passion for Africa: Missionary and Imperial Papers on the Evangelization of Uganda and Sudan, 1848-1923* (Kampala: Fountain Publishers, 2004), pp. 361.

3. Fr. Tarcisio Agostoni, *The Comboni Missionaries: An Outline History, 1867-1997* (Rome: Bibliotheca Comboniana, 2003), p. 210, note 25.

4. Annette Seegers and Robin E. Walker, "Securitisation: The Case of Post-9/11 United States Africa Policy," *Scientia Militaria: South African Journal of Military Studies* 40, no. 2 (2012), pp. 22–45.

5. Marcel Proust, *Remembrance of Things Past*, Vol. I, trans C. K. Scott Moncrieff and Terrence Kilmartin (New York: Vintage Books, 1982), p. 13.

6. Interview with Sr. Martha, p. 2.

7. http://al.nd.edu/about/ (retrieved February 25, 2015).

8. John Casey, *Pagan Virtue: An Essay in Ethics* (Cambridge: Cambridge University Press, 1990), pp. 211 and 225–6. What Casey refers to as "pagan" is largely Aristotelian.

9. Invisible Children, *Kony 2012*, at https://www.youtube.com/watch?v=Y4MnpzG5Sqc.

10. Invisible Children, *Invisible Children: The Rough Cut* at https://www.youtube.com/watch?v=kLHOh-9f8xI and https://www.youtube.com/watch?v=tLDDRspWZNY. *Jackass* was a television reality show (2000–2) and then movie (2002), where it characters carried out crude stunts. Proving that you can never have too much of a bad thing, the principals released further movies.

11. There would have been between approximately 200,000 and 250,000 such refugees in Uganda out of a total population of over ten million people in southern Sudan.

12. Invisible Children, *Invisible Children: The Rough Cut.*

13. Such claims ignore the experience in 2008–9 of the failed Ugandan military effort—assisted by seventeen US advisers and $1 million in US financial support—to bomb Kony's basecamp in the DRC in an operation called "Lightning Thunder." The camp turned out to be empty, and the bombing succeeded only in spurring the rebels to kill close to 1,000 Congolese civilians in retaliation. See Jeffrey Gettleman and Eric Schmitt, "U.S. Aided a Failed Plan to Rout Ugandan Rebels," *The New York Times* (February 6, 2009), accessed at http://www.nytimes.com/2009/02/07/world/africa/07congo.html?ref=lords_resistance_army. The Kony 2012 video make it appear as if the arrest or killing of Joseph Kony can be surgical in its precision.

14. Ronald R. Atkinson, *The Roots of Ethnicity: The Origins of the Acholi of Uganda Before 1800* (Philadelphia: University of Pennsylvania Press, 2009).

15. Chris Ocowun, "Museveni Hails Gulu Archbishop Odama," *New Vision* (October 22, 2006), p. 1.

16. Human Rights Watch, *Unfinished Business: Closing Gaps in the Selection of ICC Cases* (September 2011), p. 25.

17. Duncan Miriri and Andrew Roche, "Uganda's Museveni Calls on African Nations to Quit the ICC," *Reuters* (December 12, 2014), at http://www.reuters.com/article/us-africa-icc-idUSKBN0JQ1DO20141212.

18. See "African Union Members Back Kenyan Plan to Leave ICC," *The Guardian* (February 1, 2016), at http://www.theguardian.com/world/2016/feb/01/african-union-kenyan-plan-leave-international-criminal-court; and Henry Owuor, "AU adopts Uhuru's call to abandon ICC," *The Monitor* (February 9, 2016), at http://www.monitor.co.ug/News/National/AU-adopts-Uhurus-call-to-abandon-ICC/-/688334/3067758/-/kr2qhp/-/index.html.

19. "Museveni Tells ICC to Leave Kenya Alone," *The Daily Nation* (December 12, 2013), at http://www.nation.co.ke/news/Museveni-tells-ICC-to-leave-Kenya-alone/-/1056/2110008/-/xpanyoz/-/index.html.

20. See APA, "Ugandan Leader Pledges Co-operation with ICC in Ongwen's Case," *StarAfrica* (March 3, 2015), at http://en.starafrica.com/news/ugandan-leader-pledges-co-operation-with-icc-in-ongwens-case.html.

21. International Criminal Court, *SITUATION IN UGANDA: WARRANT OF ARREST FOR DOMINIC ONGWEN* (Public redacted version), paragraph #22; available at http://www. icc-cpi.int/iccdocs/doc/doc97201.pdf. On the exclusive focus of the warrant on Uganda, see also #6, 18, and 19. More, the warrant gives the ICC prerogative because, "the Government of Uganda has been unable to arrest" Ongwen," but, as mentioned, the Ugandan government itself had him in custody. Cf. #25.

22. See Mark Kesten, "Why the ICC Won't Prosecute Museveni," *Justice in Conflict* (March 19, 2015), at http://justiceinconflict.org/2015/03/19/why-the-icc-wont-prosecute-museveni/.

23. International Criminal Court Press Release, "ICC President Meets with President of Uganda," at https://www.icc-cpi.int/Pages/item.aspx?name=PR1279.

24. The Africanist Richard Joseph describes the "new breed" of African leaders with some enthusiasm as having "adopted structural adjustment reforms, benefited from large inflows of development aid, introduced partial political liberalization, given early emphasis to human rights and popular participation at the local level, used military force to enhance state cohesion and stability without overt repression." See Richard Joseph, "The Reconfiguration of Power in Late Twentieth-Century Africa," in *State, Conflict, and Democracy in Africa*, ed. Richard Joseph (Boulder: Lynne Rienner Publishers, 1999), p. 67.

25. Joseph Oloka-Onyango, "'New-Breed' Leadership, Conflict, and Reconstruction in the Great Lakes Region of Africa: A Sociopolitical Biography of Uganda's Yoweri Kaguta Museveni," *Africa Today* 50, no. 3 (Spring 2004), p. 46. See also Aili Mari Tripp, "The Changing Face of Authoritarianism in Africa: The Case of Uganda," *Africa Today* 50, no. 3 (Spring 2004), pp. 29–52.

26. US military personnel regularly carry out trainings in Uganda, and the last major offensive by the NRM/UPDF against the LRA was supported by seventeen US advisers and $1 million in fuel. On US advisory support for the UPDF attack on the LRA in the December 2008, "Operation Lightning Thunder," see Jeffrey Gettleman and Eric Schmitt, "U.S. Aided a Failed Plan to Rout Ugandan Rebels." "Operation Natural Fire 10" is an October 2009 joint exercise in northern Uganda where the US trained military teams from Uganda, Kenya, Tanzania, Rwanda and Burundi. See Kevin J. Kelley, "Uganda: Big U.S. Military Exercise for Northern Region," *The East African* (October 12, 2009), available at http://www.globalresearch.ca/index.php?context=va&aid=15641.

27. Eric Schmitt, "U.S. Strategy to Fight Terrorism Increasingly Uses Proxies," *New York Times* (May 29, 2014), at http://nyti.ms/1ka36fl.

28. Morgan Winsor, "Trump's Directive on Offensive Airstrikes in Somalia Could Fuel Terrorism, Experts Warn," *ABCNews* (April 1, 2017), at http://abcnews.go.com/US/trumps-directive-offensive-airstrikes-somalia-fuel-terrorism-recruitment/story?id=46490369.

29. Observer Media, LTD, "46 Ugandan Soldiers Killed in Somalia," *The Observer* (April 2, 2018), at: http://observer.ug/news/headlines/57363-46-ugandan-soldiers-killed-in-somalia.html

30. The countries that withheld aid were the Netherlands, Sweden, and the United Kingdom.

31. See Human Rights Watch, *"Keep the People Uninformed": Pre-election Threats to Free Expression and Association in Uganda* (January 2016), p. 1, at https://www.hrw.org/sites/default/files/report_pdf/uganda0116web.pdf.

32. See Ayiswa Issa, "US govt says Ugandan People 'Deserved Better,' Raise Concerns Continued Dr. Besigye House Arrest," *Of Uganda* (February 21, 2016) at http://www.ofuganda.co.ug/articles/20160221/us-govt-says-ugandan-people-deserved-better-raise-concerns-continued-dr-besigye. On the Kerry phone call, see US Department of State, "Secretary Kerry's Call with Ugandan President Yoweri Museveni" (February 19, 2016), at http://www.state.gov/r/pa/prs/ps/2016/02/253069.htm#.VsdlF-6pT2E.facebook.

33. Russia's Foreign Ministry announced after the 2016 election that it "hails the successful general election in the friendly Uganda, which has proved broad national support for the government's course." See Frederic Musisi, "Russia hails Museveni win," *The Monitor* (February 22, 2016), at http://mobile.monitor.co.ug/specialreports/elections/Russia-hails-Museveni-win/-/2471424/3087220/-/format/xhtml/-/7e68ksz/-/index.html. For the bind in which Russian and Chinese support for Museveni places the United States, and the continued US aid support, see Jeffrey Gettleman, "Instead of Democracy, Uganda Moves Toward Dictatorship Light," *The New York Times* (Febrau[y 17, 2016), at http://mobile.nytimes.com/2016/02/18/world/africa/uganda-firmly-under-one-mans-rule-dusts-off-trappings-of-an-election.html?_r=0.

34. For a detailed critique of the Ugandan government's corruption practices and the role of donor nations in enabling those practices, see Human Rights Watch and the Allard K. Lowenstein International Human Rights Clinic, Yale Law School, *"Letting the Big Fish Swim": Failures to Prosecute High-Level Corruption in Uganda* (October 2013).

35. Helene Cooper, "More U.S. Troops to Aid Uganda search for Kony," *New York Times* (March 23, 2014), at http://www.nytimes.com/2014/03/24/world/africa/obama-is-sending-more-resources-for-joseph-kony-search.html

36. See "America Confirms Military Aid to Uganda and Burundi" (June 28, 2011) at http://pressrelease.co.ug/pressuganda/?p=4497; and Michael Poffenberger, "Senate committee approves funds to help stop LRA" (June 17, 2011) at http://www.theresolve.org/blog/archives/3071029201.

37. Karen DeYoung, "On the Hunt for Joseph Kony," *Washington Post* (March 23, 2014), at https://www.washingtonpost.com/world/national-security/2014/03/23/aa468ca6-b2d0-11e3-8020-b2d790b3c9e1_story.html. The next month, the United States recalled the aircraft. See John Vandiver, "Air Support Gets Pulled Out of Effort to Counter Lord's Army," *Stars and Stripes* (April 10, 2014), at http://www.stripes.com/news/airlift-support-gets-pulled-out-of-effort-to-counter-lord-s-army-1.277314. Africa Command's General David Rodriguez "did not rule out" the return of the aircraft to East/Central Africa in the effort to find Kony.

38. Samuel Okiror, "End of Jospeh Kony Hunt Raises Fears Lord's Resistance Army Could Return," *The Guardian* (May 1, 2017), at https://www.theguardian.com/global-development/2017/may/01/end-joseph-kony-hunt-fears-lords-resistance-army-return; Jason Burke and Alon Mwesigwa, "Central Africa Fears Return of LRA after Hunt for Joseph Kony Ends," *The Guardian* (May 1, 2017), at https://www.theguardian.com/world/2017/may/01/central-africa-fears-return-of-lra-lords-resistance-army-after-hunt-for-joseph-kony-ends?CMP=Share_iOSApp_Other.

39. Petra Cahill, "Donald Trump Befriended these Strongmen in 2017," *Reuters* (January 1, 2018), at https://www.nbcnews.com/news/world/donald-trump-befriended-these-strongmen-2017-n831391; Declan Walsh, "As Strongmen Steamroll Their Opponents, U.S. is Silent," *The New York Times* (February 1, 2018), at https://www.nytimes.com/2018/02/01/world/middleeast/trump-sisi-egypt-strongmen.html

40. Jina Moore, "Uganda Lifts an Age Limit, Paving the Way for a President for Life," *The New York Times* (December 20, 2017), at https://www.nytimes.com/2017/12/20/world/africa/uganda-president-museveni-age-limit.html.

41. Elias Biryabarema, "Uganda Lawyers Seek to Quash 'Museveni for Life' Law," *Reuters* (January 15, 2018), at https://www.reuters.com/article/us-uganda-politics/ugandan-lawyers-seek-to-quash-museveni-president-for-life-law-idUSKBN1F4280.

42. "I love Donald Trump says Ugandan President Museveni," *The East African* (January 23, 2018), at http://www.theeastafrican.co.ke/news/I-love-Trump-says-President-Museveni/2558-4275118-8pnfwcz/index.html.

43. The nearly 100 million viewings was as of June 23, 2014. On the funds raised, see Sam Sanders, "The 'Kony 2012' Effect: Recovering from a Viral Sensation," *National Public Radio* (June 14, 2014), at http://www.npr.org/2014/06/14/321853244/the-kony-2012-effect-recovering-from-a-viral-sensation.

44. Adam Branch, "Dangerous Ignorance: The Hysteria of Kony 2012," *Aljazeera* (March 21, 2012), at http://www.aljazeera.com/indepth/opinion/2012/03/201231284336601364.html.

45. An Al Jezeera reporter present at the event writes: "People I spoke to anticipated seeing a video that showed the world the terrible atrocities that they had suffered during the conflict, and the ongoing struggles they still face trying to rebuild their lives after two lost decades. The audience was at first puzzled to see the narrative led by an American man—Jason Russell—and his young son. Towards the end of the film, the mood turned more to anger at what many people saw as a foreign, inaccurate account that belittled and commercialised their suffering, as the film promotes Kony bracelets and other fundraising merchandise, with the aim of making Kony infamous. The event ended with the angrier members of the audience throwing rocks and shouting abusive criticism, as the rest fled for safety, leaving an abandoned projector, with organisers and the press running for cover." Malcolm Webb, "Ugandans React with Anger to Kony Video," *Aljazeera* (March 14, 2012), at http://blogs.aljazeera.com/blog/africa/ugandans-react-anger-kony-video.

46. In December 2014, citing a drop in funding, the American headquarters of Invisible Children closed, and handed over its Uganda operations to local partners. See Eleanor Goldberg, "Invisible Children, Group Behind 'Kony 2102,' Closing Because Of Funding Issues," *Huffington Post* (December 16, 2014), at http://www.huffingtonpost.com/2014/12/16/invisible-children-closing_n_6329990.html.

47. I paired publication of the original article making the case that Museveni and his forces have committed genocide with publication of one of the documents that Ocena Charles gave me. Much of the ensuing debate focused on whether the document was authentic or not and took attention away from the overall genocide case. Given that the case stands without the document, in this presentation of the argument I simply place the document in the notes. The original article appeared as Todd David Whitmore, "Genocide or Just Another 'Casualty of War'?" *Practical Matters* 3 (Spring 2010), at http://www.practicalmattersjournal.org/issue/3/analyzing-matters/genocide-or-just-another-casualty-of-war. A copy of the memo is below.

My own inquiry—the process of seeking confirmation or counterevidence for the authenticity of the memo—took place on three levels. First, I had to seek out former members of the administration who at some point fell out with Museveni and who were still alive. I found one who was willing to talk to me, a former high-ranking official, who testified to the memo's authenticity. Still, such testimony, by itself, was not sufficient to go forward, it seemed to me, because the official, though he had no possibility of regaining any power, likely had an interest in seeing Museveni's reputation damaged. It was at this point that I decided to research more deeply than I had previously into the patterns of activity of Museveni, his brother, Salim Saleh, and the NRA/UPDF in northern Uganda, a process that led to the writing of the article. On this second level, my question was whether and to what extent such patterns of activity align with the account in the memo. Then, for a third level of assessment, I sent the memo and article to a journal for review, and they were both affirmed by two of the most respected scholars of northern Uganda.

In the memo, "Tremor 1," according to my source, is the current Ugandan president, Yoweri Museveni, and "Meteor Plus One" is his brother, General Salim Saleh, whom both the ICJ and the UN have named as a key operative in the Ugandan government's crimes and plunder in the DRC. (See United Nations Expert Panel on Illegal Exploitation of Natural Resources and Other Forms of Wealth in the DRC, *Report of the Panel of Experts on the Illegal Exploitation of Natural Resources and Other Forms of Wealth of the Democratic Republic of the Congo*, at http://www.un.org/News/dh/latest/drcongo.htm; ICJ, *Armed Activities on the Territory of the Congo (Democratic Republic of the Congo v. Uganda* No. 2005/26 (December 19, 2005)), available at http://www.icj-cij.org/docket/files/116/10521. pdf.).

The memo:

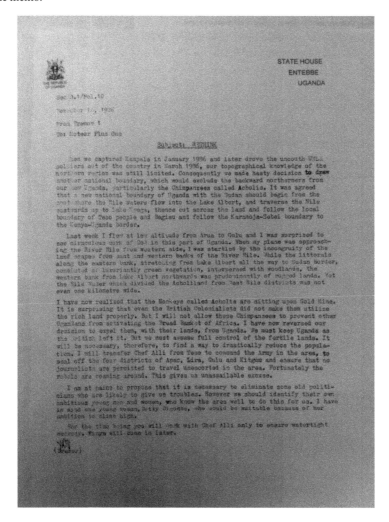

48. See http://www.un.org/millennium/law/iv-1.htm. The "in part" language of the Convention is deliberate and significant. A pattern of intent and activity does not have to have as its objective the elimination of *all* members of a particular ethnic group to qualify as genocide. Given that so many Acholi were negatively and even lethally affected by NRM policy, the "in part" clause may seem unnecessary, but it is important to keep it in view in anticipation of possible (and inaccurate) objections that only a few Acholi suffered. Once again, the UN mapping report cites cases and decisions from ICTY as precedent:

"The intention to destroy a named group, even in part, is sufficient to constitute a crime of genocide provided that it is the group or 'a distinct fraction of the group' that is targeted and not a 'multitude of isolated individuals belonging to the group.' Furthermore, the section of the group targeted must be substantial and thus reflect 'both the mass nature of the genocide and the concern expressed in the Convention as to the impact that the destruction of the section of the group targeted would have on the group as a whole' (emphasis in original)." See United Nations Office of the High Commissioner for Human Rights, *Democratic Republic of the Congo, 1993-2003*, par. 506. The report cites *Brdanin* decision, ICTY, Trial chamber, no. IT-99-36-T, September 1, 2004, par. 700; and *Kristic* arrest, ICTY, Appeals chamber, no. IT-98-33-A, April 19, 2004, par. 8.

49. Elijah Dickens Mushemeza writes, "On assuming power in 1985, General Tito Okello Lutwa invited all fighting groups, including the NRA, to join together and form a united government in the spirit of reconciliation and nation building. The NRA did not respond and this led to Tito Okello's Government seeking a negotiated political settlement with the NRA. This resulted in the Nairobi Peace Agreement (December 17, 1985), detailing power sharing arrangements and the composition of the Military Council. All parties also agreed to a ceasefire within forty eight hours including the UNLA and the NRA." Elijah Dickens Mushemeza, "Policing in Post-Conflict Environment: Implications for Police Reform in Uganda," *Journal of Security Sector Management* 6, no. 3 (November 2008), p. 4.

50. Adam Branch, "The Political Dilemmas of Global Justice: Anti-Civilian Violence and the Violence of Humanitarianism, the Case of Northern Uganda" (Columbia University Ph.D. dissertation, 2007), p. 146.

51. The best work on male-on-male violence, including sexual violence, during the conflict in northern Uganda is by Chris Dolan. See, for instance, "Collapsing Masculinities and Weak States—a Case Study of Northern Uganda," in *Masculinities Matter!: Men, Gender, and Development*, ed. Frances Cleaver (London and New York: Zed Books; Cape Town: David Philips, 2003), pp. 57–83.

52. It would not be the last time Museveni would use the tactic. Carlos Rodriguez Soto—who is hardly pro-LRA, calling its leader, Joseph Kony, "satanic"—provides a detailed account of the government's handling of his own efforts at peacebuilding. In order to mediate with the rebels, the man popularly called "Father Carlos" had, on each individual occasion, to receive prior approval from the UPDF, which he did. However, in one instance in particular—it was late August 2002—the army used Rodriguez Soto's peacebuilding efforts to track the LRA. The UPDF attacked the site, with Rodriguez Soto there, where the priest was to meet the rebels. The government forces beat and kicked him and his priest companions, took them to remote barracks, and refused them sustenance. They were not released until they signed documents that said that they had failed to secure official approval for the mediation. The army spokesperson issued a statement claiming that Fr. Carlos and his colleagues were found transporting rebels and drugs. See Carlos Rodriguez Soto, *Tall Grass: Stories of Suffering and Peace in Northern Uganda* (Kampala: Fountain Publishers, 2009), p. 65 and chapter 5 ("The Trap of Tumangu"). Occurring in August 2002, this incident can be investigated by the ICC if it so chooses.

53. Jan Egeland, *A Billion Lives: An Eyewitness Report from the frontlines of Humanity* (New York, London, Toronto, and Sydney: Simon and Schuster, 2008), p. 201.

54. ARLPI, *Let My People Go: The Forgotten Plight of the People in Displaced Camps in Acholi* (Gulu: ARLPI, 2001), p. 9.

55. ARLPI, *Let My People Go: The Forgotten Plight of the People in Displaced Camps in Acholi*, p. 9.

56. For further documentation on the unwillingness of the NRM/UPDF to protect camp residents against the LRA, see Civil Society Organizations for Peace in Northern Uganda, *Nowhere to Hide* (December 10, 2004), p. 2. Refugee Law Project, "Statement on Ethnic Violence" (February 27, 2004), p. 25, at http://www.internal-displacement. org/8025708F004CE90B/(httpDocuments)/300CBA7CC2650F55802570B7005A5725/$file/ RLP+Position+Statement+on+ethnic+violence.doc.

57. United Nations Office of the High Commissioner for Human Rights, *Democratic Republic of the Congo, 1993-2003: Report of the Mapping Exercise documenting the most serious violations of human rights and international humanitarian law committed within the territory of the Democratic Republic of Congo between March 1993 and June 2003* (August 2010; Released on October 1, 2010), par. 366.

58. United Nations Expert Panel on Illegal Exploitation of Natural Resources and Other Forms of Wealth in DRC, *Report of the Panel of Experts on the Illegal Exploitation of Natural Resources and Other Forms of Wealth of the Democratic Republic of the Congo*; and ICJ, *Armed Activities on the Territory of the Congo (Democratic Republic of the Congo v. Uganda* No. 2005/26 (December 19, 2005). See also Gerard Prunier, "Rebel Movements and Proxy Warfare: Uganda, Sudan, and the Congo (1986–89)," *African Affairs* 103 (2004), pp. 359–83.

59. United Nations Office of the High Commissioner for Human Rights, *Democratic Republic of the Congo, 1993-2003*, par. 522.

60. Ibid., par. 349.

61. Caroline Lamwaka, "4,000 UPDAs in Peace Centres," *New Vision* (April 8, 1988).

62. For instance, the Acholi often supplement their diet by hunting *anyeri* or "giant rat," a groundhog or muskrat-sized rodent. Stewed well, it is tender and tastes very good.

63. One important study puts the matter this way: "The land which a family owns is not considered as being totally 'theirs': it is their heritage and the future heritage of their children. Since they see that a family exists only as a part of a wider community, so its land is held within the wider structure of a community (clan) and as clan's land. Land is the fundamental productive asset, without which one cannot survive, and so one's social obligations and claims are intimately connected to claims and rights over land. These obligations extend to the next generation: land must therefore be protected for them and if anyone who leaves the village and fails to survive in the urban economy, the customary land is a safety net, because they can always return and be allocated a plot. Land is also the link with people's heritage – quite literally, since it is on the family land that one is buried." Judy Adoko and Simon Levine, *Land Matters in Displacement: The Importance of Land Rights in Acholiland and What Threatens Them* (Kampala: Civil Society Organizations for Peace in Northern Uganda (CSOPNU) and Land and Equity Movement in Uganda (LEMU), 2004), p. 5; available at http://www.land-in-uganda.org/assets/LEMU-Land%20Matters%20in%20 Displacement.pdf.

64. ARLPI, *Let My People Go*, p. 10.

65. Adoko and Levine, *Land Matters in Displacement,* p. 16.

66. Two years later, the ARLPI criticized the Divinity Union proposal. "During our consultations with people in the camps many expressed the fear that the policy of putting the population of Acholi in camps was a well-calculated move in order to grab their land. A project proposal two years ago by the Divinity Union Ltd., owned by Major General Salim Saleh, highlighted some large chunks of land in Acholi to be used for large-scale commercial farming." The situation with Saleh and Divinity Union, according to the religious leaders, "deepens the

already existing rift between the people of Acholi and the National Resistance Movement (NRM) Government." ARLPI, *Let My People Go.*

67. Given the present lull in the NRM-LRA conflict, at least within Uganda, Museveni and Saleh cannot any longer use military force, at least in the same way as before, as a means to cause and take advantage of social disruption in order to procure wealth. They must at least appear to be taking normal political channels, and this Museveni and others in the NRM have tried to do. Starting in 2007, Museveni sought to allocate 40,000 hectares of land in the north to the Madhvani Group for a sugar cane plantation, a number which he reduced to 20,000 hectares when faced with opposition. If such a deal goes through, the central government will have a 40 percent stake in the plantation. Another case occurred when the central government gave one billion Ugandan schillings to twenty army officers and government officials to take land in the north that was already under customary tenure, resulting in the eviction of families from their land. A case of local officials getting in on the act occurred when the members of the Amuru District Land Board applied for 85,000 hectares of land for themselves, an application that, if successful, would have evicted—that is, again, displaced—10,000 people from their land. In yet another case, Museveni, Saleh, and Museveni's son, Lt. Col. Muhoozi Kainerugaba, have been cited by the anti-corruption NGO, Global Witness, for arranging "security" for newly found oil deposits in ways that enhance themselves financially. See "Kakira Offered 20,000 Hectares of Land in Amuru," *The Monitor* (November 13, 2008); and, more recently, Solomon Arinaitwe, "The Madhvani Quest for Amuru Land," *The Daily Monitor* (July 31, 2013), at http://www.monitor.co.ug/SpecialReports/The-Madhvani-quest-for-Amuru-land/-/688342/1932108/-/11u75b9z/-/index.html.

   For a careful account of these cases and of the issue of land in northern Uganda generally, see Ronald R. Atkinson, "Land Issues in Acholi in the Transition from War to Peace," *The Examiner: Quarterly Publication of Human Rights Focus (HURIFO)* 4 (2008), pp. 3–9, 17–25. My account is directly indebted to Atkinson's. See also Samuel B. Mabikke, "Escalating Land Grabbing in Post-conflict Regions of Northern Uganda: A Need for Strengthening Good Land Governance in Acholi Region," at http://www.google.com/url?sa=t&rct=j&q=&esrc=s&source=web&cd=1&ved=0CB0QFjAA&url=http%3A%2F%2Fwww.future-agricultures.org%2Fypff-conference-resources%2Fdoc_download%2F1280-escalating-land-grabbing-in-post-conflict-regions-of-northern-uganda-a-need-for-strengthening&ei=_2HBU4EIi6bIBJ_xgagB&usg=AFQjCNHHq4afPLsK7q3uStIrjUVh77u24Q&sig2=EBdN2LfiiNyiCeW_6DHPuQ; and Yasiin Magerwa, "First Family 'Too Close' to Oil Sector," *The Monitor* (November 16, 2010), available at http://www.monitor.co.ug/News/National/-/688334/1051166/-/cl9icez/-/. For a more recent account of Museveni, oil, and land on northern Uganda, see "Oil and Land: Acholi Struggles with an Uncertain Future," *The Monitor* (March 12, 2013), at http://www.monitor.co.ug/Magazines/PeoplePower/Oil-and-land--Acholi-struggles-with-an-uncertain-future/-/689844/1715420/-/item/1/-/38r60s/-/index.html.

68. I am indebted to Ronald Atkinson for making the 2003 brochure that had these pictographs available to me.

69. United Nations Office of the High Commissioner for Human Rights, *Democratic Republic of the Congo, 1993-2003*, paragraph 310.

70. Matthew Green, *The Wizard of the Nile: The Hunt for Africa's Most Wanted* (London: Portobello Books, 2008), p. 41.

71. Ministry of Health, The Republic of Uganda/World Health Organization, *Health and Mortality Survey Among Internally Displaced Persons in Gulu, Kitgu, and Pader Districts, Northern Uganda* (July 2005), p. ii.

72. United Nations Office of the High Commissioner for Human Rights, *Democratic Republic of the Congo, 1993-2003*, par. 505.

73. United Nations Office of the High Commissioner for Human Rights, *Democratic Republic of the Congo, 1993-2003*, par. 500. The report cites *Jelisic* decision, ICTY, Appeals chamber, no. IT-95-10-A, July 5, 2001, para. 49; and ICJ, decision on genocide, para. 189: "It is also necessary to distinguish the specific intention from the other reasons or motives the perpetrator may have."

74. "Museveni Directs Final Lakwena Offensive," *New Vision* (November 6, 1987).

75. Ibid.

76. Ronald Kassimir, writes that the Ugandan president is "not shy" in using such terms as "primitive" and "backward" to refer to the Acholi. Kassimir, "Reading Museveni: Structure, Agency and Pedagogy in Ugandan Politics," *Canadian Journal of African Studies/Revue Canadiennedes Etudes Africaines*, 33, nos. 2/3 (1999), p. 654. Museveni's making such statements at the installation of an Acholi bishop indicates that he is hardly ashamed of such language.

77. See http://www.monitor.co.ug/artman/publish/Kalyegira/Understanding_the_NRM_and_its_impact_on_Uganda.shtml.

78. Gregory H. Stanton, "The 8 Stages of Genocide," p. 1; available at http://www.genocidewatch.org/8stages.htm.

79. See David Livingstone Smith, *Less Than Human: Solving the Puzzle of Dehumanization* (New York: St. Martin's Press, 2011). See also the Facebook community by the name, Less Than Human: Solving the Puzzle of Dehumanization.

80. *Shariat* (a weekly Ugandan newspaper), Vol. II, No. 15, April 15–21, 1998); Museveni repeated the comments to the East African Law Society. Cf. "Watch Out, M-7, Uganda is Unkind to Dictators," *The East African* (June 9, 2003).

    It is noteworthy that his use of the terms "backward" and "primitive" to apply to the Acholi bridges Museveni's switch from Maoist/Marxist guerilla to World Bank neoliberal. The one constant is his affirmation of what anthropologists describe as a unilinear view of social evolution. Museveni makes clear in his autobiography that, in his words, "the laws of social evolution" drive his policies. The language of evolution is here a means of distinguishing peoples—more basic to Museveni's lexicon than the differences between Marxism and neoliberalism. Primitive versus modern is simply the *social* evolutionary articulation of the *biological* evolutionary distinction of nonhuman versus human species. See Yoweri Kaguta Museveni, *Sowing the Mustard Seed: The Struggle for Freedom and Democracy in Uganda* (Oxford: Macmillan Education, 1997), p. 26.

81. Gregory H. Stanton, "The 8 Stages of Genocide," p. 2.

82. On the Holodomor, see James E. Mace, "Soviet Man-made Famine in Ukraine," in *Centuries of Genocide: Critical Essays and Eyewitness Accounts*, 4th ed., ed. Samuel Totten and William S. Parsons (New York: Routledge, 2012), pp. 157–90; and http://www.artukraine.com/famineart/unknhol.htm.

83. Sven Lindqvist, *"Exterminate All the Brutes": One Man's Odyssey into the Heart of Darkness and the Origins of European Genocide* (New York and London: The New Press, 1992), pp. ix–x and 3.

84. Unilinear evolutionism accounts for differences between cultures not by pointing to differences in space—"They are different because they developed over there"—but by constructing differences in time—"They are different because they are from earlier and lower

stages of evolution." The theory of unilinear evolution has been used to justify and animate racist policies of exploitation.

85. On indirect rule, see Mahmood Mamdani, *Citizen and Subject: Contemporary Africa and the Legacy of Late Colonialism* (Princeton, NJ: Princeton University Press, 1996).

86. Thomas Ayodele, Franklin Cudjoe, Temba A. Nolutshungu, and Charles K. Sunwabe, "African Perspectives on Aid: Foreign Assistance Will Not Pull Africa Out of Poverty," *Economic Development* 2 (September 15, 2005), at http://www.cato.org/pubs/edb/edb2.html; and Andrew Mwenda, "Foreign Aid and the Weakening of Democratic Accountability," *Foreign Policy Briefing* (July 22, 2006) at http://www/cato.org.

87. The irony is that Museveni describes himself as anti-colonial even while he mimics colonial dehumanizing speech and economic exploitation. In 1987 he writes, "It is inevitable and desirable that a clash of this type between the forces of patriotism and modernization, on the one hand, and the remnants of colonialism and forces of backwardness, takes place in order to ensure a stable Uganda." See "NRA to cover rebel areas," *New Vision* (August 21, 1987). However, the more Museveni presses his claim in the terms of "primitivity" versus "modernity," the more he mimics colonialism.

88. Zack Baddorf, "Ordered to Catch a Warlord, Ugandan Troops are Accused of Hunting Girls," *The New York Times* (May 14, 2017), at https://www.nytimes.com/2017/05/14/world/africa/joseph-kony-lords-resistance-army-uganda.html?hp&action=click&pgtype=Homepage&clickSource=story-heading&module=second-column-region&region=top-news&WT.nav=top-news&_r=0.

89. Ministry of Health, The Republic of Uganda/World Health Organization, *Health and Mortality Survey Among Internally Displaced Persons in Gulu, Kitgu, and Pader Districts, Northern Uganda* (July 2005), p. 2.

90. See Internal Displacement Monitoring Centre/Norwegian Refugee Council, *Uganda: Returns Outpace Recovery Planning* (August 19, 2009), pp. 24–38; available at http://www.internal-displacement.org/8025708F004BE3B1/(httpInfoFiles)/C0C5A39A27DD6449C1257617004AA724/$file/Uganda_Overview_Aug09.pdf.

91. See, for instance, Human Rights Watch, *Uprooted and Forgotten* 17, no. 12(A) (September 2005), pp. 32–4, at http://www.hrw.org/reports/2005/uganda0905/uganda0905.pdf. The "regard for age or gender" criterion is intended to highlight that many attacks on a population focus on the adult males, who can passably be taken as combatants, and it has been mostly males who have be singled out as such by the UPDF. Death in the camps, however, concentrates most on those whom the law of war would most put in the category of the noncombatant: young children and the infirm elderly. Add to this the fact of rape as a common practice on the part of the UPDF in the camps, even after 2002, and it is evident that all camp residents suffered and many of them died under Museveni's enforced mandate.

92. It is helpful to compare and contrast my argument with that of others who have discussed genocide in northern Uganda:
    Acholi intellectuals and public figures—Olara Otunnu, Uganda's ambassador to the United Nations prior to the presidency of Museveni, and Milton Allimadi, Editor-in-Chief of *Black Star News*, perhaps being foremost among them—have tried to bring the case of Musveni's genocidal actions to public attention, but have been largely ignored by the international community. See Olara Otunnu, "Saving Our Children from the Scourge of War," Speech delivered on the occasion of the 2006 Sydney Peace Prize, Part 1, http://www.essex.ac.uk/armedcon/story_id/000290.html; Otunnu, "The Secret Genocide," at http://www.foreignpolicy.com/users/login.php?story_id=3492&URL=http://www.foreignpolicy.com/

story/cms.php?story_id=3492; and Milton Allimadi, "Ending Uganda's 'Brilliant Genocide,'" at http://www.blackagendareport.com/?q=book/export/html/10361.

Where I differ from Otunnu and Allimadi is that, in my analysis, the LRA leaders have committed genocide on the Acholi as well. Though it is not often highlighted in the legal literature, empirically it is quite possible for two non-collaborating parties to each inflict genocide on a third group of people, and this is what I see as having taken place in northern Uganda (One possible point of comparison where mutual adversaries both committed atrocities against a third group of people would be the actions of Stalin and Hitler in the region between Germany and Russia—Poland, Ukraine, the Baltic region, and Belarus—in the 1930s and 1940s: See Timothy Snyder, *Bloodlands: Europe Between Hitler and Stalin* (New York: Basic Books, 2010)). A number of scholars have demonstrated that the LRA has acted, under leadership orders, to kill Acholi people, in the words of the UN Convention, "with the intent to destroy, in whole or in part" the Acholi as an ethnic group. That the later LRA became more indiscriminate and killed members of other groups does not undo this initial fact. Also, I anticipate and understand the argument that the majority of the LRA fighters were themselves abducted, and are thus less than fully culpable (The issue of the culpability of atrocities committed by abductees, particularly children, is a complex one that needs more space to be worked out than I can provide here.). However, there is sufficient evidence to charge the LRA leadership with genocide. Ruddy Doom and Koen Vlassenroot argued as early as 1999 that after 1994 Kony felt betrayed by the lack of active (as distinct from merely sympathetic) Acholi support for the LRA, and thus turned on the Acholi themselves in what the authors term "auto-genocide." Genocide against one's own people has occurred before, such as in the case of Pol Pot and the Khmer Rouge in Cambodia. The effort on the part of the LRA was to create a "new Acholi" from child abductees. In 2007, Adam Branch drew upon extensive research in northern Uganda to argue that the LRA sought to "eradicate the external enemy" from within the Acholi. Carlos Rodriguez Soto, who has had extensive interaction with the LRA, has described their post-1994 actions as an attempt to "purify" the Acholi. Most recently, Helen Nkabala Nambalirwa has drawn on-field interviews with former LRA combatants to show how, while in the bush, they used a reading of the Sodom and Gomorrah story to justify their directly taking the life of Acholi civilians: the combatants were taught to view the civilians as sinners—they sinned against their Acholi-ness in not supporting the LRA—and thus not as persons with human dignity; the combatants could thus take the civilian lives without the actions counting as killing another person. What the ex-combatant narratives show is that the LRA did intend to kill Acholi people on the basis of their membership in a particular ethnic group. See Ruddy Doom and Koen Vlassenroot, "Kony's Message: A New Koine?" *African Affairs* 98 (1999): 26; Adam Branch, "The Political Dilemmas of Global Justice: Anti-Civilian Violence and the Violence of Humanitarianism, the Case of Northern Uganda," p. 22; Carlos Rodriguez Soto, *Tall Grass,* pp. 21–2; and Helen Nkabala Nambalirwa, "'The Lord Destroyed the Cities and Everyone Who Lived in Them': The Lord's Resistance Army's Use of the Old Testament Sodom/Gomorrah Narrative," in *Culture, Religion, and the Reintegration of Female Child Soldiers in Northern Uganda*, ed. Bard Maeland (New York: Peter Lang, 2010), pp. 181–92.

Others withdraw from applying the term "genocide" to northern Uganda out of a desire to view genocide as a rare exception in the modern world—the ICTY called it the "the most abhorrent of all crimes"—but its gravity as highlighted in international law does not entail its rarity on the ground, as Samantha Power and others have shown with regard to the twentieth century in Europe and its colonies. There is no reason to assume that the neocolonial twenty-first century is any different. See *Kristic* decision, ICTY, Appeals chamber, no. IT-98-33-A, April 19, 2004, para. 134; Samantha Power, *A Problem from Hell: America and the Age of*

Genocide (New York: HarperCollins, 2002); Samuel Totten and William S. Parsons, eds., *Centuries of Genocide: Critical Essays and Eyewitness Accounts*, 4th ed. (New York: Routledge, 2012).

It might be tempting to draw from the work of Mahmood Mamdani to argue against the use of the word "genocide." After all, Mamdani's book, *Saviors and Survivors*, criticizes the Save Darfur advocacy group for applying the term to that region. However, in the last chapter, Mamdani addresses the broader implications of the Darfur case. Here, the issue is not the use of the term "genocide," but the international community's *selectivity* in applying *all* of its own legal norms, and it is here that Mamdani explicitly addresses the case of Uganda:

> Its name notwithstanding, the ICC is rapidly turning into a Western court to try African crimes against humanity. Even then, the approach is selective: It targets governments that are adversaries of the United States and ignores US allies, effectively conferring impunity on them. . . . When law is applied selectively, the result is not a rule of law but a subordination of law to the dictates of power. . . . In Uganda, for example, where nearly a million people have been forcibly displaced in the throes of a government-executed insurgency, the ICC has charged only the leadership of the LRA but not that of the pro-United States government. . . . In Congo, the ICC has remained mum about the links between the armies of Uganda and Rwanda—both pro-United States—and the ethnic militias that have been at the heart of the slaughter of civilians (Mahmood Mamdani, *Saviors and Survivors: Darfur, Politics, and the War on Terror* (New York: Pantheon Books, 2009), pp. 276–8, and 283–4).

But why, then, make the specific charge of genocide and especially insist on following the strict legal definition when the institution which formalized the term and now claims to enforce it—the UN—itself distorts its application? Two reasons come to mind, one epistemological and the other practical. The first has to do with the importance of naming. Mamdani himself emphasizes that "the battle for naming turns out to be all-important." (Mamdani, *Saviors and Survivors*, p. 3). Mamdani's hesitancy in using the term genocide is precisely that the institutions given over to preventing it are too distorted to make good on their claim to even-handed application of the term. This is why, in one interview, he walks right up to the line of using the term specifically in the case of northern Uganda, but then steps back. In the interview, Mamdani has just cited the WHO statistics regarding mortality in the IDP camps. The interviewer summarizes Mamdani's points and asks the question: "With this crisis in northern Uganda—the forced incarceration, the years wasted, the Acholi being a select group of people, the death toll in the camps being greater than those from the violence of the LRA—at what point does a situation bear the title 'genocidal'?" Mamdani responds,

> These days we speak of not simply genocidal outcomes but genocidal intent—and that's a more difficult area. How do you tell intent? Well, you can tell it from policy. If you have camps where people are incarcerated and these camps are only for certain areas and certain people who live within those areas, then you can conclude that these policies are people-specific. If there is a gradual rate of excess death in those camps over a period of 10 years and the camps continue, you can conclude intent from it. So I think this is a case of, you know, it's a mass crime. It is a crime against humanity, in a sense. But to me, whether we call it genocide or not is not really the key question right now—simply because there is such a "politics" around naming genocide or not (Pete McCormack, "Details and Reminders: An Interview with Mahmood Mamdani," at http://www.petemccormack.com/interview_mamdani_001.htm.).

Pace Mamadani, the term "genocide" and the institutions that use it are not about to go away. My use of the term was and is an attempt to call by its rightful name a reality that the international community refuses to consider even under the lesser charges of war crimes and crimes against humanity. The Convention highlights the existence of genocide as an exception to the rule; as a result, in keeping with what Judith Shklar calls the "normal" model of justice, it at the same time underestimates genocide's prevalence. See Shklar, *The Faces of Injustice* (New Haven: Yale University Press, 1990).

The U.N. Convention *further* reinforces the desire to not know because it links the identification of a situation as genocidal with an obligation on the part of the international community to do something about it. This dynamic was behind the Clinton administration's verbal gymnastics in avoiding the term genocide in the case of Rwanda (One internal document in the Office of the Secretary of Defense read, "Genocide Investigation: Language that calls for an international investigation of human rights abuses and possible violations of the genocide convention. Be Careful. Legal at State was worried about this yesterday-Genocide finding could commit [the US government] to actually 'do something.'". See Samantha Power, "Bystanders to Genocide," *The Atlantic* (September 2001), at http://www.theatlantic.com/magazine/archive/2001/09/bystanders-to-genocide/304571/.). Combine the dominant international and Western power narrative with regard to Uganda (Museveni = "new breed of African leader") already in place with the deep reserve that those powers have in understanding situations as genocide in the first place, and the result is a multilayered systemic resistance to the idea that the actions and intentions of Museveni and his forces during the conflict in northern Uganda are most accurately described as genocidal.

This leads to the second, practical reason for my use of the term. Mamdani's concern is that such use oversimplifies what has happened on the ground, and this indeed is the case in the instance of the Save Darfur campaign. However, I am actually using it to *complicate* the received narrative of the conflict in northern Uganda. Again, that narrative is one of a singular madman—Joseph Kony—and has the policy corollary that if we can just take him out, the other issues besetting northern Uganda will just go away. In my judgment, using the terminology made available to name the actions of Museveni—in this case, the term "genocide"—illuminates the distorted international superstructure around the LRA conflict more fully than not doing so.

93. Alfred Nyongesa Wandera, "Otunnu Unleashes Dossier on Alleged Acholi Genocide," *The Daily Monitor* (January 5, 2011), at http://www.monitor.co.ug/News/National/-/688334/1083922/-/cjdbu4z/-/index.html. In the photo, Otunnu is holding up an issue of *The Christian Century*, in which he published his own argument that Museveni has committed genocide in northern Uganda. His point at the press conference was that the memo and my article confirmed his argument. See Olara Otunnu, "Death of a People: Genocide in Northern Uganda," *The Christian Century* (April 18, 2006), at http://www.christiancentury.org/article/2006-04/death-people.

94. See Olara Otunnu, "Saving Our Children from the Scourge of War," Speech delivered on the occasion of the 2006 Sydney Peace Prize, Part 1, http://www.essex.ac.uk/armedcon/story_id/000290.html; Otunnu, "The Secret Genocide," at http://www.foreignpolicy.com/users/login.php?story_id=3492&URL=http://www.foreignpolicy.com/story/cms.php?story_id=3492

95. Miranda Fricker, *Epistemic Injustice: Power and the Ethics of Knowing* (Oxford and New York: Oxford University Press, 2007), pp. 170 and 173.

96. I am far from the only Western white, and not the most important one, to write on the Ugandan government's abuses in northern Uganda. See also Sverker Finnström, *Living with Bad Surroundings: War, History, and Everyday Moments in Northern Uganda* (Durham: Duke University Press, 2008); Adam Branch, *Displacing Human Rights: War and Intervention in Northern Uganda*, reprint edition (Oxford and New York: Oxford University Press, 2013); and Sverker Finnström and Ronald Atkinson, "Building a Sustainable Peace in Northern Uganda," *Horn of Africa Bulletin* (April 2008).

97. What perhaps took most of my psychological and even physical energy in discerning whether or not publishing the article was the right thing to do was the fact that the University of Notre Dame and its affiliated associations have many ongoing programs and projects in Uganda as part of the University's own global expansion. Some of these programs and projects are indeed "good works" insofar as they benefit Ugandans. Would publishing the article threaten them?

    After careful deliberation, it seemed to me that in all likelihood there was little threat to the project and programs of Notre Dame and its affiliated organizations as a result of publication of the article. First of all, Museveni likely does not know about the programs and projects; but most importantly, he is quite specific to the threat in his retaliation, and the directors and participants in the programs and projects in question have a long-standing history of nonthreatening silence on issues of human rights abuses in the country. I might be kicked out of country or barred from re-entry, but the other programs and projects would not. I figured that Ugandan intelligence might contact the religious house that it had visited four years prior when it had tapped my phone conversation with a dissident, and that upon hearing that the community knew nothing, would move on, which it did (I was later told that the intelligence officer and the member of the community he spoke to are in fact acquaintances, and that it was a friendly phone call.). So my discernment on this score was correct. Still, my publication of the article strained some friendships at Notre Dame, some perhaps irreparably, and this was something that was, and is still, painful for me. The colleague who insisted that I withdraw from the public debate in Uganda also thought that it was presumptuous of me to involve others—whether in their persons or their projects—in any risk at all. I have thought about this question the most, and I have to answer that, yes, my actions did potentially involve them, even if the risk was remote. I did not ask or inform the members of the religious community in Uganda in advance (I informed them the day of publication) precisely so that they could answer in all honesty to Ugandan intelligence (if asked) that they knew nothing about my writing of the article. I did not ask my Notre Dame colleague in advance about publication of the article in part because I knew that he would have opposed it and argued to suppress it, something that his subsequent actions confirmed.

    The reverse of my actions involving my colleagues is also true: no one told me in advance that the presence of Notre Dame and affiliated projects in Uganda would involve pre-set limits on what a researcher can make public of his findings. The claim of one person's actions affecting another cuts both ways. We are bound up with each other's decisions.

98. Peter Van Agtmael, "Look Back, in Danger," *The New York Times* (May 27, 2014), at http://lens.blogs.nytimes.com/2014/05/27/look-back-in-danger/?_php=true&_type=blogs&_r=0.

99. Denis Johnson, *Resurrection of a Hanged Man* (New York: HarperCollins/Perennial, 2001), p. 230.
    The protagonist in Donna Tartt's *The Goldfinch* sets out similar options: "Is Kitsy right? If your deepest self is singing and coaxing you straight toward the bonfire, is it better to turn away? Stop your ears with wax? Ignore all the perverse glory your heart is screaming at you? Set yourself on the course that will lead you dutifully toward the norm, reasonable hours and regular medical check-ups, stable relationships and steady career advancement, the New York Times and brunch on Sunday, all with the promise of being somehow a better person? Or—like Boris—is it better to throw yourself head first and laughing into the holy rage calling your name?" Donna Tartt, *The Goldfinch* (Back Bay Books/ Little, Brown and Company, 2013), p. 761.

PART IV
RETURN

CHAPTER 8
AN OFFERING: BRINGING THE ETHNOGRAPHIC ENCOUNTER HOME

The brick pit latrine with the corrugated tin roof behind Ojara's home in Lokung IDP camp is a step up from the roofless ones shielded by only a curtain of woven bamboo. It has molded cement flooring with a keyhole-shaped opening. I wonder how the elderly squat after their knees begin to go, but the walls and door are close enough, I suppose, to put one's hand out to keep from toppling over.

Twenty-two thousand forcibly displaced persons live in the camp. "Lokung started in 1997 when the LRA killed five hundred fifty Acholi," Ojara has told me. "Then the government bombed the camp to get the rebels and killed 417 more. It is a curse." The government treats those unwilling to move to the camp as rebels.

At least Ojara's latrine has a lock. Only members of his extended family can use it. This has kept the inside mostly clean. Usually there is a woven bristle broom to sweep if one misses, sometimes newspaper or old exam books for wiping. There is a can of ash to sprinkle down into the hole to cover the excrement to keep both the smell and the number of cockroaches down. Still, at night, the roaches come out of the pit, spotlighted by my headlamp on the walls wherever I look, as if in a vaudeville show. Ojara's words return, "All human efforts have failed. It is only through the Sacred Heart of Jesus that this will end."

The roof of the building with the winner of "America's Best Restroom" for 2002[1] is topped with a dome that is gilded with 23.9 karat gold.[2] Winner over the Seattle Bon Marche powder room and so a member of the restroom Hall of Fame, the facility features patterned blue, green and white Stovax Victorian tiled flooring imported from England. Marble-finished interior partitions with solid oak doors ensure privacy.

Though a mural in the hallway leading to the bathroom depicts American Indians freely bowing down before Christopher Columbus, in the case of Notre Dame the way was cleared by the displacement of almost all indigenous persons in a forced march to Kansas shortly before founder Reverend Sorin arrived.[3]

The person who nominated the Notre Dame restroom writes that it is "impeccable, and the floors are clean enough to eat off! No odors are present as these restrooms are clean!" Appropriate to a campus style that *The New York Times* describes as "manicured,"[4] the sink fixtures feature designer accented chrome and brass illuminated by classic 1800s-style frosted reflector-bowl lighting suspended from the ceiling, all, the University states, to return the setting "to its original splendor and glory." The nominator effuses, "These restrooms are shinier than the Golden Dome for which Notre Dame is famous!"

In Chapter 5, I spoke about the gap between the self and the other in the doing of anthropological theology. The gap between northern Uganda and the University of Notre Dame, felt acutely upon return to campus, can be vertiginous. That gap regards not only material infrastructure—squat pit latrines versus Hall of Fame bathrooms—but spiritual infrastructure as well. For as much as the Arts and Letters website might claim that Notre Dame is the "preeminent Catholic university in the world,"[5] and, as we will see, as much as the university's commercials feature what are indeed the good works of some of its students and professors, closer examination brings into focus an institutional logic not unlike that of the Comboni missionaries during the British Empire: concern with maintaining a pattern of expansion has foregrounded a particular understanding of organizational "prudence" that makes the kind of witness carried out by the Little Sisters—"burning love of Christ to attend to the most vulnerable people," with the concomitant risk that that often involves—seem to be ill-considered if intelligible at all.

It seems that there are a variety of ways in which the university institutionally inhibits efforts to practice gospel mimesis. This is a sharp criticism, so I must be clear on three things. First, like I indicated last chapter, I myself do not have a sustained habit of self-abnegation in the spirit of the Little Sisters. In the twenty years leading up to the publication of my article criticizing Museveni, I had been quite "at home" at Notre Dame. And I am still, like I was in the first chapter, the rich (not so) young man who turns away from Christ when told to sell all he has and follow. Nothing about my home social location has changed. Second, in saying that Notre Dame inhibits gospel mimesis, I am not saying that it is unique in higher education in having this problem; rather I am saying just the opposite: despite its appeals to a panoply of Christian symbols, there is little in the university's operational practices that is distinctive. And third, I intend this chapter, as sharp-tongued as it sometimes is, to be an invitation to the university community and its representatives to consider the kind of witness evidenced by the Little Sisters. If it is objected that, "Well, they were in a period of deep social conflict; our situation does not require that kind of witness," I suggest a return to the first moment of anthropological theology—that of attention—because due attention would establish that similar witness is indeed demanded by our situation.

I am aware that my critiquing Notre Dame and its representatives brings its own risk. Other universities have retaliated against professors critical of institutional practices; it could happen here.[6] There are compelling reasons, however, for moving forward with critique. Most published ethnographies end before the ethnographer returns home. The result, despite efforts to be reflexive, is portrayals that continue to an unexamined degree to exoticize and therefore objectivize the other. The aim of reflexivity is to turn our knowledge back on ourselves so as to place a check on our knowledge's critical manipulation of the other, yet most ethnographies that begin through fieldwork in another culture conclude with some statement about the implications of Yanomani or Nigerian or American Indian culture, and fail to discuss *as part of the that same ethnographic project* the implications of the ethnographer's ensuing writing about that culture in her home context. Even those anthropological treatments of higher education (as a separate anthropological project) tend to lack the specific focus on the *particular* institution that the researcher herself inhabits. There are few "home" or "native" anthropologies specifically of Duke or Berkeley or Notre Dame.[7]

Pierre Bourdieu is something of an exception to this trend,[8] and he terms his practice of reflexivity, "objectification objectified."[9] What he means is that, although it is my "home" institution, I must treat Notre Dame as in some sense "other" by examining its behaviors as artifacts, and this as part of the same ethnographic project that interprets the Acholi. In the end, my turning the analytical eye on my home institution is made necessary if I am to claim faith in Jesus Christ. In the words of Michel de Certeau, whose faith grounds his social analysis more than any other canonical postmodern thinker, "If the site from which I speak were above suspicion, were placed beyond question, my analysis would cease to be evangelical and would become the establishment of a 'truth' with a religious content."[10] In other words, if we do not turn the critical eye on ourselves, we fail to proclaim the Gospel, no matter what symbols and rituals we might draw upon in the attempt to assure ourselves of our faithfulness.[11]

The colleagues who insisted that our disagreement over publication of my article on Museveni was simply a matter of prudential judgment on the application of shared principles were wrong. The Little Sisters whom I tried to imitate inhabit a world quite different than that inculcated at the University of Notre Dame. In the first part of this chapter, I lift up the two cases that convinced me of this reality, both which evidence that the university's tolerance for risk on behalf of human rights is nearly nonexistent. The second part of the chapter delves deeper into the dynamic of commercialization at Notre Dame whereby faith becomes subsumed under the university's "brand," thus minimizing any willingness to risk for the Gospel. The chapter's third part shows how such branding of faith fails to exhibit not only Christian practice, but even the best of secular—in this case, Aristotelian—practices. In each of these first three parts of the chapter, I am not making the case that all individuals at the university behave in this way—there is important variation in this regard. Rather, the point is that the interlaced symbolic and material institutional practices that structure persons' lives at Notre Dame inhibit and strongly discourage gospel mimesis. This is what became clear to me upon my return.

The question that arises is how to make the case for another way of life. Here, I draw on two tactics that Jesus of Nazareth utilized. Jesus often used outsiders—Samaritans, Syrophoenicians, hemorrhaging women—as exemplars of faithfulness. In this chapter's fourth part, I focus on the actions and writings of anthropologist Nancy Scheper-Hughes and make the case that she exemplifies what John Paul II means by charity-infused solidarity of the sort where the practitioner is willing to lay down her life for the vulnerable. Christians and anthropologists have been in conflict with each other ever since the professionalization of the latter led to tensions in the field. Scheper-Hughes therefore makes a good candidate for the role of the Samaritan.

Another of Jesus's rhetorical techniques is to utilize images familiar from the daily lives of his listeners—for instance, sheep and goats (Mt. 25:31-33)—in order to display for them unexpected patterns of thought and practice, such as visiting those in prison and clothing the naked (Mt. 25:34-46). Therefore, with some help from Bourdieu, in the fifth and last section of this chapter I draw upon sports in general and football in particular to talk about anthropological theology as "playbook and gamefilm" of the sort that helps display just what charity-infused solidarity, now expressly shaped in imitation of Christ, might look like. Given that I teach at Notre Dame, sports images are indeed familiar at my home institution. I suggest that the lives of the Little Sisters of Mary Immaculate of Gulu serve as good gamefilm for a life of the Gospel, and they invite us to join that particular "field of play." First, however, it is necessary to show why a Catholic university needs to be convinced of the attraction of a Gospel way of life.

University expansionism and risk aversion

One of the most frequent phrases appearing on the Notre Dame website and its various tributaries is a quote attributed to the university's founder, Reverend Edward Sorin, that Notre Dame strives to be a "powerful force for good in the world." A search of the university website in May 2016 yielded sixty-six mentions of some variation of this phrase in the first twelve search pages, indicating that the phrase has become something of an institutional slogan. Sorin first came to the United States in the middle of what historians have called the nation's "Age of Manifest Destiny" (the era from the end of the War of 1812 to the start of the Civil War), and the idea of such destiny dovetailed well with—Weber might say it had an "elective affinity" with—the prevalence, even dominance, of the theme of Providence in Sorin's writings.[12] Being a powerful force in the world requires institutional expansion.

A liability of such thinking—that Providence is at work in our actions to back our being a powerful force for good—is that it can lead to overlooking the trade-offs that are in play even in what are good works. The abiding assumption in the "powerful force" quote is that that force and the works it inspires are unequivocally good. (Some of the university's projects and programs abroad do in fact do good for the local people; others, perhaps most, serve more for the "experience" and certification of our students and professors.) I understand that sometimes there can and must be a trade-off in favor of preserving projects and programs when the risk that confrontational human rights discourse brings to them and to the broader common good is too high. My concern is with the deep resistance to trade-offs in the other direction, in favor of human rights, such that any risk to university projects and programs is deemed to be too much. At this point, university expansion of its "powerful force" borders on becoming an absolute, overlooking the real risk that Notre Dame, like the Comboni missionaries a century earlier, will cooperate with evil. Two cases of particular relevance will have to serve to illustrate my concern. The first is germane because it also took place in relation to Ugandan governmental practices and displays that Notre Dame's tolerance for risk to its projects in the country is close to zero; the second is pertinent because the university president misuses the very principle—that of cooperation with evil—in play in the colonial practice of the Comboni missionaries in their alliance with British expansionism. The president uses the principle to *justify* university expansion—in this case for the production of university consumer goods in China—at the expense of Catholic teaching on human rights. But first, the Notre Dame and Uganda case.

Initially nicknamed the "Kill the Gays" bill because early iterations called for capital punishment for homogenital acts, the Uganda Anti-Homosexuality Act of 2014 in its present form calls for life imprisonment for offenders, extradition back to Uganda for Ugandan citizens who commit homogenital acts abroad, and imprisonment of up to three years for people, organizations, and corporations that do not report offenders within twenty-four hours.[13] When the draft bill still included capital punishment, a Notre Dame alumna who had spent time in Uganda approached the relevant university administrators and asked them to release a statement condemning the bill.[14] They refused, indicating that it was not their place to enter into public debate about Ugandan politics. She was told by one representative that that is "not how Notre Dame does things." At least one university representative specifically mentioned that any such statement would jeopardize Notre Dame's good works in Uganda. The alumna, joined then by ten other Notre Dame graduates who had worked in Uganda, returned to the administrators with the request that the university's liaisons with each of its Ugandan partner organizations approach the latter in a low-key, non-public way to inform them of Notre Dame's already-crafted "Spirit of Inclusion" document. That university document reads:

> The University of Notre Dame strives for a spirit of inclusion among the members of this community for distinct reasons articulated in our Christian tradition. We prize the uniqueness of all persons as God's creatures. We welcome all people, regardless of color, gender, religion, ethnicity, sexual orientation, social or economic class, and nationality, for example, precisely because of Christ's calling to treat others as we desire to be treated. We value gay and lesbian members of this community as we value all members of this community. *We condemn harassment of any kind.* . . . The spirit of inclusion at Notre Dame flows from our character as a community of scholarship, teaching, learning and service founded upon Jesus Christ. . . . *For Notre Dame, Christ is the law by which all other laws are to be judged* (emphases added).[15]

The students simply wanted the university to inform its partners of its own policy by making the university's "Spirit of Inclusion" document available to them. Nothing would be public. Again, the administrators refused, even though the risks to the Notre Dame projects, their maintenance and expansion, were low to nonexistent. It appears that almost *any* risk to the university's projects, even when the possible goods in trade-off are palpable, is considered to be too high.

University expansion eclipsing concern about human rights occurs on a commercial as well as educational level, as is evident in the case regarding the university's relation with China. In 2015, the executive vice president invoked the "powerful force for good" quote in an ultimately successful effort to reverse the university's long-standing policy, designed in light of Catholic social doctrine, against the production of Notre Dame goods in China, a country that does not recognize workers' right to organize. The officer said in a public forum, "One of Notre Dame's missions is to be a force for good in the world. . . . There's a huge amount of manufacturing that goes on in China whether we like it or not."[16] Here again, there was no risk to Notre Dame in continuing to refuse to cooperate with China's anti-freedom of association policy. The university's own previous policy of no production in China had been in place for fifteen years, and during that time there was no shortage of Notre Dame-logoed apparel or geegaws like "ND" stenciled doggie rawhide bones and beer bottle openers that play the fight song. Yet the university reversed its previous policy anyway.

In making the reversal of university policy official, President John Jenkins invoked the "principle of cooperation with evil" to argue that the reversal did not involve Notre Dame in cooperating with the evil of China's policy and practice, but his reasoning profoundly distorts that principle, and it evidences that the "powerful force for good" ethos as it has developed at the university can warp the discernment of even our best administrators.[17] The principle or question of cooperation with evil regards third parties whose actions just happen to overlap with the evil actions of a primary acting party. The principle raises the question of the culpability of the third parties in those bad acts. However, in the case of the production in China, Notre Dame is not a third party; it is Notre Dame (and no one else) who is contracting to have the work done in China. Those contracts do not "just happen." In other words, Notre Dame, along with the government of China, is a primary party to the act. (There can be more than one primary party.)

Sometimes it is helpful to use a dramatic example to illustrate. Mr. Smith wants to go to a shooting range to practice his riflery. However, the owner of the range says that they use only human targets. Mr. Smith decides to shoot anyway, and signs whatever papers are necessary to do so. Is he a third party simply because he didn't make the rule that there be only human targets? This is an extreme example, yes, but the exculpatory logic is the same as that given in President Jenkins's statement. Both the University of Notre Dame and the government of China are primary parties in the production of Notre Dame apparel in China. The argument that Notre Dame is some kind of bystander fundamentally misdescribes the real situation.[18]

In light of the concern regarding the overall trajectory of an unchecked "powerful force for good" logic, it is important to note that in appealing to the principle of cooperation with evil to navigate around the human right of the freedom of association in China, President Jenkins effectively guts the whole of the university's licensing code of conduct. If it is legitimate to apply the principle in the way that President Jenkins does to the freedom of association in China, then it is also legitimate to apply it to situations there and elsewhere where there is compulsory overtime, unsafe working conditions, or forced labor, because, the reasoning would go, Notre Dame does not create those conditions, we only make consumer items in them.[19]

The question that arises is that of why President Jenkins put such energy into what turns out to be a deeply troubled—contorted, really—account of the principle of noncooperation with evil. The answer, as best I can discern it, seems to be that given his position as the symbolic and real juridical head of a Catholic university, once he has accepted the university's expansionist ethos as instantiated in the executive vice president's proposal to reverse policy on the production of Notre Dame goods in China, he has to try to square that reversal of policy with Catholic teaching on human rights. That the two do not square is by now evident. It would have been much more direct to say that the university has simply decided not to follow Catholic teaching in this instance,[20] but for Jenkins to acknowledge as much would be for him to voluntarily sacrifice his and the university's symbolic capital as representing Catholicism. Once the expansionist ethos is adopted—and in this case it is commercial, not educational expansion, through the cheaper production of Notre Dame consumer items—President Jenkins has to make the teaching on rights seem to fit with it. This is not an enviable position to be in. Best and simplest of all given the minimal (if existent at all) sacrifice it would have required, would have been to continue the university's policy of fifteen years of not producing in China. That that was not the course taken is evidence of the "powerful force" of the expansionist ethos at Notre Dame. It appears that President Jenkins is, like most of the rest of us at the university, trapped in the interchange of symbolic and economic capital—think of Mary atop the Golden Dome and the expanding $11.8 billion endowment (2017)—that structures Notre Dame's operations. If any Holy Cross priest as president did not allow expansionist policies such as the production of consumer items in factories that violate Catholic social doctrine, he would not be allowed by the board to be president for long.[21]

In such an institutional structure, even what are intended as "good works" are ultimately monetized, and when faith is monetized, no risk to capital is tolerated. This is the Notre Dame that sets the context for and drives—or at the very least severely delimits—everything else that happens here, and it is worth detailing its specific constitutive elements.

What would you fight for?: The branding of faith

The video begins with a shot of a sharp mountain peak, then a Buddhist monastery. The narrative voiceover is female. "When people come to Nepal, they see breathtaking beauty." The video shifts to an old woman and a young girl sitting on a pile of gravel. "They see abject poverty." The narrative continues, "What I saw was an opportunity."

A different narrative voice, male, comes in as the scene changes to what appears to be at once a classroom and clothing shop. "Since 2006, Notre Dame industrial design professor, Ann-Marie Conrado has brought students to Nepal to collaborate with local artisans in the design and development of fair trade products."

Shots of a rice patty, working oxen, a man hammering out a copper ornament, a woman working at a loom. Back to Professor Conrado: "In Nepal you have this incredible tradition of hardworking and talented artisans, and yet for years jobs were disappearing. The problem was simply that they lacked an understanding of what people in the rest of the world wanted to buy, and that's where we've been able to step in and help. We opened up markets all over the world. In one artisan community, we've seen jobs and sales triple. But creating jobs and opportunities is just half the story. Our students are taking insights gained from that immersion and translating them into products that help people's lives."

A return to the male narrator and a screenshot of a hand sketching on a pad: "Social design products developed by the Notre Dame in Nepal Program include an umbilical cord cutter that requires sterilization before reuse, thereby minimizing birth-related deaths, as well as a three-dollar washing machine that preserves clean water sources and improves the quality of life for women."

A student at a sewing machine who we are told is Edel Crowe, together with her voiceover: "Coming here has given me more a sense of purpose, and now I'll try to look at my design beyond the actual physical appearance of it and try to think of some way it can impact somebody else."

Back to Professor Conrado: "Our work is based on the belief that one design can transform an industry, a village, a life."

The screen shows the mural of Jesus on the library from the reflecting pond at his feet. The male voice returns, "The University of Notre Dame asks, "What would you fight for?"

Crowe: "Fighting to create opportunity."

Conrado: "We are the Fighting Irish."

* * *

It is difficult to dispute that the iconic ritual at the University of Notre Dame is played out six times a year on autumn Saturdays.[22] Evidence for this is in part monetarily quantifiable. The contract with NBC for exclusive rights to televise the football games brings $15 million a year to the university. The relationship between Notre Dame and NBC dates back to 1991, and includes television coverage even during lean years on the field. When asked whether the typically five-year contract would be renewed after a particularly bad stretch, then NBC Sports Chair, Dick Ebersole, responded in the affirmative, commenting that Notre Dame is "the most *powerful* brand in college sports."[23] The university itself does not shy away from the marketing language, as its own website echoes and amplifies Ebersole's words: "Notre Dame athletics is the most *powerful* and recognizable brand in college athletics" (emphasis added).[24] Nothing is said about the good here, only about being a powerful force. Notre Dame football linebackers coach and recruiting coordinator, Mike Elston, comments, "We have a brand, and we want to get our brand out there. We want to change people's conceptions of the brand. So we have a tremendous amount of resources going into our social media."[25] A central part of that flow of resources is Notre Dame's contract with Bleacher Report, an online outlet which the university turned to after the Showtime series, "A Season with Notre Dame Football," did not get the hoped-for response from the youth demographic.[26]

And what is the content of the Notre Dame "brand"? Bleacher Report editor-in-chief Joe Yanarella sites the "key principles" of "tradition, faith, academics, and athletics," but the article in which he makes that claim focuses more on the financial payoff. In other words, the brand is about money. The article displays as a featured graphic a tweet from the Notre Dame football program (@NDFootball) about the "Notre Dame Effect": "A visit from Notre Dame can nearly DOUBLE ticket prices for the opposing home team. THAT is the Notre Dame Effect."[27] Similarly, after the 2016 National football League draft, @NDFootball put out a tweet that said, "Our 7 draftees in the first four rounds earned an estimated $51 million. The value of the Notre Dame brand. #NDinTheNFL."[28] That brand has also led to a contract with the Under Armour sports apparel company that brings $90 million to the university over ten years.[29] The arrangement allows the corporation to have its logo on the university's sports uniforms, the Under Armour brand paying for and thereby gaining some of the symbolic capital identified with Notre Dame's brand. To put the monetary perspective in a different way, the university's nine-year buyout agreement with a former head coach, Charlie Weis, who was fired for poor performance, amounted to almost $2.1 million per year, or roughly twenty-seven times what a newly tenured, and thus successful, professor in the humanities earns.

The pull of the football games goes well beyond the material capital of money to the symbolic capital of iconography, with the 134-foot mural of the resurrected Jesus with upraised arms on the library visible over the north end of the stadium being popularly called "Touchdown Jesus," and the statue of Moses, one hand holding the Ten Commandments tablet and the other pointing with a single finger to the sky, as "First Down Moses."[30] The 1993 movie, *Rudy*, about a blue-collar non-scholarship player who gets into his first game on his final day with the team and makes a tackle, continues the iconography: Roger Ebert of *The Chicago Sun-Times* wrote that the film "has a freshness and an earnestness that gets us involved, and by the end of the film we accept Rudy's dream as more than simply sports sentiment. It's a small but powerful illustration of the human spirit."[31] A month later, symbolic capital feeds back into material capital when Notre Dame's game against Florida State receives a viewership rating that as of this writing remains the highest of any regular-season college football game to date. The main rivalry games, like those against Michigan and USC, bring viewerships of between 8 and 16 million people.[32] The spiritual-material capital nexus and interchange is half-joking and wholly serious.[33]

Aside from not having to share the television revenues, the advantage of having its own network to show its games is that Notre Dame can take more programming time than the typical university for what is now a standard kind of commercial, that narrating the virtues of the universities sponsoring the teams. Notre Dame titles its campaign, "What Would You Fight For?," which has produced separate commercials on this theme for every home game since 2007. The presented people and projects are impressive, and include, for instance, an effort to eliminate lymphatic filariasis (elephantiasis) in Haiti by 2020, a project that uses ionic liquid to absorb the carbon dioxide that emits from fossil fuel use, and leadership in peacebuilding activities in Columbia. The commercials, when coupled with awareness of the size of the university's nearly $12 billion endowment and the amounts of money spent on football facilities and exchanged in contracts points toward what is perhaps the central institutional conviction at Notre Dame, that one can do good on the way to doing well, that conscience and capital do not collide. The strong version of the conviction is that such capital is in fact *necessary* to perform good works, a perspective that is more ancient Greek than Gospel-oriented, which is evident when we compare Aristotle's virtue of magnificence (μεγαλοπρέπεια/megaloprépeia) to Jesus's primary account of exemplary giving. We will see that, ultimately, the university's institutional logic does not stand up even under Aristotelian scrutiny, but first the Greek-Christian comparison to illuminate how the university constructs and understands its good works.

Of neither Nazareth nor Athens: The Notre Dame brand

> He looked up and saw rich people putting their gifts into the treasury; he also saw
> a poor widow put in two small copper coins. He said, "Truly I tell you, this poor
> widow has put in more than all of them; for all of them have contributed out of their
> abundance, but she out of her poverty has put in all she had to live on."
>
> — *Lk. 21:1-4*

* * *

The first section of Book IV of Aristotle's *Nicomachean Ethics* discusses the virtue of liberality, that is, of giving away wealth correctly. We are to "give for the sake of the noble, and rightly . . . give to the right people, the right amounts, and at the right time."[34] Liberality is practicable by anyone, as long as he or she practices it within their means (giving away too much would be prodigal or foolish), "for liberality resides not in the multitude of the gifts but in the state of the giver, and this is relative to the giver's substance."[35] At this point, Aristotle would argue that even the poor widow can be liberal, though to give away her last mite would be foolish, excessive. "For it is said, he is liberal who spends according to his substance . . . and he who exceeds is prodigal."[36] The kind of excess that Jesus lauds, as exhibited by the widow, violates Aristotle's doctrine that the virtuous action is always the mean between two extremes.[37] The philosopher would go light on the widow, however; she is foolish, but not wicked, and thus can be taught better.[38]

What the widow cannot do—even if she could become a man[39]—is be magnificent. The virtue of magnificence, which Aristotle takes up in the second section of Book IV, is a subspecies of that of liberality, and it requires wealth, vast amounts of it. "The man who in small or middling things spends according to the merits of the case is not called magnificent . . . but only the man who does so in great things."[40] Again, it would be a vice, even if not a wicked one, for the widow to try to practice this virtue, because "a poor man cannot be magnificent since he has not the means with which to spend large sums fittingly; and he who tries is a fool, since he spends beyond what can be expected of him and what is proper, but it is the *right* expenditure that is excellent."[41] The gifts of the magnificent man, in contrast, are both "large and fitting."[42] In excess or directed to the wrong things, the gifts are "vulgar"; too little and they are "niggardly."[43] Aristotle leaves unambiguous the relative merit of the gifts (even when in proportion) of the poor and the rich man. In direct contrast to Jesus' testimony regarding the widow's mite—"Truly I tell you, this widow has put in more than all of them"—the large gifts of the magnificent man, according to the philosopher, "are the greatest and the most honorable."[44] A poor person simply cannot be as virtuous as a wealthy one.[45]

Notre Dame's announcement of its "Campus Crossroads Project"—a $400 million bid to involve academic space in a plan to expand the football stadium with luxury seating—triggered online and on-campus debate about whether the project is magnificent or vulgar,[46] indicating that the assumed *terms* of the conversation, as set up by the administration and appropriated even by many critics, are decidedly Aristotelian. The official billing of the project as the "Campus Crossroads" underscores the centrality of the autumn rituals that are to take place there. The university makes the case for its "large and fitting" magnificence in the official launch video. The voice is that of President Jenkins: "This is the most audacious building project the University of Notre Dame has ever undertaken. *We simply refuse to dream small*."[47] The video considers "small" to be lesser, unworthy—acts like that of the widow with her mite are not worth our notice. The video also uses the term "audacious" three times to describe the project. The debate is precisely whether the audaciousness in this case is magnificent or vulgar.

The social stratification and Aristotelian-like superiority of the well-to-do over the ordinary and the poor is architecturally symbolized in the "best" seats being the highest ones and shaded from sun and rain. Buy-in for the most exclusive seating is a $1 million opening donation plus annual $120,000 gifts over the ensuing twenty years for a total payment of $3.4 million for a pod of eight seats. A university brochure promises "exclusive" access to a private club in their part of the stadium, where one does not have to mix with regular ticketholders.[48] In the meantime, skyrocketing ticket prices—average price for a regular ticket is $115[49]—mean that many staff cannot afford to go to the games at all. The 2016 starting salary for departmental office staff is as low as $20,837, well below the poverty line for a family of four. At $18,943 and $17,539, the 2016 starting salary for the grounds and custodial crews that prepare the campus for the games and clean up afterward is well below the poverty line for a family of three.[50]

The social structure reenacted in the material structure of the Campus Crossroads Project reflects an ethos of encouraged sharp economic stratification that increasingly serves what is called the "velvet rope" economy. In reference to the people behind that rope, Norwegian Cruise Line's chief executive states, "That segment of the population wants to be surrounded by people with similar characteristics." The *New York Times* reports, "Behind a locked door aboard the Norwegian Cruiselines newest ship is a world most of the vessel's passengers never see. And that is exactly the point. In the Haven, as this ship within a ship is called, about 275 elite guests enjoy not only a concierge and 24-hour butler service, but also a private pool, sun deck and restaurant, creating an oasis free from the crowds elsewhere on the Norwegian Escape." Such "elite segmentation" is part of an overall "money-based caste system." Royal Caribbean cruise line has also "become more comfortable with heightening the contrast between the treatment meted out to ordinary passengers and the level of service reserved for the top tier." In the words of the chief executive, the higher paying customers, "are looking for the constant validation that they are the higher-*value* customer."[51] In short, Notre Dame, as embodied in the Campus Crossroads Project, the most expensive project in the university's history, reflects more the ethos of a luxury cruise ship than that of a community of believers. Reversing the biblical adage, in the symbolic-material nexus that is Notre Dame, the first shall remain first.

That Notre Dame not only architecturally mirrors, but materially fosters an extreme economic stratification that actively keeps out the poor is evident in those most important of collegiate velvet rope acts: the admissions and financial aid that permit (or not) enrollment. In 2017, professors from Brown, Stanford, and the University of California-Berkeley—three of Notre Dame's institutional "aspirational peers"—published a study on the role of colleges and universities in intergenerational mobility.[52] Notre Dame is one of thirty-eight colleges and universities—thirteenth overall—that have a greater proportion of admitted students in the economic top 1 percent (15.4 percent in Notre Dame's case) than in the bottom 60 percent (10 percent). In terms of admitting and enrolling students in the bottom economic quintile, Notre Dame ranks at 2,383 of 2,395 schools measured. Therefore also, when the focus is on the number and percentage of students who move from the economic bottom 40 percent to the top 40 percent as a result of going to a school, Notre Dame comes in at 2,190. Importantly, those poor students who *are* admitted and attend do quite well financially after graduating from Notre Dame, which ranks twenty-third on this measure. The problem is that of the velvet rope: the university lets in too few students from the middle and lower economic quintiles for it to register when measuring *overall* mobility. Thus the low—scraping bottom—overall mobility index, 2,114th of 2,137 schools measured. The middle and lower classes cannot improve at Notre Dame if they are not let in and given adequate aid packages to attend in the first place. The optics do not change even when we are comparing Notre Dame only to other elite schools, where it ranks 63rd of 65 among such colleges and universities in terms of students from the bottom economic quintile, and thus 58th of 64 relative to overall mobility upon graduation.[53] Given the importance of education for a person's future social and economic mobility, it is clear that university policy institutionally contributes not only to maintaining, but to *widening* the gap between rich and poor. And the last shall remain last.

This is the social structure that circumscribes and binds any acts that might be termed "good works" at the University of Notre Dame. *This* is what must not be risked. And it is the cost of the university's expansionism. To be clear, it is not as if all or even most members of the university community operate with the idea of furthering such a social structure foremost in their minds. It certainly is not what consciously drives those faculty and students featured in the "What Would You Fight For?" commercials, and my colleagues who insisted that I withdraw from public exchange on human rights in Uganda would not characterize themselves in this way. What I am setting forward here in providing an account of the university's institutional dynamics is *social* theory, not *conspiracy* theory; that is to say, the social stratification is not always intentional, but neither is it an accident. Specific policies set forth by specific people—for instance, that prescribing an inordinate proportion of legacy admissions (Harvard and Cornell at

16 percent, Notre Dame at 24 percent)[54]—shape the institutional structure and dynamic. *These* are the driving institutional structures that set the background for and serve to delimit virtually all of what we do at Notre Dame, and it functions at various levels of conscious intent depending on the person and her location within the university. Professor Ann-Marie Conrado certainly has the good of the poor of Nepal in mind in her project with the artisans there, but for others at the university, her work is primarily a *selling* point. For most of us at Notre Dame, the socioeconomic stratification that is the most powerful institutional "powerful force" operates at a level of which we are often scarcely aware and do not readily acknowledge, preferring to deflect consideration of it by thinking of it as ancillary to our work. Nevertheless, it continues to shape our practices and our sense of what is possible in profound ways.

It is worth noting that while the projects portrayed in the "What Would You Fight For?" series constitute only a relatively tiny portion of the university's operating budget, they carry much if not most of its symbolic capital. In other words, though the Aristotelian argument posits that the poor need Notre Dame to be as wealthy as it is so that it can serve them, the reverse is also most certainly true: symbolically, the university needs such projects and the poor, even though comparatively little is spent on them, because otherwise the "powerful force for good" argument appears to be simply about the accumulation of power.

That said, given that an Aristotelian ethic allows for and even requires wealth and power for one to perform significant moral acts, it is still worth examining whether Notre Dame, in its institutionally structured operations, can be said to be Aristotelian. Magnificence is, in the Aristotelian tradition, a virtue. The accumulation of wealth here is not immoral; in fact it is, in this tradition, the precondition for a superior kind of morality. It is *not* generally disputed that the spiritual-material capital nexus and interchange around giving at Notre Dame ultimately also supports projects like those depicted in the "What Would You Fight For?" campaign, which are given a high profile— two minutes is a long commercial—in front of millions of people. Few people—none that I know of—dispute that these projects, again to use Aristotle's words, are, at least for those who carry out the projects, "for the sake of the noble."[55] Again, Notre Dame's Aristotelian argument—sometimes explicit, often tacit—is that the projects featured in the campaign would not be possible without that nexus and interchange of spiritual and material capital. Indeed, the campaign portrays the projects themselves *as part of* the larger project of magnificence. The people who head up such projects fight, the campaign claims, "to bring solutions to a world in need." The spiritual-material capital nexus and interchange that takes place around football is the gift of Notre Dame to its faculty and students, and, according to the campaign, the projects which those faculty and students fight for are, by extension, Notre Dame's gift to the world.[56]

The unidirectionality of the giving, with the poor being defined simply by their neediness, does deny the significance of the widow with her mite, therefore disqualifying the university's from being a Gospel ethic. The operational logic of the university and that of the Gospel are simply different.[57] From a Gospel perspective, the Campus Crossroads Project is but one particularly salient moment in an ongoing experiment as to whether a camel really can get through the eye of a needle (Mk 10:25; Mt. 19:24; Lk. 18:25). We have to acknowledge the likelihood that if Jesus were to come to Notre Dame today and preach the flip side of the beatitudes on the quad in front of the main building—"Woe to you who are rich, for you have received your consolation. Woe to you who are full now, for you will be hungry" (Lk. 6:24-25a)—university security would escort Him, perhaps politely, off campus. And if He were to upend merchandise tables in the official "bookstore," shattering ND-engraved martini glasses and bottles of "Lady Irish Eau de Parfum Spray," we would handcuff Him, face down on the floor, and turn Him over to the authorities. In the meantime, we proceed as before: artificial turf has replaced the natural sod of the old football field, which the university has sold to fans for $150 per 2′ × 5′ sheet.[58]

But could there be an Aristotelian ethic here? Aristotelian-oriented criticisms from the university community have questioned the need for things like another indoor rock climbing wall or a 500-person ballroom like the ones planned in the Campus Crossroads Project, but members of the academic departments gaining much-needed space counter that such funding could only have come under the aegis of stadium expansion, and thus is rightly ordered funding of a sort. Besides, Aristotle goes on to note that the magnificent man, "will also furnish his house suitably to his wealth, for even a house is a sort of public ornament."[59] Everything about the Campus Crossroads Project is well-appointed. President Jenkins's language in the video borders on the mystical, referring to the "spirit" and "magic" of Notre Dame, and this, too, is in keeping with gifts of magnificence, which, according to Aristotle, "bear some resemblance to votive offerings."[60]

Ultimately, however, Notre Dame's "powerful force for good in the world" ethos, structured as it is by seemingly limitless growth fostered by the symbolic-economic capital interchange, runs afoul even of Aristotelian ethics, and this becomes evident when we extend the analysis beyond magnificence (again, μεγαλοπρέπεια/megaloprépeia) to another Aristotelian virtue, that of "greatness of soul" (μεγαλοψυχια/megalopsuchia).[61] For the sake of the good, the great-souled person is willing to undertake considerable risk. "He does not run into trifling dangers, nor is he fond of danger, because he honors few things; but he will face great dangers, and when he is in danger he is unsparing of his life, knowing that there are conditions on which life is not worth having" (1124b7-10). Given the institutionally structured aversion to risk at the university as pointed to earlier—a risk-level of nearly zero—it appears that the most that can be said is that the university structures the moral lives of its members such that it perhaps encourages them to be magnificent with regard to wealth, but not to be great-souled. Such persons, Aristotle claims, "imitate the great-souled man without being like him, and this they do where they can; so they do not act excellently. . . . They attempt honorable undertakings, and then are found out; and they adorn themselves with clothing and outward show and such things, and wish their strokes of good fortune to be made public, and speak about them as if they would be honored for them" (1124b3-5; 1125a29-32). Given Aristotle's view of the unity of the virtues—the idea that to possess any of the virtues in any significant way, one must exhibit all of them at least at a basic level— it is not possible to be authentically magnificent without to some extent also being great-souled.[62] Structurally, in the end, Notre Dame is of neither Nazareth nor Athens. Rather, the dominant functioning institutional ethics, whatever else we may say we represent, appears to be whatever combination of practices that expands the institutional "brand," to use the operative language, without risk. Once faith is monetized into a brand, it is not something for which we risk; rather, it is something to be managed.

I still think that Notre Dame remains much like what I said regarding the Comboni order in early twentieth-century Uganda: the university participates in evil (Notre Dame in a wider variety of ways and perhaps more profoundly than the Combonis). Yet, like the Combonis of that time, often it also, despite itself, creates space for persons to reappropriate the religious symbols the university itself distorts, and such persons live out this reappropriation in a way more true to the Gospel. And again, the two—distortion of the Gospel by an institution's structure and representatives and the reclamation of true witness by persons formed in the context of that institution—do not cancel each other out, whether we are talking about Comboni cooperation with British colonialism in relation to the witness of the Little Sisters of Mary Immaculate of Gulu or the acquisitive expansionism of Notre Dame in relation to the witness I see in some of my students and colleagues. Most of the rest of us in the community are of some admixture of the two options. When I finish my current work in northern Uganda and South Sudan, I will turn to the university for funding of my next research project in the hope of becoming a full professor someday.

Still, it is important try to render gospel mimesis intelligible to persons in an institution that claims to be Christian and yet is shaped so dramatically by consumerism. As a first step to offering an invitation to faithfulness, I draw on Jesus's shock tactic of using outsiders as exemplars. I refer to anthropologist Nancy Scheper-Hughes, and interpret her writings and actions in light of John Paul II's account of charity-infused solidarity. Here, charity involves the willingness to lay down one's life, something that from the point of view of Notre Dame's normal institutional functioning will necessarily seem excessive. Such charity-infused solidarity highlights the fact that when our institutions fail, we have only ourselves to offer.

The excessive virtues of ethnographic solidarity and Christian charity

Scheper-Hughes may seem to be an odd choice to exemplify Christian virtue. Though educated by nuns in Queens and Brooklyn, she acknowledges a "loss of faith" by high school.[63] There are indications that that first loss was not complete. More recently, however, the Roman Catholic Church sex abuse scandal prompted another instance of loss, and her articulation of her attempt to turn to anthropology as an alternative:

> I am grieved and not relieved by my loss of a faith that once gave beauty, richness and fullness to my life. The secular humanism of anthropology offers an alternative form of discipleship, built around the practice of studied observation, contemplation and reflection. I know that anthropology is a powerful tool capable

of taming unruly emotions, replacing disgust with respect, ignorance with understanding, hatred with empathy, and a practice of compassionate and modest witnessing to human sorrows. But it is cold comfort for the former believer, when the mystery is gone and with it the light has gone out of one's soul.[64]

But here is where the analogy between Scheper-Hughes and the Samaritan is perhaps most apt. Though Jesus refers to a Samaritan whom he heals of leprosy as a "foreigner"— the Greek term, *allogenēs*, literally means, "of another race" (Lk. 17:18)—some in the nation of Israel considered Samaritans to be "half-Jewish," distinct from other Gentiles.[65] Scheper-Hughes's identity trajectory is one of being "half-Catholic" and "half-anthropologist," and as her words above indicate, these two identities do not always sit flush with each other.[66] More, her at least temporary apostate status with regard to Christianity secures her position as more than a run-of-the-mill foreigner—those who leave the faith are from the perspective of the self-described orthodox more abject than the simple nonbeliever. Still, Jesus repeatedly (Lk. 10:25-37; 17:11-19) uses the example of the Samaritan precisely to portray what faithfulness looks like, and that is what I will do here.

Scheper-Hughes writes about how the demands of her research subjects that she cease simply observing their activity and join in the aims of their community prompts her turn to a committed anthropology. The impoverished women whom she had been studying in Brazilian shanty towns, "turn[ed] their anger against me. Why had I refused to work with them when they had been so willing to work with me? . . .I backed away saying . . . 'I cannot be an anthropologist and a *companheira* at the same time.' . . . And they gave me an ultimatum: the next time I came back to the Alto do Cruzeiro it would be on their terms, that is, as a *companheira*, 'accompanying' them."[67] The pattern of the call to commitment coming from outside the anthropologist, indeed, from her research subjects, is not unique to Scheper-Hughes. Dana-Ain Davis writes of her own research subject, "Sherita asked me what I was going to do with all of the information I collected. She made it very clear that she was only a 'case file' at social services and that it was my responsibility to tell 'people' how difficult life was and share the problems women faced while on welfare. What Sherita was asking of me was to move my work as an anthropologist from the margin of my own personal achievement, that of being awarded a degree and facilitating my employment as an academic, to a center of relevance, to the realm of policy. In return for the 'gift' of her life story and the stories of other women, I was asked to do something that might make a difference. My work as a politically engaged anthropologist began at that moment."[68] In other words, Sherita was asking Davis, like Olum of the Teachers' Drinking Club asked me, that her research not be another instance of cultural plunder. "What are you going to do for *us*?"

Scheper-Hughes decides to join the Brazilian women, and doing so shifts her understanding of her discipline. "If we cannot begin to think about social institutions and practices in moral or ethical terms," she writes, "then anthropology strikes me as quite weak and useless." In her article, "The Primacy of the Ethical: Propositions for a Militant Anthropology," she calls for persons in her discipline to embody "solidarity" with the subjects of their research.[69] She dramatically illustrates in a different setting what she is talking about by telling of her intercession in the disciplining of some thieves in the Chris Hani camp—a South African shanty town—in 1993. The camps resisted policing by the white security forces because of the latter's many brutalities. Therefore, members of the camps attempted to police themselves. Without a written or strong oral basis for self-regulation, the communities administered their versions of justice in uneven and often capricious ways. In other words, the institutions of justice were dysfunctional. In Chris Hani, three boys were caught stealing 400 Rands (about 125 dollars). A crowd quickly gathered that was going to "necklace" the boys. Necklacing is the practice of putting a tire full of gasoline around the neck of a person and setting it on fire, a modern form of witch-burning. Members of the African National Congress did intervene to get the punishment reduced to fifty lashes. However, it was not considered to be adequate: as a continuation of the discipline, the boys were not allowed to eat or drink. Fearing that the smallest of them was going to die, Scheper-Hughes, knowing that she could not do so openly, sneaked a doctor into the holding cell to check on him and then secretly evacuated him to a hospital.

Scheper-Hughes is aware that solidarity with one's research subjects, particularly if they are marginalized persons, brings risks. After taking the smallest thief to the hospital, she received an anonymous phone call. "'Stay away from Chris Hani camp,' the heavily accented brown-Afrikaner voice warned. 'People there are angry that you interfered with their discipline. Your safety cannot be guaranteed.'"[70] However, she did return to the camp, and her testimony in a communal meeting helped change the camp's disciplinary practices. She recognizes that, given the social context—that of dysfunctional dominant institutions—she was in all likelihood the only one with the social location to act in the way that she did.

When she attempts to articulate her commitment, Scheper-Hughes calls her actions, "witness," and it is here that she comes closest to recognizing her convergence with a discipline that anthropology has long rejected.[71] She writes, "It is the act of 'witnessing' that lends our work its moral, at times almost theological, character." This is because to speak and act in light of the "primacy of the ethical" is to "suggest" certain "transcendent" grounds for moral norms.[72] It appears that situations of extreme violence and risk often press anthropologists, if they answer their research subjects' calls to join in solidarity, to interpretive language that finds significant points of contact with a committed Christianity. Anthropologist Philippe Bourgois is similar in his appeal to human rights that transcend specific cultures and even more so when the horror of a massacre of peasants by the Salvadoran military that he witnessed prompts him to conclude by describing the victims in terms with deep theological resonances: "We should not forget that our 'informants' continue to be crucified."[73]

John Paul II introduces the concept of solidarity as a contrast term to that which he calls "structures of sin": "'Sin' and 'structures of sin' are categories which are seldom applied to the situation of the contemporary world. However, one cannot easily gain a profound understanding of the reality that confronts us unless we give a name to the root of the evils which afflict us." A world in which the "desire for profit on the one hand and the thirst for power on the other" dominate "can only be a world subject to structures of sin." John Paul also recognizes that the reality of such structures where the normal institutions of justice are dysfunctional presses upon us the requirement, if we are not simply to look away, to act in a way that the worldview of "normal" institutional functioning[74] considers excessive: "These attitudes and 'structures of sin' are only conquered—presupposing the help of divine grace—by a diametrically opposed attitude: a commitment to the good of one's neighbor with the readiness, in the gospel sense, to 'lose oneself' for the sake of the other."[75]

That "diametrically opposed attitude" is one which John Paul, like Scheper-Hughes, calls solidarity. In his rendering, it has three aspects. Unpacking these aspects reveals strong similarities between the pope's theology and the anthropology of Scheper-Hughes. The first aspect of solidarity is simply the descriptive fact of human interconnectedness. Solidarity is, "a question of interdependence, sensed as a system determining relationships in the contemporary world, in its economic, cultural, political, and religious elements." Secondly, however, awareness of interdependence can and ought to generate concern that the relationships between and among peoples be shaped for the common good. Interdependence must be accepted as a "moral category." Noteworthy here is John Paul's warning against abstractness and his insistence that solidarity be grounded in encounters with specific people. Solidarity, "is not a feeling of vague compassion or shallow distress at the misfortunes of so many people, both near and far. On the contrary, it is a firm and persevering determination to commit oneself to the common good; that is to say to the good of all and of each individual, because we are all really responsible for all."[76] Third and finally, when solidarity has a transcendent referent, it exemplifies itself in one's willingness to sacrifice one's own life for the other, even for one's enemy. Such cruciform justice is nothing less than charity rightly considered.

> In the light of faith, solidarity seeks to go beyond itself, to take on the specifically Christian dimension of total gratuity, forgiveness and reconciliation. One's neighbor is then not only a human being with his or her own rights and a fundamental equality with everyone else, but becomes the living image of God the Father, redeemed by the blood of Jesus Christ and placed under the permanent action of the Holy Spirit. One's neighbor must therefore be loved, even if an enemy, with the same love with which the Lord loves him or her; and for that person's sake one must be ready for sacrifice, even the ultimate one: to lay down one's life for the brethren.[77]

If we turn to Scheper-Hughes's account of solidarity, we find strong analogues to each of the three aspects or moments in John Paul II's treatment. First, there is an acknowledgment and even affirmation of human interdependence. In Scheper-Hughes' words, "What draws me back to these people and places is not their exoticism and their 'otherness' but the pursuit of those small spaces of convergence."[78] Like John Paul, Scheper-Hughes takes this recognition of connectedness as an occasion for commitment. Again, "If we cannot begin to think about social institutions and practices in moral or ethical terms, then anthropology strikes me as quite weak and useless." Her accounts of her work in Brazil and South Africa provide precisely the kind of specificity that John Paul points to when he speaks of solidarity as a "firm and persevering" commitment to "the good of all and of each individual." Finally, in her actions on behalf of the thieves we have a love of "enemy" even to the point of the willingness to risk her own life. Christ was crucified alongside thieves, and Luke's gospel has him tell one of them that they will be together "in Paradise" (Lk. 23:43).

If we are to follow Scheper-Hughes and John Paul II, then we must insist that the witness of both engaged anthropology and an authentic Christianity involve, when the situation calls for it, the willingness to risk our lives. Such willingness is considered excessive by the normal view of what is required. This is why, as has been made more widely known by the movie *Hotel Rwanda*, when situations become, as the locals say, "difficult," most (white) Westerners vacate. In contrast, when the usual solidarity is infused with and by charity it, in John Paul's terms, "seeks to go beyond itself." The response of solidarity/charity still involves the exercise of *phronēsis*, or "practical wisdom," in assessing risk, as is well displayed in the lesser-known films *Beyond the Gates* and *Of Gods and Men*, where white Westerners discern and debate about whether to stay, and some do remain. What is different is the horizon against which the assessment of risk takes place. Normal understandings of justice act against the horizon of the world's institutions, such that when they fail, it is time to leave. Charity-deepened solidarity, which doubts the efficacy and integrity of the world's institutions, operates against the horizon of the resurrected Christ, where, again in John Paul's words, all persons are "the living image of God the Father, redeemed by the blood of Jesus Christ and placed under the permanent action of the Holy Spirit." Against *this* horizon, the willingness to lay down one's life is not excessive, but is rather the very thing that is proportionate to the gift we have received.[79]

It is important to keep clear that the aim is love-deepened solidarity, not risk itself; thus the necessity of *phronēsis*. Still, a life where risk—real bodily risk—on behalf of solidarity is never at stake raises questions about the commitment to solidarity. As John Paul II points out, oppression is structural violence; if we never become exposed to the violence, then this is an indication that our commitment is questionable. Willingness or what John Paul calls "readiness" to risk is a mark—even if it is not the only one—of commitment to love one's neighbor. In the Gospel context, the key moment is when Jesus "set his face to go to Jerusalem" (Lk. 9:51). He had already given offense, been driven from his hometown, and experienced threat (Mk 6:1-6; Mt. 13:54-58; Lk. 4:16-30), and while there is debate in New Testament scholarship regarding whether and how accurately he predicted his own death, it is unlikely that he did not know that going to Jerusalem increased his risk. So central is this moment in the Gospel narratives, that it seems that a life characterized by following Jesus must also display an analogous "Jerusalem turn." And what is not generally debated in biblical scholarship is that, once in Jerusalem, Jesus's actions in the Temple cleansing (Mt. 21:10-17; Lk. 19:45-46) precipitated his death and that he likely knew that this was a distinct possibility.

Scheper-Hughes's actions exemplify the Gospel and John Paul II's claim in *Veritatis Splendour* that martyrdom—or even the willingness to lay down one's life—"confirms" moral truths in "a particularly eloquent way." It is the "high point of witness to moral truth."[80] In other words, as virtue theory insists, we reason with our bodies as well as with our words. What we gain from the conversation between engaged anthropology and committed Christianity is the insight that perhaps the most elegant argument for human rights is a life of a certain sort well-lived, and, as a result, a willingness, when the circumstances call for it, to let that life go for the sake of someone else and something more.

We have come full circle back to the scene with which this book began. In that scene, LRA rebels are coming toward the town of Magwi, South Sudan. Father Joseph Otto tells us what happens next. "People from all around came to our compound. They were saying, 'Father Joseph, the LRA are coming! Help us!' I did not know what to do. We could not protect them. Father Maurice was here. So I asked him what we should do. He said, 'Let's get a motorcycle and ride toward the LRA. Let's try to talk to them. Maybe they'll talk. And if they kill us, at least the others will have more time to get away.'" Father Joseph later explains his actions, "We were the only ones. The SPLA was not there to protect. They did not come until after Easter. And the people, they are just people of the village. They did not know what to do. There are no activists, no community leaders. There is no one who can be in the middle and try to talk with the LRA. Someone maybe they can trust. It is hard. These LRA are not very dependable. But I am a man of peace, and so I seek to make peace wherever I am. I am a priest, and I am supposed to be an image of Christ. So we just got on the motorcycle and went."

I have argued that a particular understanding and practice of *mimesis*—of the imitation of Christ—enables the kind of action taken by Fathers Joseph and Maurice. What Scheper-Hughes's example shows us is that, as Jesus knows in telling the story of the Good Samaritan, the best exemplification of what it looks like to be faithful sometimes comes from outsiders. Scheper-Hughes, in effect, "just got on the motorcycle and went." True, she may no longer believe in the specific *psst* of the Holy Spirit bearing Christ's charism, though her grief at that loss indicates a desire for its recovery.[81] In the meantime, I would suggest that it is, in part, her *anthropological* affirmation of the "transcendent" and, in her words, the "almost theological" nature of her connection with her research subjects that enables her to do like Fathers Joseph and Maurice.

The remaining question is how, beyond shocking and perhaps shaming us with the exemplarity of outsiders, to bring *insiders*—that is, we who are self-described Christians—into the pull of the example of persons like Fathers Joseph and Maurice and the Little Sisters of Mary Immaculate of Gulu. For this, Jesus draws upon a second rhetorical tactic, that of utilizing images from the common life of his audience—planting mustard seeds, fishing with nets—to convey both the glory and the demands of the Gospel. Given, to take a key instance, that over 114 million people in the United States—the largest audience in US television history—watched the 2015 Super Bowl, the example of sports perhaps works best for contemporary American culture for providing images from common life.[82] And, as we have seen, sports, and especially football, are central to identity at Notre Dame. Sports and images from sports appear, therefore, to be the best way to bring the Christian ethnographic encounter home. Following this approach will also provide another opportunity to articulate the role of anthropological theology in the Christian life. This will be, for now, my closing effort to invite the community of Notre Dame and Christians more broadly to a life of gospel mimesis. That this is an invitation and not a conclusion is both because summary conclusions made as if we can stand outside of things and tie them up neatly without remainder are an illusion, and because efforts to so summarize kill the dynamic of mimesis that, if allowed to be, is always on the move. An invitation is never a final word, but a call for further response.

Anthropological theology as gospel playbook and gamefilm

I grew up in Kitgum mission.
I studied my primary in Kitgum girls primary school.
As I was living with the sisters, the Little Sisters of Mary Immaculate of Gulu,
I started to admire them.
Yeah, their way of life actually, struck me and I started to share with them what I feel. I wanted to become like one of them, the kind of life the sisters were living. Community life.
And they were so lovable, charitable, they could move around the community
The way they were also caring for the girls.
Really I feel that it was . . .
I don't know how to say it because the sisters were living very very close directing them to do this and that, both spiritual and physical. They train us how to work in the field, how to cook, how to knit and all this.
And the kind of love they were showing us.
That is what I really admired.
And the prayer life of course.

The best prayer was rosary.
They taught how to say the rosary, you know how to lead the rosary in the church and every evening when the bell

Perhaps the single most significant intellectual error in the history of theology is its appropriation of philosophy's separation of theoretical and practical reason, and its own frequent self-categorization as a mode of the former.[83] Once they separate the two, thinkers of all sorts must design ways in which they come back together—or at least relate to each other—and theologians feel compelled to identify their project as first and foremost one or the other. This kind of taxonomization has been less than helpful for doing theology. Typically it has led to the elevation of the theoretical over the practical, a hierarchicalization that has given rise to mistakes like the idea of there being "applied" areas of theology and ethics as a distinct thing that we do after we do theology or ethics proper. Pierre Bourdieu's attempt to discern the "logic" and develop a "theory" of practice is a significant relatively contemporary non-theological attempt to bridge the two while protecting practice's autonomy from the tendency to reduce it to what can be explained by theory. Showing the shortcomings of his approach helps to limn what a theology looks like for which the theory/practice separation is a non-factor. This is the kind of theology that, if we can pull it off, can be a proclamation of the Gospel.

Though Bourdieu stakes out his "theory of practice" over against both subjectivism and objectivism,[84] it is the latter that he develops

*goes we run to the church, each one
of us wants to what? to lead the
prayer.*

*After completing P7, we were invited
in the convent. That was completely
prayer life.*

*They were now training us in prayer
life and also to know more about the
congregation.*

*You could go to school and then you
come back in the convent.*

*During the school you do the academic
work.*

*When you come to the convent you are
being formed spiritually.*

*It was a very nice thing because we were
really taught deep in the spiritual life,
deep in the spiritual life.*

More even the social life.

*How when you become a Sister how
you behave outside there with
the what?*

With the community.

How do you do your work.

*So they prepare us actually how to
interact with the people.*

After novitiate I took my first vows.

My first work was teaching.

We were brought in 1987 to Kitgum.

*From Kitgum we stayed some three
days, and we were asked to go to
Padibe.*

*In Padibe there was nobody. The
missionaries were in Kitgum.*

All of them were in Kitgum.

In Padibe, things were not easy.

Things were not easy.

*Many of the people around were living
in the mission, so all of us were in the
mission.*

*I cannot remember the number because
all those buildings in Padibe, they
were filled up.*

most fully as a threat both to the development of an accurate theory of practice and to practices themselves. Objectivism attempts to isolate the object of inquiry from the investigator so as to bring the former under the rational control of theory. Objectivist theory is totalizing in that it presumes to explain and anticipate everything about a practice, and it presupposes that correct practice follows logically, even mechanistically, from the application of the theory.[85] Bourdieu finds the social presuppositions of objectivism in the Greek word *skholè*, which originally meant "leisure" or "free time"—that is, time away from activity—and, while maintaining this meaning, came also to indicate "time for intellectual discussion" and ultimately intellectual discussion itself. The problem with the split between the *theoria* which takes place in *skholè* and the *praxis* which takes place everywhere else, according to Bourdieu, is that it has from the beginning been articulated as a valuation of the former over the latter.[86]

Bourdieu cites Plato, but it is also evident in Aristotle, who mounts multiple arguments, each of which reinforces the others, that *theoria* is better than *praxis*: *theoria* pertains to *nous* (the intellect), the best part of us; it is self-sufficient and carried out for its own sake; and it takes place during leisure, upon which our happiness depends.[87] Bourdieu also emphasizes that, historically, writing both facilitates the development of *theoria* and has served as a crucial mechanism through which literate cultures that preference *theoria* at the expense of *praxis* dominate predominantly oral cultures. He warns of the "total or partial monopolizing of the [previously oral] society's symbolic resources in religion, philosophy, art and science, through the monopolization of the instruments for appropriation of these resources (writing, reading and other decoding techniques), henceforward preserved not in memories but in texts."[88]

In the hospital, the health center, people
were there in the school, and then at
the sisters.'
You find people really suffered. And you
could not eat twice a day.
During the evening they come. We eat
once a day.
Because the people are there we said,
'Now we are sent there,' which means the
congregation wants us to die together
with the people.
We are not going to leave them.

In Padibe at least we have one hour
Adoration. We used to do one hour
Adoration before the Blessed Sacra-
ment. We would close all the doors so
people don't know where we are.
Just once they wake.
But we do as a group . . .
When we were going for prayers we tell
our people.
Because there was no—you could not predict
when things may not be okay at that
particular moment.
. . . Because there was no
communication outside.
Padibe was very risky.
So we were confined in Padibe.
And once in a while, maybe twice in
the month, we footed from Padibe to
Kitgum together with the catechumens.
We come to Kitgum to get the what?
The Blessed Sacrament.
When it was consecrated then we carry
together, we move on foot with the
children in back.
That was the Sacrament we put in the
tabernacle for daily Holy Communion.
Sometimes we were scared.

But knowing we were going back with
the Blessed Sacrament we keep on
praying praying praying . . .
We were just praying

I share Bourdieu's concern about the oppressive uses to which writing has been put, and I agree that, historically, writing has arisen in the context of and in turn has reinforced a set of presuppositions about the primacy of the intellect understood as a kind of disembodied aspect of ourselves.

The problem is that in accepting the *theoria/praxis* separation to begin with, even as he tries to relate the two, he, in an act that he would term a "misrecognition," reinforces both the presuppositions and, in the end, the value system of that split. As *theoria* is opposed to *praxis*, writing, according to Bourdieu, is opposed to mimesis. Whereas particularly oral societies engage in learning by mimesis, a kind of "practical reactivation which is *opposed* to both memory and knowledge," and is "never detached from the body," all theoretical schemes, particularly where writing is involved, "intervene between the individual and his/her body." Bourdieu draws from Weber in calling writing a tool of "disincarnation." The theoretical models that arise through writing therefore have "*nothing* in common with participation in practical experience." In fact, trying to teach about practice in schools—the etymology of the latter is traceable to the idea of *skholé*—directly and conclusively interferes with practice. "Excellence (that is, practical mastery in its accomplished form) has *ceased to exist* once people start asking whether it can be taught, as soon as they seek to base 'correct' practice on rules extracted, for the purposes of transmission" (emphases added).[89] This outright separation of theory and practice (which Bourdieu then tries to overcome) carries with it an exoticization of the practitioner over against the theorist whereby the former becomes a re-creation of early twentieth-century anthropology's "noble savage." This is most evident in Bourdieu's insistence that the practitioner is not consciously aware of the true

'O Sacrament Most Holy,
O Sacrament Divine, all praise and all
thanksgiving be every morning thine.
O Blessed Sacrament.'
Just like that.

So when we reached somewhere in the
middle we were almost approaching
Kitgum mission.
That is when we met the rebels. For the
first time . . .
They took us and moved in the bush.
We moved throughout the night until the
next morning throughout the day and
then at six o'clock that is when they
release us. And we came back.
What we were usually—when we were
coming to Kitgum we would keep on
saying rosary.
At that time we were also saying rosary,
we had not yet finished the what?
The decades.
So as soon as the rebels stopped us,
I jumped out and I raise my arm and
the rosary was there.
They came and snatched it, you know,
picked away the rosary.
Say 'Bring it here.'
So as we were moving, going,
I was not even scared.
I don't know why.
I was not scared because I say, 'Now Jesus
we have not done anything wrong.'
I was the first Sister for the first time to
be taken in the bush by these people.
So now when they took us in the bush I
just moved with them.

One time when the rebels entered in the
convent the sisters were beaten.
I had come to Kitgum town.
I was preparing myself to go to school
now, in '88 September.
But now when I heard that they have
entered the convent,

rules of her actions. Learning and re-creation of correct practice "tend to take place below the level of consciousness" and have "nothing in common with an imitation that would presuppose a conscious effort to reproduce a gesture." In an act of what Bourdieu calls "learned ignorance," participants "conceal, even from themselves, the true nature of their practical mastery." Such *docta ignorantia*, "does not contain knowledge of its own principles." The only time that there is reference to any explicit rules is "in cases of misfiring or failure" in the practice itself.[90]

I understand and share Bourdieu's concern with the *ideology* of theory and writing that separates both from the body, but the fact of the matter is, as Ecclesiastes tells us, conscious intellectual activity and the body are deeply intertwined: "The sayings of the wise are like goads, and like nails firmly fixed are the collected sayings that are given by one shepherd. Of anything beyond these, my child, beware. Of making many books there is no end, and much study is a weariness of the flesh" (Eccl. 12:11-12). Recent studies tell us what all scholars know: writing contributes to back pain, eye strain, and carpal tunnel syndrome. In short, writing and theorizing *are* bodily practices. The question for Christian theologians is not how we can relate them to practice, but how to practice them such that they can be taken up as integral parts of proclaiming the Gospel.

Bourdieu himself gives us an avenue for doing so by describing practice as "practical participation in a game."[91] He draws upon the game analogy precisely to distinguish practice from objectivist theories about practice, and it is here (and elsewhere) that he stresses the lack of practitioners' consciousness about their practices. However, if we look at actual games, we can see that writing and other techniques that abstract from on-field action are very much a part of the practice. During timeouts

I took my motorcycle.
I told the sisters in Kitgum
I'm going back.
We had been so close together all along,
suffering together and now I am away
from them. I felt that I should go
again, we be together
I was praying,
'God allow me, let nothing happen to
me, let nothing happen to me. Just let
nothing happen to me.'

When I went back to Padibe,
I did not even feel bad because I know
my Sisters are there, and they are
those who I have been working
with.
They are there.
So if they are suffering, why can't I suffer
together with them?
So I did not feel actually so bad, and I
did not even complain,
'Now why are you taking me back
where I've been suffering?' and the
rest of it.
But I knew those are the people;
I have been suffering with them;
I think that is where my happiness also
will come.
That trauma is still disturbing me.
And sometimes because, now as I talk,
I move to Padibe every week. Whenever
I reach that spot where the rebel picked
me and went with me to the bush, that
thing always come back in my mind,
much as I was not hurt.

I was not even beaten by them.
They did not even use any bad words
on me.
But still I think,
'Why?'
And going to Padibe and now I'm living,
I'm going, I sleep in the same room
where they broke the door.

in basketball, the coach typically crouches with a dry-erase clipboard to diagram the next play for the team huddled around him. When the players return to the court, they are *consciously* aware of what they are trying to do. In baseball, the third-base coach sends plays to the batter and runners through a series of abstracted signals—touching his nose or cap, brushing his sleeve—for such plays as the "squeeze bunt" and the "hit and run." Again, the players are very conscious of what they are trying to do. And all of these explicit plays take place not "in cases of misfire or failure" in the practice, as Bourdieu would have it, but precisely to increase the likelihood of performative success. If the practice of abstracting from practice to improve practice did not work in practice much of the time, there would be no courtside dry-erase boards or third-base line signals. Instead, we find that the condensed abstractions constitute, to use Alasdair MacIntyre's phrase, "internal goods" for the practice of the sport.[92]

The role of abstraction through writing and other means for enhancing the practice of a sport is perhaps most thoroughly developed in American football. When a new player arrives at pre-season camp, one of the first things he receives is a thick "playbook," which he is required to "study" and memorize. Though, technically, what is called the "game" takes place later, the practice of football for a new arrival begins with study of the playbook. When the quarterback or the defensive captain calls out a play on the field through coded names—say, "wing right, twenty-three dive"—the player is supposed to know what to do from having studied the playbook. The conscious practice of abstracting gameplay and memorizing the abstracted text are *assumed as part of the game*. To be sure, the player is to memorize the play such that he does not have to think consciously much at all about it, and playbooks without on-

*Sometimes it all comes back as a sort of
dream, like where somebody says, a
day-dream.*
You can dream when your eyes are open.
So that is still a fight.
That is still a fight.
*In fact the most help that I'm getting is
being close to the Sacrament, from the
Eucharist, the Body of Christ.*
*I know that that one is the one that
sincerely is helping me to push ahead.*
*Because I meet Christ and he is always
in me.*
I never—
I used to say 'Communion';
I say now,
'You are with me.
Everywhere I go.
Whatever I do.
You are here within me.
*I'm not praying, but the whole of you is
in me.*
I move with you.'

*And I say that it is really very very
important that we unite with Jesus in
the Blessed Sacrament.*
The whole of Jesus is in me.
'I'm moving with you.'
*Whenever I receive the Holy Sacrament,
the Holy Communion,*
I feel protected.
I feel protected.
*Much as those things—because it was
really something that has touched our
lives directly.*
*And it is not easy because we need to be
full in order to make others also keep
hope.*
Without which, things will not be easy.

*Then the sisters decided to bring me
back to Kitgum.*
*They didn't tell me anywhere but they
brought me to a school, and this
school had just started.*

the-field experience are next to useless, but the
movement during this segment of activity is
clearly from explicit symbolic practice (which
still very much involves the body; players will
say how playbook study is tiring) to on-field
practice in order to raise the excellence of the
latter.

It is also true that much of what goes on
on the playing field takes place, as Bourdieu
stresses, below the threshold of consciousness,
and that there are virtuoso players who cannot
fully articulate the "logic" of their play. For
both better and worse, far from all of what goes
on on the field goes according to explicit plan.
The on-the-field practice is not reducible to
the practice of abstracting from that in order
to improve it in the future. Yet the on-field and
off-field practices are deeply interrelated—not
as practice and theory, but as two moments in
the overall practice of the game, as is evident
when the quarterback calls out the abstracted
signals *on the field*. Study of the playbook is
part of the larger field of the sport. Practitioners
of American football account for and bridge
the gap between what is usually recognized as
on-field play and the playbook by watching—
players refer to it as "studying"—gamefilm.
Someone who watches a lot of gamefilm is
called a good "student of the game." What the
gamefilms provide are the designed plays in
action so that the observer can diagnose what
makes the play work or not work on the field
more narrowly conceived.

The practice of theology, when it works,
is Gospel playbook and gamefilm. The more
abstracted sections—like the one that I am
writing right now—are like a playbook. They
present in schematic form the outlines of what
a good "play" (or a bad play) in the game of the
Good News looks like. It can be difficult for the
reader to integrate the schematic presentation
with the broader practice of the Gospel, and for
this the theologian draws upon a more time-

And the school was started for
   abductees.
The girls who had come back from the
   bush.
Secondly, girls who were living in the
   camp around here.
IDP camp.

Then the priest collected these girls and
   brought them here.
And says, 'Sister come and help.'
I sit down and make tea for the priest.
   He says,
"God has something for you." Much
   as I've been traumatized with this
   war, he wants me again to help the
   traumatized.
So we started this school with the
   twenty-one girls.
There were bush mothers.
Very young girls, like this, and this girl
   having a child with her.
Others are big, big, but because they went
   in the bush, and they remained there,
   they came back with kids.
And it is not easy: this is a woman,
   this is a girl who is completely
   traumatized. You need to mold them,
   talk to them, show them the way how
   to behave and the rest of it.

And I was thinking,
I said,
'I think God has something for me.'
Because I would have said no, I would
   have said no to the what?
To my superiors:
'Please you take me somewhere else.
Because I am also traumatized,
   and I have to come and help the
   traumatized.'
[But] I say, 'No, He has something
   for me.'
And the first group went out and now
   some of them are becoming nurses.

sensed, narrative mode of presentation, like that on the left side of these pages—our version of gamefilm. The Gospels themselves tack back and forth between playbook and gamefilm when they move from Jesus's sayings to his parables/stories and back again. Erich Auerbach notes in *Mimesis: The Representation of Reality in Western Literature* that the biblical narratives are "visually concrete," even though they do not provide much in the way of descriptive detail. Such fine detail was not initially necessary because the original hearers of the message to a large extent had a fund of shared cultural experiences, so the language of the stories could be metonymic and therefore still be, as Auerbach says, "fraught with background."[93] The hearers could fill in the details themselves. Globalization and the fragmentation and hybridization of cultures mean that we can no longer rely on such metonymic communication in the same way, and therefore must employ what Clifford Geertz calls "thick description."[94] The role of ethnography in theology, then, is that of helping to provide a particularly rich, fine-grained account of God's actions and of Christian practices (and of practices that are otherwise) in response for consideration for reenactment or rejection.[95]

Describing theology as playbook and gamefilm is also to suggest that the theologian is analogous to the coach of a sports team. To the extent that this is true, we can learn from the case of sports. For instance, in almost every case of professional and collegiate sport, the coaches, particularly head coaches, were, at least at one point in their lives, players of the sport at a relatively high level, whether in high school, college, or even professionally. This suggests that to understand how to abstract the rules of practice so that they can in turn enhance the practice itself requires some degree of on-the-field familiarity with the practice. It also suggests that one reason why

*One already a qualified nurse. And I think
    that is something God has spoken to me.*
*But out of twenty-one, only seven
    succeeded with life. The rest are now
    there in the villages.*
And I said,
'No, I think God will work a miracle.'
*I want to call those very good who come
    back from the what?*
From the bush.
I want them by next year.
*I want them to come back so that we train
    them how to do tailoring.*

*Because with the tailoring you can sit
    with your machine somewhere, even
    in the village. She can get some one
    hundred, two hundred, even more.*
*A woman can have something if every
    day she is having two hundred shillings,
    which she made with the dress, she is
    able to buy salt in her house.*
She's able to buy the soap for the washing.
*So this is the thing that has been, you
    know, disturbing me.*
Sometimes I ask
'Why, why God again, why?
I am traumatized.
*And you want me again to work with
    the traumatized. Am I going to help
    them anyway?'*
But I've seen that I am helping them.
So I praise the Lord for that.
And that's why I told you my experience.
What is helping me is
Holy Communion.
Because I know that
Jesus is in me whole, not part of him.

*Maybe if I am the one who, you know,
    stops my work, my heart falls to the
    side . . .*
But He is whole.
With him, and him now,
I have become one at my working place.

Charlie Weis—the fired Notre Dame football coach mentioned earlier—has failed as a head coach at Notre Dame and elsewhere is that he lacks that on-the-field experience.[96] The other lesson to be drawn from the world of sport and the coaching analogy is that while coaches typically have played at a relatively high level, it is almost never the case that good coaches were on-the-field *virtuosi* in the sport. Magic Johnson and Isiah Thomas were failures as coaches; Michael Jordan knew not to try. Most good coaches were "role players" as athletes.[97] Doc Rivers, Phil Jackson, and Steve Kerr come to mind.

Exceptions would have to include Larry Bird (who found coaching so frustrating that he had to stop after three seasons) and Bill Russell (and whether he was a good coach can be debated). Joe Torre might be an example. If the analogy from sports holds, then it appears that most good theologians have some significant on-the-field experience, but are not among the saints.

Theology as gospel mimesis rejects the idea of theological knowledge for its own sake both because Jesus of Nazareth, the one whom we are to imitate, was, whatever else he was, not a gnostic,[98] and because of the problematic implications—the denigration of the body, of everyday practice, and of cultures deemed "backward"—that inevitably operate under the knowledge-for-its-own-sake model. Still, the aim of writing anthropological theology is not simply (though it includes) the defense of the cultures encountered against the onslaughts of modernity and postmodernity; it is also, through vivid mimetic re-presentation of what it looks like,[99] to prompt you, the reader, to step onto the "field" of the Gospel, first through allowing you to enter into the lives of the people depicted, and then through inviting you to put this book down and to enter the Gospel game, again, yourself.

Notes

1. The America's Best Restroom contest is run by the Cintas Corporation, which "designs and implements full service restroom programs for businesses that combine superior service with top line products." See http://www.bestrestroom.com/us/sponsor.asp.

2. The dome at the University of Notre Dame has been regilded ten times, the last time in 2005 at the cost of $300,000. See William G. Gilroy, "Golden Dome to be Regilded for Tenth Time," at http://news.nd.edu/news/7572-golden-dome-to-be-regilded-for-the-tenth-time/.

3. In summer 2017, the university promoted the "Notre Dame Trail"—a re-creation of the route that Father Sorin took to the land where he would found Notre Dame after he had a falling out with the bishop in southern Indiana—as a pilgrimage route in advertisements, on banners, and with a website (https://trail.nd.edu/). Sorin had, without permission from Bishop Célestine de la Hailandière of the Diocese of Vincennes, started a school that directly competed with the diocesan school. Offering the land in northern Indiana was a way for Bishop Hailandière to move Sorin farther away.

   What the Notre Dame Trail promotion masks is that what freed up land in the region was another trail, the "Potawatomi Trail of Death," and other forced displacement of the Potawatomi American Indians (http://www.potawatomi-tda.org/). In fact, the two trails—the Notre Dame Trail and the Trail of Death—overlap considerably, only with the two populations moving in opposite directions. In 1838, the Potawatomi Indians were forced southward from Twin Lakes/Plymouth, through Rochester, Logansport, and Lafayette, Indiana, before shifting westward to Kansas. Four years later, Sorin and his followers went northward from Vincennes up through Lafayette, Logansport, Rochester, and Plymouth. Sorin at first thought that he had a calling to minister to the indigenous people, but soon found them to be too burdensome. This shift in attention allowed him to give full focus to building Notre Dame. The present promotion of the Notre Dame Trail as a divine calling and without acknowledgment of the pre-history of displacement is a consistent extension of the Manifest Destiny ethos found in Father Sorin's writings. The current mural on the first floor of the administration building depicting American Indians voluntarily kneeling before Columbus expresses the same sentiment.

4. Dan Barry, "Notre Dame President Stands Firm Amid Shifts in College Athletics," *The New York Times* (September 10, 2015), at http://www.nytimes.com/2015/09/11/sports/ncaafootball/notre-dame-president-stands-firm-amid-shifts-in-college-athletics.html?_r=0. For a response in the same publication the next day that questions the university's firmness, see Joe Nocera, "Notre Dame's Big Bluff," *The New York Times* (September 11, 2015), at http://www.nytimes.com/2015/09/12/opinion/joe-nocera-notre-dames-big-bluff.html. Supporting Nocera's point are student responses to a question that I ask each semester: "Agree or disagree: Notre Dame should drop Division I football if this guarantees the University becoming a top three academic institution." On average, about 80 percent of the students disagree.

5. http://al.nd.edu/about/ (retrieved February 25, 2015).

6. Charles Huckabee, "U. of California to Pay Surgeon $10-Million in Whistle-Blower Case," *The Chronicle of Higher Education* (April 23, 2014), at http://www.chronicle.com.proxy.library.nd.edu/blogs/ticker/u-of-california-to-pay-surgeon-10-million-in-whistle-blower-case/76415; Nick DeSantis, "Judge Increases Award to Whistle-Blower Who Sued Chicago State U." *The Chronicle of Higher Education* (March 12, 2014), at http://www.chronicle.com.proxy.library.nd.edu/blogs/ticker/jp/judge-increases-award-to-whistle-blower-who-sued-chicago-state-u; "University of California Davis: Retaliation Against Medical School Professor Over Newspaper Column," *Fire* (no date), at https://www.thefire.org/cases/university-of-california-davis-retaliation-against-medical-school-professor-over-newspaper-

column; Doug Lederman, "School May Have Retaliated," *Inside Higher Ed* (September 4, 2014), at https://www.insidehighered.com/news/2014/09/04/central-michigan-faces-charges-retaliation-against-professor; Colleen Flaherty, "Wesleyan Settles With Professor Who Alleged Harassment," *Inside Higher Ed* (September 9, 2016), at https://www.insidehighered. com/quicktakes/2016/09/19/wesleyan-settles-professor-who-alleged-harassment; "Dealing With School Retaliation," *Know Your IX* (no date), at http://knowyourix.org/dealing-with/ dealing-with-school-retaliation/.

7. See Wesley Shumar and Shabana Mir, "Cultural Anthropology Looks at Higher Education," in *A Companion to the Anthropology of Education*, ed. Bradley A. Levinson and Mica Pollock (Malden, MA and Oxford: Blackwell Publishing Ltd., 2011), pp. 445–60.

8. Pierre Bourdieu, *Homo Academicus* (Stanford: Stanford University Press, 1988); Bourdieu, *The State Nobility: Elite Schools in the Field of Power* (Stanford: Stanford University Press, 1996). Other exceptions include Brian McKinley Jones Brayboy, who writes on elite schools like that from which he earned his doctorate, the University of Pennsylvania, and Susan Blum, who gives over nine pages of her monograph treatment of higher education to the University of Notre Dame, and clearly views Notre Dame as part of the larger trends she discusses. See Brayboy, "Hiding in the Ivy: American Indian Students and Visibility in Elite Educational Settings," *Harvard Educational Review* 74, no. 2, pp. 125–52; Brayboy, "Transformational Resistance and Social Justice: American Indians in Ivy League Universities," *Anthropology and Education Quarterly* 36, no. 3, pp. 193–211; and Susan D. Blum, *I Love Learning, I Hate School: An Anthropology of College* (Ithaca, NY: Cornell University Press, 2016).

9. Pierre Bourdieu, *The Logic of Practice* (Stanford: Stanford University Press, 1990), pp. 30–41.

10. Michel de Certeau, "The Weakness of Believing: From the Body to Writing, A Christian Transit," in *The Certeau Reader*, ed. Graham Ward (Oxford: Blackwell Publishers, Ltd, 2000), p. 215.

11. Certeau also gives us the language to talk about another reason for turning my critique to Notre Dame. It is no secret in the academy that in recent years faculty participation in university governance has systematically been dismantled by administrators. Such marginalization of participation leaves faculty with little else but the possibility of what Certeau calls "tactical" responses—reactive, on-the-fly maneuvers typical of the disenfranchised, such as when faculty organized in response to administrators at Notre Dame moving, without due consultation or consent, the faculty's own retirement funds from one provider to another. Given that faculty, as faculty (as distinct from faculty who become administrators), have little or no decision-making power at Notre Dame, they lack the institutional base to have what Certeau calls "strategic" input—that is, input from institutionally established social locations that allow for advanced planning. In an institutional setting in which the advancement markers for research, teaching, and university service are, as one senior faculty member put it to me when I first arrived at Notre Dame, "Write, write, write; teach well enough; and don't be weird," the one strategic location granted to the professor is her written work. We are negligent if we do not bring the work that arises from this strategic location to bear on our home institutions. Michel de Certeau, *The Practice of Everyday Life* (Berkeley and Los Angeles: University of California Press, 1988). On the decline of faculty governance see, for instance, Larry G. Gerber, *The Rise and Decline of Faculty Governance: Professionalization and the Modern American University* (Baltimore: Johns Hopkins University Press, 2014); and Benjamin Ginsberg, *The Fall of the Faculty: The Rise of the All-Administrative University and Why It Matters* (Oxford and New York: Oxford University Press, 2011).

12. The closest quote to that given on the web pages that I could find in Sorin's own writings is this: "This college will be one of the most powerful means of doing good in this country."

Edward Sorin, *The Circular Letters of the Very Rev. Edward Sorin*, Vol I (Notre Dame, IN: Congregation of the Holy Cross, 1885), p. 261. The quote appears in a letter from Sorin, in the United States, to his religious superior, Basil Moreau, in France, in which the former justifies his informing the latter of the founding of Notre Dame only after the fact (otherwise an act of disobedience) by appealing to Providence. "Providence permitted that an offer should be made to us of a section of excellent land. . . . I waited from day to day the dispositions of Divine Providence in order to be able to give you some definite and positive information" (259). It is also precisely Providence that ensures that Notre Dame will be a force "for good."

Some critics of recent university practice cite the turn to lay leadership of the Board of Trustees and the forging of the Land O' Lakes agreement, which claimed that the university has independence from, "authority of whatever kind, lay or clerical, external to the academic community itself," as the source of the university going awry. I think that this interpretation is historically too shortsighted. The key turning point, in my judgment, is Sorin's blackballing of Basil Moreau in the Holy Cross congregation and his shift from Moreau's spirituality of the Cross to an emphasis on Providence that dovetailed too readily with the American Manifest Destiny ethos. This is the fundamental source of current university commercial expansionism. To be sure, corporate lay leadership of the Board has turbocharged the expansion, but the trajectory was there already. What this implies is that setting Notre Dame on a better track will require a turn to Moreau, not Sorin, as the primary source of inspiration. For the view that the key moment was Land O' Lakes, see, for instance, Charles Rice, *What Happened to Notre Dame?* (South Bend, IN: St. Augustine's Press, 2009). Ralph McInerny and Alfred J. Freddoso, also Notre Dame faculty, wrote the preface and introduction, respectively. See also, Patrick Reilly, "The Land O' Lakes Statement Has Caused Devastation for 49 Years," *The National Catholic Register* (July 20, 2016), at http://www.ncregister.com/blog/reilly/the-land-o-lakes-statement-has-caused-devastation-for-49-years.

13. On August 1, 2014, the Constitutional Court of Uganda ruled that the law was invalid because there was not a quorum. The government plans to appeal to the Supreme Court of Uganda to have the ruling overturned.

14. My account is based on the alumna's testimony.

15. The University of Notre Dame, "The Spirit of Notre Dame," from The University of Notre Dame, *du Lac: A Guide to Student Life*, at http://studenthandbook.nd.edu/university-mission-and-vision/spirit-of-inclusion/.

16. See Katie Galioto, "Worker Participation Committee Issues Official Recommendations," *The Observer* (September 1, 2015), at http://ndsmcobserver.com/2015/09/worker-participation-committee-issues-official-recommendations/. The article quotes the administrator as saying that Notre Dame is a "source" for good in the world, but, in keeping with institutional practice, he said "force." The structure of the logic is the same, however: appeal to the saying in order to reverse Notre Dame's enacted position on the right to organize in China.

17. President Jenkins made the announcement in a campus-wide letter. The letter refers to a "Worker Participation Committee (WPC), consisting of students, faculty and administrative leaders" from the Notre Dame community. However, two of the three research faculty who served on the committee voiced strong opposition to the proposed change in policy, and the one student who served on the committee while I was on it did not support the reversal of policy, but rather saw it as a foregone conclusion given committee dynamics. He threatened to step down from the committee unless it changed its initial grossly misleading name of, "Freedom of Association Committee." I myself stepped down from the committee because I could not in good conscience support what I also came to see as the fixed conclusion of its deliberations. The trajectory of the *administrators* on the committee was to reverse

the protection of freedom of association in the production of Notre Dame consumer goods, and the administrators were the primary drivers of the committee proceedings and recommendation. This is information that I can disclose because Executive Vice President John Affleck-Graves, the committee chair, made clear at a number of points that the committee's deliberations were not confidential. I do not know how much of the information about the lack of support for the policy reversal was given to President Jenkins. The full text of President Jenkins's letter is as follows:

Dear Students, Faculty and Staff,

As we begin the second half of the semester, I welcome students back from break and wish everyone well. I write to inform you of a decision that is explained briefly in the paragraph below and more fully in subsequent paragraphs.

Notre Dame is undertaking a pilot program with selected factories in China for the manufacture of University-licensed products to see if they can meet and sustain worker treatment standards in keeping with Catholic social teaching. The WPC, consisting of students, faculty and administrative leaders, recommended the pilot program in a report that can be found here. I have accepted the WPC's recommendation to establish a pilot program, through which Notre Dame seeks to further observance around the world of the full set of workers' rights recognized by Catholic social teaching. I summarize below the history of Notre Dame's policy and the reasoning which led to my decision to accept the WPC's recommendation.

The mission of Notre Dame calls us to live up to high moral standards, even as we admit our limitations and failings. I am proud, then, that under Fr. Edward Malloy, C.S.C., my predecessor, Notre Dame played a leading role in efforts to improve wages and working conditions in factories that manufacture Notre Dame-licensed products. In 1997 we were the first university to adopt a labor code of conduct for such factories. Notre Dame was also a founding member of the Fair Labor Association and a member of the Worker Rights Consortium. Today we remain committed to continuing this tradition of fighting for the rights of workers.

In Catholic social teaching, work is considered "a fundamental right and good for mankind," and workers have rights, such as the right to a just wage, reasonable work hours and appropriate rest, safe and healthy working conditions and pensions (Compendium of the Social Doctrine of the Church, 301). Catholic social teaching also recognizes an indispensable right of workers to form associations, such as labor and trade unions, to defend their vital interests and promote social justice (305).

The University of Notre Dame unequivocally recognizes workers' rights to associate in unions, and so in 2001 it implemented a policy that "prohibit(s) the manufacture of licensed products in all countries, without exception, which do not recognize the legal rights of workers to organize" (Notre Dame Report, February 11, 2000). Factories in eleven countries around the world were precluded by this policy from the manufacture of our licensed products. Among these was the People's Republic of China, by far the largest in population and manufacturing capacity.

The University's decision at that time was bold, principled and widely applauded. It was hoped that Notre Dame's action would encourage other institutions to follow, and that collectively pressure could be put on countries to reform their labor laws. However, as we look back, we find that no other universities have adopted similar policies, and Notre Dame's action has had no discernable influence on the practices of nations that deny freedom of association. It was reasonable, therefore, for the WPC to ask whether some other policy might be more effective in expressing the values of Notre Dame and furthering the recognition of workers' rights.

While still holding to the principle that freedom of association ought to be allowed and independent unions permitted, and recognizing that in the People's Republic of China such rights are denied at the level of national laws and practices, the WPC considered whether there might be other criteria we should employ focused on the policies and practices of particular factories, and whether adopting these criteria might encourage meaningful participation for line-workers in the factories with which we partner. Specifically, the WPC considered the character of communication, consultation and participation in decision-making that these workers enjoyed in factories under consideration.

The committee selected six factories and hired a nonprofit, internationally-recognized organization, Verite, to assist in evaluating these factories. Working with Verite, it formulated a list of 71 criteria on which six selected Chinese factories would be evaluated through online and in-person visits. In the assessment, Verite interviewed both management and workers, and great care was taken to ensure the anonymity of responses. In addition, members of the WPC committee traveled to these factories to observe conditions and speak to management and workers. The WPC concluded that two of the six factories met acceptable standards of worker participation as defined by the criteria, two required some improvements and two needed substantial improvements.

On the basis of their extensive deliberations, the committee recommended, first, that Notre Dame undertake a pilot program with factories that met our standards to see if they sustain a standard of performance acceptable to Notre Dame, and we can confidently verify such performance. The University will work with other factories that fell short of our standards to see if they can improve to an acceptable level. Second, Notre Dame should undertake a similar assessment of factories in countries that do allow freedom of association and which have been manufacturing Notre Dame-licensed products. The committee saw that, even with the formal, legal right to form and join an independent union, worker participation may be below what is acceptable, and the University can use its leverage to encourage improvement. Moreover, the review of factories in different countries could establish a useful benchmark as we deliberate about acceptable standards.

Third, the committee recommended that during the pilot program, the University should review and, as necessary, revise Notre Dame's Licensing Code of Conduct to see if it should address other human rights concerns, whether it should be revised to include a richer understanding of worker participation and, in general, that it reflects the best practices and the principles of Catholic social teaching. Fourth, a forum for continuing campus participation in these deliberations should be established, and a student subcommittee to the WPC should be formed.

Some have written to me urging that I reject these recommendations, arguing that the manufacture of our licensed products in a nation that does not allow freedom of association, which Catholic social teaching calls "an indispensable element of social life," is morally unacceptable. This is a complex question, and I will summarize my thinking.

In a world that is in many ways morally compromised, we often are faced with vexing questions about the morally acceptable degree and manner of cooperation with imperfect, objectionable practices. The means for evaluating such questions in the Catholic moral tradition comes from what is called the principle of cooperation with evil. According to this teaching, one is not allowed to cooperate with the unjust situation if one intends to support or sustain the injustice. This is called formal cooperation, and it is never morally licit. Certainly, in this case, Notre Dame does not intend to support the prohibition against freedom of association. One must then ask though, whether one contributes something essential to the evil action or situation in question. This would be called immediate material cooperation, and it is not morally licit. Again, it is clear that the prohibition against free association preceded our involvement, and Notre Dame will contribute nothing essential to its enactment or continuation.

Finally, we must ask whether our involvement contributes something, even if that contribution is not essential to the evil action or situation. This is called mediate material cooperation and may be morally justified. It can be argued that Notre Dame's involvement strengthens the Chinese economy and thereby contributes to the perpetuation of unjust laws. This contribution, however, is clearly insignificant when compared to the whole of the Chinese economy, and so involvement would be mediate and minimal. In such a case, one should then ask whether there are compelling reasons to justify participation, and it seems there clearly are—namely, participation allows us to affirm those factories that have high standards of worker participation, and to encourage other companies to meet these standards. Whether this in fact occurs is something about which a pilot program will give us valuable information.

For these reasons, I have accepted the recommendations of the WPC and directed the pilot program to begin.

I emphasize that this change in policy in no way signals a lessening of Notre Dame's commitment to the full set of workers' rights recognized by Catholic social teaching. On the contrary, with the WPC, we are trying to develop a policy that is as effective as it can be in furthering the recognition of those rights around the world. We will work with factories to encourage worker participation with the hope that, with time, the full set of workers' rights will be recognized and respected.

I thank the members of the WPC who have worked conscientiously to review our policy, formulate an alternative and engage our campus community in discussions. I also thank those who have, equally conscientiously, expressed criticism of the WPC proposals and have urged me to reject them. Discussion of difficult moral questions is healthy for any community, and particularly welcome here at Notre Dame. The WPC will continue to provide a forum for discussion as we undertake the pilot program.

In Notre Dame,

Rev. John I. Jenkins, C.S.C.
President

My response after the letter appeared as "China policy violates Catholic Social Teaching," *The Observer* (November 5, 2015), at http://ndsmcobserver.com/2015/11/china-policy-violates-catholic-social-teaching/.

18. More, President Jenkins wrote with gravity regarding the situations that prompt the appeal to the principle of cooperation with evil: "In a world that is in many ways morally compromised, we often are faced with vexing questions about the morally acceptable degree and manner of cooperation with imperfect, objectionable practices" (see note 17 above). Phrasing the issue this way makes it appear as if Notre Dame did not have other options. The fact of the matter, however, is that, again, the policy against production in China had been in place for fifteen years, and Notre Dame had successfully been making product elsewhere. There was no shortage of Notre Dame product. Therefore, the university was under no compulsion to produce in China. The principle justifies cooperation with evil if and only if there are no other viable options. President Jenkins's use of the principle, therefore, is again a misappropriation of it. President Jenkins and others suggested that the motive was to improve the conditions of workers in China, but this reasoning is problematic. Notre Dame produces a finite amount of product. To produce in China (where there is no recognition of freedom of association) therefore takes away from production in those countries where there is recognition of the freedom of association. In other words, if our concern is the overall well-being of workers, then the new China policy actually makes things worse.

I do not in any way doubt President Jenkins's sincerity or intellectual acuity (how many university presidents offer tradition-grounded arguments at all?), and there can be legitimate differences in the application of a principle, but that principle is not infinitely pliable.

19. During the debate over whether to reverse the policy of no production in China, advocates of the "powerful force for good" argument for reversal often appealed to the claim that it was

important to be "engaged" with a country in order to change it, the implication being that to openly advocate for the right of freedom of association was to be disengaged. What the "engaged" claim masks is that, as we have now seen, it implements a selective disengagement of its own: silence on human rights issues in favor of institutional expansion of university programs, projects, and now consumer goods. If Notre Dame really sought to be "engaged" in China in a fully Catholic manner, a good place to start would be to find ways to support the underground (because suppressed) Catholic Church there. Again, I do not doubt that one can sometimes legitimately make specific, occasion-dependent trade-offs in favor of programs and projects (I have my doubts in the instance of trade-offs in favor of the production of consumer goods); my concern is that the institutional trajectory of expansion appears to presumptively override human rights concerns whenever the two come in conflict.

The other term (in addition to "engagement") that those who wanted to reverse the policy often brought up was that of "leadership." The term, drawn heavily from the business world, is currently in high use among academic institutions in explaining their missions. In the present case, the argument was that, given that no other schools followed Notre Dame in refusing to make product in China, the policy must be necessarily mistaken: no one followed us; therefore we were leading wrongly; therefore the policy is wrong. The language in President Jenkins's own letter (see note 17 above) was, "As we look back, we find that no other universities have adopted similar policies" to Notre Dame's against production in China. With its prime indicator being what *other* schools are doing, such a view of leadership is vacuous, empty of any substantive content. The lack of content is even more evident when interrogated on Christian grounds: Was Jesus's crucifixion a mistake because his disciples did not follow him immediately to the Cross? The policy of no production in China cost Notre Dame far less than going to the Cross; it cost the university almost nothing. The irony is that the claim of "leadership"—like the claim of "engagement"—masks that in practice it really is its opposite, in this case a form of *following* other schools in violating the right of worker freedom of association. They are doing it, the hidden logic goes, therefore so should we.

20. In fact, at one point in his statement, President Jenkins writes that the Executive Vice President's recommendation followed "other criteria" than those of Catholic teaching on human rights. See note 17 above.

21. The only mode of resistance on the part of the Holy Cross congregation that I can imagine is if the priests and brothers, in an effort to reclaim their original charism, refused to forward any candidate for the presidency who did not see the importance of curbing the expansionist commercial ethos.

22. There is a seventh game each year that is called a "home" game as part of Notre Dame's "Shamrock Series," but it actually takes place on a neutral site elsewhere in the country as part of an effort to expand the Notre Dame brand.

23. http://news.nd.edu/news/6806-nbc-notre-dame-extend-football-agreement-through-2010/. Retrieved June 26, 2014.

24. http://www.und.com/sponsorship/nd-corporate-sponsors-opportunities.html. Retrieved June 26, 2014.

25. Mike Vorel, "Notre Dame Football Stays Ahead of the Curve on Social Media," *NDInsider, South Bend Tribune* (August 29, 2016), at http://m.ndinsider.com/football/notre-dame-football-stays-ahead-of-the-curve-on-social/article_f3029a62-6e1b-11e6-8cc4-7bd8a7383e71.html. At the time of the statement, Elston was linebackers coach; at present (June 2017) he is the defensive line coach.

26. Ibid.

27. Ibid., Coach Elston suggests the social media push is less about fundamental principles as usually understood and more about attracting recruits. "A kid is tweeting. What's his interests? OK, well he likes Jay Z. When he comes to campus, what can we do for him with Jay Z?" This is the plan even though Jay Z has rapped in the song, "No Church in the Wild": "We formed a new religion/No sins as long as there's permission/And deception is the only felony/So never fuck nobody without telling me."

28. May 14, 2016; saved in screenshot.

29. http://espn.go.com/college-football/story/_/id/10328133/notre-dame-fighting-irish-armour-agree-most-valuable-apparel-contract-ncaa-history. Retrieved June 26, 2014.

30. With the statue at Notre Dame in mind, it is worth noting that when Moses came off of Mt. Sinai, he had to plea with Yahweh not to punish his people for their idolatry: "So Moses returned to the Lord and said, "Alas, this people has sinned a great sin; they have made for themselves gods of gold" (Exodus 32.21).

31. Roger Ebert, "*Rudy*," *The Chicago Sun-Times* (October 10, 1993).

32. http://www.mlive.com/wolverines/index.ssf/2013/09/michigan-notre_dame_nets_an_av.html, and http://espnmediazone.com/us/press-releases/2012/11/notre-dame-usc-abcs-most-viewed-regular-season-college-football-game-since-2006/.

33. Evidence of the seriousness of the spiritual-material nexus in the university's relationship with its contracted companies is in the fact that when the university appointed an "anti-sweatshop task force" to recommend worker rights policies for the licensees who make Notre Dame-branded products, the administration took up every one of the task force's recommendations except one that called for a "conscience clause" that allows athletes to opt out of wearing the contracted company apparel (an alternative in all other ways similar to the contracted jersey would be provided) if the athlete, with an informed conscience, objected to the labor practices of the contracted company. In that instance, at any rate, the spiritual-material nexus is such that while conscientious objection is allowed in war, it is not in collegiate sports.

34. Aristotle, *Nichomachean Ethics*, in Jonathan Barnes, ed., *The Complete Works of Aristotle*, Vol. II (Princeton: Princeton University Press, 1984), pp. 1120a24–25.

35. Ibid., pp. 1120b7–9.

36. Ibid., pp. 1120b23–24.

37. See W. F. R. Hardie, "Aristotle's Doctrine that Virtue is a 'Mean,'" in *Articles on Aristotle, 2: Ethics and Politics*, ed. Jonathan Barnes, Malcolm Schofield, and Richard Sorabji (New York: St. Marin's Press, 1977), pp. 33–46; and J.O. Urmson, "Aristotle's Doctrine of the Mean," in *Essays on Aristotle's Ethics*, ed. Amélie Oksenberg Rorty (Berkeley, Los Angeles, and London: University of California Press, 1980), pp. 157–70.

38. Aristotle, *Nicomachean Ethics*, pp. 1121a20–29.

39. Aristotle intends the *Ethics* for citizens, which for him excluded women.

40. Aristotle, *Nicomachean Ethics*, pp. 1122a26–29.

41. Ibid., pp. 1122b26–29.

42. Ibid., pp. 1122b2–3.

43. Ibid., pp. 1123a19–31.

44. Ibid., p. 1122b35.

45. Aristotle's reference to the large gifts as being the "most honorable" indicates his central focus is not on the giving per se, but on the honor that redounds upon the person who

gives. This is why I follow Jonathan Barnes's translation of μεγαλοπρέπεια/megaloprépeia as "magnificence" as more apt than "beneficence" or "magnanimity," the latter two of which place focus more on discrete acts of good toward the other rather than the full life of honor and the quality of the person who gives. Put another way, the central purpose of acts of magnificence, in Aristotle's account, is less to give to others than to contribute to the honor of the person who gives, rendering the giver magnificent. See, for instance, Jonathan Barnes, ed., *The Complete Works of Aristotle*, Vol. II (Princeton: Princeton University Press, 1984), especially *Nicomachean Ethics*, 1122a ff.

46. For opinions that hold that the Campus Crossroads Project is vulgar, see, for instance, Nathaniel Gotcher, "An Ill-conceived Bragging Point," *The Observer* (January 30, 2014), at http://ndsmcobserver.com/2014/01/ill-conceived-bragging-point/; Colin Fleming, "Redirect Crossroads," *The Observer* (February 13, 2014), at http://ndsmcobserver.com/2014/02/redirect-crossroads/.; Robert Alvarez, "Beyond the Crossroads," *The Observer* (February 25, 2014), at http://ndsmcobserver.com/2014/02/beyond-crossroads/. For an editorial that argues that the project is beneficial—in Aristotle's terms, "magnificent"—see Observer Editorial Board, "Campus at a Crossroads," *The* Observer (January 30, 2014), at http://ndsmcobserver.com/2014/01/campus-at-a-crossroads/. In the face of ongoing campus criticism of the project, the editorial board wrote a second piece. See Observer Editorial Board, "Building a Better Future," *The Observer* (March 27, 2014), at http://ndsmcobserver.com/2014/03/building-better-future/.

47. See http://crossroads.nd.edu/. The narrative continues, "We dare to be uncommon," though there are questions as to just how uncommon the Campus Crossroads Project is. Florida State University and the University of Nebraska already have stadiums which have added-on academic space. In all three cases, there is also question as to just how much in the way of "connections," as the video puts it, between the football activity and the academic activity actually takes place; but again, the point here is that the conversation is in Aristotelian rather than Christian terms.

48. *Campus Crossroads* (brochure sent to major university donors; the PDF copy I obtained listed no specific author or publisher information, and contains no date of publication).

49. Tyler James, "New Prices for Notre Dame Football Tickets Range from $45 to $250," *NDInsider* (February 4, 2017), at http://www.ndinsider.com/football/new-prices-for-notre-dame-football-tickets-range-from-to/article_8b05240a-ea32-11e6-8cc3-6b666ef25c7a.html.

50. The 2016 poverty line for a family of three is $20,090. The poverty level for a family of four is $24,250. For poverty levels, see https://www.parkviewmc.com/app/files/public/1484/2016-Poverty-Level-Chart.pdf. Again, the 2016 starting salary for grounds crew at Notre Dame is $18,943; that for custodial workers is even lower, $17,539. See http://hr.nd.edu/compensation/overview/#/facilities/grounds and http://hr.nd.edu/compensation/overview/#/facilities/custodial. The 2016 starting salary for departmental office staff is as low as $20,837. See http://hr.nd.edu/compensation/overview/#/general-administration/department-administration. The arrangement that requires $3.4 million for a pod of eight of the best seats for football games comes to $21,250 per seat per year. That amount is over $2,300 to $3,700 *more* for a single season football ticket than is paid in the entire starting annual salary of the grounds and custodial workers.

In February 2017, the university announced new ticket pricing, lowering the worst seats for the least desired games to $45 so as to make going to at least some games affordable. It is important to read this move against the longer trend. Staff, many who otherwise would not be able to attend games, used to get season tickets (and thus decent tickets to *all* games) 50 percent off. Later that was reduced to 20 percent off. Still later, they were required to pay full price, pricing them out of the market for season tickets. So what began as being able to afford decent seats to all of the games has become affordability of bad seats for games likely to be lopsided and performed in the cold rain of November. See Alex Carson and Renee Griffin, "University announces changes to football ticket structure, lottery system," *The Observer* (February 4, 2017), at http://ndsmcobserver.com/2017/02/university-announces-changes-football-ticket-structure-lottery-system/.

51. Nelson D. Schwartz, "In an Age of Privilege, Not Everyone Is in the Same Boat," *The New York Times* (April 24, 2016), at https://www.nytimes.com/2016/04/24/business/economy/velvet-rope-economy.html?_r=0.

52. Raj Chetty, John N. Friedman, Emmanuel Saez, Nicholas Turner, Danial Yagan, "Mobility Report Cards: The Role of Colleges in Intergenerational Mobility," at http://www.equality-of-opportunity.org/assets/documents/coll_mrc_paper.pdf.

53. For easily accessible data, see, "The Upshot: Some Colleges Have More Students From the Top 1 Percent Than the Bottom 60 Percent. Find Yours," *The New York Times* (January 18, 2017), at https://www.nytimes.com/interactive/2017/01/18/upshot/some-colleges-have-more-students-from-the-top-1-percent-than-the-bottom-60.html?action=click&contentCollection=Opinion&module=Trending&version=Full&region=Marginalia&pgtype=article; and "The Upshot: Economic diversity and student outcomes at Notre Dame," *The New York Times*, at https://www.nytimes.com/interactive/projects/college-mobility/notre-dame.

54. Suzanne Monyak, "Legacy Tips Admissions Scales," *The Hoya* (March 20, 2015), at http://www.thehoya.com/legacy-status-tips-admission-scales/.

55. Aristotle, *Nichomachean Ethics*, p. 1120a24.

56. Aristotle adds that "gratitude" is the proper attitude of the beneficiaries. Ibid., pp. 1120a15–17.

57. This is the case even though Thomas Aquinas and Pius XI pick up Aristotle's concept of magnificence. See Aquinas, *Summa Theologica*, II-IIae, q. 134; and Pius XI, Quadragesimo Anno, 51.

58. The sale included a Facebook page with the heading, "OWN A PIECE OF THE FIELD: An exclusive opportunity to own an authentic piece of the grass field from historic Notre Dame Stadium." People were supposed to post what they did with the sod ("Where will you put it in your Domer Den?"). However, most of the page's comments, suggest that the sale is more vulgar than magnificent. Examples: "Historic? Since the field was sodded 2x last year, the sod's about as historic as the plastic cups"; "I am a proud ND alum, but right now I am hanging my head in shame. The stupidity of this is mindboggling"; "The only way to salvage this debacle a little bit is to donate the proceeds to charity"; "The university should be embarrassed with this one"; "$9 billion endowment and we're selling grass?"; "Is Notre Dame really that desperate for $$$. Cheesy idea from a small mind"; and "This is a joke, right?" https://www.facebook.com/FightingIrish/photos/a.420430759704.182747.112669694704/10152491848774705/?type=1&relevant_count=1 and http://fidm.nd.edu/grass/. The university did not heed the comments, and is now (June 2017) selling the old wood seating benches as the new benches are put in. See Alex Carson and Renee Griffin, "University announces changes to football ticket structure, lottery system," *The Observer* (February 4, 2017), at http://ndsmcobserver.com/2017/02/university-announces-changes-football-ticket-structure-lottery-system/.

59. Aristotle, *Nicomachean Ethics*, pp. 1123a6–7.

60. Ibid., pp. 1123a5–6.

61. Whereas magnificence relates to the giving of large amounts of wealth, "greatness of soul" pertains to true or justified honor per se (*Nicomachean Ethics*, pp. 1123a21–24).

The magnificent person gives in a way proportionate to his great wealth; the great-souled person is due—and views himself as due—honor in proportion to his all-around excellence or virtue, especially in relation to the common good of the *polis*. If he views himself as deserving of more honor than he is due, then he is vain, less and he is unduly humble (1123b16). Significantly, though the virtue concerns what is the rightly due honor, the great-souled person is not overly concerned with whether others consider him honorable, and is willing to speak frankly regarding what he takes to be true even if it leads to not receiving due honor. It is important for Aristotle, therefore, that the great-souled person be a truly good and just person, and not simply someone who is accounted as good or just by others. In fact, such a person "must be good in the highest degree" so as to be only moderately concerned with bestowed honor or the lack thereof.

62. Most current scholars reject Aristotle's (and by extension, Aquinas's) theory of the unity of the virtues. For an overview of the literature and a defense of a modified theory of the unity of the virtues, see Christopher Toner, "The Full Unity of the Virtues," *Journal of Ethics* 18 (2014), pp. 207–27.

63. See Cathy Cockrell, "Scheper-Hughes on her Church's Sins (and *Spotlight's*)," *Berkeley News* (February 16, 2016), at http://news.berkeley.edu/2016/02/11/scheper-hughes-on-her-churchs-sins-and-spotlights/.

64. Nancy Scheper-Hughes, "The Slow Death of the Roman Catholic Church" (titled, "What's a Catholic to Do When Her Church is Corrupt and Moribund" in the print version), *CounterPunch* (November 18, 2011), at http://www.counterpunch.org/2011/11/18/exclusively-in-the-new-print-issue-of-counterpunch/.

65. I am indebted to my colleague, John Fitzgerald, for these points on the status of Samaritans in ancient Israel. Correspondence, June 29, 2015.

66. For an excellent treatment of anthropologists who are also Roman Catholic Christian, see Timothy Larsen, *The Slain God: Anthropologists & the Christian Faith* (Oxford: Oxford University Press, 2014). After discussing the turn away from religion as outmoded by the advance of science by Edward Burnett Tylor and James George Frazer, the book has chapters on the faith of E.E. Evans-Pritchard, Mary Douglas, and Victor and Edith Turner.

67. Nancy Scheper-Hughes, "The Primacy of the Ethical: Propositions for a Militant Anthropology," in *Anthropology in Theory: Issues in Epistemology*, ed. Henrietta L. Moore and Todd Sanders (Malden, MA and Oxford: Blackwell Publishing, 2006), pp. 410–11.

68. Davis, Dana-Ain, "Knowledge in the Service of a Vision: Politically Engaged Anthropology," in *Engaged Observer: Anthropology, Advocacy, and Activism*, ed. Victoria Sanford and Asale Angel-Ajani (New Brunswick, NJ and London: Rutgers University Press, 2008), p. 231.

69. Scheper-Hughes, "The Primacy of the Ethical," pp. 419 and 418.

70. Ibid., pp. 410–13.

71. On anthropology's rejection of theology as an interlocutor discipline, see Eloise Meneses, Lindy Backues, David Bronkema, Eric Flett, and Benjamin L. Hartley, "Engaging the Religiously Committed Other: Anthropologists and Theologians in Dialogue," *Current Anthropology* 55, no. 1 (February 2014), pp. 82–104. See also Charles Stewart, "Secularism as an Impediment to Anthropological Research," *Social Anthropology* 9, no. 3 (2001), pp. 323–8; Henri Gooren, "Anthropology of Religious Conversion," in *The Oxford Handbook of Religious Conversion*, ed. Lewis R. Rambo and Charles E. Farhadian (Oxford and New York: Oxford University Press, 2014), p. 111, note 144; Claude E. Stipe, "Anthropologists Versus Missionaries: The Influence of Presuppositions," *Current Anthropology* 21, no. 2 (1980), pp. 165–79; and Joel Robbins, "Social Thought and Commentary: Anthropology and Theology: An Awkward Relationship?," *Anthropological Quarterly* 79, no. 2 (Spring 2006), pp. 285–94.

72. Scheper-Hughes, "The Primacy of the Ethical," p. 419.

73. Philippe Bourgois, "Confronting the Ethics of Ethnography: Lessons from Fieldwork in Central America," in *Ethnographic Fieldwork: An Anthropological Reader*, ed. Antonius C. G. M. Robben and Jeffrey A. Sluka (Malden, MA and Oxford: Blackwell Publishing, 2007), p. 297. Though it is not evoked in a situation of physical risk, we can add to the quasi-theological turn in language with ethnographers who seek solidarity with their subjects the otherwise anti-religious Pierre Bourdieu, when he refers, with echoes of Ignatius of Loyola, to his interview technique as a "spiritual exercise." See Pierre Bourdieu, et al., *The Weight of the World: Social Suffering in Contemporary Society* (Stanford, CA: Stanford University Press, 1999), p. 612ff.

74. For an excellent presentation of the contrasting presuppositions between the "normal justice" worldview and that of a more "skeptical" tradition regarding justice, see Judith Shklar, *The Faces of Injustice* (New Haven, CT: Yale University Press, 1992).

75. John Paul II, *Sollicitudo rei Socialis*, par. 35.

76. Ibid., par. 38.

77. Ibid., par. 40.

78. Scheper-Hughes, "The Primacy of the Ethical," pp. 418–19.

79. The response is sometimes given to the example of such a life that is willing to lay itself down that the Church is founded upon Peter, who was imperfect and even denied Christ three times; but that is the pre-Resurrection Peter, and given that we are a post-Resurrection community, the post-Resurrection Peter, who does lay down his life, is our true exemplar of what a life in Christ looks like.

80. John Paul II, *Veritatis Splendour*, pars. 90 and 93.

81. When she met Pope Francis at a Vatican conference in 2015, Scheper-Hughes came away thinking in reference to her lack of belief, "All of a sudden I felt like, 'Well, maybe I'll reconsider this [loss of faith].'" See Cathy Cockrell, "Scheper-Hughes on her church's sins (and *Spotlight's*)."

82. Frank Pallotta, "Super Bowl XLIX Posts the Largest Audience in TV History," *CNN Money* (February 2, 2015), at http://money.cnn.com/2015/02/02/media/super-bowl-ratings/. The number does not reflect those who watched the game in sports bars or at viewing parties. Including these populations would increase the number dramatically. Mark Lazarus, the chairman of NBC Sports, which broadcast the game, called the Super Bowl, "the most dominant and consistent property on television." See Pallotta, "Super Bowl XLIX Posts the Largest Audience in TV History."

83. An exception, of course, would be the minority sub-discipline calling itself "practical theology." Here, the exception proves the rule, as the felt need to use the qualifier "practical" affirms both its minority status and the theoretical/practical split.

84. Pierre Bourdieu, *The Logic of Practice* (Stanford, CA: Stanford University Press, 1990), pp. 1–51.

85. Bourdieu, *The Logic of Practice*, pp. 105 and 107.

86. Ibid., pp. 27–8 and 31.

87. Aristotle, *Nicomachean Ethics*, pp. 1177a11–b26. I am aware of the interpretation that this passage in Book X conflicts with passages elsewhere in the text, but find Arthur Adkins's argument to be convincing that, in the end, Aristotle is consistent and that Book X is the controlling view. Adkins is also helpful in noting that *theoria* is not research, but contemplation of knowledge that we already have. See A.W.H. Adkins, "*Theoria* Versus *Praxis* in The *Nicomachean Ethics* and The *Republic*," *Classical Philology* 73, no. 4 (October 1978), pp. 297–313.

88. Bourdieu, *The Logic of Practice*, p. 125.

89. Ibid., pp. 73, 104 and 103.

90. Ibid., pp. 73, 102, and 103–4.

91. Ibid., p. 104.

92. Alasdair MacIntyre, *After Virtue: A Study in Moral Theory* (London and New York: Bloomsbury Academic), p. 228.

93. Erich Auerbach, *Mimesis: The Representation of Reality in Western Literature* (Princeton and Oxford: Princeton University Press, 2003), pp. 47–8 and 11–12.

94. Clifford Geertz, *The Interpretation of Cultures* (New York: Basic Books, 1973), pp. 3–31.

95. The practitioners of the desired practices need not be people regarded as Christian; in fact, Jesus regularly featured protagonists not from the people of Israel in his stories as a means of both pointing to a reality and giving the accounts a particular rhetorical edge.

96. Weis could still be (and has been) successful as an assistant coach where he is more responsible for the abstract "x's and o's" of the playbook than embodied practice.

97. See, for instance, Ray Fitipaldo, "Hall of Fame Players as NFL Coaches are a Rare Breed," *Pittsburgh Post-Gazette* (September 6, 2013), at http://www.post-gazette.com/sports/steelers/2013/09/06/Hall-of-Fame-players-as-NFL-coaches-a-rare-breed/stories/201309060129.

98. It is generally agreed that the "gnostic gospels" were written between the second and fourth centuries. The Gospel of John, the most gnostic-like of the canonical gospels was written last and is the least historical of the gospels.

99. Michael Taussig is clear regarding the mimetic potential of ethnographic writing. Writing about the work of Stephanie Kane, he says, "I want to emphasize that unlike most ethnographic modes of representation . . . Stephanie Kame's mode relies not on abstract general locutions as 'among the Emberá it is believed that. . . . ,' but instead concentrates on image-ful particularity in such a way that . . . she creates a magical reproduction itself, a sensuous sense of the real, mimetically at one with what it attempts to represent. In other words, can't we say that *to give an example, to instantiate, to be concrete*, are all examples of the magic of mimesis wherein the replication, the copy, acquires the power of the represented? And does not the magical power of this embodying inhere in the fact that in reading such examples we are thereby lifted out of ourselves into those images? Just as the shaman captures and creates power by making a model of the gringo-spirit-ship and its crew, so here the ethnographer is making her model. If I am correct in making this analogy with what I take to be the magician's art of reproduction, then the model, if it works, gains through its sensuous fidelity something of the power and personality of that which it is a model." Michael Taussig, *Mimesis and Alterity: A Particular History of the Senses* (New York and London: Routledge, 1993), p. 16.

APPENDIX
FROM GOSPEL MIMESIS TO "THEOLOGY": HOW A DISCIPLINE LOST ITS SENSES

It is perhaps my most vivid memory from graduate school. Fifteen minutes before my first comprehensive examination—one of five four-hour marathon tests of intellectual stamina to take place over the next week-and-a-half. John Yoder would later chide me that no exam can be comprehensive, and that it was a sign of the University of Chicago's *hubris* that it designates them as such. But, I would insist, our theology and political theory exam is so extensive that we call it "From Plato to NATO," and the History of Theological and Philosophical Ethics exam—no rhyming nickname, just the reaffirming knowledge that Yale has to divide it into two exams and allow the use of books and notes—is even more extensive. That exam is where I am headed now.

I cross 57th Street from Regenstein Library to the main quad, my eyes still adjusting to the sun. Harvard's Widener Library may go six floors underground, but there is no room to study down by those stacks. Regenstein offers large tables with chairs among the columns of books in back rooms whose gray diffusion is only intermittently interrupted by hesitant dust-moted shafts of light that enter through narrow slot windows.[1]

As I enter the quad, most of the action is taking place inside my head. I am sure that the exam will ask about the relationship between the theological and cardinal virtues in Thomas Aquinas because an hour ago I came across a passage from the *Prima Pars* of his *Summa Theologica* that upended everything I thought I knew about his work.

"No. Can't be right. 'It is impossible for our intellect to understand anything actually, except by *conversio ad phantasma*, the turning to phantasms'? Knowledge of God only through comparison to sensory objects? The imagination building upon the senses?[2] *All* understanding 'makes use of a corporate organ'? "

"*What about the theological virtues?*" The oral examiner who has taken up residence in the frontal lobe of my cerebral cortex as of late is insistent.

I am ready.

"I answer that, They cannot be known through natural means; they can only be 'infused in us by God alone . . . not made known to us, save by Divine revelation.'"

Even Thomas—or at least the Fathers of the English Dominican Province— puts it in italics.

"That '*which God works in us without us.*' The Angelic Doctor says, 'God can produce the effects of second causes without the second causes in order to show his power.'"

I know this stuff. Now the quiet ox tells me that all understanding comes through the 'sensitive part'? Oh nonononono. The intellect does not need the 'corporate organ' in *this* theology. Question-objection-answer-reply to objection. Ee-i-ee-i-o! Auerbach is right. Theology turns *away* from the senses and the imagination. *Conversio **ab** phantasma. Conversio ad phantasma*? Not fair. Not now.

Then, on the quad, I catch something bright out of the corner of my eye, and turn. There is a man lying directly on the grass with nothing on but a pair of white cut-offs. His skin is translucent, the kind found almost exclusively among graduate students, and it seems as if he, too, has just emerged from the library. It is not much of an epiphany, I know. But I become aware that I am still wearing the winter coat that I got six months ago in December, when I started studying for exams; and that beneath that I have on a thick turtleneck. I become aware that it is warm out. I feel something of a distant solidarity with Nearly Naked Man.

Ten minutes to exam time.

"Suppress it. The *Prima Pars* is not on the bibliography."

The Auerbach I was thinking of is Erich Auerbach, author of *Mimesis*, a book that *Washington Post* reviewer Michael Dirda concluded was "arguably the single greatest work of twentieth-century criticism," and that prompted literary critic Fredric Jameson to insist, "To describe *Mimesis* as a classic is to offer something of a dismissive understatement." The central interpretive thread of *Mimesis* is the contrast between two traditions of representing reality. The first, rooted in ancient Greece, is marked by a "separation of styles" whereby "the realistic depiction of daily life was incompatible with the sublime." The two styles are realized in separate genres of writing: comedy, which portrays daily life, and tragedy, which depicts dramatic pendulations, yet in a manner detached from the everyday. Oedipus' twists of fate take place, "outside the usual course of events" and "affects only one person or a few people, while the rest of the world appears to remain apart from it."[3] The second tradition, developing in the Old and New Testament literatures, violates, at its core, the rule of the separation of styles. Dramatic events of cosmological significance take place in and through the lives of ordinary people, and while there might not be the amount of detail as that found in a Homeric epic, the characters' roles in a larger history give them a distinctive historical-like particularity unmatched in Greek and Roman literature.[4]

The hybrid style, Auerbach laments, would not last. It "very soon happened" that "interpretation reached such proportions that the real vanished" from Christian literature.[5] What happened? Auerbach recognizes that there were Hellenistic influences in the gospels, but argues that such influences were at first limited because the subject of the gospels—God acting through an ordinary and even lowly person—did not fit the received separation of genres.[6] However, resistance to the gospel message in Jerusalem required Paul's redirection of the mission toward the Gentiles, and the flow of influence reversed. In adapting the message "to the preconceptions of a far wider audience" the new kerygma reduced the dramatic and particular characters of salvation history to a "series of figures" of legend. "The total content of the sacred writings was placed in an exegetic context which often removed the thing told very far from its sensory base, in that the reader was forced to turn his attention away from the sensory occurrence and towards its meaning." In such a context, "the sensory occurrence pales before the power of the figural meaning."[7]

Such a loss of dramatic particularity would be of only (though importantly) aesthetic consequence were it not for the way in which, as Auerbach makes clear, form and substance, style and doctrine, combine:

> The Scripture stories do not, like Homer's, court our favor, they do not flatter us that they may please us and enchant us—they seek to subject us, and if we refuse to be subjected we are rebels. Let no one object that this goes too far, that not the stories, but the religious doctrine, raises the claim to absolute authority; because the stories are not, like Homer's, simply narrated "reality." Doctrine and promise are incarnate in them and inseparable from them. . . . *Doctrine and the search for enlightenment are inextricably connected with the physical side of the narrative—* the latter being more than simple "reality"; indeed they are in constant danger of losing their own reality (emphasis added).[8]

Auerbach also makes clear that the primary doctrine at stake in the stylistic shift from sensory concreteness to a mode where the "real" vanishes is the Incarnation—a point that has all the more force when we realize that Auerbach is Jewish.

> Of course, this mingling of styles [in the gospels] is not dictated by an artistic purpose. On the contrary, it was rooted from the beginning in the character of Jewish-Christian literature; it was graphically and harshly dramatized through God's incarnation in a human being of the humblest social station, through his existence on earth amid humble everyday people and conditions, and through his Passion which, judged by earthly standards, was ignominious.[9]

In doctrinal terms, the shift away from sensory concreteness in Christian literature entails a de facto (however much objections to the charges might be raised) docetism (the belief that God in Christ only seemed to, but did not really, become human). It may be the case that Thomas Aquinas *claims* that all understanding is acquired through the senses, but he does not *write* as if this were true. Thus my confusion as an anxious graduate student.[10] The style of writing in what came to be known formally as "theology" beginning in the twelfth century is indeed characterized in its representation of the world by a determined turn *away* from the senses, a *conversio ab phantasma*, and with such a turn it commits an ongoing doctrinal performative contradiction: incarnational doctrine conveyed through an abstract disembodied writing style. More, given, following

Gregory of Nazianzus, that "what is not assumed is not redeemed,"[11] writing theology in a mode that vanishes the real (to use Auerbach's terminology) denies the doctrine of redemption as well.[12] To put the point directly, if Auerbach is right, then the genre of "theology" as it is practiced in the academy is itself a performance of doctrinal error.

This performative problem currently takes place even among those theologians who insist on the specificity of the Christian narrative and the importance of the depiction of embodied Christian practices as a necessary mode of doing theology. Catherine Pickstock identifies and groups these theologians when she comments, "It seems to me that there are no sharp boundaries between radical orthodoxy and other identifiable tendencies within what one might generically call post-secular theology: one can mention, for example, the Yale School [and] Radical Traditions at Duke University."[13]

The "Yale School" includes, foremost, Hans Frei, who died in 1988, and George Lindbeck, who passed in 2018. Frei's most well-known book decries the "eclipse of biblical narrative," and his later writings, in part influenced by Auerbach, call for the recovery of the *sensus literalis*—the literal sense—of scripture.[14] Retrieving the literal sense, Frei argues, would mean, among other things, doing theology in a way that involves Christian "self-description" that "is closer to the social sciences than to philosophy," and similar to "Clifford Geertz's view of ethnography, or cultural anthropology, as 'thick description.'"[15] In keeping with Auerbach's linkage of correct doctrine and the realism of biblical genre, Frei distinguishes his proposal from much of cultural anthropology by making clear that it is precisely the particular Christian narrative that drives his case for concrete particularity. "I am not proposing or arguing a general anthropology. I am precisely *not* claiming that narrative sequence is the built-in constitution of the human being phenomenologically uncovered. That may or may not be the case. Rather, I am suggesting that it is narrative specificity through which we describe an intentional-agential world and ourselves in it. If there *is* a 'narrative theology,' the meaning of that term in the context of the self-description of the Christian community is that we are specified by relation to its particular narrative and by our conceptual redescription of it in belief and life, not by a quality of 'narrativity' inherent in our picture of self, world, and transcendence at large."[16] Frei here is consonant with Lindbeck's "cultural linguistic" epistemology: ethnography makes sense only to elaborate the Christian story.[17] So far so good; but then Frei (Lindbeck does not directly confront the issue of the necessity of concreteness) bails out on the project he proposes. His writing remains, in his words, "a strictly second-order affair, commenting on theories pertinent to the past as well as present and future *conditions* for the literal reading as a religious enterprise; it is neither an exercise within that traditional enterprise, nor even an argument on behalf of its continued viability" (emphasis in original).[18]

Though he is now no longer at the institution, Stanley Hauerwas is the chief representative of what Pickstock calls the "Radical Traditions at Duke University." Like Frei, he stresses the importance of narrative for shaping the life of Christian communities. In particular, he gives priority to Jesus' life as an exemplification of what it means to live in accordance with the Kingdom. Hauerwas is clear that relating the life of Jesus to God in this way in no way denies that Jesus is the Christ, only that claims about his being the anointed one and the son of God, "are subsequent to the whole life of this man whom God has claimed as decisive to his own for the presence of his kingdom in this world." When Christians seek to imitate Jesus, they find themselves "distinctive," "apart," "peculiar," "interesting," and even "entertaining" in relation to the world. The result is "a polity unlike any other."[19]

Hauerwas insists that this polity, the church, is "an empirical reality." Thus Christology is socio-Christology. He pushes the emphasis on the lived imitation of Christ even further and declares, "The church does not have a social ethic; the church *is* a social ethic."[20] However, Hauerwas, like Frei, does not make use of the social sciences to aid perspicacious depiction of that social ethic which the church embodies. Despite his emphasis on the necessity of the narrative display of Jesus and Christ-like people for readers and listeners to learn to "imitate a master," there is little descriptive detail in his work. He sometimes tells of an incident to launch an article, or, in homiletic style, to illustrate a point, but there is no sustained account, nothing approaching a "thick description." The article most like an ethnography in its analysis of lived detail is his account of a novel, *Watership Down*.[21]

There is a moment near the end of *Theology and Social Theory* when John Milbank, the foremost progenitor of the self-named intellectual school "radical orthodoxy," compares the "well-made deed" to a picture which "admits the sublime within the scope of its beauty."[22] If we imagine a film rather than a single snapshot, we get the kind of narrative that, together with a more speculative form of theology, Milbank endorses.[23] Detailing a narrative "elaborates also a distinctive practice . . . which cannot be fully dealt with in the style of theoretical theology." In fact, speculative theology, "properly understood," not only does not turn away from the particular—a *conversio ab phantasma*—but, on the contrary, "*demands* a return to the concrete, narrative level" (emphasis added).[24] When we encounter such concrete narrative, "we are invited to enter into it as an opening to what lies beyond it. And this opening must entrance us, we must be seduced. . . . It is not just that the infinite calls out to our freedom to affirm its own incomprehensibility, but also that the infinite is opened out along a particular path, and *within* the scene we become a free, but concretely desiring subject" (emphasis in original).[25]

For Milbank, Jesus of Nazareth, as depicted in the gospels, enacts this narrative such that it becomes possible for the church to do so as well in the form of a re-narration—a "Christian emergence"—in its practices. Theology here goes beyond Frei's mere *use* of social science; theology, according to Milbank, *is* a social science.[26] All rightly executed speculative theology is "meant to call our attention to, and to reinforce, a discovery in the 'shape' of Jesus' life and death, of the exemplary practice which we can imitate and which can form the context of our lives together, so that we can call ourselves 'the body of Christ.'" The "point of the incarnation" is less to provide fodder for speculation and "more to communicate to human beings the idiom" for imitating Christ. "We need the stories of Jesus for salvation, rather than just a speculative notion of the good, because only the attraction exercised by a particular set of words and images causes us to acknowledge the good and to have an idea of the ultimate *telos*."[27] Milbank here is preciously close to Auerbach's claim that the Good News is "graphically and harshly dramatized through God's incarnation in a human being of the humblest social station, through his existence on earth amid humble everyday people and conditions" because "doctrine and the search for enlightenment are inextricably connected with the physical side of the narrative."

But Milbank refuses his own "demand" for a "return to the concrete, narrative level." There is one paragraph in the 480 pages of *Theology and Social Theory* that refers, generically, to the Church as the place where just economic exchanges take place, and there are scattered references to mutual forgiveness (except that Milbank follows Augustine that Christians can coerce others when "necessary"), but there is nothing approaching a "scene," photographic or filmic in quality, whether of Jesus or of the Church's re-narration of Him.[28] In other words, the very mode in which Milbank writes violates his own criteria for speculative theology "properly understood."

The problem runs deeper than the oft-proffered and more or less *ad hominem* criticism that Milbank's sometimes pugnacious style runs counter to the Christian narrative of peace and love that he espouses.[29] Rather, it is that the very genre in which he writes, even if it were executed in a more irenic tone, *cannot*, by his own standards, be an instance of and evoke that peace and love. There is no return to the imitable concrete narrative, either in *Theology and Social Theory* or any of Milbank's subsequent work to date. He simply concedes, in one response to a critic's concern about what Milbank himself identifies as the danger of "a new kind of narrative essentialism," by noting that, yes, his attempts at concrete, "judicious" narratives have been "rather minimal." He then proceeds on in later writings as if this—by his own standards—fundamental flaw was never brought to his attention.[30]

What is happening here? The stakes are high. We have three leading theologians, two with outsize reputations—an article in *Time* magazine named Hauerwas "America's Best Theologian," and one in the *Chronicle of Higher Education* featuring Milbank called radical orthodoxy "the knife's edge of a broader movement called postsecularism that may well become the biggest development since Martin Luther nailed his 95 theses to the church door."[31] All three theologians call for—indeed, "require"—social science-like descriptively particular narrative depiction of both the biblical Jesus of Nazareth and actual church practices so as to enable mimetic reenactment on the part of Christian communities. Yet all three ignore (avoid?) their own prescriptions. Why?

There are likely multiple reasons. Pickstock's—and, later, the *Chronicle of Higher Education*'s—grouping of the three under the title "post-secular" suggests one possibility. Post-secular thinkers cite complicity with modern secular rationalism—including and even especially how such rationalism has been manifested in the social sciences— as at the core of what has gone wrong with theology. Frei argues that the "eclipse of biblical narrative" began in the eighteenth century. Hauerwas more broadly cites "the Enlightenment" as the problem. Milbank tracks the fault line back somewhat earlier and identifies Duns Scotus as the prime precursor and progenitor of a form of thinking that divorces rationality from the Christian narrative only to reinsert, surreptitiously, its own, violent narrative. All three reject the rationalist idea that one can speak from a neutral, trans-narrative perspective. The forceful rejection of social science as it has predominantly been practiced—the first ten of the twelve chapters of *Theology and Social Theory* are negative critiques of modern rationality—therefore may bring with it a certain skittishness in actually taking up social science-like description, even on behalf of the Gospel. It may seem too much like fraternizing with the enemy to risk undertaking. Instead, they offer a broad "alternative" or "counter-history" to the narrative of rational progress; that alternative history—one of Christian theology gone awry in the modern era—underwrites the effort to re-narrativize theology. The result, however, is a theology that remains every bit as abstract as the rationalist model it critiques. In failing to move to the kind of descriptive particularity that can provide, again in Milbank's words, "the type of exemplary practice which we can imitate," post-secular theology inadvertently mimics its more secular nemeses.

The critique of the Enlightenment does have considerable merit. Kant insisted that "imitation has no place at all in moral matters," and Milbank's account of modern rationality suppressing narrative and yet sinisterly inserting a narrative of its own has strong similarities with Max Horkheimer and Theodor Adorno's argument in *Dialectic of Enlightenment* that scientific rationality suppresses mimetic knowing and at the same time displaces it with a violent mimetic alternative.[32] In yet another twist, then, it can be said that post-secular theology in its determination to avoid the ostensibly but falsely neutral reasoning of modern secularism fails to make use of social science methodologies that, by post-secular theology's own account, can facilitate the elaboration of imitable concrete narratives of both Jesus Christ and the church that is His body.

As helpful as this account of post-secular theology's failure might be, however, I want to suggest that much earlier developments are closer to the root of the problem for Christian thought and practice, making it an issue of concern not only for post-secular narrativists, but for all theologians. Writing in genres that neglect the gospels' own way of depicting salvation history as manifesting itself through the lives of ordinary and even lowly people is the consequence of a *habitus* that shapes all us theologians, and that all of us contribute to in turn. Post-secular theology is simply the most obvious case with which to exemplify the problem because of its staunch call for imitable narrative depictions of what it means to follow Jesus Christ. Its failure is more blatant, but the failure is all of ours, and does not track simply along the polemical lines that shape contemporary theology. I single out post-secular theology—and later in this appendix Milbank and radical orthodoxy specifically—because it dramatizes the problem with greater acuity: if even those who call for imitable narrative particularity fail to follow through, then the obstacles to such particularity must run deep in the substructure of the discipline.[33] The problem is much more than a problem of nerve on the part of post-secular theologians (though it might include that too). Auerbach is right. The critical shifts come much earlier than the Enlightenment or even the thirteenth-century Scotus.

I will supplement Auerbach in two ways. The first arises out of the fact that the complex of traditions that constitutes what is called "mimesis" is made up of two main strands. Auerbach's work addresses that strand that has to do with the representational arts; thus his subtitle—*The Representation of Reality in Western Literature*. The other strand is more anthropological in its set of concerns, and involves, in Michael Taussig's words (following Walter Benjamin), the human "compulsion to become the Other" (I am less resistant to anthropological generalizing than is Frei). Gregg Daniel Miller explains, "As the basis of an anthropology, mimesis means *making oneself similar*, or *speaking in the voice of another*, or *acting as another would act* (emphases in original).[34] Milbank touches on this relation between the representational and anthropological meanings of mimesis when he writes that "the point of the incarnation was more to communicate to human beings the idiom, the *logos* of an adequate return, so that it could be made more universally."[35] I understand mimesis to be a communicative act of knowledge and authority through the reenactment of an Other. The Other might be God, nature, a person (real or fictional), a spirit, or another culture. Because knowledge and authority, in this view, is a reenactment, it requires the use of the senses. Through sense-embedded reenactment, the knower participates in the reality of the known and thereby draws upon and re-presents its authority. Another way to understand mimesis, then, is as the revivification of someone through reenactment. The aesthetic and the anthropological meanings come together in the art of theater and the theater of life, where the representation is in and through the reenactment.

But, like Auerbach says, it is important to not let definitional issues get ahead of—and thereby separate from—the story, and here is where I wish to supplement his work in a second way. Auerbach offers an external explanation of how Christianity goes awry: rejection at Jerusalem forces a turn to evangelization of the Gentiles, where a shift in style and message away from the corporeal is requisite. I find a more internal explanation to be more adequate: contestation over religious authority *within* the Jesus and, later, Christian traditions leads to the establishment of conceptual distinctions—for instance, inner versus outer, faith versus sight—that allow religious leaders to allegorize into abstraction those parts of the Jesus narrative that challenge their authority. By the time that we get to the specific development of the discipline of theology in the twelfth century, there is no incentive—in fact, there is considerable disincentive—for the new social class of academic theologians to trade at all in the realistic representation of the life of Jesus Christ and the lives of those who follow him.[36] I am offering, then, what might be called an alternative to the alternative account of the history of Christian thought and practice set out by post-secular theologians. Here, the pivotal personages are not Scotus, Descartes, and Kant, but Paul, Ignatius of Antioch, Athanasius, and Abelard.[37]

Paul provides the critical distinctions for the development. In order to counter the Jerusalem apostles, who base their authority on having sensorily witnessed the earthly Jesus—they saw, heard and touched him—Paul must discount somatic experience. He does so by introducing sharp distinctions between flesh and spirit, seen and unseen, external and internal, and associating what is "true" and "real" with the latter of each of these couplings. "Hope that is seen is not hope" (Rom. 8:24). These distinctions allow later interpreters to select which parts of the life of Jesus they wish to highlight as meriting concrete imitation and which parts they prefer to spiritualize in a way that does not challenge their authority.[38] Bishop Ignatius of Antioch's insistence on the road to Rome where he is to be killed by imperial officials that true discipleship does not even begin until, minimally, one is captured and harmed at once underpins his own authority and his argument for monepiscopacy and casts doubt on the, to him, anarchic prophets who thought of themselves as imitating Jesus' itinerant life. The authoritative leader to be obeyed is the sedentary bishop, not the wandering visionary. Two centuries later, the premium on martyriologically-based authority threatens the bishopric of Athanasius of Alexandria, who flees multiple times in the face of threat. Also drawing on Paul's distinction between the external and internal, Athanasius makes the case that not the last part of Jesus' adult life, but the first, when he flees into the desert, is worthy of literal imitation. In this account, the anchorite, Antony of Egypt—a monk who, in this telling, is obsequious to episcopal authority—is the prime living exemplar of the proper imitation of Christ. The argument allows Athanasius to forge a monastic-episcopal alliance that lasts over a millennium. That alliance, and its control over what is considered acceptable imitation of Jesus, is so strong that the purveyors of the new scholastic discipline of what is coined "theology" in the twelfth century—Abelard is the critical figure here—find it most supportive of their own claims to authority to operate with highly abstract logic and not try to narratively depict the life of Jesus at all. It is in this way that theology, at its inception as a scholastic discipline, has already "lost its senses." This original *sitz in leben* of what we call theology still profoundly shapes how we write today.

Some clarifications before we start: to argue that Paul started a process whereby Christian thinkers turned away from Auerbach's "the real" is *not* to claim that such thinkers were not epistemological realists of some sort or did not attend to concrete issues of their day, but rather that their *representation* of reality—in particular the reality of Jesus Christ—turns allegorical and more abstract especially when addressing those aspects of the scripturally narrated life of Jesus that challenge their own claimed religious authority. This *conversio ab phantasma* to secure authority need not be—and often is not—conscious on the writer's part.

Also, it needs to be clear that to draw upon contestation as an interpretive lens is not to reduce theology or its object—God—to contestation; nor, conversely, is it to portray contestation as an intrinsically evil activity that we could somehow avoid if we imitated Christ adequately. Scripture displays Jesus contesting with a variety of religious authorities—priests, Pharisees, and scribes—in forms of challenge and riposte typical of the day. My point is simply that the dynamic of intra-tradition contestation illumines how theology went wrong better than alternative interpretations.

I suggest that contestation over religious authority provides a more adequate—because more illuminative—account of how Christian theology has turned away from the kind of concrete narrative depiction that the Gospel offers than the explanations given by Auerbach (who cites the failure of the Jerusalem apostolate and resulting need of the Jesus movement to evangelize Hellenistic culture to survive) and the post-secularists (who blame the Enlightenment and its precursors). Radical orthodoxy, as a corrective, turns, according to Milbank, to "the catholic vision of the Patristic period through to the high Middle ages";[39] yet I will make the case that it is precisely during this span that intra-tradition contestation leads theology awry. There is no pre-Enlightenment "safe space" for theologians to go. The Christian suppression of "the real" in the Gospel begins much earlier, with Saint Paul.

Appendix

The Pauline gambit: Sacrificing the earthly Jesus for apostolic authority

In those days, Peter stood up among the believers (together the crowd numbered about one hundred twenty persons) and said, "Friends, the scripture had to be fulfilled, which the Holy Spirit through David foretold concerning Judas, who became a guide for those who arrested Jesus—for he was numbered among us and was allotted his share in this ministry. . . . So one of the men who have accompanied us during all the time that the Lord Jesus went in and out among us, beginning from the baptism of John until the day when he was taken up from us—one of these must become a witness with us to his resurrection."

So they proposed two, Joseph called Barsabbas, who was also known as Justus, and Matthias. Then they prayed and said, "Lord, you know everyone's heart. Show us which one of these two you have chosen to take the place in this ministry and apostleship from which Judas turned aside to go to his own place." And they cast lots for them, and the lot fell on Matthias; and he was added to the eleven apostles.

—Acts 1:15-17, 21-26

"Am I not an apostle?"

—Paul, 1 Cor. 9:1

Paul's question regarding his status as an apostle presupposes his answer, and he reasserts his religious authority repeatedly in his letters.[40] He is "sent from God" (2 Cor. 2:17), and thus "called to be an apostle, set apart for the gospel of God" (Rom. 1:1). He further claims that among the various kinds of religious authority, apostleship is the highest (1 Cor. 12:28). Such lofty claims for himself were bound to enter him into contestation with the apostles as described in Acts 1, and interpretation of early Christianity in terms of conflict between the representatives of the Jerusalem church and Paul runs from the work of F. C. Baur in the first half of the nineteenth century through to the present in the research of scholars as different as Michael Goulder, Laura Nasrallah, and James Tabor.[41] What I am adding to this literature is an analysis of the ways in which that contestation led to innovations by Paul that, in Auerbach's words, "removed the thing told far from its sensory base" such that what it might mean to follow and become like Jesus Christ of Nazareth becomes increasingly difficult to discern. The story is all the more interesting precisely because it is Paul who introduces the noun *mimitís* to early Christian literature when he tells the Thessalonians, "And you became imitators of us and the Lord . . . so that you became an example to all the believers," (1 Thess. 1:6-7) and admonishes the Corinthians, "Be imitators of me as I am of Christ" (1 Cor. 11:1; cf. also 4:16).

Given the nature and scope of Jesus's mission as received by the original twelve disciples and the reconstituted twelve apostles after them, it was all but inevitable that Paul's claim to apostolic authority would lead both to contestation with the twelve and to his mission to the Gentiles. Scholars like John Meier are correct in thinking that Jesus deliberately chose twelve core leaders to represent the twelve tribes of Israel in large part because he saw his own mission as that of the restoration of Israel (cf. Mt. 10:5-6). The account in Acts of the deliberations and procedures that went into replacing Judas reinforces this interpretation of Jesus's mission. There is no room for a thirteenth apostle, at least as this office was initially constituted. There is no such thing as Weber's utterly unique charismatic individual, particularly in the collective community-orientation of the ancient Mediterranean world; for authority to manifest itself at all, it has to be intelligible to the people toward whom the authority is to be exercised. Given the identification of apostolic authority with leadership of the tribes of Israel, Paul's claim to be an apostle had to have been first interpreted either as too strange to comprehend or as a threat to displace one of the twelve (Acts 9:26 has the Twelve at first refusing to meet with him). Thus the contestation.

The subsequent identification of Paul's mission with the Gentiles was a negotiated way of allowing his claim to be an apostle such that it was at once intelligible and less threatening. Philip had already been preaching to Samaritans, a practice affirmed by the Jerusalem apostles in their consequent sending of Peter and John to the region (Acts 8),[42] and unnamed Christians were also evangelizing Greeks in Antioch, which the Jerusalem church affirms by sending Barnabas (Acts 11:19-26).[43] The arrangement that Paul describes and attributes to God in Galatians—"for he who worked through Peter making him an apostle to the circumcised also worked through me in sending me to the Gentiles" (2:8)—was, among other things, an effort to resolve a conflict over religious authority by parceling the evangelical turf. Paul acknowledges such a division of labor when he writes to the Corinthians, "For we were not overstepping our limits when we reached you; we were the first to come all the way to you with the good news of Christ. We do not boast beyond limits, that is, in the labor of others; but our hope is that, as your faith increases, our sphere of action among you may be greatly enlarged so that we may proclaim the good news in lands beyond you, without boasting of work already done in someone else's sphere of action" (2 Cor. 10:14-16). The formula that the Jerusalem apostles will focus on Jews while Paul attends to Gentiles was a first-century apostolic version of the later Augsburgian *cuius regio, eius religio* ("Whose region, his religion").[44]

The agreement did not last long. The Jerusalem apostles thought at first that Paul was, for the most part, preaching the same message as they were, only to a different audience, but another level of disagreement opened up. The new point of argument was not, to put the matter bluntly, whether Gentiles could become (what soon would be called) Christians, but rather whether they had to become Jews, adopting all of the practices that this involved, to become Christians. Disagreement on this point meant to the Jerusalem apostles that the original deal was off and that they could then preach anywhere, particularly where they felt people had previously been led astray. Paul, in turn, complains in Galatians that "certain people" who "came from James," a "circumcision faction," have entered *his*—that is, Paul's—sphere of action and "bewitched" his converts (Gal. 2:12 and 3:1). Later, in 2 Corinthians—the letter within which he makes the point regarding "spheres of action"—he lashes out at "super-apostles"—likely Jewish Christians—who undermine his authority in churches he has founded.[45]

From the perspective of an analysis in terms of contestation over religious authority, then, the fundamental dividing point between Jerusalem and Paul was not circumcision per se—Paul even has his co-worker, Timothy, circumcised so as not to offend Jews (Acts 16:3).[46] Rather, disagreement over circumcision marks the collapse of an already uneasy *détente* that the two parties had forged over religious authority. In Paul's view, James' people violated the apostolic nonaggression pact. In the Jerusalem apostles' view, Paul had violated the authority which they had granted him through their initial approval.[47] That the issue went beyond specific questions of circumcision and food is evident in the fact that Paul's opponents questioned his very mission, prompting his retort, "Am I not an apostle?"

The contestation decidedly shaped Paul's thought such that he gave articulation to the first significant moves in theology's *conversio ab phantasma*, its turn away from the senses. This is first of all evident in the fact that, other than a brief reference to the words of the Last Supper, most likely in the form of a pre-Pauline prayer (1 Cor. 11:23-26), and one reference to the Son as "descended from David according to the flesh" (Rom. 1:3), there are no references to the life of the earthly Jesus except—and this in very formal, or as Auerbach would say, "figurative" rather than descriptive terms—to his death on the Cross. There are only three places where Paul cites Jesus as the source of a teaching (1 Cor. 7:10-11; 9:14; 11:23-26). What Hauerwas refers to as "the whole life of this man whom God has claimed as decisive to his own for the presence of his kingdom in this world," has disappeared from view. The real, in Auerbach's sense, has vanished. As a result, though there are many parallels between the lives of Jesus and Paul from prophecy of the Kingdom to wonderworks to imprisonment and death at the hands of the authorities—patterns of life that are imitable—we are left to conclude, with biblical scholar Patrick Gray, "As intriguing as his biography may be, Paul's life has had less influence than his thought" in the letters.[48]

James Dunn argues that we ought not to make much of Paul's inattention to the life of Jesus by suggesting that Paul is simply assuming that his mission communities already know the gospel stories in oral form. Paul's theology, therefore, provides "a kind of shorthand" for something the listeners already know.[49] This argument overlooks the fact that Paul *cannot* draw attention to the earthly life of Jesus without undermining his own authority: to stress the earthly life of Jesus is to throw into relief the fact that Paul did not know him whereas the Jerusalem apostles did, and this in a culture where eyewitness is paramount. To stress the earthly Jesus as important is to accept that Paul's authority can only be second-order, received from the Jerusalem apostles. Paul wants none of this—which is why he repeatedly claims that his authority as an apostle is "by the will of God," and not derived from any relationship with the Jerusalem apostles (2 Cor. 1:1; cf. also 2:17; 3:5-6, 13:10; Gal. 1:1, 10-12, 15-17).

Note the contrasting accounts of Paul's immediate post-conversion activity. Acts has Paul dependent on Ananias' gesture of the laying on of hands to restore his sight and bring the Holy Spirit to him. *Ananias* brings Paul the word that his mission is to the Gentiles. Immediately thereafter, Paul is "with the disciples in Damascus," after which he attempts "to join the disciples" in Jerusalem (Acts 9).[50] Paul himself, in sharp contrast, places the source of his mission and his knowledge of it elsewhere, with a defensiveness that betrays the fact that accounts like that in Acts were circulating even before they were written down:

> But when God, who had set me apart before I was born and called me through grace, was pleased to reveal his Son to me, so that I might proclaim him among the Gentiles, I did not confer with any human being, nor did I go up to Jerusalem to those who were already apostles before me, but I went away at once to Arabia, and afterwards I returned to Damascus. Then after three years I did go up to Jerusalem to visit Cephas and stayed with him fifteen days; but I did not see any other apostle except James the Lord's brother. In what I am writing to you, before God, I do not lie! (Gal. 1:15-20)

In order to claim his status as a primary rather than Jerusalem-community-mediated apostle—"those leaders contributed nothing to me" (Gal. 2:6b)—Paul has to disvalue the firsthand knowledge others gained from following the earthly Jesus as a source of religious authority. It is no longer of utmost relevance: "even though we once knew Christ from a human point of view, we know him no longer in that way" (2 Cor. 5:16b). Paul shifts the grounds for primacy in religious authority from experience in following the earthly Jesus to direct—that is, unmediated by any human being—witness of the resurrected Christ. He then secures his position by adding that he is the last to have so witnessed Christ; there will be no more (1 Cor. 15:8). And though he comments that, as last, he is "the least of the apostles," he rhetorically reverses this claim by again insisting that his appointment is "by the grace of God," and that he has "worked harder" than any of the others (1 Cor. 15:9-10). He gives no quarter. In another rhetorical reversal, he later responds to concerns about his authority by turning the blame on the Corinthians, "Indeed, you should have been the ones commending me, for I am not at all inferior to these super-apostles" (2 Cor. 11:15).

Shifting the basis of authority from witness of the earthly Jesus to that of the resurrected Christ does not automatically entail a turn away from the senses, particularly in a culture characterized by, in John Pilch's words, a "densely populated spirit world and ready interference of those spirits in human life."[51] The accounts of the appearances of the resurrected Christ in the gospels are rich with sensory detail. In Matthew, the women at the tomb witness an angel dressed in white who "rolled back the stone and sat on it" (28:2b) before telling them to inform the disciples to meet up with Jesus in Galilee. Jesus himself appears to the women, and they, in a very tactile turn, "took hold of his feet" (28:9b). Luke tells of the resurrected Jesus' extended walk and conversation with two disciples in Emmaus, and how he breaks bread with them. In his appearance to the disciples in Jerusalem, Jesus himself stresses the physical senses: "Look at my hands and my feet; see that it is I myself. Touch me and see" (Lk. 24:39). He then eats—note the detailed specificity—broiled fish with them. Even the Gospel of Mark, with its abrupt ending, has a "young man dressed in a white robe" appear to the women at the tomb, and the typically more ethereal Gospel of John features the account of doubting Thomas and the resurrected Jesus's response: "Put your finger here and see my hands. Reach out your hand and put it in my side" (20:27).[52]

The accounts of Paul's experience of the resurrected Christ stand in stark contrast to those in the gospels. Acts has a flash of light from heaven causing Paul to *lose* his sight. The aural message could hardly be more brief. "I am Jesus, whom you are persecuting. But get up and enter the city, and you will be told what you are to do" (9:5b-6). Again, Ananias, not Jesus, later restores Paul's sight and gives him the details of his mission. Paul himself has the opportunity to expand on his experience of witnessing the resurrected Jesus when he defends his authority to the Galatians by recounting his conversion story, but his account provides little descriptive detail except for the fact that he "did not confer with any human being" (1:16b). Paul did not give the author of Acts, which was written later, much to build on.

The interpretive lens of contestation over religious authority helps account for the differences in the depictions of the resurrected Jesus Christ. The Jerusalem apostles and those who knew them grounded their authority in eyewitness of the earthly Jesus. Luke makes this clear when he bases the "truth about which you have been instructed" on accounts "handed on to us by those who from the beginning were eyewitnesses and servants of the word" (1:2). Sensory detail of the resurrected Jesus was a way of making the case that the death of Jesus did not end, but, because of the resurrection, rather confirmed the kind of eyewitness his followers experienced during his earthly life and the authority that comes with it. Paul's lack of sensory detail is therefore not inadvertent, as is evident by his claim that he was "set apart" even before birth (Gal. 1:15), that is to say, even before his entrance into the physical world upon which the Jerusalem apostles rely so much for their authority. Paul gives more formal articulation to his turn from the senses when he sets up a binary opposition over against them, "because we look not at what can be seen but at what cannot be seen; for what can be seen is temporary, but what cannot be seen is eternal . . . for we walk by faith, not by sight" (2 Cor. 4:18; 5:7b). For the Jerusalem apostles and their followers, it was precisely by sight—and sound and touch and even, with the sharing of meals with the resurrected Jesus, smell and taste— that they know that this is the same one whom they have been following all along, and it grounds their hope that he will return again. Paul counters, "Hope that is seen is not hope" (Rom. 8:24).

Paul's rhetorical use of faith in binary opposition to the senses extends beyond specific physical senses to the body generally. I am aware of the argument that "the flesh" for Paul is not equivalent to the body, and of the occasional passage where he affirms that the body can be a vehicle of the Holy Spirit (for instance, 1 Cor. 6:13b-20).[53] However, in the vast majority of passages, Paul links the earthly human body to the workings of "the flesh," and all of its negative connotations. This is clear in Romans: God sent his Son "in the likeness of sinful flesh" (8:3), that is, as an embodied human being. "Flesh" and physical body again forcefully come together when Paul admonishes, "if you live according to the flesh, you will die; but if by the Spirit you put to death the deeds of the body, you will live" (8:13). Paul systematizes the relationship through, again, oppositional binaries when he associates what is "true," with what is "inward," "real," and "spiritual," contrasting it with what is false, "external" or "literal," that is, physical: "For a person is not a Jew who is one outwardly, nor is true circumcision something external and physical. Rather, a person is a Jew who is one inwardly, and real circumcision is a matter of the heart—it is spiritual, not literal" (2:28-29).[54] Paul's shift of the basis of religious authority from the earthly to the resurrected Jesus therefore brings with it a shift of the "real" away from what is sensed by the earthly body to something other, far away from and most often in opposition to the physical body. This is why he says, in 2 Corinthians (where he associates the body with the sense of sight and its rejection), "So we are always confident; even though we know that while we are at home in the body we are away from the Lord—for we walk by faith, not by sight; we do have confidence, and we would rather be away from the body and at home in the Lord" (5:6-8).

Similarly, reduction of the full life of Jesus to figurative references to the Cross brings with it a premium on suffering as evidence of authority. 2 Corinthians, for instance, begins not with the usual thanksgiving that heads letters, but with Paul's account of the pain he has endured as a result of the actions of others (1:3-11). And in case his point is not clear, he returns to it later in the letter when he compares himself directly to the "super-apostles": "Are they ministers of Christ? . . . I am a better one: with far greater labors, far more imprisonments, with countless floggings, and often near death . . . in toil and hardship, through many a sleepless night, hungry and thirsty, often without food, cold and naked." (11:23, 27; cf. 11:23-33 and 1 Cor. 15:30-32). And Paul supplements these externally caused sufferings through, he writes, a severe asceticism: "I punish my body and enslave it" (1 Cor. 9:27). Most noteworthy is that the virtually exclusive focus on the Cross of Christ brings with it, for Paul, a theology that celebrates the senses only when they, and he, are suffering. He tells the Corinthians, "I am filled with consolation; I am overjoyed in all our affliction" (2 Cor. 7:4). This is a quite different witness from that of Jesus, who enjoyed his meals and wine, and showed no signs of elation over—even while he did not seek to avoid—his own sufferings and impending death. Jesus built his constellation of practices—both demanding (for instance, itinerancy) and lenient (eating on the Sabbath) around the exigencies of ministering to the poor and the wicked in *their* suffering, not his. In Paul, the joy in the suffering of his body follows upon his reduction of the life of Jesus to the latter's death on the Cross. The senses are trustworthy only when they sense pain.

Paul's turn away from the incarnated human Jesus (except in reference to suffering) as accounted in the gospels and toward the (very thinly described) resurrected Christ in a way that bolsters his own authority in contestation with the Jerusalem apostles sets up the framework in which apologists in subsequent intra-Christian contestations—I focus on Ignatius of Antioch and Athanasius—can enter in whatever traits and actions to depict the imitable Jesus that work to support their own authority. More, Paul's visible/invisible and outer/inner distinctions—even dualities—allows later interpreters to read out whatever concrete demands of discipleship contravene their accounts of their own authority as having simply "spiritual" as opposed to literal meanings and implications. The early turns away from concreteness, therefore, do not so much deny embodied particularity altogether—in fact, their accounts are sometimes quite vivid, even lurid—but involve a high degree of selectivity regarding which aspects of Jesus' mission are to be taken literally and which are not, a selectivity driven in large part by how such demarcations affect public perceptions of the writer's religious authority. The early apologists offer narrative accounts of the Jesus to be imitated, but they are truncated, and Paul provides the conceptual wherewithal for them to do this. Such a dynamic sets up the circumstances in the twelfth century where, in a move that bolsters their own authority, the practitioners of the newly named academic discipline of "theology"—I highlight Abelard—determine that narrativized, sense-filled and embodied imitation is irrelevant to their professional calling.

The Ignatian usurpation: Martyrdom and prophecy leverage monepiscopacy

> Now there are varieties of gifts, but the same Spirit; and there are varieties of services, but the same Lord; and there are varieties of activities, but it is the same God who activates all of them in everyone. To each is given the manifestation of the Spirit for the common good. To one is given through the Spirit the utterance of wisdom, and to another the utterance of knowledge according to the same Spirit, to another faith by the same Spirit, to another gifts of healing by the one Spirit, to another the working of miracles, to another prophecy, to another the discernment of spirits, to another various kinds of tongues, to another the interpretation of tongues, All these are activated by one and the same Spirit, who allots to each one individually just as the Spirit chooses.
>
> —Paul, 1 Cor. 12:4-11

> I did not learn this from any human being. No, the Spirit itself was preaching, saying these words: "Do nothing without the bishop."
>
> —Ignatius of Antioch, Letter to the Philadelphians, 7:2

> The one who does anything without the bishop's knowledge serves the devil.
>
> —Ignatius of Antioch, Letter to the Smyrnaeans, 9:1

Weber was wrong. The first thing that happens following the death of a charismatic leader, and after the shock of that death wears off somewhat, is not simply the "routinization" of charisma, but also, and at first even more forcefully, its outward dispersion, its radiation. Weber writes that in the aftermath of the death of a charismatic leader, "the tide that lifted a charismatically led group out of everyday life flows back into the channel of workaday routines," and the followers turn the charismatic community "into an 'institution.'" Charisma then is "captured by the interest of all economic and social power holders."[55] However, Paul's recognition that the Spirit continues to work directly through a range of people in a host of different ways evidences the reality of another dynamic, the dispersion of charisma: varieties of gifts, but the same Spirit; varieties of services, but the same Lord. *The Didache* (the Teaching), an anonymous early church instruction document reflects similar diversity. Likely compiled in the late first century—closer to the time of Ignatius of Antioch—the document instructs Christians on, in addition to other things, the proper attitudes and practices toward itinerant "apostles"(teachers) and prophets as well as sedentary bishops and deacons.

The source of such dispersion of charisma is the fact that charismatic persons, rather than being, again in Weber's words, "alien to tradition" and therefore "absolutely unique" and "unprecedented," are in fact bundles of traditional symbolic action and meaning combined in new ways. This is why Jesus appealed to and offended people from such a wide array of social locations. He was teacher, wonderworker, prophet, agitator, and more. With his death—and that of any other truly charismatic leader— the bundle of charisms releases with centrifugal social force. Call it spiritual fission. Recombining the social actions and meanings in a similar way as fully as the now dead (and resurrected) leader is immensely difficult and indeed rare. More common, as 1 Corinthians testifies, is a community within which various persons reenact the different spirit-infused roles that the leader once forcefully brought together in and through himself. The result is that there is no one leader, no singular authority. Rather, the community as a whole enacts the charism bundle that the now gone leader brought together.

Efforts to organize the relationships between the bearers of these different charisms do begin quickly thereafter. Paul himself offers an early example in the very letter in which he testifies to the plurality of callings. "And God has appointed in the church first apostles, second prophets, third teachers; then deeds of power, then gifts of healing, forms of assistance, forms of leadership, various kinds of tongues" (1 Cor. 12:28). Still, it is the fact of the dispersion or fission of charisms that prompts the efforts to relate in an ordered way the persons who bear them. More, it is significant that Paul lists those people with the charism of organizational leadership close to last—seventh out of eight. *The Didache* agrees with Paul that such leadership is still a display of charisma, and also provides evidence of the fact that it was a charism that was often, even typically, not well regarded at the time. The author-collator of the document feels compelled to remind the community that bishops and deacons carry out a necessary ministry, and admonishes, "You must not, therefore, despise them, for they are your honored men, along with the prophets and teachers."[56]

Ignatius of Antioch's genius was in his ability to draw upon the highly respected charisms of martyr and prophet to leverage the ascendency and even totalizing leadership of the episcopacy. Paul uses the term *episkopoi*, literally "overseers," to refer to the sedentary—that is, non-itinerant—leaders of specific local churches, but these were typically groups of leaders, not singular heads, and they did not as a matter of practice reside over all of the churches in a city as bishops would later. Acts uses *episkopoi* interchangeably with that of *presbuteroi*, that is, "presbyters" or "elders" (20:17-35), as do 1 Timothy, Titus, and 1 Clement, the last written at the close of the first century.[57] Acts also testifies that traveling "prophets and teachers" came to Antioch, the young Ignatius' home, and initiated the community there, the first whose members were referred to as "Christians." With regard to community officers, at most the itinerants appointed presbyters, but not singular bishops as we understand them today (13:1-3; 14:23).[58]

Ignatius' letters—written around 115—reflect deep tension with and animosity toward the itinerants.[59] He cautions the Ephesians against "those who are accustomed to carrying about the Name"—that is, itinerant prophets and teachers preaching the gospel of Jesus Christ—because they do so "maliciously and deceitfully while doing other things unworthy of God." He goes on to warn, "You must avoid them as wild beasts. For they are mad dogs that bite by stealth" (Eph. 7:1).[60] William Schoedel notes in his commentary on the letters that there is little in this and surrounding passages evidencing a concern about a specific doctrine under threat, indicating that while Ignatius does attack elsewhere those whom he considered docetists (Eph. 18–20; Trall. 9–10; Smyrn. 1–6) and Christians whom he thought were too attached to Judaism (Magn. 8–10; Phil. 5–9), his fundamental concern in the present instance is to thwart those who pose a threat to his understanding of the unity of the church as being constituted under the bishop. When Ignatius warns the Trallians to "keep away from every strange plant, which is heresy" (Trall. 6:1), Schoedel translates "heresy" as "faction," and comments that, given the lack of specific doctrinal referent, "heresy" is "still basically a matter of people who disrupt unity and create 'faction.'"[61] Ignatius gives credence to Schoedel's interpretation when he describes himself as a "man set on unity" (Phil. 8:1) and tells his fellow bishop, Polycarp, "Focus on unity, for there is nothing better" (Pol. 1:2). And again, unity for Ignatius involves a particular church structure.

Ignatius' strategy is to make the case that only bishops—of which he is one—have the authority to command others in the manner of the original apostles. This is evident in the fact that although he indicates his own deference to the first apostles—"I do not give you orders like Peter and Paul: they were apostles, I am a convict" (Rom. 3:3)—he writes that the bishop of a church ought to be regarded "as the Lord himself" (Eph. 6:1). This last phrase is meant to recall Jesus' words upon sending the disciples out on mission: "Whoever welcomes you welcomes me, and whoever welcomes me welcomes the one who sent me" (Mt. 10:40; cf. also Jn 13:20). Francis Sullivan comments that the claim that the bishop ought to be regarded as the Lord, "shows that for Ignatius, bishops are 'sent' by the Lord."[62] In other words, Ignatius' aim is to make the bishop the one who is sent by the Lord without, unlike the itinerant apostles and prophets of his day, the prelate's literally having to go out anywhere, with all of the attending disciplines that such going out involves: "Take nothing for your journey; no staff, nor bag, nor bread, nor money—not even an extra tunic." The bishop has the office of apostle without having to undertake the mission. This is already a fundamental break with authority as understood by the Jesus of the gospels. In James Dunn's words, "*It was only as they shared in his mission that his disciples shared in his authority and charismatic power. In short, as Jesus did not live for himself but for the kingdom and others, so it had to be with his disciples. . . . Those who gathered around him did so to share in that task, to follow him in his mission, and for no other reason*" (emphasis in original).[63]

The apostle Paul's death—along with those of Stephen and James[64]—created a strong linkage between apostolicity and martyrdom in many Christian communities. Ignatius is in fact credited as being the first to attest to the martyrdom of Paul, and he draws upon this apostle-martyr linkage to turn what otherwise was an occasion of shame—his failure as bishop to bring unity to the Antiochene community—into a victory that is at once personal and institutional. His early efforts to install a monepsicopal structure in Antioch fail, and the ensuing commotion—not any active persecution of Christians—leads to his arrest by the authorities and to his eventual death at their hands in Rome.[65] However, he dramatizes his fate as that of a martyr, and in doing so uses the authority of the latter to leverage his view of ecclesial unity under the monepiscopacy.[66]

Important here is that although Ignatius takes on the roles of martyr and prophet—and in so doing recombines some of the dispersed charisms in himself—it is evident in his defense of the less outspoken and even "silent" bishops elsewhere (Eph. 6:1; Magn. 8:2; Phil. 1:1) that he is aware that few bishops at the time are capable of doing likewise. His monepsicopal strategy is grounded, therefore, in the conviction that, given the absence of the kind of communal cohesion made possible when all of the relevant charisms work *in and through* one leader—namely, Jesus or one like him in the ability to bundle charisms—the next best thing is to enforce an order where those charisms can be brought *under* one leader. Thus the charge, "Do nothing without the bishop." Ignatius retrieves this model of unity from the Hellenistic political culture around him,[67] but uses the role of apostle-cum-martyr and that of the prophet to try to bring it about in the church, and this combination dramatically alters what it means to draw upon the senses to imitate Christ.

Ignatius, even more than Paul, to whom he is indebted,[68] emphasizes suffering as *the* identifying characteristic of the life of Jesus. Though opposition to the docetists leads Ignatius to stress the Incarnation, he, like Paul, says little about Jesus' life—there is one mention that he "ate and drank" (Trall. 9:1)—except for the fact that he was born, baptized, suffered, and died. In fact, the point of Jesus's birth is so that he could suffer. "He was born and was baptized in order that by his suffering he might cleanse the water" (Eph. 18:2). A proper Christian community therefore "rejoices" in Jesus's cleansing suffering (Phil. salutation), and it is precisely "through his suffering" that Jesus calls Christians (Trall. 11:2). The first of the two prime ways that Christians imitate Christ, then, is precisely through this suffering. "Let us be eager to be imitators of our Lord, to see who can be the more wronged, who the more cheated, who the more rejected" (Eph. 10:3). When Ignatius appeals to the Christians in Rome to not interfere with his impending death, his request gets directly at this dominant motif: "Allow me to be an imitator of the suffering of my God" (Rom. 6:3). So central is suffering to Ignatius's understanding of the paramount Christian life, that he describes his discipleship as not even starting until after his arrest. "Now at last I am beginning to be a disciple" (Rom. 5:3). His mistreatment at the hands of his guards makes him even "more of a disciple" (Rom. 5:1). More, he claims that it is only upon and as a result of his death that he will "truly be a disciple of Jesus Christ" (Rom. 4:2).

At this point, suffering and death become not simply a regrettable because unavoidable consequence of discipleship, but—even more so than in the case of Paul—its *proof*. Ignatius begs the Christians in Rome not to intervene on his behalf "so that I may not merely be called a Christian, but actually prove to be one" (Rom. 3:2; cf. also 4:2 and Pol. 7:1). In ensuing decades and even centuries, Ignatius's martyrological theology becomes so influential that it plays a central role in shaping what Judith Perkins calls the formation of the "suffering self" in Christian consciousness and literature, where aspirations of suffering and death become "not only normal but normative."[69] Ignatius wants desperately—"Let me be food for the wild beasts" (Rom. 4:1)—to be killed (cf. also Rom. 1:1-2:2). "I am passionately in love with death as I write to you" (Rom. 7:2). Again, this is in contrast with the witness of Jesus of Nazareth, who knew and bore the painful and lethal consequences of his mission, but did not seek them. The point of his mission was to attend to the suffering of the poor and the wicked, not to highlight his own.

Though Ignatius attacks the docetists, his stress on suffering leads, in a way that supersedes even as it depends upon Paul, to the view that the sensory world, other than when one is sensing pain, is a hindrance to the imitation of Christ. "I take no pleasure in corruptible food or the pleasures of this life" (Rom. 7:3). The themes of corrupt/incorrupt and impure/pure appear repeatedly in the letters, with the former in each dyad alternatively referring to the sensory world and to the influence of those whom Ignatius considers his enemies,[70] and the latter referring to Christ and to those who obey the bishop (for instance, Eph. 10:3; Trall. 7:2; Rom. salutation; 4:1, 6:2, 7:2; Phil. 3:1; Pol. 2:3). In what may seem like an odd statement for an anti-docetist who seeks to imitate Jesus Christ, Ignatius proclaims, "Nothing that is visible is good" (Rom. 3:3), and that he will be a "true disciple" only "when the world will no longer see my body" (Rom. 4:2). The incarnation simply serves the purpose of the crucifixion. Again, Jesus is born most importantly so that "by his suffering" he can "cleanse" corrupt/impure humanity.

And it is precisely when Ignatius imagines his own death that he invokes the senses and provides the most evocative—even provocative—descriptive detail:

> Let me be food for the wild beasts, through whom I can reach God. I am God's wheat, and I am being ground by the teeth of the wild beasts, so that I may prove to be pure bread. Better yet, coax the wild beasts, so that they may become my tomb and leave nothing of my body behind. . . . Fire and cross and battles with wild beasts, mutilation, mangling, wrenching of bones, the hacking of limbs, the crushing of my whole body, cruel tortures of the devil—let these come upon me, only let me reach Jesus Christ (Rom. 4:1-2; 5:3).

Ignatius' prose perhaps seems lurid and his actions extreme. Why not take up the offer that he anticipates from the Christians in Rome to secure his release through bribery or other means? Why not flee and hide, just as Athanasius would later, in order to live and continue his fight? But two factors are at play. First, he is convinced that only his death—a death portrayed as martyrdom—will win his case for monepsicopacy. While he often depicts singular rule by a bishop as already the norm in what he is the first to call the "Catholic" church, his account less provides a description of reality than seeks to shape it. At the time of his arrest, he is already of advanced age, perhaps seventy years old or older. Time—unlike in the case of Athanasius—is not on his side, and he judges that what time he would have if released would be ineffective. In begging the Christians of Rome to not interfere with his death, we writes, "For if you remain silent and leave me alone, then I will be a word of God, but if you love my flesh [by securing a release], then I will again be a mere voice" (Rom. 2:1).

The phrase "again be a mere voice" indicates the second reason that Ignatius undertakes what to modern readers might appear to be excessive measures. In his account, the bishop is not to be a "mere voice," but rather *the* authoritative voice. His failure to secure assent to this vision of authority in Antioch is an occasion of great shame on his part. His frequently voiced humility is much more than rhetorical convention (Eph. 3:1; 12:1; 21:1; Magn. 11:1, 12:1, 14:1; Trall. 3:3, 4:1-2, 5:1-2, 12:3, 13:1-2; Rom. 4:3; Smyrn. 11:1, 13:1). In borrowing, consciously or unconsciously, from the surrounding political culture for his model of church structure, he also absorbs the former's ethics of honor and shame with its emphasis on male household and civil authority. Ignatius was arrested because of the ruckus that ensued when he had failed to rule his ecclesial household adequately. Because honor codes relate not just to individuals, but to the social standing of whole groups, Ignatius' failure, in his judgment, brings shame not only on him, but on other bishops and the whole of the Christian community as well.[71] His death, particularly if it can establish (his understanding of) order in the Antiochene community, is the preferable option. Schoedel notes that when Ignatius hears that "peace" is restored to Antioch (Phil. 10:1; Smyrn. 11:2-3)—meaning not a cessation of persecution, which is not at the time taking place, but the installation of church order along Ignatian lines—his articulations of humility lessen. "Ignatius sees the achievement of unity in the churches of Asia as certification of his ministry and a sign that there is no more question about his worthiness."[72] By then, Ignatius's martyrological drama and his model of the church are so deeply intertwined that there is no question but that he follow through with his death. Doing otherwise would nullify the victory. More, though earlier Ignatius voices doubts about not only his social worthiness but also his own ability to hold fast to the martyr role that he has taken on (Trall. 12:3; Rom. 3:2), by the time that he hears of the peace in Antioch he fully inhabits his adopted character.

Ignatius strengthens his case for monepiscopacy by assuming the role of prophet as well as that of martyr. He tells the Christians in Rome, "I write to you not according to human perspective but in accordance with the mind of God" (Rom 8:3). The claim echoes Paul's insistence that he does not speak from "a human point of view" (2 Cor. 5:16b) and that therefore he is sanctioned "neither by human commission nor from human authorities" (Gal. 1:1, cf. also 1:10-12, 15-17), but rather by "by the will of God" (2 Cor. 1:1). In the letter to the Philadelphians, Ignatius is even clearer in signaling that he is enacting the prophetic role in a way that backs his model of church order:

I called out when I was with you; I was speaking in a loud voice, God's voice: "Pay attention to the bishop, the council of presbyters, and the deacons." To be sure, there were those who suspected that I said these things because I know in advance about the division caused by certain people. But the one for whose sake I am in chains is my witness that I did not learn this from any human being. No, the Spirit itself was preaching, saying these words: "Do nothing without the bishop" (Phil. 7:.1-2).

Here again is a place where Weber's theory of charisma and its routinization is misleading. It implies that, after the death of the charismatic leader, those institutionalizing the charism add nothing to its content. Weber, and others after him, therefore spend much time counterposing the prophet with the priest. This way of setting up the ideal types, however, masks the way in which the priestly type continues to invent the tradition; the priest does not so much oppose prophecy as usurp it. And prophecy does not so much decline over the course of early Christianity, as some narratives would have it; it is taken over. Ignatius' primary prophetic addition to the tradition is that the bishop, not the itinerants, is the true apostle and prophet and thus the singular head of the Christian community.[73] Though Ignatius does often mention presbyters and deacons, he leaves no doubt about who is the first and final authority. "For your council of presbyters, which is worthy of its name and worthy of God, is attuned to the bishop as strings to a lyre" (Eph. 4:1). And though there are no mentions of either the presbyters or deacons without the bishop, there are many of the bishop alone.

Wherever the bishop appears, there let the congregation be; just as where Jesus Christ is, there is the catholic church. It is not permissible either to baptize or to hold a love feast without the bishop. But whatever he approves is also pleasing to God. . . . It is good to acknowledge God and the bishop. The one who honors the bishop has been honored by God; the one who does anything without the bishop's knowledge serves the devil (Smyrn. 8:2; 9:1).[74]

Just how innovative and even disruptive Ignatius' model is becomes evident when we note that *presbuteroi* means "elders," and that in insisting on the primacy of a singular bishop, Ignatius is upsetting tradition. Up to this point, writers such as Clement of Rome had been drawing on the idea of apostolic succession to give Christian articulation not to monepsicopacy, but to the rule of plural elders, in Clement's words, "reputable men," those who have lived long and well enough to gain the respect of others (1 Clem. 44:3).[75] Ignatius's admonition to the Magnesians betrays the fact that the community is *not* receptive to singular bishops, particularly young ones, appointed over the heads of the elders. He warns the community, "not to take advantage of the youthfulness of your bishop but to give him all the respect due to him, just as I know that the holy presbyters likewise have not taken advantage of his youthful appearance but defer to him as one who is wise in God" (Magn. 3:1). Here are echoes of *The Didache*'s counsel, in the face of contrary experience, to respect bishops and deacons as well as prophets and teachers.

At the same time that Ignatius is leveraging his model of monepsicopacy through his enactment of one kind of *imitatio Christi*—that of suffering unto martyrdom—he *reinforces* this ecclesiastical model by exploiting the motif of imitation in a second way. Here, the bishop imitates God the Father who issues commands, and the faithful imitate the Son by obeying the Father. "You must follow the bishop as Jesus Christ followed the Father" (Smyrn. 8:1). That to "follow" here involves not imitation of an exemplar but rather obedience to a superior is evident in other passages that couple the bishop with God the Father. "Let us, therefore, be careful not to oppose the bishop, in order that we may be obedient to God" (Eph. 5:3). The close association of the bishop with God the Father, with little if any slippage between the two, runs throughout the letters. When Ignatius calls upon the Magnesians to obey their youthful bishop, he argues that such obedience is "not really" to their bishop, but rather "to the Father of Jesus Christ, the bishop of all" (Magn. 3:1). The passage continues in a way that echoes Paul's seen/unseen—"hope that is seen is not hope"— dichotomy: "It is right to be obedient without any hypocrisy, for it is not so much a matter of deceiving this bishop who is seen but of cheating the one who is unseen. In such a case he must reckon not with the flesh but with God" (Magn. 3:2). The bishop here represents—is a stand-in for—the God, or that part of the Godhead, who does *not* become human.

Elsewhere, when Ignatius details the roles of the various church offices, he does so by relating them to God the Father, the apostles, and Jesus Christ. Here the deacons take the place of the laity in imitating Christ: "Be eager to do everything in Godly harmony, the bishop presiding in the place of God and the presbyters in the place of the council of the apostles and the deacons, who . . . have been entrusted with the ministry of Jesus Christ" (Magn. 6:1; cf. also Trall. 3:1). In his immediately preceding sentence, Ignatius tells his audience that performing the ministry of Jesus Christ means that the deacons are to "please everyone in every respect" (Trall. 2:3). In other words, the basic interpretive structure that couples the bishop with God the Father (and the presbyters with the apostles) remains, and someone else—whether deacon or lay—plays the obedient Jesus Christ whose role it is to please others. "Therefore, just as the Lord did nothing without the Father, either by himself or through the apostles (for he was united with him), so you must not do anything without the bishop and the presbyters." (Magn. 7:1; cf. also 13:2).

The implications for the use of the physical senses in imitation in the Christian life are significant. The lay Christian, in imitating Christ, is *not* to attempt to be like the bishop.[76] That would be a category mistake. The bishop here is not like Christ, who is born into this world, but rather, again, is representative of "the one who is unseen." To encounter him is to deal "not with the flesh but with God." The physical senses, with the possible exception of hearing so that one can obey the bishop, are irrelevant. And it is clear that when, as quoted above, Ignatius says for the Christian to "follow the bishop as Jesus Christ followed the Father," such following—such discipleship—leads not to imitation through extended contact with an exemplar, but rather is reduced to obedience to a distant—fleshless and unseen—authority.

Regarding the use of the physical senses in the imitation of Christ, then, Ignatius's theology moves along two mutually reinforcing tracks. On the first, imitation of the suffering Christ leads to vivid, even garish, sensory detail of the passion—Ignatius was the first to use the Greek *pathos* to refer to Jesus's suffering and death—at the expense of any depiction of Jesus's life before arrest. Again, for Ignatius, a Christian does not even begin to become a disciple until arrest and maltreatment. Other than birth and baptism, what happens before—whether in Jesus' life or our own—is not relevant. Given that this form of imitation comes into play literally only in extremis—even in periods of persecution, the vast majority of Christians do not suffer in this way—the use of the senses in imitating Christ is rarely in need of activation. Reinforcing this first track is a second that reduces the imitation of Christ to obedience to the bishop, occluding any inclination to use the senses to direct the Christian life. "Nothing that is seen is good." Simply obey the bishop, who stands in for the unseen God the Father. Later in the second century, Irenaeus appropriates the proto-doctrine of apostolic succession and applies it to the bishop alone as the singular ecclesiastical leader of the churches in a city, and monepiscopacy becomes the norm.

The Athanasian compromise: The obedient monk as imitable ideal Christian

Pace the received interpretation, Constantine's conversion does not end the persecution of Christians; it simply is inflicted by other Christians. Though the emperor calls and resides at the Nicene Council (325) that condemns Arianism, he himself later moves closer to the heterodox position and banishes Athanasius—bishop of Alexandria and staunch opponent of Arius—to Gaul. After Constantine's death, Athanaius returns to Alexandria, only to have opponents, supported by Constantius II, name Gregory of Cappadocia as bishop. Athanasius flees in the ensuing violence. Gregory dies, and Athanasius returns once again, but is condemned at two separate councils.[77] When imperial police storm the church in Alexandria, Athanasius flees once more. His supporters lynch the installed alternative bishop; his opponents torture female ascetics of Alexandria in an effort to extract information regarding Athanasius' whereabouts. Five times he leaves his see; five times he returns. While the idea of monepiscopacy is by now secure, any given bishop is not.

Against the backdrop of the witness of a building list of martyrs, many of whom, like Ignatius, not only do not flee execution but even seek it, Athanasius' multiple instances of flight bring challenges to his authority. During the Diocletian persecution (303), one of Athanasius's episcopal precursors, Peter of Alexandria, goes into hiding, and Bishop Melitius of Lycopolis installs alternative church officials in Alexandria and elsewhere, resulting in rival episcopal claims. After the persecution, Melitius and his followers insist on an extended period of penance for those who fled and, particularly, those who abjured the faith during persecution. Though the Council of Nicea attempts to reconcile the Miletians with the Petrine hierarchy, the conflict continues into the episcopacy of Athanasius. The Melitians refer to themselves as the Church of the Martyrs, and view themselves as the true heirs of those like the apostle Peter, Paul and Ignatius. Athanasius, with his record of flight, can only be a fraud.[78] In an alliance of convenience, the Melitians join with the Arians over against Athanasius.

More, a new kind of Christian emerges in Egypt: the desert ascetic. Known for his discipline, wisdom, and even intercessory wonderworks, the monk becomes a revered figure, and thus a new kind of rival for religious authority. The challenge to monepiscopacy is already strong from the presence of individual ascetics and their devoted followers and beneficiaries, but, even more, the pattern of ascetic practices becomes a large-scale movement when Pachomius founds several monasteries with a total of as many as nine thousand adherents. At this scale, monasticism threatens not only the spiritual supremacy of the bishop, but also his financial control of the church. Patrons, moved by the ascetics's practices and in hopes of the latter's spiritual intercession, give directly to the monasteries. Athanasius first makes various tactical moves to control the monks and recruit them over against the Arians and Melitians, including ordaining them and installing some as bishops, often overriding their concerns that day-to-day engagement in ecclesial politics will obstruct their ascetic vocations.[79] However, his opponents simply ordain and install monks of their own. Stalemate.

While in his third exile (356–62), during which he is hidden by monks in the Egyptian desert, Athanasius recognizes that he must wage a more effective rhetorical battle. Like Ignatius before him, he draws on developing symbolic resources in the tradition to turn a problematic situation to his favor, only this time in the opposite direction as Ignatius: Athanasius makes flight, whether into hiding or into the desert—or, in his case, both—a virtue. His *Apologia de Fuga* ("Defense of his Flight"), cites Moses's flight from Egypt as his imitable model, and his *Life of Antony* hagiographizes the anchorite Antony of Egypt. The *Life*, in particular, becomes a widely received, for the time, weapon against Athanasius's enemies. Multiple competing oral accounts of the words and deeds of the ascetic Antony are already in circulation, and Athanasius is aware of them: "Each tells what he knows." Though in all likelihood Athanasius met Antony only once,[80] he insists not only to have met the latter, but to have been a disciple of sorts. He claims that he can provide a "fuller narrative" than others because he has seen Antony "often": "I was able to learn from him when I followed him more than a few times and poured water over his hands."[81]

Rhetorically, then, Athanasius is drawing upon the tradition of firsthand eyewitness discipleship found with the Jerusalem apostles of the early Jesus movement and, consistent with that movement, he provides a narrative account of Antony for emulation by the reader. Like the biblical narratives and Ignatius's description of his anticipated confrontation with the coliseum lions, it is an account rich in detail, particularly when describing Antony's battles with demons. Athanasius's use of the first person for Antony at once provides immediacy for the reader and works to underpin the bishop's claim to firsthand knowledge of the monk's life. He writes, in the voice of Antony:

Lest you think that I am talking about these things in general terms, and in order that you might be sure that I describe these matters from experience and fact. . . . I am telling you what cunning pursuits of the demons I myself have seen. . . . Once they came with their threats and encircled me like warriors in battle array. On another occasion they filled my dwelling with horses and beasts and serpents. . . . Once they came in darkness, having the appearance of light, and saying, "We have come to bring light to you Antony." . . . And after a few months they came as ones chanting and quoting from the Scriptures. . . . Once they shook the cell. . . . And after these things, when they visited again, they made crashing noises, they whistled and leapt about. . . . Once a very tall demon appeared in an apparition and had the daring to say, 'I am the Power of God," and "I am Providence; what do you wish that I would give you?" . . . Once while I was fasting, the cunning one even came as a monk, and he offered me counsel, saying, "eat, and stop your many labors; you too are a man, and you are about to grow weak". . . . Many times he whipped me, and I said, "Nothing *shall separate* me *from the love of Christ*." After that they lashed each other instead (emphases in original).[82]

Antony, according to Athanasius, is the exemplar Christian, and all other Christians, to greater or lesser degree, are to imitate him, monks with as much exactitude as possible, laity through almsgiving and periodic fasts from food and sex. Christ, in this view, is the exemplar of bodily control.[83] The result is a program that emphasizes restraint with food (in contrast to Jesus, who feasts and drinks regularly and plucks grain on the Sabbath) and abstention from sex (whereas Peter, the first among the disciples, is married). The controlling metaphor in Athanasius's work as a whole is that of "withdrawal" (*apósyrsi*), and the *Life* presents us with the irony of a text that provides the kind of narrative detail necessary for *imitatio* while stressing the withdrawal of the senses from the basic human activities involving taste (food) and touch (sex).

And withdraw is what Athanasius has Antony do. The overall trajectory of the story is that of Antony moving further into the wilderness and even deeper into his last mountain refuge. In the face of the ongoing authority of the witness of the martyrs, particularly over against his own flight, Athanasius interrupts the narrative to have Antony go into the city to seek martyrdom yet get refused by authorities. This turn of events signals to the reader that the age of martyrdom is over, and that the true heirs of the martyrs are not the Melitians, but rather are those who flee into the desert. "When finally the persecution ended, and Peter the blessed bishop [of Alexandria] had made his witness, Antony departed and withdrew once again to his cell, and was there daily being martyred by his conscience, and doing battle in the contests of faith. He subjected himself to an even greater asceticism, for he was always fasting, and he had clothing with hair on the interior and skin on the exterior that he kept until he died."[84] Later in the fourth century, St. Jerome will make the link terminologically, calling the ascetics "white martyrs," the heirs of the "red martyrs" who literally shed their blood for the faith.[85] The extent of the dominance of the narrative of the monk as ideal imitator of Christ is evident in Jerome's own depiction of the missionary apostle as "Paul the first hermit," in an effort to leverage authority for the monastic way of life.[86] If, for Ignatius, discipleship does not begin until arrest, for Athanasius, it never gets beyond the trials in the desert; in both cases Paul's turn away from the senses and the life of Jesus creates literary room for the re-narration of the ideal Christian in a way that sits crosswise with the life of Jesus the Nazarene the Christ.

Athanasius draws from Paul's inner (real)/outer (false) distinction in depicting Antony moving to the "inner" mountain of his retreat in order to get away from people, even other monks, and be closer to God.[87] Monks, following the counsel of Jesus and the example of Antony, are to give away all of their possessions, but not to go out and preach the reign of God to crowds of people. In particular, and in contrast to actual monastic practice of hospitality at the time,[88] followers of Christ are to stay well away from the wicked, in this case the Meletians and Arians. Athanasius has Antony warn, "Do not approach the Meletian schismatics, for you know their evil and profane reputation. Nor are you to have any fellowship with the Arians, for their impiety is evident to everyone. . . . Rather, keep yourselves pure from contact with them."[89] Instead, when Antony, like Jesus, performs acts of wonder—healings, prophecies, exorcisms and nature miracles—in the presence of others, Athanasius uses the events not to highlight the authority of the anchorite, but rather follows the acts up by pointing out Antony's obedience to the authority of the bishop. Stories of Antony producing water in the desert, rendering well a woman whose mucus turned to worms, divining the needs of his visitors, and driving out a demon that made a man eat his own excrement do not, as in the case of Jesus, lead to challenge and threat from authorities because Athanasius uses the accounts to *buttress* episcopal authority. In the paragraph following the long section depicting the wonderworks, Athanasius describes Antony as one who "felt no shame at bowing the head to the bishops."[90] This is the nub of the Athanasian compromise: allow monastic *spiritual* superiority in exchange for securing episcopal *juridical* primacy. In the end, it is not much of a compromise at all. The *Life* concludes with the dying Antony instructing those with him to give his sheepskin and cloak—his mantle—to "Bishop Athanasius," thereby conferring all of the spiritual and ecclesial payoff for the ascetic life and its wonderworks to the latter. "For even seeing these is like beholding Antony."[91]

In the meantime, any call to the kind of witness that might lead to a literal ignoble death is analogized and interiorized. Athanasius picks up Origen of Alexandria's innovations with regard to the "spiritual sense" of scripture and takes it in a moral—what later interpreters will term "tropological"—direction.[92] He is concerned with the development of virtue through imitation of exemplars, but beyond the ascetic who renounces all wealth, the model of Jesus of Nazareth is not to be taken literally. Gone—interpreted away as having only "spiritual" meaning—is the journey into Jerusalem and the kind of witness to the poor and wicked that gets Jesus killed. Athanasius—creating an Antony who gets turned back from his desire for martyrdom—tells the reader that attempts to imitate the kind of witness that might lead to one's getting killed is misdirected and no longer relevant to what it means to follow Christ. If your witness does per chance lead to threats to your life, run. The *Life* soon reaches Western Christendom, where it—and its compromise of joining monastic spiritual superiority with episcopal juridical primacy—is a major influence on thought and practice for the next millennium.

Appendix

Abelard's abstraction of authority

> In cities and castles, darkness is being spread in place of light; everywhere poison is being put forward to everybody in place of honey. . . . A new gospel is being forged for peoples and communities, a new faith is being propounded, a foundation that is different from what has been established. There is disputation that is immoral . . . everything is served up to us as perversity, everything beyond what is normal and different from what we accept.
>
> —*Bernard of Clairvaux, Letter to Innocent II*[93]

> Jerome: . . . it would be sacrilege to argue about the words of God, using human understanding.
>
> Gregory: . . . we desire heretics to be checked by catholic priests, always with vigor and reason.
>
> —*Peter Abelard*, Sic et Non[94]

Bernard is no fool. He knows exactly from where the new challenge to monepiscopacy comes in the twelfth century: not from the countryside or any desert, but from the new and growing cities. These densely populated (for the time) centers of human activity indeed do become loci of new claims to authority, religious and otherwise. Abelard's *Sic et Non*, written in the aftermath of the first condemnation of his work at the Council of Soissons (1121), only fuels concerns by juxtaposing different traditionally authoritative claims to demonstrate their (at least prima facie) incompatibility with each other. Reason is both sacrilege (Jerome) and to be used against heretics (Gregory). In preparation for the Council of Sens (1141),[95] Bernard draws up a list of nineteen statements of error found in Abelard's *Theologia "Scholarium,"* a rewrite of his *Theologia "Summi Boni"* condemned at Soissons.[96]

Up to this point, the episcopal-monastic alliance initially forged by Athanasius has been flourishing. The collapse of empire in late antiquity had required in the immediately following centuries an even more central role for monasticism as the bearer of Christian heritage and learning against waves of invasion from outside. Monasteries also formalized the religious practices of holy men who—the Pachomian movement aside—prior to John Cassian's *Institutes* and *Conferences* (early fifth century) and Benedict's *Rule* (sixth century), often lived alone and enacted their own rigorous forms of ascesis beyond ecclesial control. Now in the eleventh and twelfth centuries, the monks continue to understand themselves and to be portrayed as the ideal Christians and the heirs of the martyrs, but with still no imperially sponsored persecution, they have to manufacture their own suffering. If anything, they go even further than their Egyptian forebears in moving beyond self-deprivation in a literal desert to active self-infliction of suffering. Practices include, among others, self-flagellation, the wearing of iron plates and shirts (*lorica*), immersion in water, and extended sessions of repeated genuflection. The aim is precisely to thwart one's sensual desires—to swap out what is considered gluttony and lust for pain—all in the effort to expiate one's sins and, in the process, imitate the suffering of Christ. Peter Damian, writing in the eleventh century and not long before Abelard's birth, provides an apt summation of both the motive and the means: "I would like to undergo martyrdom for Christ, but I have no possibility for it now that the [persecuting] zeal has ceased. I show at least the desire of a fervent soul by destroying myself with beating."[97] More, the eleventh century Gregorian Reform and what Giles Constable calls the "reformation of the twelfth century," seek to extend the monastic vision not simply as an ideal to be imitated remotely by other walks of life, but, much more than with Athanasius, as something to be lived out more fully by all. In Constable's words, the twelfth century reformation is, "an effort to monasticize first the clergy, by imposing on them a standard of life previously reserved for monks, and then the entire world."[98]

Now an ersatz monk[99]—Abelard—with insufficient appreciation of monasticism's contribution to Christendom—according to Bernard—seeks to upend the heritage by throwing the traditional sources into contradiction with each other. Or so it seems. In the prologue to *Sic et Non*, Abelard goes to great lengths to argue that he is not suggesting that the authorities in fact disagree with regard to the truth, rather that reason is necessary to come to a correct understanding of what only appears to be fundamental inconsistencies. "Let us not denounce them as liars, or disparage them as erroneous," he says in reference to the authorities. Rather, "let us believe that it is due more to our lack of understanding, than to their failure in writing."[100] And Abelard proceeds to set out various criteria for the interpretation of accepted texts,[101] criteria through which reason can reconcile the seemingly opposed statements: be sure to check whether an erroneous text was in fact written by the titled author rather than attributed to that author for the sake of gaining authority; be aware that words can have different meanings so as to be clear whether the two seemingly conflicting authors are in fact writing about the same thing; be on the alert for scribal errors; note that writings are shaped by their audiences and that apparent differences of opinion can be simply a matter of the authors attending to the needs and capacities of different audiences; check to see if the author of a questionable statement elsewhere retracts it; consider the fact that authors sometimes include in their own commentaries even "the conjectures of heretics" in order to be complete in their presentation; know that authors sometimes purposely leave a question in doubt in order to more fully engage the reader; distinguish time periods, because something properly affirmed in one era may be properly condemned in another. When all of the aforementioned criteria fail, go with the "older and better" authority.

But Bernard is having none of it: "A new gospel is being forged . . . a foundation that is different from what has been established." And closer reading of Abelard's prologue bears the Abbot from Clairvaux out. The criterion of interpretation that holds the reader to an awareness that traditional authorities occasionally "say some things through ignorance, rather than duplicity," does *not* presuppose that the sources can be reconciled, but rather that one of them is simply wrong. At such points, Abelard counsels that the reader assess "more according to the intention of the speaker than the quality of speech, paying attention not so much to what happens as in what spirit it happens."[102] Here, Abelard shifts the ground from the question of the objective truth of the authority's claim to the intention of the author. Sometimes, the authorities can be not just misleading or opaque, but objectively *wrong*. More, Abelard elaborates on his last resort appeal to the "older and best" authorities in ways that undercut those very authorities. Citing Augustine, he specifies the "older and best" criterion of interpretation by making a distinction between the "canonical Scriptures"—the Old and New Testaments—on the one hand and the "holy fathers" on the other. With regard to the former, "it is heretical to declare anything departs from the truth"; however, as to the latter (quoting Augustine), "the reader or listener has *free judgment* to agree with what is pleasing or to disagree with what is offensive." Abelard here also claims that Jerome held the position that non-canonical authoritative books, "should be read *in order that we might judge between them rather than follow them*" (emphases added).[103] At points, Abelard goes even further to question canonical—that is, scriptural—authority: "Even in the gospels, some things seem to be more in accordance with human opinion than truth."[104]

Abelard's criteria for adjudicating conflict between textual authorities shift authority away from the traditional sources and give it to the dialectician. This is the case even where he is simply claiming that the conflict between authoritative sources is apparent rather than real. The dialectician—and, it seems, the dialectician alone—can reconcile sources when they are not really in conflict and judge between them when they are. It is no wonder, then, that when Abelard requests to have his theology discussed at the Council of Sens, he is expecting not a juridical procedure, but a disputational exchange in the academic mode, with the rule of argument, not that of bishops.[105] That the bishops, at Bernard's urging, actually come to their judgment against Abelard in a closed meeting the night *before* the Council itself indicates that they, and Bernard with them, think otherwise. At that meeting, Bernard simply reads from the compiled list of Abelard's putative errors, and the bishops respond, *Damnamus*—"We condemn it"—after each one. When Abelard senses the next day that he has been caught in a snare that he has done much to construct, he appeals to the pope in a move that highlights the fact that multiple forces are in play.[106]

The question for our purposes arises as to why the disputational method in question at Sens does not develop in a way that is more concrete and narratological.[107] Why the abstraction of dialectical thought? There is nothing in disputational method—which is conducted orally in the cathedral schools[108]—that necessitates abstraction from the concrete narration of the lives of exemplars. In fact, the gospels use Jesus's disputations with Pharisees and scribes precisely to launch his teaching on a wide array of topics from Sabbath laws (Mk 2:23-3:6 and 3:19b-30; Mt. 12:1-42; Lk. 6:1-11 and 11:14-32) to fasting (Mk 2:18-22; Mt. 9:14-17; Lk. 5:33-39) to the source of religious authority itself (Mk 2:1-12; Mt. 9:1-8; Lk. 5:17-26), all in the context of the narration of his life. Abelard himself comes close to narration—at least to the extent that he provides arguments through representative figures, if not quite enfleshed persons— in his dialogues between a philosopher on the one hand and a Jew and a Christian on the other.[109] The scholastic disputational style, with its objections and replies, gestures toward a setting where embodied interlocutors engage. Why, then, the abstraction in the scholasticism of the twelfth century and beyond? Why does it not describe more concretely—or describe at all—the settings and persons, almost palpable upon close reading of the texts, who make the arguments? It would seem that doing so by embedding the arguments in a thick account of an apostolic life in imitation of Jesus Christ could serve to strengthen Abelard's position relative to Bernard and the bishops.

Close attention to the full set of dynamics at play at the Council of Sens shows that the ecclesial authorities present are in fact worried that the dialectical method has *already* found a setting in just such a concrete narrative. When Abelard appeals to Rome, Pope Innocent II in turn condemns not only him, but also Arnold of Brescia, whose teachings are not explicitly at issue at the Council. Why, then, the papal condemnation? Northern Italy in the twelfth century is the scene not only of urban growth, but of multiple republican movements in those cities where bishops previously had extensive temporal jurisdiction. The republican movement draws largely from the artisan and merchant classes, and Brescia at the time is second only to Milan as a center of cloth manufacturing in the Lombard region. Some cities work out compromises allowing for juxtaposed coexistence of episcopal and republican authorities, but in Brescia such an arrangement does not last due to the fact that, for the most part as a result of Arnold's preaching, the challenge to episcopal authority is not only political, but also theological.

Arnold is first of all a church reformer. To him, the Gregorian efforts against lay investiture, simony and clerical marriage are inadequate. The church and its leadership must renounce all of its property holdings and undertake a life of apostolic poverty in imitation of Christ—living only on tithes and alms, and not income from feudal landholdings—if it is to recover and preach effectively the Gospel. Arnold conveys his teaching not only in word, but by living the apostolic life himself. Unlike the monastic model, this is not an *imitatio Christi* that halts at the point of the desert temptations, but rather carries, as Bernard warns, into and then between the cities, the Jerusalems of the day. Arnold's leadership in Brescia takes place prior to the Council of Sens (1141). When the Second Lateran Council (1139) condemns his activity and expels him from Italy, he goes to France to become Abelard's student. He then appears at the Council of Sens in support of his teacher.[110]

Abelard appeals his case to Rome, and Bernard writes to the pope, urging him to condemn not only Abelard, but Arnold as well. Bernard's concern is that Arnold's popularity will serve as a conduit for Abelard's methods to reach an audience beyond the schools. He writes to Innocent II of Abelard and Arnold, describing Abelard as "the new Goliath, tall of stature and clad in war apparel, preceded by his armor-bearer, Arnold of Brescia. Scale is joined so closely to scale that not a breathing space is left between them. The bee of France has buzzed to the Italian bee and together they have advanced against the Lord and against His Christ."[111] Bernard pushes his concern regarding Arnold, even after Abelard's death, through letters to whomever is the ordinary or secular ruler where Arnold happens to reside—Paris, Zurich, Constance. When Arnold arrives in Passau, Bernard writes the legate there, "Arnold of Brescia, whose conversation is honey and whose doctrine is poison; whose head is a dove's but whose tail is a scorpion's; whom Brescia cast forth, Rome abhorred; whom France has rejected, Germany curses and Italy will not receive, is said to be with you."[112] Bernard maintains his Javertian pursuit until his own death.

At Sens, if Bernard is concerned that Arnold will serve to spread Abelard's methods, Abbot Suger of Saint-Denis worries that Ableard's academic status will give Arnold's call to apostolic poverty intellectual credibility. Experiments in republican governance analogous to the Italian cases have been developing in France under the banner of *compagnies*—urban "communes." Suger is counselor to Louis VI, and in 1138—precisely when Arnold is ascending to a leadership role in Brescia[113]—advises the king to crush the commune in Poitiers. Bernard does not at first plan to attend the Council of Sens, much less serve as its key prosecutor, until he is urged to do so by what he refers to only as "great people." Recent scholarship suggests that one of those people, and likely the most important, is Abbot Suger.[114] For Suger, to have Abelard condemned is to cut off what he fears will otherwise become the intellectual head of the commune movement.[115]

Whether the Council of Sens serves to disrupt the spread of Abelardian ideas (Bernard) or to deprive the commune movement of intellectual capital (Suger), both of the major players on the prosecutorial side are driven by the concern that the disputational methods of Abelard have already found a home in the specific narrative of communal revolt both as it is actually taking place at the time and as aspiration, a revolt inspired by the life of apostolic poverty lived and preached by Arnold of Brescia in imitation of Jesus Christ. Arnold is never formally convicted of heresy, even following Sens, only of political schism. He is ultimately executed in an alliance between pope and emperor when he takes a leading role in the rise of the commune in Rome, the central city for both papacy and empire. The executioners have his body burned to ashes and set afloat on the Tiber so that followers do not harvest it for relics that might inspire further apostolic mimesis.

The Council of Sens and the subsequent actions against Arnold serve to make clear to theologians the marshaling of violence that will take place against any threat to the monastic monopoly on what constitutes proper imitation of Christ, a monopoly that does not challenge the church's extensive feudal income. Later that century and into the next, Francis of Assisi will have to make clear his obeisance to ecclesial authority. Subsequent adherents of apostolic poverty who do not do so—from the Waldensians to the Spiritual Franciscans—will meet with violence; some of these cite Arnold as a precursor.[116] And so, from the beginning, church and state work together to warn the theologians of the schools not to set their musings in the context of a narrative of concrete gospel mimesis.

We should not be too quick, however, in placing the theologians simply as among the oppressed. There are reasons *internal* to the practice of academic theology, then as today, that inhibit and perhaps even prohibit living out and narrativizing gospel poverty for further imitation. Prior to the mid-eleventh century, most land holdings are by free smallholders. While there is slavery, most laborers who constitute the first third of the tripartite social order of *laboratores* (those who work), *oratores* (those who pray), and *bellatores* (those who fight), are free. Land consolidation, sometimes through purchase, other times through tilted judicial processes or even force, severely reduces the number of free landholders.[117] Without land of their own, by the twelfth century the vast majority of laborers become serfs working property held by others.[118] The arrangement is highly oppressive, as the landlords, acting through their bailiffs and *castalans*, exact a wide range of taxes and duties on the workers.[119] Due to endowments gifted to it by nobles, the church, through the monasteries, itself serves as a major landlord.[120] Bernard underwrites the practice by articulating a spiritual economy whereby secular rulers can gain heavenly advantage through their quite literally earthly gifts to the monks.[121] It is no wonder that Arnold's call for ecclesial renunciation of property is a threat.

Of point here is that the increased production—particularly of cereal grains—made possible by the creation of serfdom in turn makes possible the non-materially productive activity of not just monks, but also scholars. While the Counsel of Sens is often cast as a battle between monasticism and scholasticism, the latter depends on the increased agricultural productivity bought through the enserfment of previously free laborers every bit as much as the former. Their fight is an intramural one among opponents who presuppose the feudal economy and their place within it. They even draw from the same stock of people—non-firstborn sons of nobility—to supply their ranks. And while the early years of the cathedral schools are ones of political and economic precariousness for scholars, the very growth of both ecclesial and secular administration, demanded and made possible by the increased agricultural production and development of the cities, make knowledge of numbers and letters—and thus teachers in the schools— indispensable. By the end of the twelfth century, scholars regularize the curriculum so as to produce clerks who can serve anywhere in most any administration.[122] The school theologians do not challenge the social order with calls for the church to embody apostolic poverty in large part because they, like the monks, live in symbiotic relationship with that order. However uncertain their beginnings, they rapidly become scribes for church and empire.

The appeal to "reason"—abstract reason without reference to embodied biblical narrative—by Abelard and subsequent school theologians, then, is an attempt to acquire religious authority in a context where monasticism has a monopoly on what counts as the imitation of Christ and appeals to apostolic poverty otherwise bring ecclesial and civil threat of censor and violence. We do not so much have a "flight *from* authority," to use Jeffrey Stout's phrase for the development of Enlightenment philosophy from Descartes to Kant, but a bid *for* authority in a context where other avenues to religious authority are cut off from the scholar.[123] Abelard, too—and 450 years before Descartes—begins with doubt, though he proceeds not by building a freestanding system modeled on mathematics, but by relentless application of Aristotle's logic, so as to wrest authority from both prongs of the monastic-episcopal alliance: "Indeed, through doubting, we arrive at questioning; in questioning we perceive the truth."[124] The effort is to offset and even eliminate the partial (in both senses of the word) accounts of the life of Jesus Christ that either halt in the desert (Athanasius) or do not begin until the Passion (Ignatius) as sources of religious authority; the price is the loss of concrete narrativization altogether, well before Frei's "eclipse" of the biblical narrative and even radical orthodoxy's Duns Scotus. Reason so constructed places the scholar in the position of determining which statements from the tradition are authoritative while deflecting, as irrelevant, attention away from the material conditions which make such practice possible. Under the banner of free inquiry, proponents of the Enlightenment will find in Abelard a precursor figure who, like them, is hounded by hidebound traditional authorities. In this context, the Kantian Friedrich Schiller writes that Bernard, "hated and suppressed all progress as much as he could and favored the greatest stupidity of monks."[125]

The practice of writing and a stress on texts contributes to and socio-technologically reinforces the trend toward abstraction. Brian Stock argues that the twelfth century witnesses not simply a growth in literacy, but a reconstituting of culture such that literate norms shape practices even in those cases where a text is not present. "Oral tradition accepted without question nature's physicality, tangibility, and concreteness." It "required the tactile, the seen, the heard, and the performed." The development of literate culture, such that the *non*literate becomes the *il*literate, "implied a turning away from ritual and symbol and toward an intellectualism inseparable from the study of texts." [126] This is the case even for Bernard, who, although he includes a role for the physical senses over against Abelard's rationalism, draws heavily upon Paul in making a sharp distinction, even separation, between "outer" sensed reality and the true "inner meaning," the visible and the invisible, in any experience of a text.[127] Even with Bernard, there is, according to Stock, "a movement away from the performance of rites and from devotion to representational objects and towards the consideration of both primarily in terms of an inner meaning, or kernel of truth."[128] This allows Bernard to stress the human Christ while allegorizing away all those aspects of the life of Jesus of Nazareth that do not fit the monastic model of *imitatio Christi*. It is then not a large step for the scholastics to deem such imitation not relevant for their enterprise at all.

One of Stock's sub-arguments is that ecclesiastical concern for the prosecution of heretics is one of the prime movers in the turn toward texts. Such prosecution is an "attempt to fit a new, troubling experience, for which there is only a verbal record, into an acceptably conventional framework involving texts."[129] Constant Mews details how fear of textually based prosecution shapes Abelard's writing between the Council of Soisons, the site of his first condemnation, and the Council of Sens, where he is judged a second time. Mews notes that in the original version of his *Theologia*, the *Theologia "Summi boni"* condemned at Soissons, Abelard frequently appeals to the reader/listener directly through the second person singular. His citation of authorities is loose, even casual, evidencing a background context of oral exchange, where the participants recognize the authorities without their having to be explicitly named. The objection to the *Theologia "Summi boni"* at Soissons is not that it has been written, but that it has been read aloud in public. The written text is merely an aid for the oral delivery of lectures. The burning of Abelard's text at Soissons is symbolic; the prosecutors know that there are other copies. The meaning conveyed through the burning is that such ideas are not to be discussed in public again. In subsequent versions of the *Theologia*, Abelard provides detailed textual support for his reasoning, rendering the text, "torturous to read aloud." Mews concludes, "The pressure placed on him at Soissons to justify controversial theological arguments with long and learned marginal notes changed a treatise which could easily be delivered aloud to a work of reference accessible only to an educated elite. This in itself rendered the *Theologia* less dangerous as a work of theology."[130] This change in direction in Abelard's writing, as much as the convergence of forces at Sens itself, is what makes him—after Paul, Ignatius, and Athanasius—the fourth pivot point in the development of a form of theological practice that has "lost its senses." Despite many subsequent events and fluctuations, theology remains marked by this last turning, this completion of the *conversio ab phantasma*.

Stock and Mews draw from the work of Jack Goody and Walter Ong on orality and literacy I discuss in Chapter 2, and it becomes evident that the prosecution of heresy in literate culture is an effort to nail down, as if to a backboard, what Ong calls the "winged words" that "are constantly moving" in oral culture. Together with Eric Havelock, Goody and Ong show how literate culture seeks to bring fixed order to words by placing them in the context of systematic lists of topics presented as comprehensive, and it comes as no surprise that prosecutorial literacy in the twelfth century results in the production of theological texts similarly intended to be exhaustive, first Peter Lombard's *Sentences* and then the *summae* of various authors. On this account, the overall literate systematicity of Aquinas' *Summa* eclipses the putatively dialectical internal structure of each question, and an overarching abstract neo-Platonic *exitus et reditus* schema displaces the centrality of the narrative of a God-man from Nazareth.[131] The placement of the dialectic in a comprehensive and exhaustive text, to shift to Havelock's metaphor, "fossilizes" the give-and-take of the disputational setting.

This textualization of culture has particular implications for theology as a scholarly discipline in relation to the findings earlier in Chapter 6 regarding Jesus of Nazareth's twin missions to the poor and the wicked. Both Stock and Mews note how, with the ascendance of literate culture, what is nonliterate becomes suspect. Stock highlights that it is precisely the development of literate culture that gives rise to "new distinctions between religious literates and nonliterates." Such distinctions, "implied a questioning of the status of popular culture." Nonliterate as illiterate. Mews adds that even in the scholarly context, arguments made, and the persons who made them, without explicit and detailed reference to accepted texts, "soon acquired the taint of heresy."[132] When, beginning with Abelard, theologians appropriate literate culture via their detailed documentation of sources, they also absorb this embedded prejudice against the nonliterate. With close to 140 endnotes in this appendix alone, I am aware of the self-indictment in saying so, but it needs to be said: far from involving missions to the poor and the wicked, the fundamental presupposition of academic theology, with its certifications for membership and authority by citation, is that the poor—especially the orally centered, nonliterate and therefore uncertified poor—*are* the presumed wicked. This is our birth story as theologians, and our heritage.

* * *

Room 309 of the Hynes Convention Center in Boston is windowless, even cave-like, and matches the other meeting rooms, all done in browns and grays with recessed bulbs above that throw more shadow than light. The American Institute for Architects' *Guide to Boston* describes the "severe gray interior" of the Convention Center itself as "reminiscent of an early twentieth-century German railroad station." Weimar Republic gray.

But this morning, Room 309 is filled beyond capacity. People are standing in the doorway and out into the hall, and the moderator will suggest during a break between speakers that those in the back can come up front to sit on the floor, literally at the feet of the presenters, to listen to the prime articulators of a theology that claims to be at once new and deeply traditional.

It is the 1999 Annual Meeting of the American Academy of Religion, and the three editors of a recently published volume under the title, *Radical Orthodoxy*— John Milbank, Catherine Pickstock, and Graham Ward—are listed to present.[133] This is their stateside book launch. They intend the title of their introduction to the volume, "Suspending the Material" to connote not a getting rid of "the material," but a preservation of it precisely by a setting of it in its proper theological context. They write, "Only transcendence, which 'suspends' these things in the sense of interrupting them, 'suspends' them also in the other sense of upholding their relative worth over against the void." They promise a theology attentive to "embodied life," a "more incarnate" theology "allowing finite things their own integrity," thus "safeguard[ing] their worldliness" by highlighting the "density" of such material things and the "sensuality of all human thought." They promise a theology that will "turn us" not away from but "towards the body."[134] Just yesterday, in another session, Milbank warned that there was a "danger" that the "tradition was never concrete enough." And he chided modern philosophy's examples of "the real" for referring to "walking the dog" or "butter in the refrigerator," rather than more substantive matters like the "slaughter of Tutsis."[135] Perhaps there has been a turning, an effort to make good on correcting the problem that concrete depiction of the embodied church is, in Milbank's own words, "rather minimal" in his earlier *Theology and Social Theory*.

Milbank is—like in the edited volume—first up after the introduction, and marks an interesting beginning as he refers to the book-launch purpose of his visit by suggesting that doing three sessions at the conference might be "overkill from a marketing perspective." Discussion of the case of the marketing of the neologism, "radical orthodoxy," could indeed constitute not just economic, but interesting theological reflection. The book introduction claims radicality in its "return to patristic and medieval roots, and especially to the Augustinian vision," but in order to be truly radical should not such roots, if it is a matter of "return," go back to the person through whom God first uniquely self-revealed—*radix* meaning "of the root"? But there is scant reference in radical orthodoxy to the shape of Jesus of Nazareth's life as first narrated orally and then written in Scripture. Orthodoxy? It refers to "commitment to credal Christianity" and again to the primacy of patristic and medieval theology over against both earlier and later articulations—with patristic meaning for the most part Augustine and thus the middle or late stages of the era depending on one's dating.[136] At first blush anyway, radical orthodoxy does not appear to be particularly radical, and perhaps not even orthodox. Clearly then, there is marketing going on in the self-titling, perhaps the appeal of apparent opposites seemingly brought together, like the name of the American psychedelic rock band from the 1960s, Iron Butterfly.

Two floors below, anxious near- and newly minted PhDs take part in another sector of the theology and religion market in the Employment Information Service or EIS Center in Exhibit Hall D. They all know that their twenty-minute interviews with schools with position openings will not, of themselves, get them a job, but that the conversations can lose them one. Reflection on the market down there and the one up here in light of what it means for the church to be the Body of Christ could be illuminating of the concrete context in which academic theology is practiced. But Milbank's reference to market overkill is a throwaway line. It elicits the desired laughter, and finds no substantive place in the production.

The rest of the presentation repeats the pattern: Milbank reads directly from a paper that will be published word for word less than a year later, and occasionally punctuates it with concrete asides that could be theologically interesting if probed, but are not and so do not make it into the written record. He looks up from the paper after reading that radical orthodoxy can appeal to both Roman Catholics and Protestants, and says, "One thing that I have noticed in America is that all the Protestants in the South really want to be Catholic because they have Catholic weather down there, whereas all the Catholics in the North—all the Irish and Polish immigrants and Italians and so forth—are all trying to be Protestants because they have cold Protestant weather. I think that's the most fundamental problem about American religion." Again the desired laughter but, despite a claimed emphasis on the "concreteness of the gospels," there are no other displays of concreteness in Milbank's presentation other than that of the humorous aside. There is no exploration, for instance, of the role of climate in the shape of Jesus's remembered and later written words and deeds. The itinerant life prioritized there as that which embodies most fully obedience to God might be more difficult in the cold of the upper regions of Scandinavia; should the Church as the Body of Christ re-order the priority? The reference to weather is for other purposes: laughter, and that common thing that we talk about when we have nothing else to say, like walking the dog.

The concrete quotidian can be theologically significant—we mark ordinary time as part of the liturgical year—or it can be simply mundane. Or it can be the humorous. But because *all* of Milbank's concrete references are for only this— mundane humor and not that of the divine comedy—they also become the oral, the unwritten, the unofficial, the low-brow, the off-color (jokes about Poles and Italians), the heterodox. For all of its gestures toward it, radical orthodoxy does not and cannot, because of its other commitments, accept what Milbank calls "the real." In practice, the "suspension of the material" means that all that is material has been kicked out for bad behavior.

There is not much more to tell here. You can go to the article, titled, "The Programme of Radical Orthodoxy," for the rest of the written record.[137] But know: in it, "the material" is suspended.

Notes

1. I am aware of the renovations of Regenstein Library, which include a half-tube shaped glass-paneled reading room full of light. A wag might conjecture that there is a direct correlation between this development and the weakening of the previous demand—five four-hour closed-book examinations—of the Divinity School's comprehensive exam structure.

2. This is the case even when knowledge of God is by remotion, that is, by imagining God as *not* a corporeal object. See Thomas Aquinas, *Summa Contra Gentiles*, trans. Anton C. Pegis (Notre Dame, IN: University of Notre Dame Press, 1991), I.14.

3. Erich Auerbach, *Mimesis: The Representation of Reality in Western Literature*, Fiftieth Anniversary Edition (Princeton and Oxford: Princeton University Press, 2003), pp. 22 and 29.

4. Auerbach, *Mimesis*, 18: "Fraught with their development, sometimes even aged to the verge of dissolution, they show a distinct stamp of individuality entirely foreign to the Homeric heroes." Cf. 17–20.

5. Auerbach, *Mimesis*, p. 15.

6. Ibid., p. 45.

7. Ibid., p. 48–9.

8. Ibid., p. 15.

9. Ibid., p. 41.

10. Only later did I realize the distinction between how a virtue is acquired and whether it can be known by the intellect. One can acquire a virtue by divine infusion and still know it via the intellect working with and through phantasms.

11. Gregory's full statement is, "That which was not assumed is not healed; but that which is united to God is saved" (*to gar aproslepton, atherapeuton ho de henotai to theu, touto kai sozetai*).

12. It is noteworthy that Thomas Aquinas argues that angels do not need to be redeemed because they are pure spirit and thus not physical and marked by sin. *Summa Theologica*, Ia, 50, 2.

13. Catherine Pickstock, "Reply to David Ford and Guy Collins," *Scottish Journal of Theology* 54, no. 3 (2001): 406.

14. Hans W. Frei, *The Eclipse of Biblical Narrative: A Study in Eighteenth and Nineteenth Century Hermeneutics* (New Haven: Yale University Press, 1980). For the literal sense of scripture, see the chapters, "Theology and the Interpretation of Narrative: some Hermeneutical Considerations" (Chapter 3), and "The 'Literal Reading' of Biblical Narrative in the Christian Tradition: Does It Stretch or Will It Break?" (Chapter 4), in Frei, *Theology and Narrative: Selected Essays*, ed. George Hunsinger and William C. Placher (New York and Oxford: Oxford University Press, 1993). For the influence of Auerbach on Frei, see William C. Placher, "Introduction," in Frei, *Theology and Narrative*.

15. Frei, *Theology and Narrative*, pp. 96 and 100.

16. Ibid., p. 112.

17. George Lindbeck, *The Nature of Doctrine: Religion and Theology in a Postliberal Age* (Louisville: Westminster John Knox Press, 1984).

18. Frei, *Theology and Narrative*, p. 119. The passage continues, "That viability, if any, will follow excellently from the actual fruitful use religious people continue to make of it in ways that enhance their own and other people's lives, without the obscurantist features so often and unhappily associated with it. And even if, as may be expected, there is a continuing decline of the felt pertinence of this way of reading among those who do not make a direct religious use of it, this in no way alters the case for its viability in principle to Christian people, no matter how distressing it is bound to be to them as an actual cultural fact." The odd thing about this passage is that after he makes the case for a theology that combines biblical narrative particularity with lived Christian particularity, Frei writes himself, the theologian, *out* of the process of generating such a theology. He refers to "actual fruitful use of religious people" and "their" lives as if he were not a member of the community. Christian people are all of a sudden "them" in this passage, not "us." What I am trying to do in this chapter is make sense of this seemingly abrupt departure.

19. Stanley Hauerwas, *The Hauerwas Reader*, ed. John Berkman and Michael Cartwright (Durham, NC: Duke University Press, 2001), pp. 117 and 119; 72–3, 77, and 378.

20. On the claim that the church is an empirical reality, Hauerwas, *The Hauerwas Reader*, 382; for the claim that the church is a social ethic, see Stanley Hauerwas, *The Peaceable Kingdom: A Primer in Christian Ethics* (Notre Dame, IN: University of Notre Dame Press, 1991), p. 99.

21. Examples of using short descriptions of incidents to launch stories or illustrate points, see Hauerwas, *The Hauerwas Reader*, pp. 75, 246–7, 255, 265, 540, and 556–7. The one possible example of more extended descriptions begins in Chapter 5 of *Resident Aliens*, which is a coauthored book with William Willimon. The first four chapters are a broad social analysis consistent with Hauerwas's style. The later chapters reflect the firsthand knowledge of a minister, raising the question of whether Hauerwas is the primary source for the first parts and Willimon for the later chapters. For Hauerwas's treatment of Watership down, see Hauerwas, *The Hauerwas Reader*, pp. 171 ff. There may be deep theological reasons for this limited use of empirical detail. It might rest in a resistance to the kind of use of the social sciences that one finds in Walter Rauschenbusch, who Hauerwas criticizes for putting theology—funneled through the social sciences—at the service of making the world a better place. Or the source of concern could be that he not accept "experience in itself" as a moral category, but rather affirm that all experience is interpreted through particular narratives, and the relevant narrative for Christians is that of Jesus Christ. The social and natural sciences often presuppose that there is an "experience in itself." For Hauerwas's critique of Rauschenbusch, see *The Hauerwas Reader*, p. 57; for his critique of experience "in itself," see pp. 267–71 and 283–4.

22. John Milbank, *Theology and Social Theory: Beyond Secular Reason* (Oxford, UK and Cambridge, MA: Blackwell Publishers Ltd., 1993), p. 431.

23. Milbank perhaps nods to the filmic analogy when, after appealing to the idea of a picture, comments, "To 'refer' things to the infinite is to arrange them in their proper place in a sequence." Milbank, *Theology and Social Theory*, p. 431.

24. Milbank, *Theology and Social Theory*, pp. 422–3 and 385; cf. also 384–8 and 430.

25. Ibid., p. 431.

26. The full title of the last chapter of *Theology and Social Theory* is "The Other City: Theology as a Social Science."

27. Milbank, *Theology and Social Theory,* pp. 396–8.

28. For the economic reference, see Milbank, *Theology and Social Theory,* p. 422; for the references to mutual forgiveness, see pp. 409, 411, and 421. On the necessity of coercion, see pp. 418–21. It should be added that Milbank's appropriation of Scripture is also very thin. See David F. Ford, "Radical Orthodoxy and the Future of British Theology," *Scottish Journal of Theology* 54, no. 3 (2001): 394–5, and 397–9.

29. For the criticism that Milbank's tone is too pugnacious to be an exemplification of a peaceful and loving narrative, see Christopher J. Insole, "Against Radical Orthodoxy: The Dangers of Overcoming Political Liberalism," *Modern Theology* 20, no. 2 (2004): 220–3; and Scott MacDougall, "Scapegoating the Secular," in *Violence, Transformation, and the Sacred: "They Shall Be Called People of God,"* ed. Margaret R. Pfeil and Tobias L. Winright (Maryknoll: Orbis Books, 2011), pp. 87–8. While far from all pugnaciousness is loving, it is, I think, worth noting that Jesus did not say to have no enemies, but to love them, and that in his last visit to the temple he was more or less looking for a fight. The consensus among biblical scholars is that he must have anticipated that the action in the temple would lead to his death. Loving is not the same thing as being nice.

30. John Milbank, *The Future of Love: Essays in Political Theology* (Eugene: Cascade Books, 2009), pp. 134–5. Even though the book is sub-titled, *Essays in Political Theology,"* Milbank offers us nothing of the kind of particularity that enables, in his earlier words, "the type of an exemplary practice which we can imitate." *Theology and Social Theory,* p. 396.

31. Jean Bethke Elshtain, "Theologian: Christian Contrarian," *Time* (September 17, 2001), retrieved on February 1, 2013 from http://www.time.com/time/magazine/article/0,9171,1000859-2,00.html. Elshtain herself does not use the term "best," but the article is part of *Time*'s annual "America's Best" listings; thus the lead word "Theologian" refers to "America's Best Theologian." Multiple subsequent media outlets—including, among others, the Duke Divinity School and United Methodist Church websites and *Wikipedia*—cite *Time*'s designation of Hauerwas as "American's Best Theologian"; Jeff Sharlett, "Theologians Seek to Reclaim the World with God and Postmodernism," *Chronicle of Higher Education* (June 23, 2000), retrieved on February 1, 2013 from http://chronicle.com.proxy.library.nd.edu/article/Theologians-Seek-to-Reclaim/1937/. James K. A. Smith's assessment, made in 2004, of both *Theology and Social Theory* and radical orthodoxy more generally is probably more accurate, giving due recognition to their importance while not engaging in hyperbole. "While not quite a Barthian bombshell. John Milbank's *Theology and Social Theory* did land with considerable impact on contemporary theology. In retrospect, it was this tome that became something of a manifesto for an agenda that would later be described as Radical Orthodoxy." Smith, *Introducing Radical Orthodoxy: Mapping a Post-Secular Theology* (Grand Rapids: Baker Academic, 2004), pp. 33–4.

32. Immanuel Kant, *Grounding for the Metaphysics of Morals,* (1993), p. 21, cited in Miller, *Mimesis and Reason,* p. 150, note. 54. Max Horkheimer and Theodor W. Adorno, *Dialectic of Enlightenment: Philosophical Fragments,* ed. Gunzelin Schmid Noerr, trans. Edmund Jephcott (Stanford, CA: Stanford University Press, 2002). Gregg Daniel Miller argues, correctly in my judgment, that "rationality has been built up [during the Enlightenment] against its other, mimesis." See Miller, *Mimesis and Reason: Habermas's Political Philosophy* (Albany, NY: SUNY Press, 2011), pp. 33.

33. I have addressed Hauerwas's work in more detail elsewhere, where I also critique the work of James Gustafson, indicating that the problem of lack of imitable narrative particularity is not limited to one contemporary school of thought or another. See Todd Whitmore, "Crossing the Road: The Case for Ethnographic Fieldwork in Christian Ethics," *Journal of the Society of Christian Ethics* 27/2 (Fall/Winter 2007): 273–94.

34. Michael Taussig, *Mimesis and Alterity: A Particular History of the Senses* (New York and London: Routledge, 1993), p. 33; Gregg Daniel Miller, *Mimesis and Reason: Habermas's Political Philosophy* (Albany: State university of New York press, 2011), p. 14.

35. Also, the "exemplary narratives of Jesus show us the 'shape'" of the life to be imitated "so that we can call ourselves 'the body of Christ.'" Milbank, *Theology and Social Theory*, pp. 396–8.

36. To put it in terms of Pierre Bourdieu's social theory, religion constitutes a "field" of competition over power via "symbolic capital," generating a misrepresentation—or what he would term "misrecognition"—of religious authority. "Field" here is translated from the French word, *champs*, meaning, for instance, a sports field. Bourdieu's absolute reduction of all religious practice (and social practice generally) to questions of self-regarding power and misrecognition is overdrawn, but the idea that the Jesus tradition and Christianity have been, among other things, fields of competition will help delineate how dynamics within these traditions themselves have given rise to a practice of theology forged in the context of the suppression of a mimesis that seeks to reenact Jesus Christ. Pierre Bourdieu, "Genesis and Structure of the Religious Field," in *Comparative Social Research: A Research Annual: Religious Institutions*, Vol. 13, ed. Craig Calhoun (Greenwich, CT and London: JAI Press, 1991), pp. 1–44; Bourdieu, "The Forms of Capital," trans. Richard Nice, in *Handbook of Theory and Research for the Sociology of Education*, ed. John Richardson (New York: Greenwood Press, 1986), pp. 241–58; Bourdieu, "The Market of Symbolic Goods," trans. Rupert Swyer, *Poetics* 14 (1985): 13–44; Bourdieu, "Symbolic Power," in *Identity and Structure: Issues in the Sociology of Education*, trans. Colin Wringe (Driffield: Studies in Education, Ltd: 1977), pp. 112–19.

37. I do not suggest that the writings of these persons by themselves determined history. Though Paul was decisive for what followed, for instance, Abelard is noteworthy more for the fact that, although his writings did have impact, he was the theologian taken up in the paradigm event—the Council of Sens—where contesting claims of authority clashed; there were other theologians writing in a similar genre as Abelard. Ignatius and Athanasius fall somewhere between Paul and Abelard in terms of their singular impact. The four taken together, however, represent crucial pivot points in the development of Christian theology.

38. To be clear, I am not arguing that all of the material in the gospels ought to be taken literally; that would clearly constitute a misreading of Scripture. Rather, my aim is simply to show how certain theological moves—particularly the visible/invisible and external/internal distinctions, later formalized in theories of the spiritual or allegorical meanings of scripture—serve to deflect those parts of scripture that *ought to be* taken more literally, but that prove problematic to particular claims of religious authority on the part of the author in question. The tendency is for Christian writers to describe as simply "spiritual" but not "literal" those parts of the life of Jesus that, if taken more literally, would threaten the authority of the writer or those on behalf of whom he is writing.

39. John Milbank, "The Programme of Radical Orthodoxy," in *Radical Orthodoxy—A Catholic Enquiry*, ed. Laurence Paul Hemming (Aldershot, Burlington USA, Singapore, and Sydney: Ashgate, 2000), p. 36.

40. For purposes of this analysis, I am limiting myself to the undisputedly authentic Pauline letters.

41. For an early articulation, see F. C. Baur, "Die Christuspartei in der korinthischen Gemeinde, der Gegensatz des paulinischen und petrinischen Christentums in der ältesten Kirche, der Apostel Petrus in Rom," *Tubinger Zeitschrift* (1931); and later, F. C. Baur, *Kritische Untersuchungen über die kanonischen Evangelien, ihr Verhältness zu einander, ihren Charakter und Ursprung* (Tubingen: Fues, 1847). For more contemporary interpretations of early Christianity in terms of contestation between the Jerusalem representatives and Paul (but without Baur's Hegelianism or specific historical claims and dating of documents),

see Michael Goulder, *St. Paul versus St. Peter: A Tale of Two Missions* (Louisville, KY: Westminster John Knox Press, 1995); Laura Nasrallah, *An Ecstasy of Folly: Prophecy and Authority in Early Christianity* (Cambridge, MA: Harvard University Press, 2003), pp. 61–94; and James D. Tabor, *The Jesus Dynasty: The Hidden History of Jesus, His Royal Family, and the Birth of Christianity* (New York: Simon and Schuster, 2007); and Tabor, *Paul and Jesus: How the Apostle Transformed Christianity* (New York: Simon and Schuster, 2012).

42. Some in the ancient Near East referred to Samaritans as being in part Jewish, but the Gospel of Luke has Jesus refer to the Samaritan as "foreigner" (Lk. 17:18). The Greek term *allogenēs* literally means, "of another race." More, there was an inscription on the Jerusalem temple that forbade entrance to such persons. I am indebted to John Fitzgerald for this point and for many others in this section on Paul. Any mistakes, of course, are my own.

43. It should be clear, then, that in highlighting Paul's turn from the senses, I am not endorsing a Harnackian sharp distinction between Jesus' Judaic roots and Hellenistic early Christianity. Dynamic interaction with and influence from Hellenism within Judaism predates Jesus. Cf. Gerd Theissen and Annette Merz, *The Historical Jesus: A Comprehensive Guide* (Minneapolis: Fortress Press, 1996), pp. 126–41.

44. The phrase *cuius region, eius religio* was first formulated as part of the Peace of Augsburg in 1555, and taken up in the Treaty of Westphalia in 1648, though in both of these cases, the reference is to the realm of political rulers. My point is that, structurally, the agreement between the Jerusalem leaders and Paul was similar, with the exception that the focus is on apostolic authority.

45. I am aware of the debate concerning whether the "super-apostles" to which Paul refers are his opponents in 2 Corinthians, and that most scholars view them as the same. There is also debate as to whether the super-apostles and opponents are associated with Jerusalem. Many scholars do make this link, but the evidence is thinner.

46. There is scholarly debate regarding whether Paul would have Timothy circumcised. He does not have Titus circumcised (Gal. 2:3). The main point for our purposes is that Paul did not find circumcision finally relevant for membership in the Christian community.

47. That the fundamental issue is the question of Paul's authority and status as an apostle is often lost in large part because most scholars work off of the assumption that Paul's account of a meeting in Jerusalem in Galatians 2 and the account in Acts 15 of the "Jerusalem Council" are the same event, but Ben Witherington has effectively shown that they cannot be. Galatians 2 refers to an earlier meeting with the leaders of the Jerusalem church, one in which there is a quiet agreement that Paul and Barnabas will go to the Gentiles while Peter and the others will proclaim to the Jews. Beyond that, those attending agree on no particulars. When Paul returns to Antioch, he sees Peter, under the influence of James' "people," withdraw from table fellowship with the Gentiles because the food may not be kosher. The same year, he finds out that the circumcision party has infiltrated his churches in Asia Minor, prompting his writing of Galatians. The Apostolic Conference of Acts 15 follows, wherein the Jerusalem leaders agree that circumcision is not necessary, but insist that certain religious (against idolatry), moral (against fornication), and dietary (against the eating of meat containing blood) prohibitions be kept. Paul's writing against the "super-apostles" in 2 Corinthians is an indication that even the Council of Jerusalem agreement was unstable in the mission field. See Ben Witherington III, *The Paul Quest: The Renewed Search for the Jew of Tarsus* (Downers Grove, IL: InterVarsity Press, 1998), pp. 314–18. I am aware that most biblical scholars still reject Witherington's account.

48. Patrick Gray, *Opening Paul's Letters: A Reader's Guide to Genre and Interpretation* (Grand Rapids, MI: Baker Academic, 2012), p. 13.

Among biblical scholars and scholars of early Christianity, my emphasis on contestation over religious authority is perhaps most like Elisabeth's Schüssler Fiorenza's "model of struggle." See Schüssler Fiorenza, *Jesus and the Politics of Interpretation* (New York: Continuum, 2000), pp. 149–73; *Rhetoric and Ethic: The Politics of Biblical Studies* (Minneapolis: Augsburg, 1999); and "Re-Visioning Christian Origins: *In Memory of Her* Revisited," in *Christian Origins: Worship, Belief, and Society*, ed. Kiernan J. O. Mahoney (New York: Sheffield Academic Press, 2003).

49. Dunn, *Jesus Remembered*, p. 183; cf. 181–4.m

50. It should be noted that in the third version of Paul's conversion in Acts (22:15-18), Ananias is absent; Jesus speaks directly to Paul.

51. John J. Pilch, *Flights of the Soul: Visions, Heavenly Journeys, and Peak Experiences in the Biblical World* (Grand Rapids: William B. Eerdmans Publishing Company, 2011), p. 134.

52. Though note Jn 20:17, when Jesus says to Mary, "Do not hold on to me, because I have not yet ascended to the Father." Also, the Gospel of John goes on to have Jesus say, "Blessed are those who have not seen and yet have come to believe" (20:29b), though only *after* it feels compelled to establish that Jesus could be seen and touched. John is also the least reliable of the gospels with regard to the historicity of the sayings it attributes to Jesus.

53. In most passages where Paul gives a positive connotation to the term "body," he metaphorizes it—typically in reference to the community as the "body of Christ" (1 Cor. 10:16-17; 11:24, 29; 12:12-27; 2 Cor. 12:4-8)—in a way that generalizes it in a direction away from specific human bodies.

54. The inner/outer distinction in part reflects Paul's usage of concepts from Middle Platonism. See also 1 Cor. 15:35-56, where he links the heavenly to the imperishable, honorable, spiritual, powerful, and immortal, while he attaches the earthly to what he describes as a perishable, and thus dishonorable state of existence.

55. Weber, *Economy and Society*, pp. 1121–2.

56. *The Didache*, 15.2, in Michael W. Holmes, ed., *The Apostolic Fathers in English*, third edition (Grand Rapids, MI: Baker Academic, 2006), p. 171.

57. Francis A. Sullivan, S. J., *From Apostles to Bishops: The Development of the Episcopacy in the early Church* (New York and Mahwah, NJ: The Newman Press, 2001), pp. 64–5, 72–3, and 100.

58. Scholars debate the presence of presbyters in Antioch at this point because Paul's undisputed letters do not mention them. If they were there early on, there may well have been the kind of initial lack of respect for them found in the community addressed by *The Didache*.

59. I accept the dominant scholarly consensus that the seven letters described as the "middle recension" are authentic. The seven include the letters to the Ephesians (Eph.), Magnesians (Magn.), Trallians (Trall.), Romans (Rom.), Philadelphians (Phil.), Smyrnaeans (Smyrn.),and to Polycarp (Pol.).

60. Unless otherwise noted, all quotes of Igantius's letters are from Michael W. Holmes, *The Apostolic Fathers in English*, third edition (Grand Rapids, MI: Baker Academic, 2006).

61. William R. Schoedel, *Ignatius of Antioch: A Commentary on the Letters of Ignatius of Antioch*, ed. Helmut Koester (Philadelphia: Fortress Press, 1985), pp. 59 and 147.

62. Sullivan, S. J., *From Apostles to Bishops*, p. 108.

63. Dunn, *Jesus and the Spirit*, pp. 81–2.

64. Peter's death as a martyr is not attested to until around 200 A.D., by Tertullian.

65. On this point, see Schoedel, *Ignatius of Antioch*, 11; and Allen Brent, *Ignatius of Antioch: A Martyr Bishop and the Origin of Episcopacy* (London and New York: T & T Clark, 2007), pp. 19–22.

66. It is, I think, significant that while dozens of persons who died at the hands of authorities in the first century were quickly attested to as martyrs, Ignatius was not until over a hundred years later when the monepiscopal structure was more the norm. Perhaps not everyone agreed at first with his portrayal of himself as a martyr.

67. This is the main argument of Brent, *Ignatius of Antioch*. See also John-Paul Lotz, *Ignatius and Concord: The Background and Use of the Language of Concord in the Letters of Ignatius of Antioch* (New York: Peter Lang, 2007); and Schoedel, *Ignatius of Antioch*, pp. 74, 116, and 269.

68. Michael Holmes notes Ignatius' "heavy use of the Pauline tradition," and Albert Barnett writes, "It is clear that Ignatius knew 1 Corinthians, Romans, Ephesians and that he probably knew Galatians, Philippians, and Colossians. He may also have known 2 Corinthians, 1 and 2 Thessalonians, and Philemon." Holmes, *The Apostolic Fathers in English*, 93; and Albert E. Barnett, *Paul Becomes a Literary Influence* (Chicago: University of Chicago Press, 1941), p. 170.

69. Judith Perkins, *The Suffering self: Pain and Narrative Representation in the Early Christian Era* (London and New York: Routledge, 1995).

70. There is question as to whether the Christian communities that Ignatius addresses consider those whom he identifies as docetists and Judaizers to be enemies and therefore outside the bounds of the communities. Schoedel argues that the "flat denial of Jesus' fleshliness" was "not common," such that the teachings he attributed to his enemies, "they would have rejected out of hand." In addition, Ignatius construes the Judaizing tendencies "as a greater threat than they were." Finally, the link between docetism and Judaizing tendencies was "invented by Ignatius." Schoedel, *Ignatius of Antioch*, pp. 118, 125, 155.

71. For anthropological treatments of honor/shame societies, see D. Gilmore, ed., *Honor and Shame and the Unity of the Mediterranean* (Washington, DC: American Anthropological Association, 1987). For a treatment of the theme by a New Testament and early Christianity scholar, see Bruce J. Malina, *The New Testament World: Insights from Cultural Anthropology*, 3rd edition (Louisville: Westminster John Knox Press, 2001), pp. 27–57. For a critique of the use of the honor/shame rubric by anthropologists, see Michael Herzfeld, *Anthropology Through the Looking Glass: Critical Ethnography at the Margins of Europe* (Cambridge: Cambridge University Press, 1987). In my judgment, Herzfeld is correct in his criticism that at least some anthropologists use the rubric to read the Mediterranean region as somehow "backward," but it does not follow that every analysis identifying honor/shame patterns follows suit.

72. Schoedel, *Ignatius of Antioch*, p. 29; cf. also pp. 13 and 249.

73. Again, given the "silent" bishops elsewhere, Ignatius is realistic about the possibility of there being many bishops who can also enact the apostolic or prophetic roles in any robust sense— that is, through their persons—but at least all Christians who claim such roles will be under the office of the bishop.

74. For other references to the bishop that do not mention either the presbyters or the deacons, see Eph. 3:2, 5:1, 5:3, 6:1; Magn. 3:1-2, 4:1, 13:2; Phil. 3:2; and Pol. 6:1.

75. Clement uses the term *episcopoi*, "bishops" in the plural, in this passage, but he uses the term interchangeably with that of *presbuteroi*. The key point here is the fact of plural leadership by elders.

76. This is the case despite Ignatius's statement early in his first letter, that written to the Ephesians, that the congregation should be "like" their bishop (1:3). At this juncture, Ignatius is just referring to the fact that their bishop, Onesimus, visited him, and that he would like other members of the congregation to do so as well. The structural differentiation with the bishop being God the Father and the laity being the obedient Christ is predominant in the letters.

77. The Council of Arles (353) and the Council of Milan (355).

78. This was held to be the case even though Bishop Peter was eventually captured and executed. The pertinent fact is that he first fled.

79. David Brakke, *Athanasius and the Politics of Asceticism* (Oxford: Clarendon Press, 1995), pp. 4, 83, 103–6, and 109. My interpretation of Athanasius owes much to Brakke.

80. Brakke, *Athanasius and the Politics of Asceticism,* pp. 204–5.

81. Athanasius, *The Life of Antony* and *The Letter Marcellinus* (Mahwah, NJ, 1980), Introduction.

82. Athanasius, *The Life of Antony* and *The Letter Marcellinus,* pars. 39–40. I follow the paragraph rather than page numeration as given in the text.

83. Brakke writes, "According to Athanasius, the incarnate word made a successful ascetic life possible again: by dwelling in a human body, the Word granted corruption to other human bodies. . . . The incarnate Word granted incorruption to human bodies through a series of 'achievements' in his bodily career (for example, the ordeal in the Garden of Gethsemane), by which he conquered the destabilizing 'movements' in the body that post-lapsarian had been unable to control. . . . As the Word perfectly controlled his assumed body and remained untouched by its passions, he transformed the body itself, rendering it incorruptible, both morally and physically. . . . Moral courage and control of the bodily passions were once again possible for human beings because they shared a 'kinship of the flesh' with the Word's assumed body." Brakke, *Athanasius and the Politics of Asceticism*, pp. 149–50.

84. Athanasius, *The Life of Antony*, par. 47.

85. St. Jerome, *The Life of Paul, the First Hermit*, ed. Charles Kingsley (Whitefish, MT: Kessinger Publishing, 2010).

86. Saint Jerome, *Three Biographies: Malchus, St. Hilarion and Paulus the First Hermit* (CreateSpace Independent Publishing Forum, 2013).

87. Cf. Athanasius, *The Life of Antony*, par. 91.

88. Cf. Brakke, *Athanasius and the Politics of Asceticism*, pp. 131 and 134.

89. Athanasius, *The Life of Antony*, par. 89.

90. Ibid., 67. The accounts of the wonderworks run from pars. 54–66.

91. Athanasius, *The Life of Antony*, pars. 91 and 92.

92. On the senses of scripture, see, for instance, Pauline A. Viviano, "The Senses of Scripture," *Catechetical Sunday: September 21, 2008* (Washington DC: United States Conference of Catholic Bishops), pp. 1–4.

93. Bernard of Clairvaux, *The Letters of St. Bernard of Clairvaux* (Collegeville, MN: Cistercian Publications, 2003), letter 189.

94. Peter Abelard, *Yes and No: Peter Abelard's Sic et Non*, trans. Priscilla Throop (Charlotte, VT: Medeival MS, 2007), 1.18-19 (p. 34).

95. For this dating of the Council of Sens, see Constant Mews, , "The Council of Sens (1141): Abelard, Bernard, and the Fear of Social Upheaval," *Speculum*, 77, no. 2 (April 2002): 342–82.

96. Although the nineteen technical points on which Abelard was charged are drawn from his theological works, Constant Mews is correct in concluding that what was at issue for

Bernard was the dialectical pedagogy. There is question as to whether Bernard even read the *Theologia "Scholarium."* William of St. Thierry provided the first list of objectionable substantive teachings, which he sent to Bernard. Bernard then farmed out the task of reading the full text to an assistant, who drew up his own list. The final list is a compilation of the two. Mews, "The Council of Sens (1141)."

97. Peter Damiani, cited in Giles Constable, *Culture and Spirituality in Medieval Europe* (Farnham: Variorum, 1996), p. 20. Under Damian's influence, "the discipline" of whips—self-flagellation—first used as punishment for specific bad acts, becomes a general-purpose tool. Ultimately, through the influence of Dominic de Guzman, the founder of the Dominican order, the "discipline" inspires a distinct religious order, the Disciplinati, formed for the specific purpose of self-flagellation (16). My treatment of monastic ascesis is indebted to Constable's presentation, especially in Chapter 9, "Attitudes Toward Self-Inflicted Suffering in the Middles Ages."

98. Giles Constable, *The Reformation of the Twelfth Century* (Cambridge: Cambridge University Press, 1996), p. 6.

99. Some scholars cite his liturgical creations and biblical commentaries to make the case that Abelard had an authentic monastic vocation, but even he acknowledges that he did not make a very good monk: "It was my shame, I will admit, my guilt and my confusion [over having been castrated] rather than any commitment to the religious life that brought me to the refuge of the cloister." And elsewhere: "I was remanded to the abbot of Saint Médard and dragged off to his cloister as if to prison." Peter Abelard, "The Calamities of Peter Abelard," in *Abelard and Heloise: The Letters and Other Writings*, ed. William Levitan (Indianapolis and Cambridge: Hackett Publishing Company, Inc., 2007), pp. 20 and 27. Abelard's own account of the scandals of his not fitting in at either Saint-Denis or Saint Gildas indicates that he did not develop much of a monastic vocation later in life either. See Levitan, ed., *Abelard and Heloise: The Letters and Other Writings,* pp. 28ff and 37ff.

100. Peter Abelard, *Sic et Non*, Prologue, p. 11.

101. In *Sic et Non*, Ableard includes an appendix with a decretal on "authentic books" that he attributes to Pope Gelasius for his list of legitimate sources.

102. Abelard, *Sic et Non*, pp. 19 and 21.

103. Ibid., p. 23; citing Augustine, *Contra Faustum*, xi.5; PL 42.248-49.

104. Abelard, *Sic et Non*, p., 16. Elsewhere Abelard says that even the prophets, "sometimes lacked the gift of prophecy, and have uttered, through their own spirit, false things" (p. 19).

105. See Constance Mews, "The Council of Sens (1141): Abelard, Bernard, and the Fear of Social Upheaval," and Wim Verbaal, "The Council of Sens Reconsidered: Masters, Monks, or Judges?, *Church History* 74, no. 3 (September 2005): 492-3.

106. Wim Verbaal writes of the Council, "Western history has seldom known a comparable moment in which practically all the evolutionary developments of a period came together in one place, each represented by one of the most singular and influential personalities of the time. There was a multiplicity of tensions at all levels between all the parties involved. . . . Increasingly, the Council of Sens now resembles a test case for the claims to authority made by the different institutions coming to maturity in twelfth century society. . . . The confrontation between Abelard and Bernard became the crystallization point that brought all these tensions to the fore." Wim Verbaal, "The Council of Sens Reconsidered: Masters, Monks, or Judges?," pp. 462-3.

Unfortunately for Abelard, Bernard and the others involved in his condemnation take his either/or of Jerome's "it would be sacrilege to argue about the words of God, using human understanding" versus Gregory's "we desire heretics to be checked by catholic priests, always with vigor and reason" and make it into a both/and by claiming both that Abelard has committed sacrilege by questioning authoritative sources *and* that present authorities are to use the best of their reasoning—Bernard drew up a list of nineteen errors in Abelard's work—to censor him. It appears that, at least on a practical level in this case, Bernard succeeds in reconciling the sources far better than does Abelard.

107. It might be pointed out that Abelard's *History of My Calamities* is both concrete in its detail and narratological. What is most significant here, however, is that even though he couches it as a letter of advice and claims in the first sentence, "The force of example often does more than words to stir our human passions or to still them," the force of the writing is to highlight the author's singularity—that is, the inimitability of his example. See Peter Abelard, *The Calamities of Peter Abelard*, in William Levitan, *Abelard and Heloise: The Letters and Other Writings* (Indianapolis, IN: Hackett Publishing Company, Inc., 2007). Throughout the piece, Abelard highlights the singularity not only of his intellectual acumen—"I was always quick in spirit with superior intelligence" (p. 1)—but also of his sins ("I got easily what I wanted," p. 11), of his ability to write love songs ("sung throughout the country," p. 12), and even of the calamities that beset him ("made the whole world shudder," p. 18). Though he denies any real vocation to monasticism—"It was my shame, I will admit, my guilt and my confusion rather than my commitment to the religious life that brought me to the refuge of the cloister" (p. 20)—he also highlights his singular capacity to excel in certain monastic pursuits: "It became clear that God had given me a gift for scripture no less than for secular learning" (p. 21). Though in the immediate account of his love affair with Heloise and his subsequent castration, he gestures toward theological lessons—"As I was weighed down by lechery and pride, the grace of God brought me relief from both" (p. 10)—these lessons quickly drop out as he returns to the kind episodic accounts of his brilliance and others' envy that characterize the first pages of the piece (pp. 3, 5, 8, 9, 21).

In other words, when Abelard is theological, there is no concrete narrative, and when he offers a concrete narrative, there is little if any theology. The *Calamities*, then, is not a confession in the tradition of Augustine, where the story builds theologically. Rather, it is a presentation of the self, a proto-modern autobiography more akin to Rousseau and Thoreau than to Augustine. Rousseau wrote, "I have resolved on an enterprise which has no precedent, and which, once complete, will have no imitator. My purpose is to display to my kind a portrait in every way true to nature, and the man I shall portray is myself. Simply myself." Jean-Jacques Rousseau, *The Confessions* (New York: Penguin Classics, 1953), p. 17. This seems to be the intent, as exhibited by the genre, of Abelard's *Calamities* as well. On the development of the autobiography as a genre, see Linda Anderson, *Autobiography* (Oxford: Routledge, 2001).

William Levitan makes the insightful suggestion that the *Calamities* is Abelard's "campaign of public rehabilitation" after the scandal involving Heloise (Ibid., xiii); as such, it is much like the rehabilitation projects of twentieth- and twenty-first-century politicians after sexual scandals.

108. See Constant Mews, "Orality, Literacy, and Authority in the Twelfth-Century Schools," *Exemplaria* 2, no. 2 (October 1990): 475–500.

109. Peter Abelard, *Dialogue Between a Philosopher, a Jew, and a Christian*, in Peter Abelard, *Ethical Writings*, trans. Paul Vincent Spade (Indianapolis: Hackett Publishing Company, Inc, 1995). The preface to the dialogues has the philosopher, the Jew, and the Christian come to Abelard in a dream and request that he serve as arbitrator of the conversation. They say together, "After conversing and disputing with one another for a long time about our different religious faiths, we have finally submitted to your judgment" (p. 59).

110. For an extended treatment of Arnold and his context, see George William Greenaway, *Arnold of Brescia* (Cambridge, UK: Cambridge University Press, 1931).

111. Bernard, Letter 189, col. 355: "Procedit Golias procero corpore, nobili illo suo bellico apparatus circummunitus antecedente quoque ipsum ejus armigero Arnold de Brixia. Squama squamae conjungitur, et nec spiraculum incedit per eas. Siquiden sibilavit apis quae erat in Francia, api de Italia: et venerunt in unum adversus Dominum et adversus Christum ejus."

112. Arnaldus de Brixia, cujus conversation mel, et doctrina venenum: cui caput columbae, cauda scorpionis est; quem Brixia evomuit, Roma exhorruit, Francia repulit, Germania abominator, Italia non vult recipere, fertur esse vobiscum." Bernard, Letter 196, col. 363.

113. Greenaway, *Arnold of Brescia*, pp. 51–2.

114. Constance Mews, "The Council of Sens (1141): Abelard, Bernard, and the Fear of Social Upheaval," *Speculum*, 77, no. 2 (April 2002): 342–82; Wim Verbaal, "The Council of Sens Reconsidered: Masters, Monks, or Judges?"

115. This is despite the fact that Abelard has made no statements in support of the communes, though he roundly criticizes clerical abuses in his *Ethics*. Peter Abelard, *Ethical Writings*, tr. Paul Vincent Spade (Indianapolis and Cambridge: Hackett Publishing Company, Inc., 1995), pp. 50–8.

116. See Greenaway, *Arnold of Brescia*, pp. 190–204.

117. See Pierre Bonnassie, "The Banal Seigneury and the 'Reconditioning' of the Free Peasantry," in *Debating the Middle Ages: Issues and Readings*, ed. Lester K. Little and Barbara H. Rosenwein (Malden, MA and Oxford: Blackwell Publishers, Inc., 1998), pp. 115–18.

118. See R. I. Moore, *The First European Revolution: c. 970-1215* (Malden, MA and Oxford: Blackwell Publishing Ltd., 2000), pp. 30–64.

119. Bonnassie concludes, "Growth of production no longer profited the peasants, who, after countless exactions, *toltes*, and other *acapes*, were left only the bare minimum for survival." Bonnassie, "The Banal Seigneury," p. 133.

120. See, for instance, Lester K. Little, *Religious Poverty and the Profit Economy in Medieval Europe* (Ithaca and New York: Cornell University Press, 1978), pp. 61–9.

121. Little, *Religious Poverty and the Profit Economy in Medieval Europe*, pp. 94–5. Even the Cistercians, initially critical of monastic physical sloth and material excess, depend on *conversi*, lay brothers, for field labor so that they themselves can attend to chanting the office. By the thirteenth century, the Cistercians, too, become known for their vast wealth. Little, *Religious Poverty and the Profit Economy in Medieval Europe*, pp. 90–6.

122. See Moore, *The First European Revolution*, pp. 113–45.

123. Jeffrey Stout, *The Flight from Authority: Religion, Morality, and the Quest for Authority* (Notre Dame, IN: University of Notre Dame Press, 1987).

124. Peter Abelard, *Yes and No: Peter Abelard's Sic et Non*, p. 25.

125. Quoted in Adriaan H. Bredero, *Bernard of Clairvaux: Between Cult and History* (Edinburgh: T & T Clark, 1996), p. 179.

126. Brian Stock, *The Implications of Literacy: Written Language and Models of Interpretation in the Eleventh and Twelfth Centuries* (Princeton, NJ: Princeton University Press, 1983), pp. 525 and 524.

127. Stock, *The Implications of Literacy*, pp. 408–9, 438, and 452.

128. Ibid., p. 525.

129. Ibid., p. 119.

130. Constant Mews, "Orality Literacy, and Authority in the Twelfth-Century Schools," *Exemplaria* 2, no. 2 (October 1990): 475–500; esp. 481.

131. Interestingly, there remains a vestigial life of Jesus in Aquinas's *Summa*, but it is, for the most part, only that. The treatment of the life of Jesus comes late in the work, in a section toward the end of the third and last part of the *Summa*, and of the thirty-three questions that pertain to it, only one is on Jesus' "manner of life" (In contrast, there are eight questions on the Immaculate Conception and Virgin Birth.). More, the juridically oriented *summa* genre, with its heavy citation and parsing of distinctions—a style of writing indebted to the ecclesial and broader social forces that first played on Abelard—stymies the cumulative narrative impact of the telling of the life of Jesus that takes place in oral reenactment. The story of Jesus's baptism, for instance, becomes a debate whether he should have been baptized in the Jordan or the Red Sea. And it is through careful parsing that Aquinas neutralizes any substantive difference his account of Jesus's "manner of life" might have on the lives of Christians. He first determines that, unlike the monk, Jesus did not lead a solitary or austere life. However, after careful reasoning, he adds, "Now both of these lives are lawful and praiseworthy—namely, that a man withdraw from the society of other men and observe abstinence; and that he associate with other men and live like them" (IIIa, q. 40, a.2). Similarly, Aquinas states that the life that seeks to imitate Christ is "impossible for those who are possessed of wealth." Such a claim, taken by itself, would threaten the fiefdom-based episcopacy; but Aquinas, after further reasoning, determines that followers of Christ can support themselves "by possessing riches" (IIIa, q. 40, a. 3). In other words, Aquinas, after first describing a life of Jesus that would threaten both prongs of the monastic-episcopal alliance, works diligently to neutralize the implications of such a life. The ultimately juridical literary aim of the recounting the life of Jesus in Aquinas' *Summa*—an aim shaped by the kinds of forces Abelard faced at the Council of Sens—is evident in the fact that the whole sequence of questions culminates with the question of the nature and extent of Christ's judiciary power (IIIa, q. 59). While there is little doubt that, as Joseph Wawrykow has argued, Aquinas in the *Summa* likely also *thought of* Jesus as "the model for emulation" in living the virtues, the combination of the late appearance of the exemplar Jesus in the work and the juridically parsed neutralization of what following such a Jesus might mean renders the life of Jesus seemingly inoperative and therefore extraneous. That, in any case, is the interpretation of later scholastics, who, like the earlier Abelard, drop altogether the attempt to render the life of Jesus. To that extent, Abelard, not Aquinas, sets the pattern of subsequent theology. See Joseph Wawrykow, "Jesus in the Moral Theology of Thomas Aquinas," *Journal of Medieval and Early Modern Studies* 42, no. 1 (Winter 2012): 13–31.

For the observation that later scholastics do not appropriate even the vestigial life of Jesus found in Aquinas, see Mark D. Jordan, *Rewritten Theology: Aquinas after His Readers* (Oxford and Malden, MA: Blackwell Publishing, 2006), and Leonard Boyle, *The Setting of the Summa Theologiae of Saint Thomas* (Toronto: Pontifical Institute of Medieval Studies, 1982).

It could be argued that the scholastics could *assume* the narrative of Jesus's life as part of Christian culture, and so did not need to spell it out (similar to the argument taken on above that Paul could assume, and so does not have to unfold, the life of Jesus for his audiences), and Wawrykow presupposes that this is the case when he argues that although the treatment of Jesus's life does not come until the end of the *Summa*, Jesus still "provides the model for emulation" in the life of virtue for Aquinas. Again, I do not deny that Aquinas likely thought of his account of the life of Jesus as central and exemplary of the life of virtue, but Wawrykow's argument fails to take into account the larger social and economic setting of the *summa* literature. In light of the response by ecclesial and civil authorities to Peter Abelard and Arnold of Brescia at Sens and afterward, there is a strong interest on the part of the scholastics in not putting forth a vision of the life of Jesus that directly contests the reigning, if truncated, version of Jesus's life articulated by the monastic-episcopal alliance. Abelard responds to the pressures by dropping the life of Jesus altogether; Aquinas does by postponing and then defusing it. The fact that later scholastics also drop the life of Jesus indicates that theology went the Abelardian rather than the Thomistic route.

132. Stock, *The Implications of Literacy*, p. 99; Mews, "Orality, Literacy, and Authority in the Twelfth-Century Schools," p. 491. R. I. Moore concurs with Stock and Mews when he writes regarding the rise of literacy of the "equation of illiteracy with notions of paganism, rusticity and heresy itself." See Moore, "Literacy and the Making of Heresy, c.1000-1150," in Little and Rosenwein, ed., *Debating the Middle Ages*, 367.

133. Pickstock could not attend, and someone else read her paper.

134. John Milbank, Catherine Pickstock, and Graham Ward, *Radical Theology: A New Theology* (Oxford and New York: Routledge, 1999), pp. 3-4, 6, 10, and 12.

135. I reconstructed Milbank's oral comments through a combination of written notes taken from the sessions and recordings of the sessions that the American Academy of Religion made available, thus allowing a degree of what Jack Goody calls "backward scanning" that is generally not available with oral communication. See Goody, *The Domestication of the Savage Mind* (Cambridge: Cambridge University Press, 1977), pp. 76 and 128.

136. Milbank, Pickstock, and Ward, *Radical Orthodoxy*, pp. 2-3.

137. John Milbank, "The Programme of Radical Orthodoxy," in *Radical Orthodoxy?—A Catholic Enquiry*, ed. Laurence Paul Henning (Aldershot, England, Burlington VT: Ashgate, 2000), pp. 33-45.

INDEX

Index

Index

Index

Index